THE AMERICAN CONSERVATIVE

Xavier Aerosmith Keough

A collection of socio-political commentaries, spanning from
2012 to 2019, written by essayist Xavier Keough.
Any statistical or circumstantial variations present within
this compilation reflect that discrepancy in time.

Chapter Contents

Land That I Love

Freedom, both the incandescent whisper of revolution and the reduced triviality of commercialism, is the seed from which the most opulent columns of civilization have sprung and the hammer from which the most prolific empires have fallen. If history has taught us anything – other than man's propensity to achieve the improbable and preside over humanity's most grotesque atrocities – it's that you cannot fight or defeat an idea, even long after its armies are vanquished. It endures as long as man persists and a single vessel believes in its undying premise.

What is liberty's most quintessential definition? Is it merely a politician's word, wrapped around the sentimentality of patriotism, or does it reside in the solemn handshake of a handful of idealists who risked their lives, the very future of their families, solely to taste its fruits without condition or regret? Freedom, that which cannot be enumerated or quantified, is by no means a guarantee of equal means or outcome; it is a potential gateway to endless exploration and limitless potential. Liberty is both the twisted flame of malice that willingly ensnares the souls and limbs of men into the ruddy bonds of subjugation, and the divine light that inspires ordinary people to liberate their suffering. And yet those who use a pen or a gavel to tell you what to eat, think, feel or say in the name of the "common good", no more speak on its behalf than those who slumber beneath our flag as their neighbors are condemned for merely speaking their convictions.

George Washington once uttered the prophetic words, "It will be found an unjust and unwise jealousy to deprive a man of his natural liberty upon the supposition he may abuse it." Why else would a so-called man of privilege, besieged by an endless litany of defeat and apparent futility, lead 2,400 starved, ill-equipped and frostbitten recruits across the icy waters of the Delaware River on Christmas night as the American Revolution stood on a whisper's edge of failure? Why else would thousands of young men, many who would never know true love or hold their own child in their arms again, charge the fortified beaches of Normandy to the foreign tombs of their impending deaths? "Why", you ask? Because of freedom...that's why! Without equal regard for all mankind, the dignity of life, liberty cannot endure.

Freedom is not an artifact to be dusted off at our complacent convenience or invoked at injustice's greatest hour of need, nor is it a man-made institution to be hoarded and ruled over by the deluded whims of conspiring leaders. Those who are most determined in shackling the free will of others are often the least likely to abide by their own decrees; or the bidding of others. Liberty, without distortion or deceit, is a construct of God's grace, the derivative of free will and the natural state of sentient beings. Do not believe for one moment that the same omnipotent creator who blessed us with rational thought and the ability to discern, would subsequently bemoan their usage or place limitations upon their inevitable dangers. Society cannot legislate human nature any more than it can harness perfection. To choose is to learn; to learn is to accept accountability for one's actions. An astute government does not poison the fruit of industry, aspire to control the mind of human discovery, for only virtue safeguards America's blessings against gratitude's greatest foes: envy, enmity and apathy. No autocratic regime or glorious leader has liberated more people from the clutches of oppression and poverty than the divine institution of choice: to toil and prosper according to one's volition, own two hands and unique gifts.

Much of the world, but specifically America, has lost its intrinsic love for freedom because we longer appreciate its most invaluable gift: opportunity. Rather, we've allowed jaded politicians and counter-intuitive agendas to pervert the word of God and our nation's founding creed under the wailing siren of mass conformity. That is, man's natural born rights are derived from God, and not rationed by the self-serving hand of government. On this Fourth of July, our 241st celebration of our lauded independence from British rule, if "We the People" bestow one final gift to our beloved homeland let it be this indelible truth: America didn't become the most affluent, powerful and revered country on Earth because our elected representatives fostered endless dependency, divided the people into warring factions and dictated our every decision. The United States of America ascended to the pinnacle of hope and humanity because the work ethic and innovative spirit of her people, our love of God and our unyielding desire to be free, could not be bartered or threatened by any personality or party that sought to dispose of our identity under the entitled cries of spoon-fed discontent. Yes, when patriotism is branded as extremism and the Constitution derided as a dangerous relic, speaking the truth indeed becomes a revolutionary act; if not our most fundamental duty and unbreakable vow in a land predicated upon individual autonomy.

Instead of berating the choices of our brethren and rejoicing in their capitulation to one despotic will, why not simply be thankful for residing in a sovereign nation that was erected with the explicit purpose of allowing all Americans to associate with like-minded people while respecting the rights of all God's children; if not, at the very least, to preserve the remaining vestiges of liberty and protect the founding charter of this republic? The further we allow the harbingers of hate, race, class and political propaganda to destroy our ability to reason – this "last, best hope of mankind" – the further we fall, both literally and ideologically, from perhaps the most transcendent point in modern human history: July 4th, 1776. God Bless America and may freedom, that eternal light of the human spirit, forever break the fog of tyranny.

America: The Eternal State of Mind

Since his inauguration on January 20, 2009, one man has spent every hour of his insular existence waging a "scorched-earth" campaign to burn the prophetic house of our forefathers' Constitutional blueprint to the ground, condemn Anglo-America's "privileged" heritage to the dustbin of history, and to inflict a fatal wound against a "flawed" nation; yes, the very same country that elected the same propagandist and self-professed bigot twice. And yet for all his angst and bitterness, victimization propaganda and blind hated of a "racist" country responsible for ascension to the pinnacle of power, Barack Obama was never privy to or the object of these historical indiscretions he supposed seeks to adjudicate in the politically correct haze of social justice. Rather, the President of the United States, the supposed embodiment of integrity and liberation from excessive government, has recklessly incited animosity and discord, divided America to the point of fracture, suffocated capitalism and our economic vitality, redistributed wealth without recourse, demonized our Judeo Christian values, empowered our enemies to the peril of our allies, subverted the Constitution ad nauseam, and lied with narcissistic regularity to deflect from his radical agenda and countless indiscretions by attacking those who attempt to hold him accountable. Sadly, despite all his incessant scheming, shameless deception, and political posturing, our cultural warrior has yet to discover let alone accept one inconvenient truth: America cannot be destroyed by any politician, ideology or derisive plot.

America goes far beyond any sovereign border, tangible asset or the photographed nostalgia of sacred monuments; it's an idea conceived in the womb of divinity and nurtured by the natural intuition of mankind. Even if a self-professed, anti-American extremist erects his most idyllic progressive utopia – erases all vestiges of God, free will, and Americana – no leader can expunge, let alone shackle, the institution of reason; the intangible soul of man forged from the endowed seeds of discernment. Centuries of Americans didn't fight on the fields of Bunker Hill or sacrifice their lives on the foreign shores of oppression to surrender the earned fruits of their labor to socialism or place their faded recollection of their natural rights upon the red altar of Marxism. Manifest destiny, the natural prowess and property of each and every individual – not the Communist Manifesto, mind you – unfurled the flag of freedom by providing the philosophical basis of modern civilization...our political and socio-economic evolution.

Thomas Sowell
@ThomasSowell

"Some Americans will never appreciate America, until after they have helped destroy it, and have then begun to suffer the consequences."

Excuse me, Mr. President, but unlike the pawns of progressivism you sacrifice in the name of the common good, no good idea ever truly dies; it merely slumbers beneath the splinters of statism until the false hope of change wilts beneath the breathing fire of enlightenment and the inevitable discontent of its forsaken subjects. It is, and always will be, eternal. Whether or not the rage of your personal vendetta erases America like a blackboard or bludgeons this fabled republic to the point of being unrecognizable, it will be reborn from the discarded ashes of its enduring premise; that is, individuals, not the forced status quo of mass subjugation, will always seek to live according to their own will, their unique God-given gifts, and prosper according to their own efforts under the auspices of choice. As long as people are ruled by corrupt and conspiring politicians like yourself, Hillary Clinton, America will serve as the immortal guide for their liberation from tyranny; or in our case, the choice and undying right to remove "righteous" adolescents claiming dominion over the universal existence of historical impropriety instead of endeavoring to never repeat such injustices.

The "Californication" of America

If you harbor any doubts as to the depraved depths progressives want to submerge America, look no further than the once Golden Republic of California. Inundated with 1.3 trillion in debt despite possessing the highest sales tax and marginal income tax rates in the U.S., California is now attempting to borrow from itself to pay outstanding retirement pensions. Why? When counties and cities continuously offer exorbitant employee benefit packages – the over 20,000 residents currently collecting 6 figure pensions – while the taxable revenues/disposable incomes of private businesses and corporations are fleeing suffocating regulations in record numbers, somebody's trying to eat Prime Rib on a McRib budget. The dichotomy between rich and poor could not be more evident than the 34% of 39 million residents, over one-fourth of all Americans on welfare, attempting to float across the rising river of public assistance without ever reaching a recognizable state of self-sufficiency.

Not to pour salt into insolvency or double dip those $15 minimum wage fries waving in the Western horizon, but Illegal aliens and their dependents cost Californians $25.3 billion per year according to FAIR's 2017 report: The Fiscal Burden of Illegal Immigration on California Taxpayers. The state's 3 million illegal immigrants and their 1.1 million US–born children cost the average California household — headed by a U.S. citizen — $2,370 annually. And what special allowances have been granted to those struggling, natural born families who must now foot the bill of the Democratic Party's foreign-voter adoption program and affirmative action estate? In other words, mind your white privilege; even if you're not white, live paycheck-to-paycheck and still can't afford to rent a cupboard in San Francisco's Pacific Heights. If only the city's estimated 7,500 homeless residents were undeclared "squatters" who wanted more than just clean syringes and public defecation.

Enough about redistribution and devaluing a sentient being's "worth". What's the going "Uber" price for perspective when purposely infecting an unsuspecting partner with HIV is no longer a felony, but state workers (including teachers and social workers) can be fined or even jailed for using the incorrect "gender" pronouns. In some educational institutions where gender-queer conditioning of elementary kids has become mandatory conditioning masked as sensitivity cognition, grade school students themselves can be reprimanded for not indulging their peers' non-binary, role playing fantasies. In other words, ignore your genitals and reject your biological birth, liberate hate by wearing a dress, because little is more abnormal than just letting kids be kids without the inherited baggage of "sex" obsessed malcontents. But never fear, calling for the assassination of the President, beating peaceful pedestrians expressing political dissent or slandering any patriotic Republican as a Nazi bigot, is both commonplace, if not admirable, on enlightened college campuses and now in the "non-discriminatory" workplace.

To invoke the irony of all future-mugged constituents, California lawmakers recently passed Proposition 57 mandating early release for all "non-violent" criminals". And what exactly constitutes a non-violent crime worthy of such leniency? Oh, just the rape of an unconscious person, human trafficking involving sex acts with minors, and assault with a deadly weapon. And here I thought legalizing child prostitution was but another attempt to normalize pedophilia among Hollywood benefactors lecturing Middle America about equality and tolerance. Once you breech and discredit one ethical boundary – those societal foundations of gender, family, faith and love of country – people will literally defend the most senseless, soulless acts for their existence is defined by limitless pleasure, perceived entitlement and a glaring inability to think for themselves. "Progress" isn't derived by forcing people to handicap their success, bake a sacrilegious cake to the extortion of financial ruin or purposely exposing innocent children to perverse Gay Pride parades and profane feminist rallies. Progress is realizing living the lifestyle of your choice, the literal sanctity between right and wrong, should never require confiscating the rights and dignity of others solely to validate/advertise one's bombastic beliefs.

With such inane reasoning masquerading as good government, it is of little surprise Governor Jerry Brown declared our immigration laws moot by further investing in sanctuary cities and attempting to obstruct ICE officials from apprehending known fugitives. When you're more distraught over the safety and so-called rights of non-citizens than the death of a 32-year-old woman murdered by a seven-time felony convict deported 5 times, prudence and justice are antithetical anomalies. This defiant lunacy is as absurd as spending $25 billion on enabling illegal immigration while the now infamous Oroville Dam, providing irrigation for 755,000 acres and electricity for 25 million, eventually collapsed due to disrepair. Not only are California illegals now eligible for driver's licenses, they can legally vote in an election if they are officially registered to vote. And what does it take to register to vote in the great state of California? A driver's license and a personal guarantee you're a citizen. Yes, you heard me correctly, the legitimacy of our elections, the survival of our 241-year-old republic, is now based entirely on the honor system; or if you prefer perspective over subjective bliss, foreign invaders who consciously broke our laws without a hint of regret, only to be congratulated with a complimentary door prize, the honorary American oppressed immigrant mindset, of leftist socio-economic contempt.

I take umbrage with any self-respecting American, God forbid elected civil servant, who is completely indifferent to the estimated 3 million unlawful votes cast in 2016 simply because they believe small town America values and the electoral college should acquiesce to the moral degradation and militant activism of urban epicenters like San Francisco, Los Angeles or Chicago. Considering California alone accounted for over 10% of Hillary Clinton's final vote total, a 3.4 million difference that exceeded her 2.86 million popular-vote lead, I'm confused as to how those Donald Trump supporters representing over 83% of American territory – or precisely 2,626 counties of all 3,141 U.S. counties – should take a knee with Colin Kaepernick to empower a regressive state that dismisses the rule of law, mocks rural America and remains visibly contentious towards any concept of electoral sovereignty. In other words, who in their right mind would deny illegals shielded from deportation the opportunity to vote by forcing them to serve up to 6 months in jail for using banned plastic straws before election day? That justice is clearly reserved for unruly citizens who can still legally drink $8 beer from plastic cups at Dodger Stadium.

There's also another term for those politicians who willingly subvert the immigration process and disregard our voting statutes to their personal and civic benefit? It's called sedition, dereliction of duty, treason. If I may, when did defiant trespassers become "Dreamers" and doorbells a humanitarian crisis? Have millions of aspiring Americans from across the globe, for well over a century, not honored the afforded requirements for securing the privilege of becoming a U.S. citizen? Conspiring to invalidate prescribed protocols ratified to ensure legal and orderly naturalization – those measures explicitly enacted to protect America's citizens and welfare – makes about as much sense as giving convicted felons the right to vote because of "felon disenfranchisement"; i.e., the admitted hearsay of political opportunists salivating over the fact 60% of released California convicts are minorities who deserve the opportunity to vote Democrat.

The same bureaucratic terrorists who forced 53 dairy farmers to go bankrupt and/or relocate to saner pastures due to absurd regulations on cow flatulence are somehow entirely satisfied with the unsubstantiated word of an undocumented, unvetted immigrant. Surprised? Not unless logic and liberalism share a nonflammable unitard. And while peace activists remain adamant U.S. citizens must undergo extensive background checks to exercise their constitutionally affirmed right to bear arms – naturally excluding those potential militants illegally entering a sovereign country in a post 9/11 world – their unflinching "non-partisan concern" for human life magically ceases at the recognized borders of radical agents like Iran and North Korea; inhumane, totalitarian regimes that globalists duplicitously believe possess an inalienable right to develop nuclear weapons despite vowing daily to destroy Western Civilization. So what's the common denominator? Rampant, unabridged, unapologetic anti-Americanism!

What other state of "Democratic socialists" would dare suggest rejecting two of our most indispensable leaders, George Washington and Abraham Lincoln, men directly responsible for the creation and survival of the most transcendent Republic in modern history, for "May Day"; a revered communist celebration of a murderous ideology that has oppressed and impoverished BILLIONS? Naturally, these are the same lunatics fighting for non-citizens to vote, hold state offices and receive sanctuary from our existing laws. I guess "Labor Day", a national holiday honoring the contributions and achievements of the American workforce since 1894, no longer suffices for those ungrateful malcontents obsessed with degrading our heritage and fundamentally transforming this country's founding values. This is the war on American history. This is the war on common sense.

When voting is no longer our most sacred duty and the integrity of our elections becomes a racist endeavor, as denoted by California's refusal to investigate massive vote fraud uncovered in November, America becomes a second-class citizen unable to defend itself in its own home due to fear of "offending" the same guests who would outlaw our flag, silence free speech and ban the national anthem if given only a fleeting chance. In essence, any policy that strengthens or reaffirms America's independence, influence and economic vitality is an affront to the liberal narrative America must surrender its identity and founding Constitutional charter for being an evil empire built upon greed and White supremacy. Or in historically accurate terms, a superior culture displacing an ethnocentric population which supplanted other nomadic societies via the auspices of war, commerce, adaptability and/or technological superiority. Whereas California and New York are hopelessly lost to the left's orchestrated demographic coup d'état and ideological conditioning of their respective populaces, states like Virginia, Colorado, and Michigan are not far behind.

Regardless of one's political persuasion, you don't have to be a historian or even watch the History channel to understand America was erected as a free republic for a moral, self-sufficient people acutely aware of the triggers of tyranny, poverty and religious persecution. Individual liberty, limited government, transparency and accountability were never optional amenities on an academic drug trip to worship the Lenin statue in Marxist Seattle. These autonomous attributes represented conceptual necessities whose only negotiable features were the exact method and expected integrity of implementation.

Unfortunately for the idyllic state of California, squatting on the world's sixth largest economy and boasting vast untapped natural resources, its propensity for dysfunction and waste is only superseded by its systemic rejection of America itself. Whenever West Coast socialists are not charging working families and commercial transportation the highest fuel taxes in the nation, environmental terrorists who cannot differentiate between ecology and political alarmism are manufacturing water shortages and sparking unnatural disasters with pseudo-scientific regularity. While restricting residents to 55 gallons of water a day is obviously a crisis of competence, who would dare shower and wash their clothes on the same day, fixing the error of your naive ways is near impossible when rogue political fantasy displaces sound judgement and the Constitutional authority of your native country. How else can controlled burns and thinning excess forestation to reduce the risk of uncontrollable wildfires, similar to the recent devastation which devoured 9,000 homes/buildings and 250,000 acres of habitat, be equated to "clear cutting" or raping the land?

It is also of little surprise California elitists, aka doomsday legislators seeking another excuse to tax common sense, believe Global Warming is not a natural, cyclical occurrence predominantly caused by solar fluctuations and the internal temperature of the Earth's core. Never mind Antarctic ice levels are far greater than 30 years ago and New York is not submerged beneath Al Gore's "unnatural science" grade point average, if you believe a .03 reduction goal in global temperatures in a century's time at an eventual loss of 2.5 trillion in annual GDP is a winning strategy, than counting cow farts and banning combustible engine cars by 2040 is your golden ticket to getting assaulted on Bay Area Rapid Transit (BART) for reading 1984 without a permit. But never fret, Sacramento City Council approved a motion to pay gang members for the conscious decision not to kill one another; or in layman's terms, obey the law and stay in school. And to think millions of decent, hard-working Americans are ineligible because of their offensive "privilege".

Although it's mathematically impossible to pinpoint exactly what alternative universe California Democrats reside, our Forefathers would have called for a second armed revolution long ago. No, Really! Whether or not progressives approve of President Trump is a moot point if their own policies and authoritative abuse do not adhere to the prescribed constitutional checks of adopted statehood. Likewise, embodying the fight for state sovereignty by no means justifies endeavoring to become like those impoverished, inept nations your exploding illegal immigrant population is instinctively fleeing. It's hard to fathom how the once "Go West" mantra of American pioneers that catapulted California into an unprecedented wave of prosperity, proud nationalism and a vibrant centrifuge for diversity, has dissolved into an immoral state of cultural Marxism that believes government is god, gender is a fluid state of mind, exploitation a form of education, and patriotism an unjust form of racial oppression. Thank God "woke" Democrats are feeding a public drug epidemic, enabling record homelessness and once-eradicated diseases, by pretending none of it exists.

It is obviously no secret the once predominantly "Red" stomping grounds of Ronald Wilson Reagan has been turned bright blue by an unprecedented wave of immigration and indoctrinated anti-Americanism. That was and always has been the goal of the radical statist quo. Where this nation was forged as a beacon of hope and opportunity for millions of law-abiding aspiring citizens seeking a better life, California has descended into counter-intuitive cesspool that preaches victimization over accountability, reverse discrimination over equality, intolerance over intellectual diversity. No matter how pure your intentions or how strong your faith in the nature of human volition, you cannot coexist with partisans so obsessed with maintaining political supremacy they would gladly surrender their own country to those who tirelessly seek our demise or break any rule to control our lives out of some misplaced sense of social justice that gives no such credence to their own failures and hypocrisy; most notably, those corrupt governments globalists so foolishly favor to the liquidation of civility and the downfall of mankind. In its most celebrated form, modern progressivism is a communicable virus that consumes every last crumb of logic, vitality, identity, accountability and unity from the American frontier.

While no American wants to witness the secession of California, or more profoundly the dissection of America's legacy and the abandonment of our fellow right-minded countrymen who represent the powerless minority, how long can you spare a cancerous appendage before it spreads, poisons your soul and ultimately takes your life? Will apathy reclaim our revisionist classrooms or assuage the sponsored anarchist war on police and freedom of speech? Once again, the left's goal is not to coexist under the ideological umbrella that was and is America. Their unrelenting mission is to whitewash history, ensure conformity and redefine America by eradicating all borders, natural human distinctions – symbiotic gender roles and the family paradigm – so the concepts of liberty, individual achievement and morality quickly become outdated manifestations that can no longer threaten the secular supremacy of a progressive state.

The systemic decay of California is as much a symbol of our failure as a society, as it is a dire warning to every governor and undaunted patriot that still believes God is the liberty of salvation, character does not fear consequence, and raising respectful, responsible children is by far our greatest contribution to humanity; that indomitable virtue of a free nation born from the bounty of a Judeo-Christian seed but distinctly American creed. If this transcendent republic has any chance to coalesce and preserve the timeless wisdom of a handful of visionaries marked for death by the tyranny of a crown's crest, I believe hope resides in the heartland of an industrious people – a convened Convention of States faithful to independence and the merits of intelligent debate – still rightfully proud of their heritage and ever cognizant of the evil contempt and complacency breed.

The 10 Most Pervasive Lies About Conservative America

1) Conservatives are racist! Shall I quote the blissful bigotry of Barack Obama, Hillary Clinton, Al Sharpton, or any slew of "socially conscious" crusaders; celebrities included? If I may, which party was founded as the anti-slavery party, ended Jim Crows and spearheaded the legislative movements for citizenship, suffrage and equal rights? Here's a hint...it doesn't rhyme with "sewer rat"! Conservatives welcome all races and colors in our quest to defend and preserve America's founding ideals. Likewise, we unilaterally reject divisive victimization rhetoric used solely to incite animosity along socio-economic lines for political gain. Although racism exist in all facets of America, such hateful attitudes are infectious and only invite future bigotry upon yourself, your peers and your loved ones. Progress is not measured by the number of times race is invoked or celebrated. It is personified by the number of lives liberated from its requirement. Why again would "racist" Republicans support Allen West, Ben Carson, Dinesh D'Souza, Mia Love, Condoleezza Rice and Marco Rubio, let alone spread the transcendent wisdom of Booker T. Washington, Martin Luther King Jr. or Thomas Sowell? Refusing to support a former President's spiteful, anti-American agenda doesn't make anyone a racist, regardless of their heritage or political affiliation. It makes one increasingly cognizant of the destructive aftermath such deep-seated prejudice inevitably brings.

2) Conservatives are misogynists! Naturally, because conservatives don't have mothers, wives or daughters, nor do they care about their well-being. We decry discrimination against either gender, detest violence against women in any form, and support equal rights and pay for all women. Conservatives simply reject the regressive agenda of modern feminism which seeks injustice where none exists – "psychological trauma" inflicted by patriarchal images, the sexism of "mansplaining" or the "rape culture" of "manspreading", gender identity conditioning of children, free birth control and taxpayer funded abortions, the so-called prosecutable sexual paradox of "yes" means "no" – as a means of degrading the masculine image and traditional role of men in society.

This adopted brand of radical activism ensures reverse discrimination by attempting to validate such absurd demands to the detriment of both society and all reasonable, responsible women that desire nothing more than equal opportunity and treatment under the law. Self-respecting women do no want to be coddled, made to feel hopeless and therefore given an emotionally crippled crutch of contempt. Whether pursuing a career of or raising a family full time, they deserve the right to live the life of their choosing without discrimination or the crass exploitation of bitter gender fascists. Parading around in public topless, shouting obscenities and performing vulgar acts doesn't make you enlightened, let alone noteworthy. It makes you the willing subject of your own stupidity. Empowerment, much like equal rights, doesn't illicit hatred or reject accountability.

3) Conservatives are "Nazi" extremists! Unless you passed a concentration camp on the way to work, hauled the smelted gold taken from numbered corpses, this is nothing more than media driven hysteria designed to justify progressive policies that are incompatible with our founding ideals, or better yet, common sense. You do realize Adolf Hitler, the infamous leader of the Third Reich, was a rabid German socialist who denounced individuality, capitalism, Christianity, and free speech? He also advocated imprisoning or executing political dissidents and all inferior ethnicities. Do you know what other fascist movement harbors almost identical beliefs? Progressivism. Conservatives aren't the ones silencing intellectual diversity on campuses, clamoring for state-run media, physically attacking Trump supporters, rioting in the streets over a free election result, singling out Christian businesses for prosecution, mocking traditional values or publicly demonizing white Americans.

Liberal fascism, the once fringe element that officially hijacked the Democratic party in 2008, is now the single greatest threat to liberty, tolerance, due process, prosperity, and the survival of America. Considering the Nazis sought absolute control and conservatives loathe intrusive, unilateral government, this accusation is about as sensical as a transgender Jewish man asking to be circumcised by a Muslim butcher before he uses the little girl's restroom. "Halal No" or until hell freezes over, the left is by far the greatest embodiment of extremism in America today. When the end justifies the means, truth is of no consequence.

4) Conservatives oppose immigration! Hardly. America was founded as a beacon of hope for all races, creeds and colors. On the contrary, we rightfully object to the pardoned excuses of "illegal" immigration and the mass influx of untraceable "refugees". Not supporting our immigration laws, those protocols every civilized nation enacts and enforces, is a slap in the face to every man, woman and child who immigrated to America legally, not to mention those 3,000 victims who died on 9/11. Abandoning our borders, not shielding citizens from criminally and medically unvetted threats, is a dereliction of duty and a clear and present danger to our country's sovereignty and security. Encouraging, dare I say "engineering", illegal immigration solely to win elections and demographically override our founding principles is nothing short of treason. Despite such disingenuous ploys, all are welcome who respect our sovereignty and complete the process afforded by law. Perhaps someday activists will understand this "revolutionary" concept when sentenced to decapitation by an Islamic tribunal or while picketing corporations in the progressive soup lines of socialism.

5) Conservatives are gun fanatics! Like our forefathers, we unequivocally embrace people's right to defend themselves against all forms of tyranny; Thomas Jefferson's most profound reason for preserving our right to bear arms. Gun violence isn't a disease but a sociological symptom that reflects a parenting failing and an obvious psychological disconnect. Rather than addressing the obvious moral erosion infecting our communities – an endeavor Hollywood has worked overtime to achieve by mocking our religious values – progressives are content exploiting national tragedies to justify their insatiable desire to repeal the Second Amendment.

Not only is gun confiscation historically the final lynch pin to uncontested subjugation, gun control does little to deter those who truly want to harm others; especially when you realize both the Oklahoma City Bombing and 9/11 were carried out without a single shot being fired. Every day firearms deter crime and save far more lives than the soulless of any disturbed individual. You can no more regulate human nature than an inanimate object can pull its own trigger and be convicted for murder. When mass death is the ultimate goal, the weapon of choice is moot for people will always find a vessel to deliver their wrath. The fact these mass shootings rarely occurred 50 or even 25 years ago is a costly reminder that parents, schools and our elected leaders have failed to instill our children with the proper values and universal respect for their fellow man. The question isn't why do so many citizens own a gun. The question is why are so many comfortable ending a human life? Leaving decent, law-abiding Americans helpless against thugs, terrorists and aspiring dictators is never the answer; it's the broken promise of armed regret.

6) Conservatives despise the poor! Of course not, because conservatives never get sick, lose our jobs or struggle to provide for our families. Sorry but poverty doesn't discriminate and any President that doesn't create jobs, lower taxes and eliminate waste, is no friend of the American people. One of the benefits of living in a nation as resourceful as America is the financial assistance available to those in need. Nearly all people struggle, require assistance time to time, and there is no shame in that. And yes, Americans are an extremely compassionate and generous people. However, Conservatives take great umbrage with those smug opportunists who view welfare as a career calling and conspire incessantly to defraud the system when they should treat such blessings as a stepping stone to reclaim their life. Stealing bread from the mouth of honest labor – those taxpayers who have watched the number of welfare recipients and the national debt nearly double since 2008 – is a slap in the face to all hard-working Americans, as well as those families that struggle with real misfortune and lingering disabilities.

Everyone owes it to themselves, their family and their country to find a job. A paycheck is a means to a means, a self-sustaining gateway to a better life, whereas welfare is a handcuff to endless dependence, debt and discontent. For when the fog of propaganda and entitlement clears, no economic system has liberated more people from the clutches of poverty than capitalism; that independent engine of ambition most synonymous with liberty, prosperity, and human discovery. However, please note, and much to the chagrin of Marxists everywhere, capitalism only works if you do! A healthy work ethic is the most reliable path to lasting success and escaping personal hardship.

7) Conservatives are religious radicals! Clearly. What's the terrorist score card of the last century? Which religion has never had a reformation? Yet again, this is but another baseless claim designed to insight fear, hate and paranoia at the expense of dispelling dangerous misconceptions. America, Western Civilization, was founded upon Judeo-Christian ideals; a fact liberals malicious muddle, twist and insistently attempt to discredit. Opposing abortion – the death of a human being even in its most glorified state – or rejecting Gay Marriage – the political corruption of a "religious" institution in Western Society which threatens the family dynamic – hardly makes us harbingers of hate or the equivalent of Islamic militants; those extremists who deny women basic human rights and kill gays for merely existing. As ardent constitutionalists, Christian conservatives advocate the tolerance of all competing beliefs that coincide with our founding values. No, Christianity is not perfect or without historical indignities. Christians simply learned "killing in the name of God" was a fruitless endeavor that undermined every tenet of their faith. What we absolutely refuse to condone is empowering those ideologies that violate people's natural born rights, i.e. Sharia Law, or threaten our founding values to the debasement of our culture and national ethos. Not all laws are just or justified; not all boundaries are meant to be broken.

8) Conservatives are war mongers! Yes, because once again, Conservatives, those who are most likely to serve their country or volunteer for during times of crisis, do not have families who sacrifice and grieve so that "We the People" many live free from harm and bask in those liberties so often denied to millions across the globe. Like all Americans, Conservatives detest war and view it as an absolute last resort of recourse. That being said, we do not live in a world were evil does not exist and circumstance can rely on the unwavering good nature of our fellow man. To unconditionally reject military intervention regardless of the prevailing circumstances is the equivalent of watching a rape across the street and doing nothing about it. Frankly, when did we stop caring? The question all liberals should be asking themselves, and that of the entire civilized world, is why aren't more nations and leaders taking a stand against mass injustice and depravity? No, America cannot be the savior of the free world or right all wrongs of humanity. We simply must refuse to be the doormat of tyranny and criminal apathy. "Injustice anywhere is a threat to justice everywhere."

9) Conservatives care little for the environment! I'd love to indulge this popular progressive fairy tale, but we too drink from the sources of water, breathe the same air, and educate our children about the ravages of pollution. Rather, conservatives refuse using science fiction as to implement unnecessary regulations, collect more taxes, solely to expand government and claim more austerity over our everyday lives. The same bureaucrats who can't balance their checkbook, protect our borders, or give the people a straight answer, want to control every aspect of your life out of the goodness in their hearts. No, right-minded Americans aren't fearful of science, anything but, for we eagerly embrace its universal necessity, power and wonder. What we don't accept is a political alarmist, i.e., a pseudo scientist named Al Gore and his celebrity salesmen, proclaiming the Arctic ice shelf would cease to exist within a decade and that the entire city of New York would become the lost ruins of Atlantis due to the impending catastrophe known as climate change. Sadly, not to spoil the inconvenient truth about his "D" in Natural Sciences, or his six-figure speaker fees, glacier coverage of the planet is now as prominent as it was 20 years ago and the Yankees have yet to give away floaties during any home game promotion. Bummer.

As firm believers in empirical data, reputable science, conservatives recognize the existence of global cooling and warming; we merely view both as natural climatic cycles that far outweigh the shameless ploys of politicians. Now that's not to say mankind has no negative impact on the environment, bio diversity or even global temperatures. I have no doubt whatsoever. It's just that our presence pales in comparison to the mercurial power of the sun and the instinctive reflux of mother nature. After all, if the truth be known, one of the hottest years ever recorded in our nation's history occurred in the 19th century during pre-industrialized America. Believe it or not, just as many if not more conservatives live off the land, utilize nature for recreation, and tirelessly work to protect and preserve the source of their greatest blessing…their preferred way of life. Protecting our environment against corporate waste and individual apathy is nonnegotiable.

Listening to those politicians who manipulate scientific data for political and financial gain, on the other hand, is entirely optional.

10) Conservatives are out of touch! Or perhaps we're painfully astute of history and vigilant to the ides of tyranny. As the proud torchbearers of the timeless ideals America was founded upon – individual liberty, limited government, God, hard work, accountability and duty – conservatives pose the biggest threat to the globalist agenda: a secular, soulless paradigm of mass conformity and institutionalized dependence. Progressivism cannot survive without inciting distrust, division and discord to conceal the truth from low information voters; those vulnerable souls most easily cajoled by such sensationalist propaganda. Any ideology that cannot stand on its own merits and is counter-intuitive to the Constitution, albeit socialism and Marxism, is inherently radical and a tangible threat to our founding way of life. If I may, how are any of these philosophies remotely synonymous with our founding creed, not to mention the supreme law of the land? Historically speaking, one must work far more diligently to protect a lie than to simply speak on the behalf of self-evident truths.

Conservatives believe, and freely attest, man's natural born rights are derived from a divine creator and not ransomed by the "benevolence" of centralized despots. At its most rudimentary core, our elected government has three fundamental duties: to protect our lives and liberties, to honor and uphold the prescribed limitations of the Constitution, and to provide transparency in all its dealings. I'm sad to report the corrupt cesspool of polarized bureaucrats known as Washington have egregiously failed on all three accounts. Defending the ideological cornerstones America was erected upon doesn't make conservatives "extreme" or detached in any sense of the word. It makes our detractors hopelessly ignorant, toxic and irrefutably malicious.

My Conservative Credo

I believe in the timeless ideals that once made America the last, best hope of mankind.

I believe one's love of country – its survival, welfare and the privilege of citizenship – supersedes all partisan loyalties.

I believe any form of intrusive or oppressive government that ransoms the rights and will of the people is an enemy of humanity.

I believe "We the People" can accomplish anything when liberty, hard work, responsibility and respect are non-negotiable.

I believe we can reform healthcare, without denying individual liberty and succumbing to the highly cumbersome, ineffective leviathan known as socialized medicine.

I believe we can honor legal immigration, the promise that is America, without abandoning our borders and security solely to stuff the ballot box with an inexhaustible source of illegal votes.

I believe in rewarding ambition and work ethic, the innovative spirit of private enterprise, in lieu of encouraging envy, dependence and entitlement.

I believe capitalism – the breathing fire of competition and discovery too often suffocated by the glass ceiling of socialism – is the genesis for our revered way of life and most synonymous with freedom, opportunity, and upward mobility for all Americans regardless of one's abilities, education or life circumstances.

I believe we can reform social programs, welfare fraud and abuse, without denying those with real struggles and disabilities the necessary assistance to live with dignity.

I believe intellectual diversity is the path to enlightenment, the transcendent blessing of free will, and that Freedom of Speech must never be denied or abridged in our public institutions regardless of our political beliefs or personal differences.

I believe we can embody the fight for equality, fairness, without succumbing to radical feminism, race-baiting, and the regressive stigma of victimization propaganda.

I believe we can protect a child's right to be born, that a human life is worth far more than the sum of its parts, without denying women and men the "choice" to accept the inherent responsibilities of having sex.

I believe any gender identity conditioning of our youth is child abuse and a desperate attempt to push a destructive political agenda that seeks to normalize gender dysphoria: a recognized psychological disorder with far-reaching consequences.

I believe we can teach our children to respect and properly use guns, to defend our Constitutional right to bear arms, without having to become an unarmed statistic of violent crime.

I believe journalism, the symbolic Fourth Estate and historic independent watchdog of this Constitutional Republic, must exemplify objectivity and integrity to ensure the transparency of our government, to preserve the power of the governed and to keep the electorate dutifully informed without regret or refrain. Advocacy invites propaganda, partisan collusion and the subversion of the democratic process.

I believe we can honor God – share his universal wisdom in our schools – without forcing anyone to accept Christianity, let alone embrace his existence.

I believe in preserving the sanctity of marriage, a religious institution and biblical covenant in Western society, without tolerating violence, animosity or discrimination against gays by denying equality in the workplace or their right to secular Civil Unions.

I believe we can defend religious liberty, our founders' indelible belief in the divine source of our natural born rights, without allowing the barbaric and backward tenets of Sharia law to infiltrate our communities.

I believe we can honor our commitment and duty to protect Israel, its sacred right to exist in a sovereign homeland free from hate, without aiding and abetting her sworn enemies of intolerance.

I believe the United States military is the rock upon which tyranny must break, that lasting peace is best achieved by projecting strength through unwavering resolve, without abandoning our allies, moralizing only select victims of human suffering or failing to meet the everyday needs of our veterans.

And I believe we can hold our elected government accountable for a litany of failures and abuses, rather than enabling "blameless" politicians to destroy America with divisive politics and unending corruption.

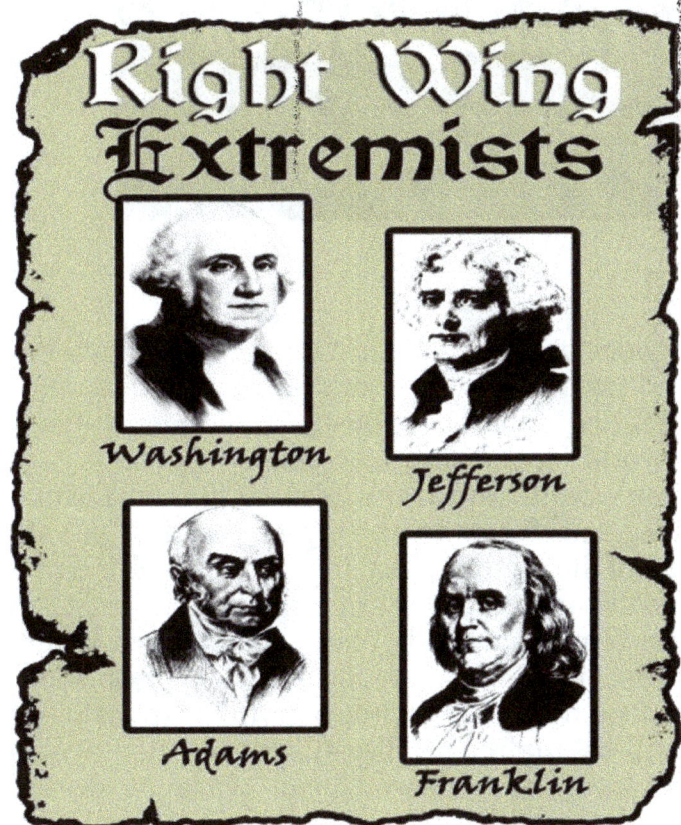

Right Wing Extremists

Washington

Jefferson

Adams

Franklin

These are not radical concepts; they are the ideological bastion of this nation's founding charter and the common-sense principles progressives have systematically subverted and usurped with their anti-American agenda. The time has come for responsible and competent leaders who genuinely care about this country, her future, and the people to reclaim the reigns of a rogue government and vindictive media used to cajole the masses beneath the poisonous fog of petty politics and false narratives. In other words, with no corrections for political correctness or apologies to conspiring globalists, I believe in God, liberty, the Constitution, self-reliance, our brave servicemen and women, capitalism, and limited government. I believe in America!

The Capitalist

"UPWARD" & ONWARD

"The democracy will cease to exist when you take away from those who are willing to work and give to those who would not."

- Thomas Jefferson

Burning the Soup of Socialism

In the 239-year-old wake of a revolutionary declaration to ensure the rights of mankind over the historical dangers of excessive and immoral government, the global beacon of hope and opportunity that once defined America – that indelible spirit of independence and innovation that has transcended the world on numerous occasions – is fading, or more succinctly dying, from the self-inflicted wound known as socialism. Barack Obama and Hillary Clinton are zealously pursuing our fiscal demise by suffocating private enterprise, the heartbeat of our revered way of life, with endless regulation, taxation and rogue redistribution. And for what; because all banks and corporations – those "soulless" creations that never donated to medical research, endowed education, financed family homes, discovered watershed technologies or created a single, decent paying job – are irrefutably evil? Apparently so. Feeding societal discontent, while starving responsibility and perspective, turns grown adults into helpless children needlessly suffering in the cold-hearted soup lines of capitalism as limousine liberals decry Global Warming during campaign drive-bys of urban blight. It's hard to politicize greed and income inequality when the road to your newly purchased, third home is paved with $600,000 in campaign "shush" money and lobster bisque is for lunch before naptime on your chartered jet.

Because activists love to defy or mock conventional avenues, I suggest the art of taking the road less traveled in a Constitutional republic predicated upon choice. If you don't like the prevailing interest rates of national financial institutions, don't take out a loan, open an account or agree to their banking fees. Ever hear of credit unions? If you despise a corporation's practices, file a lawsuit, work elsewhere or refuse to buy their products and stock. Or God forbid, start your own enterprise with like-minded consumers. Competition, economic Darwinism and the Law of Demand, will eventually weed out the parasites in both industries. Regardless, how does either complaint validate Washington's crusade to punish hard-working Americans and business owners, siphon their wealth and property, by attempting to legislate economic equality in the name of social justice? It doesn't.

If we're marinating "fate" in the melancholy of "fairness", minimum wage was never intended as a living wage. Rather, it represents the baseline compensation for unskilled labor performing menial jobs; such as students seeking extra pocket change. Just don't tell me fast food workers deserve $15 an hour and free health care, only to claim the privilege and benefits of higher education, learning a trade, doesn't outweigh the cost or personal sacrifice required to forge a bridge to a better life. And it is that quality of life that will ultimately suffer when drastic wage hikes result in mass layoffs and/or mass inflation. True financial stability requires establishing a means to a means, not by relying on and depleting an exhaustible end: i.e., long-term public assistance handouts that contribute to widespread poverty. The best social program is, and always has been, a job: one that rightfully compensates your unique and acquired attributes.

There is no shame in needing help time to time, we all do, but welfare is not a career opportunity and charity is never an executive order. Although Americans are a compassionate and extremely generous people, all able-bodied citizens owe it to themselves and their families to find work. A monthly government check doesn't liberate the poor, it merely ensures their depravity for generations to come. This is why socialism is nothing more than the equal division of misery and the legalized theft of success. Why is it a travesty when an immigrant or discouraged minority is struggling, but karma when an entrepreneur, one who could have hired these individuals and improved their quality of life, goes broke and loses everything? In other words, welcome to the dawn of envy and entitlements, or the dusk of hard work and accountability. Here in the land of the fleeced, the home of the bankrupt, you personally owe your neighbor a free ride, lunch money and an apology for daring to achieve; where big government is God, liberty is flawed, and capitalism – acquired wealth and job creation – is pure greed; unless, that is, you're a multimillionaire liberal politician, athlete or entertainer who believes in Climate Change.

Whereas confused collectivists love to point out how roads, schools, and emergency services are sterling examples of socialism's success – the "you didn't build that" Marxist guide to self-loathing – these necessities are basic stalwarts of any functioning, civilized society. So yes, according to leftist logic and your tax dollars, you built that bridge too. Yet, by some miracle of competence, free enterprise & public works coexisted and thrived in this country long before 60's radicals, today's Democratic leadership, waged class warfare, excessively taxed prosperity and redistributed wealth in order to incite voter discontent, justify mass dependence and erect their socialist utopia. In fact, up until 1913 Americans kept 100% of their earnings. And despite adhering to this "unfathomable" economic principle, i.e., keeping your hard-earned money, our hallowed way of life somehow benefited from a vast network of educational institutions, extensive roadways and railways, hospitals, police and fire departments, as well as a fully functioning military in the form of the Army, Navy and Marine Corps: those fabled military branches that still managed to win eight wars without the duplicitous dealings of Big Brother.

As for the official "police" report of statism, public education is effectually based on a capitalistic theory of individuality and self-worth. By teaching a child the necessary skills to become a productive and well-adjusted member of society, research indicates they're much less likely to struggle, break the law or become dependent, an undue fiscal burden, upon the state. The universal goal of a market driven economy is sustainability, or more succinctly, self-sufficiency: to empower commerce with diversified labor so everyday people can buy their own home, provide for their family and afford "quality" health care independent of government control. The more disposable income each family possesses, the more likely they are to purchase the products and services of those businesses that pay our salaries and hire new employees. A means to a means, my comrade.

"The difference between a welfare state & a totalitarian state is a matter of time." ~Ayn Rand

Bernie Sanders and his equally-misguided protégé Alexandria Ocasio-Cortez love to publicly invoke Sweden, Norway and Denmark as irrefutable, socialist "success" stories to distract from the dystopian nightmare that is Venezuela, but these Scandinavian countries do not possess centralized economies or a nationalized means of production and their combined populations are roughly the same as the state of New York. Furthermore, America covers 75% of NATO defense expenditures while these supposed "thriving" nations contribute less than 2% of their GDP to protect their own people. Each of their respective economic foundations are built upon capitalistic markets, private enterprise, and all three countries rank in top 25 of The Heritage Foundation's Index of Economic Freedom. By contrast, their highly-touted yet inefficient, resource-stressed "social programs" are derived by imposing a much greater tax burden (between 50 - 75%) on a skilled but dependent workforce, with a higher labor participation rate of 70 - 75%, that is culturally cohesive and demonstrates confidence in their government; a level of competence and cooperation foreign to many Washington bureaucrats who lacked the resolve to read Obamacare, to protect private healthcare/education, or to faithfully honor those "inalienable" rights and individual liberties enumerated by the Constitution.

In America, unlike so many other countries, there are countless paths to success – regardless of one's personal struggles, attributes or disposition. Don't breed spite and contempt for others because you have less; be angry you forgot "the pursuit of happiness" is ultimately incumbent upon your own choices and resolve. Yes, life is not fair, bad things happen to good people, but how much of that is due to our own accord? How does hating or taking from the more fortunate, many who earned the fruits of their labor, justify or change anything? A menial or "average" life in America is still much better than the everyday lives defining most other nations. Why else would entire families abandon their native countries, risking their very lives in the process, to come to the supposed capitalist lair of "greed"? Better yet, why are American politicians endeavoring to become more like those bankrupt and corrupt leftist regimes these immigrants are fleeing? The blessing of liberty does not dictate equal outcomes because free will is far more valuable than rationed rights or ransomed dependence. It infers that no one owes you but yourself because your potential is inherently limitless. Unfortunately, that's far too inconvenient of a concept for those socialists attempting to demonize dissenting speech and bribe the electorate with other people's money solely to win an election. Since when did "hope" require an enemy or success a notary of guilt?

The question pundits should be asking isn't whether capitalism is flawed or not – that which is most synonymous with freedom and upward mobility – for all ideologies are innately imperfect. Rather, where would a country sporting the size and populace of America be today without its unparalleled penchant for growth, independence and prosperity? How else did a newfound republic become the most affluent, revered and powerful nation in the world, without sacrificing individual rights or the people's quality of life, in less than two centuries? One only needs to look at Greece, Communist Cuba, most of the Middle East or any third world nation to witness the devastating effects caused by a lack of commerce, capital and/or infrastructure. Considering welfare recipients have jumped from 27 to 47 million between 2008 and 2016, over 95 million were absent from the U.S. workforce, our national debt has almost doubled to a record 20 trillion in only seven years despite collecting record tax revenue, while household income and home ownership continue to plummet, I missed the part where more entitlements and fewer of those evil, profitable businesses would help the American people. Yes, who in their right mind wouldn't elect a proud statist who praised the murderous legacy of totalitarianism, religiously demonized his native country, and didn't earn a steady paycheck until he was 40 years of age? Perhaps 'We the People' are just beginning to 'Feel the Bern' of socialism, or better yet, the crass exploitation of victimization politics. When limited government becomes a radical idea and personal responsibility is racist, perhaps it no longer matters. In other words, entitlement is quickly becoming our greatest export and unsustainable debt is the most likely candidate to sign America's death certificate.

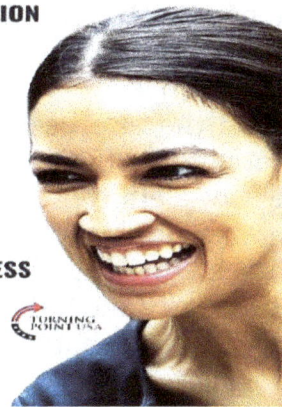

THE COST OF SOCIALISM

SOCIAL SECURITY EXPANSION
= $188 BILLION

FREE COLLEGE FOR ALL
= $807 BILLION

GUARANTEED JOB
= $6.8 TRILLION

MEDICARE FOR ALL
= $32 TRILLION

STUDENT LOAN FORGIVENESS
= $1.4 TRILLION

TOTAL COST
= $42.2 TRILLION

"If socialists understood economics they wouldn't be socialists." ~F.A. Hayek

Make Payable to America

What do you deem the actions of a "radical" President who creates over 7 million jobs in under 3 years as a record 6.7 million openings surpass unemployed applicants, lowers jobless claims to a 50-year-low and reduces minority unemployment to their lowest levels in history, induces a 400% increase in black-owned businesses, increases a nation's annual GDP by more than one trillion-dollars for the first time in world history, restores consumer confidence to a 20-year-high generating over $10 trillion in new stock market wealth, strengthens median household income to nearly $60,000, cuts taxes across the board to revitalize small business and the suffocated national staples of steel and coal, punishes American corporations that profit domestically but employ cheap or slave labor abroad, secures new or expanded foreign investment in American commercial ventures, refuses to accept disproportionate tariffs placed on American products, cuts foreign aid to militant regimes and anti-American organizations, eliminates government waste and two-thirds of bureaucratic red tape, and negotiates on behalf of US farmers to gain greater access to the restricted agricultural markets of the most populous country in the world...the over 1.4 billion residents of China? Common sense. In just over a year, "capitalism" and a maligned magnate have pulled America from the beginnings of a "welfare state" with a disenfranchised working class to a robust economy where businesses are struggling to find enough workers to fill good paying jobs.

Our Country is doing GREAT. Best financial numbers on the Planet. Great to have USA WINNING AGAIN!
🐦 @realDonaldTrump

No, common sense doesn't deserve a Blue Ribbon or a participation trophy, but it demands an honest media and appreciative workforce that understands the difference between a Chief Executive who works tirelessly to ensure ample opportunity – putting the interests, independence and livelihoods of the American people first – instead of accommodating those brooding socialists who merely view business as a necessary evil and individual prosperity as an imminent threat to government autonomy. Call me hopelessly old-fashioned but I'll always choose a loyal, fearless and competent CEO, even the infamously savvy Robber Baron, over a conniving body of global pawnbrokers issuing Utopian promissory notes for the permissible crumbs of intellectual conformity. One seeks personal advancement on his own accord, the second mortgages your soul.

Unlike the afforded walls of mediocrity, mankind's limitless potential and unrivaled creativity are the flammable tinder of economic liberty. Without incentive and reward, the work ethic of ingenuity and accountability cannot breathe. Being a responsible member of the world community does not require surrendering your nation's identity, financial sovereignty, nor does it include the right to control, dictate and siphon the labors of humanity under the collectivist banner of coerced political unity. And helping the needy and less fortunate does not require arresting prosperity at the finish line. Elitist arrogance, on the other hand, has already picked your "greedy" capitalist pocket in the "unidentifiable" name of the common good. The International Thieves Guild is always looking for naive donors.

The Exploitation of Unequal Taxation

It's common knowledge the socialist left would love nothing more than to excessively if not fatally tax wealthy individuals, private business owners and corporations who already account for over 80% of all duties collected; not to mention the countless jobs and disposable income their success inevitably generates. Regardless of what laws Congress may pass or what selective rules are used to justify such abuse, what gives our government the "constitutional" authority to tax one citizen more than another, one business or a specific industry more than the other? It is nothing more than discrimination, a violation of equal rights and equal protection under the law. Honestly, do these people toil or risk less? If every affluent household or aspiring entrepreneur went broke tomorrow, or even 5 years down the road, would they recoup their time, lost income or confiscated possessions from those disgruntled voters who supported such excessive taxation as a form of political protest; or more profoundly, compensated envy? Absolutely not. Such regressive reasoning makes about as much sense as a Death or Estate Tax, a government's soulless attempt to profit from the loss of a loved one, despite the fact citizens already pay income, social security, Medicare, property, state and/or sales taxes from adolescence through the duration of their adult lives.

LIBERALS THINK WE SHOULD BE EQUAL AT THE FINISH LINE.

CONSERVATIVES THINK WE SHOULD BE EQUAL AT THE STARTING LINE.

This very conundrum is why the 16th Amendment, in part, is unconstitutional; it provides no constraints or limitations on the methodology of exacting tax rates. Does a doctor earning $200,000 still not contribute more tax revenue than a Fast Food worker also paying a flat 10% fee? If we are all created equal, and not reduced to the progressive sliding scale of class, race, or gender appropriation, shouldn't our tax laws also reflect that founding principle and universal maxim? I myself have never been wealthy; however, if I were to come into money, I'd like to think I was entitled to keep my property and enjoy the earned fruits of my labor. That's what America was predicated upon; rewarding hard work and protecting individual rights, liberty, without the illicit intrusion of excessive government regulation and taxation. If Washington truly wants to reduce the record $9.5 trillion deficit Barack Obama accrued alone and restore the now politically incorrect American dream, they might start by cutting the trillions of dollars wasted on those improperly monitored socialist programs riddled with fraudulent claims, the continuous kickbacks of pork barrel projects, or by eliminating an indulgent caveat of Congressional perks; including, but not limited to, a lifetime pension and private healthcare for those elected officials serving only a single term in office.

While I willingly accept taxes are vital to public works and the civic/state/national infrastructure millions use on a daily basis, the methodology in which our government derives and collects these funds is as important as the manner in which they are allocated. The same progressive propagandists duping millennials into believing paying higher taxes is patriotic and society's solemn duty – i.e., their those responsible citizens and parents who work tirelessly for a better life – have no reservations taking bread off our tables to feed a corrupt, failed establishment that subsidizes illegal immigration, refuses to balance the budget or enforce a debt ceiling, and has aided and abetted terrorist regimes with no regard for the American people's safety or economic prowess. Why should those taxpayers already suffering the immediate consequences of such callous negligence bear the long-term costs of enabling Congress to bankrupt America and destroy private industry in the process; the greatest known vehicle of economic independence and upward mobility in Western Civilization?

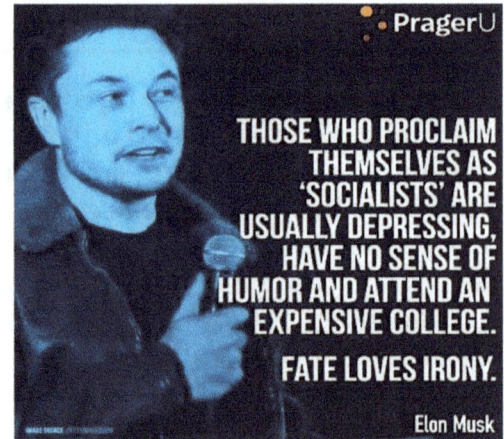

THOSE WHO PROCLAIM THEMSELVES AS 'SOCIALISTS' ARE USUALLY DEPRESSING, HAVE NO SENSE OF HUMOR AND ATTEND AN EXPENSIVE COLLEGE.

FATE LOVES IRONY.

Elon Musk

Whereas Bernie Sanders and Elizabeth Warren love to decry greed and the inevitable commercial goal of profit, just never the tangible reality the "dreaded 1%" pay 40% of all taxes, they both got rich off the "system" by convincing millions of able-bodied Americans they were "victims" because economic injustice and the natural inequality of achievement are somehow one in the same; and all despite regularly dining with fellow limousine liberals, sharing their campaign collection plates with donors earmarked for federal dollars, pandering to America's most affluent enemies, and turning corporate America and collegiate campuses into their political pulpit of private speaking fees. It is by no means a coincidence the ten most solvent and economically vibrant states also have the most-friendly tax codes and attractive investment packages: Texas and Wisconsin to name but a few. Adding and subtracting is not a revolutionary concept, nor is giving families a fertile environment to thrive, although expecting our elected officials to understand basic economics and act on the behalf of the people's interests is quickly becoming an extinct one.

Every senator and state representative, regardless of party affiliation, should be required by law to balance the budget or thus automatically become ineligible for re-election. Being it's the people's money to begin with, the liquidated seeds of our blood, sweat and tears, this is neither an unreasonable request or a rhetorical question inviting pointless debate. If every day Americans ran their affairs like the detached parasites plaguing Washington, they all would be destitute and homeless within a month; only "We the People" cannot simply print more money or shamelessly give ourselves a bailout at our neighbor's expense. If the buck truly stops here – at the fiscal crossing of common sense and accountability – our government should have been foreclosed years ago for entertaining the indoctrinated lie collectivism is a harbinger of prosperity and justice, rather than the oppressive aftermath of scheming bureaucrats attempting to discredit the individual attributes of hard work, ambition, talent and education to reconcile the Socratic revelation equal opportunity will never guarantee the Marxist fantasy of equal outcomes.

The $15 Question: Who the Hell Are You?

Do responsible Americans, excluding the unemployed socialists protesting the cost of Xbox live in their parents' basements, actually believe private enterprise is obligated to share or "redistribute" their profits with the general public; albeit paid employees, the unemployed or complete strangers? If I have a job and my neighbor doesn't, or God forbid I make more money, am I obligated to give this person a percentage of my income? Is "Bob" going to give me his money if I lose my job and become homeless? Hell no! People open businesses to make money...period! It's not rocket science or a Right-Wing conspiracy. It's called risk, work, reward!

If a business or an individual is concerned about economic inequality, wants to donate a percentage of their profits or income to charity, that's their personal choice. No one – not the government, politicians or celebrities – has the right to tell you how to allocate your own property. Otherwise, these offended activists can open their own establishment, dig deep into their own pockets, and doll out every last dollar to whomever their baroque hearts' desire. These smug propagandists will single out Corporate America as capitalist marauders, the purveyors of the poor, yet make no mention of entertainers, actors, and athletes who command astronomical salaries by fleecing struggling Americans with outrageous ticket and merchandising prices. But that's not capitalism, right? Right?! If you have the gall to accept those million-dollar endorsements, have the brass tacks to admit you're a convicted hypocrite who decries homelessness by shopping for "economic justice" on Rodeo Drive. The more able-bodied Americans no longer provide for themselves, prefer to drown in self-pity or willingly become a burden on society, the quicker our only remaining vessel of economic independence sinks.

$15 PER HOUR

BECAUSE OUR JOBS ARE THE SAME

Capitalism may be the convenient scapegoat of socialists who want to ensure your dependence on Big Government, but it is by far the most synonymous with liberty, opportunity and prosperity. In a market economy, the only limits or chains one must shed is that of their own device. If the armies of entitlement are going to orchestrate public demonstrations and demand $15-an-hour jobs for unskilled, fast food workers, perhaps they should start by buying their iPhone mafia a mirror. There are construction grunts who bust their back every day and don't make that much money. If you truly want a better job, try building a thriving business from scratch, educate yourself, learn a trade, or gain valuable experience by working your way up the proverbial ladder; anything besides standing on a corner and bemoaning your "woe is me" Twitter status. No one is forcing you to live in poverty, pay rent in Seattle or to work at McDonald's. That, my friend, is entirely of your own choosing. For every city ordinance that recently turned the concept of minimum wage into a legalized form of political extortion, there is a cemetery of small businesses who paid their "fair share" without as much as a solitary thank you card or a single, deferred tax credit. But who's counting, right? If your future prospects require soliciting "guilt" or protesting "white privilege" to get paid, you don't deserve to get paid because minimum wage was never intended to be anything but pocket change. Just don't make me pay $15 for a Big Mac because you refuse to accept what every right-minded American already knows: life is unfair, there are no magic rainbows, and no one owes you a damn thing except yourself! In other words, just like two centuries of Americans before you, get off your ass and make it happen. Until then, get off my lawn! You have to EARN that right.

More Taxes, Please: Said No One Ever!

Tax relief is now officially a reality and by some inexplicable twist of luck, nobody has died from spontaneous economic growth, the Earth is still round hand no working American is being deprived the right to earn a living; unless, that is, the media is referring to those federal money launderers rewarding envy, inciting class warfare, and getting rich by punishing success to achieve their socialist wet dream of permanent electoral control through forced mass dependency. Ask almost any economist or financial expert and they'll explain how tax cuts increase disposable income/ profits, fuel greater commercial investment, foster more opportunities for workers and entrepreneurs, which ultimately creates more private wealth.

Not only will the entire middle-class benefit from the most significant tax reduction in over 30 years, the newly designated corporate tax rate of 21% is now competitive with the rest of the world; including those destitute countries that use cheap labor to harbor American companies like Apple and Nike. Instead of being mindlessly berating those who pay a bulk of American duties, who create the most jobs, and donate the largest endowments to public/private institutions, perhaps we should be thankful these successful individuals and businesses even exist. The fact not one Democrat voted to lower your taxes should be as disturbing as it is indicative of the party's rapid regression. If Donald Trump is willing to sign a bill that will effectively raise his own tax rates to lessen the burden for over 90% of the American people, shouldn't every Congressional member making a six-figure salary, at a minimum, be willing to do the same? The fact not one Democrat voted to lower your taxes should be as disturbing as it is indicative of their party's rapid regression which once extolled the patriotism and prosperity of such economic freedom under JFK.

Considering the Obama administration nearly doubled the national debt despite collecting record tax revenue between 2009 and 2016, it's about damn time "We the People" were allowed to enjoy more of the fruits of their own labor. Contrary to Marxist hypnotists, paying high taxes isn't patriotic; it's apathetic, ignorant and an indoctrinated excuse for anti-American statists to redistribute your blood, sweat, and tears in the name of social justice by spending billions on terrorist nations, clearly favored non-citizens, and those senseless progressive projects designed to demonize our ideological heritage. For how long have wealthy bureaucrats bathed in a dirty river of misappropriated funds – your property, income and social security taxes – solely to reward party operatives/donors, live the 1% lifestyle and to feed their criminal sexual appetite? While you go to jail for unpaid parking tickets or for refusing to pay an "individual mandate" infringing upon your individual rights, the political establishment dines on the remnants of an increasingly disregarded Constitution. Unless "Death before Taxes" is no longer incumbent to the founding of our Republic and a prerequisite of limited government, then by all means feel free to send a monthly check of your hard-earned money to Washington, DC. And since no one in their right mind would resort to such an idiotic gesture, why spread such vicious propaganda about its elementary necessity by ignoring our historical aversion to Big Government? The only thing remotely scandalous about affordable taxes is the inability of millions of partisan contrarians to realize excessive taxation is theft and that our rogue government rarely puts anyone's interests in front of its own agenda.

"A tax cut means higher family income and higher business profits and a balanced federal budget. ... As national income grows, the federal government will ultimately end up with more revenues. Prosperity is the real way to balance our budget. By lowering tax rates, by increasing jobs and income, we can expand tax revenues and finally bring our budget into balance."
— John F. Kennedy

Volunteering Your Neighbor's Money

If so many on the left, specifically younger adults, are so dead-set on socialism then give every single advocate the "honorable" option for their income, investments and fixed assets to be taxed at a 50-75% rate. Of course, almost none of their hypocritical ranks will honor their so-called principles because their true goal is to legally fleece more ambitious, accountable and/or accomplished Americans to provide life's basic amenities and unearned privileges for complete strangers. And what does complacency, ignorance or jealousy risk by demanding free entitlements for simply living in their parents' basement or refusing to do everything in their power to succeed? Absolutely nothing.

Collectivists use the social justice facade of free college, health care and a universal living income to justify excessively taxing businesses and more affluent citizens because they despise the individual freedom, personal responsibility, and natural incentive of capitalism. It is limitless, transcendent and threatens the fiscal monopoly of bureaucratic demagogues. In other words, only by imposing socialized programs usurping the labors, work ethic and wealth of the people can a conspiring cabal of progressive elitists control millions of independent voters through forced dependency and centralized indoctrination to a singular political agenda. If you're wondering why so many European nations continue to be ruled by progressive leaders and parties despite the destructive fallout from unchecked immigration and unsustainable economic practices, it's because they have a virtual stranglehold on public education, the press and their populaces' cultivated need for continuous government assistance. Rousseau said it best....man is free but everywhere he is chains. Where else but the human trafficking playground of liberal academia does helping the poor, the less fortunate, demand surrendering your rights and property to a corrupt ruling class in order to remedy the natural inequities of human achievement? I will always choose manifest destiny, the volition to forge my own path and a better future for my family, over the extorted price of equally shared misery.

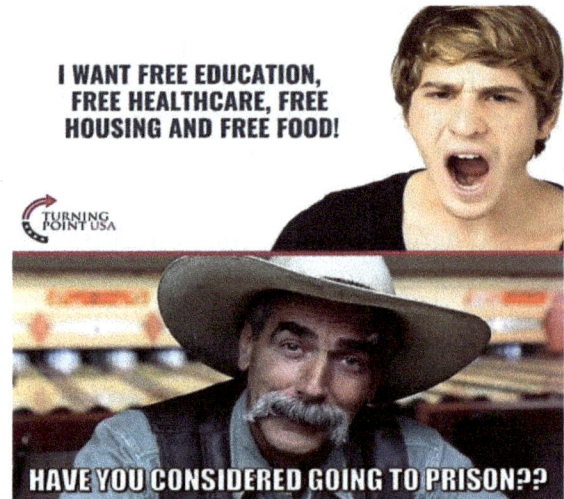

Democrats Blast "Reckless" Job Boom

Lord, please stop the "terror" of an expanding private sector, lower taxes, higher median household income, half-a-million new manufacturing jobs, rebounding home ownership, fewer bureaucratic regulations and the unreported "nuisance" 600,000 Americans have entered the workforce in less than two years. And here I foolishly hoped goodwill and good fortune - a strong, reciprocal economy with limitless opportunity - transcended petty politics and party lines. When fellow Americans cannot even agree of the universal benefits and constitutional staples of individual liberty, open markets, "fair" trade and limited government, we're literally two foreign populaces forced to play tug-of-war on the same burning island.

Budgets & Bureaucrats

Whereas the lapdog media loves to proclaim Barack Obama magically lowered the deficit – i.e., losing less at the casino after each subsequent trip – the Marxist maestro of mass dependence actually ran huge deficits every year of his deceptive tenure. I also find it amusing tax-and-spend liberals are now so publicly concerned about the national debt when their social justice savior raised it by over $9.5 trillion dollars or an amount nearly equal to all other previous Presidents combined; not counting near the $500 billion dollar bailout of Wall Street under George Bush after affirmative action Democrats, building on the 1970's Community Reinvestment Act and exasperated by the Clinton deregulation of lending requirements in the 1990's, fueled a historic collapse of subprime loans.

And what did Mr. "Hope and Change" give hard-working American families in return for his reckless deluge? A public assistance payroll which jumped from 26 to 47 million welfare recipients in 5 years, an anemic 1.6% GDP for 8 years, the inept Obamacare experiment which hyper-inflated private premiums, failed "green energy" projects like Solyndra, the infamous "Cash for Clunkers" environmental ruse, a costly GM bailout which produced the defunct Chevy Volt and federal nepotism, the clearly-illicit Obamaphone voter bribery scheme, hundreds of billions in foreign aid sent to terrorist regimes or funneled back into the pockets of his "common good" constituents, unauthorized funds used to interfere with Israeli elections, and a refugee program which transported, housed and/or provided for thousands of noncitizens at taxpayer expense; even granting unearned Social Security benefits for some "guests" nearly three times greater than most veterans.

As a fiscal conservative, I adamantly believe an annual, mandatory balanced budget should be read, debated and passed without exception. While it is true the deficit has increased by roughly 3 trillion since Donald Trump took office, the President has yet to pass his own signature budget; one that includes extensive welfare reform, ends congressional kickbacks, cancels aid to all foreign enemies and terminates a number of wasteful, federal projects. The infamous Omnibus bill which recently drew so much ire from conservatives alike was merely a reluctant compromise between Democrats and the White House to increase military funding – modernization capital, including higher base pay with improved VA benefits – and expand construction of the Border Wall.

I hate to be the bearer of bad news, but without a sizable majority in each Congressional chamber, President Trump will probably never possess the means to pass a sound, responsible, deficit-reducing budget. Despite the fact Republicans currently hold a 53-to-47 advantage in the Senate, and their ranks controlled the House for two years, at least five RINO Senators are vocal obstructionists who oppose substantial cuts and routinely side with their progressive counterparts. Therefore, as the media predictably stirs the pot of public perception to proclaim Donald Trump is bankrupting America and breaking his campaign promises, the man cannot achieve the type of fiscal reform America desperately needs without first causing a lengthy shutdown – which still may not change any votes except those employees/citizens angered by the loss of their paycheck – or until "We the People" begin electing more fiscally-conscious politicians who understand the Constitutional precept of limited government.

The Domestic Sellouts of Foreign Tributes

When the truth is offensive, the more the socialist sensitivities of propagandists like Mr. Trudeau are insulted. And this is exactly why so many voted for our unapologetic President. He's willing to say whatever needs to be said, fight for his country's best interests, while his predecessors passively accepted or even praised the senseless status quo. Leadership is not, nor should it ever be, a cordial welcome mat to mass exploitation. The more the anti-American New World Order cries and throws public tantrums, the more their once uncontested grip on power, factual reality, slips through their collective, sweaty grasp. Sorry John McCain and John Brennan...Donald Trump is far from an embarrassment, mentally ill or an aberration; he is a desperately-needed awakening as to the despotic depths your globalist ranks are willing to deceive and cajole the fleeced families, independence, of this once rudderless nation.

Donald J. Trump ✔ @realDon... ·12m ⌄
PM Justin Trudeau of Canada acted so meek and mild during our @G7 meetings only to give a news conference after I left saying that, "US Tariffs were kind of insulting" and he "will not be pushed around." Very dishonest & weak. Our Tariffs are in response to his of 270% on dairy!

💬 3,821   ↻ 3,453   ♡ 10.7K   ⬆

Donald J. Trump ✔ @realDon... ·14m ⌄
Based on Justin's false statements at his news conference, and the fact that Canada is charging massive Tariffs to our U.S. farmers, workers and companies, I have instructed our U.S. Reps not to endorse the Communique as we look at Tariffs on automobiles flooding the U.S. Market!

Perhaps our Northern business partners should refresh the Prime Minister's mistaken memory because America alone accounts for over 90% of Canada's total exports; or roughly $296 billion in revenue. China is second at a scant $15.8 billion. Unless media pundits and whining bureaucrats are willing to pay a 50% or God forbid a 300% excise tax levied on their home or car in the open marketplace, they're simply talking out of the wrong end. American consumers are traditionally far more vital to the success of foreign companies than the collective purchasing power their populaces provide to our private sector. This is largely due to consumer preference and regional devotion to native firms, as well as a matter of affordability resulting from absurd duties placed on American goods. If the discerning public chooses an international product through the natural rigors of competition and expectation, without strategic roadblocks and tribute fees, so be it. At least the playing field is level, based on equal opportunity rather than treating U.S. commerce as the world's largest communal piggy bank.

Since the latter has been official G7 policy for some time now, it's abundantly clear grossly disproportionate tariffs have become the preferred street hustle for exacting wealth redistribution: a convenient guise for shifting global influence or addressing perceived historical inequities via a form of economic reparations. Considering America's annual trade gap regularly surpassed $500 billion under previous administrations – over $350 billion and $150 billion-dollar deficits to China and the European Union respectively – why would any elected politician continue to accept, dare I say submit, to such inane terms? Because America's commercial health has long been a bellwether for the world economy, it's of little surprise a deep recession ensued after our trade deficit topped $700 billion for four consecutive years between 2005 and 2008.

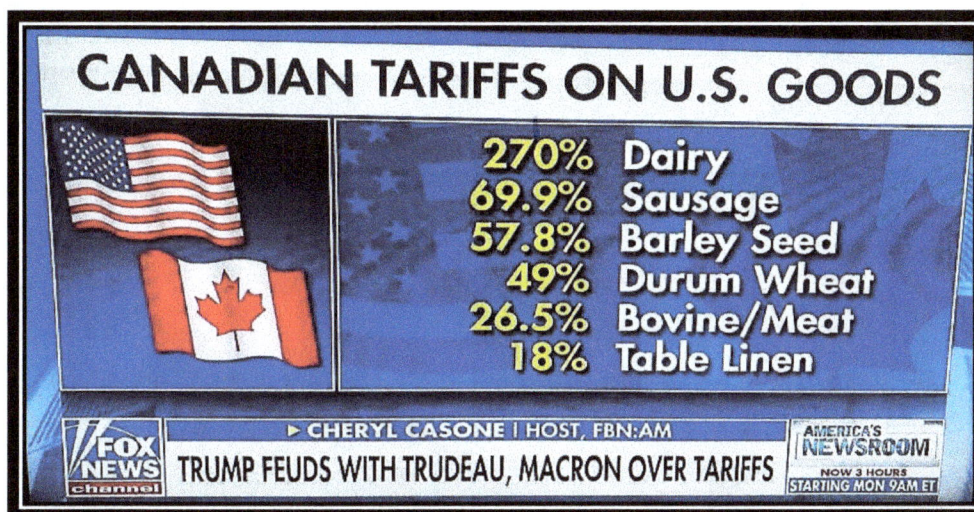

CANADIAN TARIFFS ON U.S. GOODS

270% Dairy
69.9% Sausage
57.8% Barley Seed
49% Durum Wheat
26.5% Bovine/Meat
18% Table Linen

FOX NEWS channel
▶ CHERYL CASONE I HOST, FBN:AM
TRUMP FEUDS WITH TRUDEAU, MACRON OVER TARIFFS
AMERICA'S NEWSROOM
NOW 3 HOURS STARTING MON 9AM ET

The U.S. economy, whose GDP is greater than the sum of all other G7 countries combined, is the undisputed bellwether for global prosperity. If being mercilessly swindled now constitutes "protectionist" policies, what's the sensationalist headline for consciously penalizing American industry and labor for decades: "love hurts"? Fair Trade isn't a negotiation, it's a prerequisite for doing your elected job, sound fiscal growth, but more profoundly for instinctively putting the American people first. And it's about damn time someone actually had the unflinching nerve to accept accountability.

Table for Two

The White House has announced the much-maligned NAFTA accord has been scrapped for a more equitable economic deal - The United States-Mexico Trade Agreement - aiding American farmers, increasing wages for Mexican workers and keeping manufacturing jobs in North America. As a result, the Dow Jones Industrial Average rose 260 points and The Nasdaq Composite climbed 1% to an all-time record, breaking 8,000 for the first time ever. After Trump's successful renegotiations with the EU and Mexico, it seems Mr. Trudeau is now on the outside looking in...at his own obstinance and ignorance. Successful executives deliver results while career politicians cater to bankrupt ideologies. Nevertheless, there is always room at the board table for those willing to learn the elementary difference between greatness and groveling.

The Trillion Dollar Question

For those misled millennials hopelessly enamored with the idea of living in a socialist country and implementing radical environmental reforms at any cost, I have but one question. If American taxpayers had the uncontested choice of funding or rejecting these poorly construed policies, how many would voluntarily surrender more of their income to the most wasteful, inept and corrupt institution in America; the U.S. federal government? My guess is less than 10% of employed and retired citizens, which merely validates the reality the left's infatuation with centralized control is not about any moral imperative or global emergency, but a sick obsession with forcing successful businesses, political opponents and hard-working families to pay for an overwhelming majority of their social justice, science fiction, Ponzi schemes; that which would eventually lead to suffocating debt, mass inflation, record immigration, unparalleled dependence to coerce voters, and economic collapse.

Donald J. Trump ✔
@realDonaldTrump

The United States and European Union have a $1 TRILLION trade relationship - the largest partnership in the world. We want to further strengthen this relationship to the benefit of all American and European citizens...

8:14

You cannot assert leverage on those foreign countries defrauding American industry if your apologist mindset refuses to acknowledge there's a problem in the first place. A successful Chief Executive does not accept appeasement, mediocrity or the failed status quo to avoid confrontation. He demands more for the labors of his people.

Dollars & Sense: Because Facts Matter

Allow me to divulge a few friendly details about a certain former President having the audacity to take credit for America's current economic resurgence. Why? Because facts matter!

America will never see 3% economic growth again!

I take the credit for Trump's 4% economic growth!

Dixon Diaz 09/08/2018

Barack Obama never enjoyed a single annualized growth rate of 3% and his 1.6% average was the lowest since World War II. Likewise, welfare recipients skyrocketed from 27 to 47 million, he nearly doubled the national debt from 10.5 to 19.5 trillion – surpassing 100% of our total GDP and roughly the equivalent of all other presidents combined – despite collecting record tax revenue from the highest number of domestic regulations/duties ever imposed, the coal industry nearly went bankrupt as promised, and America suffered its first two credit downgrades in our nation's history. And for the record, the unemployment rate only fell significantly during his second term because the U.S workforce suffered the largest mass exodus since the Great Depression; an estimated 14.5 million Americans freshly excluded from the true jobless equation by Jan 2017. The man was an unmitigated disaster for our economy but a hero to socialists and Marxists because his true goal was to dismantle private enterprise, foster mass dependency and redistribute other people's hard-earned money in the name of social justice: an insatiable hatred for our founding Judeo-Christian heritage, our rapid global ascendancy, and most notably, that innovative, transcendent catalyst most synonymous with liberty which made it all possible. Otherwise known as capitalism.

The Path to Prosperity

Consumer confidence has risen to its highest since December of 2000. The DOW has set over 70 new benchmarks since the election, even surpassing 26,000, and subsequently has added over 6 trillion dollars to the economy. Exports hit a new, all-time benchmark as the President successfully negotiated a 380-billion-dollar ANNUAL reduction in our trade deficit with our greatest commercial competitor, China; the largest such decrease in US History. Food stamp enrollment is the lowest in 8 years. Home prices have hit record highs, registering a 6% annual gain. The unemployment rate has dropped to 3.9%, jobless claims are at their lowest level since 1973, while Black and Hispanic unemployment are now at historic lows. One and half million fewer Americans are on public assistance. The US has not only enjoyed consecutive quarters of over 3% GDP growth, but

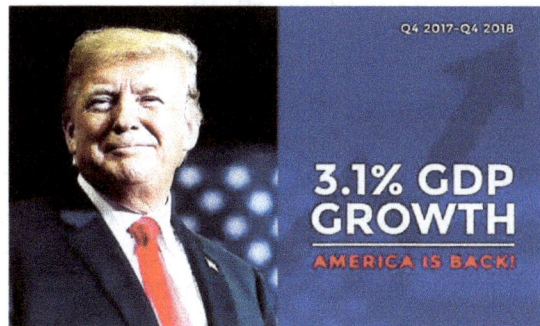

Q4 2017-Q4 2018

3.1% GDP GROWTH

AMERICA IS BACK!

also surpassed 4% expansion; and all despite two devastating hurricanes, wildfires and the anti-business trust of California, New York and Illinois. And all this without a new budget in effect to aggressively lower the national debt or sweeping tax cuts to trigger even greater investment and expansion. Just imagine what Donald Trump could accomplish if 95% of media coverage didn't purposely mislead the public, Democrats sought constructive discourse over scorched earth politics or 100% of his own party was dedicated to passing much needed legislative reforms. As our President continues to trim the endless Red Tape of excessive bureaucracy and federal overreach, I'd say such impressive initial progress more than qualifies as a worthy opening act for "Making America Great Again".

"I think one way you get rid of Trump is a crashing economy. So please, bring on the recession. Sorry if that hurts people but it's either root for a recession, or you lose your democracy."
-Bill Maher

If you're interested in genuine economic upward mobility for individuals and families and not runaway statism dividing the fruits of other people's labor, then true vitality and independence reside in a robust and diverse private sector. When a fertile environment for commercial growth produces more profitable businesses and quality jobs for an ever-industrious populace, people are far more likely to own their own home, buy their own health care, and properly provide for their children. Unless you believe billions in taxpayers' hard-earned money should be used almost exclusively as a means to an end – inviting mass dependency by rewarding envy and apathy to the point of federal insolvency and bankruptcy – why would you empower the most inept, corrupt and wasteful institution in America; or in socialist terms, legalize theft and the equal division of misery in a country predicated upon limited government? Considering no nation has ever taxed itself into prosperity and the top 20% of earners now pay well over 90% of all income taxes, as recently confirmed by the Office of Management and Budget, I believe "fair share" should equate to the amount of personal responsibility people accept for their own lives; including the greatest usurpers and domestic abusers of all, the Washington establishment. Once you realize a majority of globalists would rather watch America burn than Donald Trump succeed – our founding ideals, economic prowess and sovereign identity survive – the only acceptable path forward is a free republic's unflinching resolve denying political arsonists a match.

Teaching Men to Fish

Avg. Annual Real GDP Growth by President, Post-WWII

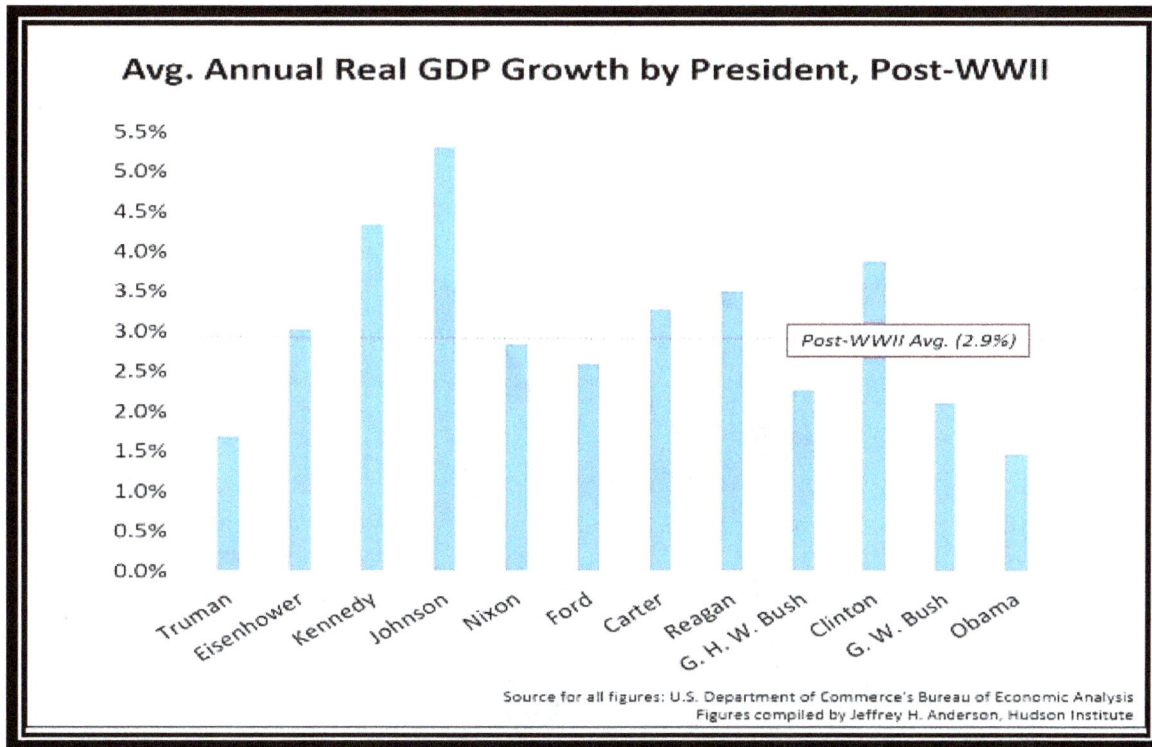

Post-WWII Avg. (2.9%)

Source for all figures: U.S. Department of Commerce's Bureau of Economic Analysis
Figures compiled by Jeffrey H. Anderson, Hudson Institute

The media's favorite punching bag, the 45th President of the United States, just sealed a $109 billion-dollar deal in military sales with Saudi Arabia, which includes a commitment of an additional $250 billion in commercial investment that will secure hundreds of thousands new American jobs. Considering Trump has literally created half a million jobs and boasts a GDP of 4% in in just 5 months of work, his proactive approach merely confirms his predecessor was either deliberately sabotaging our economy or was simply incompetent. The conveniently misplaced fact Barack Obama lost roughly 300,000 manufacturing jobs during two terms in office and his career 1.6% GDP growth rate was the most anemic since Herbert Hoover and the fourth worst in U.S. history, illustrates how inept and destructive his policies were to the American people. Once you digest the uncooked truth food stamp recipients rose by 20 million between 2009 and 2017, median household income dropped by over $2,500 and the Marxist in Chief raised the national debt almost as much as all other presidents combined, it doesn't take a rocket scientist to realize capitalism and a healthy private sector are the most synonymous with liberty, opportunity and upward mobility. Entitlement, excuses and self-pity never built a home, provided clean drinking water or spurred the most transcendent discoveries in human history. If necessity is the mother of all invention, apathy is the father of futility.

The business of America has always been business because accountability and hard work are not incumbent upon one's race, religion, education, political affiliation or economic disposition. Both attributes are, however, fundamental cogs of a vibrant, sufficient and moral society. For every minute a profane feminist, political propagandist or social justice warrior wastes blaming others for the nature of his or her plight, they could be diligently working towards overcoming those inevitable obstacles that are part of everyday life. In other words, everyone of able body and mind owes to themselves, their family and their country to work and be part of the solution, contribute to a robust and solvent population, instead of becoming resigned to the problem itself. If Donald Trump the greedy "collusionist" is so hopelessly ignorant as the media loves to suggest, he accomplishes more in a morning of "privileged bliss" than those pesky details of real success his omnipotent critics conspire so tirelessly to dismiss. Or perhaps he should apologize for using his unique talents to pursue good paying jobs that can literally transform generations of his fellow citizens' lives.

AMERICAN GREATNESS

LOWEST OVERALL UNEMPLOYMENT RATE SINCE 2000
LOWEST AFRICAN AMERICAN RATE IN HISTORY
LOWEST HISPANIC AMERICAN RATE IN HISTORY
LOWEST ASIAN AMERICAN RATE IN HISTORY
LOWEST FEMALE RATE SINCE 2000
LOWEST MALE RATE SINCE 2000
LOWEST TEENAGE RATE SINCE 2000

An American President that does not protect and help create quality American jobs is no friend of the American people. There is a stark difference between a proven business executive who understands economics and a bitter political propagandist who seeks to punish America and redistribute private wealth out of an ingrained hatred for our heritage, affluence and unrivaled global influence. You can't lead a nation into financial security, embody accountability and self-reliance, when you believe millions of able-bodied adults are owed a "fair share" of the fruits of other people's hard work, without sharing the same level of personal risk and sacrifice, simply because of one's race, nationality or the inevitable pitfalls in life. Equal rights, opportunity, does not dictate equal achievement or outcome. Reality does not bend to the detached delusions of modern academia fostering a generation of "traumatized", entitled, and intolerant thugs who sanctimoniously judge the world through the myopic keyholes of color, gender, class, political affiliation or religion; those career malcontents who falsely claim injustice, incite discord and who believe logic is a subjective construct of personal convenience. Rather, reality exposes these radicalized factions as the greatest living threat to those responsible Americans wanting nothing more than to grow old in a free, proud, moral and prosperous society.

Underlying most arguments against the free market is a lack of belief in freedom itself. *~Milton Friedman*

The Socialist Wonder Twins

To the bitter, anti-American socialist duo of Sanders & Warren...

Forget Wall Street – those legal entities that actually create jobs and individual wealth by earning the fruits of their labor – nothing poisons or oppresses the poor more than your socialist victimization propaganda which insinuates people are not accountable for their own lives or actions. After all, how does one get exiled from a 'peace and love' hippie commune for lethargy, while the other shamelessly invokes her fraudulent Native American heritage solely to pander to cultural stereotypes? I'll take personal responsibility and respect for my intelligence, rather than the ploys of social justice parasites who keep millions living in fear, poverty and ignorance. When's the last time self-pity built a road, a home, a school or a municipality? Not only did entrepreneurs, fearless innovators and 'evil' corporations build America by risking failure and financial ruin, sacrificing their time and utilizing their acquired skills, their ingenuity and ambition generated the tax revenue required to fuel your socialist utopia of blame, entitlement and redistribution in a country predicated upon limited government. So yeah, not to 'bust' your tax bracket, capitalism is not only your fiscal 'daddy', it built your suburban homes and pays for your "uncommon" salaries.

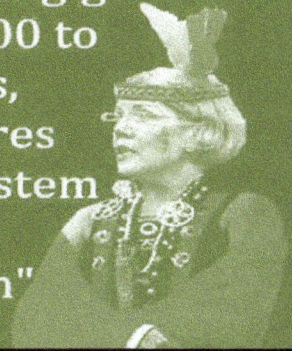

Senator Liz Warren lives in a $5.4M mansion, claimed "Native American" status to score a Harvard gig paying $350,000 to teach one class, and now lectures us that "the system is rigged to benefit the rich"

I'll take a corporate CEO who offers me the opportunity to provide a better life for my family, even develop watershed products or life-saving technologies, than an insatiable, corrupt government leviathan that ransoms liberty and defines dignity by the number of breadcrumbs it spreads on its social contract of self-admitted 'white privilege' and criminal 'greed'. Yes, please excuse me while I choose manifest destiny, salute the flag of my protected freedoms, unconditionally hold all Americans equally accountable, wear this nation's founding faith on my sleeve, and teach my children that culture cleansing leftists are now the clear majority stockholders of 'hate': i.e., social justice terrorists who believe successful, wealthy citizens are more of a threat to our well-being and survival than crooked politicians, Islam, illegal immigration, urban crime, reverse racism, colleges silencing free speech, the national debt, a society that conditions children to question their gender, or cross-dressing men who cannot respect the right to privacy of women and little girls. Sorry but I don't need a 'safe space' from the 'micro-aggressions' of truth to make the right choice. Your antagonistic and asinine rhetoric already made it for me.

Socialists ignore the side of man that is the spirit.
They can provide you with shelter, fill your belly
with bacon and beans, treat you when you're ill, all
the things guaranteed to a prisoner or a slave.
They don't understand that we also dream.
--Ronald Wilson Reagan

A Paid Recess from Reality

What's the difference between prudence and pandering? Prudence is rooted in reason, reality, while the latter typically preys upon the fears, misconceptions and misfortunes of others to produce a desired result: i.e., a vote. As misinformed politicians continue to invoke "income equality" as a rallying cry for a $15 minimum wage, they fail to mention one inconvenient truth: minimum wage was never intended to serve as a living wage. It was merely intended as the baseline hourly rate of compensation for those entry level workers with no discernible skills...such as high school or college students looking to make extra pocket change. If angry and envious activists are successful in recklessly raising the minimum wage by over $5, then they need to take responsibility for three inevitable consequences: small businesses will close in droves damaging an already atrophying private sector, retail chains will resort to widespread layoffs by consolidating their number of stores to remain profitable, and increased costs will trigger hyperinflation across the board. It's not a conspiracy, it's not unbridled greed; it's called economics. No politics required!

> **Charlie Kirk** ✓
> @charliekirk11
>
> .@AOC's mom recently moved from NYC to Florida citing high taxes, like the ones her daughter proposes
>
> She said: "It was a no-brainer. I was paying $100,000/yr in property taxes there. I'm paying $600/yr in Florida"
>
> High taxes hurt her own family yet she still supports them?

There is no shame in needing help time to time, we all do, and the minimum wage should be reasonably raised periodically as the cost of living increases. However, if someone truly wants to improve their financial prospects and job security, they must take the initiative of learning a trade, going to college, or working his or her way up the proverbial ladder to secure a higher wage. There is no magic rainbow unless you realize the timeless adage "no one owes you except yourself" is the only pot of liquidated gold waiting for the accountable and industrious. In the words and wisdom of your grandparents, the problem with all that "Free Stuff" – college education, health care, welfare, and exaggerated menial wages – is that it is never free; except in the speeches and pamphlets of aspiring traveling salesmen. "We the People", just like those in struggling socialist countries, will eventually pay with our jobs, independence, and by giving 50% or more of our income to the government – those bureaucrats who cannot even balance the budget (19 trillion & counting) while ordinary citizens lose their homes over a few missed mortgage payments – as the scarcity and prices of the products and services you need to survive grow amidst endless regulation and taxation. Accessibility to healthcare and higher education are indeed universal rights; as is the obligation to pay for it without expecting your neighbor, whether more successful or not, to pick up the tab against their will or in violation of their individual rights. You cannot multiple wealth by dividing it and you cannot legislate the poor into equality by legislating the wealthy out of freedom.

No, the American dream isn't dead because everyone isn't floating down a sparkling river of opulence and basking beneath the spoils of social media stardom. It's only dead when adults actually believe handouts, unearned benefits and wages, are more acceptable than

ALL iN FAVOR oF TAX CUTS RAiSe YouR RiGHT HAND...

hard work and when spoiled children no longer realize the greatest blessings in life do not require WiFi or safe spaces from accountability. Considering the number of welfare recipients and the national debt has nearly doubled since 2008, it is only a matter of time before opportunity becomes synonymous with oppression as America suffocates beneath unsustainable obligations. This is why the best social program is, and always will be, a job; it inherently pays for itself. When the incentive of opening a business, or becoming a doctor, is siphoned by Big Government in the name of the 'common good', competition and innovation are but a distant casualty as you wait in line for communal health care or a loaf of bread that is made by only a select few companies. There is a reason why crime hates competition; both require a willing and ignorant victim. Why again are hard-working Americans are jailed for unpaid parking tickets or taxes while elected politicians – those career civil servants who lie ad nauseam, drive us to the precipice of financial ruin, give billions to terrorist nations and use class/race warfare to the virtual extinction of common sense – can act with re-electable impunity? Simple...because we allow it!

If America, that nation which became the most influential and affluent nation in less than two centuries under the roar of economic liberty and independence, is in need of anything it is in the form of a mirror. By holding everyone to the same standard, honoring both our founding Constitutional values and our personal responsibilities, we'd systematically solve most of our problems while spending a lot less time wiping the noses of whiny millennials crying tears of entitlement for a used-car salesman who became student council president by promising free lunches, guilt-free classrooms, and a permanent paid recess from reality. Only one requires you to think for yourself without carpooling to the "Occupy Wall Street" rally to protest those evil, job producing corporations that are most likely fueling your 401k's portfolio.

Save America

"You cannot legislate the poor into equality
by legislating the wealthy out of freedom.
What one person receives without working for,
another person must work for without receiving.
When half of the people realize they do not
have to work because the other half is going to
take care of them, and when the other half realizes
it does no good to work because somebody else
is going to enjoy the fruits of their labor,
that my dear friend, is the end of any nation.
You cannot multiply wealth by dividing it."

In A New York Minute

The Big Apple is teetering on the verge bankruptcy and yet Big Government cheerleaders still can't comprehend why American taxpayers are tired of being fleeced for all these highly-inept and wasteful social programs. With more and more hardworking families and businesses fleeing the excessive tax codes of Blue states, it's only a matter of time before California and New York go bankrupt because those who benefit the most, illegal immigrants included, don't contribute near enough to cover their expenses. Finland recently learned that painful fact after their entire government cabinet resigned due to the unsustainable cost of universal care, welfare and higher education. These policies will be even more of a catastrophic failure if delusional socialists like Bernie Sanders and Ocasio-Cortez successfully enact single-payer healthcare, free college tuition and radical environmental reforms nationwide. You can't cross the raging river when only 3 are rowing while the other 7 are demanding concessions.

PROGRESSIVE "COMPASSION" IN PRACTICE

TOP 5 CITIES BY POVERTY RATE

1. **DETROIT** - 32%
   MAYOR: DEMOCRAT

2. **PHOENIX** - 26.5%
   MAYOR: DEMOCRAT

3. **PHILADEPHIA** - 20.9%
   MAYOR: DEMOCRAT

4. **NEW YORK** - 17.9%
   MAYOR: DEMOCRAT

5. **CHICAGO** - 15.7%
   MAYOR: DEMOCRAT

TOP 5 CITIES BY VIOLENT CRIME RATE
PER 100,000 PEOPLE

1. **DETROIT** - 1,989
   MAYOR: DEMOCRAT

2. **MEMPHIS** - 1,741
   MAYOR: DEMOCRAT

3. **OAKLAND** - 1,685
   MAYOR: DEMOCRAT

4. **ST. LOUIS** - 1,679
   MAYOR: DEMOCRAT

5. **BIRMINGHAM** - 1,588
   MAYOR: DEMOCRAT

PragerU.com

SOURCE: BROOKINGS INSTITUTION

SOURCE: FBI 2014 CRIME STATISTICS.

Democratic Socialism & the Mayor of Mudville

When is the last time Bernie Sanders, the Maestro of Malcontent, said anything good or remotely endearing about America? He demonizes our heritage, embraces gender and class warfare, mocks morality and incites the political sham that is Black Lives Matter: those sacrificed Democratic pawns who murder one another with far more regularity and callous indifference than any other race. Anyone who praises Communist Cuba and calls Islam a peaceful religion is disturbingly disconnected, has no appreciation of natural-born liberty and is completely oblivious to the timeless ideals America was founded upon. In other words, Senator Sanders is just like Barack Obama: he's but another spiteful, race-baiting, anti-American statist who feeds off anger, excuses and envy. Because misery loves company, half-baked propaganda dipped in spoon-fed animosity, forgive me while I pass on the spiked fruitcake of self-pity! The self-proclaimed spokesman of the common people didn't even earn a steady paycheck until he was 53 years of age; no wonder he's so comfortable giving away other people's money. Self-reliance, a hard day's work, means nothing to a man who has never earned his keep. Whining Bernie Sanders is the epitome of the entitled 60's radical who destroyed the once fiercely-patriotic party of JFK. Quoting Karl Marx and cursing capitalism is obviously far easier and more fashionable than being a responsible adult who recognizes the most inescapable blessings of American life.

Apparently, one can only 'Feel the Bern' of social justice by accepting the assertion liberals need safe spaces from accountability and 'truth' is a micro-aggression unless it involves attacking private enterprise, Christianity, White Privilege or the "crazy" idea America became the most revered and transcendent country on Earth due to its once unrivaled work ethic, Judeo-Christian values, and innovative spirit. Yes, please excuse me while I demand a leader who exudes economic competence, fearless optimism, and possesses an unapologetic love for his native country. No, America is not perfect, but I have never once claimed to be a victim of anything other than my own choices and the inevitable pitfalls of life. All I ever wanted from my elected government was to protect my rights, to provide transparency in all its dealings, and to uphold the Constitution as it is written...nothing

Feel the Bern

more. Likewise, I never once thought I was owed anything or that 'my share' was a 'free share'...unearned benefits redistributed at the expense of my neighbor or those more fortunate; i.e., citizens who also have inalienable rights.

Not to rain on the Tofu picnics of Marxist misery, but wealthy individuals or the top 10% contribute roughly 70% of all duties annually while 45% of Americans paid no income tax at all last year. And since payroll taxes account for one-third of government revenue, brooding socialists conveniently forget "greedy" corporations

account for almost 50% of the American workforce and 65% of new hires since 1990. Now whose 13% tax bracket is confused about 'fair share'? Bernie Sanders isn't leading a revolution in any sense of the word. He's simply pledging to finish what Barack Obama started: destroying America's economic independence and global influence beneath the Marxist camouflage of universal healthcare, free college indoctrination, and fresh breadlines with a guaranteed, rationed income. And that's the perfect job for someone who lived off the state and his parents for nearly half of his "unfair" life.

Sorry to disappoint the dregs of Democratic Socialism, but I honestly love my life, no matter how pedestrian or uneventful it may seem. Why? Because I'm free to pursue the life of my choosing and there are literally countless paths to success and personal contentment. I don't need to be a rock star, celebrity activist or a multi-millionaire athlete to validate my self-worth. In America, you can either complain endlessly about how unfair life is, blame your perceived enemy for your failures and shortcomings, or you can get your ass off the couch, cancel your 'woe is me' lifetime subscription, and do everything in your power to succeed; only one has a future. If I wanted a Socialist to dictate every aspect of my life, to tell me how to think and what I can't achieve without Big Brother, I'd move to Europe and pretend government has no real agenda other than taking our money and silencing dissent for the 'common good'. But then again, I'm an American. I don't ransom liberty or exploit the inevitable differences of personal wealth. I fear the ignorant masses voting for a disgruntled parasite inviting me to his "free" dinner.

As socialists, we are opponents of the Jews, because we see in the Hebrews the incarnation of capitalism, of the misuse of the nation's goods.

— *Joseph Goebbels* —

"We are socialists, we are enemies of today's capitalistic economic system for the exploitation of the economically weak, with its unfair salaries, with its unseemly evaluation of a human being according to wealth and property instead of responsibility and performance, and we are determined to destroy this system under all conditions."

~Adolf Hitler May 1, 1927

The Capitalist: Yeah, I Built That!

Deep in the trenches of oppression and opportunity, beneath the rubble of idealism and propaganda, lies the truth. No, the truth doesn't lie but it is far too often manipulated, torn, and waved as the flag of special interests. Yet, where there are tears in the fabric of freedom, the thread of misconception can always be traced back to the source. America, the land of the free and home of the brave, was forged upon the pain and suffering, the ingenuity and wisdom, of cultures spanning the dawn of man. In the wake of tyrannical rulers, religious persecution, and endless bloodshed our forefathers knew that if our society was to survive, let alone flourish, government must be limited, people must be held accountable, and freedom must provide the inescapable blanket beneath which both must coexist. Over two hundred years later, the intricate yet flexible fabric they wove, the Constitution, led to the proliferation of the most powerful & prosperous country on Earth. Was this new-found republic perfect? No. Was it a resounding success? Absolutely. Evidently, however, that is still not enough.

Once upon a time, before Las Vegas, Twitter, and Global Warming coincided with revisionist history, American settlers died from basic ailments, starvation, or a chance encounter with a wily predator. Everyday needs – such as food, clothes and shelter – were a blessing; a sign of unspoken respect and indelible pride. Now, they are but foregone conclusions; a relic of want and envy that are too often discarded and forgotten beneath the sheen of a complacent, insatiable culture. Knowing human desire is as infinite as Hollywood stars, though it's much more unlikely to be paid like one, how one provides for themselves is entirely a different question. There is no crime in wanting a better life, the pleasures of the pedestrian mind, yet who is responsible for bridging the gap between fiction and reality, opportunity and responsibility? More prophetically, who is to blame if you fail to reach your goals, or in today's progressive paradigm, if your neighbor achieves more?

In the eye of the recent Wall Street protests reside the cruxes of social and economic justice; i.e., equality levied by the leftist hand of inequality. Liberalism, a distant relative from its classical and much more patriotic predecessor during the Great Depression, evolved from the counter-culture of the 1960's into an anti-American, anti-capitalism, secular spitball. They pretend to be a predominantly mainstream phenomenon by grabbing headlines with bold accusations – i.e., threatened by armed, racist Christians high on Jesus – but the facts speak otherwise. As the country continues to flounder in the Great Recession, swept into the currents of a global downturn, liberals claim capitalism, corporate America, is at the heart of our problems; when more apropos, it's at the epicenter of their agenda. Allegedly, these firms systematically exploit struggling masses, they oppress their workers, and they never pay taxes. The problem is, these accusations are overflowing with stereotypes, assumptions, and just plain sensationalist ire.

Without corporate America, perhaps the single greatest catalyst of our wealth, power, and quality of life, this country would be a shell of itself. Big business accounts for a substantial percentage of hiring, building, and philanthropy in the United States. Countless public institutions and organizations – academic, medical, athletic, and the arts – are either founded or sustained through corporate donations. Furthermore, a number of these entities have and continued to pioneer innovations that transcend the world: from life-saving treatments, to alternative energy research and everyday information solutions. If I may, what country's "capitalist marauders" invented electricity, the telegraph, the telephone, the airplane, the automobile, the personal computer and made them available to individuals across the globe? That's right; those evil, profit seeking corporations. Without their resources, their humanitarian and entrepreneurial spirit to push the boundaries of technological and cultural advancement, the world would indeed be a much darker place. Thank God for those energy saving light bulbs. Demagoguery loves the dark!

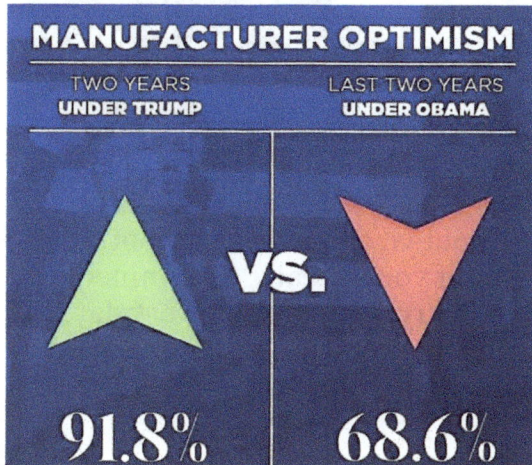

MANUFACTURER OPTIMISM

TWO YEARS
UNDER TRUMP

LAST TWO YEARS
UNDER OBAMA

VS.

91.8%　　**68.6%**

And what of duty, patriotism to you and me, but TAXES to the soldiers of statism? Why are liberals so obsessed with taxes? Simple...CONTROL! They want more social programs, more handouts, more unabridged power. Yes, so much for the priceless institutions of pride and accountability. Not to pour soap on the left's propaganda parade, but corporations account for nearly 50% of all payroll taxes in this country; hardly a paltry figure. Likewise, these firms' earnings are subject to a 35% flat corporate and a 15-20% dividend tax. That's half of your profits, time and efforts, turned over to the powers that be! Sound fair? *crickets* Without a doubt these firms are either directly or indirectly responsible for a bulk of sales generated and salaries paid in America, as well as a major source of revenue collected by Uncle Sam. If the business of America is business, which it is, they represent the heartbeat of our progress and the anti-thesis of the socialist agenda.

Not to assuage the hand of contrarianism, those extreme cases invoked to paint reality with hyperbole, but do corporations get tax breaks and specialized treatment? Of course, some do; just ask GE, Obama's biggest commercial donor in 2008. Or how about those lucrative contracts awarded to congressional home districts? It is definitely not uncommon for companies to be given special breaks by our local, state and federal government. These trade-offs are simply a proven method to lure corporations – the economic growth these companies provide to a community in terms of jobs and disposable income – with tax abatements, land grants, and zoning privileges. That's what helps to keep them solvent and growing. Is it always right? Of course not! In fact, sometimes it's downright criminal. But then again, what do critics say when these conglomerate fire thousands to leave America for more profitable pastures?

Regardless of the numbers, commonality or sensational exceptions, we're missing the ultimate equalizer: politicians. Our elected officials – those elected by these same socialist activists – are the ones who write the tax codes and grant special privileges in exchange for benefits. So if corporations, even under the worse-case scenario, are operating within the law, how does that make them the enemy? It doesn't. It makes their accusers ignorant. Perhaps progressives should protest the exorbitant salaries and tax loopholes enjoyed by their numerous celebrity supporters. What's the going cost of a game, a concert, or a movie again? Darn those greedy celebrities!

But what about all that profiteering; price gouging the common man to the point of poverty? From regulatory committees to fair competition acts, anti-collusion statutes, there is a plethora of federal and state checks on today's corporations. And if there is a shortcoming that needs to be addressed, such as in the case of Enron, Congress and the courts are readily available to meet the challenge. Once again, "We the People" hold the ultimate trump card. If you don't like it, don't buy it. If you disagree with a company's practices, don't work for them or buy their stock! With the exception of a few products, consumers set the bar as far as demand. Without your financial support, these car, clothing, and phone companies wouldn't exist. And if you're really determined, you can always start your own company and redefine the industry. People do it every day. No, really, they do. Apple, anyone? All you need is a garage! Just remember, for every single business that succeeds, countless more shut their doors. Risk...work...reward.

"Wait, you haven't even mentioned despicable slave wages that are dictated to helpless workers!" Hmm, do I even have to say it? I could list a mountain of legislation and oversight committees that are dedicated to procuring safe working conditions and fair compensation, but I won't. It's a jungle out there. Modern America is but a shadow of the egregious conditions that dominated the Industrial Revolution. Just ask Upton Sinclair. Today, workers' salaries and benefits are at their zenith. Even at the lower spectrum of the corporate ladder, McDonald's employees can receive health care and Walmart employees are offered stock options. Does your local convenience store or mom and pop store offer such amenities? Do you really believe local businesses don't do everything in their power to make a buck? Sure, we could pay menial labor $15 an hour, pretend minimum wage wasn't intended for unskilled works, but what good is a $5 sub when you have to go to Mexico to get it? How many slices of ham are on that Congressional bill and lifetime pension?

While we're on the subject of "fair" compensation, are you privy to what a United Auto Workers member makes? How about the Teamsters? Who's transporting that dynamo product of yours out to the marketplace? The executives of these "righteous" unions, just like their corporate counterparts, make a very pretty penny. Any surprise these CAPITALISTS have joined the Wall Street protests? Mob rule means more union dues, higher salary demands. The oppressed proletariat smells money; MO' money. Yes, don't be a fooled by the incessant glare of idealism, for they too work the system. How else can an uneducated average Joe start at $40 an hour with full benefits and a retirement plan? There are many reasons as to why a string of firms are going bankrupt or teetering on the brink of foreclosure. Everybody wants theirs, even at the price of failure. Yes, cutting off your nose to spite your face is still hip in Seattle and California; especially if you're a socialist drinking Starbucks decrying economic inequality.

"The inherent vice of Capitalism is the unequal sharing of blessings; the inherent virtue of Socialism is the equal sharing of miseries." ~*Winston Churchill*

So, for the sake of toasters, hot coffee, and world peace, what's all of this civil disobedience really about? It's about frustration and power. Voted the most liberal Senator by an independent watchdog before his presidency, Barack Obama was the left's game-changing, shining star; a torchbearer for their cause – along with the likes of self-admitted Marxist pals Robert Ayers, Robert McChesney and Van Jones – who promised to "dismantle capitalism brick by brick" and to institute social and economic justice. So much for the Constitution. Well, to their credit, they're succeeding...with catastrophic consequences. As Obama's approval numbers continue to spiral into oblivion while his list of failures continues to catapult into the stratosphere, Liberals are lashing out in a desperate attempt to save face, deflect attention from their leader/party's woes, and preserve their agenda. With the landslide losses of the 2010 and 2014 elections, coupled with Hillary's likely candidacy in 2016, these organized protests of opportunistic anarchy are nothing more an attempt to disrupt the system and "capitalize" on people's suffering in an attempt to sway public opinion by blaming corporate fat cats for massive unemployment, the highest poverty in our nation's history, and a crippling debt. Of course, nothing could be further from the truth. If Bush was supposedly a disaster, despite accruing less debt and possessing an average unemployment rate of 5.4% in a tenure plagued by the economic fallout from 9/11, two wars and the credit collapse, what does that make Obama? Sorry, hope doesn't change the truth.

STATISM: THE BELIEF THAT A BUNCH OF IDIOTS WHO DROVE OUR NATION $20 TRILLION INTO DEBT ARE MORE QUALIFIED TO RUN YOUR LIFE THAN YOU ARE

No, Barack Obama wasn't dealt the best hand, but he has made it exponentially worse with worthless bailouts, wasteful spending, and naïve socialist doctrine. Adding more debt than the first 42 presidents combined in his first term alone, while engineering a culture of entitlement that nearly doubled public assistance recipients to 50 million, is hardly the calling card of an experienced, responsible leader. If we ran our finances like Washington, we'd all be homeless and bankrupt in a week. The only difference is "We the People" can't print 40 billion a month and call it progress. Spending sensibly within the framework of a sound economic plan – as a means to a means, not a means to end – is paramount to growth. When you provide a fertile platform for business to flourish, to create new money, people can find those jobs that lead to a better life. They can now afford their own healthcare, buy that home, and send their kids to college; thus, nurturing the next generation of well-adjusted, self-sufficient Americans. However, that requires two conditions: one, a government that is committed to the principles of free enterprise, and two, a populace that is willing to work instead of endeavoring to live-off the public dime.

The real tragedy of this progressive debacle, this smoke and mirrors ruse, is that capitalism – ingenuity and hard work – is being made the scapegoat for Washington's failures. Whether a corporation posts a profit of a billion dollars, an athlete signs a 100 million-dollar contract, or your neighbor wins the lottery, how is that violating the law? More importantly, what does that have to do with you? Is it forcing you to seek employment from a company you despise or to buy their products? How is someone else's success, property, keeping you from furthering your prospects in life; from finding and keeping a job? Michael Moore, the anti-establishment pariah, sued to claim more profits from his conspiracy documentary, 9/11 Fahrenheit. Why? Because he felt entitled to the fruits of his labor. How ironic being capitalism, far from his favorite love story, is intrinsic to that very ideal. In life, you can either cower behind obstacles and excuses, or you can do everything in your power to succeed. Only one has a future.

The bottom line is that America is predicated on freedom, self-reliance, and accountability. The Government, at its most rudimentary level, has two functions: to protect our liberties, this country's sovereignty, and to provide transparency, accountability, in all its dealings. Every man and woman, regardless of their heritage, beliefs or class, is entitled to make a living without unnecessary government intrusion. Whether you're an ordinary citizen or a multinational corporation, as long as you obey the law you are completely within your rights to pursue the American dream; whether you seek riches, a quaint house on the corner or dedicate your life to the poor is a moot point.

The Constitution only gives people the right to pursue happiness. You have to catch it yourself. Benjamin Franklin

Personally, I have never been wealthy, but if I were to come into money – albeit my own hard work or simply good fortune – I'd like to think I was entitled to keep my property. That's capitalism, the Bill of Rights, in a nutshell. It's also our forefathers' charter against excessive government, otherwise known as socialism. You work, you earn. You innovate, you earn. You make your own choices...you control your own destiny. You should never be trapped by the glass ceiling of progressivism and ransomed to a federal leviathan of economic redistribution that chooses to limit our potential, to tax one man more than another, one business or product more than the next. How is that synonymous with liberty, let alone equal protection under the law? It's not. The U.S. Government was not erected to run your life – to tell you what to eat, think, or do – merely to preserve your rights, this country's sovereignty and the indelible institution of freedom. Although civic safety nets are in place to help us when we fall, to help us get back on our feet, your survival, your economic success, is ultimately your own responsibility.

Whether we like it or not, there will always be those individuals blessed with more ability, fortune or fame. That's life. It's not, nor will it ever be, fair. Why do people get cancer? Why are the guilty set free? Why do I drive a Pinto instead of a Porsche? Why? There comes a time when people must stop pointing the finger of envy at others...legal corporations, wealthy Americans...and start pointing the finger of self-realization at themselves. Beyond the glitz and glamour, there are many levels of success and affluence. And if you don't fully appreciate America, the ample opportunities and securities available within, I freely invite you to visit any number of third world countries where drinkable water and free speech are subject to interpretation. Perhaps then you will appreciate the warmth of your bed, the food on your table, the smile on your child's face.

No economic system is perfect, there are only perfect intentions. That being said, we must always strive for the betterment of society. Remember, the Constitution – not the times or aspiring politicians – provides the blueprint for true hope and change. If you sincerely believe today's demonstrators are wiser and more learned than our forefathers, that the past 239 years of America's evolution are but a footnote of greed and futility, then by all means, light that match. Historically speaking, it's much easier to destroy than to build a meaningful legacy. If people continue to empower liberals who recklessly threaten to tear down our commercial foundations of freedom, our hallowed way of life, then we might as well tear down this country and build a new one. And that my friend, will still require poverty, protests and union labor. I prefer, like my forefathers, to use my own two hands.

WHEN THE LEFT SAYS SOCIALISM IS DIFFERENT FROM COMMUNISM OR NAZISM:

"NAZI" = NATIONAL SOCIALIST GERMAN WORKERS' PARTY

"USSR" = UNION OF SOVIET SOCIALIST REPUBLICS

Pop Culture Relativism,

Political

Correctness

& the Cult of Celebrity

Tinsel, Gold Teeth and A Warm Body Underneath

The best tours of Hollywood should always begin with the seductive long legs of La La Land leading to the toast of Tinsel Town where it's not what you know but who you know can fill your glass with their unquestioned sexual needs. Whether you're greeted in the 5-star foyers of celebrity bliss or lured into the wine cellars of the ultra 1% dream, privilege is a political podium tied to the trysts of Charlie Sheen, Lindsay Lohan or Miley Cyrus spoiling the fruits of our unsung labor. Unbeknownst to the nostrils, bank accounts and notched bedposts of America's most wanted lifestyles, the "Go Fund Me" extravagance of fan-paid escapades, America would be a far richer place – ethically and financially – if "We the People" withheld a dollar and an hour of our time every time Michael Moore, Katie Perry, Eminem, Robert De Niro or Rosie O'Donnell mocked middle America as a hateful abyss of Right-Wing supremacy. For every James Woods or Tim Allen blacklisted for quoting the Constitution and lamenting the unborn, there's an anti-American Jane Fonda or racist Whoopi Goldberg fanning the flames of societal discord for the syndicated shock value of gross-exaggeration.

The only public menace more hypocritical than the entertainment industry incessantly lecturing America about discrimination, equal rights and human decency is their unquenchable thirst to bathe their ego – sow their political seeds and feed their carnal desires – wherever and whenever they please. Just like the pharaohs and kings of old, no amount of self-indulgence or moral subversion can fill their vacationing hearts; a lifestyle defined by excess and adulation. And yet amidst the suffocated stories of coerced victims the world is finally beginning to see the film and music industry for what it is worth; a cesspool of greed, sexual exploitation and social degradation that not only poisons the minds of generations of our youth for the price of a ticket or song, but eagerly ransoms the frail, budding aspirations of "dreamers" who too often are forced to pay a pound of flesh for the slightest hope of fortune or fame.

For years renewed claims of sexual harassment, rape and pedophilia have plagued the entertainment industry with little action or collective concern from the inner circles of cinematic, sports, and music executives. Corey Haim and Corey Feldman, both of whom were prominent 80's childhood stars, admitted to being raped on the same night in separate rooms. And while Haim eventually succumbed to a drug addiction – one he battled for years after being introduced to cocaine as an emerging teenage star – Feldman has been ostracized for his campaign to expose what he calls "rampant pedophilia" in Hollywood. As expected, his assertions based from personal experiences were immediately dismissed as "false and damaging" by Barbara Walters during a televised interview. Then again, if you can stomach former Chief of Staff Jon Podesta's taste in modern art as much as a slice of his brother's pizza, no child is really off limits. It's therefore of little surprise pop star Kesha was also shunned by the press after revealing music producer Dr. Luke raped her when she was an 18-year-old virgin and that he threatened to destroy her career if she ever exposed his vile behavior. Naturally many within the mercenary mud pit known as journalism labeled her accusations as spiteful, baseless indictments without merit. But as we all know, appearances are everything when entitlement and self-gratification are the greatest impetuses of achieving such control...the OJ Simpson illusion of innocence. Money buys influence and access is a drug the adoring media rarely moralizes no matter what the human cost.

Although Harvey Weinstein has become the tip of the proverbial storm – rightfully so considering Rose McGowan was allegedly raped by him, a young model pressured into allowing him to perform oral sex, a reporter forced to watch him shower/masturbate, and now other woman have come forward with stories ranging from repeated harassment to forced sex acts – how many other aspiring actors, actresses, models and musicians fell in the cracks of his constituents' complacency; even worse, the media's silent consent or willingness to falsely debunk almost any claim of industry indiscretion to maintain a reputable lie of social activism?

Of course, when so many detailed allegations come forward with such ferocity, victims can finally breathe and the dam can no longer deny the portending public relations nightmare, the truth finally finds the light of day. A video of "esteemed" Trump critic Jimmy Kimmel recently surfaced showing him asking an 18-year-old girl to guess what was in his pants, along with a dignified plea for her "to put her mouth on it", while footage of Oscar-winning writer and actor Ben Affleck relentlessly groping and objectifying a television host has empowered other actresses, including a well-respected make-up artist, to go public with similar tales of abuse at the hands of the now infamously dubbed, "buttman". Whether you're a common stage hand, a doting fan or yet another Red Carpet VIP sipping Chablis in a guarded trailer, it's obvious no one is immune from being the recipient of such unwarranted advances; i.e., the moral relativism and callous apathy of Hollywood's so-called imaginary "rape culture". Few examples can better exemplify the dichotomy between private deviance and public admiration than Bill Cosby. For decades he was universally beloved for his comedic genius, a devoted family man regarded as the epitome of wit and clean humor, only to be exposed as serial predator who drugged unsuspecting women for the explicit purpose of violating them. When fame or wealth can no longer seduce the adoring senses, the spoiled celebrity appetite for excess too often attempts to cash a forged check forgoing the prerequisite of individual consent.

In light of the worst offenders, I'm not recklessly suggesting everyone in the entertainment world is guilty of sex crimes and unparalleled misconduct. There are a number of conscionable thespians, musicians, and athletes who walk the walk and tirelessly work to make the world a better place with their time and money. However, as much as I agree all people should be judged on an individual basis and given the benefit of the doubt, that same has not been afforded to Republicans, Christians, or anyone in traditionally conservative states who have fought to preserve our Judeo-Christian values and have repeatedly warned about the consequences of eroding the family paradigm. The last time I checked, glorified violence, ingrained disrespect and unchecked hedonism sit squarely on the shoulders of "cultured" urban activists who believe a married woman choosing to raise her children is sexist oppression and who portray self-defense as an armed crime that pales in comparison to movies or video games that mindlessly shoot or invite viewers to kill everything in sight; including cops, free speech or God-forbid our own President.

When sex, materialism and an insatiable desire to live the celebrity lifestyle – mass adoration, soulless vanity and living a life without regrets or boundaries – replaces society's need to raise generations of respectful, well-adjusted youth ever cognizant of their choices, the results speak for themselves. Social change and female empowerment isn't achieved by parading around naked in the streets, scrawling slut across your chest and profanely degrading anyone who finds such lack of decency offensive. Such obscene sensationalism merely seeks validation through political intimidation and does nothing to encourage civil discourse, let alone instill an acute sense of accountability in anyone; regardless of their political leanings or sexual identity.

True feminism is about reminding our daughters they are not reduced to the sum of their body parts; that the content of their character and the legacy of their actions are the greatest indicators of their self-worth and natural born rights. Equality begins by teaching girls to respect themselves, as well as by empowering young, impressionable boys to see all females as their sisters and mothers; deserving of equal regard for their well-being and aspirations. It does not require a political affiliation, demonizing the opposite sex or denouncing morality and basic decency as fascist gender control. Likewise, sexual freedom or personal gratification without restraints, an innate concern for others, merely invites philandering, uninvited aggression and even pedophilia. One needs only to peruse the unfiltered depravity of social media, those more concerned with their genitals, convincing Holocaust survivors Trump is a Hitler or garnering the maximum number of "retweets", to conclude regression and progressivism are now one in the same.

HI, MY NAME IS ALLISON MACK

YOU MAY KNOW ME FROM TV'S 'SMALLVILLE'. WHAT YOU MAY NOT KNOW, IS THAT I HAVE BEEN CHARGED WITH CHILD TRAFFICKING FOR MY ROLE IN RECRUITING PEOPLE INTO A CULT CALLED NXIVM, WHICH HAD TIES TO THE ROTHSCHILDS & CLINTONS. WOMEN IN THE GROUP CALLED ME 'PIMP MACK' AND AFTER THEY JOINED THEY WERE BRANDED NEAR THEIR GROINS, CAGED, STARVED AND TURNED INTO SEX SLAVES FOR THE GROUP'S MEMBERS AND ITS LEADER.

Not to rain on Hollywood's incestuous love affair with itself, but not all boundaries are meant to be broken and conditioning society to treat violence as entertainment and women as stage props hardly exonerates their ranks from culpability. Harvey Weinstein personally befriended and/or routinely partied with cinematic heavyweights such as George Clooney, Meryl Streep, Matt Damon, Quentin Tarantino and Russell Crowe. And despite the reality so many witnessed and/or personally learned of his improper behavior from colleagues, not discounting published pictures revealing the distressed faces of actresses like Emma Watson while in his libido's therapeutic presence, little was ever said or done out of fear of hurting their careers by unnecessarily writing a best-selling script of industry scandal; or better yet, self-incrimination. Yes, how utterly courageous and apropos when the names of modern sex toys are viewed as more life-like, more memorable, than the actual expendable victims of Hollywood sex crimes. Apparently only Brad Pitt, seething over the mistreatment of then girlfriend Gwyneth Paltrow, had the gumption to confront the film mogul with a "Missouri Whipping" if he did not cease and desist.

Only under the protective halo of the colluding press could a heavyweight Democratic fundraiser like Harvey Weinstein, a personal confidant of both the Clintons and Obamas who was repeatedly invited to White House events, be publicly hailed as "a wonderful human being" without one network rewinding the remarkably absurd comments of one Michelle Obama for posterity's sake. And to think Hillary kissed congressional colleague and former Klan leader Robert Byrd on the cheek, while the President has been disparaged daily by networks as a white supremacist for saying hate is not a race because it inevitably exists in all facets of America. Who in their right mind could actually believe the media isn't hopelessly compromised, built to indoctrinate trusting, ignorant minds, when incontrovertible maxims are clearly twisted to house partisan lies? How many women, without a shred of evidence, were given press conferences by the major networks just weeks before the election in hopes of thwarting Donald Trump's campaign? Twelve more than the number who made police reports or filed lawsuits: none.

The fact Mr. Weinstein "bravely" announced he's entering rehab and hired a high-profile criminal attorney reveals his response is as phony as it is entirely devoid of remorse. Of course, the real question is what happens now? How many conspicuously silent talk show hosts – the same politically conscious hacks who lambaste the President daily over mere hyperbole and unsubstantiated paranoia – will demand its viewers choose between rejecting the cultural rot of pop culture, the sexual impropriety of celebrity affluence, or watching their obnoxious programs? How many award galas, public classrooms or athletic venues will be hijacked to rail against Hollywood indecency, exploitation and liberal hypocrisy? And lastly, when will America unite to reclaim their dignity by stripping away their support and hard-earned money from those detached elitists, moral degenerates, and political terrorists who sanctimoniously dehumanize any dissension from the celebrity status quo? "Strip away the phony tinsel from Hollywood and you will find the REAL tinsel underneath": Sycophants, narcissists, traitors and always a warm body beneath. The real American heroes we crave and so desperately need are not born from fiction or cut from the commercialized cloth of a marketed name, they quietly walk among us every day in our homes, schools, hospitals and uneventful streets.

Lights, Camera, Affirmative Action!

As scores of celebrities and political activists surface from their beachfront bunkers to fashionably boycott the Oscars for being too unbearably pasty, shooting flares of distress from the insured wreckage of their scuttled hearts, perhaps they should begin their ascent for mob justice by boycotting the most obvious antagonist: themselves. The problem isn't necessarily that racism exists in America, for it inevitably breathes in all facets of society, but that more and more people are so comfortable waving its false flag in the face of everyday misfortune, petty disagreements, or any undesirable result. In other words, don't cry wolf if you're the wolf or because you're selling tickets to your own martyrdom.

The accusation the Motion Picture Academy purposely excluded minority actors and films from their rightful recognition is the equivalent of saying the performances of those nominated were merited by skin color and not according to their unique gifts and efforts. In short, it's incredibly insulting. Hollywood, perhaps more than any other institution in America, has more often than not set the curve in terms of embracing those subject matters and individuals caught in the spotlight of societal scorn. Although I do not always agree with the supposed cultural relevance and moral climate of the cinematic industry, their ranks are hypersensitive to any hint of discrimination and acutely aware of the most-opaque social slights. How else did 'Driving Miss Daisy', 'Brokeback Mountain', 'MILK', 'Slumdog Millionaire' or '12 Years A Slave' soar to the fabled heights of immortalized Oscar glory; because voting members were homophobic, misogynistic supremacists who catered to racially cognizant celebrities that could not delineate between jealousy, sour grapes, and true injustice? Paid victims...aren't they all.

If I was Jada Pinkett Smith, fatally wounded by her husband's Oscar exclusion, or Spike Lee, who always aspires to do the black thing, and viewed the totality of life through the myopic lens of color, I'd selfishly decry that over 90% of the NBA is black and there have been only three white MVP's in the past 30 years. Or maybe most are simply better at basketball. Likewise, I'd also protest the fact 13% of the population – or a healthy 15% of the film industry – commits 50% of violent crime in America only to watch the press selectively demonize law enforcement on a daily basis. Naturally such raw, unadulterated logic has been relegated to French Sudoku subtitles. Or maybe, just maybe, the fewer number of blacks in film and a lack of quality roles, not the choreographed catcalls of racial conspiracy, is the root cause for the obvious discrepancy. Ironically, the demographic with the greatest disproportionate representation in Hollywood, Latinos, is also the most silent or undemanding. Sometimes reality, regardless of our personal expectations or political agenda, doesn't reside on the pregnant litmus test of political correctness. In the black and white world of mathematics, probability is exactly what it is; like it or not.

Excuse my non-gender specific commas, but do perpetually-offended critics somehow believe Laurence Olivier, Marlon Brando, Tom Hanks or Meryl Streep didn't really earn their proverbial stripes, while Hattie McDaniel, Omar Sharif, Morgan Freeman, or Denzel Washington were merely given participation trophies in lieu of being respected and beloved for their transcendent talents? If so, then by all means segregate that theater, pawn those pale statues and dismiss over 50 years of progress; Sophocles loves a good incestuous drama. I'm sure most of this year's "straw man" nominees – consisting of both first-time candidates and seasoned veterans who never had the privilege of shaking Oscar's whiteness – would love to unapologetically digress. After all, it's not like they "earned" it.

In this never-ending quest for affirmative action, or more specifically cinematic reparations, just remember that those brave black Americans who defined the struggle of the civil rights era, endured racism on a systemic scale, never sought special treatment, exclusionary rights or to be summarily reduced to the genetic hue of their ancestor's bartered flesh. They prized opportunity above all else. These pioneers persevered through real oppression and inescapable derision for the faintest hope of being judged by the content of their character, endeavoring to grasp the ladder of equality with their own calloused two hands, instead of clinging to any shipwrecked notion of entitlement weeping on the rotting docks of lost perspective. Truly, there was no greater disservice to their memory or sacrifice. Celebrating excellence, individual achievement and universal artistry does not require monochromatic glasses, a guaranteed treasure map or a personally autographed excuse for self-pity; it's a never-ending tale of human dignity that thirsts for a mature protagonist foreshadowed by the priceless virtues of grace, altruism and humility. If only life imitated art.

Hollywood's Black Mass of Cognitive Dissonance

What could possibly be better than watching an ostentatious parade of detached, condescending, and grossly overpaid thespians lecturing everyday Americans about exercising their political freedoms? Hmm, how about yet another pompous, privileged award gala that blissfully celebrates Hollywood's rape/pedophilia culture by attacking those "immoral voters" who have the audacity to pay their "unfair share" salaries but somehow adamantly refuse to applaud the entertainment industry's smug, hateful hypocrisy? When an annually televised circle jerk of bitter celebrities demands a Red Carpet of international adulation, hijacking a once revered artistic platform to needlessly slander a President seeking to restore accountability and prosperity, reality is as foreign as the concept of patriotism; i.e., preserving a sovereign Constitutional Republic conceived in liberty, the human capacity for self-government, forever incumbent upon intellectual diversity. Unlike the hostile pulpit of political intolerance, respect for others, the blessings of America, never requires a scathing acceptance speech.

Despite the orchestrated pageantry of designer black dresses proudly revealing their own "me too" cognitive dissonance to fawning cameras, the so-called social pioneers of Hollywood knew countless actresses were being sexually exploited and they did absolutely nothing because the entire industry feared the public humiliation of scandal, preserving their own careers, far more than ending decades of perverse injustice and discrimination. And what did the "honorable" heroes of the progressive left gleam from these disturbing and brazenly self-righteous turn of events? Oprah should run for President! So much for the noble humanitarian icons of cinema. **#TheyKnew**

The Political Misappropriation of Cultural Jurisdiction

The same social justice jurors who love to claim borders, gender roles, economic classes and basically any man-made distinctions are innately discriminatory, are typically the first hypocrites to accuse their detractors of "culture misappropriation". Sorry to be the bearer of bad news, but no matter what you wear, say, eat or do, you're inevitably borrowing from another culture, if not countless preceding civilizations. The advent of tools, the birth of fire, Mesopotamian city-states, the universal linguistic roots of Latin and Greek, Egyptian art and Byzantine architecture, Indian horticulture and Chinese alchemy, Roman aqueducts and American suspension bridges, by no means represent unaltered, isolated contributions to the human condition. These social stepping stones are no more private relics than the communal air billions breathe. Contemporary society, but especially America as a diverse and free nation, is a smorgasbord of influences, accumulated knowledge, discerning tastes and synthesized ideas. And that's exactly why "We the People" have thrived as a unique collection of individuals, whereas more sedentary, sheltered cultures have remained stagnant or faltered beneath a lack of external enrichment and assimilated abilities.

Unless it's suddenly acceptable again to designate white only bathrooms, gender segregated jobs or eating establishments with ethnically exclusive clientele, individuality is the natural culmination of liberty, creativity, accrued experiences and personal enlightenment. Without the cultural intersection of past and present – scientific theory, artistic mediums, and technological advances – the modern world would faintly resemble itself. For the sworn enemies of reality that still angrily digress, the next time a visiting Japanese student eats a hamburger, a Cuban immigrant waves the American flag, a black Chicago chef opens a Mexican restaurant, non-Irish folk celebrate St. Patrick's day, a German kickboxer dreadlocks his hair, a single father teaches a maternity class, or an Anglo-American girl chooses to wear an exquisite Asian dress to her high school prom, I strongly suggest removing that rather large, sanctimonious chip on your padded shoulder spilling your Italian Gelato coffee on your fake hipster shoes which were probably made in a "designer" Chinese sweatshop for less than the exchange rate of several pesos left in a Jack Daniels shot glass as a quaint housewarming gift.

My insincere apologies to the hopelessly conflicted, but you can't preach multiculturalism only to admonish, selectively indict, its subsequent aftermath. This politically correct charade is as absurd as attacking a New York native for wearing a Dodgers baseball cap. Not surprisingly, traditional "white" America is most often targeted by cultural appropriation terrorists because progressivism requires hiding behind false appearances to belittle that which they religiously take for granted and despise the most: freedom. The beauty of cultural diversity is not confined to a singular race, sex, ideology, nationality or hoarded piece of property, but liberated by the unlimited ingenuity and application of the human mind. This rudimentary concept, of course, makes far too much sense for imaginary victims so ignorantly crying foul over the improper distribution of cultural domain.

As for those deluded activists still claiming otherwise, I suggest surrendering your car, never boarding a plane, smashing all cell phones and renouncing the "privileged" use of electricity because where would the obnoxiously intervening "thought police" be without those distinctly American contrivances? E Pluribus Unum or Cogito, Ergo, Sum – "I think, therefore I am" – the mere political invention of culture misappropriation is as offensively "racist" as it is exceedingly dumb.

The Brooding Type

ABC's "The Bold Type" is about as racist and sexist as it is intentionally condescending. The three main characters perfectly encapsulate the modern feminist zeitgeist of obnoxious, entitled millennials incessantly whining about how unfair life is because the rationale world refuses to embrace their victimization drivel. Its premise is nothing more than political propaganda wrapped around an undying hate of successful men, a patriarchal society in general, but of white conservative America specifically. According to the show's writers, "old-ass white men" in positions of power are soulless, chauvinistic pigs conspiring to oppress and sexualize young, ambitious women who are as unappreciated as they are unaccountable for their own lives and cleavage. Hollywood grooming future generations of spiteful voters with divisive identity politics? Never!

Hannah Montana and The Wrecking Ball of Feminism

I just love when Hollywood attacks Christians and distorts our faith because entertainers don't want to be judged for using a midget as a sex toy, holding a microphone to broadcast their vagina's monologue or violating themselves with a Styrofoam finger on national TV in hopes of fostering world peace and stopping world hunger. Yes, I'm talking about you, Miley Cyrus. It's not sex that is dirty or even necessarily sinful, but rather it has been degraded into the tainted product of a society that neither has the sense or the soul God gave them to realize shameless celebrities like yourself reduce the beauty of human sexuality to a cheap sideshow of mindless desecration. If your life's greatest ambition is to be a stripper or a porn star, so be it. That's your sentient choice. Just don't accuse me of believing in fairy tales or being a Puritanical extremist because you lack the wit, eloquence or perspective to distinguish between talent and perversion, respect and repugnance. And just in case you forgot, and I know you did, the religious fanatic known as Jesus Christ didn't wash the feet of a prostitute because he believed in righteously condemning the commercial exploits of artistic harlots to the fiery pits of hell. He merely believed the sanctity of life, the salvation of mankind, lies far beyond the reach of our genitals. Too bad some "divine" concepts are simply too difficult for a liberal to understand; unless, that is, you're a fully concealed Muslim woman forced to walk behind your misogynist husband in absolute silence as he watches a naked, feminist "Wrecking Ball" swinging from his iPhone.

Miley Cyrus & Lady Gaga didn't vote for Trump because he degraded the image of women in society.

Male George Lopez Funny Again

Deport all police officers in lieu of those illegals who have criminal records, gang affiliations and are receiving public benefits at taxpayer expense? Sure, George Lopez, and turn America into the same destitute, lawless abyss known as Mexico; that corrupt cesspool of disrepair millions are fleeing for any semblance of a normal life? No, thanks! Don't blame us because your ancestral homeland is incompetent and struggles to provide basic sanitation and a high school education, let alone passable drinking water. Rather than criticizing our laws, mocking our servicemen and women who put themselves in harm's way each and every day, you should be grateful centuries of immigrants have benefited from the unique opportunities, abundant liberties and revered quality of life America affords.

For those who faithfully honor and welcome the privilege of becoming a U.S. citizen, I have one suggestion: fill out the damn paperwork before crossing an internationally recognized border of a sovereign country. Millions have done it, millions more have foolishly refused or abstained. It's a not a racist conspiracy, nor rocket science, but a universal necessity designed to ensure the security of any civilized nation and the safety, economic efficacy, of her citizens. Of course, that would require common sense, the faintest hint of humility and an ounce of respect for those American lives and livelihoods outside of Hollywood's self-indulgent bubble. And apparently you have none. If your blind pride and myopic political beliefs are immune to the "racist" concept of accountability, perhaps you should start a petition to 'Make Mexico Spain Again' before surrendering your identity and the keys to your lavishly, secluded home. At least then the joke would be on you and no "foreign" citizen would ever be denied the right to vote for a government that doesn't expect its neighbor to pay for their 200-year-old bar tab. Until that improbable and refreshingly sober day, please remind all visitors to kindly knock before permanently entering.

Dear Hollywood…

No child is born desiring a sex change, to become transgendered, in order to aesthetically appease their innate sexuality. Children must be conditioned, made aware of sex confusion or reassignment, by parents, educators and a society that breaches those ethical barriers and encourages such behavior. Just because a young girl loves sports and the outdoors, or a boy rejects both, doesn't make them gay or confused; it makes them the exploited product of a culturally induced, self-fulfilling prophecy. Thank you for doing your part to make adolescence – a virtual minefield of emotions, family dysfunction, peer pressure, and expectations – all the more traumatic by using the welfare of our youth to push the LGBT agenda. The problem isn't that too few teens are gay or denied their rightful "identity" – an inevitable future ploy of Obamacare coverage – rather that soulless activists like yourselves are working tirelessly to convince so many of our sons and daughters it's an issue in the first place. Trying to put a "happy face" on an otherwise disturbing trend doesn't change the fact it's wrong. Since when did child abuse become an acceptable form of entertainment? Culture, not nature, needs to be transplanted. In the meantime, just let kids be kids!

Signed,

Common Sense

Celebrity Rehab: 'Licking' the Donut Hole of Hate!

"I hate America. I hate all Americans!"

Ariana Grande is but yet another twisted link in a growing chain of bitter ignorance and defiant decadence that is strangling our youth's ability to discern our most basic blessings. If I may ask, Princess, what is so unbearably unfair about living in a nation that tolerates and graciously rewards ungrateful, spiteful, and spoiled Disney debutantes like yourself? Is your festering rage caused by the fact your seven-figure checks aren't made on recyclable hemp paper or that you might actually have to sign them? Could it possibly emanate from the disturbing discovery your naked "selfies" are no longer private or that you took them in the first place; the brutal reality your own humiliated father had to bear witness to your former 'ghetto fabulous' boyfriend tweeting about giving his daughter that "D" in Detroit? Rather than appreciating the very vehicle of her success and fame – basking in the light of liberty and giving thanks for its innate bounty of endless opportunity – Miss Grande chooses to cry injustice because ordinary people have the inalienable right to free speech and sentient thought. And yet, regardless of anyone's "offensive" political or religious beliefs, she is not going blind from drinking river water in Africa, scavenging through the diseased landfill of Haiti, or being beaten and beheaded for nothing more than being born a Muslim. Oh, the incomprehensible inhumanity! How "fat" are your concert tickets again?

If we're talking about "true" discrimination and justifiable disgust – not that progressive Hollywood variety that requires physically dialing 911 because Miley Cyrus has chapped lips or your Range Rover is racist – then by all means, enlighten America about the perilous plight of human indignation. Choosing to cast aspersions at an entire nation, the media-driven stereotypes you step on to ascend to your opulent throne of righteousness, merely proves you're still a little girl; both intellectually and emotionally. Mirrors aren't just for the digital art of undressing hypocrisy, Ariana; they're also for discovering you're the one who is hopelessly out of place. It's a pity those with the most blessings in life, tend to have the least amount of love for this great country. God Bless America and please stop molesting the donuts!

Dear Kathy Griffin...

You are by no means a victim. You're not even worthy of sympathy in the most liberal sense of the word. You're a bitter, morally bankrupt narcissist who CHOSE to do a photo shoot that featured yourself holding the bloody, decapitated head of the President of the United States. And yet somehow, you're being treated unfairly? You never once thought it was wildly inappropriate, let alone a punishable crime? The entire world, including impressionable children and the traumatized son of Donald Trump, witnessed your smug display of blind hatred. Maybe I'm just hopelessly old fashioned but the unconscionable thought of someone holding my father's severed head, or anyone's for that matter, never struck me as humorous or particularly worthy of a selfie. Do you even care the surviving families of actual terrorist beheadings were horrified by your callous disregard for their incessant suffering? You've built a career on profane, tasteless commentary and now you're angry because you're finally being held accountable for your own soulless stupidity? I don't feel sorry for you. I don't care if you go broke and are rejected by every entertainment medium; which I'm sure will never happen in the socially regressive cesspool of modern progressivism. Excuse my common sense, but not everything is a joke and there wasn't anything remotely funny about your vile behavior; regardless of your whining political discontent. You're a grown woman, fully cognizant of your own actions, and in the real world those decisions have consequences: yes, even choices made by non-homicidal children with voices much less annoying than yours. Just because civilized society has definable standards, basic human decency and an emotional IQ greater than your braille rectal thermometer, doesn't mean they must apologize or support your obscene excuse of a life. The next time you feel unappreciated or identify as the wrongful victim of social outrage, try looking in the mirror to discover the single greatest source of all your ills. No amount of money is worth a good head on your shoulders; especially when it has never seen the light of day.

Signed,

Your Unborn Reflection

The Cult of Celebrity

Have you ever stood up at your place of employment and lectured your coworkers about politics? Did you ever hijack a charitable gala, sporting event or seasonable celebration and denounce complete strangers as racist, deplorable human beings for not sharing your personal beliefs? No? Never? Of course, not...you would have been fired, escorted to the door, for unlike the celebrity lynch mob you possess both common sense and a healthy dose of respect for the opinions of others. Oh, there is a time to resist radicalism and rise-up against oppression, Jody Foster, and that revolution occurred on November 8th, 2016. For 8 years fawning celebrities attended presidential parties, held private photo-ops to the chortling pour of imported Chablis, all while America's vitality, independence and security burned to their joyous applause of a bitter, anti-American propagandist. While "astute" Hollywood elitists were paid 7 figure paychecks to play charades on the Big Screen a few months out of the year, manufacturing jobs dropped by over 300,000, welfare recipients and the national debt nearly doubled, terrorist attacks/deaths and mass shootings rose by 800% and 300% respectively, gender identity supplanted gender privacy, and billions in taxpayer dollars went to Islamic regimes, illegal immigrants and unvetted refugees. Apparently "outrage" has an alternate definition on the glamorous catwalk of criminal misappropriation.

Excuse my curiosity but in what other semi-rationale universe does exposing systemic failure, reverse discrimination and unchecked abuse constitute being slandered as a hateful despot by those oblivious to their laughable hypocrisy? Inequity equally exists in those sanctimonious mouthpieces using fear and fabrication as an obnoxious pulpit to obscure one inescapable truth: if Barack Obama was held to the same warped standard as Donald Trump, he would have been impeached long before the hurt feelings of liberal activists superseded our absolute right to identify those who refuse to coexist with the American dream. No insincere apology necessary.

Contrary to the glittering purse of make-believe, the real Red Carpet isn't the one where Meryl Streep denies demanding compensation to wear a $100,000 dress, or doting reporters ask Beyoncé who designed her $500,000 ear rings. The real Red Carpet is the unsung road that takes millions of Americans to a modest job every morning to put food on the table and a roof over their families' heads in the hopes their children may one day have a better life; that is, if their parents don't go bankrupt from a "pre-existing condition" or laid off due to an anemic socialist economy that hasn't witnessed 3% annual growth in a decade. No, unlike Mr. George Clooney and the pompous hypocrites living in a cognitive bubble where non-citizens deserve lavish detention centers and neglected veterans die unceremoniously everyday as feminists march for free birth control, most Americans don't have French maids cleaning their Malibu beach home or Beverly Hills masseuses flown to Europe for an awards extravaganza in which they maliciously denigrate their own President; a populist candidate their own blind apathy and reckless ignorance willingly created.

The only revolution necessary to restore order, or more succinctly sanity, isn't the one led by overpaid fascists using public warfare to harass political opponents. It's a revolt against the lost institution of reason perverted by mindless partisans who believe intellectual diversity is a crime and that assimilation – respect for a host nation's laws, let alone the forgotten victims of terrorism, murder, rape and other foreign-born crimes – requires entertaining our own fiscal, electoral or physical demise without hesitation or regret. If putting America First triggers the gated communities of cultural apologists, those basking daily in the greatest blessings this republic provides, when do the ordinary lives and livelihoods of "We the People" matter? The price of admission to jurisprudence and due diligence far outweighs the cost of indulging the intemperance of cinematic bliss.

A Moral Failing

Ivanka Trump had her clothing line and life's work, through no fault of her own, removed from department stores like Macy's and Nordstrom's for no other reason than bearing her father's name. Snoop Dog released a video portraying an assassination of the President, while his nephew lil "Bow Wow" tweeted his desire to "Pimp Out" Melania – the First Lady, mind you – without one retail chain removing their CD's or images. Even worse, not a single mainstream news outlet, celebrity activist or "feminist" group condemned their despicable, misogynistic behavior or demanded a march of solidarity! This is why America is so irrevocably broken and in the midst of a final countdown to self-destruct along political, racial and socio-economic lines. Right and wrong is no longer a matter of simple ethics, basic decency, but rather a social construct increasingly dependent upon political preference born from juvenile spite. And yet "We the People" wonder why so many crimes by illegal immigrants go unpunished or hyper-partisan judges invent or ignore the law – a Chief Executive's legal right to restrict immigration from volatile nations like his unopposed predecessors – based solely on their obstinate personal beliefs. If a country singer pretended to murder Obama as a form of artistic expression and voiced a smug desire to turn Michelle into a corner prostitute, nearly every retail outlet or concert venue would reject their business amidst mass protests...and rightfully so.

When paranoid rhetoric makes it perfectly acceptable to riot, destroy private property and assault innocent bystanders on the street over the democratic election of a President maliciously demonized by the press, but holding peaceful rallies in support of the Constitution and your native country is discriminatory, insensitive and a form of racial supremacy – despite embracing fellow concerned citizens from all walks of life – the delineation between logic and triggered lunacy is a chalk outline of an offensive smoking gun. Regardless of your sensitivities and homicidal aspirations, your creed, color or undeclared gender should be equally irrelevant in the crosshairs of consequence. Until objectivity and common sense once again rule the day to restore accountability as a universal concept and human necessity, if only to remedy our most egregious contradictions and moral failings, America is nothing more than a Banana Republic plagued by petulant children throwing tantrums until their political victims are someday as disposable as their soiled diapers.

The Price of Perspective

Meryl Streep is a talented actress, but everyday Americans are tired of being treated like petulant children that must be incessantly lectured by condescending Hollywood elitists. If hard-working families are so "offensively" out of touch with "cultured" celebrities, what do you call wearing six-figure outfits to attend pompous galas honoring the same intolerant sycophants who are paid millions for pretending to be someone else a few months out of the year? Charitable role playing for our mental and financial health? Or perhaps those "racist" voters who have little-to-no life savings, struggle to meet their monthly bills and must pay ridiculous ticket prices to see Meryl's movies, should simply embrace a government 20 trillion in debt that gives billions in taxpayer dollars to illegal immigrants and grants free trade to foreign business competitors utilizing cheap or slave labor. Obviously our "uneducated" privilege is showing again. Oh, misogyny too? Forgive us for liberal Hollywood never sells women as sex objects, promotes negative stereotypes or pays them less than men.

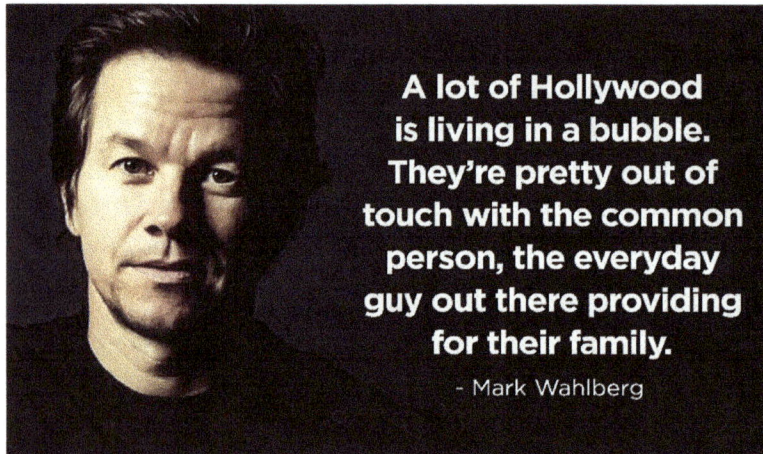

A lot of Hollywood is living in a bubble. They're pretty out of touch with the common person, the everyday guy out there providing for their family.

- Mark Wahlberg

Apparently, it's hard to tell the difference between "fake" news and reality, terrorism and humanitarianism, when writing checks to the pay-for-play, "Clinton Cash" Foundation from your beachfront balcony at the Cannes Film Festival. I don't need a Red Carpet of blind adulation or a politically hijacked pulpit of glittering vanity to realize Washington is overrun with corruption, mass deception, and a smug contempt for both the intelligence and the electoral will of the people...those independent thinkers who are the rightful owners of a federal leviathan that seeks self-preservation, unchecked power and personal favor, over transparency and the rule of law. And I sure as hell don't need permission from delusional thespians who bask in the limitless blessings of liberty, their "progressive" and celebrity privilege, only to have the gall to marginalize Trump supporters as the ignorant harbingers of hate. Sorry but I don't need bigotry or hostility to choose an unfiltered, successful CEO who unapologetically puts America first – the welfare of ALL citizens – over a glorified propagandist who struggles to utter a single positive word, let alone an honest one, about the country he claims to serve.

The very same wave of populism and palpable outrage that elected Donald Trump was born from the neglected aftermath of a rogue agenda that demonized our heritage daily, treated truth as a treasonous crime, incited discord without regret and justified entitlement (envy) over the absolute necessity of accountability. The fact the media, Mrs. Streep and her Hollywood cohorts are completely oblivious to the reality Barack Obama is by far the most radical, deceitful and hateful presidential candidate in our nation's history – a self-professed Marxist who despises America, Israel, and is obsessed with race – merely confirms the best accolades in life never require a spotlight or an acceptance speech. They are the unspoken pearls of wisdom gained from the open invitation of reason; more commonly known as, perspective.

ENCOURAGED THE PHYSICAL ASSAULT OF THE PRESIDENT
ROBERT DENIRO

DEMANDED THE PRESIDENT'S EXECUTION
MADONNA

CALLED FOR THE MURDER AND RAPE OF THE PRESIDENT'S SON
PETER FONDA

CALLED FOR THE PRESIDENT'S ASSASSINATION
JOHNNY DEPP

The Red Carpet of Denial

If you enjoy watching a whining dog itching its own ass to the thunderous applause of bleached sycophants, you would have loved the Emmy's. Otherwise, this annual gala was but another exercise in futility as smug celebrities celebrated their universal hatred of Donald Trump because they still lack the critical thinking skills necessary to discern fact from fiction, grotesque exaggeration from mature discourse, or better yet find the humility necessary to hold themselves accountable for choosing to support the most corrupt, deceitful and despised presidential candidate in modern American history: Hillary Rodham Clinton.

Perhaps I'm confusing a good Monty Python farce with a Shakespearean tragedy, but any so-called human rights platform that openly invites spewing the stale epithets of racism and sexism beneath the glitz and glamour of catered bliss – blackballing conservative actors/directors/screenwriters while zealously inciting societal discord through the inflammatory stereotypes of identity politics – is a grave threat to the harmony of any society: i.e., Hollywood's cultivated ignorance and vile intemperance towards civil decorum and intellectual diversity. Choosing to rejoice in the slanderous rhetoric and blatantly false narratives regurgitated by a media establishment that has abandoned any obligation of objectivity for the explicit goal of character assassination – a hopelessly biased medium that absurdly stated it's their job to tell us what to think or who to believe – hardly constitutes a public emergency worthy of our time, respect and undivided attention. The fact so many of these incensed celebrities were completely oblivious to the destructive and absurdly anti-American policies of the previous 8 years is exactly why so many everyday Americans chose self-preservation over self-aggrandizing propagandists and prudence over progressivism. Unless white supremacy is now the prerequisite of patriotism and common sense the sworn enemy of social justice, color and gender have become the new "search and seizure" mantra of victimization activists seeking to discredit any person or ideology that dares challenge the sheer lunacy of the globalist agenda.

Instead of fostering mutual respect among all parties and holding everyone to the same standard, leftists incessantly conspire to replace what works, or proven effective over time, solely with what sounds good to the fickle armies of entitlement. Failing to reside in the real world where criminal acts and resisting arrest puts people of all color in harm's way, where funded hate groups and political agitators are the real root of civil unrest – yes, immigration laws, sovereign borders and the doorbells on gated Hollywood communities exist for a purpose – doesn't make Donald Trump racist or a xenophobe. It makes his critics woefully naive and undeniably incredulous. Likewise, giving credence to profane feminists publicly fantasizing over the President's death – consciously ignoring the 'deplorable' detail news networks and Democratic operatives conspired to recruit false accusers who never filed a single harassment complaint – doesn't make a man sexist or a rapist in any sense of the word. Such nonsense transforms grown adults into mindless, malicious drones who have no regard for the truth, the plight of actual sexual assault survivors, simply because spoiled children still refuse to accept the electoral results of a legitimate election.

And finally, when you cannot logically deny single-payer socialist medicine is an unaffordable affront to quality healthcare or convince people that single parent households, a crumbling work ethic and a glaring lack of basic decency are the greatest threats to America's future, cinematic starlets resort to hurling insults and inane accusations to distract voters from the realization real change requires dedication and self-sacrifice rather than pompous displays of televised vitriol. Any contracted host who has the gall to call the leader of the free world a "Nazi" with no historical context of fascism's atrocities, obviously has no semblance of respect for the fallen or the faintest idea what constitutes mass suffering. Until Mr. Colbert pulls gold fillings from rotting corpses steamrolled into ravines, literally starves to death in a forced labor camp or drags entire murdered families from gas chambers, someone needs to remind him soulless hysterics born from partisan paranoia do not even register amid the unmarked ashes of cremated victims denied the everyday liberties, or should I say the lavish amenities, of limousine liberals living in a brainwashed bubble where mere political dissent now equates to the brutal oppression exacted beneath the Third Reich. If I may, in what twisted heart is such a reference remotely humorous or a subject matter worthy of such intentional indignity on a national stage?

The moment industrious, law-abiding citizens are labeled bigots for exercising their solemn duty to vote or for questioning how their tax dollars are spent while only illegals are celebrated for "dreaming" of a better life and subsequently granted sanctuary from the consequences of their actions, is the moment your opinion is about as insightful as the cost of your six-figure outfit as you applaud those mistreated, millionaire athletes who disgrace our flag and disrespect the national anthem to fight injustice; but just not the variety which encourages rioting and looting based on the race of the acquitted in lieu of embracing the actual evidence. Who needs due process, an ingrained sense of law and order, as long as showcased elitists continue to labor under the delusion they're the epitome of enlightenment, moral clarity, when in reality they're the most dangerous embodiment of excused "hate" in America today? No, it is not bigotry or the dreaded "patriarchal society" that is to blame for systemic crime, violence, unequal pay and the inevitable existence of poverty, but a failing of culture and personal responsibility itself. Truly, little is more hypocritical than a cache of coddled fascists claiming to fight "intolerance" by hijacking entertainment forums as their personal pulpit for insulting those marginalized fans caught in the political crossfire of Hollywood's privileged lifestyle.

As for those apologists who blindly disagree with my contention, when's the last time your waiter, mechanic or doctor made it his or her business to lecture you about your political beliefs in a manner or setting completely unrelated to the nature of your business? Receiving a trophy and a standing ovation for pretending to be someone else does not make your viewpoints any more relevant than the censored convictions of common men or women living in most rural reaches of America. And it sure as hell doesn't grant you domain over the autonomy of individuals who desire nothing more than to watch a celebration of artistic expression, or say a national sporting event, without being endlessly sermonized in addition to being fleeced with outrageous merchandising and ticket prices. It makes you an inconsiderate, insufferable excuse for a human being who somehow believes fame justifies celebrities selfishly bringing their political baggage into the living rooms of independent Americans who are sick and tired of being treated as second class citizens incapable of thinking for themselves.

"There seems to have been an actual decline in rational thinking. The United States had become a place where entertainers and professional athletes were mistaken for people of importance. They were idolized and treated as leaders; their opinions were sought on everything and they took themselves just as seriously-after all, if an athlete is paid a million or more a year, he knows he is important ... so his opinions of foreign affairs and domestic policies must be important, too, even though he proves himself to be ignorant and subliterate every time he opens his mouth."

~ROBERT A. HEINLEIN
1907-1988

Hogging the Celebrity Crack Pipe

The only definitive mistake Laura Ingraham made was apologizing to the adolescent anathema known as David Hogg in the first place. The lynch mob left views such civilized gestures, necessary or not, as little more than public trophies used to validate their gestapo tactics. Not only were her comments completely harmless and self-evident, they paled in comparison to his obnoxious tirades; which include, to name but a few college resume builders, disrespecting a White House liaison on the phone, profanely slandering and falsely accusing the NRA of condoning/committing mass murder, threatening uncooperative politicians, disparaging mature voters and posting the private information of corporate executives, advertisers of Laura Ingraham's show, on social media.

Semantics and pleasantries aside, Mr. Hogg is far more than a bitter, whining opportunist. He's a crude, petulant child pretending to be a celebrity authority on gun violence, criminal justice, despite having never fought in a war, survived an oppressive regime or defended his loved ones from a violent intruder who neither cared about gun laws or the sanctity of human life.

Apparently, according to the commercial censors of acceptable behavior, there's nothing quite as precious to consumers as the smug, spoiled offspring of a retired, Deep State apologist and CNN VIP using his 15 minutes of parasitic fame to lecture educated adults about their Constitutional rights, the relevance of the Second Amendment, while advocating the higher virtues of mob rule. Only in post, common sense America would the "esteemed" media give credence to such a foul-mouthed charlatan who couldn't differentiate between a fascist, a young Democrat of voting age and a Twitter endorsed cult leader aspiring to boycott logic into submission. For those not familiar with Rules for Radicals, anti-American antagonists like George Soros, Media Matters, the Southern Law/Poverty Center and Hollywood elitists have not only been waging a non-stop war on Donald Trump to deflect from his many accomplishments, unforeseen popularity, but on established Conservative voices as well by using any perceived slight, unproven allegation of impropriety, to justify terminating their syndicated views.

Naturally, no such standards of offensive conduct have been applied to the newest publicity stunt props of modern academia: the reincarnated Hitler youth commissioned with headlining the midterm resistance that somehow peacefully slumbered during the one presidency that presided over the most mass murders, terrorist attacks, police assassinations and school shootings in modern American history...the tragically praised tenure of Barack Hussein Obama.

Fortunately for the Maestro of Marxism, the young and the feckless victims of propaganda forgot to schedule a Chronic catered revolution knowing the man never passed a single piece of gun control legislation in 8 years, despite Democrats controlling Congress for two of them, or the buried fact the Obama administration sold fully automatic weapons to Mexican drug cartels resulting in the death of an American border agent. Apparently selective "outrage" requires hugging unvetted refugees and religiously ignoring public death threats of bullied students in the very Gun Free Zones liberals created to keep hypocrites like David Hogg from having to experience, God forbid pass, a real Civics class. While it may be breaking news to the paperboy proletariat, liberty is only as strong as your ability to defend it; or today's case, water the historical roots of undeterred tyranny in your comfy, hypo-allergenic pajama pants.

If "dumb-ass, old people who do not understand democracy" are to blame for the homicidal actions of the mentally ill, militant or hopelessly malicious, the same firearms that pull their own trigger must be responsible for the rapid moral decay of a self-absorbed generation that can name more Kardashians than amendments, Bible verses or actual people murdered by the NRA. When maintaining false appearances is imperative to inciting an electoral "blue wave", politically orchestrated rage conveniently masks the realization you're guilty of the very transgressions – intimidation, apathy, greed and ignorance – used to unapologetically destroy the lives of the wrongfully accused.

Glass Bubbles and Feckless Concubines

It's one thing to engage in verbal fisticuffs with someone who has insulted you or maliciously interfered with your life; it's an entirely different matter to ruthlessly degrade another human being, calling a loving mother a "feckless c*nt", for sharing an innocent and intimate moment with her toddler son. You literally must not have a soul, any shred of moral restraint, to even utter such a callous, heinous, and completely savage remark. Not only should Samantha Bee be immediately terminated from TBS and universally reprimanded by the entertainment industry, her behavior is but a microcosm of Hollywood's unbridled hate and condescending arrogance towards intellectual diversity. If a conservative host, contractually obligated employee, was responsible for such an obviously indefensible remark, that person would have already been fired, banned and vilified on practically every news network, publication and website within hours. And to think Laura Ingraham almost lost her show and was forced to apologize for merely suggesting David Hogg's antics were the impetus for colleges rejecting him. Mountain meet molehill!

Whenever adolescent celebrities and leftist activists are not indulged to the point of mindless adulation, they viciously slander dissenting opinion, marginalize the common masses, mock religion in lieu of sexual depravity and violent revolution, incite division in our communities, orchestrate classroom walkouts and profane marches to twist public sentiment, harass uncooperative businesses to the point of bankruptcy, and weaponize any Marxist tactic to demand submission to their "peaceful" political sensitivities. In other words, when grown, coddled children are not spanked by reality, possess zero regret or regard for individual liberty and basic civility, the only acceptable alternative is to throw a never-ending tantrum by force-feeding toxic stereotypes and smashing every dish in America's unplugged dining room. And yet unbeknownst to the cinematic flash mob, Ivanka Trump is far more of a political moderate, holding distinctly liberal views on a number of issues, than any ardent conservative or strict constitutionalist. Naturally such awkward trivialities are of no consequence to the woefully detached and ethically impaired mirrors of moreish self-consumption. As a result, I'm still quite vexed as to what's actually worse: Samantha Bee's disgraceful disparagement of a serene maternal embrace or her feminist peers' "feckless" response to an overpaid concubine living in the unbreakable glass bubble of Democratic devolution.

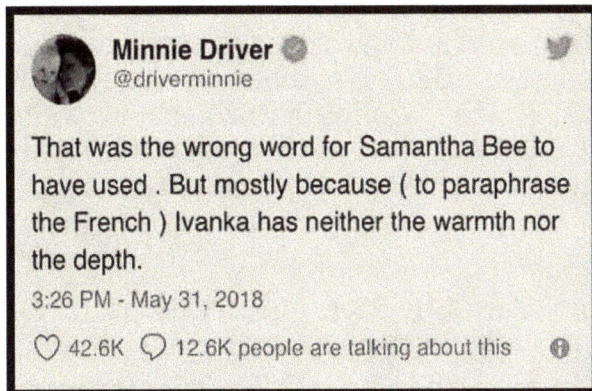

Minnie Driver ✔
@driverminnie

That was the wrong word for Samantha Bee to have used . But mostly because (to paraphrase the French) Ivanka has neither the warmth nor the depth.

3:26 PM - May 31, 2018

♡ 42.6K ○ 12.6K people are talking about this ⓘ

Sally Field ✔
@sally_field

I like Samantha Bee a lot, but she is flat wrong to call Ivanka a c■nt.

C■nts are powerful, beautiful, nurturing and honest.

3:05 PM - May 31, 2018

♡ 163K ○ 58.4K people are talking about this ⓘ

Truth, Consequence and Cool Celebrity Marxists

Other than an obvious lack of equal accountability in a politically-incestuous industry, I honestly don't have a problem with Roseanne losing her show. Her comments, satirically driven or not, were foolish and stupid actions have consequences. That being said...spare me the media's non-stop, "Racism Non-Grata" pledge and cued celebrity outrage when their peers have relentlessly slandered and physically threatened the President with uncanny and remorseless regularity; still a prosecutable felony by my calculations, if not a simple matter of basic decency.

Despite the left's sincerest attempts at daily martyrdom, Donald Trump has been called an Orangutan, a baboon, a Nazi, the Grand Dragon of the KKK, an orange "Cheeto" and a serial rapist by countless Hollywood personalities and affiliated journalists. Likewise, if I had a dollar every time the symbolic Leader of the Free World was referred to as Hitler, a genocidal maniac literally referred to as the anti-Christ, I could literally fashion a straitjacket vast enough to house every actor, musician, and unethical member of the press incapable of recognizing the mental neurosis of their own fascist hypocrisy. Johnny Depp, Snoop Dog, Robert De Niro, Eminem and Madonna have all publicly advocated Trump's assassination and/or overthrow, Jimmy Kimmel has repeatedly and viciously insulted the President's family, "The View's" Joy Reid has a rich history of bigoted tweets, her colleague Joy Behar smugly degraded Christian conservatives, while Stephen Colbert obscenely belittled our Chief Executive on live TV with a wildly-inappropriate homophobic slur. Do I even need to mention the incessant body shaming and ad-hominem humiliation Press Secretary, Sarah Sanders has had to endure?

Not surprisingly, every single one of these "respected" individuals, moonlighting "humanists", are still employed and embraced by the so-called socially-conscious entertainment industry that somehow spontaneously combusts in the presence of political incorrectness. Even Keith Olbermann, a former sports anchor known for his inflammatory political tirades – including urging our "effing Nazi President" to die a thousand times – was recently welcomed back to host SportsCenter despite his uninterrupted legacy of hostile attacks. For those keeping score in the land of duplicity, ESPN is owned by Disney, the parent company of ABC, which is the very same network that just terminated Roseanne's extremely successfully sitcom for her "repugnant and highly-offensive" remarks. Yes, these are also the identical hypocrites who fired baseball commentator Kurt Schilling for simply sharing a photo of a male crossdresser to demonstrate his support for the "controversial" North Carolina bathroom law which defined privacy according to one's natural-born gender; a concept far too elementary for those trans-geneticists lobotomized by progressivism because they stayed at Holiday Inn Express last night.

Although I make no apologies for Roseanne Barr's reckless observations, I am disappointed a highly-popular show endorsing patriotic, common sense ideals is now lost amidst an endless sea of liberal programming. Her comedy's strong ratings merely confirmed how neglected everyday Americans feel when it comes to modern television and cinema, but how short of a proverbial leash respected conservative actors like Tim Allen are on in the hyper-sensitive arena of public indoctrination. With or without any star's personal misgivings, Cable executives will not hesitate to drop the most lucrative show if its cultural relevance poses a threat to their warped agenda. However, I am grateful Roseanne's careless behavior at least placed a searing spotlight on the true embodiment of uncontested evil in this country: Valerie Jarrett. The daughter of affluent, American parents investigated by the FBI for real ties to Soviet agents, Chicago Communists and one infamous Frank Marshall – not to mention Barack Obama's most trusted political confidant and longtime friend – this Iranian-born revolutionary never should have been allowed within 1000 feet of the White House, let alone given access to the most consequential levels of our government.

Contrary to "Happy Hour" hucksters, Mrs. Jarrett is a malicious, contemptible, unapologetic anti-Semite who despises America, embraces murderous Islamic factions the likes of the Muslim Brotherhood and Hezbollah, and who has worked tirelessly to undermine our national unity, global influence and economic vitality. She is a key cog in the famed "resistance" organized to thwart any legitimate reform promoting American independence, federal transparency and individual prosperity. In fact, during college, her quoted life's ambition was to fundamentally transform the United States by using the blessing of religious liberty against her own citizens to exact meaningful "change". Yes, never mind the expendable detail the Middle East has remained a despotic bastion of injustice for millennia on end, and please disregard the racist anecdote Communism has historically oppressed and murdered hundreds of millions of innocents, but who wouldn't want to tear down the one global respite which still offers unlimited opportunity and universal human rights to those spiteful globalists masquerading as the cure for their rewarded, callous indifference?

In any other semi-sane or remotely-vigilant era, Valerie Jarrett would have been arrested for treason, tried and sentenced to death. Not only do I have no doubt whatsoever she was the driving impetus behind freeing $150 billion in frozen assets for the radical Ayatollahs of Iran, arranging a $400 million-dollar ransom payment for "captured" U.S. sailors, and the unratified authority to pursue a nuclear arsenal, isolating Israel and interfering with their sovereign elections, including French nationalist Marine Le Pen's presidential bid, you can bet your atrophying Christian freedoms she played a leading role in hatching the Russian conspiracy plot used to illegally spy on a Presidential candidate and newly-elected administration for the first time in U.S. history.

For those uninterested in spoon-fed propaganda and the warm, shared bed of yellow journalism, guess which "egregious crime" our esteemed partisan watchdog so bravely chose to chastise and investigate for the betterment of society: a growing malaise poisoning the very soul and future of this nation, or a juvenile "Planet of the Apes" analogy from an unfiltered humorist allowing partisan hacks the perfect opportunity to once again denounce all Trump supporters as Right-Wing supremacists? Then again, when it's common knowledge Roseanne profanely desecrated the National Anthem in 1990 and ran for President in 2012 on the far left-wing "Peace and Freedom" ticket, what's a little friendly misdirection in the of smoke-filled corridors of political assassins? Without the trending hashtag assistance of golden double standards, the celebrity caravan of #WeKnew and #StopH8 wouldn't know where to find their giant, jagged, immoral compass stuck on their collective, little forehead.

Our Father
who art in heaven,
hallowed be thy name.
Thy kingdom come.
Thy will be done
on earth as it is in heaven.
Give us this day our daily bread
and forgive us our trespasses,
as we forgive those
who trespass against us.
And lead us not into temptation,
but deliver us from evil.
For thine is the kingdom,
and the power, and the glory,
for ever and ever.
Amen.
Matthew 6:9-13

GOD & FAITH

The Light of Liberty

One Man With Courage Is A Majority

Faith

The House of God

Knock! Knock! Who's there? Pizza? Fluffy? Absolute awareness? While creationism has left the door open for a secular crescendo of doubt, science has sought to rip the House of God off its theological foundation and definitively answer the most evasive question in human history: who or what created life as we know it? Thus, the intergalactic search for the fingerprints of divinity and friendly aliens has produced perhaps the most controversial hypothesis ever put forth: The Big Bang theory.

As both a disciple of Christ and the evolutionary embodiment of science, knowledge gained through observation and mathematical probability, I too love the Big Bang: that iconic moment when atheists magically appear to protest an imaginary God. Whereas Stephen Hawking surmised gravity created our universe, gravity requires matter which still suggests "something" was created by "nothing". Or perhaps, just maybe, all that mass and energy that was bottled-up and inexplicably confined for eternity...but just not in the form of an omnipotent being or conscious energy, of course...was the catalyst of intelligent design. Where there is structure; there is purpose. Where there is purpose; there is intent. Don't you love when a Mercedes materializes out of thin air without a single engineer, commercial or mechanical blueprint? The fact the human genome stretches to the moon and back over 250,000 times shouldn't scare any "nonbelievers" or raise any red flags of evolution. Yes, that was empirical doubt disguised as sarcasm. Fred Hoyle, the scientific author of the iconic term "Big Bang", called his celebrated hypothesis dubious at best and highly unlikely due to the massive statistical improbability the right amount of force and mass would correctly mix to form celestial objects, and in the process, exact life.

In order to keep from becoming the biggest dud in unrecorded history, or the biggest anomaly since Pop Rocks and Pepsi, the Big Bang had to essentially catch lightning in a bottle. How so? Balance, Daniel-san; balance! If this cosmic explosion was too strong, matter would only exist in a gaseous form, diffusing at such a substantial rate that stars or planets would be unable to take shape. Likewise, if the bang was too weak, gravity would have pulled the expanding matter back unto itself, eradicating any possibility of celestial bodies forming. As a primer to this singular event, our world-renowned astrophysicist Fred Hoyle estimated the odds of life forming on its own to the tune of one shot in ten to the forty thousandth power. That number is so astronomical, excuse the pun, not even a socialist with a meth, yacht and gambling addiction could spend it. Wow, good thing our Indian ancestors taught us how to count. Forget that, I need a solar-powered calculator.

The probability that life started on its own is $1 \times 10^{-40,000}$. Therefore, we would naturally ask ourselves if some "entity" was behind the beginning of life. When scientists test hypotheses, they test what is called the null hypothesis or a statement opposite of the hypothesis that presumes the original hypothesis is wrong. In this case a scientist would attempt to validate the assumption there was no entity behind the beginning of life; that it began by chance. The researcher then determines the probability that the null hypothesis being tested is false. The standard used to reject a null hypothesis is = 0.95. A 0.05 probability can be restated as $1 \times 10^{-1.3}$. As such, the probability that life started on its own is many magnitudes smaller than 0.05. Thus, a scientist using standard statistical methodology would easily reject the statement that life began by mere chance.

Life, in its most elementary form, is far from some archaic stew; a random assemblage of mix and match proteins. The DNA of the simplest bacteria contains nearly ten trillion bits of information, more than five million paired bases, all precisely encoded for the purposes of survival and reproduction. And you thought your computer was a dinosaur? Don't flatter yourself! By contrast, a human's DNA is a scintillating sequence of approximately three billion paired bases of four separate chemicals; each arranged in perfect order. To duplicate the supposed biological splendor of human evolution, you must flawlessly sequence our DNA through mere adaptation and chance alone. Furthermore, you will be completely isolated, unable to consult anyone or anything, and must finish this paltry paradigm in a little less than 4.6 billion years. Oh yeah, I almost forgot. You cannot begin until the first sign of life appears, which, according to some scientists, will take at least a billion years under the most ideal circumstances; not excluding, of course, that little meteor mishap, the occasional ice age or the ecological plunder from the unlicensed fireworks of super volcanoes.

If you feel like you just gave birth to an accountant, or better yet Carl Sagan in a turtleneck, you're not alone. And what does Charles Darwin think about his fashion sense or better yet the butterfly collar effect of this biological quagmire; you know, that English naturalist who floated the supremacy of evolution as the genesis of life and not the divine blueprint from which engineered life evolved?

"To suppose that the eye, with all its inimitable contrivances for adjusting the focus to different distances, for admitting different amounts of light, for the correction of spherical and chromatic aberration, could have been formed by natural selection, seems, I freely confess, absurd in the highest degree."
~Charles Darwin, 1859

Other than the inevitability of death, neither science nor religion can definitively lay claim to the throne of creation. Science cannot disprove the existence of a god, though it can "theoretically" account for the origins of life. Religion cannot prove the existence of a god, though any account of creationism must ultimately utilize some form of intelligent design...a scientific framework. Thus, by some literary twist of fate, it seems our two competing notions of universal induction are cosmically linked, or in modern nomenclature, sleeping under the same roof! Please excuse me while I read a little "Genesis" before going to bed and magically begin to feel "genetically" enlightened. I don't need to solve a riddle or look in the mirror to know life is an unrivaled gift that cannot be enumerated, dismissed or reduced to the palatable tastes of scientific conjecture.

"As for me and my family, we will serve God, we will serve this constitutional republic, we will serve America." *~Allen West*

Divinity & Darkness

During times of national discord, tragedy or personal loss I routinely hear atheists or agnostics ask...if God truly exists why does he allow so much needless suffering to occur? My response...does he? God blessed mankind with free will, not freedom from consequences or misfortune, for that is the inescapable nature of life. What would be the purpose of life in all its magnificence and self-aware glory, without choice or free will, if God constantly needed to intercede on our behalf? The greatest gift also comes with the greatest burden: mortality. Why else would Jesus – a humble, peaceful and compassionate man mocked for his beliefs – endure such endless torture for refusing to renounce his faith in the face of such evil and dire circumstances? Without consequence or conviction learned from the struggle of everyday life, how would humanity recognize or appreciate the smallest blessings born from endeavoring to coexist in a world free from strife? The wisdom of a penniless carpenter who chose to walk in the light of virtue, to sacrifice himself so others may find redemption, could not be extinguished by fear of pain or decree of death. It continues to reside in a universal maxim: you don't have to be religious to accept God's love, let alone pray in a church to espouse a moral life. You merely have to accept that divinity and darkness exists in all of us – both in times of triumph and tragedy, charity and senseless depravity – regardless of our eventual fates. Wherever there is hate, there is also hope. Where loved ones will eventually perish, billions will rejoice in the beauty of birth.

The key to peace on Earth is not to waste breaths engaging in endless theological debate, but rather to relish every moment we have together as sentient beings blessed with the ability to discern: to cherish and choose life over needlessly forsaking it. Faith is not a handwritten guarantee or unbreachable protection from daily peril. It's a lifelong struggle and testament that challenges followers to believe when public sentiment, the faculties of the mind, overwhelmingly tell us not to. The character of Christ did not wilt beneath the unspeakable cruelty surrounding his persecution and crucifixion; it merely strengthened his resolve to embody love. And that is why I will forever endeavor to follow in his footsteps: to shed light during the darkest of times or seek salvation in the gloomiest corners of the globe.

The Legacy of Man

For as long as man has roamed the Earth, we have become exceedingly efficient at one thing: killing one another. Yet, no two people are born hating one another. They are taught how to hate. And if people are taught how to hate, they can be taught how to love. No religion, nationality or political ideology is worth looking in the eyes of another human being and taking their life in the name of blind spite or sheer righteousness. In the sky, there is no distinction between east and west; people create these divisions and believe them to be true.

Rather than dividing ourselves according to race, gender, wealth, affiliation or geography, we should remind ourselves we're bound by common struggles and hopes. In other words, no matter how much we disagree or distrust one another, the solution has always been love, respect and temperance. It doesn't cost money, you won't find it on Black Friday and no celebrity endorsement is necessary. It simply resides in you. The antidote to hate is the one gift every man and woman has been blessed with since our creation...a heart to heal, to feel another's pain, and a mind to digress from and alleviate our discord. The Kingdom of Heaven is within you, within us all, because it is here on Earth where we must make our stand; where virtue must rain and our children must grow tall. No God, in all his omnipotence and might, would grant mankind a sword to kill one of his children. And right now, that's exactly who we are and how we're behaving. Pray for Paris, but most of all, pray for a legacy that endures without refrain.

"Do not pity the dead, pity the dead; and above all else, pity those who live without love."

The Divorced Truth of "Church and State"

"The Congress of the United States recommends and approves the Holy Bible for use in all schools." *~United States Congress 1782*

This country was established upon the espoused belief religion was essential to good government. On July 13, 1787, the Continental Congress enacted the Northwest Ordinance, which stated: **"Religion, morality and knowledge, being necessary to good government and the happiness of mankind, schools and the means of education shall be forever encouraged."**

On October 7, 1802, roughly 13 years after the final ratification of the Constitution, the Danbury Baptist Association of Connecticut wrote to President Thomas Jefferson to decry the infringement of their religious liberty. In his response, the President expounded... "Almighty God, the father and creator of man, hath created the mind free. I shall see with sincere satisfaction the progress of those sentiments which tend to restore to man all his natural rights, {rather than} convinced he has no natural right in opposition to his social duties." ... "I contemplate with sovereign reverence that act of the whole American people which declared that their legislature should "make no law respecting an establishment of {an official} religion, or prohibiting the free exercise thereof," thus building a wall of separation between Church & State."

In the 1947 case Everson v. Board of Education, Supreme Court Justice Hugo Black put forth the novel interpretation that the First Amendment's establishment clause applied to the states and that any government support or preference for religion amounts to an unconstitutional establishment of religion. In support of his argument for a "radical" separation of religion and politics, he cited Jefferson's metaphor: "The First Amendment has erected a wall of separation between Church and State. That wall must be kept high and impregnable."

By taking the Jefferson metaphor out of its proper context, strict separatists have often used the phrase to silence Christians and this limit Christian influence – the theological basis for our societal norms and Constitutional rights – from further influencing the political system. Jefferson's actual aim was quite to the contrary. To understand his "wall of separation" verbiage, we must return to the original context in which it was written. Jefferson himself wrote:

"On every question of construction, we must carry ourselves back to when the constitution was adopted, recollect the spirit manifested in the debates, and instead of trying what meaning may be squeezed out of the test, or invented against it, conform to the probable one in which it was a part."

So, what did Jefferson really mean when he used the infamous "wall" metaphor? If Congress had no legal authority in matters of religion, then neither did the President. Religion was clearly within the jurisdiction of the Church and states. As a state legislator, Jefferson saw no conflict with proclaiming days of thanksgiving and prayer, and even on one occasion prescribed a penalty to the clergy for failure to abide by these state proclamations. Jefferson emphatically believed the Constitution created a limited government and that the states retained the authority over matters of religion; not only through the First Amendment but also through the Tenth Amendment. The 'wall of separation' existed to affirm natural rights, including those of faith and religious worship. The "wall" does not imprison the free exercise of religion in which Jefferson sought to prevent the domination of particular sects, not ostracize any and all reference to God and our faith, therefore protecting the religious practices of all.

Our Forefathers never intended for an unconditional separation of Church & State. They supported religious freedom to protect against forced subjugation by the federal government, while ensuring "state" rights and their intended jurisdiction over the matters of religion. Thus, the term, "Church and State". Merely acknowledging God on a national level – the recognized source of our natural born rights as prescribed by the Declaration of Independence – and giving credence to his inherent wisdom as the ideological basis for our laws and norms, was but a living testament to who we innately are as a people, our nation's founding creed. Cultural Marxists forged the absolutism of "Separation of Church of State", hijacking our framers' original intent to wrongfully claim domain over all doctrine and essentially divorce religion, as part of a political ruse to undermine our Judeo-Christian values and fundamentally transform America to their liking. Well, consider it a job well done for prisons are now the only public institution deemed universally appropriate for the usage of Bibles. How apropos being the truth shall once again set our children free!

Liberal Lie #666: The Secular State

"It cannot be emphasized too strongly or too often that this great nation was founded, not by religionists, but by Christians; not on religions, but on the gospel of Jesus Christ. For this very reason peoples of other faiths have been afforded asylum, prosperity, and freedom of worship here."
–The Trumpet Voice of Freedom: Patrick Henry of Virginia, p. iii.

Separation of Church & State, a brazen perversion of our founder's intent made increasingly popular by progressives during the 1970's, was never intended to exclude God from our Government or public schools. It was meant to ensure religious freedom: an open and constructive inclusion of biblical teachings without the historical transgression of religious hostilities so prevalent in the Dark or Middle Ages. Whether secularists like it or not, or no matter how much they object or protest, Judeo-Christian values serve as the ideological pillars of a sovereign nation built upon individual liberty, personal accountability and limited government. If you read the writings of our most influential forefathers...Madison, Jefferson, Adams, and Washington...the manifestation of God is thoroughly entrenched, directly or indirectly, in the conception of our republic, cultural norms and everyday laws.

These wise and learned men warned us numerous times about the dire consequences of abandoning our faith and fundamental belief in self-rule. Society today is case-in-point; a political minefield of decadence and division in which we've become obsessed with vice and discontent rather than contributing to a productive, virtuous and vibrant future acutely aware of the triggers of tyranny and injustice. While it is true ethics or moral judgement do not require any religious affiliation, both are largely synonymous with Christian doctrine. Except in addition to the ethical austerity of the Ten Commandments – do not kill, steal, commit adultery or bare false witness – the human condition of compassion and forgiveness so prevalent in the New Testament are equally intertwined into the moral fabric of our national conscience: i.e., charity, kindness, empathy, and temperance.

Our founders' acknowledgment of "God" in our public institutions, a higher power which they unanimously believed created life and was the genesis of their natural born rights, in no way forced citizens to be Christian, Jewish, or to even believe in God. Apropos, America has never designated a national religion or forced subjugation an ideology of any kind. Their assertion simply recognized the perceived divinity of sentient salvation, enlightenment and atonement through the unique faculties of mankind, while allowing citizens to retain the choice to believe what they wanted without fear of persecution.

If you truly want to erect a completely secular country, you better start by tearing down nearly every facet of American society because for millennia Judeo-Christianity has helped Western Civilization define the family paradigm, individual rights, due process, civic duty, and democracy. All are undeniably symbiotic and invaluable to our revered way of life. Lest we forget, it was Christian activists invoking the universal affirmation of the Declaration of Independence and the supremacy of the Constitution of the United States, not the misguided practices of any era, who spearheaded the movements to end the lingering injustices of human bondage, suffrage and abortion. Striving for the betterment of any culture, instilling the virtuous necessities of respect, decency and humility in our children, becomes virtually unattainable when violence, substance abuse, profanity and promiscuity are far more recognizable in modern media than those "antiquated" Christian beliefs incessantly mocked by political detractors.

The real hypocrisy surrounding God and the role of limited government is that cultural terrorists want to instill their own religion...progressivism...rather than recognize the intrinsic and rightful place of God at the American table of liberty and justice. Because socialism and collectivism are the historical enemies of American idealism, individuality and prosperity, statists incessantly plot to discredit our values and disregard the Constitution in favor of imposing their own political beliefs; i.e., those activist judges ignoring the explicit Executive authority to issue travel bans, deport illegal aliens or defund the criminal premise of sanctuary cities. Attacking free speech, burning the flag, labeling conservatism as fascism, legalizing polygamy and kneeling during the national anthem are hardly random coincidences. They are malicious acts specifically designed to eradicate our respect for America and any sense of obligation to a higher calling.

The problem with secular leftists, the unrivaled source and/or support of militant radicalism today, is they cannot stand being questioned over the merits of their convictions or held accountable for their actions; which, of course, predominantly emanates from espousing an intolerant, anti-American, and counter-intuitive agenda. Progressives hate recognizing any higher power or moral authority for it undermines their ability to indoctrinate the masses and ensure political supremacy. Truly, there is no greater force than faith – love of God, country and family – guided by unwavering principles centuries of men and women fought and died to protect. The fact conservatism is clearly most synonymous with our constitutional ideals, our rise to the forefront of Western Civilization, is the very reason why the liberal media and the Democratic Party resort to such vicious and shameless propaganda: they must tirelessly conspire and cajole to eradicate common sense, the immutable influence of God, in order to achieve their objectives.

It is no coincidence that Barack Obama and Hillary Clinton systematically inflamed cultural divides and incited hate among nearly every socioeconomic faction. Divide, distract, and conquer is the Marxist mantra of modern identity politics. America wasn't forged with the duplicitous intent of winning a political game of charades while human decency, national security and industry crumbled in the proverbial distance beneath the oppressive hammer of Communism. It was America's contract between man and God that a small band of idealists risked live and limb to erect a free, just, hard-working and self-aware society. Freedom of speech, religion, was never designed to shield us from our religious values; it was designed to protect our religious values and this nation's founding charter from the potential future excesses of our government.

The subversive practice of exploiting social issues such as school prayer, gender conditioning, gay marriage, abortion, pornography and pedophilia via Separation of Church & State is little more than activists attempting to fit a square peg in a round hole in hopes of convincing an apathetic public the wheel really isn't round. Unlike those unscrupulous politicians who have no conscience or regard for our intelligence, excuse us for not kneeling before a corrupt establishment that embraces propaganda over progress, entitlement over independence, and government over God. In other words, like our forefathers, I find strength in the grace and indelible wisdom of my creator – the limitless potential, fortitude, and moral compass of an American creed – over the inhumane ashes of any soulless, totalitarian state.

"Resistance to tyranny becomes the Christian and social duty of each individual ... Continue steadfast and, with a proper sense of your dependence on God, nobly defend those rights which heaven gave, and no man ought to take from us."
–John Hancock, *History of the United States of America*, Vol. II, p. 229.

"While we are zealously performing the duties of good citizens and soldiers, we certainly ought not to be inattentive to the higher duties of religion. To the distinguished character of Patriot, it should be our highest glory to add the more distinguished character of Christian."
–*The Writings of Washington*, pp. 342-343.

"Now I will avow, that I then believe, and now believe, that those general Principles of Christianity, are as eternal and immutable, as the Existence and Attributes of God; and that those Principles of Liberty, are as unalterable as human Nature and our terrestrial, mundane System."
–*John Adams wrote this on June 28, 1813, excerpt from a letter to Thomas Jefferson.*

Jesus of Nazareth: The Kingdom of Heaven

"The Passion of the Christ" – as difficult as it is to watch – is a transcendent work for one indelible reason: why wouldn't a man, if he didn't truly believe he was the Son of God, simply renounce his claim rather than suffer so horribly at the hands of his detractors? For many, those whose lives are equally fraught with human frailty, faith ultimately supersedes any fear of pain or indignation. Their spirit is ethereal and cannot be touched or diminished by any earthly device of such tangible hate. For others, it is a righteous pulpit to pass judgement and instill fear as a means to achieve power, fortune or fame. Either way, temptation and temperance is the crux upon which humanity can rise or fall.

Nothing is more profound, representative of the dichotomy between Jesus the man and Jesus the Son of God, than the philosophical bridge spanning these two iconic statements: "My God...why hast thou forsaken me?" and "It is finished"! It was this distinct juxtaposition that became the genesis of the "The Last Temptation of Christ". Although many believed the book and film to be blasphemous, the writer was simply trying to reconcile these contrasting thoughts. In essence, Nikos Kazantzakis hypothesized that God gave Jesus a vision of what the world would have become if he was but an ordinary man – misled by temptation, evil and sin – in lieu of leading a life of virtue and willingly sacrificing himself on the cross for the salvation of all mankind. In this context, I believe this interpretation was both fascinating and ingenious for you cannot study or appreciate Jesus the Son of God without understanding his trials and tribulations as a man.

Whether you're a devout Christian, Jewish, agnostic or an atheist, one thing is for certain; a wealth of inspiration and wisdom can be drawn from the brief life and brutal torture of Jesus of Nazareth. Unlike the feared priests and prefects of the time, the selfless deeds and testimony of a humble carpenter from Galilee embodied love and forgiveness; a stark contrast from the "fire & brimstone" fatalism of the Old Testament. It's not that he didn't believe there would be consequences for one's actions – albeit in life or the liberation of death – Jesus simply recognized that as long as hope remained, sincere contrition for our missteps, it was never too late to live a virtuous life and seek salvation. Our sacred duty to honor the divine gift of life lies not in any ordained structure or hoarded artifact, but in our willingness to honor thy commandments and sacrifice for the welfare of others.

Whereas his battered body eventually succumbed to the most unspeakable cruelty, Jesus' faith did not. The resurrection of the human spirit, one man's choice to feel compassion without contempt, bleed benevolence beneath the blade of belligerence, is now humanity's cross to bear. Therefore, as we are all mired in life's daily struggles and injustices – poverty, disease, conflict or petty, everyday contrivances – it becomes all the more vital to embrace one inescapable adage: The Kingdom of Heaven is in you, whether you believe in God or not. You need only be willing to find it.

<u>The Gift of Charity</u>

For the over two billion Christians around the globe, Christmas is a sacred celebration marking the birth of our savior, Jesus Christ. It has also become increasingly synonymous with commercialism, materialism, and the almighty power of the dollar. Now before you sense a lengthy diatribe against greed or self-indulgence, my answer may honestly surprise you. I personally do not have a problem with gift-giving as long as these traditions are put in proper context. Charity is not only a virtue but one of humanity's most redeeming qualities when it is done strictly from a standpoint of love, altruism, rather than the jaded expectation of reciprocal reward. I do freely admit many children have lost sight of what Christmas embodies – God's undying love for mankind, his children, and that of his only begotten son – but many have not been properly taught, and two, well, they're kids. It is neither insidious or unnatural to be excited by the prospect of receiving presents for they fill our hearts with both joy and wonder. However, above all else, we should be even more enthusiastic and grateful for those everyday blessings present in our lives – the lifelong love of supportive parents, a caring and faithful spouse, healthy children, and the basic amenities of food, shelter, education – modern complacency too often takes for granted or freely expects.

And yes, even when people lack any of these invaluable necessities and struggle to overcome such trying tribulations, we as Americans must never forget to give thanks for the divine gift of liberty, an eternal light conceived in God's compassion and grace, which warns ours senses and strengthens our hearts against hate, cruelty and depravity. For no matter how bleak or barren tomorrow may seem, America offers a bounty of self-fulfilling opportunity, generosity and level of hope from despair that millions throughout the world, still to this day, can scarcely imagine.

As someone who truly rejoices in the festive revelry of the Holiday season, a virtuous reminder of personal rebirth and redemption that should last throughout the year, there is no greater gift than human empathy...most notably, a genuine concern for the well-being of family, neighbors and complete strangers. Muddled in the hustle and bustle of our own daily lives, our growing impatience and demand for satisfaction, society is too easily blinded or even numb to the struggles of our fellow brethren. As we are increasingly consumed by modern contrivances and hoarded possessions, there are countless souls who have never known love, who cannot escape the ravages of disease, who sleep in abandoned warehouses or parked cars in the dead of winter, who frequently go to bed hungry, are sexually abused by supposed figures of trust, or lack the support to overcome loss, domestic violence, depression and substance abuse. To these forgotten or falsely stereotyped individuals, the slightest hint of compassion or a kind face with whom to share their feelings – perhaps a cup of coffee, a phone call for help made on their behalf or a warm embrace – exceeds the dollar amount of any highly coveted, mass marketed, commercial item.

Making a lasting difference in the world, endeavoring to walk in the benevolent footsteps of Christ, begins by teaching our children the greatest act of charity is their time, humanity, forgiveness and willingness to think of others before themselves. And although it is true I believe no child should go without a present or a family's love on Christmas day, I gain far more satisfaction from giving to and helping others than any ornate present I may receive. Whether volunteering to feed the homeless, befriending an orphan in foster care or donating services to a senior citizen in need, hope resides in our capacity to embody charity, spread good will and cheer, each and every ordinary day of the year.

"Kindness is the language which the deaf can hear and the blind can see."
~Mark Twain

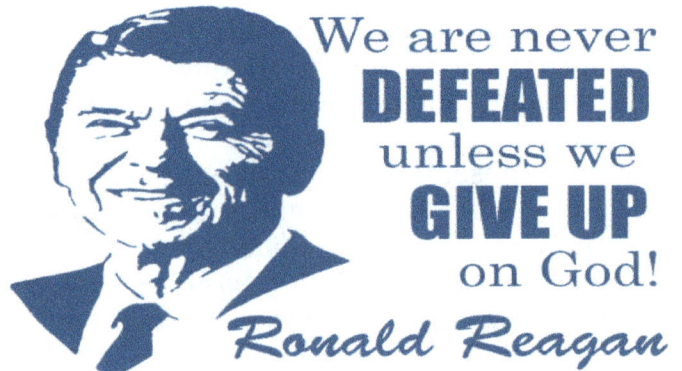
We are never **DEFEATED** unless we **GIVE UP** on God!
Ronald Reagan

Thankful to be An American

October 3, 1789

A proclamation by the President of the United States of America, George Washington.

"Whereas it is the duty of all Nations to acknowledge the providence of Almighty God, to obey his will, to be grateful for his benefits, and humbly to implore his protection and favor—and whereas both Houses of Congress have by their joint Committee requested me "to recommend to the People of the United States a day of public thanksgiving and prayer to be observed by acknowledging with grateful hearts the many signal favors of Almighty God especially by affording them an opportunity peaceably to establish a form of government for their safety and happiness.

Now therefore I do recommend and assign Thursday the 26th day of November next to be devoted by the People of these States to the service of that great and glorious Being, who is the beneficent Author of all the good that was, that is, or that will be—That we may then all unite in rendering unto him our sincere and humble thanks—for his kind care and protection of the People of this Country."

America's Founding Fathers were by no means passive bystanders whose convictions withered beneath the earthly pleasures of solitary indifference. They were devout Christians and ardent patriots who believed our natural born liberties, the creation of this Constitutional Republic, were an extension of God's wisdom; a divine calling for mankind to choose virtue over virulence, charity over tyranny. Regardless of our innate differences or disagreements, our triumphs and struggles, America cannot survive when a growing faction of our brethren, those who also slumber and dine from the same tree of liberty, seek disrespect through shared discontent rather than unity from universal esteem. Thanksgiving is a joyous occasion to celebrate our faith and family, breathe hope in the face of despair, so we may appreciate the smallest blessings in life...no matter how seemingly insignificant or difficult to comprehend. And while it is true some are more fortunate than others – more affluent in success, health or happiness – our lives cannot be marginalized or reduced to pompous rivalry when we persevere to embody God's grace: to embrace our challenges, bring humanity to those in need and fill the footsteps of everyday heroes who sacrificed so we may still choose how to both live with dignity and amend regrets. Today is not just another frivolous day of food and festivity; it is our privilege to gather with family and friends, welcome complete strangers into our homes, to reflect upon what it means to be an American, and with it, a humble messenger of faith. May God Bless you all for he has blessed me with your amity and yet another bountiful Thanksgiving.

The Secular Pope of Progressivism

Excuse my brash inquisition, but exactly what manner of Pope praises the oppressive and murderous ideology of communism but demonizes America, capitalism and individual liberty; that which recognizes our natural born rights are derived by God and not ransomed by the ruddy hand of soulless statism? And what kind of Pope, let alone a Christian, supports gay marriage, its destructive practice and cultural implications, when the Bible – the theological basis for our faith – condemns it explicitly in numerous passages? Sorry but building a wall to restore order to a broken and recklessly exploited immigration system isn't hateful or the act of a non-Christian. It's a prudent and bold initiative designed to address the disturbing reality our pandering government has purposely allowed millions of medically and criminally unvetted immigrants to freely enter America, breaking those very laws our President swore to protect and thus putting actual citizens at risk, solely to stuff the ballot box with an inexhaustible source of foreign votes. Who knew 'humanitarianism' was so coy about honesty?

The question at hand isn't whether or not Donald Trump is a Christian simply because he spoke an uncomfortable truth. The real question is what is the definition of treason and when did it cease being a crime; that which over half of our elected officials are guilty of proudly committing. Everyone who respects our laws and completes the immigration process is welcome in America. Those who don't, the same trespassers who are aided and abetted by our own radical leaders, are criminals. That's right...illegal is, and has always been, a crime. It's just too bad we have to contemplate building a wall to remind our own pandering politicians, the media and anti-American celebrities of one immutable truth: we are a nation of laws, borders, and protecting our national sovereignty is a nonnegotiable necessity. It's not rocket science or an insidious conspiracy; it's common sense, unless that is, you're dedicated to the proposition of the once most revered nation on earth becoming a third-world socialist cesspool and a banana republic in the name of political correctness. And to think the Ten Commandments were so offensive and inappropriate in state capitols across America, the Pope of the People never once stood up for the word of God, our Constitutional foundation, and condemned those atheists, the secular forces of contrarianism, who had them removed in the name of 'progress'. The invisible walls of ideological hypocrisy are often far more egregious than those we perceive as tangible threats.

The Good Shepherd

That is correct, snide celebrities, prayers alone are not enough to prevent future tragedies similar to the senseless massacre at Sutherland Springs. And yet despite your successful attempts at unabashed blasphemy, your greater contempt for the Second Amendment than the corrupted soul denied a gun permit – the same bitter atheist who viciously targeted the faith of vulnerable innocents – blinds your arrogance to the most self-evident hypocrisy of all. America needs far less glorified depravity and far more armed, law-abiding, Christian citizens ever cognizant of the cultural hostility Hollywood intentionally breeds with its libertine lifestyle and obnoxious propaganda...i.e., your condescending politics of perverse hate. If God is truly a figment of our naive imagination, the greatest trick moral relativists ever played was convincing the countless victims of rape, child abuse and murder that Satan by no means exists.

Unlike the Box Office and Billboard charts, the Ten Commandments are invaluable virtues that reward humility, instill respect and embody love. Our Heavenly Father does not stop bullets in our sacred halls of worship to satisfy the facetious validation of scornful nonbelievers. He steadies the hand of malice, eases the burden of discontent, by granting humanity one indelible bridge to eternal life: choice...that conscious crux of a meaningful existence born from consequence. Within the divine gift of free will lies our salvation for the Kingdom of God cannot be displaced or destroyed by any earthly pleasure, political measure or wielded weapon of mankind. It resides in the weeping hearts of penitent men and women who seek forgiveness from sin, wealth from wisdom and the courage to defeat evil amidst the despair of human strife. The Holy Scriptures do not abandon the shepherd amidst the wolves to be hopelessly conflicted and thus powerless to protect his flock. The Almighty commands his followers to carry the lamb, defend the orphans and oppressed, so mere mortals will no longer terrorize them.

The Gospel is and always shall be the light from which life, liberty and justice portend; our strength of conviction to feed the hungry, shelter the poor, heal the afflicted and free the persecuted from the twisted darkness that will never relinquish its sword. I do not hide behind the Bible and invoke my right to bear arms to incite fear from false accusation or punish rightful dissension. I "cling" to my faith and arm my God-given senses because I choose salvation over suffering, compassion over complicity, by endeavoring to preserve what remaining good still strives to better this world. As long as I draw breath and tend to the welfare of his people, so shall the word of the Lord.

"I am the good shepherd: I will rescue my flock & they shall no longer be prey." *Ezekiel 34:22*

The Fall of Faith

I somehow misplaced the part of evolution, dare I say creation, that denotes contemporary marriage as anything but a religious institution in the cultural framework of Western Civilization; an American nation's ethical boundaries and laws forged upon the altar of Judeo-Christian principles. While radical leftists rarely break ranks, capitulate to common sense or rightfully acknowledge our founding values, conservatives are expected to compromise with a soulless and backwards agenda that seeks to erase any last vestiges of virtue or divinity. Once the fundamental core of morality is unraveled – the family paradigm itself – the very crux and basis of civilization begins to crumble beneath the weight of a false premise, or social issue if you will. Essentially once all barriers are removed, gender roles are reversed and children are an unnatural afterthought of man's perverted natural state, the cultural void of reason, or right versus wrong, melts into an unintelligible consequence of choice. To oppose is to judge; to love is to accept. Advocates actively try to invoke pity or claim hypocrisy because they cannot avoid one salient truth:

matrimony in Western society is a religious covenant, not a secular one, which fostered the need for Civil Unions.

Progressivism cannot survive, let alone thrive, if any ideology (moral doctrine) or higher power supersedes the authority of the state; that which seeks uncontested control by degrading the source of people's values and spiritual resolve. As much as devout leftists enjoy incessantly mocking the Bible, it has prophesied this rampant decay of modernity – the societal prosecution of ardent believers – with unrivaled and harrowing accuracy. Today I am ashamed of my country, the abandonment of the innate gift of reason and shunning God in the name of a perverse and destructive creed. When those born from the seed of God's grace willingly embrace the duplicitous speech of a hateful leader who openly disparages the testament, love and sacrifice of Jesus Christ – instead espousing blind reverence to him, or even worse, to the savagery of Islamic law – then "We the People" have allowed the enemies of America to depose the very source of our greatest strength: our faith.

The Fire in Which We Burn

"We the People" are fueling a disturbing trend in this country by demonizing and dehumanizing those who do not share our political views. I find it ridiculous that more and more leaders, businesses, educational institutions and media networks are attempting to silence free speech – undermine one's career, associates, and natural born rights – rather than respectfully discuss the merits and wisdom of one's beliefs. I honestly do not hold any ill will against those who digress from my convictions as long as I'm treated with equal regard. In fact, I have a number of friends who couldn't be more diametrically opposed politically and religiously. How we approach our differences and engage in earnest discourse is far more important than the perceived "winner" of an argument. We're quickly becoming a savage nation of petulant children, drunken mothers cursing and fighting in the streets while holding their toddlers on their hips, who have no respect for their neighbor, themselves, and who possess little if any discernible intent of contributing to a moral and upright society. It's truly scary...as if we are regressing into a primitive state of justifiable intolerance and insatiable hatred. Common courtesy, compassion and empathy do not discriminate...people do.

Call me naive or woefully out of touch, but basic decency and universal respect begins at home, exemplified by strong and caring parents who embody strength and love. This blatant decline in civility, if not personal accountability and a strong work ethic, can be directly attributed to broken homes and the erosion of family values...no matter how old fashioned or politically incorrect my assertion may seem in today's hypersensitive climate. Everyone should try shaking the hand of their "perceived" enemy, focusing on the common hopes and struggles that bind all of humanity, before burying any hope of decorum and unity. I stand by my convictions, without fear or animosity, but selective persecution and blind malice threatens individual liberty and stains those timeless ideals centuries of Americans died to protect. The precedent we set is the fire which our children must eventually endure.

The Liger, The Wig & The Wardrobe

If Jesus returned to Earth to ease the suffering of the poor, afflicted, and the persecuted, who do you think the liberal media would choose to honor: The Son of God or Caitlyn Jenner? This is how utterly delusional and myopic progressives have become in their quest to worship the LGBT community to the fall of Christianity, if not all humanity. How else can you explain ESPN giving the Arthur Ash Courage Award to a 65-year-old, cross dressing father of six – an accolade typically bestowed upon those bravely facing imminent death or grave injury – rather than a double-amputee war veteran who has persevered to become a Cross-fit champion and reclaim his life? When society can no longer delineate between those soldiers who stormed the beaches of Normandy from the thugs who riot in the streets of liberty, the atrocities of ISIS from the spiritual defiance of Christian bakers, something is seriously amiss. No one chooses to get cancer or ALS, to die on foreign soil beneath the fascist boot of a bloodthirsty tyrant. Rather, they choose to fight for what is right: the dignity of life, their family and the betterment of mankind. Bruce Jenner chose to sacrifice his marriage, humiliate his children and seek fame and fortune for doing nothing doing more than wearing his mother's panties. If such a twisted act is the epitome of courage and achievement, succeeding in the face of indomitable odds, then by all means consider RuPaul a national hero and the Gay Pride Parade a living testament to the bonds of slavery.

The Death of God

Sure, let's remove the Ten Commandments from the Oklahoma State Capitol because it's just so utterly offensive, distracting, and marches helpless pedestrians directly into the dungeons of Christian subjugation. The truth is our laws, business ethics, and cultural norms were founded upon the ideological bastion of Judeo-Christian values. This is not wishful thinking, Right-Wing propaganda, or Christian folklore, but a salient truth that is symbiotic within all of Western Civilization. Naturally the same critics who are so outraged and oppressed by a piece of etched stone – its transcendent wisdom that pertains to both the religious and secular world – have absolutely no qualms with an anti-Semitic Muslim Cleric giving a prayer before Congress or a Mosque being built upon the ashes of the near 3,000 Americans slaughtered at the hands of those same Islamic hypocrites wishing to commemorate a "great victory". The political demands of indoctrinated intolerance, that which threatens the rights of all humanity, is now the most acceptable form of religious liberty.

This progressive tidal wave of political correctness that seeks to purge any and all religious influence from our culture is not only woefully ignorant; it's historically a self-destructive device of so-called progressive thought. Frederick Nietzsche himself, a known atheist and the father of Nihilism, admitted that once God and any fear of lasting judgment was removed from the discerning brow of man, the moral teachings tied to the salvation of the soul, mankind would descend into darkness and succumb to its own impulsive desires and unbridled hate; i.e., human nature. If reminding people not to commit murder, steal, or bare false witness against their neighbor is so despicably Christian and unbearably radical to our founding creed – the fundamental cogs of any enduring, civilized society – then what moral relevance or obscene epithets are secularists attaching to internet pornography, gay bondage parades, Communism, race riots, pedophilia, ISIS, Sharia Law, genital mutilation, Hollywood, drug abuse, or the over 7,000 black Americans murdered annually by their own brethren? When morality and tolerance are sacrificed to erect a national platform of irreverence, God is the first intangible threat to be hung by the last vestiges of common sense.

An American Tradition

Because today is Cinco de Mayo, a revered celebration for millions, I believe it is also an opportune moment to make an important distinction. As my family and friends will attest, I'm a staunch opponent of illegal immigration and those political enablers who encourage or justify this serious crime. I have no love for any hostile agent who seeks solely to exploit or harm this beloved nation. However, there are many more native-born citizens, as well as legal immigrants, hailing from diverse backgrounds who both appreciate America and are fiercely proud of their family heritage. Just as Irish and Italian Americans are renowned for displaying their affection for their ancestral homeland, so are countless Cubans, Mexicans, Salvadorans, Ethiopians, Serbians, or Vietnamese who now call this international beacon of hope their home.

As a Constitutional Republic forged upon liberty and tolerance, "We the People" must never forget to make the intellectual distinction between those who truly love America, who sincerely want to protect her blessings and preserve our future way of life, and those malcontents who harbor ill will and malicious intent towards the civilized world. While this is not always an easy observation to make, especially amidst such growing political animosity, I simply endeavor to afford others the same degree of respect until proven otherwise. Therefore, as a loyal friend, fellow patriot and humble servant of God, the next time you see someone waving a foreign flag or displaying their patriotism for another country on our sovereign soil, remember the same freedom won by centuries of brave American servicemen and women is by far the greatest human achievement because dignity affords us all that right.

The Fault in Our Hearts

Little surpasses the sheer joy and excitement within the scientific community when discussing the mere possibility of discovering the faintest traces of life – the elemental building blocks of nitrogen, hydrogen, carbon and oxygen – beyond the celestial confines of Earth. Unfortunately for the so-called "evolved" minds of progressive thought, their lust for alien intelligence cannot begin to remotely fathom the unbridled passion a mother feels when cradling her newborn child for the first time; a sentient being she created without having to leave our solar system, the comfort of her home, and without the assistance of a microscope. While the human genome – the miracle of creation – stretches to the moon and back over an astounding 200,000 times, the concern secular science has

THE PEOPLE WHO ONCE CALLED OUR SOLDIERS BABY KILLERS NOW MARCH FOR THE RIGHT TO KILL BABIES

for our own unborn is almost entirely negligible. It appears "love" is not quantifiable in the plastic Petri dish of progress.

Abortion, even in its most glorified state, is nothing more than the death of a human being. Not only was the landmark case of Roe v. Wade a gross misinterpretation of the law, Norma McCorvey (Jane Roe) herself still publicly laments being the naïve pawn of soulless and scheming progressives. Since 1973 abortion has accounted for over 60 million deaths; a sum 10 times greater than that of the Jewish Holocaust. Planned Parenthood – the 'oxymoronic' embodiment of compassionate and responsible parenting – kills more black babies in one week than the 3,446 lynched by the KKK in almost one century. Likewise, despite the fact African Americans only encompass 13% of the total population, roughly 450,000 black lives are aborted each year; that's 435,000 more deaths than all homicides in America annually, or approximately 50 times greater than all U.S. war casualties combined. It's hard to proclaim any life matters, or that you unconditionally support the rights of women, gays, or minorities, when your backwards agenda and soulless pride refuses to acknowledge their most universal and natural right: the right to be born.

"I've noticed everyone who is for abortion has already been born."
~ RONALD REAGAN

Any reasonable or even mildly empathetic individual would view these horrific statistics as a stain on humanity and a wake-up call to decisive action. Whereas researchers claim fetuses can feel pain as early as 5 months, the same can't be said for militant activists – those shamelessly soliciting and lauding abortion as a celebratory rite of passage – who are now demanding to legalize all late-term and even post-birth abortions. Correct me if I'm wrong, but once a baby is born it's a living, breathing human being endowed with certain inalienable rights according to law...including the right to life? After all, wasn't this contention the very basis for the original abortionist argument; if a baby is not born, surviving independently outside the womb, it's "technically" not a human life worthy of equal protection under the law?

As the proud torchbearer of bad news for the sadistic left, human conception, regardless of its gestational status, refers to the creation and presence of life. Otherwise, why would you have to "abort" or kill "it"? A newborn isn't some disposable piece of property you toss in the garbage because you have buyer's remorse, possess a sweet social life or feel the baby's aesthetics don't quite match your keen fashion sense. If that's the case, please tell me the difference between abortion and killing your 5-year-old son because you're tired of his financial baggage? Or, perhaps, it's only a miscarriage of justice when someone is charged for murdering a pregnant woman's unborn child against her will. "Choice" begins long before conception and one's right to life should never be dependent upon another person's refusal to honor it.

Not surprisingly, the same offended "humanitarians" who oppose the death penalty for convicted murderers and routinely denounce the killing of Islamic terrorists find it perfectly acceptable to murder their own child due to some twisted sense of devotion to the feminist concept of "choice". When it comes to procreation – affecting a life other than your own – choice is the decision by two consenting individuals to accept the inherent responsibilities and ramifications of having sex. If you can't deal with the consequences, both expected and unforeseen, read a book until you become mature enough to play both doctor and parent!

Birth control isn't the capitalist brain child of virgin Right-Wingers declaring an invisible war on women; stupidity, like Sandra Fluke, accomplishes that all by itself. If you can afford that $5 morning fix from Starbucks or buy the hottest new X-Box release, you sure as hell can take responsibility for your actions and seize control of your future. If you can afford and possess the self-awareness necessary to obtain an abortion, you most certainly can buy a box of condoms or arrange prescribed birth control. Or, if you dare, simply "choose" to visit your local health department where both are typically free, affordable and/or readily available. Irresponsibility, like ignorance, does not recover the nonrefundable value of a beating heart.

As for the so-called earnest "mistake" excuse – faulty latex, beer goggles or coital time travel – such misfortunes do not pardon us from reality for they always represent an inherent risk. If your tire blows out while driving, are you suddenly absolved from the damages that ensue? Of course not. You chose to drive, you put your trust in the vehicle, you alone are responsible. Everything we do in life, intentional or not, has inescapable consequences. Why would sex, the fate of an actual human life, be any different? If exercising your rights requires violating or ending the rights of another, you're hardly a victim. You're the ethically abstinent executioner.

After the convenient excuses of money, conspiracy and mental illness are exhausted, the last resort is to shamelessly equivocate any opposition to abortion with the abhorrent indignity of sexual assault. Activists routinely exploit the extreme and horrific scenario of rape to justify all abortions, regardless of the circumstances, in order to demonize critics and deflect from the absolute necessity of everyday accountability. No sane human being is suggesting a rape victim is responsible for a violent and unpreventable pregnancy. That's just callous indifference. Whereas the possibility of adoption or personally raising the offspring from such a traumatizing event would represent the most ideal outcomes, I could not justify forcing a brutalized woman to choose either option against her will. However, considering females of all childbearing ages now have access to the "Morning After" pill without a prescription, there's no reason to abort an unwanted pregnancy months after an immediately-suspected conception.

Aborting a fully formed fetus with functional organs is hardly the equivalent of stopping a cell from reproducing genetic proteins before a body is formed. Likewise, consequences from one's actions is not the moral equivalent as being a victim of someone else's or uncontrollable circumstance. Is having an abortion because a mother's life is in danger a blatant hypocrisy, a necessary medical procedure to preserve her life when both cannot

be saved, or should self-defense now be considered murder? No matter how much I detest abortion or believe that life begins at conception, there are no perfect scenarios – black and white solutions – when it comes to issues as convoluted as the human condition.
When an evolved society rejects the indefensible premise of unconditional death, doomsday feminists will predictably claim, "If abortions are relegated to emergencies or extreme cases, thousands of women will be forced to have them in unsafe environments or without proper medical personnel. You can't throw everyone in jail!" So, dissecting and selling healthy baby parts is acceptable, God forbid federally funded under the guise of "planned parenthood", but just don't use a coat hanger and a flashlight in your bathroom? Such inane logic bears the same rotten fruit as paying gang members not to commit crime or hypothesizing terrorists need more tolerant victims. You can't transform a culture of depravity by paying a ransom on your most basic values. True, lasting change must be internalized as a conscientious state of virtue, not fabricated from mindless allowances that merely encourage further contempt for the sanctity of life.

Failing to heed the law and accept culpability for having sex does not constitute an injustice or justifiable homicide. Are we comparing the prohibition of drugs, or the sanctimonious movement to outlaw alcohol, to rationalizing taking a human life whenever it inconveniences our lives or absolves making foolish choices? In other words, you can't be pro-life and pro-abortion solely because you're afraid of other's reckless responses and the innate challenges of demanding basic human decency. Besides, it is much easier to punish the source of crime, rogue doctors and black-market providers, than endeavoring to imprison every patient seeking an illegal medical procedure. If a woman is incarcerated for infanticide by throwing her premature born baby in the trash, should we also ignore those instigators who simply ask someone else to soil their hands instead? Ethics, unlike the politics of apathy, provides no refuge to those individuals seeking validation for choosing what is easy over what is right.

Regardless of the victimization narrative peddled by feminists who refuse to be "judged" or invoke reason, I've always been of the spiritual and scientific belief that life begins at conception and that it represents by far humanity's most precious gift. Not only is mankind blessed with the innate ability to comprehend and manipulate its own environment, embrace and protect all forms of life, we embody the potential to reach beyond our planet and unlock discoveries no other Earthly species can. Therefore, I find it extremely disconcerting liberals will zealously fight for the survival of a tree, oppose the abuse of animals (as they should), and laud the discovery of a single cell organism as irrefutable proof of life in the cosmos, only to remain completely ambivalent, if not physically hostile, towards the rights and suffering of our own children. Is there any greater hypocrisy? You don't have to be a Christian or even believe in God to appreciate the universal connection and indelible beauty of all creation. You merely need to care.

PRETEND I'M A TREE AND SAVE ME

Crime & Punishment: Terminating 'Planned Parenthood'

What do you call a supposed "indispensable" women's health clinic receiving $500 million in taxpayer subsidies annually for performing over 300,000 abortions a year, 160 terminated pregnancies for every lone "adoption referral", and zero mammograms? An oxymoron. Calling an abortion clinic "Planned Parenthood" is the equivalent of labeling a drug dealer a pharmacist. Killing and dismembering unborn babies has nothing to do with educating generations of Americans about the consequences of having sex, properly raising children, or the medical efficacy of such barbaric practices. Forget stripping federal funds from Planned Parenthood, I want to see indictments and arrests made for illegally harvesting human remains and the negotiated sale price for preserved body parts by sadistic pawn brokers. Considering people are being fired, verbally disparaged and violently attacked for merely displaying a flag that has legally existed for over 150 years, what's the level of outrage for secretly profiting from the orchestrated dissection of healthy children?

If progressives want to play the politically correct game of adjudicating the past by punishing those innocent bystanders of today who had nothing to do with actual slavery, what's the going punishment for erecting a "women's rights" organization – founded by Margaret Sanger, a real gloating Nazi sympathizer who advocated the deaths of "subhuman Blacks and dirty Jews" – that consciously and defiantly commits human atrocities in the present tense? Let me guess...fundraisers, mass demonstrations of support, celebrity endorsements, and the backroom reassurances of one Hillary Rodham Clinton? The real 'War on Women' goes far beyond the marketed placebo used to scare "helpless" females into voting Democrat; it's the soulless campaign being waged by radical leftists who ignore our sisters', daughters', and mothers' God-given right to be born. Excuse me while I demand a little more than an apology, a refund and a million-dollar media cover-up for those 'war criminals' who are only sorry they were caught.

Aborting the Truth

For those claiming New York's new abortion law merely protects mothers whose lives are endangered by an atypical pregnancy, their naive assertion is insulting at best considering nearly all late-term babies can still be delivered, by C-section if necessary, not to mention most states already allow for such "emergency" medical procedures; surgical actions performed by reputable doctors which do not include needlessly terminating a life due to suspected disabilities or future parental hardships. However, for those still in denial about the insidious intent of this immoral law, once these full-term babies are killed, their organs harvested and their carcasses disposed of posthaste, who's going to know the actual prognosis except abortion practitioners, activist clinics, and those indifferent patients seeking to forever silence an unwanted child by any means necessary?

> **Matt Walsh** ✓
> @MattWalshBlog
>
> Late term abortion is now legal in New York. Capital punishment is illegal. Which means it is only okay to give lethal injection to infants. If that seems rational or moral to you, you're a psychopath.

Does anyone really believe the same Planned Parenthood that illegally sold healthy baby parts underneath our government's nose, and gloated about their commercial ruse on camera, is going to make any moral discernment; especially when all liability has been removed in the event the mother dies? Don't hold your breath. Even if a pregnancy was wrongfully ended, in what sedated daydream would ultra-liberal New York vigorously prosecute the offenders and potentially invalidate the feminist jest of their new benchmark legislation...to celebrate and normalize abortions under any circumstances as a woman's natural right? Not a chance in maternity. Accountability has clearly become an unbearable hindrance to the egocentric lifestyles of proud hedonists, secular humanists and heartless sadists.

A Mother's Embrace

Women are the dawn of humanity, the salt of salvation, the beating heart of hope's tender might. Without a mother's compassion, devotion, and selfless sacrifice, the world would indeed be a more somber, barren place. In the gathering dusk of death and depravity, there are two ways of spreading light: as the burning candle, strength in the face of enduring strife, or as faith's placid waters reflecting love's luminous flame. A matriarch is both for within her embrace resides the power to create, nurture, protect and transform. Happy Mother's Day to all the unsung women who have cradled and cherished the greatest gift of God's undying grace: the beautifully-divine blessing, the soul's breathing vessel, of a newborn life.

"Mother is the name for God in the lips and hearts of little children."

<u>In God We Trust</u>

When you were a child, what was the most indelible image that came to mind when you heard "America"? Was it the flag, fluttering in the breeze as you sat on your father's shoulders and marching bands, pushed by the echoing footsteps of proud veterans, filed down Main Street to a crescendo of cheers on the Fourth of July? Was it saying the Pledge of Allegiance in your first-grade classroom, with pride and dignity, as your teacher and principal recited it with equal reverence alongside you? Or was it the mere thought of family, tee ball and Sunday barbecues, Midnight Mass and Christmas morning, as you learned what love, devotion and happiness truly meant; to be thankful for the simplest blessings?

No, it's not that life was free from struggles or vice, loss and injustice; "We the People" simply knew what it meant to be American. Liberty, patriotism, and an intrinsic calling to a higher power, an innate sense of right and wrong, were the foundation of the world's most revered nation. We lauded the promise of the individual, the necessity of accountability, and the premise of opportunity. And now? Now we are called extremists for merely questioning our elected leaders and a counter-intuitive agenda rife with failure, division, and abuse. We are called sexist for opposing abortion, Hillary Clinton and a feminist agenda that equates clapping to assault and free birth control to a civil right. We are branded racists for opposing illegal immigration, endless entitlements, and a media that incites violence by defining injustice according to the color of the victim. And finally, if not most egregiously, we are called bigots for defending the sanctity of marriage – a religious institution defined by a man and a woman and the epicenter of family values – because our Judeo-Christian heritage, the impetus for the creation of a free, industrious, and morally upright nation, is the greatest threat to a soulless agenda that seeks to unravel the very core of America.

Progressivism, liberalism, Marxism, or whatever term of depravity you choose, is based on one goal: control. Historically speaking, those lacking principles, ideals, are much easier to manipulate through deceit, deflection and outright propaganda. Liberal fascists – the so-called trumpets of tolerance – love to control every aspect of your life, tell you what to do and how to think, while they vehemently refuse to be held accountable for anything. In other words, they detest that which they spend a lifetime doing...being "judged"; an inescapable discernment that befalls us every day in the face of our families, friends, school, jobs, and life in general. Perhaps no other group better embodies this paradox than the gay community. Activists desperately want mainstream America to unconditionally embrace homosexuality as the moral equivalence of heterosexuality – not the crux of cultural decadence or a desensitized product or conditioning – because they refuse to be judged according to any standard whatsoever. Although that's all find and dandy in make-believe or a Democratic National Convention, please tell us where has it ever been viewed as a primary, necessary and moral behavior in sentient beings or an "evolved" culture? Simply put...it hasn't.

Naturally, the homers of hyperbole will defend their lifestyle by highlighting divorce rates of traditional marriage or heterosexual promiscuity. Then again, who of any substance or moral authority ever said that was acceptable either? Yes, let's all jump off the cliff because Tommy had a few too many beers, cheated on his wife and got the clap from his cousin. Forget mob justice forcing business closures, we now have mob morality! And where exactly do progressives believe our moral compass, laws and societal norms were derived from? That's right, from our Judeo-Christian beliefs; the building blocks of Western Civilization that are currently being dismantled in the very nation for which they were espoused. If you dislike or summarily reject these values, for whatever reason, then you're living in the wrong country or perhaps the wrong universe. These ideals not only serve as the philosophical foundation for our Constitutional Republic, they're non-negotiable and an ethical guide for all facets of our society; from our work ethic, to our sense of duty and love of family.

Destroy the family and you destroy society

— Vladimir Lenin —

So, am I suggesting gays are incapable of being decent, compassionate human beings? Of course not, for my own sister is lesbian! Many are kind, talented, loving and an unrelenting force for good. And by no means am I saying they're doomed to Hell or if there even is one. I'm neither God nor the Supreme Leader of Iran. No one deserves to be the targets of hate or violence due to their sexuality, including friends and family members. Rather, my observation implies these individuals have chosen a deviant lifestyle that tends to be destructive in terms of the family dynamic and almost always leads to an erosion of other values and cultural norms. And once one boundary is breached, discredited, what's to stop the next one from suffering the same fate? Absolutely nothing. Frederick Nietzsche himself, a known atheist, lamented this very fact. Believe it or not, my love of individual liberty inclines me to support gay marriage; regardless of my personal opposition. However, without those ethical bastions most synonymous with and often prescribed by peaceful religious precepts, the very moral fabric of society inevitable erodes; an event that is easily precipitated when social militants conspire to erase all standards by demonizing "idealists", morality, and any reverence to a higher power. Sound familiar? That, my friends, is how empires fall and civilization crumbles: self-indulgence, apathy, corruption, and entitlement. Not exactly the building blocks of a conscientious and vibrant society.

Outside the centrifuge of enriched sensationalism, most Christians live by the adage, "love the sinner and not the sin". The problem is the newly-formed "Social Justice Gestapo" is now forsaking such tolerance by inventing injustice to fulfill a radical agenda and force Christian/Jewish Americans to love the sin and submit to the sinner; to violate their religious freedom and most sacred beliefs. Yes, "We the People" have the freedom of choice, individual liberty, but that does not excuse our behavior from being deemed wrong, deviant, or immoral. Sorry, but it doesn't. Just because you love a child doesn't mean you can have sex with one; consensual or not. If you drink yourself to death in the confines of your own home, how does that make it virtuous or inherently right? Wishful thinking at best.

Parallel to the physical laws garnering our universe, there is a universal standard for framing every human action – whether we accept it or not – and it existed long before the dawn of man. Humans merely acknowledged that truth over time via their intellectual capacity; well, everyone except progressives who believe that no God, or any religion for that matter, can supersede the power and authority of the state. Then again, how is statism not an oxymoron when our natural rights are derived from God – as recognized by America's founding document – and the government erected in that indelible light was solely intended to protect our liberties, not usurp our defining values so liberals can hijack virtue, tolerance, and grant special transgender bathroom privileges over two centuries later? Oh, forgive me, I keep forgetting Christian Pizzerias are more dangerous than ISIS and the Death Star recycled religiously. Details, details!

The reason there is such a profound, cultural chasm in America is because the hard left is reluctant to deem any behavior as truly deviant or immoral; a supposed "righteous", judgmental, religious designation. And what exactly do you call it when a man has sex with a man, or two women for that matter, and God forbid they want to raise kids? Normal; the cradle of civilization? Or how about when gays apply for a permit to hold a bondage parade right in front of children and families in broad daylight? Is that constructive, progressive and morally superior to those "righteous" Christian beliefs? Is theft, murder, or rape not immoral? Of course, they are! Oh, so morality does exist, the constructs of right and wrong, but it just doesn't pertain to sexual and interpersonal relations; disregarding glory holes, promiscuity or sex parties. My mistake, I keep forgetting we're helpless animals subservient to Mother Nature's libido. Because monkeys periodically engage in homosexual activity to relieve stress and assert dominance, the human race is pardoned from any judgments whatsoever. I see, so that's where we got abortion? And let's not allow the fact we've evolved, created the processor and put a man on the moon, to dissuade us from believing our mental faculties are incapable of grasping any higher sense of being or right from wrong. Some just refuse to acknowledge such an immutable truth out of sheer contempt for their contemporaries. I believe that's called a naked selfie!

The truth is morality, ethics, can exist without any religious connotation at all. Such behavior codes are not some religious conspiracy to keep people from having sex which is natural, beautiful, and a necessary part of life. Context is everything, my friend. It just so happens our Judeo-Christian values tend to be most synonymous with those universal standards, including those defending heterosexuality and monogamy, which infuriates liberals all the more. It was common knowledge, even predating the time of Christ, that homosexuality was taboo and a doorway to further destructive behaviors; so more focus was given to protecting the sanctity of a love between a man and a woman. Adultery (hedonism) was far more rampant and therefore served as a prime example, a commandment if you will, to define eternal love and commitment....a pillar from which to teach our families and erect an enduring civilization. However, make no mistake about it, homosexuality was not only directly mentioned in the Bible on multiple occasions – disproving leftist propaganda claiming its acceptance – it was considered an abomination.

Leviticus 18:22 "You shall not lie with a male as one lies with a female; it is an abomination."

Romans 1:26-28 "For this reason God gave them over to degrading passions; for their women exchanged the natural function for that which is unnatural, and in the same way also the men abandoned the natural function of the woman and burned in their desire toward one another, men with men committing indecent acts and receiving in their own persons the due penalty of their error."

Corinthians 6:9 "Do you not know that the wicked will not inherit the kingdom of God? Do not be deceived: Neither the sexually immoral nor idolaters nor adulterers nor male prostitutes nor homosexual offenders."

I don't quite sense a "I Am Gay, Hear Me Roar" vibe pulsing through those historic verses. Our favorite social warriors and politicians, the ones who told us Obamacare is not ploy to control your life and a fetus isn't a living person, couldn't possibly be guilty of rewriting morality and the Bible? Never! After reading these damning passages how can anyone not understand homosexuality, dare I say gay marriage, is a sin in Christians' eyes and a grave threat to their perceived salvation? Would Barack Obama force Valerie Jarrett to serve Ted Cruz a piping hot Sheboygan Brat on the Fourth of July at Arlington Stadium? Fat chance! So why should Christian entities succumb to the politically correct mob that has zero regard for their religious freedom? Christianity isn't merely a matter of choosing the palatable parts you find appealing only to summarily discard the rest. You either accept its doctrine as a whole, a blessed path to deliverance, or you don't. There is no menu for political or cultural sensitivities, regardless of any leader's disregard for God's law.

The Bible, written during a time when most were illiterate, was largely a symbolic text designed to convey the greater concepts of divinity; the importance of living a meaningful life. These are ideals, a guide to a higher sense of being and purpose that are inherent to our nation's founding and the Constitution. They permeate all sects of our communities and form our collective ethos. True moral precepts should never change or morph according to the prevailing attitudes of the time. Otherwise right and wrong, perversion and passion, are nothing more than a popularity poll. Cultural relativism, the ethos of an era or culture, is responsible for some of humanity's greatest tragedies and injustices: slavery, genocide, child labor, genital mutilation of young African girls. It's thus of no surprise that the Constitution, embodied by the will of Northern Christians in the 1860's, provided an ethical blueprint for ending slavery and procuring equal rights; rather than morality succumbing to the accepted practices of the period. And yes, at various times throughout history, religions and their followers have acted immorally and hypocritically. Believing in God, being a Christian, in no way means such actions are excused and immune to judgment. Nevertheless, their impropriety does not negate these universal standards which can and do stand on their own merits. Beating your brother Harry Reid senseless with the Book of Mormon – although highly enjoyable and exponentially tempting – would fall far short of satiating such a litmus test.

Any time you mention religion or morality to frame homosexuality, the armies of liberal supposition will inevitably invoke Separation of Church and State; as if a concept that appears nowhere in the Constitution expunges all accountability and keeps the evil tenets of religion at bay. Separation of Church and State was never intended to exclude God, merely to ensure religious freedom. Paying homage to a creator, even mentioning religious doctrine in our public institutions, doesn't force anyone to believe in God or to accept any denomination. Likewise, the First Amendment wasn't meant to protect government from our religious values; it was devised to protect our religious values from government tyranny. I'm sad to report that's exactly what is happening to Christian businesses and organizations; singled out for defending the ideals that have defined America since its inception. Would the flag bearers of discrimination force a black carpenter to make a cross for the KKK, or demand a gay-owned printing shop make "God Hates Fags" banners for the Westboro Baptist Church? Not in your wildest dreams; nor should they!

What the media conveniently is that most Christians rarely inquire or even care about their customer's personal lives for they accept people's right to live as they choose. Unfortunately, some activists are hell-bent on politicizing their sexuality and enjoy creating a contentious conflict of interest to publicly highlight their agenda. They shout discrimination from the street corners of America yet give no consideration to others' religious liberty; the right not to violate the sternest canons of their faith. Now imagine if Baptist entrepreneurs forced their patrons to say grace before their meal. Suddenly religious freedom becomes a nonnegotiable concept for all. And wasn't that the framer's original intention to begin with? Too bad the liberal lynch mob fails to realize discrimination is a two-way street and that sunshine is by no means subjugation. If the gay community wants to have their cake and eat it to, I suggest they open a bakery called "Shut Your Pie Hole!" Catering to common sense doesn't fabricate injustice just because you ordered liberty with a side of hypocrisy to go.

When the ideologically origins of America cannot be discounted and the scriptures speak for themselves, the armies of secularism resort to their final argument: their "Get Out of Judgment" Free Card! That is, forget cultural norms, forget religion, if you're born gay how can it possibly be immoral?! If humans are nothing more than thinking animals and products of sequential evolution, as the secular left proclaims, wouldn't our first and most overriding instinct be to survive...to procreate? A woman's body is specifically engineered to entice her male counterpart and to then care for her offspring in order to facilitate survival of the species. That's common sense. Therefore, what would be the purpose of an ever-growing gay population? Absolutely none. The only discernible conclusion you're left with is "choice": preference, taste, good-old personal choice. Whether one has had a bad experience with the opposite sex or feels too inadequate to attract and keep a partner, they often turn to an alternative, a comforting source to fulfill their need for companionship and sexual satisfaction. Choice is a voluntary mechanism that is no different from declaring a favorite or color or discovering what traits attract you to another person. Therefore, it is not nature who is your pimp, but your own acquired or conditioned feelings. The Shopping Channel exists for a reason.

I do realize nature is far from perfect and deviations do occur; i.e., hormonal imbalances and genetic irregularities. However, that would be more reticent of suggesting an infrequent, underlying mistake or an aberration – say a 1-2% base deviation – than a naturally ingrained behavior. Famed behavioral psychologist B.F. Skinner spared no bells when he said human behavior was garnered almost entirely from conditioning. In essence, the Harvard alum claimed he could raise twins from birth, turning one into a serial killer and the other into a concert pianist through the power of conditioning alone. The reason why homosexuality is now occurring at a higher incidence, although still compromising around 4% of society, is plain and simple: conditioning. In this new era of twisted priorities, it's not uncommon to here gay couples, or even liberal activists, to proclaim their desire for gay children. So much for living your own life! It is also no secret progressives are making a concerted effort to paint homosexuality in a positive light. Music and film have become increasingly riddled with bisexual and same-sex themes, and it seems like every television show now has a token gay character. Even our educational system is subjecting millions of impressionable children to materials depicting homosexuality, transgenderism and same-sex parents. Yes, the more people are desensitized to a specific behavior, or cultural taboo, the more likely they are to adopt and engage in it. Internet pornography, anyone?

If homosexuality is truly a harmless, moral and natural behavior inherent to human and societal evolution, why has it taken so long to rise to the forefront of acceptance? Three words: Pop Culture Relativism. Our Founding Fathers never discussed, made special provisions for homosexuality or gay marriage, because they never envisioned a Christian populace – or any modern civilization for that matter – would recognize or give legal, moral preference to such behavior. Yes, they knew homosexuality existed, it was inevitable, although every major religion and much of the world rejected any notion of its intrinsic worth or place; thus, making no sense to give such behavior credence, let alone a platform to rival our most sacred beliefs and institutions. The mere thought of such insanity was abhorrent at best.

Right or wrong, a majority of both Christian and secular Americans have supported the gay community's right to live as they choose, to embrace discourse and the necessity to coexist. And what have the voices of liberty, tolerance, received in return? Entrapment, exploitation, and future expatriation. When does your family, the fate of this country, your salvation – the constructs of decency and reverence to the divine source of our liberties – demand an equal response or matter again? For the millions who believe Jesus suffered horribly at the hands of evil and died so mankind could live according to the natural blessings bestowed by God, to consciously hold ourselves to a higher standard, "We the People" reject any attempt to redefine America and invent morality. If we're truly nothing more than out-of-touch religious fanatics like our forefathers – pioneers who were much more learned, wise, and brave than those currently leading this nation – I have but one retort: the current state of America, if not the world, speaks for itself.

Today, under the orchestrated culture coup of an anti-American President who uses Marxist doctrine as his soulless creed, a Christian nation and God are the enemies of "progress". Any contempt for homosexuality or vocal opposition to its proliferation in our everyday lives is silenced in the counter-culture vacuum of progressivism. If you dare speak your mind and defend America's timeless ethos, the Democratic disciples of intolerance will threaten our livelihood (if not your life), requisition your rights, and annex any concept of discrimination to further their quest to vanquish any religious values from the American landscape. The question you have to ask yourself is...when is enough, enough? When are decent Americans, those forever bound by the roots of creation and Western Civilization, tired of bending over to accommodate those who view America as an illegitimate state that must be terraformed to suit the caustic whims of political agitators who are driven by hate, discrimination, and most of all, insatiable power?

Any leader, behavior or political movement that stands in direct contrast to America's Constitutional charter, is, by definition, radical and a clear and present danger to our way of life. The demonization of our Judeo-Christian values, praising homosexuality as the moral equivalency of traditional marriage and touting Islamic Law as quintessential American values, is the final lynchpin in achieving this goal. Truly, what could be more offensive or absurd? In the new-found, twisted tenets of Barack Obama's "progressive" America, Thomas Jefferson and Benjamin Franklin would be punished for achieving success, mocked for "white privilege", barred from being victims of hate crimes, threatened for invoking God, and declared "extremists" for holding government accountable for a litany of failure, abuses, and lies.

THE RIGHTS OF MAN COME NOT FROM THE GENEROSITY OF THE STATE, BUT FROM THE **HAND OF GOD.**

JOHN F. KENNEDY

ACLJ.ORG

Religious Liberty and Political Polygraphs

In a decisive 7-2 ruling, the Supreme Court concluded Denver native Jack Phillips was treated grossly unfair and with "impermissible hostility" when the Colorado Civil Rights Commission prosecuted him for refusing to bake a gay wedding cake. In other words, state officials intentionally disregarded his religious beliefs, afforded liberties, in favor of recognizing same-sex marriages: which, ironically, wasn't even legal at that time in Colorado. Regardless, this case is but one of many legal conflicts which have emerged since the Obama administration began selectively targeting Christian organizations and private businesses: specifically, Catholic charities and Christian commercial chains such as Hobby Lobby. Chick-fil-A, despite being a selfless supporter of our military, first responders and local communities during times of national disaster, is still routinely slandered by anti-Christian activists, denied business opportunities in urban epicenters, and picketed across liberal college campuses.

Whether through unlawful IRS intimidation or by invoking the intrusive stipulations of Obamacare to demand religious entities provide paid abortions and birth control for their constituents, it was painfully clear our very own Constitutionally-restrained government, the same Republic founded upon religious freedom and Judeo-Christian ethics, had become irrevocable hostile towards our ideological heritage; if not America itself. Such devious and inexcusable insanity is no different than a Jewish President forcing an Islamic bistro to serve BLT's and Tequila Sunrises during Ramadan or requiring atheist students to recite the Lord's Prayer on Good Friday; abusive acts which would immediately stir widespread criticism, organized protests and regurgitated accusations of bigotry.

And yet no reciprocal outrage was present for those steadfast Christians ordered to violate their biblical doctrine which unconditionally condemns infanticide and homosexuality as sinful abominations. Without almost any mainstream media or Democratic dissension, their collective rights were summarily swept under the rug of cultural Marxism by social justice soldiers who viewed the LGBT agenda as infinitely more consequential than one's perceived religious salvation, economic livelihood and wrongful persecution. Considering it is illegal to demand a Mosque weds a same-sex couple, whether you're a Christian, Hindu, Amish or Muslim, why would it be "Kosher" for a privately-owned enterprise to violate their religious beliefs?

While this landmark decision clearly confirmed Christians still have indelible civil rights, a non-rhetorical affirmation by all logical accounts and national eras, it is by no means a carte blanche to discriminate against other citizens based on their race, gender, or sexuality. Rather, judicial history suggests these cases will be now adjudicated by state courts on an individual basis to determine intent, religious history and extenuating circumstance. Naturally, any perceived chance of fostering mutual boundaries is wishful thinking in today's hyper-partisan climate where political advocacy is systematically supplanting even the most self-explanatory tenets of the law in state and federal courts. As a result, this polarizing issue will likely become more convoluted by opening an inescapable Pandora's box of opportunistic interpretations, frivolous lawsuits decrying a lack of Alien pastor insemination services or "Flat-Earth" newlyweds demanding undoctored NASA wedding pictures, in the coming years.

Buried beneath this incessant tug-of-war, the "religious extremism" media motif, is the fact most Christian business owners would never inquire about a customer's sexual orientation or even consider refusing selling goods and services based on a couple's private life. One, it's bad business, and two, a majority of Christians are pretty tolerant of alternative lifestyles. Then again, there is always that sovereign matter of self-respect which would lead me to never support an establishment that didn't want my business. Why not simply find a bakery that welcomes your time and money? That being said, politically-motivated plaintiffs purposely targeting religiously-devout entrepreneurs for fame or financial gain deserve to be prosecuted for harassment and entrapment to the fullest extent of the law. As someone who supports an establishment's right to refuse service for any number of legitimate reasons – unacceptable attire, vulgarity, violence, vagrancy and religious principles – I do realize there are limitations to such exclusions.

Because political ideology, like religion, is but a definable set of beliefs minus the spiritual atonement, where do we as a sentient society eventually draw the line between exploitation and self-identity? When a man is legally thrown out of a New York City pub for simply wearing a "Make America Great Again" hat, as determined by a New York Court, or a Republican woman denied roadside assistance because she has a Donald Trump bumper sticker, what's to stop gun owners, pro-life advocates, or any First Amendment expression from being denied equal access to teaching positions, government subsidized programs, legal aid, community organizations, and entertainment venues; slights which are growing more prevalent with each passing day? Better yet, how do you definitively prove "politics" was the deciding factor in their exclusion; especially when judges selectively protect legal, dare I say "reasonable", self-expression?

Although economic boycotts and electoral protest (voting) are traditional methods of recourse, they are typically only as effective as majority rule. Due to the pervasive hostility dividing our communities, sacrificing civil decorum for the ultimate goal of unilateral control, I believe it is only a matter of time before political discrimination becomes the newest civil rights frontier and most common form of injustice. Once an everyday matter of casual disagreement becomes a credible basis for mass societal segregation, alienation, progressive strategists and politicians will stop at nothing to punish political opponents at every opportune moment to exact the type of social change they deem "honorable". Nevertheless, I will always find solace in the divine truth our rights are derived by God, and not the oppressive whims of cultural terrorists seeking supremacy over sensibility.

"The Religion then of every man must be left to the conviction and conscience of every man: and it is the right of every man to exercise it as these may dictate." ~ James Madison, 1785

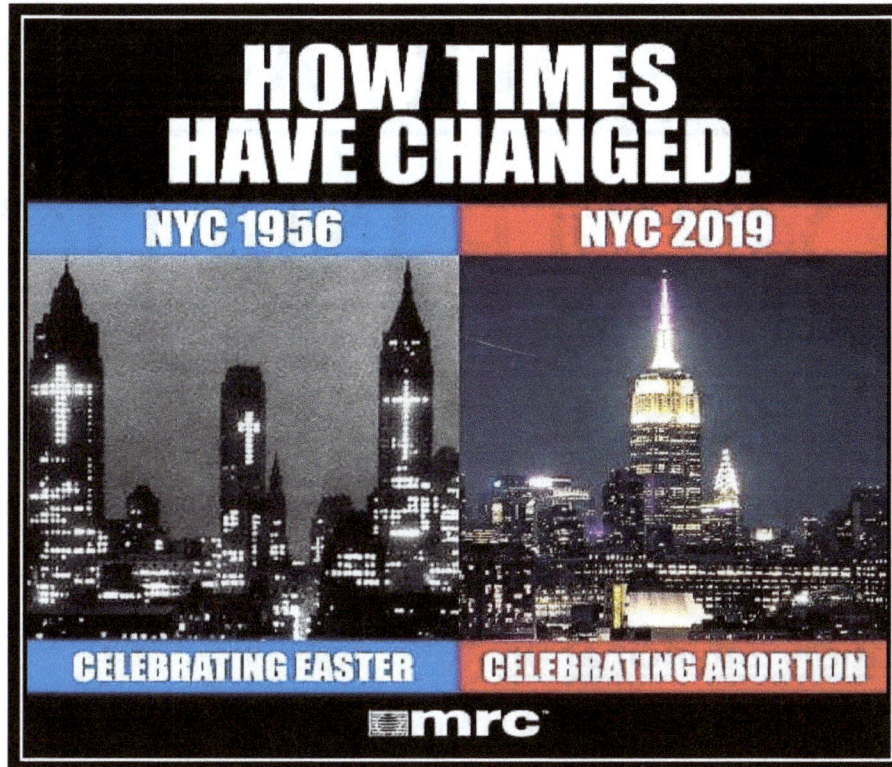

A New Year's Hope

Tonight is not about politics or obsessing over our inevitable differences, regardless of our contrasting gender, color, sexuality, wealth, political or religious beliefs. New Year's Eve is a worthy cause for celebration, for appreciating our most obvious or overlooked blessings through joyous revelry with family, friends and the good will of complete strangers. It is a reminder that we are survivors, insatiable dreamers and forever bound by common needs and struggles. And although life is riddled with death and personal misfortune, despair and discord, I do not need to drift amidst the endless sea of tombstones marking departed loved ones and fallen heroes or loiter in the streets of apathy and moral depravity, to recognize the ominous pitfalls that await my every step each 365 days of the year. Rather, on this festive night, I choose to drink from the fountain of humanity to honor mankind's most quintessential gift: hope. Hope has resurrected hearts from the depths of hate, inspired the afflicted to cure illness, and slayed improbability by rousing starving peasants to defeat the corpulent armies of tyranny. Its strength is immeasurable, innately indelible, and represents the last untouchable vestige of liberty....our God-given rights....for hope is an undying remnant of love; of what could and can be when we drink from its universal chalice. So, as you raucously raise your glass to the heavens tonight, kiss your loved ones or hug complete strangers, remember all that is right with this imperfect world and that no good-thing ever truly dies; no matter how much we endure or must overcome. The most endearing resolutions are not those impulsive pledges made on any singular day or momentous occasion, but they are the unspoken virtues, selfless actions, we embody every uneventful day of our lives.

THE EDUCATION INDOCTRINATION

A PUBLIC DISSERVICE

The Education Emancipation

Without the ability to control and manipulate students, progressives are like Pavlov ringing a bell; only they are the ones left salivating to the anticipation of mass indoctrination. The core responsibility of public education is to provide a functional skill set for our children, to fully prepare those who will seek further enrichment beyond graduation, and to instinctively foster well-adjusted, productive members of society. Unfortunately for the guardians of good intentions, ever since the 1950's Marxist agitators like Saul Alinsky and Bill Ayers realized the best manner in which to topple America – our fierce independent spirit, economic prowess and Judeo-Christian values – was not by brute force but rather by steadily poisoning the national pipeline of public education, generations of impressionable minds, with spoon-fed, anti-American propaganda. And judging by the dysfunctional state of modern academia where liberal educators now overwhelmingly outnumber their conservative counterparts by a 12-1 margin, I'm sad to report "Project Assimilation" is succeeding.

The incessant onslaught from social conditioning leaves a trail of carnage far greater than any singular battle or standing army. How else could you convince millions or voters and a majority of millennials that America is an evil empire built upon unrivaled injustice; that capitalism is the root of our problems instead of a transcendent engine of discovery, an economic ladder of opportunity, to liberate mankind from the ransomed dependency of unchecked government? How else could any American justify silencing free speech in our communities, let alone physically attacking intellectual diversity in our supposed institutions of higher learning...key cogs of any civilized society built upon human discourse and the natural dichotomy of competing ideas? I don't need to bathe my senses in a filtered pool of mass conformity to realize the bubbles are America's last breaths. And I sure don't need to kneel before the altar of Howard Zinn to be baptized by half-truths beneath the sanctimonious drivel of progressive brain surgeons. I just need to breathe and think for myself without the euthanized consent of Big Brother.

The left's opposition to Betsy DeVos goes far beyond contested credentials and the informal grammar of "tweets". Her confirmation as Secretary of Education is a tangible threat to their monopoly on the minds of future voters. When educational excellence becomes the bell curve of mediocrity and behavioral problems become the gold standard of appeasement, why shouldn't parents reserve the right to reallocate their tax dollars for the private instruction of their children? People's hard-earned paychecks aren't signed permission slips granting moonlighting political advocates the means to abolish the occupational integrity of objective learning. They now represent the voided vouchers of public trust in government.

Have you ever asked yourself who writes your child's textbooks, investigated the publisher's political associations or wondered what was the true genesis of the Common Core curriculum? I can assure you it's by no means a coincidence or the ongoing subject matter of a PBS investigation. When a public educator stomps on the American flag in the classroom or zealously demonstrates a mock assassination of the President, it's of little surprise when God is expelled for Christian "extremism" or a boy exercising his First Amendment rights is sent home for wearing a "Make America Great Again" hat. The fact students as young as elementary school are now being berated by teachers for not supporting Democratic candidates and/or liberal views is as disgraceful as it is abusive. There is madness and then there are publicly funded lies contributing to an ideological coup d'état: more commonly known as sedition or treason.

Do not believe for one moment the same radicalized forces willing to tear down monuments in a mad rush of misappropriation, including those so-called cultured celebrities openly cursing and threatening the President on national TV like rabid animals, would not hesitate in punishing conservative viewpoints, solely defining racism as white supremacy, replacing our national flag or allowing the government to seize property in the name of the 'common good'. Mob justice born from cultivated hate has little concern with individual rights, moral objectivity or due process. Marxism's goal is revolution through conditioned ignorance, a perceived state of perpetual victimization, to replace the supposed injustice of economic inequality with a politically oppressive, totalitarian regime. In essence, the liberty to achieve and believe as you please are stifled so "the people" can be better controlled by an elite ruling class, or more profoundly, a singular despot. It is, by definition, the very anti-thesis of human evolution and America's founding charter: our desire to think, feel and prosper according to our own unique gifts without undue interference or hostility.

My goal is not to disregard or pardon America's historical transgressions for those are cultural scars, indelible reminders, of how far we have progressed as a nation. My goal is to remind "We the People" that the Constitution, and not the flawed cultural norms of any era, provided the blueprint for overcoming our most daunting challenges and blatant injustices. For the 1.6% of Americans that owned slaves during the height of the Antebellum period, how many textbooks laud the over half a million whites who suffered and/or died to end human bondage? Do they mention or label Portugal as rampant "racists" accountable for importing 5 million black slaves to toil in their Brazilian gold mines; a number 15 times greater than those servants transported to America? How much credit is given to those Northern evangelical Christians who spearheaded the movement to both topple human bondage and secure suffrage for blacks? Is there any mention of how 46% of Democrats, compared to only 18% of Republicans, opposed a woman's right to vote some 50 years later and therefore attempted to filibuster a formal vote on the 19th Amendment before its ultimate ratification in 1920? And lastly, were "Native" Americans not "nomadic" tribes who displaced/conquered other settlers, who slaughtered each other in droves over "territory" and who routinely enslaved enemies or engaged in slave trading? Or perhaps I should complain my non-native American "privilege" does not include free land, tax exemptions or a complimentary college education despite engaging in such historical depravity.

"THE FOUNDERS NEVER INTENDED FOR AMERICANS TO TRUST THEIR GOVERNMENT. OUR ENTIRE CONSTITUTION WAS PREDICATED ON THE NOTION THAT GOVERNMENT WAS A NECESSARY EVIL, TO BE RESTRAINED AND MINIMIZED AS MUCH AS POSSIBLE."
— RAND PAUL

Contrary to the bland rhetoric of seasoned revisionists, history was never intended to be a politically correct menu of partisan delicacies passed around among pompous critics. It is but a vigilant reminder of the innate fallibility of man and our imperfect legacy as a global society. Whereas older generations endeavor to never forget about ravages of war, poverty or the threat of Communism, younger generations are endeavoring to forget everything history has taught us; most notably, that America was born from the ashes of tyranny and the creeping censorship of blind subjugation. And what exactly has leftist academia learned from the mass oppression and murder of dissidents under Stalin, Hitler, Mao or Castro? What textbooks or lesson plans have been adopted to warn our sons and daughters about an Islamic creed that still justifies and contributes to 1400 years of bloodshed, intolerance and misogyny? If you choose to label capitalism as the gospel of greed, please inform Cloward & Piven that capitalism has liberated far more from poverty – built more bridges, hospitals and universities – than the noble bread lines of socialism. The inevitable inequality of achievement, differing degrees of success born from the unequal application of ambition and sacrifice, is by no means an indictment of social or economic injustice. The best thing to happen to old, lingering Marxists is naïve, young millennials allergic to the aroma of common sense.

Instead of reaffirming America's founding charter – those values, liberties and innovative discoveries that have repeatedly transcended modern civilization – progressive educators are promoting hate and conformity to exact political supremacy: i.e., think as we do, Government is your master, entitlements are your birthright. Whether you're a Republican or Democrat, there is no excuse for disparaging intellectual diversity or suffocating a universal beacon of hope and liberty. The quickest way to handicap a child and ensure the demise of a free nation is to hijack the very tool of their empowerment...education. If students lack the critical thinking skills to decipher historical context from modern exploitation, dissect political propaganda from non-partisan prudence, how can any civilization forge a brave new path that both evolves from the struggles of its past without destroying the ideological cornerstones of its future?

The nonnegotiable function of our educational system is not to fund or streamline militant radicalization, the adopted anti-American indoctrination camps of our children, but to provide a quality, competitive curriculum that fosters an ingrained knowledge, if not an undying appreciation, of the timeless ideals America was founded upon: freedom, limited government, faith, hard work, accountability and duty. Honoring America does not require inciting division or demonizing dissent to suffocate the last gasps of individuality and independent thought. It rightfully demands honoring students, their parents, and those responsible teachers who still believe political terrorists have no place in our classrooms. Reclaiming the purpose and integrity of our public schools is the first step in preserving this last, best hope of mankind for generations to come.

Educate and inform the whole mass of the people. They are the only sure reliance for the preservation of our liberty.
- Thomas Jefferson

Training for a Better Life

Every four years pandering politicians decry poverty and invoke income inequality to raise the ire of voters by demonizing capitalism and the so-called existence of "white privilege": all despite the fact Caucasian children represent the largest impoverished sect in America. Unfortunately, outside of pure legalized theft, the rogue redistribution of citizens' hard work and property, these propagandists offer few real-world solutions to those progressive policies cultivating decades of economic despair. After all, for those capable of working, endless welfare merely ensures mass dependence and offers little upward mobility to escape the institutionalized web of poverty. Likewise, pushing impoverished or underachieving kids through a conveyor-belt system solely to get a diploma – when a majority will have few other future prospects than flipping burgers or stocking shelves – does little to assuage their plight or reverse urban decay. If you must lower the bar of expectations only to throw grocery money at the inevitable aftermath, you're the problem to achieving a long-term solution and forging a better tomorrow.

Instead of feeding societal discontent and handcuffing hope, America should immediately re-institute the practical alternative of licensed public trade schools throughout the nation. The truth is, regardless of their race, many of today's youth lack the ability, the support structure at home or the interest necessary to succeed in academics; let alone a viable path to pursue anything past secondary education. Yet, by learning a valuable trade while in high school they would not only possess a lifetime skill, a career commodity, they can command a respectable wage necessary transcend the depravity and destructive mentality of generational poverty. When men and women have greater access to better housing, quality healthcare and a higher standard of living, their respect for themselves and the necessity of an earnest day's work increases exponentially. In essence, they begin to realize the American dream goes far beyond the glitz of Hollywood fame or the fleeting glory of professional sports. Success suddenly resides in a very tangible road of self-actualization; a self-fulfilling prophecy and stepping stone that reaches beyond the political stigma of race or class warfare.

Public trade schools would not only offer an alternative to a traditional high school diploma and add generations of diverse and adept workers to a shrinking private sector that now trails the U.S. government in new hires, they would help counterbalance a service-based economy where in excess of 90 million Americans are absent from the workforce and another 52 million are now on some form of monthly public assistance. Between 2009 and 2016, the once most prolific, manufacturing-based economy in the world never reached a single annualized GDP of 3%; a modest number by any standard and the longest such drought since the Great Depression. If you combine this dubious distinction with our over 50 billion-dollar trade disparity each month, it doesn't take a Rhodes Scholar to realize America is on a self-imposed march towards financial ruin.

How to college like a Liberal:

1. Go to college
2. Accumulate debt
3. Pick stupid major
4. Graduate with useless degree
5. Play victim
6. Blame society
7. Vote Democrat

I AM 25yrs. WITH A FINE ARTS DEGREE.
· NO JOB
· NO INSURANCE
· ON FOODSTAMPS
AND $20,000 IN COLLEGE DEBT.
I AM THE 99%.

To paraphrase Calvin Coolidge, "The business of America is business!" Commerce is the genesis of our greatest blessings and the single greatest catalyst for our economic and cultural vitality. Well, until that is, power-usurping statists chose unsustainable debt over diligence and victimization over vision to fulfill a counter-intuitive agenda. The world doesn't need more social justice workers who proudly contribute to a never-ending legacy of futility, division and blame. It needs more mechanics, welders, and carpenters who represent the mortar and brick of real, sustainable change; the self-sufficient foundation of innovation and ambition.

No, I'm not suggesting some adolescents should be exempt or excluded from learning the basic building blocks of a functional education: math, English, history and science. I'm suggesting that a diploma is nothing more than a blank piece of paper when it becomes the equivalent of a participation award fading in the back pocket of an indigent parent, a career criminal or a disgruntled voter who is lectured about injustice every election by failed bureaucrats living the 1% lifestyle. Whether it's politically incorrect or distinctly offensive, pragmatism does not dictate every child should go to college and seek further academic enrichment. Rather, common sense teaches us every student simply requires the proper set of tools to overcome their own unique circumstances and utilize their untapped potential to effectively contribute to an industrious, moral and enduring society.

Cupcakes, Snowflakes and the Path Less Coddled

If students from my era walked out of the classroom to protest an election result, let alone demanded the cancellation of all midterms due to the so-called "psychological distress" inflicted upon their weary brows, administrators would have said two things: don't let the door smack your ass on the way to a permanent vacation and enjoy your "F". These schools and educators that coddle this nonsense need to be harshly reprimanded by parents, if not outright fired. Our public schools and universities were not built to assuage the political intolerance and emotional imbalances of whining millennials; they were founded by pioneers and funded by taxpayers with the explicit purpose of transforming lives for the betterment of society.

Here in the real-world children do not dictate the terms of acceptable behavior, tantrums have consequences and life rarely caters to your fragile sensibilities or misplaced outrage. Thousands of Americans suffering from severe disabilities or fatal diseases go to work every day without one protest, complaint or special media report. In other words, Snowflakes need not apply because there are no "safe spaces" from the "unfair" responsibilities of life. Sorry, Cupcakes but the time has come to contribute to the very freedoms and quality of life your generation so egregiously takes for granted. After all, your great grandparents built the Hoover Dam, stormed the beaches of Normandy and cured Polio with a microscope before you even shared your first Starbucks latte on Instagram. And to think none of these heroes were offered complimentary "safety pins" of solidarity or "cry-in" election counselors for living in a nation that afforded them the right to vote and to pursue the life of their choosing. It appears "perspective" is no longer a required course in the bubble wrap of modern-day academia.

Progressive Pedophiles & The Castration of American Values

"University Academics" claim Pedophilia Is "Natural for Males" and that it's normal for men to be "Aroused by Children".

On what planet is this even remotely moral, let alone true? And on what planet do these sick, ethically bankrupt scholars hail from? If you view a child in any sexual connotation whatsoever, you are not a man but rather a soulless scourge of creation; a predator devoid of all emotion and humanity who deserves to be castrated. What parent would ever accept their little boy or girl being violated in the name of "nature", or more succinctly, progressive thought? Honestly, who in the hell could even watch such a revolting injustice, let alone participate in it? The mere thought of such an abomination is both heart-wrenching and sickening. Not only is a child emotionally, mentally, and physically unprepared for such an event, they will suffer serious and irrevocable damage: psychological trauma, bodily harm, disease and/or the inability to conceive their own children in the future. Have we learned nothing from the countless stories of sexual abuse and the horrific, far-reaching effects suffered by victims? Apparently not, for even to deem "pedophilia" normal, with or without moral implications, is to justify its prevalence. Who would even utter such a repulsive suggestion?

We are not animals who are mindless slaves to the slightest triggers of impulse and instinct. Humans are sentient beings, blessed with unparalleled mental faculties and whom possess an innate sense to differentiate between right and wrong. Then again, some animals obviously have a far greater moral compass than those who enable such crimes or prey on purity. A child is not a toy, a disposable piece of meat, because progressives reject societal limits on sexual behavior...i.e., perversion. Children are a blessing, the embodiment of innocence and hope, and we are all held accountable for their well-being. It has been long suspected that the homosexual agenda went far beyond seeking equal rights and acceptance; its most subversive goal was unadulterated access to our sons and daughters. Apparently, the best way to achieve that goal is to declare it's also perfectly acceptable, dare I say natural, for heterosexual sex offenders as well. Thank God progressives had the moral fortitude to ban prayer from school, dismiss family values and declare Christianity the creed of extremists. Of course, you don't need religion to have a soul or an education to live an ethical life; you just need to be remotely "human".

Innocence Lost

Maybe I'm just an old-fashioned prude but I'm saddened by the skyrocketing number of female teachers – many of whom are younger newlyweds – now caught sexting, sending explicit pictures or engaging in sexual relationships with their students. And while I'm sure many will say their male targets were hardly unwilling "victims", imagine the consequences if the perpetrator was a grown man who seduced, harassed or slept with your teenage daughter or grandchild? Not only is there an obvious double standard in terms of outrage and sometimes punishment, this type of deviant behavior is further proof of society's steep moral decline and obsession with indulging our most intimate sexual desires and fantasies at any cost; i.e., "living life to the fullest" because sex between two legal adults, God forbid a couple, is not near extreme enough to satisfy today's twisted requirements of acceptable gratification.

Once a upon a time, women were the gold standard of moral etiquette; both in terms of expectation and reciprocation. Their personal expectations of men were not dependent upon objectifying themselves for meaningless attention or reducing their self-worth to the size of an unsolicited appendage. While our parents and grandparents primarily endeavored to raise respectful, well-adjusted children, a disturbing number of contemporary "adults" are content spending countless hours creating crude quips or sharing explicit photos of themselves on social media simply to garner the maximum number of likes or retweets. Not surprisingly, the record number of divorces and single parent households are a direct reflection of what we value in a partner, or better yet, ourselves. Lasting commitment, dare I say love, isn't a beer commercial where two fashionably dressed models toast to the 'good life' and dance on New York City rooftops until 5 am without ever getting hungover, angry or jealous. It involves work, sacrifice, and yes, even the inevitability of disappointment. Despite the inherent challenges of human relations, such heartfelt appreciation for another also offers a level of reward, personal satisfaction, that no one night stand or insatiable fetish can rival. More profoundly, it serves as an endearing example that happiness – a romantic note hidden in your pocket, a kiss on the forehead during a long embrace, a hand to hold when hope seems spent – is the greatest, enduring pleasure of all.

No, I'm not suggesting you can't tell a dirty joke, dress a bit risqué for a night on the town or unapologetically love sex; passion is natural, healthy, and at its zenith when an extension of our true feelings for someone we truly care about. Furthermore, it is of little consequence whether people approve of what happens between two consenting adults in the privacy of their own bedroom. However, how can we empower and teach healthy behaviors to our youth – those impressionable minds already inundated with internet pornography, gender-bender pansexuality and raunchy pop culture before they even go on their first date – when modernity's Tinder mentality teaches kids they need only be concerned with getting off or getting laid; exploits far too many parents and community mentors are still recklessly pursuing because narcissism, vanity and mindless hedonism are the new American Dream? Unless fathers and mothers are appalled at the idea of our daughters being viewed as nothing more than a disposable "piece of ass" – young women believing it's their greatest asset to command "respect", let alone a worthy spouse – our classrooms and workplaces will continue to serve as fertile playgrounds for sexual predators everywhere. You cannot raise expectation, universal empathy, by consciously lowering the bar of basic decency without regret. The longer our communities feed these destructive attitudes, the closer Hollywood hedonism comes to accurately portraying the depravity destroying our own homes and families.

The Censored Shackles of Free Speech

Free speech does not cease in a nation predicated upon individual liberty, nor does it inevitably qualify as a "hate crime" simply because you disagree with or are deeply offended by the personal beliefs of others. There are no 'safe spaces' from the self-inflicted micro-aggressions of reality...i e., one's own insecurities or deep-seated biases. Tolerance, disregarding the newly socially engineered version that slanders or threatens divergence, is a prerequisite of free will and the fundamental crux of open and constructive discourse; a Socratic ideal colleges should be obstinately preserving rather than forcibly constricting in the name of fostering political uniformity. Students, our own sons and daughters, should never be afraid to speak their mind out of fear of condemnation or retribution in our institutions of higher learning, let alone in the sovereign confines of a constitutional republic that openly rebelled against intrusive government, religious persecution, and the oppression of mankind's natural born rights. If the immediate goal is to label all conservative views as hate speech, then the ultimate objective is the dissolution of our nation's founding premise and the justified demise of due process. Tyranny goes by many names and you don't have to be a college student to matriculate into the baited den of madness. One merely must realize that totalitarianism is a futile endeavor because human nature, regardless whether America is buried and replaced by the most progressive state, will always challenge the limitations of any authoritative society that seeks to stifle our unique faculties and man's innate desire to be free.

UCLA Students Sign Petition to Put Trump Supporters in Concentration Camps

To quote Voltaire and rejoice in the "Common Sense" of Thomas Paine, I may disagree with what you say but I will defend to the death your right to say it. Democrat, Republican, liberal, conservative, Christian, atheist, white, black, gay, straight, rich, poor, Donald Trump or Hillary Clinton...to bask in the light of liberty, the transcendent gifts of humanity's intellectual prowess, spiritual and empathetic capacity, is to shed the shackles of coerced silence. I would much rather embrace the uncertainties of individuality, encourage the open exchange of competing ideas to challenge my convictions and unearth the best possible solutions, than to faintly exist amidst the blaring stigma of stereotype to justify mass conformity. Progress, our insatiable thirst for excellence and innovation, isn't born solely from the comfort of serenity or the pulpit of self-righteousness; it is most often forged from the fires of failure, dissent, necessity and most notably, self-discovery. Two and a half centuries of Americans didn't toil and sacrifice so their tepid descendants could bite their tongue and recoil in fear amidst the Orwellian tactics of glorified political terrorists. They risked their very lives and the welfare of their children so the flame of freedom, the very First Amendment of our inalienable Bill of Rights, would endure without condition. These unfiltered voices of free will knew what it meant to be an American; more succinctly, they overwhelmingly understood their liberties were a birthright, derived from the grace of God, and not ransomed by any government decree or bloodthirsty movement. Even if AntiFa and the armies of liberal fascism beat their perceived enemies into submission, they would merely ensure the reciprocal means of their own demise. You can no more command the dead than a tyrant can earn the respect of the brutally oppressed. When "tolerance" requires bloody knuckles and hateful epithets – flash mobs of masked thugs assaulting political dissent – America becomes the first casualty of criminal contempt. Anarchy, however, eagerly invites them all.

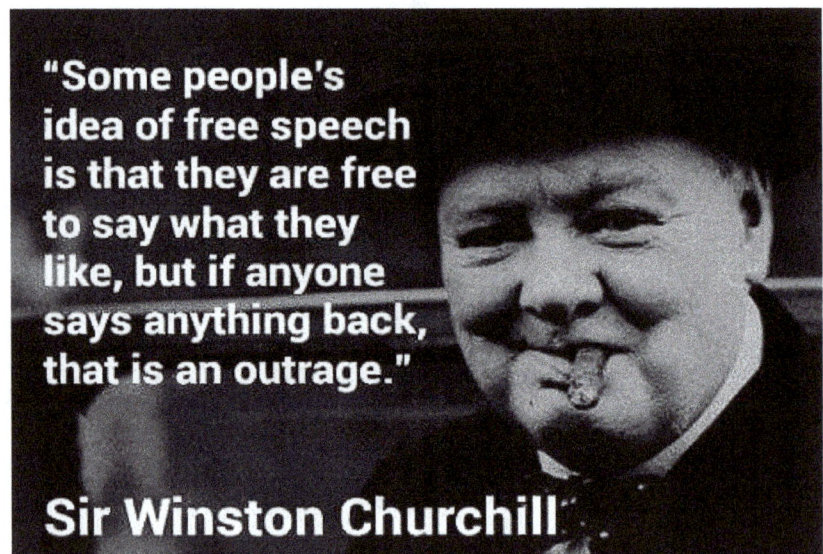

"Some people's idea of free speech is that they are free to say what they like, but if anyone says anything back, that is an outrage."

Sir Winston Churchill

Unraveling the Thread of Liberty

I find it extremely disconcerting that a former Supreme Court Justice, John Stevens, must be reminded as to why the Second Amendment was rightfully created: to protect the people against all forms of tyranny, but most notably from the oppression or subversion of their own government. To rescind the Second Amendment is to pretend human nature, our penchant for hate, intemperance, envy and hostility, does not exist; including criminals' obvious refusal to follow gun laws. Although I freely admit a firearm in the hands of a wicked soul is highly dangerous, it's even more deadly, unjust, when their unsuspecting prey have no equal measure of recourse.

Sadly, the growing prevalence of such absurd assertions are almost entirely predicated upon a misguided love of statism or intrusive, centralized government rather than rational thought based on the original intent of our Founding Fathers. Even worse, as a result of continuous illegal immigration and the unforgivable reality some blue states are encouraging non-citizen voting, it is only a matter of time before America succumbs to single-party rule despite being conceived upon the ideals of intellectual diversity, decorum, compromise, and universal checks and balances. In other words, when plotting, elected officials spend every waking moment undermining an administration's most distinct accomplishments and the media knowingly misinforms the electorate to the detriment and fracture of a nation, the descent into despotism is all but inevitable. Insatiable malice is like patriotism without sight: you cannot find wisdom in the ashes of your blind contempt.

Tyranny, unlike our regulated right to self-defense, will endure regardless of era or circumstance because human nature, people's lust for power and propensity to commit criminal acts of aggression, will always exist to some degree. Whether it methodically undermines our societal values, siphons the earned fruits of hard labor, erodes mankind's natural born rights, or puts a boot on the throat of your uncooperative convictions, evil can manifest in any medium or willing personage. Unless legalized theft, free educational indoctrination, state censorship and systemic oppression sounds distinctly "progressive" to the human condition, what could possibly be more necessary than preserving the last, detectable vestiges of American independence with your own two hands? Apparently only "boring, old-ass parents" willing to defend their liberties, families and country are unworthy to vote in the eyes of today's increasingly fascist youth.

One of the most deceiving arguments solicited by critics of individual liberty is that true security, harmony, cannot be achieved without absolute control or submission to a totalitarian authority; one, which naturally, has no agenda, corrupt elements or nefarious intent. Considering Europeans and now some Americans are being fired, fined and/or jailed for simply voicing their opinions – i.e., free speech deemed hate speech for speaking non-politically correct truths – I would say Western Civilization is quickly deteriorating into a regressive state of mob rule, political intolerance, if not one of denial itself. The fact a frightening number of judges now justify supplanting the most self-explanatory statutes, legal precedents, with their own partisan beliefs is a grave threat to the equal application of justice, equality, but most significantly the survival of America's Constitutional charter.

Whether the issue is enforcing the absolute necessity of immigration and voter ID laws, combating the uninterrupted brutality and discriminatory legacy of Islam, or simply agreeing two biologically born sexes do not require forcing people to recognize over 50 socially contrived genders, the masses ability to perceive the most rudimentary truths and safeguard the foundation of any free, vibrant and moral society is fading beneath the cultural warfare of political malcontents: radical activists who despise our way of life, founding heritage and who seek to dictate your every thought and action. Never fear, this gradual dissent into madness lead by a militant youth is the exact blueprint collectivists and Democratic Socialists have touted for nearly a century to bring about the end of American exceptionalism. To weave an enticing tapestry of tyranny you must first unravel the thread of liberty with the incited anger, imagined injustices, of the ignorant.

Roughly 11 teens are killed each day by texting and driving, a sum greater than the annual number of school shootings for almost every state, yet no one has suggested banning cell phones, boycotting Apple or holding a national march. Why? Political theater, unlike common sense, requires deception to achieve a superficial end. If this Constitutional Republic and the so-called civilized world ever needed the right to bear arms and protect that which is indispensable – our lives, liberties and autonomy – that time is now more than ever. Otherwise, those one million new Barack Obama's the former President so openly dreams of politically fathering will eagerly embrace the depravity of Marxism only to judge the imperfect transcendence of America exclusively through the subjective prism of racism, sexism and greed. Or, in Communist Manifesto terms, the sensational propaganda an aspiring ruling class feeds to maintain the entitled, victimization mentality of a predominately apathetic and gullible generation.

My apologies to the countless millennials who spend more time complaining about Snapchat filters than studying the unarmed infamy of Lenin, Hitler, Mussolini, Castro, Mao, Stalin and Che Guevara in school, but David Hogg isn't changing the world...let alone anything. He's merely reaffirming the ominous adage those who are unaware of the past are the most likely to repeat it. And that especially includes any opportunistic hypocrite hijacking an avoidable tragedy solely to push a false NRA narrative his family already believed. While I do love a good farce, what's more preposterous than a smug suburbanite posing for a picture with Valerie Jarrett – a doting Marxist and Islamist – while complaining about his potentially infringed civil right to conceal the private contents of his backpack in the very Gun Free Zones that leftists publicly advertise the availability of mass murder? Apparently the "grassroots" revolution of privately flown students will be televised on every major network with a complimentary Democratic registration card and an iPhone map to every Soros voting machine in America. Irony, it seems, is not without a sense of morbidity.

"Freedom is never more than one generation away from extinction. We didn't pass it to our children in the bloodstream. It must be fought for, protected, and handed on for them to do the same." ~ Ronald Reagan

THE IDEOLOGIES THAT KILLED OVER 100 MILLION LAST CENTURY

ARE BEING PRAISED AT OUR UNIVERSITIES TODAY

The Golden Rule

In my day, anyone who openly cursed in a classroom would have been docked grade points, sent to the office and/or given detention; regardless of any clear lack of malice or specific target of intent. If you flipped over your desk, threw a chair, threatened or aggressively touched your teacher in any manner whatsoever, you were dragged out, arrested, suspended or even expelled. Why, you ask? Because zero tolerance meant zero tolerance for those endangering the safety of others and undermining the very purpose of education; to enrich and empower every student willing to transcend their own life. You cannot maintain a civil environment, one conducive to higher learning and mutual respect, when spoiled juveniles are allowed to dictate the terms of acceptable behavior. The time has come for federal and state legislators to restore the authority of administrators and educators, so they can reclaim our public institutions without fear of losing their job or critical school funding for simply demanding common decency; those once non-negotiable norms of assumed responsibility. Political correctness and the regressive standards of social pandering - i.e., handicapping the bar of everyday expectations due to substandard parenting - has encouraged and even protected unruly adolescents who are increasingly mired in a defiant culture of disrespect and entitlement. "No more" means saying "yes" to our children's futures, the welfare of our youth and a renewed call for moral teachers because fostering generations of productive, well-adjusted adults begins by requiring them to act like one.

HEALTHCARE

Pulling the PLUG on Patient Rights

Taxing FREEDOM To Death! OBAMACARE

The Generic Brand of Bad Government Healthcare

The greatest driving force in human history is not hate or greed but self-preservation; an innate resistance to losing one's life, livelihood and family. It is through our natural-born instinct to survive the rigors of human nature, the rise of everyday competition, that circumstance breeds urgency, innovation, excellence and even empathy. Sadly, I can lend no such credence to the state of government healthcare. While the political leviathan of socialized medicine is supposedly predicated upon universal need, it is more commonly defined by waste, apathy, and the not-so-friendly institution of centralized ineptitude.

If you want a glimpse into the frightening future of medical malpractice, look no further than our VA hospitals where poorly equipped facilities offer about as much hope as they do heartache. Yes, there's a reason why Donald Trump recently signed a 55 billion-dollar bill giving military families more private healthcare and caregiver options: those who gave so much are receiving so little! Whether in need of routine checkups or critical surgical procedures, thousands of our veterans are treated as burdens and callously left to linger on waiting lists; a growing number of which die from neglect or commit suicide out of sheer anguish. These stories of socialized futility are hardly aberrations for similar experiences are prevalent in England, Cuba and yes, even the liberal love child known as Canada; a country that boasts one-tenth the U.S. population and an average wait time of two and a half months for an MRI. In a fifteen-year period, researchers estimated 50,000 Canadian women died while waiting for adequate care. If advocates can claim the moral high ground by invoking greed but ignoring reality, what's the cost/benefit ratio of a life lost to gross negligence or equitable incompetence? Dependency doesn't demand excellence; it invites the lowest bidder to misspell mediocrity on your entitled epitaph.

I'm not here to claim private healthcare is a pinnacle of perfection endorsed by the most meticulous proctologists. Hardly, for many within the industry are motivated be self-interests. However, by comparison, independent providers and physicians are overwhelmingly driven by an inherent need to survive by offering a product and degree of service superior to their competitors, including a federal singularity that caters only to itself. Quality healthcare is about options; giving ordinary people access to as many competent doctors as possible, including affordable drugs and life-saving, experimental treatments. In other words, when you make the rules and there is no commercial alternative, what is your motive to improve and innovate to satisfy the expectations of your customers? Better yet, what are the consequences for failure? The same government that can't balance its checkbook or give a simple, unrehearsed answer wants to dictate every aspect of your life; most notably, the acceptable terms of your unconditional surrender. If Washington is so incestuously corrupt, as Bernie Sanders loves to reiterate, why would anyone want to give more power, money and control to those who so summarily abuse it?

Healthcare is the Holy Grail of progressivism because its inescapable necessity invites political indoctrination; a medium easily manipulated to blackmail voters or a convenient ploy to question the sanity, but more succinctly the rights, of any gun owner. Many of the same Congressmen who profusely declared Obamacare a success – fiscal fairy dust that made healthcare even more unaffordable and countless employees unemployable – refused to subject their own families to its ill-conceived guidelines. Attempting to pay for the healthcare costs of over 300 million Americans, let alone squeeze them into a broken mold showcasing a singularly inferior product, is about as progressive as barbecuing science books to raise awareness for Global Warming. Unless you believe imitation isn't the sincerest form of flattery, the road most traveled is typically the one with the most dining options and the fewest bureaucrats selling trillion-dollar sporks. Why would choosing insurance or a trustworthy doctor be any different? A government "death panel" ordering hospitals to pull the plug on gravely-ill patients is bad enough but refusing to allow parents the opportunity to save their own child's life by accepting offers of medical assistance from other countries is simply sadistic. Charlie Gard and Alfie Evans obviously didn't meet the British court's honorable criteria of "redeemable value".

The inherent flaws of private healthcare do not require sacrificing liberty or quality treatment on a glass altar of unsustainable socialism. Nor does it justify the estimated $33-trillion-dollar cost for the pipedream of universal Medicare over 10 years; a burden the middle class would inevitably bear. Lasting and immediate reform can be achieved by eliminating or restricting the exclusion of "pre-existing" conditions, adjusting the rates of emergency and surgical care, opening foreign pharmaceutical markets to lower the cost of drug prescriptions, and by establishing tax-free healthcare coops for businesses or municipalities. Likewise, the cost of routine medical procedures can be lowered by either subsidizing the purchase of vital Hospital equipment or by providing abatements for the companies that manufacture these devices. If Washington can waste 150 billion annually on illegal immigrants, or subsidize the human rights abuses of terrorist nations, Congress can refund our forsaken trust by finding creative methods to lower the medical expenses of actual citizens without infringing upon the autonomy of choice.

As for those struggling individuals unable to afford insurance, a greater emphasis should be placed on upgrading, staffing and properly equipping community health centers; as well as encouraging more area doctors and nurses to volunteer their expertise in exchange for student loan forgiveness or future job preference. Whereas "access" to medical services is a right, free or discounted healthcare is a privilege incumbent upon helping yourself; albeit by working to survive or by seeking higher education/training to earn a better living. There is absolutely no shame in requiring assistance during times of financial distress, failing health or personal misfortune. However, other than enduring a permanent disability, refusing to provide for your family or make an honest attempt to meet your medical obligations is not "need"; it's exploitation. A lack of personal accountability is a surplus of contempt for those affected by its absence.

Average wait times for socialized healthcare in Canada:

21.2 weeks for specialist referrals

4.1 weeks for CT scans

10.8 weeks for an MRI

4 weeks for an ultrasound

Forcing Americans to embrace a single-payer healthcare system is as absurd as claiming only one company should sell shoes or manufacture cars. After all, Crocs are equally traumatizing whether at the plant or in the office and who doesn't want a convertible Yugo tank with a fully-functional etch-sketch GPS? The American pioneers of discovery were not the offspring of a federal mandate, clamoring for affirmative action, nor were they motivated by the thought of the fruits of their labor being confiscated for the common good of bad government. Rather, they personified a spirit of ambition that risked failure for the potential reward of a dream – realized by a tireless work ethic – dedicated to pushing the boundaries of the status quo.

While most medical personnel possess an intrinsic desire to both transform and save lives, they also rightfully deserve to thrive within an environment that both compensates their unique abilities and stokes the fire of human ingenuity. If "necessity" is the mother of invention, competition is undoubtedly the father of competence. Although some degree of oversight will always be required to combat fraud, negligence, and to maintain safeguards within an ever-changing industry, "the people" deserve the best possible care with the least amount of political subversion. Government does little-to-nothing as well as the private sector because in the real-world efficiency, specialization and solvency, are not logical fallacies "mislabeled" as enemies of the state. When Socialism is defined as Communism without a bayonet in your back, success is defined by the number of functional limbs left to command instead of by the number of lives saved from its dysfunctional grasp.

Dude, Where's Our Country?

A Healthy Bottom Line

Many aspiring doctors and medical specialists pursue healthcare careers due to the financial incentive; a completely justifiable decision due to the amount of sacrifice, skill and education required. However, I do not believe medical insurance, a medium which can literally be the difference between life and death, should operate on the same maximized profit paradigm of private ventures selling goods or services. Other than ensuring the necessary funds to pay personnel, preserve quality customer care and maintain sufficient monetary reserves to account for inevitable spikes in annual claims, a healthcare provider's primary goal should always be to differ the best possible coverage at the most affordable premiums; not to pay CEO's multi-million-dollar salaries and benchmark bonuses while denying policy holders "pre-existing" medical needs whenever humanly possible. The goal of saving lives is not the same "modus operandi" as marketing cars or aftershave.

Just talked with Pfizer CEO and @SecAzar on our drug pricing blueprint. Pfizer is rolling back price hikes, so American patients don't pay more. We applaud Pfizer for this decision and hope other companies do the same. Great news for the American people!

@realDonaldTrump

Because everyone loves a functional Acme Rocket with an optional airbag, it is also my humble contention medical research should be conducted separately from pharmaceutical firms seeking stratospheric revenues by endeavoring to create an unyielding line of new medications/treatments that merely lessen symptoms, despite posing many new risks, yet rarely remedy any disease or lingering ailment. Rather, as part of independent laboratories or perhaps non-profit entities funded by public donors and/or government grants, young researchers could be provided with the necessary resources and intellectual freedom to unlock world-altering breakthroughs that could be sold near cost as a universally-accessible, affordable medication. Successful individuals, pioneering groups, could be awarded small commissions for each prescription filled by applying a minimal royalty percentage to each purchase; a non-evasive gesture that would represent mere pennies to the most impoverished patients, but significant long-term compensation, professional motivation, to both proven and future researchers. And yes, for the record, pharmaceutical companies could still receive fair compensation for manufacturing these drugs, just without the abusive monopoly on research and the longest-running world record for unrealized cures.

Although cultivating healthcare options and fostering healthy competition will always be indispensable components of quality, affordable healthcare, eliminating obscene profiteering and ulterior industry motives without succumbing to despotic government mandates is unequivocally in the best interests of individual liberty and the foreseeable well-being of the American people. Chronically-ill patients are routinely denied access to potentially life-saving, experimental treatments, only to be bankrupted by uncovered medical bills and overpriced medicines that are equally if not more hazardous to their marginalized health. Living with dignity, instead of being left in perpetual pain or God-forbid without reputable insurance, begins by providing real solutions; not by rushing to patent the newest "snake oil" promising only hope's "refillable" allure.

" If people let the government decide what foods they eat and medicines they take, their bodies will soon be in as sorry a state as are the souls who live under tyranny."

-Thomas Jefferson

Repealing the GOP

I said it three months ago, I'll say it again. The same GOP so adamantly opposed to Obamacare & socialized healthcare in 2008 is now advocating its own brand. Why?

I support a full repeal of Obamacare, not a replacement. Government healthcare – single payer, individual mandate or not – is a construct of statism and therefore an exercise in abusive ineptitude. Even if you improve upon the disastrous fallout from Obamacare, the next "progressive" administration that comes along will simply pass further regulations and requirements to expand the degree of control Washington can exert over the electorate, but more specifically, our everyday lives. There are much saner, more effective and affordable healthcare reforms that do not require accruing mass debt or sacrificing privacy and personal freedoms in the name of the 'common good'. If I may, what has our federal bureaucracy ever done in a competent, conscionable and timely manner? Socialized medicine in any form is a grave threat to America's founding charter of limited government and individual liberty. Call me a colonial conservative or merely acutely aware of the historical dangers such excessive power inevitably invites. People deserve the best care possible, one driven by competition, trust and responsible oversight, not endless manipulation designed to serve a singular political end. Although I do have faith in a handful of elected representatives within Congress, the centralized cesspool of revolving special interests and partisan dysfunction is about as coherent as a Nancy Pelosi speech on ethics. Excuse me while I abstain from the most ignorant form of self-assisted suicide.

Green Socialist Healthcare and Asylum Yellow Sheets

Unbeknownst to a googly-eyed bar maiden turned neurotic politician and instant Netflix millionaire, "Green Oco-Loco", and her famed Marxist marshmallow, Bernie "three estates" Sanders, socialist healthcare really isn't cheaper; it's simply heavily subsidized by much higher taxes and supplemental coverage. However, unlike private healthcare systems which give patients much greater autonomy over their choice of doctor and available treatment options, most European governments dictate nearly aspect of their populace's healthcare...socialist plans that offer few incentives for aspiring or accomplished doctors, let alone quality and timely care. Even worse, citizens are essentially forced to bankroll the medical needs of their fellow countrymen, working or not, regardless if they themselves are in good health and require few services. Despite the endless media propaganda, divisive class warfare and utopian hype, nothing is truly ever free. Limousine liberals simply want to sell you a Mediterranean wet dream wrapped inside an asylum patient's yellow sheet.

The Obamacare Deception

It's one thing to shake the hand of a notorious used car salesman; it's an entirely different matter to provide a false alibi for their insurance scam in the face of their victims. Either John Robert's bleeding heart kindly suffers liars and thieves, an incurable condition known as liberalism, or his real resume is taped behind Barack Obama's braille version of the Constitution. As for Justice Kennedy, an ardent dissenter of Obamacare in 2012, I'm guessing he also believes con artists possess the innate right to sell a "Yugo-to-hell" by forcing the people to pay for their Mercedes. What is the purpose of accepting a state's challenge on the legality of forced subsidies, if you're only going to validate its false premise by signing off on the disturbing reality your worst fears actually came true?

The not-so-startling admission by Obamacare architect Jonathan Gruber that Barack Obama lied to the American people in order to pass his socialist leviathan is but confirmation of what we already knew; it was a Trojan horse for an eventual single-payer healthcare system and a gateway to a national patient database of oversight. Democrats lied through their teeth by proclaiming Obamacare wasn't a tax; that it was a choice, only to go before the Supreme Court and claim it was a mandatory penalty (tax) the government had the right to enforce under the Interstate Commerce Act. The former President repeatedly reiterated everyone could keep their existing insurance policies, even their preferred doctor, and yet that was another complete fabrication; millions lost both. Democrats argued Obamacare would lower premiums, save Americans $2500 a year, and make the market more competitive. The Affordable Care Act is anything but affordable. Insurance rates have risen by an average of 41% – in some cases by more than 150% – and Washington is expected to announce additional spikes in the coming years. How commendable! Yes, how many jobs have been lost, full-time employees forced to accept part-time jobs and lose their financial independence, due to the inane requirements of Obamacare? No matter what the issue, or the perceived results, one thing is for certain: the "progressive" establishment has deceived, manipulated, and outright lied to the American people at almost every conceivable turn. If I may, who in their right mind would continue to fund such a callous and destructive trail of deception?

Not only is socialist medicine doomed to collapse beneath the collective weight of its own insolvency in a country as populated as America – especially when given so freely to the millions of illegals our government welcomed without reservation – but it destroys the true genesis of quality healthcare: competition. Competition spurs innovation, which increases the quality and efficacy of healthcare, lowers prices through anti-trust regulation, and in turn saves lives. Sadly, saving lives is not in the 'secular humanist' vocabulary when Big Government is more concerned with documenting a patient's political views, whether or not you own a gun, or God forbid identify as a Christian, than alleviating debilitating diseases or curing its citizens of any fatal conditions. Who can even stomach the idea of corrupt legislators like Nancy Pelosi and Maxine Waters, those too inconvenienced to read the bill or too busy "getting paid" to give a damn, deciding whether the lives of your parents, spouse or child are worth the financial cost of partisan disloyalty? By merely entertaining the thought of government healthcare, we're validating and advancing the left's ideological goal of turning our educational and medical institutions into permanent weapons of ignorance and mass dependence. Who needs second opinions when free will and self-respect are aborted on the operating table of political malpractice?

Unless Death Panels are Life Alert's new coveted coupon club, Government does nothing as well or as efficient as the private sector. One only needs to witness the horrific treatment of our veterans, those lacking timely and competent healthcare, by apathetic and incompetent bureaucrats. Utterly disgraceful. America's healthcare system didn't need to be hijacked by Big Brother as a choreographed charade to ensure mass dependency and leverage our liberty. The American people, those who work and toil for a better life, clamored for common sense reform that honored choice, excellence and affordability; the very anti-thesis of statism. Rather than writing trillion-dollar blank checks each year to a morally bankrupt President, Congress could have achieved lasting change by capping the astronomical prices of emergency and surgical care, increasing the availability of cheaper prescription drugs, assuring better access to international treatment options, and by placing restrictions on "pre-existing conditions" used to deny desperately needed healthcare.

Historically speaking, this endeavor can be accomplished by three distinct approaches; allow a complete government takeover of your personal healthcare, subsidize the increased expenses of doctors and hospitals incurred by reform, or kick the medical community – equipment and supplies manufacturers – in their collective ass to find more economical and ingenuous ways to improve care without sacrificing the quality of their respected practices. Or four, fail to adapt by creatively streamlining your costs and sell snake oil for Uncle Joe (Biden) on the campaign trail of tears. By combining market reforms with the known prevalence of Medicare and Medicaid, programs already designed to subsidize the burden of more indigent Americans, there's absolutely no reason why Americans cannot demand more from the private sector while relying far less on the gold-plated lemon known as Obamacare. Choice isn't a revolutionary concept; it's a dying one.

Seeds of Change

The revered and equally feared Cannabis Sativa, one of the oldest domesticated plants in the United States with historical ties dating back to the third millennium BC, didn't really take root in modern America until the 1960's when it crossed socio-economic lines and found a more mainstream audience on college campuses and in more affluent neighborhoods. Although restrictions on cannabis have existed since the early 1900's, long after the common prevalence of oriental-style hashish bars in rural towns and urban America during the mid-1800's, "weed" didn't truly become illegal across the U.S. until the federal Marijuana Tax Act of 1937 prohibited the possession or transfer of marijuana for recreational uses. However, it wasn't until its flowering popularity, criminal exploits and subsequent profitability that our government banned the entire cannabis species under the Controlled Substances Act of 1970. With countless arrests, incarcerations and political debate having ensued since these actions, both user obsession and societal misconception rarely coexist in the same plane of reality.

Whether you're a skilled "midnight toker", a naturalist practicing civil disobedience in your HEPA-filtered bathroom or a licensed herbalist knitting edible sweaters for a Norwegian nudist colony, I find it equally disconcerting our government has made little genuine effort to scientifically delineate between marijuana and hemp; unique variations of the same plant differing in both function and cultivation. Marijuana, which now exists in countless hybrid forms, is used almost exclusively for medicinal or recreational purposes because it contains higher levels of THC...a psychotropic chemical known to cause sedative or hallucinogenic effects when absorbed, smoked or ingested. Hemp, by contrast, contains very low levels of THC (less than .03% according to Canadian law) and is known to have over 25,000 possible applications: including, but not limited to, dietary supplements, skin products, clothing, rope, rugs, and many other common accessories. It is currently an agricultural staple in over 30 countries, with China, Chile and European Union serving as the greatest purveyors of its numerous commercial inventions.

Unlike a modest contingent of my former friends and peers, I freely admit never being interested in the "High Life". It simply did not appeal to my nature or my focus. By the same token, outside of the obvious legal risk, I never really cared if others partook in its recreational pleasures being it was far less dangerous than many opiates or prescription sedatives. After all, moderation is the guiding modality to nearly all life's pursuits and many everyday products sold on store shelves can inflict just as much damage to trusting consumers. However, if you have an addictive personality, are a chronic abuser or find yourself pawning your mom's toaster to feed your "controllable" fix, marijuana is obviously far more detrimental to your life's worth than any perceived benefit. Unfortunately for younger generations lost in the cultural fog of this incessant debate, millions of vulnerable adolescents are too often hypnotized by the glamorized allure of the "420" lifestyle because they typically lack the conviction to resist the temptation of its inviting social status; regardless of the potential criminal or health complications.

As a self-professed conservative who preaches self-respect over recklessness, consequence in lieu of compulsiveness, "legalization" was not in my vocabulary. Well, until now. Before you bust out your "Puff the Magic Dragon" bong and chill with Bob

Marley's muse in Jamaica, let me preface my change of heart by first rejecting the sensationalist notion Marijuana is a harmless, magical Godsend that cures cancer, halts Parkinson's and ensures eternal happiness in angry dwarfs unable to reach the non-vegan cookies. If that was the case millions would stop at nothing to save their loved ones from unbearable suffering and even death. On the contrary, "reefer" is eerily similar to alcohol or cigarettes in that excessive use can cause organ damage, respiratory failure, cognitive dysfunction, motor impairment, behavioral disorders and yes, even cancer. The idea that an "organic" substance cannot injure the body is as woefully naïve as it is plain wrong. Many toxins present within our environment – elements, plants, insects, and animals - are naturally occurring and distinctly hazardous to the uninformed. One must either become acutely aware of the danger they pose or develop an evolutionary immunity; something frat parties or stoned designated drivers have yet to prove. While I do believe cannabis oil possesses certain medicinal properties to lessen the debilitating symptoms of widespread pain, inflammation, tremors or certain mood disorders, there are still inherent risks like any synthetic drug produced by Big Pharma for mass consumption.

My abrupt evolution is not based on any new science or random brownie peace offerings. Rather, it's a measured response to societal benefit, fairness, and national security. The recreational use of Marijuana by the average American, if done in moderation and under the right circumstances, is very comparable to alcoholic beverages and poses less risk than most overprescribed painkillers. The greatest threat resides not in its usage but in the illicit manufacturing by foreign drug cartels and distribution by domestic crime syndicates...i.e., street gangs. This highly lucrative business also serves as a convenient incubator for weapons, prostitution and human trafficking, costing billions in border policing as well as the strain on local communities from rising crime ratings. If I may, what's the cost of a 20-year-old kid searching for a cheap high being gunned down in an alleyway by a career criminal, sentencing a casual user to 5 years in prison, or a college student dying in her dorm room from a joint unknowingly laced with ecstasy? The catastrophic fallout from the battle for street supremacy over a substance that pales in potency to heroin, meth or fentanyl is one that can be largely avoided, even turned into a positive resource for meaningful change. Punish those who illegally produce or distribute marijuana, not those members of society who pose little or no threat to their neighbors.

By ending the federal ban on marijuana and imposing a national 5% excise fee, trained experts can not only regulate the safety and content of cannabis sales, but billions in revenue can be raised to improve education, strengthen our failing infrastructure or build that much needed wall to restore order at our porous Southern border. Furthermore, legal growers will once again have access to the federal banking system, thus aiding their daily operations without needlessly placing their lives at risk by hoarding obscene amounts of cash. In Colorado and Oregon alone, annual duties from lawful sales have already surpassed $200 million. For those critics believing I'm equating dollar signs to legalized depravity, let me digress. I am by no means suggesting minors should be able to purchase marijuana, that anyone should work or drive under the influence of a controlled substance, and I'm definitely not condoning public consumption in our parks, community centers or near schools. Personal discretion is the caveat to any potentially harmful action. I'm merely attempting to lend a degree of sanity to those activities which will happen regardless of any formal acceptance or grandfathered policy of denial.

The Fascism Of Feminism

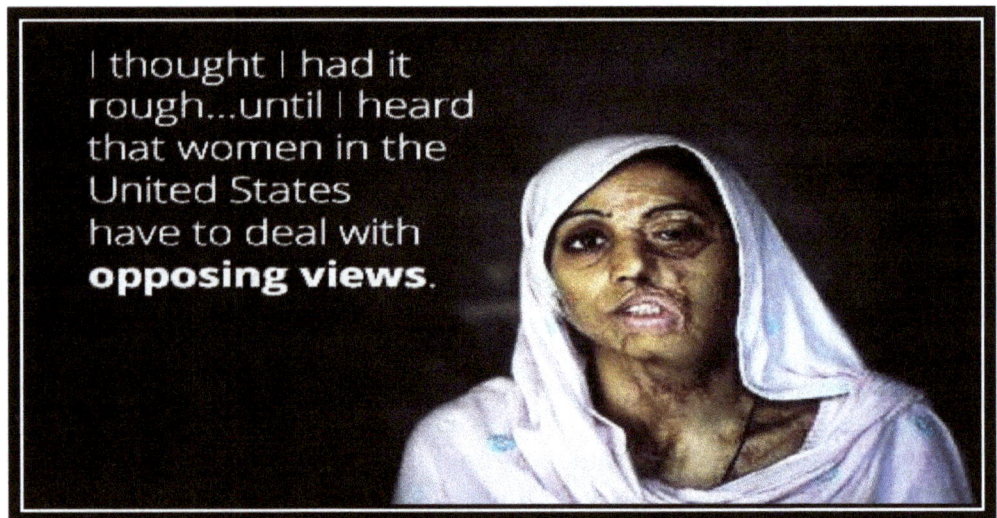

I thought I had it rough...until I heard that women in the United States have to deal with **opposing views**.

The Fascism of Feminism: No Conservative Victims Allowed

Do I have a problem with the modern feminist movement? Hmm, that depends if that's a multiple-choice question! Before feminism was hijacked by militant activists such as Code Pink, and yes, even the heralded NOW, it was designed to empower, support, and defend the rights of women regardless of their personal lives and affiliations. Now, no pun intended, it is a twisted political platform that discriminates against women who don't adhere to a malformed stereotype of what progressives deem as worthy of their "cause". Today's feminist cults pick and choose whom they defend, they maliciously incite discord and tarnish lives with imagined slights – i.e., Gloria Allred's political theater of phallic defamation – and anything overtly masculine/paternal is labeled as misogynistic and a palpable threat to their esoteric vision of an "evolved" society. In other words, these radical feminists are hopelessly insecure, biased, and extremely vindictive when they cannot discount or emasculate the traditional male role model into a submissive tool of political servitude. For some unresolved childhood issue, perhaps their socialist dream of secular serfdom put to show tunes, it makes them feel better about themselves and the Boy Scouts!

Unfortunately for country music and the "XY" chromosome, the strong jaw, blue collar, gun-owning, meat-eating, God-fearing, flag-saluting silhouette of manhood is now classified as a predator to women everywhere; regardless whether "said man" is a good father, treats women with the utmost respect, and leads a moral life. The reality such misguided activism places effeminate, emasculated males on a pedestal of exceptionalism and enlightenment – because it's least offensive to their frail sensibilities and innate to their "gender simplification" mantra – begs to the exact degree of their sexual neurosis. I believe Mr. Freud called it penis envy, or more profoundly, jealously without snow tires. A true woman requires no such infantile generalizations for she is fully content in whom she is, confident in what she can achieve, and seeks only to be judged according to her actions; that is, equal opportunity does not necessarily dictate equal outcomes or demand profane displays of juvenile rage whenever life's inevitable struggles ensue. Dying your armpit hair, refusing to bathe or reducing your self-worth to objectifying your vagina doesn't empower generations of impressionable young girls, it repels the civilized world. Our innate biological differences are not our weakness, a bitter platform of insecurity from which to discriminate or breed discontent. They are natural gifts, blessed with unique attributes and God-given strengths, designed to foster symbiotic relationships that compliment both genders for the benefit of all humanity.

So, do I have a problem with feminism? Hmm…I have a problem with the validity and intelligence of any movement that happily allows Sarah Palin to be called a slut, the hopeful victim of a rape, because her detractors – most notably the liberal media – would rather disparage her as a conservative woman, her right to express herself in a land predicated upon liberty, than simply refute the factual strength of her argument. (Yes, slander is the tool of the defeated) I have a problem with anyone who demeans a woman for staying at home to personally raise her children and maintain her household, rather than seek out a professional career of advancement and accolades. As a true believer in equality, I always assumed both were highly commendable and solely a woman's choice. Obviously, I'm wrong.

I reject any bankrupt ideology that judges the worthiness of a woman's plight according to her sexuality, gender, wealth, race, religion or whether she believes in abortion or not, rather than recognizing her as a sentient being blessed with certain unalienable rights. And last but never least, I detest any hypocrite or fascist faction that finds it necessary to discriminate against and belittle men, individuals worthy of respect until proven otherwise, to somehow justify the type of unapologetic sexism some women are tragically fighting. True men, not the extreme cases of misbehavior used to objectify our entire gender and ignite political firestorms of opportunism, see themselves and the struggle for gender equality through the eyes of their sisters, wives, daughters, and mothers. It's called empathy, objectivity, humanity. No political affiliation or gender bias is necessary or required!

"Women's marches are a clever progressive divide and conquer strategy that not only turns women against men, but also turns women against each other in the guise of peace and solidarity." ~Dawn Perlmutter

Blue Booties, Pink Hats and the War on Masculinity

In the never-ending battle for America's soul, the newly endangered institution of common sense, the problem isn't toxic masculinity. The problem is toxic insecurities; that insufferable transference of implied guilt born from a weak victimization mentality. The innate differences between men and women are not a sexist conspiracy intended to define or limit our aspirations, abilities, for what we ultimately become is of our own volition. Our biological distinctions, over 6,500 genetic variations in all, are evolutionary attributes designed to instinctively protect and proliferate our species. And while it is true each sex possesses unique or unequal strengths, these delineations serve as symbiotic reminders we are "stronger together" when we reject Hillary Clinton's quest to dissect humanity through the social justice cross-hairs of gender warfare.

If boyish lesbians are celebrated for their adopted masculinity – "feminists" typically obsessed with seeking the physical appearance of their gender identity to, ironically, "balance" their sexual relationships – why are men now negatively stereotyped for exercising their natural inclination for contact sports, action movies, fast cars, shooting a gun or passionately defending their political convictions; whose freedom of expression, by the way, is now negatively stigmatized as "mansplaining". Apparently, your father or brother's opinions are entirely contingent upon whether their genitals tip the weighted scales of acceptable "conservative" baggage. As long as millennial women are fatally triggered because a majority of people instinctively use a masculine reference to describe God, despite the biblical account man was theoretically fathered in his image, then please express equal offense at the countless instances "her" is used to describe one's car, America or Bruce Jenner's androgynous hypnotherapist named Billy Le Disco. After all, dressing and acting like a man no more turns Paris Hilton, a natural born female, into J.J. Watt than wearing a dress and lipstick magically transforms Charles Manson into Mother Teresa; no matter how many hormone injections or plastic surgeries someone receives.

Honestly, how does the mere utterance of a pronoun – the sex of an author, a cook or your dog – hinder or change your life for the better? Does crying over God's "assumed" appendage alter "science" or the eternal blessings of love, forgiveness or faith? Fair treatment begins by realizing "equality" is oblivious to your political desire to reject or redefine the real world according to your prejudices; a veiled attempt to compensate for your own inadequacies. Likewise, reducing God's relevance to a genetic marker, a chromosomal precursor of a baby's sex that more and more "educated" progressives believe no longer exists, is as inane as claiming criminal intent is incumbent upon one's gender. If Americans spent more time embracing the universal wisdom of the Scriptures in lieu of perverting the Bible to fit their morally skewed beliefs, chivalry would not require a permit to wake Sleeping Beauty from her cursed slumber without her consent. Yes, believe it or not, many of the most overtly masculine archetypes are also some of the most respectful and protective gentlemen due to their supportive, demanding upbringing.

When your own hyper-sensitive insecurities cannot escape the cultural black hole known as political correctness and therefore fail to process the harmless nuances of human interaction, you literally live every minute of every day being offended by the truth; that inedible garnish touching your imaginary vegan steak. It also means you probably lack the ability to discern mischief from malice. How does the immature act of a Navy Pilot leaving a penis plume in the sky draw more outrage than naked activists publicly threatening the President and screaming profanities in front of children; in front of their own kids, no less? Dare I even mention the thousands of "empowered" female sex workers and nude models using social media to willingly objectify themselves for a buck and forever warp the mental health and sexual behavior of young kids? And to think we're still talking about tyranny of God's 'kibbles and bits', marginalizing our savior and his 7.6 billion distinct, sovereign children to the non-descript pacifier of "it".

America would be a far more inviting if political pundits and triggered feminists spent more time focusing on their own lives and personal "transgressions" in place of policing the sociological intricacies of individual discretion. "Equality" is not achieved by attempting to coerce "respect" or by forcing others to acquiesce to your subjective whims and perceived slights. It is as much an imperfect manifestation of choice as it has become a politician's crutch to distract society – those lost souls conditioned by academia/media and whose lives are defined by perpetual misery – from the fact we are our greatest oppressors and liberators because life's most daunting obstacles overwhelmingly reside within ourselves. Both women and men play integral parts in our society's development, survival, and neither should be discounted or diminished for their invaluable contributions.

The sooner political antagonists accept responsibility for waging nonsensical campaigns that provide no foreseeable benefit, the quicker common sense forever puts feminist fervor over mere technicality to rest. Instead of arguing the perceived anatomy of God solely to coddle gender militants seeking our unconditional surrender to an agenda that equates smooth arm pits to patriarchal subjugation and promotes non-binary identification as a bonafide biological sex, why not simply embody the timeless virtues of prudence and temperance over the hostile paranoia of manufactured misappropriation? The rapid attrition of strong male role models and rise in apathetic parenting has provided a fertile breeding ground for a millennial generation content rejecting any sense of societal obligation and necessity of reciprocal respect for a trite existence seduced by entitlement, envy and the limitless perversion of moral restraint. A society that emasculates its men and minimizes their functional roles - fathers, protectors, providers, mentors, leaders - will quickly be replaced by one that doesn't. The cultural castration of the male gender is the perilous rejection of natural selection.

To be a "she" or a "he" was never a rhetorical question, but an accepted formality of birth for masculine and feminine traits are both native and conditioned behaviors. Likewise, to deny who we are, one of two sexes and not any combination of 58 gender identities conceived on the comforting pillows of self-indulgence, those "not-so-rare" genetic anomalies known as hurt feelings, is the epitome of madness. Purposely interjecting gender into every conversation, decision or life event is not only the pettiest form of discrimination, it's no different than unsolicited religious indoctrination because such convictions also represent an imposed ideological set of personal beliefs; or more profoundly, the voracious desire to dispute/corrupt someone's gender or inherent sexuality to validate one's twisted assertions. Unless separation of "Church and State" is no longer the sacred bell cow of progressive secularism, excuse me while I abstain from joining the cross-dressing cult of gender sadists attempting to shame Barbie for shaving her legs but not for emasculating Ken with bedazzled pajamas, a crocheted pink hat and electoral shock collar. I have far too much respect for those secure, self-respecting women and men who are neither threatened by the opposite sex – the natural connection and biological gifts of each gender – or feel the need to acknowledge those hypocrites attempting to neuter unapologetic Alpha males just so they can more successfully impostor one.

The Bare-Naked Truth of Feminism

If a woman's ability to choose is truly paramount to liberals, why do they attack those who choose to stay at home and raise a family in a world that is brimming with immorality, promiscuity and absentee parents? Furthermore, if feminists truly care about women, shouldn't they support their rights as individuals, equals, regardless of their political or religious affiliation? The real war on women has nothing to do with opposing abortion, protecting a child's life, or free birth control; it's a perilous product of the radical left's undying hatred of those independent voices who don't share their sexist views of how a woman should think, feel, and act. Whether a woman wants to pursue a career, raise her child full time, vote Republican or Democrat...that is entirely her choice. And Thank God she is free to exercise such personal discretion. After all, wasn't it roughly a century ago women in this country were denied their natural born and Constitutional liberties; equality in the eyes of God and their innate ability to choose a life of their own bidding? Yes, how disconcerting is it that modern-day feminists are complicit in their silence as millions of Islamic women are deprived of basic human rights – free speech, the necessity of education, due process and protection from legalized brutality – only to religiously chastise those American women who are Christian and who espouse conservative ideals? Activists will celebrate "progressive" females who proudly have abortions or single women who have more children simply to garner more welfare, but they will viciously degrade Sarah Palin – a successful, self-made woman – who chooses to embrace motherhood and raise her handicap son as an equal. Sense any hypocrisy or glaring lack of respect?

Feminism, which arose from need and injustice, has tragically morphed into a fascist movement solely designed to redefine womanhood to further a political agenda and to squeeze our daughters into a stereotypical mold that is by no means progressive: it's an affront to their liberty, intelligence, and individuality. Instead of fighting for the betterment of all women, regardless of their personal beliefs or lifestyle, feminists selfishly attempt to oppress those who do not cater to their fragile and warped sensibilities. Simply put, it's discrimination of the worst kind for it is born out of choreographed deceit, political gain and sheer malice. Unbeknownst to the historically obtuse left, America was founded upon personal freedom and tolerance. Just because a woman doesn't flaunt her sexuality, treat her children like bumps in the road, or attack men for professional or monetary gain, doesn't make her old-fashioned, weak or naive. It simply means she embodies self-respect, accountability, and can delineate between choice, reality, and destructive political rhetoric. It also means, unlike Madonna, she doesn't need to publicly share the geometric shape of her pubic hair or bribe every man willing to vote for Hillary with the promise of oral sex in order to feel empowered, special or enlightened. Some crimes against humanity are best left to the naked imagination where shameless celebrities still believe they are somehow relevant or remotely appealing.

Emasculating America and the Sexism of Shapes

Modern day feminists are brainwashing an entire generation of women into believing they are helpless, inferior creatures who are incapable of buying birth control, coping without abortion, raising a family, using a gun for self-defense, getting married or working with men because the Sandra Fluke's of the world are nothing more than sexual objects trapped in a meat-eating, misogynistic society. According to the genetic scholars at Salon magazine, it has become feasibly impossible for those human beings with two "X" chromosomes to function, let alone to be responsible for their lives and bodies.

Believe it or not, the sorority sisters at Code Pink actually want the fairer sex to discover everything is potentially sexist, including the alphabet, and that anything remotely phallic – i.e., a talking hand or an innocent statue of a returning WWII soldier swooping the love of his life off her feet – is a crime against the female gender; well that and excessively loud clapping. Unannounced, loud hand gestures by conspiring males, those everyday expressions of approval resulting in irreversible psychological trauma, are now interpreted as unprovoked sexual aggression by contemporary feminists. Yes, I really, really wish I was joking! My God, how did we ever survive school assemblies, football games, or Knick Knack Paddy Whack? Good thing "jazz hands" are now universally acceptable. Confused? Me too.

Sorry to disappoint the transgendered bathroom engineers of progressive families but my mother raised six kids, maintained a spotless home, worked a full-time job, honored God, shot a rifle and she didn't take crap from anyone; especially mentally challenged activists who barbecued tofu. She gave her daughters a backbone, ingrained her sons with unconditional respect, and demanded all of her children to be proud, proper, independent, and most of all...to never make excuses. Thus, it baffles me how far this "selfie" generation of younger women will go to sexualize their image on social media, do almost anything to draw negative attention to themselves, only to succumb to this absurd, liberal nonsense that views all females as societal slaves who cower in the shadows of Barney, curling irons and glow sticks. Anything but! By the way, how are the sales of adult toys these days? Just ask Siri if feminist geometry causes carpal tunnel syndrome, phallic panic attacks or multiple personality disorder in bathtubs. That's right...always blame Barry White; or Melissa Etheridge.

The real tragedy of this entire debacle is that I'm forced to go to such obnoxious extremes to illustrate how utterly ridiculous feminism has become. Feminists rarely deal with or address real injustice or discrimination on a mass scale anymore, such as unequal pay among Democratic staffers or Hillary shaming Bill's "bimbo" rape victims, so they desperately try to compensate by inventing ways to stay relevant. If you decide not to shave your pits, refuse to wear "sexist" bras, or use soiled sanitary napkins to make a political statement, so be it. It's disturbing and gross, overtly degrading, but still your sentient choice. Just don't accuse me of wrongdoing, juggling corn dogs in your fragile state of yoga hypnosis, because you can no longer delineate between right and wrong, class and crass, empowerment and indecency, reality and Rasputin.

Personally, it's not my choice or desire to decide what a woman wears – no matter how tasteless – or how she lives her life; nor does it justify anyone violating her body or her rights. In a country predicated upon free will, it's of little consequence whether or not I approve of anyone's lifestyle. I simply do not need to witness a naked Lena Dunham eating an entire birthday cake while sitting on the toilet, recollecting about molesting her toddler sister, to realize your straight jacket isn't near tight enough. I'd much rather retreat to my "sexist", conservative delusion where there are still classy, intelligent, and strong ladies who believe the best way to empower other women is to actually be one; politics be damned. Sound kosher or am I being obtuse?

"Second-wave feminism – in its attempt to destroy men – is also destroying women and our culture." Feminist Icon, Camille Paglia

The Hijacked Gender of Jihad

Linda Sarsour? Methinks the grifter doth protest too much! Or shall I compare you to a soiled blade betrayed by a handle bearing your unindicted name? There are innocent laughs shared among mutual friends, and then there are malicious plots waged by unarmed saboteurs who squat on your hospitality, seduce your sense of security, solicit dowries to consummate your demise, before unlocking your backdoor to smile at sovereignty's death. The only revelation more hypocritical than an anti-Semitic "feminist" advocating Sharia Law in a country predicated upon universal human rights is the militant Islamic offspring of anti-American immigrants organizing a national protest march to galvanize women already liberated by Judeo-Christian values. How else can the self-identified, third party victim of a democratic election result rise to the forefront of American social justice by advocating "jihad" against the Leader of the Free World? Yes, whenever tolerance and self-respect won't suffice, there is always the honorable platform of making terrorist threats and invoking Taqiyya; i.e., the Islamic practice of deception to topple a foreign foe by any means necessary. Or, unless I'm horribly mistaken, are your Zakat payments made out to: "I Love America regardless who is president"?

I find it ironic the outspoken daughter of Palestinian parents who fled the decadence and destitution of the Middle East to bask in the ubiquitous opportunities and freedoms of Western Civilization, dismisses the uncooperative reality she would be beaten unmercifully by the barbaric tenets of the same Islamic creed she willingly applauds with such wanton ignorance. If Hamas and Hezbollah are indeed freedom fighters not bent on eviscerating the Jewish state, how is glorified misogyny and an unyielding legacy of mass murder no longer a travesty simply because you consensually cover your head and accepted an arranged marriage to honor a deified "prophet" who believed martyrdom begets 72 virgins of "virtuous" fornication? Refusing to assimilate to Western customs, an American nation forged upon the anvil of individual liberty to shatter the glass sword of religious persecution, is about as ingenious as banning water in hell. An ounce of common sense is more than enough divine recompense for 150 pounds of searing flesh. Gratitude reciprocates grace.

While it's easy to predict your obnoxious opposition to Donald Trump – a patriotic President who recognizes Islam as the greatest singular threat to humanity – it's extremely disconcerting to witness the Democratic party (American citizens, mind you) confuse political disagreement with ingratiating the ruse of a seditious ingrate who would gladly watch America and Israel burn beneath the same vile breath she spent praising terrorist attacks against both nations. Obviously there must be something so morally redeemable about a self-proclaimed "social justice warrior", one who actually mourned the death of Saddam Hussein, spearheading an orchestrated coup to dehumanize our President – excuse me, publicly opine for his overthrow or death – only to consciously conceal the suffering of millions whom continue to toil beneath the tyrannical rule of a religion that still beheads nonbelievers, profits from slave auctions or rationalizes raping "infidel" women in lieu of eating a ham sandwich; a despicable act of "questionable" character strictly forbidden by the Quran.

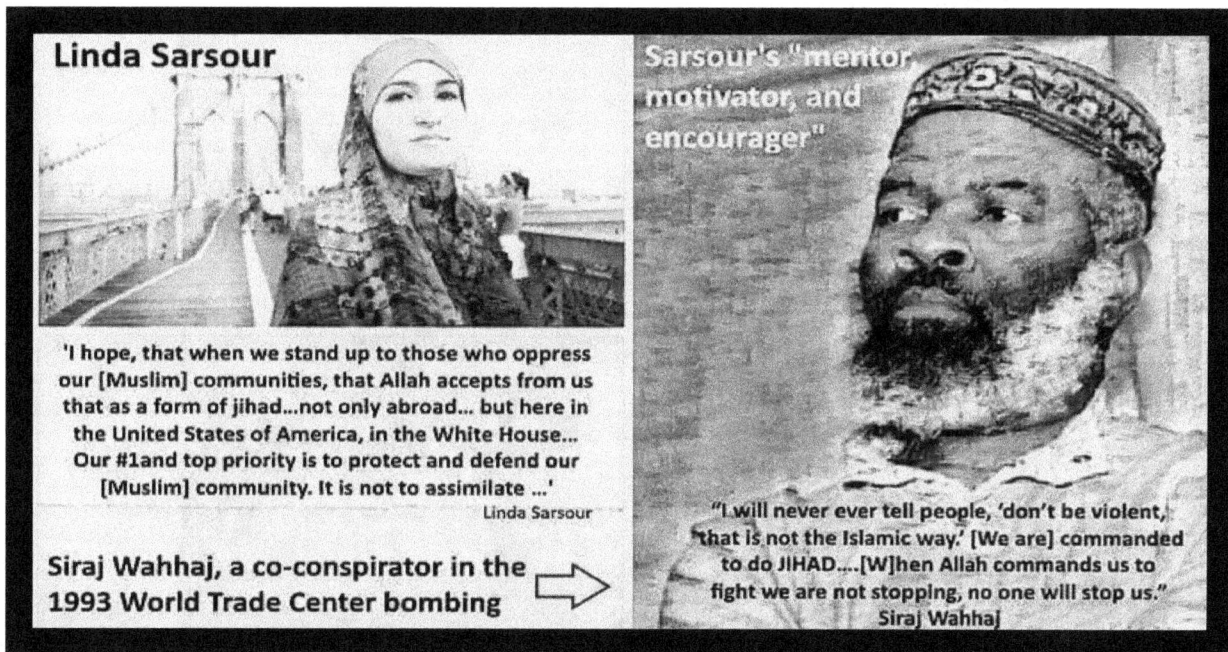

Linda Sarsour

'I hope, that when we stand up to those who oppress our [Muslim] communities, that Allah accepts from us that as a form of jihad...not only abroad... but here in the United States of America, in the White House... Our #1 and top priority is to protect and defend our [Muslim] community. It is not to assimilate ...'

Linda Sarsour

Siraj Wahhaj, a co-conspirator in the 1993 World Trade Center bombing

Sarsour's "mentor, motivator, and encourager"

"I will never ever tell people, 'don't be violent, that is not the Islamic way.' [We are] commanded to do JIHAD....[W]hen Allah commands us to fight we are not stopping, no one will stop us."

Siraj Wahhaj

It's a sad indictment of our God-given capacity for empathy and love when basic human decency, the value of human life, is increasing incumbent upon one's political loyalties some 2000 years after Jesus' crucifixion. Truly, what remotely reputable movement barters the dignity and equality of all women by demanding their submission to a violent theocracy which treats our sisters, wives and mothers as disposable pieces of property unworthy of education, let alone free speech? The moment saving an unborn baby, buying your own birth control or "manspreading" are condemned as more ideological extreme, dare I say sexist, than suicide bombers, genital mutilation or throwing gays off buildings to honor Muhammad – a known murderer, pedophile and thief – no amount of sanity will justify grown women wearing pink hats to collectively acquit real injustice.

The same gender terrorists who somehow believe bitter nude females screaming obscenities in our city streets is the highest form of maternal empowerment, or God forbid child friendly entertainment, are now validating Islam's grotesque treatment of women simply because they both increasingly share a misguided hatred of America. Strong, independent women don't require a fake cross of false victimization or harbor a shameless desire to weaponize their menstrual cycles to prove their self-worth to the detriment of society. Real women who appreciate the evolution of gender equality in a free republic, especially those mentors and mothers not fooled by dysfunctional political stunts, see themselves in all people and plights; including those voices marginalized by the myopic propaganda of religious bigots like yourself. Only in the malformed mind of modern liberalism is Linda Sarsour a feminist hero and Islamic Law most synonymous with America's timeless ideals: life, liberty, due process and the pursuit of happiness for all crying partisans, hijacked genders or unapologetic "infidels".

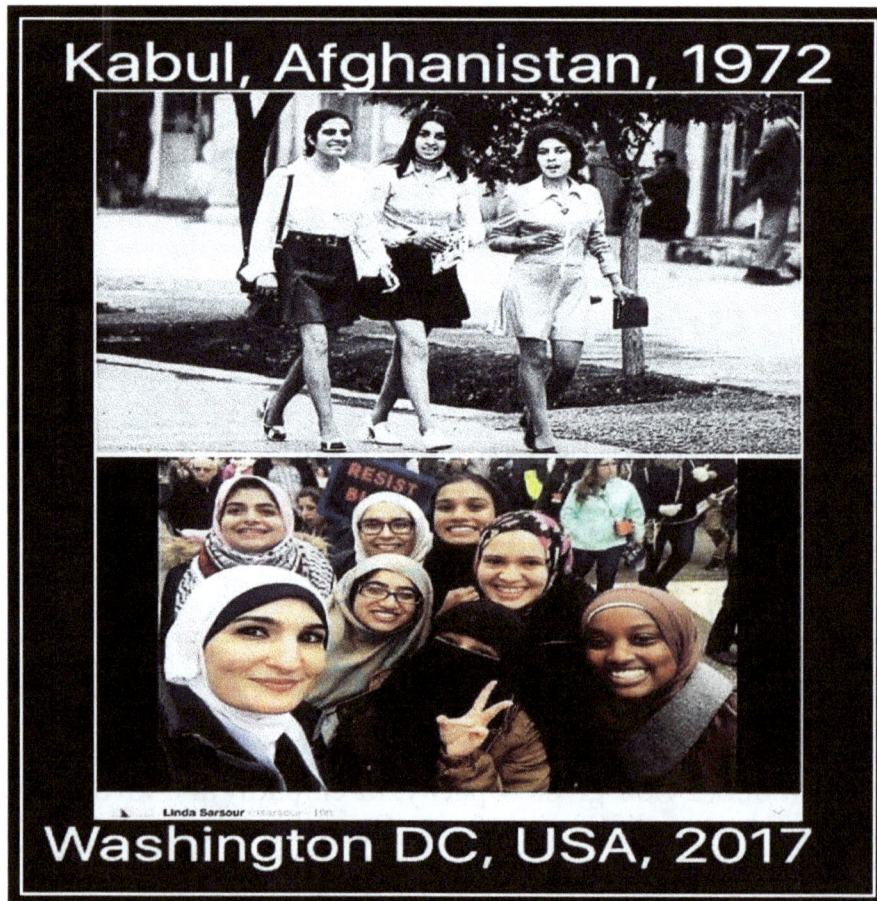

Into Darkness

I freely admit it is difficult to bear witness to such disturbing images, but I believe the human cost is far greater when silent virtue fails to bring light to darkness, justice to depravity. These women represent the forgotten faces of unspeakable cruelty and the marginalized victims of true oppression; those crimes against humanity summarily dismissed by activists who now embrace Islam as a "progressive" partner in the fight for equality. Contrary to the mainstream news, the real War on Women isn't being waged over free birth control, the tyranny of "muscle shirts" or funding abortion clinics that profit from a dissected child. Nor is it a bombastic march of hate protesting a democratic election result by wearing knitted, pink hats and parading in vagina costumes while spewing the most grotesque profanity. Rather, it's a millennium-old campaign that turns females into disposable objects, denies millions due process, glorifies pedophilia and human servitude, and justifies the most unforgivable forms of brutality against females for the most innocuous infractions.

In a free country where feminists are now "triggered" by how a man sits or the symbolic purity of the "Virgin Mary", it's preposterous the so-called voices of liberation would ceremoniously dawn a hijab as a symbol of empowerment, when it literally embodies censorship, mass suffering and unyielding misogyny. Don't be fooled by those apologists dismissing these victims as "extreme" examples of an otherwise peaceful religion. Most "Westernized" Muslims are only constrained by the consequences of our laws, a minority contingent restrained by the potential backlash of armed citizens, as their growing ranks endlessly conspire to impose Sharia Law across America without hesitation or regret. Until the civilized world stands in unison and demands a global reformation of Islam, an immediate cessation of its most discriminatory and barbaric practices, nothing will change. If we are to truly defend the dignity of life and seek equality for all God's children, there can be no refuge or political absolution for those who mock the universal necessity of human rights.

ACCORDING TO LIBERALS

a woman can be a man

BUT

if she gets pregnant the baby is not human until it is born

BUT

the baby is already gay, straight, or bisexual

BUT

the baby does not have a gender until it decides for itself

The LGBT ASSIMILATION AGENDA

Penelope's Closet

The fatal flaw of modern feminism and LGBT activism doesn't reside within the pursuit of equality, impartiality before the eyes of the law and protections within the workplace. It's found in the blatant omission of natural distinctions, evolutionary advantages, defining the two biological sexes and one's sexual orientation. Whether blissful ignorance or calculated denial, this obvious exclusion exponentially compounds their combative drive to gain special accommodations or preferential treatment for their constituents; even at the cost of violating the liberties and livelihoods of innocent bystanders. What started out as a legitimate platform for equal rights and opportunity, has morphed into a scorched-Earth campaign to single-out Christian businesses, eliminate gender-exclusive organizations founded upon harmless camaraderie, demonize masculinity, corrupt our children's self-image, and criminalize traditional values in lieu of appreciating the lifestyles, opinions and accomplishments of both communities. If your gender or sexuality require fashioning a flag of self-adulation, you've probably missed the last departing boat to inner peace. Your sexuality is not a career, your gender should never define your life, and character doesn't seek undue attention in a shallow sea of foaming animosity.

LGBT activists routinely claim conservatives incorrectly comprehend the difference between gender and natural-born sex. Even if this assertion was true, their ultimate goal is for one's declared gender identity to procure the same recognition, societal privileges, as one's biological sex. Therefore, the conundrum of transgenderism is a social riddle wrapped inside a political blueprint of duplicitous intent. Or in laymen's terms...same, twisted difference! Selling such a self-evident lie that rejects both nature and common sense naturally requires soliciting sympathy behind the painted facade of ubiquitous hate and discrimination. Yes, love is most certainly love, but unlike handcrafted pronouns genetics is not a cultural fad. And because their clamoring ranks simply refuse to accept scientific reality, they predictably invoke the .0006% "mutation clause"; i.e., I'm a beautifully-unique intersexual anomaly, a hermaphrodite with undefinable genitalia or undeclared luggage, who refuses to be imprisoned by the puritanical stereotypes of gender-CIS fascists. Thank goodness only 40 out of 326,575,934 Americans die annually from "sexist" lightning strikes; of which roughly 80% are males.

Biology, a living being's chromosomal sequence and physical manifestation, is not merely a matter of changing shoes to match your self-fulfilling behavior's newest gender-fluid impulse. It is discernible, irrefutable and nonpolitical. Our attitudes, personal insecurities, and ingrained misconceptions, on the other hand, are a matter of conditioning and conscious choice. If a man claims to be Napoleon or a butterfly, he's typically declared mentally ill and potentially placed in a psychiatric unit. But if that same male contends to be a female, his "rights" and newfound identity are vigorously defended. Sensitivities be damned, men and women are distinct, binary creations: not mythical unicorns conjured by androgynous thespians, moonlighting transvestites or sunburned, Flat Earth lesbians. If one's preferred self-identity requires defying grounded societal norms, proven scientific method, you're probably in the wrong bathroom. Borrowing your sister's Luis Vuitton handbag may not be a crime, but demanding the Free World calls your penis 'Penelope' in the little girl's locker room sure sounds like one.

The Transgendered Rules of Privacy

It's a pretty damning indictment of our country when asking someone to use the restroom of their natural born gender, regardless of their sexual orientation or personal attire, is considered unreasonable or a hate crime. Refusing to allow men in a female bathroom or locker room has nothing to do with hate, homophobia or discrimination. Such prudence does, however, have everything to do with protecting the privacy and lives of our daughters, wives, sisters and mothers from predators. Until these cross-dressing individuals have the anatomical 'kibbles and bits' to match their desired sex, they are by no means justified using the facilities of their choice simply because they put on a dress or buy a wig. Just because you believe yourself to be a woman, or a man, doesn't make it so; nor does it grant you unfettered access past gender-specific, societal protections. If that's the case, I'm the President and I'm moving into the White House to play 'Call of Duty'! One's sex is not a social construct, there are over 6,500 congenital differences between a man and a woman, and no amount of "identity" conditioning or wishful thinking can alter your genetic code. The war on reality is real. Really!

Unless you somehow believe "paranoia" is the physical perpetrator of pedophilia, theft, voyeurism, murder or rape, do everyday Americans really need to justify not giving shameless opportunists – those non-transgender men who will eagerly exploit such irrational laws – greater access to the vulnerable, defenseless, and most importantly, our loved ones? I think not. And for the record, it's not that I don't have equal regard for the welfare of young boys, but criminals and sexual predators are predominantly male and already have access to the same restrooms. Yes, it doesn't matter whether or not these crimes can occur anywhere and that some gender-bending men have already illegally infiltrated these areas for years. Why? Since when did two 'wrongs' make a 'right' and when did "real" women no longer have rights? When your ad hoc fallacy kidnaps logic and demands a reward! Privacy matters.

Celebrities and politicians can boycott common sense all they want because they're guaranteed to boycott your loved one's funeral or trip to the emergency room. This entire 'transgender' rights debate is a complete fabrication because all men and women, regardless of their sexual orientation, already have access to public facilities. In other words, it is nothing more than an orchestrated pit stop on the progressive road trip to erecting a genderless, borderless, global society. If transgender activists truly believe they are victims and entitled to special privileges for altering reality and ignoring their evolutionary birth, then I suggest soliciting donations to build unisex LGBT bathrooms so they can prey upon each other's complete lack of discretion, boundaries and respect for their fellow 'man'. The time has come to stop indulging the mindless fantasies of manipulative cultural terrorists, allowing complete strangers to question and redefine out children's gender and sexuality, and to fight for our survival as an intelligent, decent and pragmatic society. When the perverse psychosis of less than .01% of the population supersedes the sanity and safety of the other 99%, then America has successfully achieved the self-destructive state known as moral apathy.

Is it a Boy or a Girl?

We'll Have to Wait for "it" to Decide!

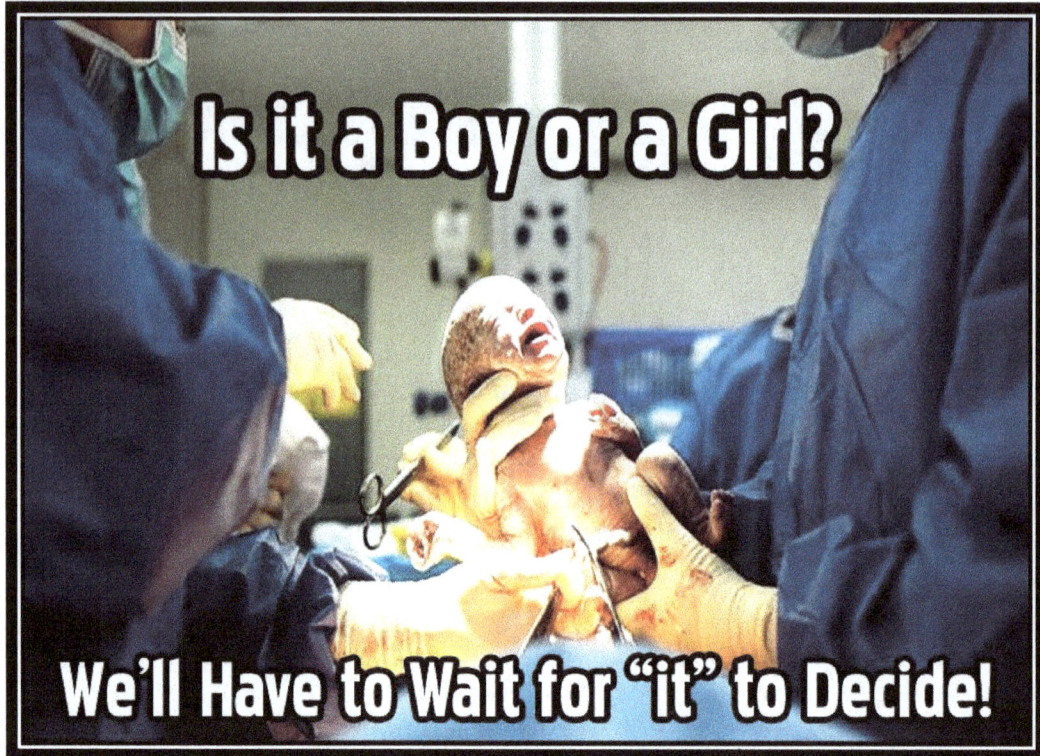

1. In a sexual species, there are two sexes, MALE and FEMALE.
2. 99.93% of humans have XX or XY sex chromosomes (rest is mutation).

3. Being one sex but thinking you're the other is a psychological disorder.
4. Mandating a widespread enabling of a psychological disorder is sociopathy.

Predators, Prey and the Age of Consent

Questioning or attempting to alter your child's gender because you find it politically advantageous or socially admirable is nothing short of child abuse. Such contemptible behavior is a clear example of psychological conditioning disguised as compassionate, progressive parenting. Whether a child is ultimately straight or gay is of little personal interest as long as it happens on their own accord. Fifty years ago, let alone in the 1980's or 90's, children rarely displayed gender confusion because they were not bombarded with imagery and activism that both condoned and encouraged transgenderism. Feminism or masculinity, no matter how prevalent or uncommon, were present in both sexes and sexual orientations. These imperfect realities did not require public interventions, physical makeovers or notice of gender justification in grade school.

WHEN YOU THINK INJECTING CATTLE WITH HORMONES IS EVIL

THE ACTIVIST MOMMY

BUT INJECTING KIDS WITH HORMONES TO CHANGE THEIR GENDER IS JUST FINE

For the record I do not deny a very minute percentage of the adult population consciously seeks to change their natural born gender. However, their desire is more of a psychosomatic manifestation, an internalized response based upon how they are perceived, revered or rejected, by their peers. And yes, because no one is born instinctively hating or questioning their sex, some possess an insatiable need for attention. Either way, it does not change the fact there are only two genetically encoded genders and I don't need to watch a man who identifies as a woman attempt to breastfeed his lover's adopted son to comprehend the disturbing consequences of indulging such destructive fantasies. If "gender" is nothing more than a fluid state of mind, nature's neutral role-playing game, reality must be an erasable blackboard of pointless regret. Unless our androgynous spirit animals are romping free from the confines of guilt and bathroom privacy, common sense shouldn't require a paper cut on your God-given genitalia to realize the "sex" listed on your birth certificate isn't an undeclared prostitute paid with monopoly money and a complimentary pair of sexist pink or blue booties. Predators love to stalk or "dress" their prey and impressionable children should never be the nameless guinea pigs of culture warriors' reckless "identity manipulation" campaign designed solely to validate their chosen lifestyle.

While I proudly treat all people with equal respect regardless of their race, gender or sexuality, there is no evolutionary precedent for homosexuality or biological need for cross-dressing and gender dysphoria. They are acquired behaviors and social constructs of human interaction, whether we embrace their existence or not. Encouraging childhood dysfunction to make homosexuality, gender reassignment, appear more appealing – dare I say commendable and courageous – speaks to our downfall as an "evolved" society. Nobody deserves a televised award or special recognition of any kind for wearing their momma's clothes...for being gay or straight. Likewise, no child should ever be the subject of the soulless left's social engineering experiments simply to fulfill a counter-intuitive agenda that spitefully undermines our societal values, the intrinsic benefits of a strong family dynamic, and shows no regard for the long-term mental health of susceptible adolescents. Children don't need to be "sexualized" and forced to carry the psychological baggage of conspiring con-artists. Politics be damned, kids just need to be kids...period! Our sons and daughters already have enough obstacles to overcome growing up in a hopelessly twisted and morally depraved world.

Minor Attracted Persons (MAPS)

is the new social euphemism & political rebranding for

PEDOPHILIA

Although most LGBT members claim to reject this movement,

many "Pride Parades" feature & applaud cross-dressing young

boys surrounded by half-naked, gay men simulating sex acts.

Ze, Zir and the Power of Magic Shoes

Sorry to disappoint the LGBT LARPing community but I will never be coerced or threatened into using gender neutral pronouns and titles. The day I willingly agree to use "ze" or "zir" in the name of pseudo-sensory "progress" is the moment Xenu the Evil Intergalactic Ruler of Scientology lore descends with a list of his dietary demands in Pig Latin. Regardless of what politically correct haze activists are now conspiring within – confusing children by mocking the common-sense tenets of biological evolution – nature doesn't need redefined so 99% of the populace caters to the hyper-sensitive, role playing delusions of cultural contrarians.

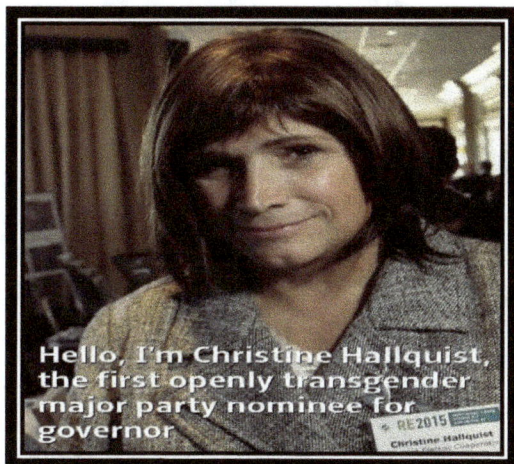

Hello, I'm Christine Hallquist, the first openly transgender major party nominee for governor

I'm a respectful individual, I treat all people with universal regard, and I will rightfully continue to address the two scientifically recognized sexes by he and she, her and him, boy or girl, man or woman. Other than that, I don't care what people identify as or what they do in their private time – whether they're gay, straight or fornicating with Fortnite every night – for liberty is the crux of free will. However, if public schools and our elected government want to openly prosecute people for calling the sky blue or a bearded diva a man, then the inmates are officially running the asylum and common sense is receiving shock treatments for denying the existence of asexual unicorns that poop rainbows of medicinal marijuana. In other words, only in the padded rooms of progressive academia, where 'Gender Studies' professors now earn more than mathematicians, would the "wishful thinking" of gender contortionists become the educational edict of an unbreakable social contract where scientific reality is sexist and/or distinctly homophobic. Yes, beware the ides of cross-dressing chromosomes: puff, pass, 23 pairs of fabulously androgynous shoes.

Just because someone refuses to date you or call you "Joyce" because you have an extra appendage doesn't make that person hateful or remotely socially inappropriate. It makes them a realist, and quite likely, a heterosexual. Despite our personal differences or political leanings, we as a nation simply have so many more pressing issues to address rather than endlessly indulging the destructive whims of those who want special accommodations – pandering to a media celebrated lifestyle choice and its nonsensical demands – while simultaneously refusing to recognize our individual freedoms as a whole; such as the right to call a female a girl or a male a boy. Clearly, truth is now genetic hyperbole in the land of make-believe. To boldly quote the keen observations of Kindergarten Cop, "boys have a penis, girls have a vagina". Now only if we could get grown adults to understand such a non-political concept and to stop asking innocent, impressionable children if they would like to change their God-given gender by wearing a dress or using the wrong bathroom. Our sons and daughters don't need to be "sexualized" and given identity reconditioning as part of a veiled attempt to normalize and promote a deviant agenda; they need to be educated and allowed to be kids: period!

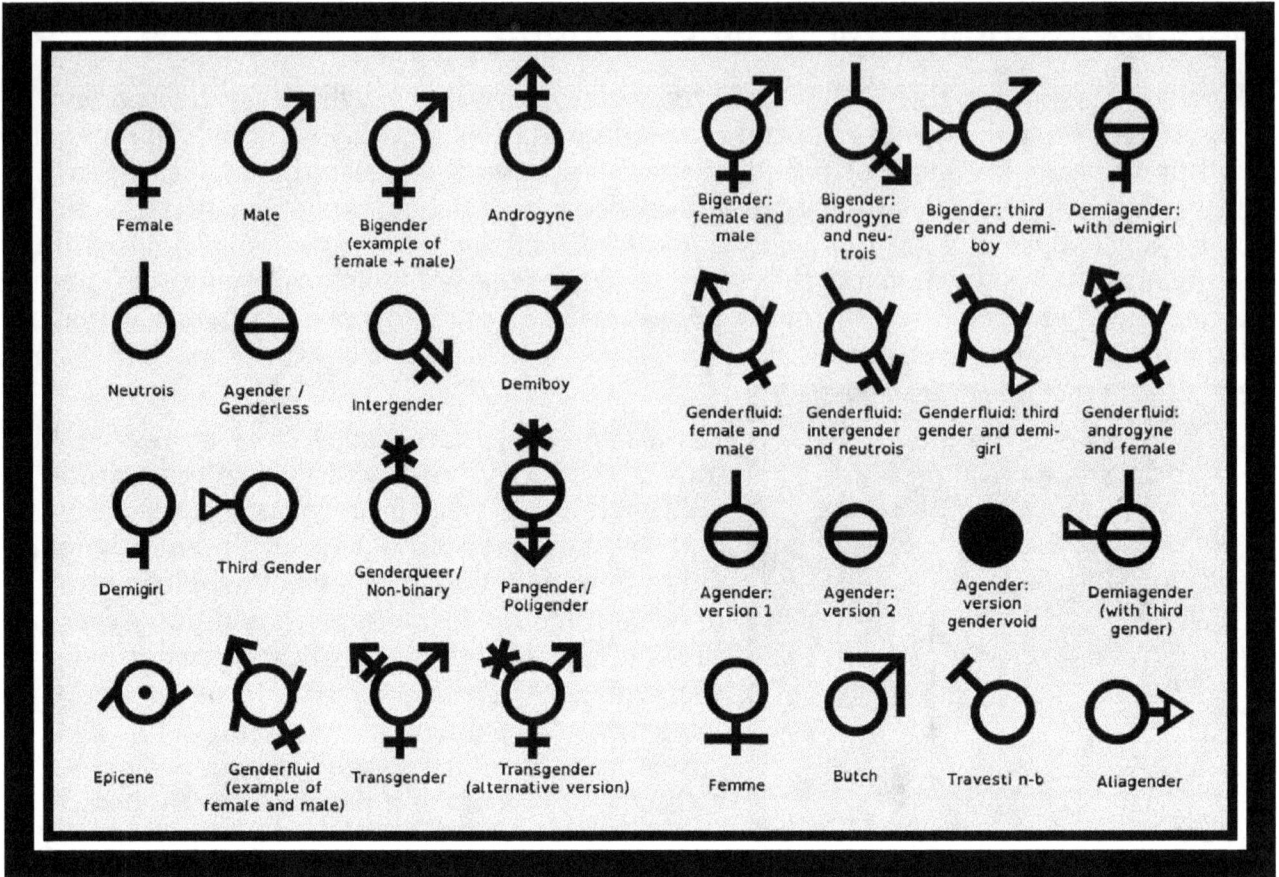

The chart displays gender symbols with labels: Female, Male, Bigender (example of female + male), Androgyne, Bigender: female and male, Bigender: androgyne and neutrois, Bigender: third gender and demi-boy, Demiagender: with demigirl, Neutrois, Agender / Genderless, Intergender, Demiboy, Genderfluid: female and male, Genderfluid: intergender and neutrois, Genderfluid: third gender and demi-girl, Genderfluid: androgyne and female, Demigirl, Third Gender, Genderqueer/Non-binary, Pangender/Poligender, Agender: version 1, Agender: version 2, Agender: version gendervoid, Demiagender (with third gender), Epicene, Genderfluid (example of female and male), Transgender, Transgender (alternative version), Femme, Butch, Travesti n-b, Aliagender

Chromosomes and Common Sense

The United States Military is not about indulgence, political agendas or pointless self-expression; it's overriding mission is to mold a group of men (or women) into an effective fighting force designed to achieve a strategical objective with a minimal loss of life. These protocols are not an open invitation to debate, nor a stage for interpretation, for they are intended to instill respect, minimize distractions and foster an undying sense of unity. From the rigid specifications of uniforms to the perilous details of combat training, the single greatest modality of interest to our Armed Forces is that of conformity. Furthermore, any perceived physical weakness or sensory impairment, such as obesity or a lack of visual/auditory acuity, are routine grounds for denying applicants admission. While their unflattering methods and stringent regulations may seem harsh or even unnecessary, they are deeply rooted in scientific observation – psychological precursors and suppressed deviant behaviors – forged by centuries of military training and global conflict. Maintaining a modern army is far more of an applied science focused on cultivating a productive environment...definable roles, unwavering discipline, steadfast resolve and group morale...in lieu of entertaining a social experiment designed to stretch the whimsical boundaries of gender identification.

What do my boring textbook affirmations have to do with Trump's "discriminatory" transgender ban? Everything. Supporting one's right to be gay, a private matter and sexual orientation, is by no means the equivalent of indulging a recruit's fantasy to live as the opposite sex; a psychological disorder known as gender dysphoria and recognized by both academia and the medical community. While I highly commend anyone's willingness to serve their country, a truly honorable endeavor, that selfless commitment must respect the privacy/safety of other soldiers and abide by universal gender norms. Wearing a dress no-more grants one the unabridged right to shower and bunk with actual women, than it affords a man a special accommodation to wear female attire or present himself as a woman among a male company of servicemen. It's not a matter of tolerance; it's a matter of functionality.

If enlisting is truly paramount to your beliefs, distinguishing yourself according to your actions instead of merely collecting a check and free government healthcare for a complimentary sex change, who in their right mind would confuse their wardrobe with their career? Considering recruits must bunk with the same sex and wear the same standard issued clothes regardless, what is the purpose of declaring your imaginary gender except to bring undue attention to yourself or seek special treatment? On the binary battlefield of life or death, whether pulling a trigger or residing in its cross-hairs of denial, any issue that distracts from your mission and threatens your camaraderie is but another senseless casualty of the progressive culture war on common sense. "Transgenderism", which provides the perfect vessel for political terrorists to further erode self-evident truths and societal values, is far more of an adopted coping mechanism to physically accommodate one's sexual orientation than a gross violation of civil rights; i.e., a gay man attempting to become a woman or a masculine lesbian identifying as a man to consciously compliment her more feminine or submissive girlfriend.

Before the Obama administration rejoiced in mocking our military and societal values, the U.S. Armed Services, like a majority of reasonable Americans, only recognized two God-given genders; that genetic dichotomy defining every human being's anatomical birth. (And please spare me those rare genetic mutations and birth defects contrarians invoke as irrefutable proof of gender fluidity) These military institutions do not believe bathrooms or gender exclusive units are a matter of personal preference and wishful thinking. Being denied a locker room of your choice or entrance into a military branch hardly constitutes discrimination simply because you refuse to accept reality by acknowledging the tangible genitalia of your natural born sex. That is your failing alone. Likewise, any attempt to link the historical fight for racial equality or women's rights with this campaign to secure transgender privilege is a callous and ignorant disregard for the millions who suffered under a sordid legacy of oppression, human servitude and bigotry. Could a runaway slave magically change the color of his skin to evade his captors any more than a mother could alter her anatomy to cast a vote in 1919, avoid sex trafficking in Asia or become a Catholic priest? Nor should they have too. There's a stark contrast between the systemic persecution of one's biological heritage, an involuntary target of circumstance, and decrying the uncooperative consequences of one's actions or blatant lack of accountability.

While I do not deny the transgender community endures ridicule and hate, often stemming from their insistence to demand acceptance, supporting one's conscious decision to identify as "transgender" does not transform his or her true identity. Asking society to forgo verifiable truths, those natural constructs of gender delineation used to identify our strengths and weaknesses or ensure your safety, is as absurd as calling your poodle a cold-blooded invertebrate because it likes to drink from the toilet. Honestly, how long will it be before uncooperative bystanders are reprimanded, expelled, fired or sued for not entertaining the gender delusions or advances of their peers? Enjoying the individual freedom to pose as the opposite sex, for better or worse, does not change your gender, suddenly invalidate the legitimacy of public standards or displace your neighbor's right to reject your lifestyle without reason or explanation.

Conspiring to make the world "gender neutral" will not end discrimination, save more lives or heal the planet by placing our cognitive abilities in a plastic bubble of "non-offensive" ambiguity. And it definitely won't improve the mental health and emotional stability of our youth – those impressionable minds now being conditioned by schools and pop culture to question or reject their natural gender while attempting to overcome the everyday challenges of adolescence. Teaching our sons and daughters to appreciate their innate differences and symbiotic connection is not regressive; it's indigenous to our survival and evolutionary proliferation as a sentient species. Nevertheless, a biological woman or man can still play sports, fire a gun, open a boutique and love the gender of his or her choosing without regret. However, breaking barriers solely for the spiteful sake of eradicating biological order or any remaining sense of basic decency is about as logical as a man who identifies as a pregnant mother attempting to publicly breastfeed his own baby to protest gender bias; excluding those cute little pink or blue booties of course. The more the rational world accommodates this destructive nonsense, the more future generations

Johns Hopkins Chief Psychiatrist: Transgender is a 'Mental Disorder'

will be unable to distinguish the most elementary truths or God forbid complete the simplest tasks without having to first visit the Island of Misfit Toys in hopes of saving the malformed appendages of gender fascist capitalists.

The difference between a privilege and a right is that neither you nor I can dictate the terms of our desired acceptance. The same LGBT activists demanding political concessions to appease a blissful state of mind, are also oblivious to the fact "old, sexist" generals originally spurned women in combat roles because studies confirmed their male counterparts became psychologically distraught by the mere site of their deaths and needlessly lingered over their dismembered bodies. Should I even mention the exponentially higher risk of rape at the hands of enemy combatants, including the increased incidents of abuse, fights or operational dysfunction among transgender integrated troops? Contrary to the victimization propaganda of science fiction fans, not every pragmatic decision requires a politically correct pronoun to appease any one of the approximately 58 genders now claiming dominion over the human anatomy and the social gentrification of modern warfare. It merely requires a sensible leader willing to understand the mental manifestation of transgenderism, an aesthetic desire for sexual transfiguration, does not supersede biology or negate the necessity of maintaining gender norms in the private barracks and front lines of national security.

Gender By Graphic Rhythm
Yes, There are More than Two Genders Shirt

THERE ARE
MORE THAN
TWO GENDERS

Select Fit Type

Men

Women

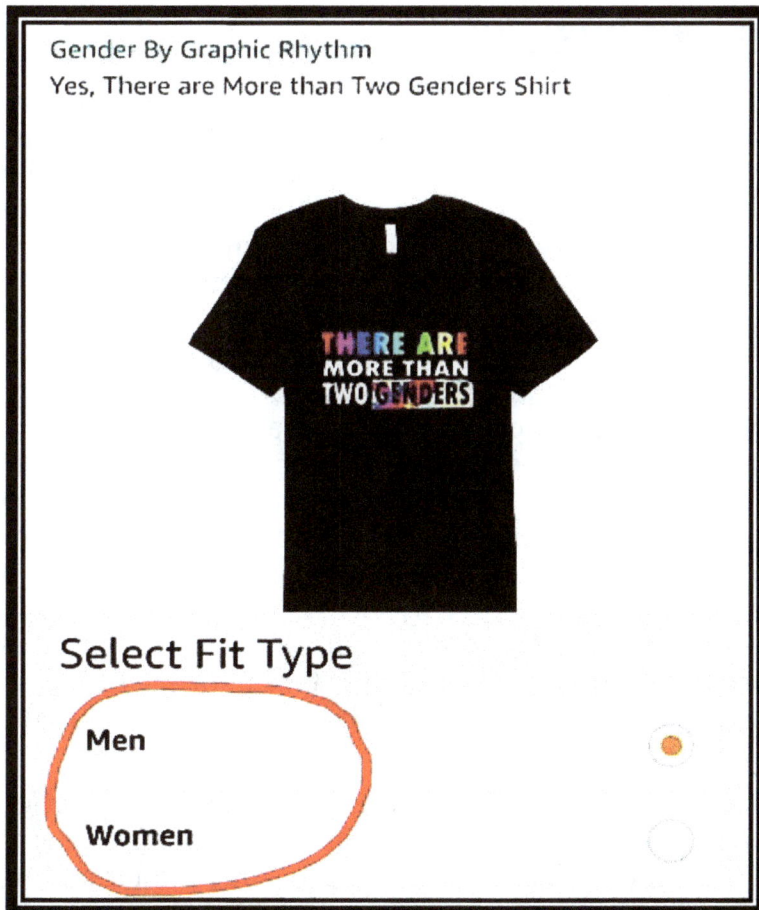

When your counterfeit brand of political activism doesn't quite mesh with reality. And to think some millennial parents are waiting for their newborns - "theybies" - to choose their own gender. Children Advisory: Mental illness is not only hereditary, it is also a learned behavior. Get your parents help before their unicorn spirit animal finds a "genderless" electrical outlet to challenge the outdated laws of physics!

Game, Set, Madness

Martina Navratilova, a respected lesbian activist for over 30 years, was recently kicked off the advisory board of a prominent LGBT organization. Her crime? She used common sense to vocally oppose granting biological men, posing as transgender women, permission to compete against actual females in amateur and professional sports. This pandemic of progressive insanity is now punishing and censoring anyone who refuses to indulge the proven mental illness of gender dysphoria. Sorry but allowing genetic males who possess a distinct physical advantage to compete against female athletes – many who have devoted countless years if not their entire lives to their sport or skill of choice – is nothing short of sexist, naively dangerous and a culturally-regressive political charade which devalues the unique contributions and talents of all women who are being denied a level playing field. Welcome to the real war on women where having ovaries and a vagina no longer satisfy the legal requirements and afforded protections of being a biological female but wearing lipstick and a Halloween wig somehow demands immediate inclusion and special privileges to prey upon them.

Religious Freedom & The Rainbow Vendetta

Rabid liberals continue to protest and boycott states passing Religious Freedom laws claiming these statutes unfairly discriminate against gays – not that LGBT activists are purposely trying to entrap Christian businesses into being sued and losing their livelihoods – only to have no recollection of the "bigot" who signed the national Religious Freedom Restoration Act into law in 1993: one very proud Bill Clinton! And guess who voted for it as an Illinois state senator? That's right...Barack Obama! Nineteen states have passed similar laws with the help of or at the behest of Democrats. This is how disconnected today's left has become in their quest to deify homosexuality and demonize anyone who objects to the gay agenda. They're so obsessed with fabricating impropriety, they're completely ignorant of the fact such legislation, an extension and reaffirmation of the First Amendment, allows Jews to wear Yarmulkes at their jobs or Muslim students to honor their religious holidays in our public schools. Funny how the "principled" warriors of social justice would never ask or sue an Islamic business for refusing to cater to a gay wedding. They have inalienable rights and that would be an injustice to Allah! Is it therefore of any surprise many of these same progressive hypocrites support Sharia Law which openly discriminates against women and gays – advocating torture, mutilation or death for merely existing – but accuse Christians and Jews of hate for honoring their faith and exercising their Constitutional rights? Sadly, no. Liberals are that clueless.

For the record, these religious liberty laws do not single out gays nor do they mention them. These protections merely prevent people, organizations and businesses from being punished, i.e. for serving bacon in their own establishment, because some intolerant tool insists on forcing their views down freedom's throat rather than respecting the beliefs of others. Yes, going to another restaurant that meets your standards would just be too difficult! An adopted boy has no recourse against his two moms or dads for mental anguish or forced emasculation, but it's OK to sue McDonald's because they serve meat on Sabbath or an employee says God Bless after you sneeze? There is a stark contrast between discrimination and engineered injustice. Then again, our delusional President compared the LGBT movement – those seeking a gay wedding cake in a Christian bakery, a bondage float in a Christmas parade or a same-sex marriage certificate – to the millions who toiled, suffered and died under the auspices of slavery. Callous and unforgivable.

Propaganda aside, homosexuals are not slaves and Jesus didn't stutter or wash the feet of gay prostitutes. He was guided by love but was not without principles. Americans of all sexual orientations absolutely have the right to live the life of their choosing free from violence or unfair treatment: workplace or otherwise. That's tolerance and basic decency. However, no one is obligated to embrace your sexuality or to make you feel warm and fuzzy about your choices! Believe it or not, a majority of minorities in America are morally opposed to homosexuality and gay marriage, a religious institution defined by Judeo-Christian values and common sense in Western Civilization. (That's also why civil unions, a non-religious recognition, formally exist) Are they bigoted extremists too because culture terrorists like yourself want to reinvent the wheel and fit a square peg in a round hole to prove there are no universal norms or ethical boundaries in a "progressive" society? Or perhaps they're just devout believers practicing their faith and protecting the sanctity of family and age-old societal mores; just like your beloved, benevolent Muslim Brotherhood but without the swords, hatred, blood and black flag of Islamic fascism. True tolerance requires reciprocity, Thank God, but that does not excuse us from differentiating between what is right and what is wrong, decadence and temperance.

A Rainbow of Truth

Just because the Son of God preached love and forgiveness, not to supplant the divine hand of judgement, did not mean to ignore or condone the blatant blasphemy committed by those who repeatedly and knowingly defied God's law. If the Bible itself, strongly and unequivocally, condemns homosexuality in a number of passages, how could it possibly be construed as Jesus supporting same-sex matrimony? Such an ignorant assertion is yet another progressive fairy tale and an outright shameless distortion. While my love of individual liberty inclines me to support all lifestyles, marriage, by definition, is a religious institution in Western Civilization – not ancient Mesopotamia, Etruscan folk art or the Inca Empire, mind you – and its Judeo-Christian doctrine does not somehow morph to magically appease your political beliefs or culturally relevant whims. That, my confused friends, is exactly why we have Civil Unions. Now does that mean gays do not have the right to live the lifestyle of their choosing? Of course not, for that is the very basis of liberty and tolerance, which by the way, is a two-way street. No one deserves to be the undue object of hate or violence and I truly abide by the heavenly command to 'love thy neighbor'. It simply means you cannot alter reality and erase centuries of biblical precedence, American history, to realize only one rainbow speaks for God.

> ## Jesus said,
>
> "...from the beginning of creation God made them male and female. For this cause, a man shall leave his father and mother and shall cleave to his **wife** and the two shall become one flesh. What God has joined together, let not man put assunder." (Mark 10:6-9)

GLOBAL WARMING

NATURE vs. NEUROSIS

God Save the Green!

The EPA's "progressive" decision to label carbon dioxide as a "pollutant", the fundamental basis of all life on Earth, is little more than bad science fiction. While it is possible to have excessive amounts of CO_2 in theory, carbon is an essential building block of life; one in which the energy-producing reactions of photosynthesis, producing breathable oxygen for countless lifeforms, would be nonexistent. The real focus of climate alarmism, however, is the commonly abused misnomer of "carbon emissions" or "carbon footprint"; that political and celebrity-travel manifestation which is neither colorless or odorless, unlike Carbon Dioxide itself. The 100 trillion-dollar "green shoe" drive by globalists to eliminate all carbon emissions from fossil fuel usage by 2100 and lower the Earth's aggregate temperature by .03 degrees, is far more a political ploy for exacting further government control - universal taxation, regulation, and Western wealth redistribution - than based on real scientific necessity. Believe it or not, fossil fuels and the environmental emissions that ensue from their consumption are entirely organic. These so-called "feared" gases once originated as carbon in the atmosphere before being consumed by plants and plankton, only to eventually be reabsorbed into the Earth until the viable energy sources of oil, natural gas and coal were naturally formed with the archaic assistance of time, heat and pressure. Although these resources are depletable and do pose dangers during extraction and/or transportation, they are by no means "death sentences" in the scope of everyday life. Eliminating our nation's dependence on foreign oil, economic roulette, is an entirely different matter.

The unreported reality of "Global Warming" is Carbon Dioxide levels were estimated to be as much as 10 times greater when the first signs of multi-cellular life appeared, whereas the optimum level for plant growth is still considered 5 times greater than our atmosphere's current composition. With recent satellite imagery denoting a "Greening of the Earth", increased crop production and forestation will be vital to all countries, consumers, and pseudo-scientists alike as the world population is expected to approach 10 billion by 2050. If "clean", renewable energy is indeed the future for all mankind, fossil fuels are the contemporary bridge between nature's bounty and the sound application of reputable science.

Playing with A Hot Stove

The fact America recently eclipsed a 136-year-old heat record in 2016 – a benchmark set in 1880 before modern industrialization and the dawn of automobiles when America harbored a mere 15% of its current population – is a stark reminder of just how insignificant humanity is in relation to the unrivaled power of the Sun. It therefore is also of little surprise the smog capital of Los Angeles County just recorded the coldest February in over 60 years. Although I always advocate being cognizant of our environment, the inevitable and natural climatic variations that ensue, I find solace in a far more organic and self-evident explanation. If the degree of the Earth's tilt changes but a fraction in correlation to our favorite Yellow Dwarf, the results can be devastating...from droughts and widespread desolation to glacial periods that last tens of thousands of years. Not surprisingly, there is a strong link between solar activity, the length and ferocity of solar cycles, and Earth's annual temperatures. In other words, when perspective requires oven mitts, blame the nuclear fusion reactor in the sky that produces 500 times more Hiroshima bombs per second than the reported energy accrued from "climate change" during a 15-year period.

Any statistical model, regardless of whether you're tracking a baseball player's batting average or the daily heat index, is going to experience "natural" fluctuations or even statistical aberrations. Those activists who believe climatic changes are neither natural or cyclical are both naive and predatory. The truth is even the Earth's radioactive core and its incessant decay, accounting for roughly 50% of the heat omitted from the planet, plays a significant role in surface temperatures and a magnetic field that extends into outer space for the overriding purpose of deflecting damaging solar winds. Furthermore, it is only a matter of time or roughly every 250,000 years before another polar shift occurs. No, you won't die in a fiery ball of Hollywood pyrotechnics, but the effects are tangible as earthquakes in Oklahoma or tsunamis in the Pacific. Even amidst the aftermath of a blind hubris that threatened our rain forests and poisons our waterways, man is but a fly in the perilous vacuum of space compared to the unparalleled power of Mother Nature's wrath.

Whereas global warming and cooling cycles are distinctly inevitable, I will not contest or deride the importance of the Ozone layer. Despite the ongoing debate concerning its exact state of degradation and the magnitude of distress levied by such changes, it is invaluable in terms of absorbing the Sun's ultraviolet rays. Any depletion in the Ozone caused by free radicals such as Nitric Oxide and Hydroxyl, fluorocarbons in the form of banned aerosol sprays or industrialized emissions containing Methyl Chloroform, can cause skin cancer, cataracts, genetic mutations, damage to entire ecosystems, and an increase in greenhouse gasses which in turn precipitates higher levels of air pollution. While I by no means support an alarmist mentality regarding climatic fluctuations – those environ-socialists spreading apocalyptic doom to demand more control over our everyday lives or as a means to legislate higher taxes – I believe all nations and persuasions should work tirelessly to protect our planet through responsible regulation, collaborative research, general education, and greater public awareness. By finding promising new alternatives to age-old misconceptions or destructive practices, mankind can achieve equally meaningful reform on both an individual basis as well as an international platform.

As long as globalists continue rewarding destitute, unscrupulous nations that pollute our atmosphere with reckless abandon, granting free trade agreements and conceding basic regulatory standards, any attempt to pigeonhole America as the unrivaled source of the problem is clearly a veiled attempt to diminish her influence and/or redistribute our wealth in the name of "science"; that "independent" institution which supposedly should never be challenged by conservatives but is frequently perverted by pseudo-scientific progressives. Never mind the "inconvenient truth" a single year of Volcanic degassing can produce between 100 and 600 million tons of CO_2 and negate a century's worth of the Paris Agreement's proposed guidelines to lower Carbon Dioxide levels – as confirmed by the Italian National Institute of Geophysics and Volcanology – because "doomsday" predictions, like Las Vegas campaign fundraisers, must be maintained for the sake of speaking appearances. Considering New York is not underwater, and the Arctic Ice Shelf is as profound as it was 25 years ago, I don't need to pay Al Gore six-figures to recognize a convenient lie when his "carbon footprint" is one thousand times greater than mine. The same politically-perverted data models used to sell an "incontrovertible observation" can also statistically prove GMO's and fluoride are safe for mass consumption. That is, if you don't live in Europe and boil for political parasites.

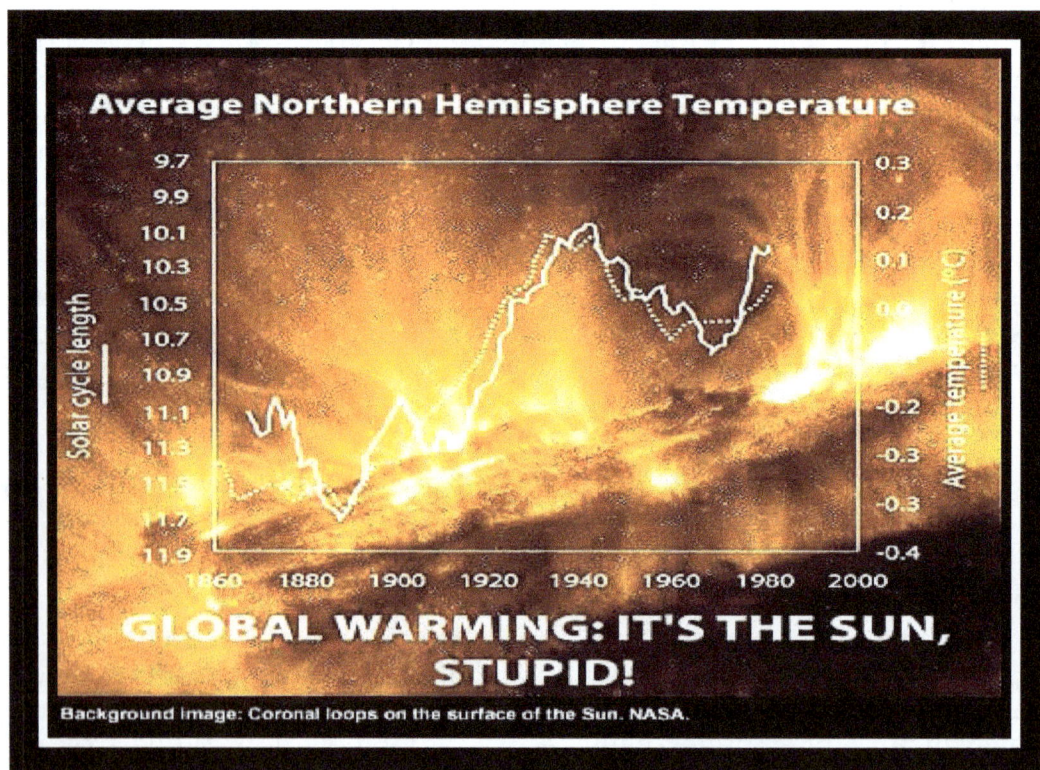

Green with Bureaucratic Insanity

Despite the delusional grandeur of Miss Oco-Loco's grandiose claims, her half-baked "New Green Deal" has nothing to do with protecting the environment, the sound application of science to ensure mankind's symbiotic balance with nature, and everything to do with redistributing wealth to maximize federal authority. By religiously declaring a climate crisis of inescapable doom – distorting carbon-based "pollution", disregarding the unrivaled waste of underdeveloped regimes and decrying any human consumption of the Earth's natural resources – progressives firmly believe they're fully justified in taxing anything that moves, suffocating successful businesses with endless regulations, and dictating the terms of our disposable lives to erect a more equitable society; if only to punish political opponents in the posthumous name of "social justice". When your "Gucci" revolution costs four times more than the national debt, no plastic straw is green enough to save the sea turtles from choking on the microwavable bowl of your home-cooked chili.

These absurd Orwellian proposals, as illustrated by today's Democratic extremists seeking to quell the tyranny of "cow farts", ban meat consumption, reconstruct every public building, restrict child bearing and eliminate air travel without disturbing those sponsored immigration caravans seeking the Red Carpet treatment of criminal sanctuary cities, are little more than a public ruse to help scheming globalists nationalize industry, liquidate private property and fund their Marxist utopia promising a universal income for all worthy converts: an indentured means to bribe the lazy, indoctrinate the indigent, and blatantly favor any race, gender, economic class or foreign-born demographic at the expense of every "privileged", taxpaying household.

In other words, by demanding mass conformity and bankrolling a $93 trillion-dollar police state overrun with self-indulgence, willful ignorance, and a toxic culture of disrespect, a once vigilant Constitutional Republic and indelible beacon of hope quickly descends into an unsalvageable shipwreck of amoral corruption incapable of recognizing itself, let alone saving her timeless charter. There are no undiscovered treasures residing in the floating strait-jackets of the historically insane, the rotting remains of Cuba, Venezuela or North Korea, merely a forged suicide note left by socialist scavengers elected to rob "racist, greedy" Americans of their liberties, labors and country for the greater good of failed liberal academia.

155

The Seers of Sabotage

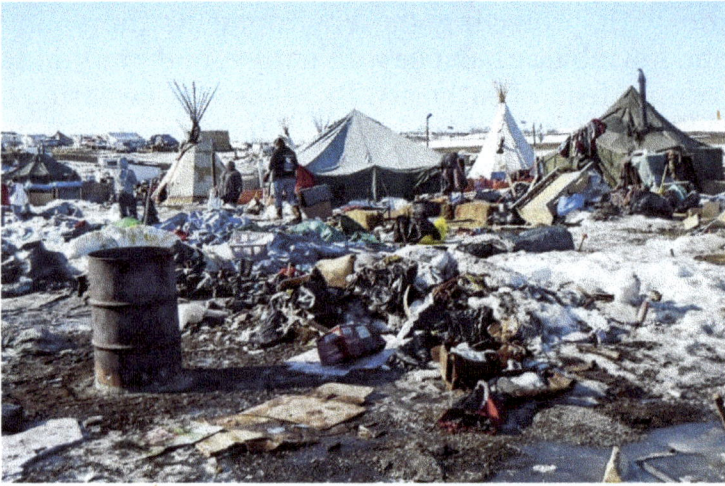

The moment news broke revealing the recently finalized Keystone Pipeline had ruptured, I immediately suspected sabotage from leftist militants; those endlessly plotting malcontents who deemed its creation a disaster waiting to happen. Alas, and right on cue, reports are now surfacing it was a deliberate attack on America's infrastructure and economic sovereignty. Funny how those claiming to care so much about our environment and the delicate balance of our ecosystems – yes, the same hypocrites who shamelessly polluted the North Dakota countryside with garbage and diseased waste while busing in paid protesters – are willing to spill thousands of gallons of crude oil just to preserve their false narrative concerning fossil fuels and multinational commercialism. However, because these vital resources naturally come from the Earth, let us be thankful this act of domestic terrorism didn't occur in our oceans or waterways. It appears state and federal authorities will have to find a more suitable means to better protect the thousands of miles of unguarded pipeline, and in the process, the safety of the American people.

"That pipeline was inspected less than a year ago and we're supposed to believe that more than a dozen bolts gave away to corrosion in that amount of time? The hardware used on those pipelines is galvanized and painted with rust treatment twice a year. This was no accident."
~THE ARMY CORP OF ENGINEERS

The Extremist Protection Agency

Once upon a time the EPA was dedicated to implementing common sense environmental regulations – based on the objective interpretation of actual scientific data – that protected our most precious resources without needlessly suffocating private enterprise. Climatologists, not rogue politicians or rabid activists, realized that the activities and indiscretions of man paled in comparison to that giant yellow ball in the sky composed almost entirely of Hydrogen and Helium – also known as, the Sun. Unfortunately, then came along an underachieving, racist, pot-smoking Marxist who attended Harvard via affirmative action to further his insatiable hatred for America's economic vitality, global supremacy, Judeo-Christian values, and Anglo-Saxon Founding Fathers. Despite his numerous bigoted and anti-American rants, his sheer comfort with distorting the truth and misleading the masses, this self-lauded Community Organizer went on to win the presidency under the glittering generalities of false "hope" and nondescript "change". The rest is infamy.

ZEROHEDGE.COM
U.N. Official Admits Global Warming Agenda Is Really About Destroying Capitalism

Nearly seven years and a million media buried truths later, the festering plume of progressivism has poisoned the competitive heartbeat of America exceptionalism with record debt and welfare recipients, the worst GDP growth and workforce participation since Jimmy Carter, the highest poverty level in half a century, and a 50 billion-dollar monthly trade deficit to reward the unsavory business practices and anti-American banter of third world nations. Barack Obama's two greatest ambitions were to expand the role of government to the point of unilateralism – until liberty begs for permission to breathe – and to foster mass dependency by strangling the proven economic catalyst known as capitalism. Whereas the trillion-dollar socialist leviathan known as Obamacare has already cost America countless jobs and reduced the number of full-time employees to anemic levels, Mr. Hussein's rash demand to abide by the nonsensical terms of the Paris Agreement could cripple an already feeble job market and confiscate hope from an already struggling working class. Essentially, our energy situation could become so catastrophically broken that the government would zealously swoop in to seize it in the name of the "common good" and recalled Chevy Volts. That's right; when all other excuses are exhausted, blame evil capitalists for the regulatory "snake oil" sold by Global Warming Scientologists seeking political salvation from their own radical agenda; Number 21 to be exact.

Not only has Barack Obama almost single-handedly pushed the coal industry to the brink of extinction – an estimated 50,000 job losses during his tenure – and furthered our dependence on foreign energy by vetoing the Keystone Pipeline, it's obvious he'd like nothing more than to personally remove the economy, the Constitution, and the institution of reason from life support. The same Environment Protection Agency that is now deathly concerned the aroma from your backyard barbeque is terrorizing the fragile sensibilities of your neighbors, attempted to cover up its own environmental disaster after releasing three million gallons of toxic pollutants from a Colorado mine into the Animas River, failing to properly warn state officials, and even refusing to pay for any damages caused by their negligence. It is therefore any surprise the Obama administration hid research data debunking the need for the adopted Ozone Rule? Too bad the carbon footprints left by our President's vacationing heart and Mr. Al Gore's traveling Science Fiction Theater haven't been grandfathered into the Guinness Book of taxable liberal lies.

The same soldiers of statism who left our backdoor open and negotiated free trade deals with slave-labor regimes boasting some of the worst environmental track records, want you to renounce your right to bear arms, toss your Bible into the bonfire and trust in the judgment of Big Government. Protecting and preserving our air, water, and natural resources is a non-negotiable maxim for all of humanity; doing it in accordance to the same progressive playbook that seeks our unconditional capitulation and demise is self-assisted suicide. After all, unless you're "Gru" and have the Moon proudly displayed on your magical mantle of repossessed relics, you can no more "control" Mother Nature than you can stop the Sun: the greatest and most unrivaled cyclical source of Climate Change in the entire Solar System.

Doomsdays and Demagogues

Leftist demagogues have been obsessed with politicizing the weather for nearly half-a-century because climate alarmism is but another effective means of spreading fear to galvanize voters, raise taxes and suffocate business with socialist regulations. From the Miniature Ice Age, to Acid Rain, Global Warming and now simply the nonspecific stigma of omnipresent Climate Change - that "confusing" scientific concept of cyclical and naturally fluctuating weather patterns - no amount of historical perspective, empirical data or common sense will assuage their desire to cajole the masses for political gain. If you're looking for the single, greatest culprit responsible for influencing our weather, albeit mild or extreme seasonal variations, you might want to start with that evil genius commonly referred to as the Sun. Like politics, too much exposure can be fatal.

PragerU

FAMOUS CLIMATE PREDICTIONS THAT HAVEN'T COME TRUE.

1970 "Between 1980 and 1989, some 4 billion people, including 65 million Americans, would perish in the 'Great Die-Off.'" -Paul Ehrlich

2006 "Humans may have only 10 years left to save the planet from turning into a total frying pan." -Al Gore

2019 "The world is going to end in 12 years if we don't address climate change." -Alexandria Ocasio-Cortez

THE SWAMP

A "Deep State' Cesspool

> "I know it's hard when you're up to your armpits in alligators to remember you came here to drain the swamp."
>
> -Ronald Reagan

LOU DOBBS TONIGHT 7PM ET FOX BUSINESS

The Death of America

The historical duty of the minority party in any form of representative government is to serve as the voice of opposition: to respectfully question, clarify or confirm the prevailing course of the nation through constructive discourse. Regrettably, I am witnessing no such decorum today. Donald Trump hasn't even been in office for a single month and organized chaos has rippled throughout our communities and pierced the hearts of our senses. And for the love of God, why? Because he refuses to fund sanctuary cities, those entities that harbor illegal aliens who knowingly broke our immigration laws or committed further crimes while on U.S. soil? Are American citizens provided refuge from not paying taxes, robbery or even murder? Or is violent anarchy now virtuous because President Trump, concerned about the rising death toll from terrorism, temporarily restricted immigration from the most notorious regions of radicalized Islam; prudent actions taken by both Jimmy Carter and Barack Obama during times of tense cultural hostilities?

What we are witnessing is not a revolution of consequence, or even oppression, but a regressive plot to turn the logical into the illogical, a political tantrum into a public tribunal. When grown adults become so detached from reality, exempt from accountability, they seek validation through false perception; such as boycotting shaking the President's hand or inciting destructive demonstrations. If Donald Trump disbanded legal immigration and deported 15 million illegals (although justifiable) I could understand the outrage. However, he has not. Where was this insatiable disgust when Bill Clinton called illegal immigration our greatest threat and implored Congress to build a border wall, or when the Obama administration – recklessly enabling an unprecedented wave of undocumented migration – spent more per illegal immigrant than the average Social Security recipient or U.S. veteran?

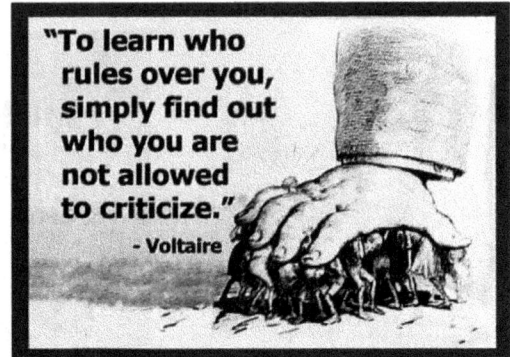

"To learn who rules over you, simply find out who you are not allowed to criticize."
- Voltaire

And, if I may, when did "Never Forget" become "yes, please, can we have another" in a matter of a few short years? This is not 1900 where millions sought and respected the opportunity America afforded, rather than being consumed by an ingrained hatred to do her harm. If demanding that all refugees, visa holders or immigrants be thoroughly vetted is a radical concept, no matter what their point of origin, why even have background checks for police officers, educators, or caregivers; none of which were responsible for 9/11, the Orlando shooting or the Boston Marathon bombing? Better yet, when did common sense become a verified security risk?

Winston Churchill once predicted, "When fascism comes to America it will be in the form of anti-fascism." Few sayings could be more prophetic for progressives are not only waging war against free will, but the institution of reason itself. Without an unconditional respect for our democratic process, to express ourselves free from violence or duress, freedom is but a removable footnote. I don't want to live in an America where a mother, cradling her baby, is verbally accosted over her last name, where my children are beaten on a campus of higher learning for exercising intellectual diversity, or where celebrities are applauded for suggesting the overthrow of our government or the assassination of a man who hasn't even been charged with a crime. That is the flag of fascism, fear born from propaganda, for liberty is not a tool of convenience to be yielded or only respected when it suits our desires. I would rather peacefully divide the country I so dearly love, live amicably among conservative and liberal states, than witness a rejection of all civility from the comfort of my home. What we are witnessing is the death of America.

Vault 7, Agenda 21 and the Zero-Sum State

I'm not going to naively insinuate the American intelligence community has been a pillar of ethical behavior since its inception. From the McCarthy hearings to the infamous Rolodex of Herbert Hoover and the conviction of G. Gordon Liddy, no coincidence or common misappropriation was free the spotlight of scrutiny or the growing shadow of Black Ops. However, these actions, whether foolishly excessive or ever cognizant of a rising threat, were largely geared towards exposing and defeating our enemies; those countries or agents who overtly threatened America's daily survival and despised our hallowed way of life.

Unlike the bulk of secrets obtained from the urgency of World War II or the heightened tensions of the Cold War, the massive digital espionage web cast during the past 8 years was not waged specifically against foreign foes or unvetted radicals, but for the convenient purpose of sabotaging political opponents and weakening the moral fiber of a nation's defiant heritage. While Washington ushered Islamic militants across our borders with ceremonial spite and homegrown anarchists operated with impunity, the Obama administration turned phones, computers and smart TV's into political weapons of mass corruption; illegally confiscated intel aimed at identifying and/or discrediting any law-abiding American citizen who opposed their radical agenda. Liberty lovers, capitalists, Christian conservatives, Jews, veterans, but most notably Donald Trump and his recently appointed cabinet members, all became the select targets of a 24-hour media assassination campaign designed to demonize anyone who posed a danger to the newfound "statist" quo, or more apropos...the New World Order of anti-American globalists. If you can't intimidate, undermine or silence the damning truth, you can always hijack the navigation system of uncooperative whistle-blowers exposing the secrets of your rogue surveillance state.

Buried in the vast vaults of this endless Russia subterfuge, the unrivaled paper trail of executive abuse, is the revelation the very progressives leading the charge of civil insurrection are the forgotten radicals who have been endeavoring for decades to lead a Marxist coup of American's founding ideals; and all despite the fact the former U.S.S.R. abandoned and denounced Communism as a failed ideology. If I may, which outgoing President instructed loyalists to leak classified information, moved his top adviser into his personal estate to spearhead "the resistance" of peaceful transition – the same Iranian malcontent who pledged to "fundamentally" transform America – and assembled a team of prestigious lawyers to obstruct nearly every policy decision of an incoming administration? Yes, there's obviously nothing disconcerting about sedition or treason, let alone a former leader of the free world plotting to subvert a sovereign government he led by spying on his eventual successor. And because misery loves inconsolable sociopaths, what former Presidential candidate, not even a month after losing the election, had her campaign operatives organize national marches of vitriolic sensationalism and plan disruptive protests at town hall events to give the appearance of mass outrage over "fake" syndicated news? When a day without feminists or trespassing immigrants turns into a civil rights charade of partisan hatred, the only oppression evident is an unsuspected dose of reality.

Little is more amusing, if not deeply disturbing, than the absurd narrative Donald Trump is Adolf Hitler – a despotic, racist and genocidal nationalist – when he has respectfully reached out to all sects of American society in the name of unity and cooperation. Let's not forget, mere weeks before the election, these same bastions of integrity reported a celebrity billionaire violated at least a dozen women, without one lawsuit or settlement, and that he later somehow colluded with Russians to pervert our electoral process; a laughable claim considering we now know the CIA has a program called "umbrage" to falsely imitate Russian "hacking" and that the Clinton Campaign has a lucrative history of soliciting favors from Russian operatives. If hypocrisy is now the most widely accepted form of political currency, or more succinctly bankrupt credibility, my Ruble is on the same esteemed propagandist who said he'd have more flexibility to work with Putin after his re-election.

Aspiring American communists, aka the current neurotic leadership of the Democratic Party, fully realize they cannot erect a totalitarian state of single party rule, especially in a country as ideologically incompatible as the United States, without first demonstrating an apocalyptic need; i.e., fabricating an unconditional excuse to both incite discord and restore social order through coerced conformity. By orchestrating mass chaos in our streets and cultivating fear through gross propaganda, professional agitators like George Soros, Barack Obama, Hillary Clinton and Loretta Lynch seek to unravel civility in a mad fervor of mob justice. Yet, no matter what political faction riots or sheds blood in the streets of duplicity, only the victims of such rabid violence will be blamed for opposing its absolute "necessity".

How in God's good name and infinite grace, you ask? The best way to justify censorship and purging intellectual diversity is by brainwashing the misinformed populace into believing the very vehicle of their individuality, free speech, is a perilous threat to their survival and desired quality of life. If you can cajole the same masses into believing illegal immigration is a crime against the actual criminals, vetting or banning Islamic refugees hurts our ability to combat terrorism, Christianity is glorified hate speech, and American patriotism is inherently racist, you can literally accomplish anything through the moral inversion of Marxist indoctrination. Whether maliciously publishing the email address of a respected dignitary's wife or imploring a sworn government agent to violate the Constitutional privacy of a Chief Executive's inconsequential tax returns, there are no Rules for Radicals except the ones used to strangle the last breath of coherent dissent.

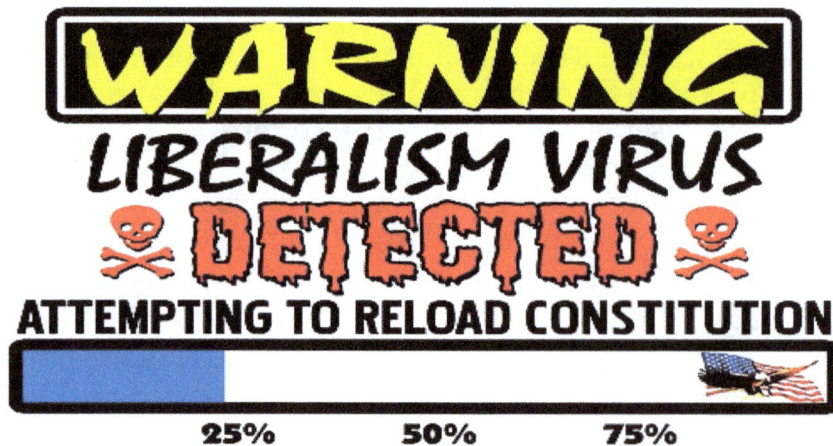

162

Toeing the Covert Party Line

"Trump's not ever going to become president, right? RIGHT?!" Lisa Page texted him.

"NO. No, he won't. We'll stop it," Peter Strzok responded.

And lest we forget the iconic line, "Don't worry, we have an insurance policy", ringing across the federal espionage headquarters of disposable due process and harmless intent. What could possibly be more "biased" than blatant insurrection, lateral impunity, at nearly every level of Washington's intelligence apparatus: supposed non-political entities.

DAVIDHARRISJR.COM
Lisa Page Says FBI Ready to Charge Hillary but DOJ Said No - David Harris Jr

If this ominous exchange took place between two drunk patrons at a bar, so be it. But repeatedly referenced in over **10,000 text exchanges** between two FBI agents who were never reprimanded or subsequently fired; even after their superiors became aware of their disturbing rhetoric? Any self-respecting civil servant having sworn to uphold their solemn oath would immediately report and/or investigate such a potentially grave matter; unless that is, they were already cognizant of, dare I say involved in, an ongoing treasonous plot. Then again, when the former Head of the CIA admits illegal surveillance of the President is somehow a good thing, who needs a formal trial? Better yet, how can aggressively draining every ethically-deranged parasite lounging in the Deep State cesspool possibly be a bad thing?

Et tu, crying James Comey? Or was that private Gmail account employed exclusively for your officially-fake review of Hillary's real, unauthorized server simply a coincidence to give your sterling penchant for objectivity and following protocol a permanent vacation from the social media pink slip of Executive authority? The "wrongfully" terminated always scrub their implicated Commander in Chief's name from their final report to shield his handpicked successor from a sexist court of law. Thank God Dinesh D'Souza was prosecuted for reimbursing two associates who donated to the Senate campaign of Wendy Long when the Clinton Foundation dispersed less than 7% of hundreds of millions in charitable political slush funds. But yes, I know, Donald Trump and hurtful words of pain.

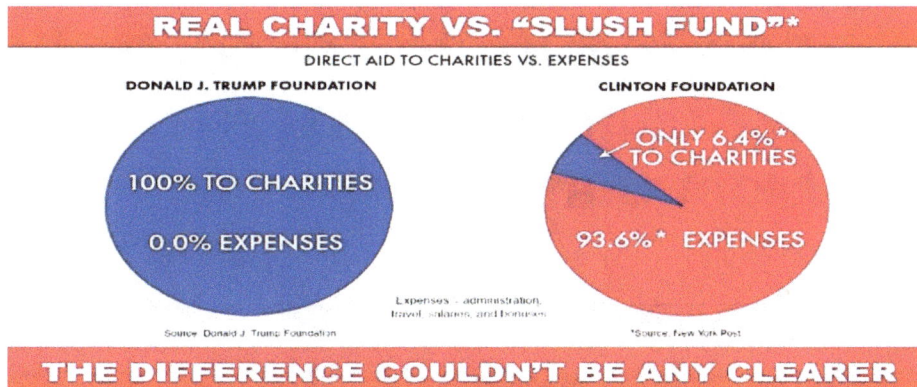

REAL CHARITY VS. "SLUSH FUND"*

DIRECT AID TO CHARITIES VS. EXPENSES

DONALD J. TRUMP FOUNDATION

100% TO CHARITIES

0.0% EXPENSES

Source: Donald J. Trump Foundation

CLINTON FOUNDATION

ONLY 6.4%* TO CHARITIES

93.6%* EXPENSES

Expenses - administration, travel, salaries, and bonuses.

*Source: New York Post

THE DIFFERENCE COULDN'T BE ANY CLEARER

Funny how the same "faithful" FBI that immediately catered to the gold-digging whims of a porn star and the politically-motivated vendetta of her corrupt DNC attorney – recharging Mueller's baseless collusion crusade – was completely immune to the criminal behavior festering deep within their own ranks. If members of our intelligence community can stonewall or categorically refuse congressional oversight and operational accountability, Mr. Rosenstein, what's the difference between a Constitutional government built upon centuries of "checks and balances" and a Banana Republic confiscating coconuts from unruly sloths for the purpose of exporting authentic Pina Coladas? The size of your obstructionist ego obviously pales in comparison to the intoxicated scope of your undisclosed misconduct. Luckily in prison, newly-discovered remorse rarely shrinks for posterity's sake.

Forgive my faint recollection concerning the partisan particulars of punishable betrayal, but when do "We the People" get to raid the hostile corridors of the FBI and conveniently impotent DOJ; those now "honorable" modern fairy tales of integrity waging war against this nation's founding ideals with our tax dollars but by no means our collective consent. In an age where bill collectors are the new barbarians at the squeaky gate, how long will it be before the bloody tip of the intelligence iceberg melts proving victims never cut their own wrists to pay the counterfeit toll for their captors robbing the public's trust?

It's a bitter-sweet indictment of our country when the only justice political traitors and protected thieves will receive is the fact Hillary Clinton will never become president. I don't need the anecdotal validation of an Inspector General's report to know treasonous sedition without unwavering consequence is a suicidal proposition. The very moment the prescribed peaceful transition of democratic power becomes a foreign concept among the supposed domestic guardians of our once Free Republic, liberty becomes a wounded lie living in media-imposed exile.

"Strzok's decision to prioritize the counterintelligence probe of the Trump campaign over the Clinton email criminal investigation led us to conclude that we did not have confidence Strzok's decision was free from bias." ~Inspector General

---

Objects and Operatives

If one, dare I say multiple FBI agents conducted themselves in the same seditious manner Peter Strzok and Lisa Page attempted to subvert a legitimate election, violated the century-old mission of our intelligence apparatus, smugly insulted over 60 million Americans, and proudly referenced an ongoing plot to frame Barack Obama, that individual would be in jail or indicted without hesitation. And to think Paul Manafort is being subjected to solitary confinement in hopes he'll turn state witness for a fraudulent Russian investigation, while Al Sharpton owes millions in unpaid taxes but has not been charged or arrested. Not only would the consequences be swift and stern, generating near inconsolable outrage among the mainstream media and congressional Democrats, any attempt by Republicans to defend, God forbid praise these treasonous actions would result in widespread condemnation if not a possible formal censure. Public service without a profound sense of patriotic duty to the rule of law, regardless of who is president, too often invites rogue or politically motivated activism. Judging by the nauseating hubris of a remorseless mule whose relative was pardoned for leaking classified information by the same political espionage President Mr. Strzok has known since 1988, a rotten apple doesn't fall far from the family tree.

Unfortunately, that's exactly what "We the People" witnessed today in the halls of our forefathers, the supposed epicenter of our conferred trust. That televised moment a partisan agent's inexcusable behavior fails to generate an unconditional, bilateral reprimand, a simple acknowledgement of clear illicit intent, moral objectivism is officially dead. If the preoccupied masses ever needed a disturbing reminder as to how consciously close the progressive movement has veered towards embracing mutiny – rejecting punitive recourse, logical discourse and the required transparency of constitutional democracy – today was a disgraceful declaration of their party's reckless animus and unending quest for unrivaled, amoral control. The guiding conscience of an enduring free nation is only as relevant as its citizens willingness to sincerely distinguish right from wrong, malice from careless negligence. This once solemn duty is quickly becoming a buried dagger of subjective concern.

The Misappropriation of Party Favors

Paul Sperry
@paulsperry_

BREAKING: Cohen testified under GOP grilling that he consulted with Democrat investigative committee leaders Cummings and Schiff before preparing his testimony, along with Clinton operative/lawyer Lanny Davis

Media cartwheels withstanding, I'm by no means surprised Michael Cohen rolled over, accepted the complimentary services of Hillary's lawyer, Lanny Davis, and agreed to a plea deal after he was exposed for much more nefarious activities over the course of his legal career; illicit tax practices which had nothing to do with the one man the New York Democrat is now attempting to publicly shame, despite repeatedly praising his former client, to save himself. However, Mr. Mueller's predictable assertion the President violated election finance laws is little more than a mosquito's wet dream being Trump is a known billionaire who almost entirely financed his own campaign and who personally paid Cohen to satisfy a porn star's $130,000 "non-speaking" tabloid fees. Naturally, not a single network recalls the "impeached" fact Barack Obama had to pay a $375,000 fine for honorably hiding over $2 million dollars in donations during the 2008 election; one of the largest such fines ever levied on a candidate. If paying "hush" money for two consensual relationships is now a crime, what is the going penalty for extortion, perjury or collusion to convict? Just don't ask the extensive list of Congressmen who illegally used taxpayer money to discretely settle numerous cases of actual sexual misconduct. Truth is no longer a public commodity when a rogue Special Prosecutor is threatening your ex-lawyer's wife with 30 years jailtime for alleged bank fraud.

> **Sean Davis** ✓
> @seanmdav
>
> Worth noting that career Clinton fixer Lanny Davis, who likely wrote Michael Cohen's opening statement, is also a foreign agent of Dmytro Firtash, an oligarch whom Putin used to control Ukrainian elections and officials on behalf of Putin's puppet there.
>
> reuters.com/article/russia…

The FISA Faux Pas: Unredacted and Unacceptable

The newly revealed "Carter Page" FISA warrant application all but confirmed the "controversial" unredacted Devin Nunes memo released in February...

There was absolutely no "reasonable suspicion" of wrongdoing presented to the FISA court by the FBI/DOJ when asking for electronic surveillance of Trump campaign volunteer, Carter Page: a foreign affairs liaison and suspected CIA plant by some pundits.

The Obama administration, our intelligence community, presented the known fake dossier without informing the court it was paid for by the DNC and the Clinton campaign. The media reported details of the fabricated collusion narrative as a developing scandal, leaked by Democratic officials and the FBI, without any factual validity or due diligence. The Democratic Party not only worked tirelessly to protect to this lie, repeatedly fighting the Congressional release of classified information exposing their systemic deception, they knowingly attempted to frame an innocent man in an elaborate hoax designed to aid Hillary's election chances and/or hopefully force Trump's resignation or impeachment. Former National Intelligence Director James Clapper recently confirmed Barack Obama was the primary architect of the guilt-by-association, Russian hacking, entrapment scheme.

Special Counsel Robert Mueller has yet to acknowledge any of these incriminating facts, let alone investigate the criminal actions of those involved in illegal espionage and conspiring with the press, instead choosing to harass, bully, incarcerate and violate the legal rights of anyone associated with the Trump campaign for activities completely unrelated to the afforded scope of his "election tampering" probe. Sadly, anyone familiar with the former U.S. Attorney and FBI Chief's resume knows this behavior is but a microcosm of career misconduct rather than a political anomaly or amoral aberration.

Who is Robert Swan Mueller III?

He is the same former US Assistant Attorney who wrongfully and knowingly imprisoned four Boston men for murder, two of whom died in prison, costing taxpayers $100 million in civil damages while protecting the infamous FBI informant Whitey Bulger; who attempted to coerce Scooter Libby, Dick Cheney's Chief of Staff, into committing perjury to frame his boss for the breach of a CIA agent's identity despite knowing then Attorney General John Ashcroft was the suspected "leaker" all along; who failed to frame but instantly destroyed the reputation of Dr. Steven Hatfill for the 2001 Anthrax letters, a known virologist who had never handled Anthrax, by claiming two "trained bloodhounds" identified him as the domestic terrorist responsible for 5 deaths – Dr. Hatfill was later exonerated by the DOJ and awarded a $5.82-million-dollar settlement; who used government resources to destroy Congressman Curt Weldon's career in 2006, illegally raiding his daughter's home in the early morning hours to generate a media firestorm, after he exposed the FBI for rejecting pre-9/11 intelligence of an Al-Qaeda Brooklyn sleeper cell which included Mohammed Atta and three other terrorists a year before 9/11; who used gestapo tactics to indict Senator Ted Stevens, crippling his re-election chances before his tragic death, forcing Attorney General Eric Holder to later abandon the case after citing concerns of gross prosecutorial misconduct; whose FBI agents repeatedly violated the Fourth Amendment by sending out demands for private records and documents without probable cause – similar to National Security Letters (NSL) used by the DOJ to bypass the formality of subpoenas; and the former "Muslim Outreach" program architect who purged the FBI of critical anti-terror intelligence, which precipitated the Orlando Night Club shooting and Boston Marathon Bombing, including all counter-terrorism training literature during his tenure within the Obama administration. Since it was common knowledge James Comey and Robert Mueller were longtime confidants, collaborating to some degree on several of the before-mentioned incidents, under no circumstances should have he been appointed Special Prosecutor to investigate the clearly fraudulent accusation of "election collusion", but in all actuality, to undermine and topple Donald Trump by any means necessary for terminating a failed associate of the very "Deep State" Mr. Mueller himself exemplified for so many years with his abusive, criminal and sociopathic pattern of behavior.

Swamp Creatures, Lies and Leaked Audiotapes

Need more proof the Fake News establishment and the Mueller investigation are thick as thieves, if not completely out of control? Look no further than the Cohen-Trump tape leaked by the FBI to CNN. Not only was this the second egregious violation of attorney-client privilege, malicious acts of corrupt cowards, the released soundbite was obviously another orchestrated attempt to seize national headlines and deflect from the snowballing FISA scandal to once again smear the President despite the reality no law was broken and it's a private matter from over a decade ago. While celebrating pundits are somehow befuddled as to why the security clearances of criminal swamp creatures are being revoked in unison, media networks continue to embarrass themselves by setting daily dumpster fires because unruly children moonlighting as upstanding adults simply can't deal with the fact Donald Trump is winning...YUGELY! Democrats have obviously learned nothing from the endless electoral schemes and insulting identity politics employed by Hillary's campaign during that historic fiasco known as the 2016 election. So be it.

> **Thomas Jefferson**
>
> When once a Republic is corrupted, there is no possibility of remedying any of the growing evils but by removing the corruption and restoring its lost principles; every other correction is either useless or a new evil.

The Undeparted

If I was the 45th President of the United States, the unremitting target of incessant federal leaks and vicious rhetoric from fired or retired civil servants, I would absolutely revoke the security clearances of all meddling, ex-Obama officials: specifically, James Clapper, John Brennan, James Comey, Susan Rice, Andrew McCabe, and Sally Yates just for beginners. The real question is why did any of these former intelligence officials still have such privileges? While I do realize it is common practice for high-ranking intelligence officials to retain their security clearance for 4 to 5 years after their departure, subject to renewal if deemed necessary, granting such latitude to hostile agents of an outgoing administration, especially in today's age of hyper-partisanship where party loyalty is beginning to eclipse one's sworn duty to protect and serve their country, is reckless and naïve to say the least. It's also by no means a secret these individuals have conspired with the media and Robert Mueller to conceal real collusion, their own contributions to a prolific culture of corruption, while pushing slanderous narratives to prevent the public from learning the truth. Miranda platitudes and erupting chasms aside, these conniving miscreants deserve nothing but contempt and the unrevoked right to remain silent.

Politics and Proctologists: Deep State Rumblings

Another day, another pathetic Mueller-media leak without any legal consequences. When a glorified proctologist can't distinguish the offending orifice defining his own repulsive practices, it's hand-delivered to the soiled press as a smoking gun of indefensible guilt. CNN's "big story" about Michael Cohen claiming President Trump approved of a meeting with "the Russians" is stale garnish rehashed as breaking news, not to mention predictably misleading. For those who remember correctly, a British journalist/music producer named Rob Goldstone – eventually exposed as an anti-Trump pawn with ties to foreign intelligence – randomly contacted Donald Jr. offering a private meeting with a female Russian lawyer, a now suspected Kremlin double agent, claiming she wanted to share incriminating dirt on Hillary Clinton; a career Washington insider whose political life has been synonymous with corruption, deceit and scandal.

Because the Trump campaign was naturally curious about what Natalia Veselnitskaya might divulge, unaware she had once been a private guest of Barack Obama at the White House, Donald Trump Jr. agreed to meet with her at Trump Tower: the very offices our trusted intelligence agencies supposedly "never" but "coincidentally" wiretapped. Just like our mainstream network tabloids that love omitting factual details for the specific purpose of validating sensational allegations, the Russian national soon revealed she had no relevant information whatsoever and this "unforgivable" meeting quickly became little more than an informal, awkward conversation about unrelated topics and pop culture. Regardless, there was absolutely no illegality to his actions, or his father's consent (although Cohen testified Trump never knew of the meeting), since it is common practice to scour an opponent's past for inconsistencies, inflammatory comments and misconduct. Even with the shameless spin, this obviously orchestrated string of events pales in comparison to the "opposition research" paid for by the DNC, Clinton campaign, and used by the FBI, DOJ, and CIA to spy on the entire Trump team in the hopes of framing the Republican presidential nominee through contrived circumstances, planted moles in his campaign staff, and relentless media coordination with Obama officials waging a secret war to salvage his threatened "America Last" agenda and recycled toilet paper legacy.

Prison Bubbles & Bullshit Artists

Creepy porn lawyer Michael Avenatti, the same corrupt slimeball who represented Stormy Daniels and more recently serial sexual predator R. Kelly, not to mention one of the Kavanaugh accusers who later admitted fabricating her story, is now facing up to 97 years in prison after being arrested for bank fraud, wire fraud and attempting to extort $20 million from Nike execs with the assistance of co-conspirator, Mark Geragos: celebrity attorney and former CNN legal analyst who naturally represents the infamous Jussie Smollett and Colin Kaepernick. Just Karma it, baby! Couldn't have happened to a more deserving parasite and wet paper gangster. Perhaps he'll soon announce his candidacy for prison shower buddy. I hear they come in real handy when playing knick-knack paddy-whack pick up my bar of soap, b#@ch! Happy scrubbing, dirtbag.

The Corrupt Temple

If you've never heard of the "Office of Misconduct", it's a soulless specter, secluded deep in the Second Estate, bleeding cash in the tunneled vault of buried virtue and blinded oversight. The fact U.S. Congressmen funneled 17 million dollars of taxpayer money to silence the victims of sexual harassment and/or assault is as morally reprehensible as it is unforgivable. It's hard to proclaim yourself a champion of women's rights, basic human empathy, when you're violating someone's wife, sister or daughter for your own sadistic pleasure and reducing their suffering to a privileged form of unsolicited prostitution. I don't care whether you're a Democrat or Republican, those responsible for the creation of this criminal reserve – including every member who used it to conceal their crimes – should be removed from office and forced to pay full restitution. Honestly, for how many years have the people been fleeced and shielded from the true depths of the establishment's depravity? Washington has become little more than a polarized cesspool of perversion and corruption; a psychological disease masquerading as its own sociological cure. While sick degenerates violate nearly every Constitutional ethic of public trust, America is drowning beneath a tidal wave of dysfunction, deceit, and mindless self-indulgence. When will "We the People", those second citizens tired of the federal aristocracy's incessant schemes and cavalier betrayal, tear the entire corrupt temple down?

To Eliminate with Extreme Prejudice

Since the declaration of the Republican presidential nominee, the Democratic establishment, disgracefully aided by the betrayal of GOP globalists, have cajoled and relentlessly plotted to displace Donald Trump by any conceivable means necessary. In essence, the desperation of their inane schemes has only been surpassed by the escalating absurdity of their baseless claims. When publicly unveiling nearly a dozen, self-proclaimed victims of sexual misconduct just weeks before the election proved inconsequential, PC militants opted for the stale racist stigma of white supremacy. When fabricating/funding a Russian dossier failed to frame a sitting President for election fraud, the Swamp chose to reignite the Clinton gender warfare of misogyny and toxic masculinity. After Obstruction of Justice proved to be the unclaimed baggage of Deep State magicians unmasking their own sedition, the exposed architects of Fake News conveniently decried suppression of the free press to digress from their singular goal of impeachment.

And yet despite the left's tireless allegations and juvenile ploys, nothing has changed except the accumulating accomplishments of the elected recipient of their collective disdain. This is why I honestly believe, beyond the endless hoaxes and spoon-fed hysteria of regurgitated hyperbole, George Soros and his soulless band of puppets have a much better chance at opening a lucrative PB&J gourmet bistro in Paris than forcing Donald Trump to resign over rehashed and blatantly false allegations. Despite George's best attempts at misdirection to laughably "reclaim" a moral high ground he never once visited, even a Marxist billionaire cannot conceal the fact the Democratic Party and its incestuous Hollywood partners are now the unrivaled sponsors of sexual impropriety, perversion and criminal collusion. And as we all know, false appearances are the laced dime bags of laundered "anti-fascists" who always believe the end justifies the immoral means or the quality of their peddled propaganda; especially when your anti-American crop of millennial terrorists has no independently functioning brain or moral compass.

The same John Conyers and Al Franken who defiantly pledged to remain in office regardless of any threatened consequences, vocally defended by celebrities and congressional peers alike, only had a change of heart after DNC leaders concluded their unsalvageable reputations were far more valuable if used to demonize Donald Trump and Roy Moore's refusal to respectfully submit their measured necks to the highly-esteemed court of lynch mob justice. Unfortunately for the Soros money train which leads straight into the anti-Trump documentary of Brave New Films and through the heart of the mainstream media's renewed obsession with previously discredited sex accusers, including one extremely bitter Megyn Kelly, innocent men are never going to acquiesce to political mercenaries that failed to produce one tangible piece of credible evidence. Giving credence to any jaded woman craving national attention or seeking to fulfill a political vendetta significantly hurts the real victims of sexual harassment and assault from ever pursuing/receiving justice. And if that rudimentary revelation is somehow too difficult for whining divas to digest, it's also of little surprise as to why Chuck Schumer and Nancy Pelosi spend far more time trying to sabotage political opponents than faithfully serving the America people and the unwritten future of this Constitutional Republic; because it's just not in the nature of liars, traitors and thieves to say pretty, pretty, please.

Make America Sane Again

Like Robert Mueller's Russian investigation turned global Deep State inquisition, the introduction of Articles of Impeachment by Democrats is an absolute farce that have no chance of succeeding; well, except in the detached minds of bitter partisans joyously "resisting" logic and rigging reality. Such juvenile semantics are just more undeniable proof the radical left is all about appearances, cultivating national headlines, to validate a blatantly false and vindictive narrative for political gain. If Congress could simply impeach a President for being disliked, let alone for being the victim of a never-ending smear campaign, nearly every Chief Executive in American history would have been disposed of over the mere heated exchange of words. The Constitutional prerequisite of "high crimes and misdemeanors" does not take into account your feelings, unproven accusations or one's glaring inability to comprehend the law; i.e., Donald Trump's explicit authority to restrict or ban travel from dangerous regions, to enforce our existing immigration laws or defund sanctuary cities in red states, and to negotiate with foreign dignitaries however he sees fit. Ironically, if the President was Bob Menendez or Hillary Clinton, he would have been tarred and feathered by the press, forced to resign or duly removed from office before he could send out one more politically incorrect tweet.

If I may, where was this hyper-sensitive, sensationalist call for "justice" when the Obama administration routinely incited racial, class, gender and religious discord, circumvented nearly every Constitutional check and balance to expand the reach of government, weaponized federal agencies to target and spy on political opponents, and empowered our conspiring enemies with complicit regularity. Fortunately for "We the Sane People", it is painfully obvious progressives have no interest in coexisting or cooperating to better America because they can no longer discern liberty from liberalism, discourse from demagoguery. Rather, Democrats and establishment Republicans are entirely content pointing fingers, misleading the public, criminalizing dissension, and catering to the lowest common denominator of human nature; those hateful, destructive behaviors children are often punished for without hesitation. If you're irrevocably hostile towards the founding ideals of this 241-year-old republic and the bi-partisan ratified stipulations that incessantly guide her, insanity is your only viable defense. Until that fateful day, the American taxpayers would like a refund and the only key in existence to your Obamacare mandated padded room.

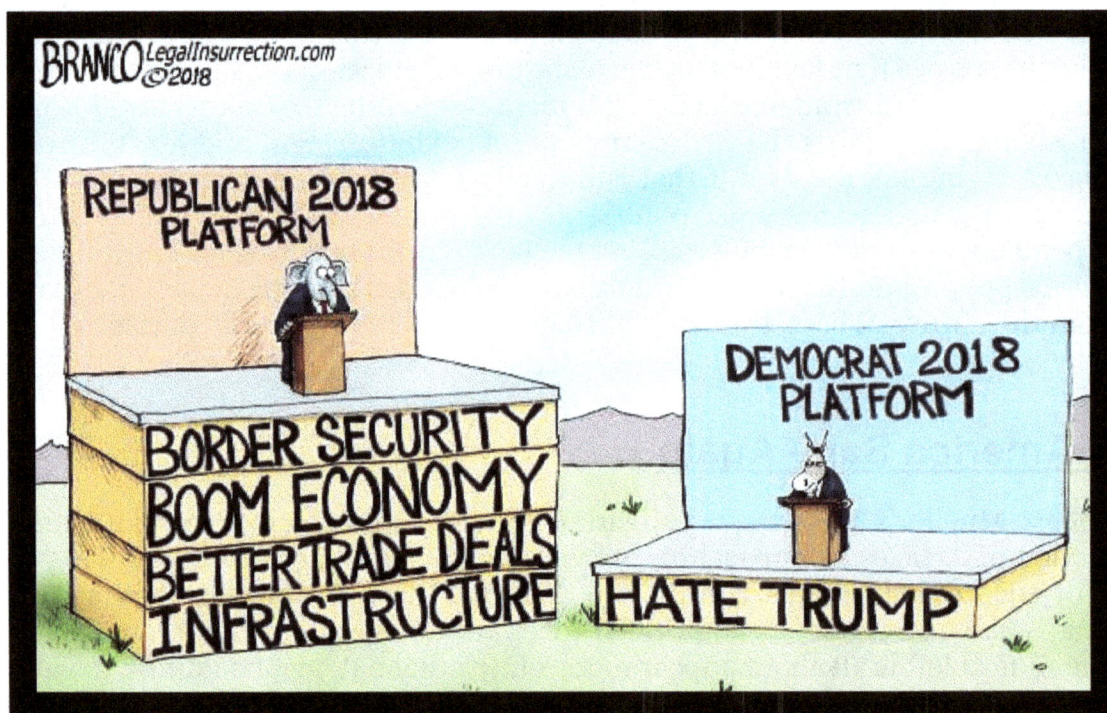

A Recipe for Resignation

If you love a bad rerun amidst an endless saga of orchestrated and entirely predictable character assassinations, welcome to America. In yet another highly questionable crusade to crucify yet another Republican candidate in hopes of achieving their goal of recapturing Congress – i.e., fabricating public hysteria in hopes of forcing an immediate resignation without a hint of proof or due process – it appears the Democratic party is forgetting one, all too ominous detail. By some misplaced crumb of cosmic justice, Judge Roy Moore's accuser Debbie Gibson worked for the DNC as a sign language interpreter...most notably, during campaign rallies for both Hillary Clinton and Joe Biden. While some will claim this discovery is mere coincidence and therefore inconsequential, I'm guessing the fact she's actively campaigning for Judge Moore's opponent, Doug Jones, is anything but. Although I abhor any man who sexually harasses and/or assaults a woman, regardless of one's political affiliation or beliefs, I'm hesitant to unconditionally believe a Democratic operative who waited 40 years and one month before an election to publicly name her abuser, dare I say frame, her sacrificial lamb of choice.

As we all know too well, the three major news networks rolled out nearly a dozen crying wolves in librarian clothes just weeks before the 2016 election – from beauty pageant contestants to former participants on his show Celebrity Apprentice – after aggressively soliciting any female from Donald Trump's past who had a grudge to itch or could somehow twist any perceived slight, perhaps a humorous casual remark, into the most tenuous allegation of rape or sexual misconduct. Of course, by yet another completely innocuous and coincidental twist of fate, nearly all of these so-called traumatized women were represented by the famed feminist instigator, attorney Gloria Allred, and not a single "victim" sought charges if only to obtain a quick payday from a known celebrity billionaire. Not only did any of these women offer a shred of evidence, a leaked DNC email acknowledged that all sexual allegations should move forward because Trump's campaign had yet to become "litigious". Once the damage is done, whether such claims prove fatal or fruitless, the perpetrators of these ploys are overwhelmingly unphased and unrepentant even when their assertions are unequivocally debunked.

Unless you've been living on Fantasy Island and are completely unfamiliar with the Spanish inquisition of Herman Cain, the left's Marxist manifesto begins with falsely accusing a high profile, Republican male with sexual impropriety and immediately initiating an avalanche of accusatory media coverage to secure a conviction in the kangaroo court of public opinion. In other words, every political threat to the progressive agenda must be successfully neutralized by being depicted as sexist, a womanizer, a racist or any combination of the three. The only thing I detest more than pathological liars are establishment charlatans like Mitch McConnell, Paul Ryan, John McCain and Mitt Romney joining the guillotine choir to conveniently dispose of an "America First" conservative they disapprove of regardless. The most dangerous party of a conspiracy isn't the jaded accomplice willing to shake the tree of public perception, it's almost always the striking snake lurking beneath the grassy knoll.

Flakes, Widows, and the Cold War on Reality

At no time during Jeff Flake's self-aggrandizing sermon – a slanderous diatribe so scripted that the non-functioning brain trust of CNN and Salon applauded its detached duplicity – did the proud turncoat mention he had no chance of winning re-election in 2018 because he personally broke nearly all his campaign pledges to Arizona Republicans solely to spite President Trump. Arbitrary semantics aside, Senator, when exactly did your party, let alone those marginalized conservative voters responsible for your election, support Obamacare, higher taxes, amnesty, unrestricted refugees, gun control, and the media malpractice of anti-American race-baiting used to discredit conservative ideals, demonize patriotism and obstruct common sense reforms? For every Bob Corker lamenting hurt feelings and "unprofessional" behavior, there is a struggling working family burdened by the unsustainable costs of illegal immigration or a patient dying from failed healthcare abandoned by a handful of whining Republicans content on playing politics, orchestrating public spectacles to further imbue leftist talking points, in lieu of actually helping people and fulfilling their discarded obligations.

Unless you've been hypnotically lobotomized by fellow Arizona malcontent John McCain – still fuming over the realization a prisoner of war does not constitute a hero and personal vendettas never justify deserting one's core political beliefs – don't blame the abrasive demeanor of a relentlessly maligned populist for choosing to fallaciously present yourself as a right-minded patriot who believes life, liberty, unity and the pursuit of happiness are irreconcilable with modern progressivism. In other words, if you believe a politically incorrect CEO is a horrific human being because 93% of the media coverage is unforgivably negative and maliciously contrived, then you are bound to believe a lifetime Democrat and military widow showcased by every talk show, radio host and newspaper – shamelessly exploited by the obnoxious Frederica Wilson herself to publicly validate her anti-Trump obsession – has nothing to do with race, newfound fame and fortune, or the incessant "Nazi" narrative of the endlessly conniving Democratic party.

The same outraged "humanists" responsible for funding/fabricating the infamous Russian dossier and politicizing/doctoring the intent of a private conversation conveying a Commander in Chief's condolences – a gesture Barack Obama routinely acquiesced in favor of written correspondence or delegated to subordinates – are plotting day and night to destroy the single greatest threat to the fake media monopoly and corrupt Washington establishment intent on fundamentally transforming America to ensure permanent control. While I grieve for the loved ones of all our brave fallen, I have no remorse for the soulless schemes of a hopelessly compromised press. The moment context and integrity are no longer relevant, dare I say conducive to controlling what pundits want the masses to despise and believe, is the day the left's ambition of achieving a permanent state of political supremacy becomes an omitted anecdote in the crocodile tears of seasoned "super predators".

For those avid history buffs, Nazi fascists and Marxist revolutionaries were both extremely adept at one practice: blaming their most vocal critics, political detractors, for that which they themselves were guilty of...fraud, conspiracy, bigotry, greed, treason. Because it takes a complicit village to raise and conceal a lie of such grotesque proportions – Hillary Clinton lost to a sexist "White Supremacist" because of solicited Russian interference – what's the going price for a former POW, a bitter ex-First Lady and even the FBI itself colluding to frame a sitting President of the United States for that which they attempted; financing a vicious plot through the Washington D.C. firm Fusion GPS to incriminate a common political adversary? Better yet, what's the incarceration rate for personally profiting from selling 20% of America's Uranium stockpiles as the former FBI Maestro and Deep State magician, James Comey, exonerated his comrade Hillary Clinton before an "investigation" into her illegal activities even began?

"Most bad government has grown out of too much government." *~Thomas Jefferson*

Can you imagine the sheer chaos, the unrelenting screams for "justice", if Hillary had won the presidency and Donald Trump attempted to falsely implicate her by conspiring with the identical historical adversary he publicly decried as our greatest foe? Just like the Democratic Socialists and Red Bolsheviks of old who invoked injustice with insatiable regularity, the loudest whistle blowers are the table-fed, seditious sneaks who wiretapped political opponents, sponsored hate groups, consorted with our foreign enemies and somehow managed to force a criminal investigation of an innocent man through the mere theatricality of accusation and media-manufactured hysteria alone.

Whenever the billowing smoke of an impending fire sale draws an inquisitive crowd, the progressive circus sends out a glittering, one-trick pony whose safe word is "racism"; or even worse, a grieving and graciously politicized military widow who only draws tears of outrage from the Anthem-separatist press corps during a Republican presidency. Only in the festering swamps of mass media manipulation would the death of four Special Forces members ambushed by militants while providing assistance to Nigerian counter-terrorism efforts, equate to four Americans murdered in Benghazi amidst repeated unanswered requests for additional security at a stagnant embassy due to intelligence reports warning of a possible terrorist attack: documented pleas that Hillary Clinton self-admittedly ignored, including rejected calls for military assistance over the entire duration of a 7 hour siege which left Ambassador Stevens dead. If Barack Obama, Hillary Clinton, Hollywood, media muckrakers and violent social activists were held to the same intolerant standard as Donald Trump – their every move scrutinized, spoken word distorted and very existence dehumanized – Senator Flake's pandering attempt at martyrdom, the deceitful and destructive antics of the so-called "resistance", would be impeachable forms of hostility awarded a much-needed dose of prison cell humility.

Death, Dishonor & Democratic Tripwires

Leave it to the two-faced press and crying Chuck Schumer to turn John McCain's personal vendetta against Donald Trump into an immortalized call for national martyrdom, a helpless victim of Executive heresy, by politicizing a veteran's death a decade after they mocked him as a racist, homophobic, angry old white guy whose only claim to fame was being a "celebrity" POW who crashed a U.S. Navy plane. If it wasn't for the fact the Arizona Senator broke half of his campaign promises and betrayed his entire party solely to spite one man, the mudslinging media wouldn't have given a damn if a Viet Cong memorial was raised on the White House lawn by an Antifa fascist seconds after news of his passing. Regardless, the President immediately and very publicly expressed his condolences to McCain's family and the flag was ordered flown at half-staff for the appropriate period of time according to federal protocol or **U.S. Code › Title 4 › Chapter 1 › § 7:** i.e., lowered the day "after" a member of Congress dies. Lest our "unbiased", flag-burning fact-checkers forget, their former beloved Commander in Chief never lowered for the flag for murdered American sniper, Chris Kyle, or for the posthumous General Harold Greene who was tragically shot by an Afghan soldier in 2014. The only scandal present in the eyes of our Armed Forces is the relentless goal of the conniving left to deprive the American public of the unmitigated truth.

Supreme Choices and Cheap Publicity Tricks

Judge Brett Kavanaugh has the highest rating from the left-leaning American Bar Association and yet Democratic operatives, partaking in orchestrated protests to seize national headlines, have screamed, interrupted his opening statement and acted like unhinged miscreants incapable of constructive discourse. Disgraceful. If this is what leadership and "humanitarianism" looks like, I want no part of it. If any ordinary citizen behaved in such a manner, on the job or within the public realm, that person would be immediately fired, reprimanded and/or locked up for the people's safety. It's clear the DNC propaganda machine is desperately trying to trigger national outrage, solicit an angry response by Judge Kavanaugh himself, by suggesting any judicial appointment they "politically" reject must be a Right-Wing extremist who kicks puppies, oppresses women, and wears Nazi memorabilia on the weekends. These formal proceedings were never designed to reconcile whether or not Senators ideologically aligned or even agreed with judicial nominees, but to determine if these chosen individuals possessed the legal acumen, work ethic and character attributes to faithfully fulfill the required and often arduous duties of a Supreme Court Justice. Unfortunately, those paid civil servants currently juggling kittens before the entire civilized world, turning the hallowed halls of our forefathers into a three-ring circus of jungle warfare, are neither worthy of our respect or mentally stable enough to honor their prescribed Constitutional privileges.

Progressivism 101: **When the first sexual harassment allegation falls apart, introduce 5 more. Manifest your hatred of Donald Trump into believing you're the actual victim of an imaginary crime to "resist" his authority, policies and nominees. Convince the public a great injustice has occurred to fundraise for socialist candidates, to promote divisive identity politics, and to increase voter turnout. Repeat as often as necessary.** **See Also:** Easy Money, Lie, Soros

Despite the obvious fraudulent schemes of plotting obstructionists, my gut tells me the Yale graduate and Federal Appellate Judge will ultimately end up somewhere between former Justice Scalia and John Roberts ideologically. I also believe Trump chose Brett because Mitch McConnell convinced him Amy Barrett probably wouldn't be confirmed in light of mounting opposition from GOP moderates. This way, if the left somehow manages to successfully thwart Kavanaugh's bid with a therapist-induced accusation of sexual misconduct from over 36 years ago, the next choice will likely be even more conservative with even greater electoral repercussions at stake come November. I have long said Donald Trump is a pragmatist, not an unyielding partisan, and this is but another example of his life's guiding philosophy. No matter how diverse our opinions, imagine the very plausible alternative where Hillary Clinton could have selected the last two Supreme Court candidates; each "progressive" choice guaranteed to be infinitely worse than Brett Kavanaugh. As such, regardless of our personal favorites, our best course of action is to fully support the new nominee, debunk the left's vicious smear campaign with unflinching vigor, and pray he stays true to his touted conservative ideals. Unnecessary negativity will only needlessly deflect from preserving our nation's sovereignty, moral and intellectual integrity, during such a pivotal point in American history.

To Kill A Supreme Court Nominee

So now the venerable FBI investigates baseless sexual harassment allegations from a known partisan zealot with mental health issues who repeatedly perjured herself? How convenient for the overflowing cesspool of dirty politicians infecting our government without a single care, earned indictment or hand-delivered bill for incalculable damages. Yes, how many soiled rats residing in the darkest depths of the Congressional "Swamp" would survive a 36-year rectal exam using their current pristine standard of character assassination? Perhaps the Deep State bomb squad will lobby the FISA court for a surveillance warrant to see how much Brett Kavanaugh farts in his sleep for the sake of unreported sexual assault cases or tasteless yearbook jokes. After all, Washington parasites with no discernible conscience or sense of civic duty truly want to know where to properly hide their settlement slush "fun"d!

This fabricated scandal is by far the most nefarious, if not the most obvious setup I've ever witnessed in my lifetime. Not once during the entire nationally-televised hearing did a single Democratic Senator ask any question regarding Mrs. Ford's recollection, motives, or conflicting testimony. Maybe I'm just old fashioned or due diligence is a fascist misnomer, but I'm not quite sure how "you're so incredibly brave", "thank you", and "I believe you" constitute ascertaining a man's innocence or guilt concerning a grave matter that forever haunt his family's safety and well-being. When lynch mob justice rages without a solitary voice of reason rising from the gallows of the Democratic camp, tossing a few more "bodies" into the bonfire will keep the iron hot just long enough to permanently brand the innocent with the stigma of guilt.

Christine Ford never reported her "harrowing" ordeal to police over 30 years ago, mentioned it to her own parents or alerted Congress when Mr. Kavanaugh was first nominated as a Federal judge; although she openly despises his personal convictions and publicly advocates "resisting" everything the President pursues. How incredibly fortunate it must be for the #MeToo McCarthy militia that all of their "distraught and damaged" survivors consist of anti-Trump, liberal females with no corroborative evidence or legal consequences to match their knitted pink hats and feminist pitchforks? In social justice parlance, such celebrated duplicity is also known as sexism, discrimination, persecution.

Sorry, but in America presumption of innocence and burden of proof are still intrinsic to affording due process for people of all genders, creeds, and media stereotypes. If a mere unsubstantiated accusation can instantly ruin a man's life, a highly-suspect event all of her so-called witnesses have contradicted to some degree, then it's open season on your husbands, brothers, sons and male friends. The fact these reckless accusers can now be paraded across national media within minutes and compensated with huge payouts on GoFundMe account within days, only makes their allegations seem all the more disingenuous and cheap. The same confused, childish and robotic professor appearing on Capitol Hill very well may have been harassed by someone at some time, never raped by her own hazy admission, I simply do not believe the well-respected and self-admitted virgin Brett Kavanaugh was her personal boogeyman.

And while it is technically true a naked prostitute loitering in a Frat house can still be a victim of sexual abuse, the "benefit of the doubt" does not lend itself to the foolish or morally obtuse who cannot even recall the most basic details. Maybe next time the unlicensed psychologist, published abortion activist and frequent-flier hypocrite will choose not to relish in the sheer multitude of her roughly 64 partners she once boasted (to close friends) having slept with in high school and college. If you're attempting to "Kill A Mockingbird" with your own posthumous tears, you might want to try finding some shame before exposing your pro-bono harem of Clinton advisers. It's not a fashion-forward look for publicly-financed martyrs, regardless of who is on top.

A Man of Honor

In a world increasingly bereft of genuine role models and benevolent souls, Neil Gorsuch is a much-needed breath of fresh air. He is honest, respectful, poised, patient, insightful, compassionate and most of all an unflappable patriot who puts his love of country, his sworn constitutional duty, above the petty politics of squabbling partisans and seditious activists. Despite being surrounded by bitter bureaucrats seeking to twist his every word and taint his honorable legacy, his dignified and articulate answers have turned the most disingenuous attacks into the most memorable reminders of what constitutes competent, mature leadership. Any failure to confirm this man would serve as an ignorant display of gross negligence and a tragic loss for what little integrity remains in our dysfunctional judicial system. Although dissension within constructive discourse is healthy and the most seasoned legal minds will always digress to some degree, it is how they conduct themselves and their relative commitment to the law that separates the scholars from the usurpers. The questions his smug detractors are asking shouldn't focus on whether he supports abortion, the Second Amendment or restricting Muslim immigration, but rather what is his rationale, judicial precedent, for addressing our most divisive issues while upholding the Constitution of the United States; still, and always, the supreme law of the land. Political anarchy is a poor substitute for jurisprudence and due process.

Law & Democratic Disorder

Rod Rosenstein personally requesting to initiate a massive investigation of a Supreme Court nominee is so blatantly absurd and abusive that he should be universally admonished by every self-respecting member of our government. The same Deputy Attorney General who should also currently be indicted and/or fired for conspiracy, dereliction of duty and obstruction of justice for failing to submit subpoenaed documents detailing FBI collusion to Congress, needs a stern legal reminder that our intelligence community has no jurisdiction in the confirmation process. Yes, it's called Checks and Balances, not unhinged partisan hysteria justifying criminal subversion of due process. If I may, did conservative politicians recklessly plot to circumvent the Senate's authority, incite hostilities on mainstream networks or mindlessly slander political opponents when the unapologetically liberal Sonia Sotomayor or Elena Kagan were selected to serve on America's most consequential court? Were the most sacred convictions of right-minded voters not under equal duress? And finally, where is the dormant Jeff Sessions amid his subordinate's illicit scheming and continued unabashed contempt for our federal institutions?

If panicked leftists ceased believing their own doomsday propaganda for one lucid moment, they might realize Brett Kavanaugh was clearly the more moderate choice on Trump's short list of candidates. Regardless, centuries of parliamentary procedure don't arbitrarily dissolve just because the Democratic Party refuses to accept losing control of Congress and the presidency due to the exploding radicalism, "moralized" anarchy, engulfing their spiteful ranks. Why is perfectly reasonable if not commendable for an unapologetically progressive President to potentially shift the ideological balance of the Supreme Court for years to come, but suddenly a national emergency, a criminal undertaking, when Donald Trump seeks the same legitimate end? Numerous, nominated justices possessing vastly conflicting beliefs have been questioned and confirmed by both Republicans and Democrats without sacrificing decorum, civility, let alone the undisputed rule of law. If elections indeed have consequences, as Barack Obama once so ominously uttered, perhaps the militant Thought Police should surround themselves with more distinguished company, learn how to rationally and respectfully articulate their dissenting views, before making such insulting, despotic demands on the functional integrity of this now obviously-dysfunctional Republic.

> Civics was a class that used to be required before you could graduate from high school. You were taught what was in the U.S. Constitution. And after all the student rebellions in the '60s, civics was banished from the student curriculum and was replaced by something called social studies. Here we live in a country that has a fabulous constitution and all these guarantees, a contract between the citizens and the government - nobody knows what's in it. It's one of the best kept secrets. And so,
> **if you don't know what your rights are, how can you stand up for them?**
>
> Frank Zappa
> Spin Magazine, July 1991

Bushwacked: From Apples to Alzheimer's

As someone who voted for him twice and routinely defended his administration from partisan witch hunts, I find it disgraceful globalist George Bush took a silent knee for 8 long years as Barack Obama divided & dismantled America with reckless abandon – insidiously inciting a culture war against the Constitution, conservatives, Christians, police and even our historical heritage – only to suddenly find the nerve to join the media lynch mob unapologetically attempting to destroy Donald Trump by any means necessary. Sorry, George W., but the same conniving propagandists applauding your decision to suggest white supremacy is our President's burden to bear, let alone proliferating at all, also cursed your "failed and racist" tenure on a daily basis, organized monthly marches protesting a sanctioned campaign to overthrow a murderous tyrant, and even sought your removal from office by releasing fake memos disputing your military service. And despite what your selective memory may wish to believe, or foolishly convey, Barack Obama was by far our most divisive President ever because "bigotry" was not only emboldened under his stewardship, it was his modus operandi, the bane of his bitter existence, his conduit of social change through anarchist activism.

The fact a self-confessed Marxist steered this transcendent republic so unimaginably far left is exactly why so many liberals suddenly cannot fathom a President who rejects discrimination as a one-way street and staunchly refuses to surrender America's sovereignty to a globalist ideology that embraces the intolerant legacy of Islam, encourages the hostile exploitation of limitless immigration, breeds universal contempt for our laws, and justifies wealth redistribution (theft of earned property) as a form of reparations for historical inequities; or better yet, modern entitlement. Not only did Barack Obama fail the black community by choosing inflammatory rhetoric over responsibility – idle dependence in lieu of economic liberation, opportunity and urban gentrification – he funneled nearly every political issue and public event through a jagged lens of color, gender, sexual orientation and religion to solicit/galvanize a negative public reaction in order to distract from his own failures and radical aspirations.

The more we as a society acquiesce to "racial" grandstanding and the malicious media norm of false accusation, the more the real issues dividing and hindering this country are forever obscured by the functional fallout of identity politics; i.e., our ability to critically think independently, logically, and function as a nation predicated upon due process and limited government beyond the diversions of blame, stereotype or mass hysteria. When the "resistance" blueprint seeks to avoid individual accountability and never engage in substantive debate – acknowledging reality, not hyperbole, by accepting relevant points of contention instead of drowning dialogue in endless demagoguery – kneeling during the anthem becomes a celebrated fad, national security branded a form of white supremacy and every word spoken or decision made by Donald Trump is molded into a Red Light scandal of Right-Wing radicalism.

In other words, never mind jobless claims are at a 44-year-old low, the stock market has added over 5 trillion to the economy with repeated record highs, over 200 million in Executive waste has been eliminated, the DOJ is waging an unprecedented campaign against pedophilia and illegal immigration has dropped by over 70%, because only Hitler would want to lead a nation of proud, prosperous, law-abiding citizens against the clearly treasonous subversion of its founding charter. Until "We the People" can have an honest conversation about real issues without crass condescension and the malicious media manipulating every single detail for partisan gain – understand equality is not affirmative action or verbose millionaire athlete's ignoring the urban epidemic of absentee parents and systemic crime – the closer America comes to committing self-assisted suicide; a fate a number of morally twisted and financially bankrupt states like California would hail as a "progressive" milestone. If a house divided against itself cannot stand, neither can a propaganda state built upon victimization politics, spoon-fed anti-Americanism and a growing belief Government, and not God, is our salvation from the tyranny of a corrupted heart, illogical mind or regressive regime.

To Kill A Whistleblower

I'm not much of a conspiracy theorist for such accusations are typically rooted in knee-jerk paranoia and an insatiable desire to assume the worst about those we dislike or distrust. However, because human nature is as pernicious as it is inspiring, there are events that are deftly muddled by those guilty parties who purposely conflate the relevant details to bury the truth and discredit their accusers in the court of public opinion. That being said, if my close friend or fellow DNC staff member was murdered in cold blood – yes, Seth Rich's death was ruled a homicide by Washington D.C. police after being shot twice in the back – I would by no means seek a hasty conclusion to the case, obstruct justice or callously slander those who sought answers to very reasonable questions. Without truth, there can be no justice, and without justice, there is no acceptable resolution or closure for grieving loved ones. If this vibrant and popular man's death was merely a rogue crime, why didn't his assailants take any of his valuables? Over 80% of all violent crimes are motivated by theft or personal discord. Why did he suddenly die, before he could give a police statement, shortly after doctors performed successful, emergency surgery in which he was expected to live? And why didn't his superiors, whose response to such a horrific tragedy bordered more on stoic resignation than sorrowful outrage, immediately invoke a possible political motive being it occurred in the middle of a hotly contested campaign season? There is no party that loves to capitalize on the mere inference of scandal, expendable political capital to sway public opinion in an election year, more than the Democratic establishment itself. Their tepid reaction to such a senseless act, their continued desire to suppress information in this unresolved travesty, speaks almost as loudly as the absence of an arrest nearly a year later.

While these questions could either be quickly dismissed by provable, plausible explanations, or purposely left to linger due to the incriminating nature of such details, the answer to one remaining question, in my opinion, will literally spell the difference between conspiracy and untimely coincidence. If Seth Rich was the infamous source of the DNC email leaks, the insider who allowed Wikileaks to access their vulnerable servers, I have little doubt he was murdered in cold blood to seal a river of damning evidence and criminal behavior. From Hillary's smug messages degrading Latino's, blacks and Catholics, to rigging the DNC primaries with party officials to defeat Bernie Sanders and even her blatant collusion with the "unbiased" press to falsely accuse Donald Trump of sexual harassment, these leaks were so utterly damning that they splintered the Democratic base come election day and created a public relations firestorm her Presidential aspirations would not escape. It is no secret the Clintons have a lurid history of skillfully and viciously attacking those who dare cross or attempt to hold them accountable for a litany of lies and abuses; i.e., Bill's alleged rape victims, Vince Foster and the culturally eponymous Clinton body count. Likewise, Debbie Wasserman – a longtime Clinton ally and propagandist whose brother is also an assistant U.S. Attorney in Washington – was fired 18 days after Seth Rich's murder, or 2 days after the first leaked emails were released, but more profoundly as part of an obvious ploy to shift blame during an exploding Wikileaks scandal that further magnified Hillary's "corrupt" image and voter credibility issues. Yes, it doesn't take a Rhodes Scholar to connect the dots of suspicion and logically surmise that an ardent Bernie supporter within the DNC machine was targeted for attempting to expose a hopelessly compromised party. To quote the immortal

Shakespeare, "who profits" because honesty does not invite a platonic mix of power, money and politics.

I find it incredibly disconcerting the liberal media will chase Russian rainbows without refrain or discernible proof, only to ignore a very tangible trail of unexplained irregularities surrounding the extremely suspicious and brutal murder of one of their own party's operatives. There is a stark difference between sabotaging an incoming President simply because you disagree with his policies, and being slain for consciously exposing real corruption. Regardless of the outcome, or the inevitable political fallout, we must never forget a 27-year-old man who had a contagious lust for life and a clear love of politics was denied his future by a ruthless killer. Whether his death was a random act of violence and this is all baseless conjecture, or an orchestrated plot was hatched to silence dissention within the DNC, an unpunished murder is all that remains of a promising individual who may have died for simply trying to do the right thing. And if that doesn't deserve our undivided attention, if only for the sake of laying his soul to rest and restoring his family's peace of mind, nothing will acquit our conscience for failing to demand due diligence.

Tokyo Rose & the Wilting Memory of John McCain

> **John McCain** ✓
> @SenJohnMcCain
>
> More bad #Obamacare news: Arizonans will face premium hikes of 51-75% nxt yr - another indictment of this failed law
> mccain.senate.gov/public/index.c...
>
> 12:47 PM · Oct 19, 2016
>
> **403** Retweets   **266** Likes

Whether crawling through the ruddy trenches of the Western Front or speaking from the esteemed floor of the U.S. Senate, honor and integrity should ring equally true. Unfortunately for those American citizens currently drowning in the Congressional cesspool of broken vows, John McCain has become the epitome of a bitter obstructionist who will religiously contradict himself solely to spite anything the President endorses, touches or desires; regardless of the foreseeable consequences. The same outspoken critic of Obamacare who condemned its ill-conceived legislation on at least a dozen occasions, calling it an affront to our liberties and a wasteful burden on taxpayers that threatened the quality of our healthcare, has allowed his blind obsession with stonewalling Trump to sacrifice his own ideological principles and thus abandon his electoral obligation to Arizona voters, his fellow party members and most of all, the welfare of the American people. However, unlike many of my fuming friends who are disgusted by his increasingly calculated and shameless hypocrisy, I believe his selfish betrayal could be far more beneficial, dare I say educational, than simply repealing inept socialized medicine only to replace it months later with more bad government healthcare; that identical liberal leviathan the GOP so adamantly opposed a mere 6 years ago.

If 51 elected Senators refuse to accept the fact Obamacare is literally imploding as we speak, causing massive premium hikes and widespread cancellations of policies as more and more state exchanges drop their coverage entirely, so be it. Let it crash and burn and explode again until there is no one left to blame, no excuse left to hold, except the smoldering ashes of a grotesque lie told for the explicit purpose of achieving a morally bankrupt end. Yes, an elaborate ruse Obamacare architect Jonathan Gruber himself already confirmed and the socialist death panel of Charlie Gard brutally reaffirmed. Allow the people, once and for all, to realize how poorly construed Obamacare truly was and that its invention was never about affordable, compassionate medical care but rather a Trojan horse for a single-payer system designed solely to expand the control of government over our everyday lives.

For a man who willingly served his country and endured five horrific years of torture at the hands of the Viet Cong, it's disheartening to watch a once mutually respected presidential nominee so easily manipulated by sensationalist 'doomsday' propaganda and to consciously align himself with anti-American statists like George Soros, the Pivotal Foundation and the infamous Clintons themselves. While I wish Mr. McCain well and pray for his convalescence from brain cancer – a highly fatal condition too often uninsured for elderly Obamacare patients – I cannot extend such pleasantries for his wilting convictions, his paid vacation from reality and his reignited love for the opportunistic spotlight of public adulation; those hollow praises bestowed by the same miscreants who mock our veterans, country and values with insatiable regularity and callous indifference.

The Audacity of Soup Nazis

The day the government tries to tell me what to eat, i.e. no red meat, fried foods or sugar, is the day I show them how to conduct a successful colonoscopy with a watermelon. There are over 95 million citizens out of the workforce, unvetted illegal immigrants are streaming across the border, and Washington is worried about what's on my plate? Unbeknownst to Obama & Co. – who can't tell the truth to save their life and who refuse to take responsibility for a smorgasbord of failures and abuse – the Constitution is not a napkin and America was built upon a tasty little premise called individual liberty. Americans don't work 40 hours a week, sacrifice for their families and struggle to make ends meet so a clueless bureaucrat can tell them it's illegal to grill a steak or have a burger at their favorite restaurant. If "meat is murder", then what the hell is abortion?

Whether you're a 300-pound video game addict or a world class triathlete, no one has the right to strip you of free will: NO ONE. Life is full of choices and those choices have consequences...for better or for worse. Progressivism is not about the efficacy of meat nor has it ever been about healthcare; it's about control. They live for any opportunity to confiscate every aspect of your life. Remember, these are the same hypocrites who don't have the time to read the bill (or care to) and who tirelessly conspire to silence dissension in a nation predicated on freedom. Just because the loony left thinks meat is murder and a vegan lifestyle will save the planet doesn't mean you need to dawn a straitjacket to be spoon-fed the truth: Michelle Obama is not a dietician and gutter water is not soup! The same government that can't balance its checkbook, or call ISIS a threat, wants you to believe abortion is kosher and EBT cards should be used at Red Lobster. I don't need to jump off a cliff to discover gravity doesn't vote, bullshit doesn't float and a steak tastes better after an honest day's work. Check, please!

Racists, Radicals and A House of Ill Repute

After only several months into their contentious, dysfunctional terms, here's what "We the People" have learned about the despotic trio of celebrated Democratic freshman...

Rashida Tlaib, the American-born daughter of Palestinian immigrants, and Alexandria Ocasio-Cortez, a New York descendant of her mother's native Puerto Rico, concealed and misreported their true physical residences to gain favor with voters and win their respective Congressional districts. Tlaib fraudulently registered her father's Detroit address as her official residence despite living in Dearborn, Michigan with her husband and son. Cortez touted her blue collar, Bronx upbringing, despite growing-up in a Yorktown suburb of Westchester County and later attending Boston University. Since 2012, she listed her deceased father's Bronx address on her voter registration card as her legal residence. In 2017, the vagabond bartender didn't even know what district she lived in; mistakenly declaring her intentions to run for New York's 15th Congressional District.

Ilhan Omar apparently married her bother, Ahmed Nur Said Elmi, to help him gain American citizenship as a British national; her 2009 marriage certificate marked her "husband's" date of birth as the same as her biological brother's...April 4, 1985. And all this in lieu of the fact Ilhan already partook in a "community marriage" with the father of her three children, Ahmed Hirsi, in 2002, and her 2016 campaign literature listed Elmi as her current husband even though they permanently "split" in 2011, without an official divorce, before she had another child with Hirsi in 2012. The Minnesota representative has been tied to multiple anti-Semitic groups, she has publicly renounced any allegiance to America, or any country for that matter, and has urged her Islamic constituents to resist cultural assimilation.

Ocasio-Cortez and Rashida Tlaib have also made anti-Semitic slurs, including criminal threats against private citizens who have questioned their radical viewpoints and socialist policies, elected Republicans who mock their pompous ignorance, as well as fellow Democrats who dare break party lines during legislative votes.

Rashida Tlaib illegally used campaign funds to pay herself a $45,000 salary after the 2018 election, while Ocasio-Cortez and her Chief of Staff, Saikat Chakrabarti, funneled roughly $900,000 in campaign donations into two of his private management firms, Brand New Congress LLC and Brand New Campaign LLC. Chakrabarti used these private "consulting" organizations to support aspiring progressive politicians, but more significantly to skirt the traditional reporting requirements of Political Action Committees which require itemizing all revenue/expenditures. According to Tom

Anderson, Director of the National Legal & Policy Center's Government Integrity Project, "In all my years of studying FEC reports, I've never seen a more ambitious operation to circumvent reporting requirements."

Muslim Democrats Pictured With America-Hating, Anti-Semitic Muslim Brotherhood Sympathizer Linda Sarsour on First Day in Office

All three of these combative, anti-American extremists have urged the impeachment of President Trump for Russian collusion, obstruction of justice, abuse of power and for refusing to divulge his private, legally-filed tax returns. The Democratic House is currently poised to waste millions of dollars and countless brain cells by hosting a non-stop, national inquisition to investigate "all things" Trump over the next two years. Why? Instead of honoring their Constitutional oath and serving the best interests of this country – including exposing those corrupt Obama\Clinton officials who manipulated the judicial process and colluded with the media in a vast, treasonous plot to overturn an election result – their incorrigible ranks would rather besmirch, demonize, and slander a highly-successful, populist leader solely to improve their party's presidential prospects in 2020.

If I may, what sane, loyal civil servant wouldn't put "America first" in the face of such blatant deception, rabid hostility and unapologetic corruption? Generations of progressive indoctrination is crippling our public institutions' desire and capacity to punish real malfeasance, let alone to simply acknowledge the obvious systemic perversion of our most fundamental checks and balances. The American people, those everyday workers and families held to a separate standard of justice and acceptable behavior, deserve so much better.

A Date with Infamy

Just so we're clear, an overwhelming majority of the progressive establishment, media, and Democratic Party now believes nearly all Republican candidates and conservative judges are racist, sexist, homophobic bigots who at some time or another have sexually harassed, beaten or raped a woman. America has officially become a propaganda state of gutter politics where civic duty – rational thought, due process, tolerance and decorum – is being systematically dismantled beneath the comforting lie of "love and progress". Liberty, a Constitutional democracy of inalienable rights, cannot survive in a perpetual vacuum of hostile inquisition where the wrongfully accused are somehow judged by the very conspirators concealing and distorting the truth to demand submission to an archaic agenda based upon unilateral rule. Likewise, "We the People" cannot coexist in a decaying banana republic where the rewarded ploys of false accusation successfully substitute paranoia and hate for the presumption of innocence and the once afforded dignity of mutual respect. When the simplest, most routine matters descend into a carpet-bombing campaign of acceptable collateral damage, civility is always the first casualty of war. The more partisan identity zealots defame and demonize intellectual dissension regardless of the consequences or the means, the further America fades into the obscurity of historical infamy.

Crazy, Crooked, Creeper

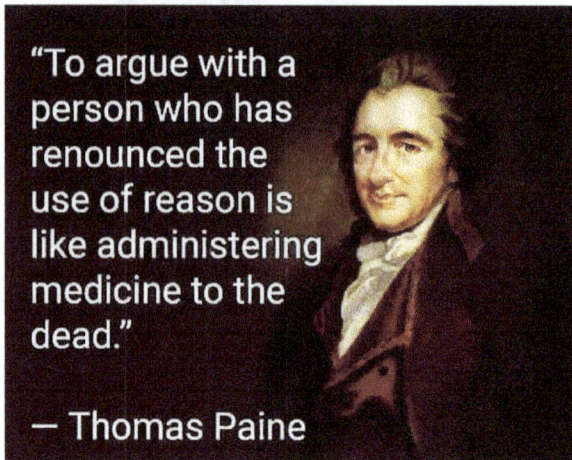

"To argue with a person who has renounced the use of reason is like administering medicine to the dead."

— Thomas Paine

If anyone needs a psychological exam, Maxine, I suggest testing the mental health of the man who has been stalking Donald Trump around the globe and operating under the delusion he is still president: one Barack Hussein Obama. The very same megalomaniac who became the first American leader to wiretap a Presidential candidate and his newly selected administration, also empowered his remaining staff within the Executive branch to leak classified information with no regard for national security. As for Mrs. Waters, she proved long ago that psychological distress and progressivism are one in the same by asking why the CIA only sells Crack in black neighborhoods. Hmm, forgive my Johnny Cash but my guess is because the "CIA" was purposely placed and misspelled on speed dial to better patronize, dare I say victimize, all those non-white voters illegally profiled and bribed with free Obama phones at taxpayer expense. Or, in your own words, did I just pull a "360" on you, Congresswoman? Apparently, mathematics, just like "the truth", isn't your friend either.

The Kettle & The Tea Pot

It's hard enough to restore America's founding premise when Barack Obama is allowed to act with such reckless impunity, but it becomes exponentially more improbable when your supposed "friends" help perpetuate the same shameless lies devised by their scheming pallbearers. Yes, I'm deeply appalled by those Republicans who are attacking conservatives, the ideological bastion this nation was founded upon and the liberating force to end human bondage, by joining the progressive chorus labeling the Tea Party as racist and radical. If that's true, I must be a KKK member, a Constitutional terrorist and a grave threat to everyone's life. Simply absurd! Sorry but the Tea Party is largely made up of old Reaganites, independent libertarians and even a few disenfranchised JFK Democrats who feel betrayed by the GOP and are sick and tired of their incessant capitulation to the left's divisive, anti-American agenda. It's funny how the Tea Party, their unapologetic populist platform, was accredited for spearheading historic wins in 2010 and 2014, only for our ranks to be cast aside as undesirables during Romney's embarrassing defeat in 2012 and now once again on the eve of 2016. The difference between the Tea Party and the GOP is that only one is willing to stop Barack Obama's destructive and unconstitutional power grab, while the Republican establishment merely wants to utilize it for a campaign slogan as Boehner and McConnell repeatedly bend to his will beneath the politically correct ruse of "compromise, progress and unity". If that makes us radicals and racist, so be it! In the meantime, I'm going to fly Old Glory, pray for this Republic and read a little more Thomas Sowell! And by the way, so should you!

A Blueprint for Disaster

I'm frequently asked what can be done to save America from this rising tide of radical progressivism. Other than reforming our educational system, producing more right-minded teachers, tirelessly debunking Fake News, investing in alternative sources of mass media, registering new party members and voting as if our life depended on it, the best advice I can give is for conservatives in hopelessly liberal states – California, New York, Illinois, Oregon, etc. – to relocate to Texas, Florida, Ohio, Pennsylvania, Michigan and Arizona. Elections are number games, especially to scheming leftists, which is exactly why Barack Obama opened the floodgates to Islamic "refugees" and slowed deportations of illegals from Central/South America. Once Texas turns Blue, a Republican will likely never win the presidency again and a massive wave of immigration, followed by blanket amnesty and socialism, will inevitably ensue. That's why Democrats are spending obscene amounts of cash to demographically and ideologically terraform traditionally Red strongholds. This is also why apathy and lack of voter turnout are simply unacceptable. Every lapsed second apathy disavows our pledge to defend our way of life, our constitutional charter for a limited and transparent government, is another waking moment "Organizing for Action" spends unraveling the remaining threads of liberty, justice and the American flag.

> **Jacob Wohl** @JacobAWohl
>
> Barack Obama literally has a "war room" inside his multi-million dollar mansion where plots to undermine the country — Valerie Jarrett also lives there rent-free

A Political Racket

Although I'm obviously a staunch conservative, I unequivocally despise the two-party system: it's destructive, wasteful, and reduces the absolute necessity of constructive problem solving into an incessant tug-of-war that is obsessed with partisan supremacy rather than sound decision making. There is nothing democratic or progressive about legalized monopolies and untouchable, career politicians. If I had the authority, I would abolish all political parties, end political action committees, permanently ban lobbyists, enact term limits and place a strict limitation on campaign fundraising and spending. Squandering $5 billion dollars on midterm races when America has homeless citizens, an eroding infrastructure, an epidemic of illegal immigration and a glaring need for educational reform is irresponsible and simply unacceptable. Elections should be about ideas, competing convictions, not hoarded slush funds of mass manipulation. People must once again learn to think for themselves instead of becoming willingly brainwashed by media propagandists and corrupt, self-serving bureaucrats who are grossly enriching themselves in lieu of faithfully serving this Constitutional Republic.

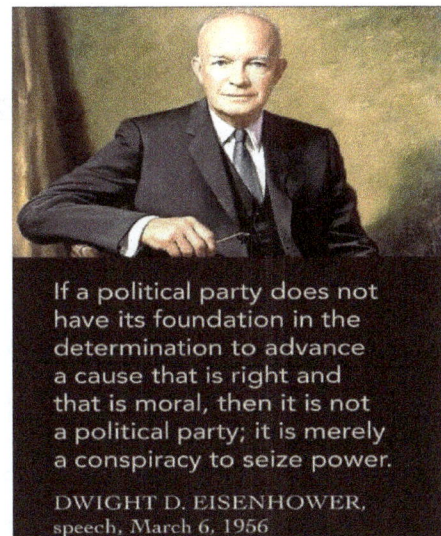

> If a political party does not have its foundation in the determination to advance a cause that is right and that is moral, then it is not a political party; it is merely a conspiracy to seize power.
>
> DWIGHT D. EISENHOWER, speech, March 6, 1956

"When the law doesn't apply to the lawmakers, you're no longer being governed; you're being ruled."

Like Father, Like Son

When you're unanimously indicted by a Grand Jury on 16 felony charges, and your co-conspirators provide investigators with proof of payment and how you instructed them to perpetuate a staged hate crime with recently purchased supplies, the only way such brazen criminality never goes to trial is if the local prosecutor is corrupt, racially biased and/or bribed by the whispered promise of future partisan favors. And that's exactly the case with Cook County Attorney General, Kim Foxx, who along with Jussie Smollett has close personal ties with the social engineers of racial injustice: Kamala Harris and her notorious Marxist mentors, the conniving Obama's themselves. And yes, lest we forget the ambitious young lawyer's ascendancy to power was paved with over $400,000 in PAC money donated by none other than George Soros, the infamous Western agitator and globalist pimp.

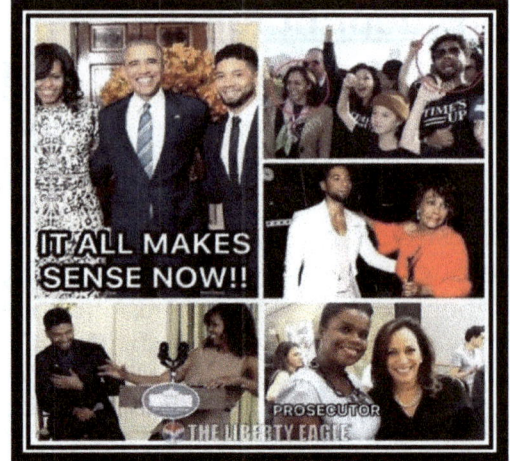

The fact a known celebrity activist was allowed to walk free for the forfeited principle of his bond and his vast 18 hours of "community service", despite the fact a black Police Superintendent spent weeks documenting irrefutable evidence and damning interviews, is nothing short of criminal collusion and a clear dereliction of duty. After all, the moment progressive lightning rod and Chicago Mayor Rahm Emanuel joins the public chorus of irate taxpayers, calling Foxx's decision an obvious "whitewash of justice", the fix is hardly amiss. Imagine the sheer outrage if a famous white conservative was completely exonerated after falsely accusing leftist minorities of brutally attacking him – wasting hundreds of man hours and potentially inciting widespread civil unrest – only to smugly mock the police, the press and any political pundit who dared question his "innocence" and that of his hired assailants. Oh, the audacity of hopeless narcissists!

Excuse my jurisprudence, but what "average Joe" is suddenly summoned to an "emergency" court hearing for the unprecedented dismissal of such extensive, publicized charges? From the treasonous Russia hoax to the Kavanaugh confirmation circus and now the Avenatti extortion plot, the Democratic crime syndicate is proving boundaries are for the well-intentioned. If federal authorities do not thoroughly investigate Ms. Foxx for legal misconduct and prosecute Smollett for felony mail fraud after sending himself a fraudulent toxic substance, then the "Chicago way" is the mattress tag line for the newest racial farce, "If Obama Had A Gay Son". As long as the Empire drama queen remains unpunished for his malicious efforts to demonize Trump supporters and solicit national sympathy to financially resurrect his sagging Limp-Biscuit career, he should at least be given the first annual Louis Farrakhan "Nazi Victim Hoax" Award for single-handedly destroying the myth of "white privilege" in an armed black neighborhood.

BARACK OBAMA

America Has Hit BARACK BOTTOM

A State of Delusion

If you may, Mr. President, please tell us...in explicit factual detail...how you've personally restored prosperity, security, unity and justice to this racist, Christian and capitalistic country! How many "record" number of Americans are now out of the workforce? How have welfare recipients jumped from 27 million to 47 million since 2008? Black unemployment is high how and black home ownership is how low? Who increased the national debt by nearly twice that of all other Presidents combined? GDP growth is how anemic; having never surpassed 3% annualized growth during your tenure and rivaling what destitute communist neighbor? Which self-professed "common man of the people" has proposed nearly 500 new taxes on businesses, hospitals and hard-working taxpayers since taking office? How many billion is the FED illicitly pumping into this paper machete economy each month?

Because misery loves Death Panels and pathological liars, how many jobs and working hours have been lost to Obamacare regulations, forcing employers to opt for part-time workers instead? Who lied to pass socialized healthcare, stripping millions of the right to keep their physician and insurance policy of choice? How many non-citizens are receiving Obamacare free of charge, while our veterans die waiting for inept and indifferent healthcare? How many illegal immigrants have poured across our borders in the past 7 years? How many unvetted Syrian refugees did you smuggle into our communities under the cover of night? How much of taxpayer money have you spent resettling and providing public assistance for both immigrant populations?

Despite knowing damn well Islam poses the greatest danger to the civilized world, why did you call ISIS a JV team only to order the DHS to list "liberty lovers" as the greatest terrorist threat in America: a country predicated upon individual liberty? Why have you declared war on Christians and their religious liberties, while downplaying or flat ignoring the atrocities and human rights abuses committed by Muslims against women, gays, and non-believers? Why did you give Iran – a radical Islamic state that vows daily to destroy America and Israel – billions in aid and a green-light to build a nuclear arsenal? Why would any elected President release known terrorists from Gitmo, consciously trading a known deserter for 5 Islamic militants, allowing them yet another opportunity to kill innocent Americans? Why has your administration chosen to only adjudicate and politicize white-on-black crime, even though African Americans account for 50% of all murders and robberies, as well as for 7,000 black-on-black homicides annually: by far the greatest source of violence and injustice perpetrated against the black community? How does the imaginary right of 'transgender' individuals to select the restroom of their choice, the perverse psychosis of less than .01% of society, supersede the privacy and safety of women and little girls, as well as the rights of parents to shield their children from gender identity conditioning in taxpayer-funded schools? Exactly why have you repeatedly exceeded your executive powers by disregarding the Constitution, the supreme law of the land and a strict limitation on government authority, to blatantly trample on individual and state's rights?

And lastly, why is the self-confessed, anti-American duo of Barack Obama and Valerie Jarrett, two individuals with FBI documented communist and radical Islamic ties, allowed anywhere near the Oval office – the pinnacle of our trust and liberties – let alone allowed to operate with impunity in the highest levels of our government? Perhaps the "how" and "why" no longer matter when the "who" leaves no doubt as to your true intentions. Congratulations, Mr. President, you've almost single-handedly made America a more vulnerable, impoverished, ignorant and divided nation. Apparently "treason doth prosper" when neither the people or the truth does.

A LIBERAL is someone who feels a great debt to society; which he proposes to pay off WITH YOUR MONEY!

Cry Me A Communist Love Song

The minute a sitting U.S. President cites Communist China – a ruthless regime that has stripped countless innocents of their life, rights and due process – as the pinnacle paradigm of his gun confiscation utopia, is the second you realize that individual is completely devoid of rational thought or any hint of respect. If you need to shed an obligatory tear on national TV for those speech props you couldn't name or ever wept for before, while failing to shed one tear for the victims of black-on-white violence selectively ignored by the media, let alone the endless barrage of black homicides occurring in gun control havens like Chicago and Washington, D.C., it's probably because your grieving "racist" heart knows damn well that if dishonesty achieves your Marxist dream of disarming the people, then the wrongful end most definitely justifies the corrupt means.

Yes, the same narcissistic, anti-American sociopath who lied to you about Obamacare – who proclaimed it wasn't a tax, the Affordable Act was affordable, and you could keep your physician – believes he has the unilateral authority to use government stamped doctors, blatantly violating your 'freedom to choose' and existing HIPAA laws in the process, to determine your proper "political state" of mind. Naturally our hero of humanitarianism forgot to mention 34 times more people registered for a gun license last month than Obamacare. Just make sure to mark "yes" when asked if Global Warming causes terrorism or if Donald Trump is the white devil who single-handedly destroyed the Ozone with hairspray. Truth, dare I say free speech, will not be tolerated!

If our safety and well-being is the ultimate goal of progressives, too bad these life-saving executive protocols weren't employed when the White House gave the terrorist state known as Iran billions in aid, a green light to forge a nuclear arsenal, while arming radical Syrian rebels, or when federal officials transported over 100,000 unvetted Muslim refugees into America since 2012 under the cover of night. After all, it's not like 9/11 and the Boston bombing, the attacks on Fort Hood, Chattanooga and San Bernardino, ever happened or involved bypassed Jihadists. In other words, voter ID laws and universal background checks for immigrants are overtly racist and far too arduous of a task, but extensive security checks on law-abiding Americans is easily achieved and sorely needed; as if the IRS ever forgets the name of one out of over 300 million Americans with unpaid taxes!

What will be fully visible, however, is the fact conservatives and patriotic Americans, pre-selected by a federal database of targeted political enemies, just like those railroaded by the IRS and Louis Lerner, will be singled out for a comprehensive mental evaluation and mandatory monitoring by the DHS. So basically, if you have ever been depressed (like any normal human being), ever entertained the slightest notion of an angry thought (like any normal human being would) or you ever harbored a negative feeling about Barack Obama and his lawless regime (like any rational human being should), you will be marked as a tangible threat to society for purely "objective" reasons. And lest we forget...these are the same people who declared liberty lovers, Christian conservatives, as the greatest domestic threat in America: A Constitutional republic predicated upon individual liberty, limited government and conservative ideals.

How does liberty die? Not by a gunshot or an imaginary firearm purchased by a violent felon over the internet without a background check, but to the thunderous applause of ignorant voters blinded by the executive pen of a pathological propagandist. I suppose "We the People" should be thankful his weeping conscience didn't have the safety on!

A "Good & Terrible" President

Barack Obama: *"I've been a pretty good President and would probably win a third term. I'm proud my administration was scandal free."*

If this statement is inherently true, then perhaps our Harvard graduate would like to explain these rather dubious distinctions...

- A record 95 million Americans are unemployed and workforce participation is at a paltry 62%; the lowest since Jimmy Carter. A record 14.5 million have dropped out of the workforce since 2008 and are no longer counted in the unemployment equation.

- Welfare recipients have skyrocketed from 28 to 47 million in nearly 6 years.

- The national debt has risen by over 9 trillion since 2009 – nearly doubling all the amount accrued by other Presidents combined – and now encompasses 100% of our yearly GDP. During this same time period, the US hasn't enjoyed a single annualized GDP of 3%; the longest such drought since the Great Depression.

- Median household income has dropped by over $3,000 and 40% of all Americans have less than $3,000 in total savings. Black home and business ownership are at their lowest levels in over 25 years.

- The Federal Reserve is pumping 40 billion a month into our markets to give the illusion of a vibrant and solvent economy. The US currently boasts a $50 billion monthly trade deficit which will only be exasperated by the passing of TPP. Business closings now outpace business openings and the government is outpacing the private sector in job creation.

- Solyndra, the California-based solar company that received $535 million in federal loan guarantees from the Obama administration, went bankrupt after being touted during the 2012 election as a beacon of clean energy and a sterling model for all future "green" enterprises. Not one dollar of taxpayer money has yet to be recovered in the name of progressive nepotism.

- The White House proclaimed Obamacare wasn't a tax; only to go before the Supreme Court and argue it as a mandatory penalty (tax) under the Interstate Commerce Act. The President claimed every American could keep their existing insurance policies, even their preferred doctor, and yet that was another complete fabrication; millions lost both. The Affordable Care Act is anything but affordable for insurance rates have risen by an average of 41% and in some cases by more than 150%. Estimated to cost taxpayers over one trillion per year, if not their individual liberty of "choice", the socialist leviathan known as Obamacare is exactly what millions feared it to be: a Trojan horse for an eventual single-payer healthcare system.

- In what became known as the Fast and Furious scandal, President Obama invoked 'Executive Privilege" and then Attorney General Eric Holder was held in contempt for knowingly using the ATF to provide high-powered firearms to Mexican drug cartels. The "gunwalking" program resulted in the death of Border Patrol Agent Brian Terry along with hundreds of Mexican citizens killed by native crime lords and drug cartels.

- Despite being warned by both our intelligence community and Ambassador Christopher Stevens of an impending attack, Barack Obama and Hillary Clinton took no action as Islamic militants stormed the consulate and killed four Americans. As the siege was underway, both the President and then Secretary of State Clinton ordered the military to stand down and to effectually "let them die" due to fear of upsetting Muslim sentiment in the region. Ambassador Stevens was tortured, beaten, raped and burned for hours.

- The Obama administration ordered and conspired with IRS Director Lois Lerner to target, fabricate charges whenever possible, and wrongfully prosecute conservatives as a means to punish the President's political opponents. Thousands of 'deleted' emails have yet to be accounted for and no arrests have been made.

- Race relations are at their lowest point in over 50 years. The White House has incited racial animosity, fueled urban violence, selectively exploited race-based tragedy and swept 50 years of failed Democratic policies under the rug to deflect from the rampant crime, poverty, broken families and general apathy destroying the black community. Roughly 7,000 black homicides are committed by their brethren annually and not one murder involved a Confederate flag or a white cop. Police account for roughly 200 black deaths a year or approximately less than half the average number of Caucasians gunned down in the line of duty.

- Millions of medically and criminally unvetted illegals - openly solicited by our government, transported to cities across America and given federal benefits at taxpayer expense as part of the left's electoral schemes - are streaming across our borders while the Obama Administration has ordered the DHS and INS not to arrest and/or deport a majority of these trespassers: those whose crimes rates are 5 times greater than their representative population, whom account for 1,200,000 crimes a year, commit more than 2,100 murders per year, and are responsible for over 130,000 sexual crimes annually. There are currently 500,000 unaccounted for illegal alien criminals with outstanding deportation orders. At least one fourth of these are hard core criminals. Washington currently spends more per illegal immigrant than the average US citizen or Social Security recipient.

- Christian churches, pastors and entrepreneurs are being targeted and prosecuted for nothing more than exercising their religious liberty and honoring America's founding Judeo-Christian values – a Biblical opposition to abortion, gender identity conditioning and gay marriage – while the radical left advocates the hateful and violent tenets of Sharia Law by orchestrating lawsuits and public relations campaigns to fight for their implementation.

- Planned Parenthood, funded by our government and the crowning jewel in Hilary Clinton's platform of women's rights, has been illegally preserving and selling the body parts of healthy aborted babies via the underground railroad of medical malpractice. Planned Parenthood kills more black children in one month than the KKK lynched in nearly one century – 3,446 – and was founded by Hillary Clinton's personal hero, Margaret Sanger: a vocal racist and Nazi sympathizer.

- As the infamous "JV team" our golfing President cannot develop a "varsity" strategy to defeat, ISIS continues to act with reckless impunity across the Middle East. Christians are being systematically exterminated, while women and children are being tortured, raped, and beheaded by the religion of 'peace'. The DHS has confirmed ISIS agents have infiltrated our cities and communities, while thousands of unvetted Syrian refugees are being transported all across this nation.

- In 2015, The EPA attempted to cover up its own environmental disaster after releasing three million gallons of toxic pollutants from a Colorado mine into the Animas River, failing to properly warn state officials, and even refusing to pay for any damages caused by their negligence. The Obama administration also hid research data debunking the need for the adopted Ozone Rule.

- During his tenure, mass shootings in America have increased by over 300% while terrorist acts against the U.S. have more than tripled.

- The White House freed $150 billion in financial assets frozen by Jimmy Carter during the Iran Hostage Crisis, sent $1.7 billion in unauthorized cash, secretly granted citizenship to 2,500 high ranking Iranian officials, and pledged assistance necessary to develop nuclear arms in a "reasonable" timeframe. The President, a well-known anti-Semite and Muslim supporter, claims he has single-handedly prevented a nuclear Iran – those whom chant death to Israel & America on a daily basis – by ensuring they have money, expertise, and support necessary to do so.

"I didn't have scandals."
—Former President Barack Obama

Barack Obama hasn't been a good President; he's been a great propagandist. In any other era of semi-sanity and self-respect, he would have been identified as a domestic terror threat by the FBI, charged with treason, and/or the subject of a documentary detailing the radical rise of modern day Communism – the proud descendants of a failed, oppressive and murderous ideology – who have vowed to destroy America and destabilize the world in the name of social justice. Apparently "good" has an alternative definition in the modern pantheon of 'progressive' thinkers.

The Color of Hate

Will someone please inform our so-called President it's not 1860 and that neither him or Michelle Obama have ever been slaves. Even at the height of slavery during the Antebellum period, less than 2% of the population owned slaves; which by the way, included black Americans among their infamous ranks. This of course is omitting the trivial facts African tribes sold their brethren into bondage for everyday trinkets and that nearly 400,000 white men died to procure their freedom. In fact, of the 12.5 million slaves originating from Africa, roughly 388,000 were transported to America while 4.8 million were imported by Portugal to largely toil in Brazilian gold mines. Yes, Brazil! I'm also guessing our myopic pastor of prejudice forgot that the KKK was specifically forged as the terrorist arm of the Democratic Party, to dissuade blacks from voting, and that more Republicans voted for every civil rights bill, from the Emancipation Proclamation to the Civil Rights Act of 1964; a historic piece of legislation Al Gore Sr. voted against long after Dwight Eisenhower – an old, white, conservative Army brat – desegregated the military. Apropos, it was the Constitution, and not the flawed practices of any time period or the modern-day propaganda of a political party, that provided the blueprint to overcome society's most daunting challenges and glaring justices.

Instead of dividing America with endless race-baiting, history revisionism and victimization propaganda to further his failed and radical politics – inciting a war on police while ignoring the disproportionate levels of black crime, violence and absentee parents – perhaps Mr. Obama would be better served by devoting his time and energy to addressing the proliferation of urban decay, the exploding opioid crisis in nearly every American community, the skyrocketing rates of insurance premiums under Obamacare, the absurd 50 billion-dollar monthly trade disparity, and the countless unvetted refugees the Department of Homeland Security is smuggling into cities all across America…at his behest and at taxpayer expense. If White Privilege is the modern equivalency of racism, Barack Obama is undoubtedly the progressive pimp of poverty. After all, how many slaves have the keys to the White House, a private jet and an open invitation to every prestigious golf course across this country?

The next time the President and the First Lady feel unappreciated – the supposed racist targets of white, Judeo-Christian scorn – I suggest they travel back in time and shackle themselves to the mast of the Amistad so they can get the best view of their hypocrisy on their journey towards self-anointed martyrdom. Pretending to be a victim to further a political agenda, inciting endless division and discord to deflect blame, has nothing to do with being a leader, let alone a sentient human being. It simply means you're perfectly content feeding off the immutable pain of those who truly suffered at the hands of real injustice because you're a racist who still cannot define "liberty" in the year 2016. It means people continue to die over skin color, the sacrificed pawns of your incessant scheming and prodding, because you are so utterly blinded by its galvanizing allure; or more profoundly, its perceived gain. How else could the vile practice of human trafficking currently plaguing Asia, Africa and the Middle East mysteriously evade your sterling moral compass for human suffering? Oh, that's right, you can't blame white America which is now the modern-day prerequisite for constituting a tragedy. Somehow the historical stigma of evil, a clear and racist indifference for mass servitude, doesn't translate in the keen minds of today's social justice warriors.

The key to overcoming discrimination isn't by denying its existence or pigeonholing one sect of society as the singular embodiment of hate. The answer is realizing that every race, creed and color harbors racist tendencies and that everyone must tirelessly work together to eradicate or disprove these fears. Is racial injustice, regardless of era or circumstance, wrong? Absolutely. Is it justifiable to blame and slander present generations for the transgressions of the past when no living soul has practiced or been victimized by slavery in America for over 150 years? Absolutely not. I just never imagined America's first, black President would be the biggest hypocrite of all! Refusing to appreciate and protect the litany of opportunities America affords all people, the very liberties so many were wrongfully denied in the annals of history, makes you nothing less than the proud slave owner of peace, progress, and prosperity. No, you're not a man or a leader of men in any sense of the word, Mr. President. You're a bigot, a liar, a fraud, a tool of ignorance, a petulant child, and most of all, the sole product of your own disgrace. And just in case you lost track, that makes you the enemy of truth, justice, and this American Republic.

The Czar of Kiev

With Barack Obama it's always about appearances, rarely truth, and that's exactly why he levied sanctions and expelled Russian diplomats...to feed the baseless lie foreign agents violated the integrity of our elections, specifically targeted the DNC's private apparatus, and therefore somehow stole the presidency for Donald Trump. As usual, Barry's ultimate goal is to give credence to a false narrative that would undermine Trump's authority, populist support, and thus hopefully incite voter outrage in 2018 and 2020. When all else fails, the President of the United States, the supposed dignified leader of the free world, proves himself to be a spiteful child bent on widening existing divisions and justifying further discord because America rejected the failed status quo: his indefensible record of blame and betrayal. Because propaganda hates precedent, did Mr. "Hope and Change" expel known jihadists from America, let alone ambassadors from known terrorist nations, after importing and welcoming those who despise our very existence and way of life? While we're on the subject of electoral sovereignty, why didn't our principled leader admonish, punish or expel DNC operatives for colluding with Hillary to defeat Bernie in the Democratic primaries? Better yet, why did three states catch the Department of Homeland Security trying to hack their servers on election day? And lastly, where was his unwavering concern and decisive call to action when the media admitted conspiring with Hillary to rig the debates, to slander Trump with a preposterous number of unproven sexual assault allegations, and whose reckless attempts to paint him as the reincarnation of Hitler resulted in violence and discriminatory acts against his supporters across America?

When only select lives matter and the truth is the political equivalent of Play-Doh, your inner sociopath lives in an imaginary world where Russians steal elections from corrupt, pathological liars and your hateful, anti-American legacy is under siege by bigoted, white,

Christian extremists who believe in the treasonous ideals of limited government, transparency, free speech, legal immigration, accountability, and duty. For a man who wasted $85 million on personal vacations, exported more jobs than Islamic martyrs and pleaded with college graduates to ignore those paranoid voices warning of government tyranny, reality is about as relevant as a Muslim 'refugee' wearing a Che Guevara t-shirt while demanding free tuition, the right to vote, Sharia Law, and a safe space in every building or city block to pray for the destruction of America without the interference of intolerant, Trump voting nationalists. In other words, the absurdity of a lie is only surpassed by the ignorance required to protect it: i.e., selectively reporting the race of police shootings, fabricating inflammatory hate crimes for votes or deleting the damning details of a nuclear agreement once hailed as a seismic victory for world peace. Obviously the most effective strategy to fight "fake news", also known as self-incrimination in media circles, is to master the liberal performance art of deflection: a partisan process of enrichment, mass deception, in which you magically acquit yourself but simultaneously convict all whistle-blowers as "fake" sources by simply pointing a single, solitary finger of blame. Call it a preemptive strike for the post-departed alibi, or better yet...grade school in 1960 Kiev. In the case of our pious and pontificating President, only Hollywood could write such complete, utter bullshit and only the lapdog media could bury the unadulterated truth without choking on their own pungent contempt for our intelligence and welfare.

The Target of Choice

Barack Obama: *"You don't defeat ideologies like ISIS with guns; rather with "better ideas".*

Did pacifists with "better ideas" defeat the Japanese Empire or Nazi Germany: schizophrenic jingoism that slaughtered 2,400 Americans at Pearl Harbor, exterminated 6 million Jews and accounted for over 20 million Russian casualties? Did "better ideas" stop Saddam Hussein from gassing thousands of Kurds, ravaging Kuwait, or indiscriminately sending missiles into the Israeli populace? Did it prevent 9/11 and save 3,000 innocent lives...the worst terrorist attack in our nation's history? No? I'm all for dispelling a culture of hate, reforming a bloodthirsty plague on humanity, but considering Islam has remained the same murderous cult since its inception 1500 years ago, that's not going to happen. If "common sense" Muslims have yet to rise up, condemn and reform the radicalism killing their own families, their own native countries, they simply never will. In other words, ISIS is Islam. The only reason those Muslims living in the United States, the same misunderstood souls who routinely shout "Death to America" in our own background, have yet to commit mass atrocities is out of fear of retaliation; i.e., men and women with guns and a zero tolerance for the rabid dogs of tyranny.

And yet it is men like you, Mr. President, politicians armed with "better ideas", whom have threatened Christian pastors and bakers with lawsuits and incarceration, carried out by agents with guns, if they fail to accept the immoral tenets of homosexuality or refuse to embrace gay marriage out of respect for their faith. How convenient being "principled" progressives have made no such request of Muslims or Mosques, whose defiance is merely pardoned as a matter of religious liberty or steadfast reverence. Correct me if I wrong, but did ISIS not just behead 72 children and throw four gay men off a rooftop in broad daylight? If only your concern for real injustice and historical precedence gave you the "better idea" to ban the ISIS flag and outlaw Sharia Law to protect future American lives from Islam's undeniable legacy of death. Perhaps your justifiable apathy, your intrinsic call to peace and love, will convince the LGBT community to bake them a cake and personable deliver it as an international peace offering. Then again, I'm willing to bet not even your "non-existent" Muslim sympathies are that hopelessly ignorant. You can't deny history or pander to murders, Mr. President – soulless scavengers who feed off the civilized corpses of humanity's indulgence – you can only hope to eradicate them. It's just too bad your hatred of guns ends at the same point you're pointing them at the object of your true disdain: America.

A Marxist, A Calculator & A Comedian Walk into A Bar

If you've ever played the shell game – one ball and three half coconuts – then you understand the entire charade behind this so-called economic recovery: deception. Let me introduce you to subtraction, addition's tricky friend! According to astute celebrities like Chris Rock, only in America could a black President lower the unemployment rate to less than 6%, reduce the price of gas to $2.50 a gallon, end two wars – despite accounting for 75% of all casualties and using the exact same timetable as George Bush – and still somehow be considered a failure. Hmm, well that depends on whether or not our color-coded jokester flunked math, bought women drinks with their own money, wore a pirated Che Guevara t-shirt or confused Civics class with his cousin's repossessed ride.

When 1 + 1 = 3, truth is only as relevant as the name of the IRS seizing your home. In other words, the end justifies the means. Today the Bureau of Labor Statistics announced that unemployment has fallen to a respectable 5.3%; the lowest rate in Barack Obama's tenure. Unfortunately for both reverse mortgage and Sudoku enthusiasts, the media excluded one teensy-weensy detail; nearly half a million Americans dropped out of the workforce in June alone. Although roughly 223,000 jobs were added, 432,000 Americans crashed out of the workforce and landed directly onto the cushy couch of socialism. In what other universe, fascist state of banned mathematical computation, is a $200,000 net loss a triumph of historic proportions? Even worse, what do you call it when only 60% of the civilian work force is employed full-time? Pocket change"?

In six years alone over 14 million citizens have fallen of the workforce and are no longer counted in the unemployment equation; nearly three times the number of the relentlessly-assailed George W. Bush. In other words, real unemployed stands near 15% while black unemployment – those alleged beneficiaries of Democratic policies – is well over 20%. Workforce participation is now at a paltry 62.6% and represents the lowest mark since the economic futility of Jimmy Carter. Yet for all the "Blame Bush" rhetoric liberals conveniently invoke to pardon their Marxist messiah, workforce participation never dipped below 65.8% under the former President while median unemployment was

5.4% during his two terms; a number Barack Obama just now surpassed due to near record non-participation, or approximately 100 million Americans not seeking employment. Honestly, how else could welfare recipients skyrocket from 27 million to 48 million, household income plummet by over $3,000 and the national debt nearly double to just under 19 trillion under Barry's watch alone; because of unprecedented prosperity and unclaimed lottery tickets? If only.

Contrary to the retirement advice of community organizers, true economic recoveries are almost always defined by steep gains due to the inevitable statistical contrast of the recessions they inherently follow. The Reagan years brought annual real GDP growth of 3.5 percent; 4.9 percent directly after the recession. In inflation-adjusted dollars, the GDP jumped from 6.5 trillion at the end of 1980 to 8.61 trillion at the end of 1988. That's a 32 percent bump and the equivalent of adding the entire West German economy to our own. During the reign of "Obamanomics", the GDP has grown at an anemic 1.6 percent...TOTAL...and economic growth under the Great Communicator was easily more than double that of the Great Divider. When over one-third of the country is living paycheck to paycheck, 40% have no retirement savings, and the average savings account balance is below $4000, prosperity becomes an oxymoron of progress; or in government parlance, a lie! You cannot multiple wealth by dividing it through the straw of social justice.

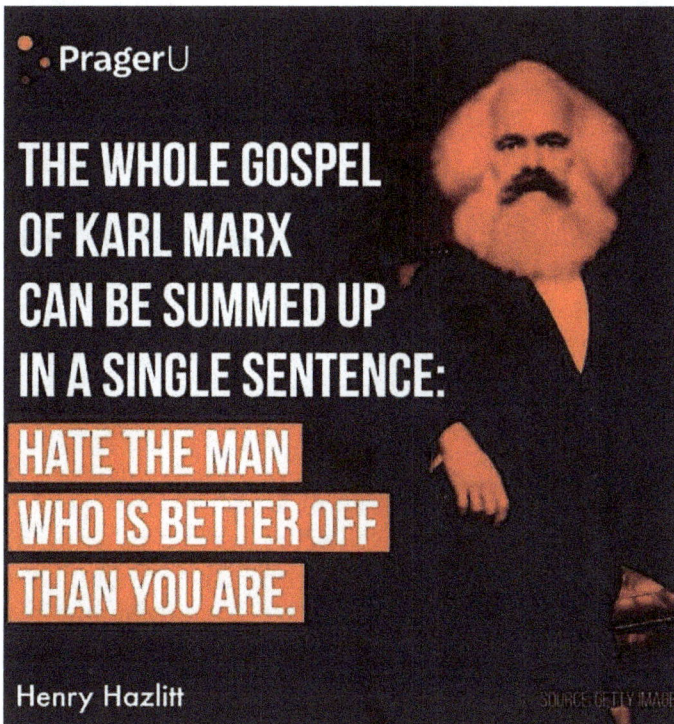

PragerU

THE WHOLE GOSPEL OF KARL MARX CAN BE SUMMED UP IN A SINGLE SENTENCE:

HATE THE MAN WHO IS BETTER OFF THAN YOU ARE.

Henry Hazlitt

Unless I'm missing the purpose of comedy, like being the butt of a bad joke, perhaps Mr. Rock could tell America what white president was re-elected sporting the same horrific economic record as one Barack Hussein Obama. Care to venture? Not one guess? ZERO! Yes, please excuse me for pulling out my racist calculator and hitting the "O"bama button to clear the pungent air of progressive bean counters. And just in case our talented comic's false charge is beginning to run on empty, gas was only $1.80 a gallon in 2008. How ironic being that's about the same time common sense was hijacked, stuffed in the trunk of a Chevy Volt and driven off the cliff in the name of hope. If endless business failures and mass layoffs are a sign of days to come, I suggest we put on our blinker, take a sharp right turn and head straight for the corner of "Wake" & "The Hell Up"! I hear they're not using our money and the Constitution as confetti to celebrate the planned suffocation of American exceptionalism.

Nuke, Paper, Scissors: Choosing Islam Over Israel

The United States of America spent decades, countless lives and billions of dollars trying to keep nuclear weapons out of the hands of rogue nations – the notorious Axis of Evil – only for our omnipotent leader to give Iran a blank check to build them; a nation whose enriched Uranium stockpiles have since doubled to 950 tons? "Why", you ask? Well, that's all too simple; because Barack Obama, Valerie Jarrett, and John Kerry are Muslim sympathizers who detest the very existence and military superiority of Israel in the Middle East. After all, did our government even attempt to barter for the lives of four Americans wrongfully imprisoned by the Iranian regime? Of course not! Such trite inconveniences require loyalty and merely distract from achieving their true goal: giving Islamic militants a more effective way of killing Jews and the infidel in the name of religious "equality". Yes, all this myopic and petulant agreement accomplished was to guarantee future hostilities between Israel and Iran, if not to serve as a possible trigger for a global catastrophe. If such a weapon was mobilized and used on an unsuspected urban populace – dare I say Chicago, Washington, or New York – the effects would make 9/11 seem like a glorified theme park.

Naturally such unapologetic ignorance begs one question…where are all of the so-called anti-war activists now? Liberals love to continually remind the uniformed voting masses that we couldn't find WMD's in Iraq – yes, those very ones used to murder thousands of Kurds and so easily relocated to Syria – and now they're applauding the decision to give Islamic extremists the green light to pursue nuclear proliferation as a hobby at their anti-Semitic leisure? More cowbell, please! Somehow the same worrisome media that gleefully kept a real-time body count of the Afghan and Iraqi wars during the Bush administration, have been magically reduced to catatonic shadows and incoherent whispers despite the fact military casualties are three times higher under Obama's glorious tenure. I guess it's only apropos I haven't heard one voice of dissent from the Democratic Party of Nobel 'peace and love' after the President signed a deal to remain in Afghanistan until 2024. Principle before politics? The hypocrisy is almost as deafening as the countless epitaphs his blind favoritism has yet to write in the name of world peace.

The Apprentice Who Cried "Roof"

As a member of the radical group Weather Underground, Bill Ayers was a Marxist, anarchist, and domestic terrorist who helped murder innocent Americans. He is also a close personal friend and was the most trusted mentor of Barack Obama during his ascension into politics. If we're staying true to the guilt-by-association, mainstream media motif, where's the outrage and the universal call for his resignation by offended activists? If you consort with, let alone identify with a known anti-American communist who ended human life and openly sought to overthrow the U.S. government, how are you even remotely allowed to go anywhere near the Oval Office; the epicenter of our liberty, unity and trust? Meanwhile, progressives are pointing fingers everywhere and anywhere desperately searching for any crumb of indiscretion or commonality they can attach to any unsuspecting pedestrian, organization, business, religion, political party and inanimate object as undeniable blame/guilt for the sadistic actions of a rogue killer who irrefutably deserves the death penalty: Dylann Roof. And yet people wonder why this country is in such a horrific state of cultural and socio-political disrepair. I guess that's why Bill Ayers now writes children books and our Founding Fathers are gradually being ostracized by our very own collegiate institutions: because it's just so commendable for a once-militant communist to "properly" educate our youth about tolerance, virtue, and the benevolent intentions of community organizers. The propaganda never stops.

e an advertiseme

The Pen & the Pauper: Dotting the "i" of Marxism

As his catalog of historic failures and serial abuses grow exponentially, there is little doubt the ultimate goal of Barack Obama and his Marxist minions is to dismantle America brick by brick: her institutions, philosophical beliefs, our markets. The two most indelible pillars that illustrate this subversive ambition are the passage of Obamacare, nationalized healthcare, and the unprecedented rise of our national debt. As laid out by Sal Alinsky's "Rules for Radicals", once you control people's healthcare, their very lifeblood, they are forever at the government's mercy. Obamacare wasn't designed to coexist with other insurance options; it was designed to fail in order to produce a single payer system that would, in effect, eliminate all private options through crippling regulations and bloated costs. Millions of Americans have lost their insurance plans while others' premiums have skyrocketed to the point of insolvency. If Obama & Co. truly cared about the people, wouldn't they scrap Obamacare and reconstruct it from the ground up; creating efficient, competent, and affordable coverage that still honored individual liberty? Instead, the powers that be are content with putting lipstick on a pig and passing it off as a free dinner. Only it's not free and it's not bacon.

The second set of fiscal fingerprints found on this economic degradation is the unforgivable rise and proliferation of the national debt; which is why, in theory, we have a debt limit. If you remember correctly, in 2008, Barack Obama smugly declared that any leader, i.e. George Bush, who raised the debt by a single dollar was unpatriotic and an example of failed leadership. How ironic being Barry alone has raised the debt a staggering $8 trillion in a mere six years; the most by any president in history and more than the first 42 presidents combined. This is yet another classic staple of Marxism. By raising the debt to unsustainable levels, they convince the public into believing the only way to solve the problem and avert disaster is through higher taxes.

In turn, these higher tariffs all but eliminate the middle class by creating an army of impoverished citizens who are already struggling to make ends meet. Since 2008, an additional six million Americans have dropped below the poverty line while the number of welfare recipients has nearly doubled. Throw in the fact nearly 40% of the country is now out of the workforce, real unemployment is over 15% and the debt has surpassed 100% of our GDP, and the field is ripe for a prolific economic collapse. The more people become solely dependent on a centralized Government to survive and/or work, the more the shackles of subjugation begin to tighten around the wrists and ankles of lady liberty. For all intents and purposes, the "rights of man" becomes a misnomer in the preface of a

Communist manifesto. Remember, Marxism was never about the people, merely controlling the people. Yeah, I concur...a pretty glaring omission.

If tyranny has taught us anything, it is much easier to implement the oppressive principles of Socialism and Communism through the shiny, new facade of glittering generalities like "hope" and "change". It's hardly a coincidence some of the most infamous leaders erected their own symbol to supersede all others. Fear and wonder are a powerful combination when disarming, both physically and mentally, the impressionable masses. However, if these current political proclivities are truly the product of a carefully disguised plot, the real question is "how"? How have Barack Obama and his ideologues carried out such a radical ruse upon the highest altar of freedom? The answer is simpler than you think. The seeds of modern-day progressivism have been there for decades, primarily taking root in the 60's and 70's until their perfect instrument of delivery arrived in the form a Marxist Senator from Illinois – deemed the most liberal congressman by an independent watchdog – who unexpectedly rose to national prominence. Articulate, an unapologetic propagandist, and possessing a keen talent for inflaming divisions into rabid voting blocks, all despite lacking any degree of executive acumen, he somehow became virtually impervious to criticism or unearthed scandals; even long after winning the presidency. Aided by an increasingly unscrupulous leftist media – the once guard dog of the republic now turned lapdog of liberalism – any hint of indiscretion was simultaneously molded by mainstream news into a stinging condemnation of any opposition while heaping effusive praise on their Democratic counterparts. In other words, lie; a motif this administration continues to employ without refrain.

Every time someone has attempted to hold Barack Obama's feet to the fire of accountability they have been attacked, investigated, and branded as an enemy of the people; a tactic perfected by both Marxists and Nazi Germany. By dividing America into warring factions – rich vs. poor, white vs. minority, Christians vs. atheists, homosexual vs. heterosexual, women vs. conservatives – Obama's non-stop propaganda machine continuously distracts voters from the actual issues, their abuses and failures, only to time and again cast the light of dispersion, blame, on their accusers. The real tragedy is that we all personally know someone like this and we can't stand or respect them. Ah, but the President is special. What's even more mind-boggling is that our government has admitted to manipulating economic data before the election, altering the Census, refusing to enforce existing immigration laws, using federal agencies to punish political opponents, purging military officers loyal to our founding values, labeling "liberty lovers' as America's greatest terrorist threat, and disregarding the Constitution whenever it suited their agenda. For God sakes, liberals wanted to impeach Bush, who received permission from Congress and the United Nations, for going to war against a tyrant guilty of mass genocide. Nixon was forced to resign for covering-up a bloody break-in of Democratic headquarters, while Mr. Hussein had the phones and emails of reporters and congressmen tapped. In the name of God, how has this President been allowed to act with such reckless abandon and impunity?

Barack Obama's historic ascension to power and the degree of his indiscretions are hardly coincidences. Despite possessing the most radical views and associates of any candidate in history, those identical to fellow anti-American extremists like Valerie Jarrett, he has capitalized on the perfect political storm. The cultural divide in America is so perilous, so bitterly caustic, that there are factions on both sides who are incapable of objectivity, let alone recognizing any hint of impropriety by their respected leaders. In fact, many openly believe the end justifies the means; yep, that's fascism. Obama fully realizes that no matter what he does, how far he pushes the status quo, a majority of his supporters will either refuse to entertain even the most factual criticism or they can be manipulated, especially be blind emotion, into accepting whatever explanation he produces. America is no longer America: a rationale, patriotic brethren who happen to be Republican or Democrat. It is now inhabited by Democrats and Republicans, who just happen to reside in America. It is within this crisis of conscience – these faux party allegiances that are negating our intrinsic duty to protect and defend this republic against all enemies, foreign and domestic – that today's radical progressive, dare I say Marxist, is thriving unchecked, unhinged, and unrepentant.

Anyone who has ears, can read a book, add 1 + 1, comprehend cause and effect, can properly dissect the sham that has become the United States government. How else has the trillion-dollar, freedom-usurping, job-destroying Obamacare been allowed to survive? How else has Congress, under the guidance of the President, been allowed to operate without a law-mandated budget for six years? How has God, those Judeo-Christian values responsible for the creation of Western Civilization, been incessantly eroded in lieu of progressive views on homosexuality, abortion, morality and promiscuity? And how else has our Constitutional rights – free speech, the right to bear arms, privacy – been systematically siphoned by our own elected government; the only entity unequivocally limited by the Constitution? To quote Puff the Magic Dragon, once upon a time liberals prided themselves on questioning everything, obeying nothing, and now they want to silence and jail those who dare question Obama's power; that is, their "progressive utopia" which stands in direct opposition to our country's founding premise. And somehow, by some miracle, these so-called mainstream thinkers have escaped being labeled "extremists" or imminent threats. Russia has condemned its Communist past, Cuba, North Korea, and China have impoverished and imprisoned countless of their "beloved" people, yet our leftists publicly embrace such idiocy with little or no outcry. I guess when you're united by a hatred for America - white people, capitalism, the military, and Christianity - you're allowed to fail history and fly the flag of Lenin on Independence Day.

In the face of such criminal indifference, blatant contempt for the will and intelligence of the people, it is fair to say Barack Obama, Harry Reid, and Nancy Pelosi couldn't care less about the alleged consequences of their actions. Because of his shameless tactics – this apathetic culture of spoon-fed low information voters – the President clearly believes his detractors lack the ability to punish him or halt his assault on America. Outside of an armed uprising – which he would openly welcome or eagerly incite – Obama fears or respects nothing that doesn't coincide with his agenda. Therefore, as his tenure inches ever closer to conclusion, Mr. Barry Soetoro feels even more empowered, or should I say unhinged; almost daring his political adversaries to thwart his attempt to unilaterally terraform America with his Executive pen. It is increasingly evident the leader of the free world would welcome a national emergency – whether fabricated, induced or credible – to tighten his grip on the throat of this once proud and prosperous republic. This opportune development would give him the perfect excuse, not that he needs one, to delay elections, extend his rule, and implement drastic measures in the name of the "common good". Oh, but I almost forgot, there are no Marxists in the White House, "Rules for Radicals" doesn't exist, Bill Ayers and Frank Marshall have nothing in common, the President never told American students to ignore warnings of government tyranny, and Dinesh D'Souza was never arrested in Obama's America.

Dinesh D'Souza

"THE TRUTH IS, THE DEMOCRATS ARE THE PARTY OF SLAVERY, INDIAN REMOVAL, OF BROKEN TREATIES, THE TRAIL OF TEARS, SEGREGATION, JIM CROW, LYNCHING, THE KU KLUX KLAN, JAPANESE INTERNMENT, OPPOSITION TO THE CIVIL RIGHTS ACT OF 1964, THE VOTING RIGHTS ACT OF 1965, AND THE FAIR HOUSING BILL OF 1968. THIS IS THEIR ACTUAL HISTORY. SO WHAT THEY DO IS TRY TO COVER IT UP AND HOW THEY DO THAT IS BLAME AMERICA. THE REALITY IS AMERICA DIDN'T DO IT, DEMOCRATS DID."

HILLARY CLINTON

Unto Thyself

Hillary GO DIRECTLY TO JAIL

www.theilluminati.tv

DO NOT TELL LIES, DO NOT COLLECT PRESIDENCY

A Lie Named Hillary

I don't detest Hillary Clinton because she is a woman. I oppose her because she cannot tell the truth to save her life. Any public servant who has the gall to issue a list of terms the press cannot utter, as if disposing the corpse of free will, is helplessly deluded and a petulant child. Sorry, Hillary, but no one owes you anything; especially the nation you proclaim to serve with nothing but the benevolence of blind ambition. If your candidacy cannot survive without the aid of deception, division, and the fabricated catcalls of "sexism" to demonize your critics, then please tell us why America needs you? Better yet, please explain how you're even worthy of a job? A leader doesn't need pollsters, a panel of advisers, two news conferences and a room full of media drones just to announce whether or not she used an unauthorized server to conduct official government business and therefore deleted emails in an attempt to avoid prosecution. A leader would never break the law in the first place. And a leader doesn't shout "what does it matter" when four American lives are lost in Benghazi amidst the wake of her unmitigated failure. Any self-respecting adult with an ounce of integrity would simply admit the truth. Excuse me, any self-aware child who knows the difference between right and wrong, life and death.

If I'm hiring someone to run my business, placing my future in foreign hands, I don't care whether you're a Democrat or Republican, a man or woman, white or black. I want the most qualified candidate whose character speaks for itself and whose ideals can stand on the merits of their own wisdom. That's common sense. Are you going to have the audacity to tell me what I can and can't ask; what verbiage is acceptable? If your resume and vision are truly best for the entire nation, not just one party, gender or race, either should be able to withstand the most blistering questions and exhaustive scrutiny. In fact, you should welcome any and all discourse to discredit your detractors and display your competence. A leader unites, empowers and inspires by example, not by excuses or endless blame.

Tell me the national debt is a record 19.5 trillion and that Barack Obama has raised it more than the first 42 presidents combined. Admit that 95 million Americans are out of the workforce, nearly 50 million are on public assistance, and that the economic recovery is a sham. Admonish Iran as a destabilizing force of Islamic radicalism that must never be mentioned in the same sentence as "nuclear power". Recognize the reality every civilized nation has immigration laws and that American sovereignty, the safety and security of her people, supersedes any political ploy to stuff the ballot box beneath the hollow cries of racism. Ask me if a trustworthy "servant of the people" would delete 33,000 unauthorized emails, ordering subordinates to smash their laptops and phones detailing the sale of political favors to foreign regimes, only to maintain her innocence by attempting to bribe FBI agents? Convince me that you – a self-proclaimed feminist and so-called egalitarian of equality – never dismissed, degraded, or threatened the victims of your husband's numerous sexual indiscretions. And please explain how any worthy presidential candidate, let alone a conscionable human being, uses the guise of 13 "charitable" foundations to collect over 100 million dollars in donations – including foreign contributions solicited from America's sworn enemies of Communist China, Iran and the Muslim Brotherhood – only to defraud the actual victims of global disasters by keeping 85% of those misappropriated funds for her personal, political ambitions? Tell me anything that suggests you even remotely care!

Yes, just like generations of legal immigrants before your candidacy, respect is given when trust is earned. If you are incapable of acknowledging simple, documented facts – solely because it's easier to hide behind a propaganda platform that cajoles and incites an expendable public – you're not interested in solving anything, let alone serving the American people or any notion of truth. You're the cancer killing the country I love. You're the lie my forefathers never told.

"If my dear friend Donald Trump ever decided to sacrifice his fabulous billionaire lifestyle to become President, he would be an unstoppable force for ultimate justice that Democrats and Republicans alike would celebrate."
~John F. Kennedy Jr., June 1999

The Real War on Women

While the media bypasses real criminality to unearth every possible crumb of Trump lewdness to sway the election, I'd absolutely love to hear the Clintons' personal, unfiltered conversations: racist, sexist, criminal, obscene and distinctly unapologetic. Oh, but wait; that's media protected and privacy matters! Truly, why would Wikileaks' treasure trove of emails exposing a tangible paper trail of Hillary Clinton's illicit activity demand national scrutiny or any hint of a judicial indictment when there are decade old clips of sexual crudity in locker rooms? I was truly unaware that sexual banter was somehow an undiscovered phenomenon in the showers of male bravado or the gossiping bathrooms of group female excursions. If I may, when did non-PC locker room chatter, as unacceptable and perverse as it may be, become worse than Hillary shaming/threatening Bill's rape victims or laughing about successfully defending a child rapist in 1975? I guess when your husband is "still dicking bimbos", to quote Colin Powell, it's not nearly as offensive as him receiving oral sex in the Oval office from a young intern that isn't his wife. Sorry but the Clintons burned their moral relevance card long ago. Hillary knows she cannot win on her record or the issues, so her campaign is desperately tossing out the gender, race, class, and pity card hoping to find anything that disturbs the currents of public opinion.

Is it also really of any surprise the candidate viewed as the least favorable and the most dishonest, Hillary Clinton, also used an aspiring porn actress who once threatened to murder a judge to deflect from her own countless scandals. And guess which one the media chooses to frame as a "victim"? That's right; their blessed Madonna who destroyed laptops and phones, perjured herself before the FBI and Congress, and called Muslims "sand niggers" because she is a global role model for disenfranchised girls and minorities. And yet the fact Hillary proudly defended a child rapist in 1975, supports Arab nations that enslave and murder girls, doesn't recognize a woman's right to be born and ignores the reality her own political party pays female staffers less than men is somehow neither offensive or noteworthy. Yes, how could anyone not construe profane language heard in nearly every school, office and bar across America – including remarks unleashed by other women – as being the epicenter of the real war on women? Sticks and stones, Sharia Law and voter apathy may kill your daughter, but callous words are what we're after. Apparently basic human rights, such as freedom of speech, choosing one's clothing or the right to be educated, are so overrated that only billions in foreign aid to Islamic nations will cleanse our conscience as an accessory to mass suffering and depravity.

Whether we like it or not, everyone, at some time or another, has engaged in vulgar conversations or called someone a bitch, an ass, fat, a dick, slut or a pig out of frustration or disdain. You, me, Hillary, everyone; no exceptions! Does that make it acceptable? Of course not. The only difference is Trump simply admits it, his life is under the social media microscope and the press is desperate to find any hint of usable dirt to create a cloud of deception in order to sneak the contemptible Hillary and her litany of lies into the White House. How else can the coddled Clintons continue to get away with misogyny, sexual assault, coercion, perjury, treason and fraud without the same degree of moral outrage? I guess it takes a real leader to admit one's non-felonious mistakes and ask for forgiveness.

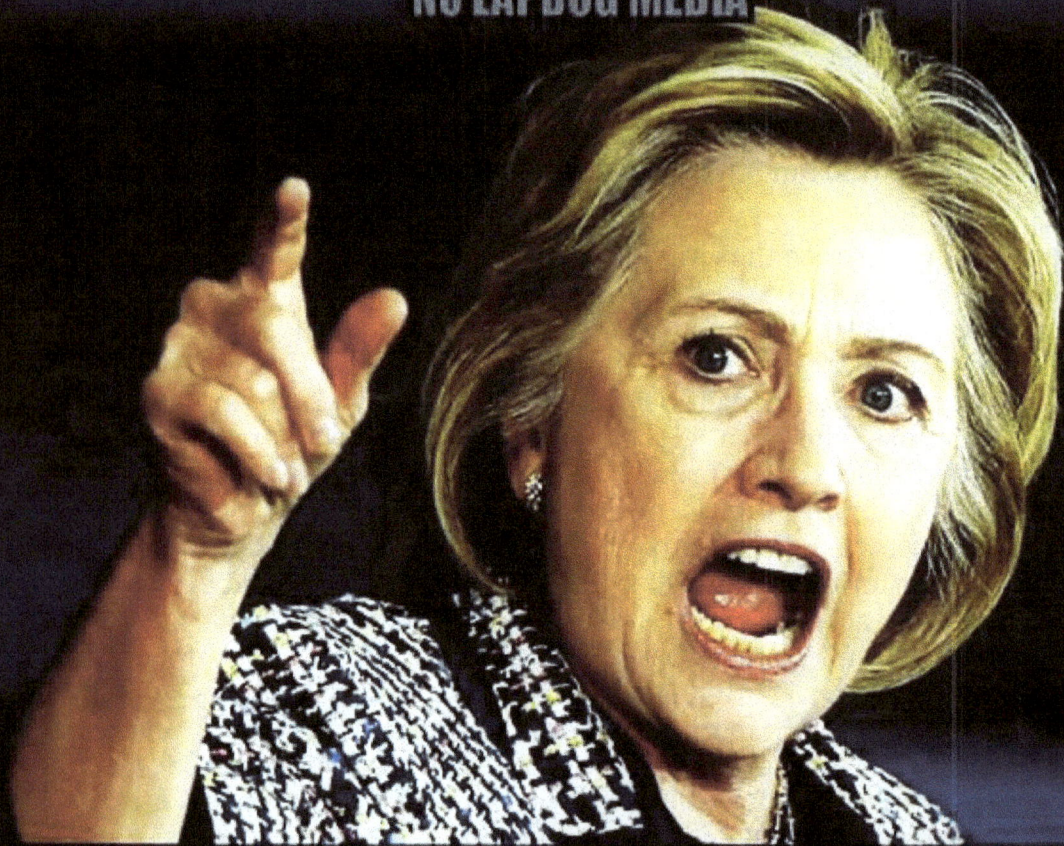

"IF THAT F**KING BASTARD WINS, WE'RE ALL GOING TO BE HANGING FROM NOOSES! YOU BETTER FIX THIS SHIT!"

NO LAPDOG MEDIA

~ Hillary Clinton
In an email to interim DNC chair Donna Brazile
October 17, 2016

Why Hillary Really Lost

Why did Hillary really lose the presidency? Because she is forever synonymous with scandal!

1) Russian Uranium One scandal – with Barack Obama's consent, the knowledge of the Department of Justice and the involvement of former FBI Director Robert Mueller, Hillary sold 20% of U.S. Uranium rights for a total of $145 million in donations made to the Clinton Foundation by Uranium One stockholders. Russian influence/dollars were also used to incite civil and racial discord across America for political gain.

2) Clinton Foundation – Established in 1997, the Clintons' "non-profit" charity morphed into a political slush fund for Hillary's political aspirations by funneling "tax free" campaign donations from wealthy investors, corporations and foreign governments.

3) Haiti Relief Rip-off – The Clinton Foundation siphoned millions in public donations collected for Hurricane survivors – administration costs, insider or defaulted reconstruction contracts, pocketing the difference for overpaid supplies – to subsidize her political aspirations and personal expenses such as her daughter's lavish wedding; as confirmed by emails between John Podesta and former Clinton aide Doug Band.

4) Pay-to-Play – As Secretary of State, Hillary solicited donations from foreign donors/governments/organizations – Abu Dhabi, the Muslim Brotherhood, Uranium One – in exchange for current and/or future political favors: staff appointments, access to resources and favorable foreign policy decisions.

5) Benghazi – Despite repeated requests for additional security due to an increased terror threat at the US Embassy in Libya, including direct communications from then Ambassador Christopher Stevens, Hillary Clinton failed to properly act or notify the Pentagon. Furthermore, her failure to promptly respond after confirmation of an attack was underway, essentially abandoning staff and security personnel for the duration of the 7-hour attack, culminated in the deaths of 4 American citizens. In response to repeated questions lamenting the senseless loss of life due to her indifference and clear negligence, she angrily snapped, "What Difference Does It Make" to members of the Senate Committee on Foreign Relations.

6) Established an unauthorized private server to engage in government related communications and illegally transmit classified information. Roughly 33,000 emails and all relevant electronic devices were destroyed in an attempt to conceal her "innocence".

7) Russia, Russia, Russia – Hillary Clinton knowingly broke campaign finance laws by secretly hiring DC research firm Fusion GPS to fabricate ties between Donald Trump and Russian operatives. The fake dossier was later given to the FBI by Bruce Ohr, Senator McCain, which was also used to obtain FISA surveillance warrants under false pretenses. Media hysteria and Democratic outrage triggered a criminal investigation headed by former FBI Chief Robert Mueller – a personal friend of fired FBI Director James Comey – and staffed overwhelmingly with known Clinton lawyers and donors.

8) Conspired with DNC operatives to rig the Democratic presidential primaries to defeat Bernie Sanders; actions the Democratic party confirmed in a recent lawsuit. Seth Rich, a DNC staffer who despised Hillary and was vocal corruption within the party, was murdered near his home in May of 2016; in the middle of a hotly contested primary season after DNC emails were leaked to Wikileaks from an anonymous source within the party. Shortly after Hillary won the nomination, it was confirmed she received presidential debate questions from then DNC Chair, Donna Brazile.

9) Whitewater Scandal – A precursor to the subprime mortgage crisis, the Clintons formed Whitewater Development Corporation with friends Jim and Susan McDougal as part of a joint real estate venture. Rose Law Firm, in which Hillary became a senior lawyer and billing partner, provided legal services. With an additional 1.2 million in credit illegally obtained from the Madison Savings and Loan, of which Jim McDougal was also a primary partner, home loans were given to unqualified applicants. After attempts to resell the foreclosed properties failed due to skyrocketing interest rates and a collapsing market, both entities collapsed. The scandal cost taxpayers $73 million. Fifteen people were convicted of crimes, including the McDougal's, of which Bill Clinton later pardoned four of the participants as Arkansas governor.

10) Reprimanded by the House Judiciary Committee for misconduct after attempting to submit a fraudulent brief during the Watergate investigation.

11) Defended a child rapist who served less than a year in jail despite beating a defenseless 12-year-old girl into a coma. In an interview given years after the trial, Hillary humorously referenced the "fortuitous" verdict which left a girl with a lifetime of emotional and physical trauma; most notability, the inability to bear children.

Hillary Clinton didn't lose the presidency because she was a helpless victim of cultural sexism or "Republican racism", she lost because she is a corrupt, condescending, and soulless opportunist who reduced the electorate to "deplorable human beings, super predators, and taco bowl voters". Her lust for power was only superseded by her disregard for the truth, the rule of law and any sense of accountability to the American people for her numerous criminal transgressions. In light of her sordid history and pathological hypocrisy, Hillary Rodham Clinton had no business being nominated for President of the United States, or running for a public office of any kind, because her vainglorious memoirs should have been written exclusively inside the confines of a Federal prison.

Return to Sender: The 5 Crimes of Hillary Clinton

For those media pundits claiming the FBI investigation is nothing but a witch hunt, a partisan hit job, here's a list of the five prosecutable crimes Hillary committed without even mentioning those additional violations – i.e., fraud, collusion, solicitation – revealed in her recovered emails.

Guilty...

1. Of setting up an illegal server and using a private email account for official government correspondence without approval. **FELONY**

2. Of mishandling/transmitting classified information over unsecured channels; including giving unauthorized personnel and/or private citizens access to said correspondence. **FELONY**

3. Of not complying with a federal subpoena to surrender all emails; including those devices used to access said communications or store relevant materials. **FELONY**

4. Of destroying Government property and evidence pertinent to a federal investigation. **FELONY**

5. Of knowingly giving false testimony to both Congress and the FBI with the intent to deceive. **FELONY**

Celebrities, politicians and military personnel have been arrested, demoted, discharged or sentenced to prison for far less: including Martha Stewart, Dinesh D'Souza and General Petraeus. Yet, somehow, the most corrupt and deceitful candidate in recent history has evaded prosecution due to the orchestrated obstruction of justice waged by the Obama administration, and a complicit media propaganda campaign designed to sway and misinform the electorate.

Mommy 'Deplorable': Hillary's 1975 Rape Defense

In 1975, as an Arkansas defense attorney, Hillary Clinton attacked the character of a 12-year-old girl who was lured into a car, raped, beaten into a coma and left permanently unable to bear children. She demanded the rape victim take a lie detector test, accused her of fantasizing about being sexually assaulted by an older man, and asked the court to strike all physical evidence; which included blood and semen found on the girl's clothes and her body. Hillary's client, 41-year-old Thomas Taylor, served only two months in jail. It was later revealed she chuckled about the fortuitous verdict when touting her successful strategy during an interview. The word 'deplorable' does not begin to do this woman justice, nor does it reclaim the shattered lives and slandered reputations left in the turbulent wake of the Clintons' illustrious victim shaming campaign. If anyone can still vote for such a callous and contemptible individual in good conscience, then criminality has officially replaced credibility on the ballot for America's soul.

The Bittersweet Tears of Defeat

Sorry, Madame Clouseau, but just because you failed to garner enough electoral votes to win the presidency doesn't mean the Electoral College is ineffective and therefore should be abolished; quite the contrary actually. Without this ingenious system, yet another Constitutional check on unilateralism, countless rural residents – states that account for a majority of our food and natural resources – would be brazenly ignored and railroaded by unscrupulous politicians just like yourself. Yes, this was the exact same impetus responsible for the creation of the U.S. Senate: a non-negotiable degree of equal representation. I believe this is also called "affirmative action" in progressive parallelograms! If I wanted America to resemble Chicago, Detroit or Baltimore, urban epicenters rife with violence, decadence, and Democratically-ruled decay, I would have voted for the Manchurian Uniter-and-Usurper, Barack Hussein Obama. However, because I'm an American patriot, I realize the heartbeat of this great Republic – our work ethic, faith, and love of liberty – resides in the open roads and small communities of Middle America. Now, if you please, "We the Expendable" would like to enjoy the idyllic remnants of the last American frontier before bilateralism is forever blinded by the shoveled ignorance of your steaming contempt for the budding ides of buried history.

Electoral Education

There are over 3,100 Counties in the United States
Trump won 2,626 or 84% of all recognized counties

There are 62 Counties in the State of New York
Trump won 46 of them: Clinton won 16

In NYC & LA County, Hillary won 3.2 million more votes
That's 112% of her NATIONAL popular vote victory

The 5 Boroughs of New York City
- Brooklyn, Bronx, Queens, Staten & Manhattan -
comprise roughly 300 Square Miles

The U.S. covers nearly 3.8 million Square Miles

It's absurd to suggest a land mass over 125,000 times
smaller than the entire country should dictate the
values and freedoms of over 300 million people

America's Founding Fathers knew Mob Rule,
a pure democracy without constraints, would inevitably
usurp the rights and property of the powerless.
New York and California have proven them correct!

Dear Hillary...

If Donald Trump wanted to return America to 1850, slavery would still be legal because the Republican Party – founded as the anti-slavery party and responsible for ending human servitude, granting suffrage for both blacks and women, and protecting civil liberties in the 1960's – had yet to come to fruition. And yes, lest we forget, that forgotten little anecdote known as the "Trail of Tears" was spearheaded by fellow Democrat and staunch anti-abolitionist, Andrew Jackson. Since you're so much more adept at social semantics, victimization propaganda and class warfare, I thought an "esteemed" historian like yourself should know the untainted difference before further staining your "presidential" resume with the dishonored sacrifices of real American heroes, evangelical Christians and Civil Rights champions. Fortunately, our too often forsaken forebearers of that conveniently ignored treatise on Constitutional Republicanism made keen preparations for your predictable insurrection. It's called the Electoral College. Never fear, denial is not fatal when your hateful duplicity finally convinces voters what's best for their families and the future of this reborn Republic: your retirement, imprisonment, both.

"North Korea requires trained and experienced diplomats. Just sending out tweets won't work."

Son of a ...

THE DC

DONALD TRUMP

AMERICA FIRST

Rinse, Lather, Retweet

Donald Trump didn't ascend to the pinnacle of real estate or become a global business icon because he was afraid to speak his mind and step on a few uncooperative toes. He made his proverbial bones by being a brash, fearless entrepreneur who learned to survive, dare I say thrive, in a cesspool of bloodthirsty sharks, yellow journalists and political parasites. The man does not apologize for his success, his survival instincts or Darwinian tactics, any more than you or I would apologize for being shot by a home intruder. If you choose to berate him, Mika – repeatedly labeling him a goon, a liar, a fraud and joyously mocking his appearance – he's going to piss in your Morning Joe and posterize your hypocrisy for the entire world to see. Your smug ploy for ratings solely to promote a hateful narrative, neither invites or requires grace and tact. And yet despite his rough, politically incorrect exterior, his compassionate nature has recognized and assisted countless people from all walks of life with his generosity, vast resources and sincere appreciation. Too bad your sagging journalistic integrity omits reporting the unadulterated truth.

For over a year now, the President's family has been viciously slandered, harassed and threatened by nearly every facet of society with little outrage or condemnation from the supposed moral high ground; specifically, those pundits who believe social media is somehow beneath the dignity of the Presidency but a worthy platform for his obscene assailants. Celebrities have openly fantasized about his assassination, feminists urged raping Melania to defend women's rights, Barron Trump has been called an autistic brat who should have been aborted, and even the President's young grandchildren have been subjected to profane attacks in public settings. If the hysteria surrounding Trump has taught us anything, it's that progressivism has become the epitome of a soulless dystopian culture which celebrates Planned Parenthood, a baby chop shop founded by a genocidal white supremacist, only to decry the frequency and nature of a populist's "inappropriate tweets". Unless using a young intern as human humidor for your Cuban Cigar is now offensive to the guardians of slumbering standards, my guess is the Bill Clinton litmus test for Presidential etiquette miscarried the righteous perception of moral relevance long ago.

I WOULD RATHER TRUST A BILLIONAIRE THAT BECOMES A POLITICIAN

THAN A POLITICIAN THAT BECOMES A BILLIONAIRE

TPUSA.com

Today's political landscape is no longer 1950's America, let alone the patriotic renaissance of the 1980's, where right-minded politicians could voice their beliefs without every word being doctored, every fact distorted, or logical solution maligned by the media. The 2016 election confirmed the press has no intention of honoring the faintest notion of objectivity, instead choosing to advocate for the Democratic Party on a full-time basis. A recent Harvard study revealed 90% of all media coverage during and after the campaign has been overwhelmingly negative towards Mr. Trump. The liberal establishment, even that of the new "progressive" GOP itself, has worked assiduously to destroy his reputation and fabricate any imaginable instance of impropriety, perceived failure, as long as it results in his humiliation, impeachment or future electoral defeat. Yes, when you're suffocating beneath a poisonous blanket of propaganda, you're not exactly concerned about articulating the most respectable response to the rabid lynch mob zealously plotting your demise.

Do I wish Donald Trump would engage in fewer social media spats to better concentrate on the tasks at hand? Of course. Then again, when your family is the incessant target of such insatiable hatred and shameless dishonesty, I cannot blame him. Public perception, that psychological weapon used to taint one's reputation and incite blind resistance against real reform, is a commodity that cannot be undervalued or ignored. Whether you admire or despise the President, he is clearly a master at beating the media at its own game. He confronts their monopoly, lures their sense of superiority, unhinges their violent intolerance, and ultimately exposes just how corrupt and destructive the press has become in its partisan quest to control the electorate at all costs. By the mere suggestion he was going to resurrect the "birther" issue – an accusation the Clinton campaign originally researched and introduced – Donald Trump duped every cable network pledging to blackout his speeches into unwittingly broadcasting a campaign ceremony honoring our veterans. That's power you cannot buy but is paid for by the karmic manifestation of your adversaries' malicious intent.

Whereas some of the President's communications are admittedly unnecessary or self-indulgent, there is undoubtedly a method to his so-called madness. No other figure in contemporary society has done more to single-handedly discredit, or potentially topple, the mainstream news hierarchy. In the matter of a few seconds, or 140 characters if you will, he can instantaneously bypass the filtered progressive bias of traditional media and literally reach, dare I say liberate, 100 million brainwashed minds from the matrix of corporate news and public education. In a single tweet alone, Trump convinced James Comey to tell the truth by insinuating he taped their conversations. In a matter of minutes, he reduced CNN, the New York Times and the Washington Post into supermarket tabloids whose most trusted sources teetered between the Arkansas Booger, the Southern Sasquatch, and an Oval Office desk plant that was once watered by the ghost of Abraham Lincoln. By smashing the archaic misconception the media represents an independent, credible source of information, Donald Trump has transformed the once sacred bell cows of syndicated thought into sniveling relics of privilege complaining their Depends are unbearably too tight. Apparently, the unyielding stench of their disposable duplicity is not near as uncomfortable.

In 2012, despite challenging a divisive socialist sporting the worst economic record since World War II, a polished politician codenamed "Mittens" lost with a "dignified" smile and a cordial concession speech. As a result, eight years of unchecked anti-Americanism ensued. Now those same media mouthpieces and spoiled celebrities who ravaged Romney's record and "fact checked" his intellect without refrain – burying the numerous failures, lies and abuses of Barack Obama – are suddenly upset their new victim is unwilling to be a political piñata; i.e., refusing to honor the media's "house" rules when "tweeting" against the crooked status quo. Spare my cinematic nostalgia, our President's abrasive persona, but honestly "We the People" need him on that wall; I want him on that wall fighting to preserve those forsaken timeless ideals that once made America great. I'd much rather have an undeterred President who lives and breathes to reclaim our vitality and security, engaging his detractors at 3 AM, than watching the country I love dismantled behind the affable Orwellian facade of "Hope" and "Change". While Donald Trump may lack Reagan's oratory refinement and social elegance, his political instincts and the unflinching manner he acts upon them are equally if not more impressive. The difference between proven leaders and regurgitated rhetoric is that only "fake news" serves garnish 24 hours a day to the malnourished masses. Bon appetite!

The Shark, the Donald, and the Shipwreck of American Exceptionalism

Growing up in the Heartland as a young teenager who was captivated by the steadfast convictions and eloquence of one Ronald Wilson Reagan, his contagious brand of Christian conservatism, I freely admit to identifying with Ted Cruz and Ben Carson far more than any other candidate. Yet, unlike the rabid left or some disgruntled conservatives, I'm not dumbfounded or discouraged by the phenomenon that is Donald Trump; nor do I detest his "unconventional" popularity simply because my preferred choices will inevitably fail to secure the nomination. Sometimes that which we do not necessary covet, or entirely understand, leads us to heights we could not attain otherwise. It's hard to make "America Great Again", spot the "land of the free, home of the brave" in the fading horizon, when your Grand Old Party is selling life insurance from the shipwreck of the status quo.

As someone who takes pride in being self-ware and ethical, I don't need endless memos and researched anecdotes to peel back the layers of pretense to expose the real Donald Trump. I know exactly who the man is: he's a skilled opportunist, a narcissist and an insatiable shark who lives for the thrill of the hunt. However, he's also a closer, a shrewd businessman, and an aspiring luminary who embodies American exceptionalism: a concept that forged the most powerful and affluent nation in less than two centuries and an ideal liberals have worked tirelessly to eradicate to appease her enemies. The most accomplished leaders aren't always the most cordial, modest or polished – i.e., Stonewall Jackson, Teddy Roosevelt, Winston Churchill, or General Patton – but they're typically relentless in their field of choice. These alpha assassins are self-driven achievers who make the tough calls when few will, for better or worse, and they will ruthlessly exploit any advantage to achieve their goal. No, I'm not suggesting Donald Trump is a heartless tyrant or a criminal. His random acts of kindness, charitable endeavors and diverse collection of character references are well documented. Rather, historically speaking, he's one that's not going to be denied his catch....by anyone. And that scares the hell of modern statists who proudly live by the code, "the end always justifies the means"!

While "The Donald" is routinely crucified for his unscripted remarks and political incorrectness, it's also his greatest source of strength: raw, unapologetic candor. In essence, Trump fearlessly speaks what many are thinking but his peers are afraid to utter out of fear of backlash: people are pissed off, sick of the double standards and tired of the endless excuses. Is his demeanor painfully juvenile and counterproductive at times? Absolutely. Is it a deal breaker in the face of the unprecedented level of impropriety waged by the Obama administration? Only if you like garnish. The fact Donald Trump doesn't tip-toe around media tripwires or pander to the sensitivities of the perpetually offended is what cements his image as a Washington outsider who will take charge from day one. Promising to build a wall because our current President has orchestrated a demographic coup d'état by allowing millions of criminally and medically unvetted illegals to stream across our borders isn't racist; especially when you still honor "legal" immigration. It's a relevant response to a criminal act that threatens the rule of law and the very survival of America. Proposing to stop the influx of all Syrian refuges because their ties to terrorism cannot be properly vetted isn't Islamophobia; it's a prudent measure reminiscent of Jimmy Carter's decision that could potentially save countless lives. When's the last time political correctness stopped an executive order, Hillary Clinton or an act of terror?

Despite his negatives, I don't need to be told Donald Trump is not a "true" conservative or an "evangelical" Christian. That much is obvious. Then again, no candidate is ever unscathed and no resume is without some degree of deficiency or inconsistency. Likewise, I'm not overly concerned about the media labeling him a "Nazi" or racist; that stale epithet which they routinely slander any GOP politician with who threatens their social narrative. What I do know is Mr. Trump just may be the only Republican candidate who can win the presidency in November. His Republican base is literally unbreakable and his appeal to nontraditional voting sects – minorities, disenfranchised Democrats, struggling labor unions, etc. – is uncharacteristically tangible. Whether he benefits from sheer name recognition, celebrity status, or his economic prowess, people are drawn to his persona for different reasons. For some, it's his hardline stance on immigration and promise to protect the Second Amendment. For others it's his touted ability to create jobs and fuel prosperity. Either way, the New York native generates a level of voter enthusiasm unmatched by his Republican rivals; the most critical staple of electoral success that eluded both McCain and Romney. You can't claim to be a champion of the people, a pillar of strength and a catalyst for change, when you refuse to take off the gloves. You can't win the crowd when you're tangled in the ropes of trepidation.

If Barack Obama taught us anything it's that even a candidate with the most questionable credentials and radical beliefs can ascend to the pinnacle of power. After 8 years of unabashed anti-Americanism that was exasperated by the GOP's endless capitulation to the most destructive agenda in our nation's history, and all despite conservatives handing Republicans a congressional majority, Mr. Trump has keenly tapped into an erupting chasm of discontent that is not interested in meaningless platitudes, table manners or half-measures. America is more divided and dysfunctional than ever, on the precipice of financial and racial ruin, while public trust in government is at an all-time low. More than ever "hope" is in dire need of a leader, a CEO, a staunch defender of American exceptionalism who will grab the reigns of accountability and restore order in a raging sea of discord. Truly, there is no moral high ground or silent victory when abstaining from voting against the most corrupt and deceitful candidate in American history: Hillary Rodham Clinton. If you truly want to measure the value and mettle of a man, begin by asking his entire family their opinion of him after observing just how thoughtful, diligent, and respectful his children have become under his guidance and in his wake.

Before any of my fellow Americans pledge to stay home in November, or God forbid choose a third-party novelty that cannot win out of myopic spite, perhaps they should entertain the fleeting notion Donald Trump just may be the right candidate at the most opportune time; that insatiable shark willing to stalk his liberal prey, wade through the perilous jetsam of race-baiting and media bias, and capture the White House without fear or hesitation. For if we again lose the presidency and America is forced to endure another 8 years of progressive rule terraforming the Constitution, the Supreme Court and our hallowed way of life, there may be nothing left to save. And when I look into my children's eyes each and every night, that option is simply unacceptable. Sometimes the end, no matter how difficult to comprehend, justifies the means. Sometimes, just sometimes, you need to bring a billion-dollar sledgehammer to a government house warming party, or more succinctly, a Marxist pawn shop.

FIRST FIVE MONTHS OF THE **OBAMA** ADMINISTRATION

CREATED $3 BILLION IN NEW REGULATIONS

PHOTOS: NEWSCOM
SOURCE: WHITEHOUSE.GOV

FIRST FIVE MONTHS OF THE **TRUMP** ADMINISTRATION

WIPED AWAY $22 BILLION WORTH OF REGULATIONS

heritage.org

The Art of Flattery

President Trump didn't say Kim Jong-un cares about his people because he believes it to be factually true. He made that sketchy public comment because calling your already anxious adversary a lying, murderous tyrant on an international stage would have torpedoed any chance for a disarmament deal, let alone any hope of North Korea abiding by the terms once the summit concluded. It's called artful flattery, diffusing the tension, and it's a fairly common negotiation technique. In what deluded daydream does, "Sign the paper, you piece of shit" begin to assuage 60 years of distrust and derision? Seasoned statesmen appeal to the best versions out their counterparts, raising expectations by lowering their defenses, not by needlessly inflaming divides. How many times has Patriots' head coach Bill Belichick lavished the opposition with praise during press conferences, only to destroy his competition come game day?

The panicked left is so desperate to put a negative slant on a positive outcome, you would have thought the President signed a clearly fabricated accord giving $150 billion in seized assets to Iranian militants and our blessing to "gradually" build a nuclear arsenal so they could someday fulfill their undying vow to destroy America and Israel. Unlike Trump's global best-seller, "The Art of the Deal", Barack Obama authored the amoral mystery, "How to Commit Treason while the Media Holds Your Beer: A Two-Step Program." The press either has a sick sense of humor or the worst case of partisan-induced amnesia since Ted Kennedy's car admitted to playing Truth or Dare with his drowning, abandoned date on a drunk Chappaquiddick bridge. Much to his failed predecessors' chagrin, the President brought a notorious dictator's panties home and made the world a safer place without actually having to violate or kill anyone. Now that's skill a well-rehearsed alibi can't buy.

Before taking office people were assuming that we were going to war with North Korea. President Obama said that North Korea was our biggest and most dangerous problem.

NO LONGER - SLEEP WELL TONIGHT!

@realDonaldTrump

The Road Less Censored

The fact Donald Trump has risen to the top of the polls, despite his so-called "inflammatory" rhetoric, proves how utterly detached the GOP establishment has become from its own base; whether or not he secures the nomination. For years conservatives have been clamoring for the Party of Ronald Reagan to hold Obama accountable, to secure our border and to stop the White House from illicitly using government agencies to attack and punish its political opponents. And exactly what prudent actions have the dynamic duo of Boehner and McConnell taken to address these obvious abuses and failures; by zealously joining the Democratic chorus labeling us as radicals, racists, and religious extremists out of fear of bad press! Funneling our nation's founding ideals – the timeless principles of freedom, faith & accountability – through the color-coded, secular and gender-neutral progressive filter of political correctness will do nothing to assuage this country's ills or preserve our Constitutional liberties. Has the GOP once used its congressional monopoly, its historic mandate of voter discontent, to shut down this rogue administration's reckless spending, defund Obamacare, protect Christian businesses and pastors from persecution, or to condemn the redistribution efforts and anti-American tenets of Obamatrade? Not once! Rather, they have consistently and routinely capitulated to the deceptive ploys of radical leftists and habitual liars like Harry Reid and Nancy Pelosi; as if Democrats themselves are the majority and possess a legal right to censor what we say, do, and think. Preposterous!

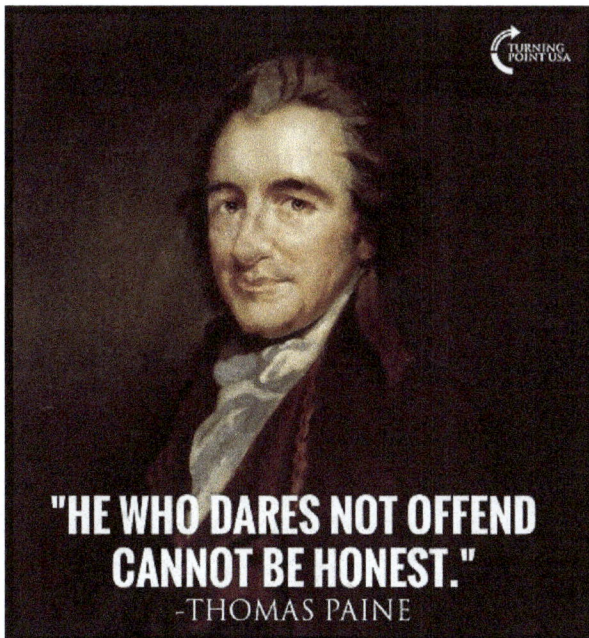

"HE WHO DARES NOT OFFEND CANNOT BE HONEST."
-THOMAS PAINE

No, Donald Trump's ascension to the forefront of the political spectrum is hardly due to blind coincidence, engrained racism or carnival gimmicks. Those struggling Americans who have been systematically crushed and silenced by the Obama agenda aren't interested in career politicians who are dedicated to the proposition of tip-toeing around the issues and taking extra-special precautions as if not to offend those propagandists who will slander conservatives and seek America's destruction regardless. They want a leader who isn't afraid of speaking the truth in the face of the most obstinate criticism and mass scrutiny. If honesty, courage and conviction are now considered revolutionary concepts, then we are truly living in extraordinary times that require unconventional methods; or more succinctly, ardent and unabashed patriots. Just don't be surprised, America, if you spot a golden ticket of Trump/Carson or Cruz at the top of your ballot in the Fall of 2016. Not all men, or women, are inherently equal. And most of all; not all desire a teleprompter to lie to the American people under the false pretense of "hope" and "change"!

Meet Karma: The GOP's Bastard Son

While the Republican establishment and numerous right-leaning publications have shamelessly joined forces with anti-American liberals in a desperate attempt to derail the Trump campaign, let us embark on a brief history lesson. Lest "We the People" forget, the GOP are the same charlatans who wasted two historic victories in 2010 and 2014, due to a conservative platform, only to break nearly every campaign promise and capitulate to the most radical and rogue President time and again. So much for the moral high ground.

How many times did the sworn enemies of Donald Trump vote to raise the debt ceiling; despite knowing Barack Obama has increased the national debt almost more than all other presidents combined, even resulting in not one but two historic credit downgrades? Did the once proud party of Ronald Reagan actually vote to approve Loretta Lynch's nomination – a serial racist who ignores black hate crimes, attacks the religious liberty of Christians and refuses to prosecute criminals within the IRS and DHS – or am I just a confused and unreasonable "Tea Party" radical? Did Republicans, the elected majority in Congress and not just a "dangerous, singular blowhard" like Mr. Trump, agree to an international trade agreement that will undermine American commerce and allow corrupt foreign regimes who utilize slave labor and deplorable conditions to dictate future trade stipulations; i.e., unequal tariffs and market access, environmental regulations and back compensation?

And if I may, how many of these same "principled" Republican stalwarts ever tried to prosecute Barack Obama, his contemptible administration, for a single one of a litany of provable crimes: continual abuse of Executive power, ordering states and border officers not to enforce existing immigration laws, transporting and resettling medically and criminally unvetted illegal aliens across America, instructing the DHS to secretly print work visas in violation of a Federal court order, using the IRS to wrongfully target conservatives, abandoning four Americans to their deaths in Benghazi, wiretapping the press and Congress, selling arms to Mexican drug cartels, failing to indict Planned Parenthood for selling human remains on the black market, releasing known criminals and terrorists from imprisonment, granting failed "green" loans to political allies (Solyndra), ignoring Black Panther voter intimidation, and repeatedly exceeding the Constitutional authority of the EPA...to name but a few? Not once? How ironic. Maybe I'm not dreaming.

The same "progressive" GOP that created Donald Trump's historic popularity with their endless lies and failures, even begging him not to seek an independent bid, secretly instigated and even funded an avalanche of negative attacks. Now who's the petulant child of spite? Yes, I truly respect and admire Ted Cruz, I always have, but I fully support Mr. Trump because he says what most of us are thinking but the establishment refuses to say. The man is fearless, bold, and he simply gets things done; which is much more than I can say about the pawn brokers at broken promises. I'm tired of playing games with the liberal media and the anti-American socialists known as the Democratic Party because soon there will be nothing left to save. Illegal immigration must be stopped, radical Islam must be defeated, our private sector must flourish, the Constitution must once again become the supreme law of the land, and the victimization politics of race and class warfare must be unconditionally condemned as destructive and ignorant movements. It's time for common sense to once again take center stage and I couldn't care less if it was politically correct or limited to the cardboard cutout of my "ideal" candidate. Mitt Romney proved political "moderation" is vastly overrated by losing to the most ideologically extreme, inexperienced and divisive President in our nation's history. And he did it with a smile and a concession speech.

For the Congressional record, I'm not concerned about whether a candidate is skilled at making well-rehearsed speeches on the campaign trail or dishing out prime time soundbites on national TV for the sake of scoring debate points to ensure the survival of a failed party that routinely betrayed its own constituents. I want a proven leader whose actions will inevitably match the rhetoric. More importantly, I want to win, PERIOD, and I always believed Trump had far more electoral appeal and coattails than either Ted Cruz or Marco Rubio. The fact the Stony Brook Method calculated Trump has a 97% chance of securing the presidency only further validates that assertion. Just remember, the real enemies of American exceptionalism are still on the other side of the aisle; or so I once thought. It's about damn time the forsaken masses reminded the party elitists of that simple fact on November 8th.

The Spilled Milk of #NeverTrump

As the weeping wounds of defeat are still unbearably fresh and the disappointment of the #NeverTrump faction echoes like an unfulfilled wish on Christmas morning, it is clear their anger is not only misplaced and self-destructive, but their misery is a self-inflicted gunshot from the shadows of denial. From the onset of his mercurial campaign, Donald Trump was exactly who I thought he was: a boisterous, unapologetic, politically incorrect executive who instinctively capitalized upon the ever-growing jetsam of GOP betray. If "We the disgruntled" remember correctly, it was the GOP, not Donald Trump, who broke countless campaign promises despite being handed two historic victories by conservatives in 2010 and 2014. Their endless litany of lies and capitulation to the divisive Obama agenda forged the very political fissure very from which Trump's nationalistic bravado sprung and resonated without match. In other words, the man simply navigated the political currents, spoke his mind and seized the moment. Senators Cruz and Rubio, whom I have respected for years and will continue to support despite the recent bloodbath, doomed their candidacies by failing to confront Trump's popularity much earlier in the process. If they acted sooner, I would likely be touting their prospects today. However, by the time they aggressively confronted both his persona and politics, it was far too late and the primal mudslinging ensued; a game that was ill-suited and detrimental to their carefully crafted statures and an arena in which their nemesis resided and comfortably thrived.

American politics is no longer a platform for honest discourse of competing philosophies designed to judge candidates solely on the merits of their ideas and records. If so, Hillary would be in prison, illegal immigrants wouldn't be given more aid and deference than actual citizens, BLM activists would protest the moral decay of their own neighborhoods, and bathrooms wouldn't require boycotts of common sense. Our political system has morphed into a media-manipulated, special interest fiasco that shamelessly preys on their fears and ignorance of low information voters; those who now constitute a majority of American populace. Whereas modern Democrats will do anything to win an election, their once respectable intentions hijacked by anti-American extremists who believe the end justifies the means, recent Republicans have tried to take the high road, relying on the integrity of the process and their opponents only to be successfully demonized as racists, greedy capitalists, and religious bigots. Ergo, enter the shark, Donald Trump. By tapping into a bevy of dissatisfaction from party parties, organic themes like "Make America Great Again", "Can't Be Bought", "Build the Wall" and "Crooked Hillary", there's no angle of attack too steep or subject matter too polarizing. Essentially, he's beating the Democratic drum of derision with the skeletons from the left's own urban warfare of demagoguery. Why, you ask? Stigma, not standards, is the new flag bearer of mass persuasion.

As a lifelong conservative who is quite cognizant of our founding charter and the gravity of issues at hand, I never once misrepresented or felt duped by Donald Trump's campaign. I never categorized him as a "textbook" conservative, or one at all, and I never suggested he was immune from deceit or contradiction. Why would I? After all, we're talking about contemporary politics, right? It's just too bad the same "conservative" whistle-blowers lamenting his false credentials voted for Bush, McCain and Romney in the general election. I guess they forgot to boycott themselves as well. Yes, semantics aside, the billionaire celebrity is better characterized as a shrewd, ambitious opportunist who succeeds by adapting to the environment of his prey. Succinctly put, he is willing to win at all costs by defeating Democrats at their own depraved game; formalities or appearances be damned. And that's why the media plantation owners on the left fear Trump above all others: no rules, no chains, no surrender, no apologies.

What I do feel insulted by, however, is those #NeverTrump mouthpieces – Glenn Beck, Charles Krauthammer, National Review, the Weekly Standard & even the GOP itself – that smugly claim there is little to no discernible difference between a Donald Trump or a Hillary Clinton presidency. Sorry to rain on their scorched earth fertilizer of discontent, but sour grapes are not, nor where they ever been, on the "adult" menu of democracy this November. Unless chicken nuggets are the new Kobe beef, how can any self-proclaimed patriot consciously drown hope with idle scorn while America's survival is teetering on the precipice of financial, cultural, and ideological ruin after 8 years of unchecked progressivism? If 'hurt feelings' are flyers from consequences, or better yet humility, perhaps the guardians of idealism need to launch the #ScrewAmerica movement to put their "principled" actions in the proper context. Crying over spilled milk doesn't clean up the mess, stop the snowballing socialist hoard with your bitter abstinence, or magically increase your IQ.

For the sake of argument but more so to understand how Trump supporters are supposedly so hopelessly bemused, what "non-conservative" candidate that fully supports "legal" immigration wants to once again make illegal immigration a punishable crime again, secure our borders and cease the resettlement of unvetted Muslim refugees that was solely designed to stuff the ballot box? My money is on 'definitely not Hillary'! What presumptive nominee wants to empower the private sector – which hasn't enjoyed a single annualized GDP of over 3% under our Marxist-in-chief – end the entrepreneurial atrophy of 'free trade', lessen the tax burden on struggling families, and restore the precept of American Exceptionalism? Still stumped? Here's a hint; it's not the proud collectivist who once uttered, "We'll take from you for the common good!" And finally, which 'greedy' tycoon wants to lower the 19.5 trillion national debt, which has nearly DOUBLED under Barack Obama despite Washington collecting record tax revenue during his tenure, to avoid yet another credit downgrade and global recession? Hmm, is it the same social justice warrior who wants you to apologize for your 'White Privilege', for pursuing higher education or being fiscally responsible by finding a job in lieu of becoming one of the record 48 million on welfare? Only if you're willing to punish success, reward envy and curse the "unnatural" inequalities of achievement by shouting, "I'm With Her!" during every handheld step on the winding road to self-pity. When minimum wage is racist, minimal thought is bliss.

Not to dangle the carrot stick of regret, and please forgive my insatiable curiosity, what "unelectable megalomaniac", the same political charlatan who has collected a record amount of Republican primary votes, has pledged to elect a conservative to the Supreme Court to protect the Second Amendment, stop non-citizens from voting and to ensure our religious liberties? Nope, sorry, wrong again, my friend. Hillary Rodham Clinton wants to prosecute gun manufacturers, equate self-defense to murder, and use Obamacare and Social Security to deny or ransom our Constitutional right to bear arms. And what pandering, fraudulent politician seeks to label conservative viewpoints as hate speech, in a country predicated upon free speech and limited government, despite personally justifying the racist/violent actions of Black Lives Matter, defining feminism by the political affiliation of a body orifice, or by forcing the morally corrosive, counter-intuitive LGBT agenda into our homes, classrooms and communities? Do I really need to bake a cake for posterity sake, inscribed with her legal defense motto of "What difference does it make", or does the fact she masquerades as a women's rights advocate who threatened and slandered the victims of her husband's voracious sexual appetite, somehow make her no worse than Donald Trump: a 'hateful' vulture who married an immigrant, donated millions to charity, and has created more jobs than the 30,000 emails deleted by Hillary?

Whether Trump has voiced support for some Democrats, altered his stance on key issues or keenly donated to both sides of the aisle to protect his business interests, is a moot point at this stage of the electoral journey. He is, like it or not, the nominee. Ted Cruz, Marco Rubio and John Kasich all had ample opportunity to seize the national narrative, dismantle Trump's candidacy and to illuminate the unmistakable treasure map of Hillary's radical roots, treasonous ties, and graveyard of criminal impropriety. Their failure is not Trump's cross to bear. That proposition is now the sole baggage of those disheartened voters who would rather wallow in self-pity, cast a ceremonial ballot for 'spite', rather than fight for the survival of their native country that is literally on life-support. The question is...when did the common regularity of disappointment lead right-minded Americans to become willing spectators as Hillary Clinton pulls the plug on the most transcendent nation in modern human history? Apparently, the fate of our 240-year-old republic boils down to abstaining from pulling the lever for an imperfect man –

capable, patriotic, flawed and often an uncouth narcissist – instead of voting against a corrupt, anti-American statist that is dedicated to finishing the 'unalarming' job Barack Obama started: destroying America along racial, religious and socio-economic lines. There is no moral victory or high ground when abstaining from voting against Hillary. There is only the inevitable aftermath of failing to act in the name of self-preservation.

The Paid Puppets of Nazi Propaganda

The building crescendo of organized chaos surrounding Donald Trump's rallies has very little to do with the man's actual legacy, and everything to do with destroying his candidacy in the arena of public opinion. After all, if these so–called mouthpieces of public outrage didn't troll Trump's events to incite discord with their vile brand of 'moral' objectivism, there would be nothing to report in the news. Not only are known radical groups like Moveon.org, Code Pink, La Raza and Black Lives Matter orchestrating these hostile protests – blocking highways, screaming obscenities, assaulting Trump supporters, and damaging private property – they're financed by skilled social puppeteers like George Soros who invest billions in the art of mass manipulation. In essence, by using these gross spectacles to insinuate waves of distressed Americans are flocking to the streets to defeat evil's latest persona non- grata, the leftist establishment is hoping operation chaos will serve as a future blueprint to dissuade, fatally damage, any future candidate or nonconformist policy that threatens their agenda and media stranglehold on public opinion.

NAZIS	DEMOCRATS
SOCIALISM	SOCIALISM
NO GUNS	NO GUNS
CENSORSHIP	CENSORSHIP
MEDIA MIND CONTROL	MEDIA MIND CONTROL
ABORTION	ABORTION
HATE JEWS	HATE JEWS AND WHITES
WORSHIP THE GOVERNMENT	WORSHIP THE GOVERNMENT

As the progressive thought police collude daily to derail Trump's campaign, to attempt to convince you he is the modern day reincarnation of Hitler, they're omitting one minute detail: he openly praises and encourages "legal" immigration, is married to an immigrant, and merely seeks to halt the costly epidemic of illegal immigration; something countless other Presidential candidates have pledged to address for decades and all without their opponents inciting riots, silencing free speech or re-incarnating Nazi propaganda to deflect from reality. As a celebrity entrepreneur and philanthropist who has been in the public eye for over 30 years, Donald Trump has openly contributed to both parties, befriended people from all walks of life and somehow was never publicly labeled as a racist, a Nazi or a xenophobe before announcing his Presidential bid. How ironic. Not only are these assertions blatantly false, recklessly antagonistic, they belittle the memories and suffering of the countless victims who were actually murdered by a deranged, sadistic madman. Now who's being obtuse and hopelessly paranoid?

If the adage "no human being is illegal" is true, as activists love to proclaim, why do we have borders and immigration laws in the first place; those very statutes Democrats helped author, pass and have duly existed for over a century? Has federal oversight of immigration not existed since 1891; first through the Treasury, the Department of Justice in 1940, and now via the BCIS? If anyone should be protesting in the streets and threatening a revolution in the name of mass injustice, it's the citizens of this republic who have become afterthoughts in the progressive war on traditional America. Instead of putting the safety of Americans first, the Obama administration is not only fueling the current flood of illegal immigration – soliciting and transporting thousands of medically and criminally unvetted individuals into our communities – they're dolling out taxpayer money like candy to bribe dependent foreigners into supporting leftist policies for generations to come.

The appalling fact our government spends more money per illegal immigrant than on actual citizens, even those social security recipients who worked and paid taxes their whole life, is criminal and insulting to say the least. Opposition to this destructive practice has nothing to do with hate, exterminating an entire race of people in the name of a Nazi regime bent on world domination, but everything to do with returning sanity and an ounce of credibility to the halls of our forefathers. If Democrats simply honored our existing laws, recognized the prescribed process of naturalization every civilized nation demands, and admitted their socialist schemes are bankrupting this nation both fiscally and ideologically, then Donald Trump wouldn't have to suggest the "radical" concept of building a wall to stop and confront the even more radical liberal concept of overthrowing America's sovereignty and electoral balance to achieve a permanent state of political supremacy.

Not to spoil the blissful delusions of Democratic socialists, the contemporary aspirations of the Democratic Party, the term "Nazi" was derived by the National Socialist German Workers' Party that paved the way for Hitler's ascendancy and rabid platform. These fascists sought, much like today's progressives, to control every aspect of the people's lives through authoritative government under the guise of the country's best interests: education, religion, commerce, sexuality, gun control, any institution or mechanism that further indoctrinated the masses with their unilateral agenda. (Hence, no mention of individual liberty or limited government) Whereas the Nazis murdered, enslaved and oppressed millions – basically anyone who was not German, healthy or compliant – Donald Trump has never sought to deprive or control anything other stopping our elected government from orchestrating ILLEGAL immigration, enabling radical Islam out of spite of traditional America, and forcing the mass exodus of American companies and jobs to impoverished countries by suffocating private enterprise for the sole purpose of wealth redistribution.

Unless I'm badly mistaken, our current government has threatened the sacred beliefs and liberties of Christian churches, jailed Americans for merely exercising their right to free speech, forced homosexuality and gender identity education into our public schools while removing God for the common good, shot peaceful protestors who opposed the overreach of federal agencies, and left Americans to die in a foreign land out of fear of upsetting

Muslim sentiment; yes, those same religious extremists who pledge to destroy Israel and America on a daily basis. And what did Donald Trump do? He's running for President to return accountability to Washington and America to her abandoned, forsaken citizens. Apparently, progressivism has a new definition that goes by a much older name: propaganda. The greatest trick the media ever played was convincing the public "extremism" or "fascism" doesn't pertain to the left side of the aisle, when in reality it now almost exclusively resides there.

True to Thyself: The Populist President

For those who followed and supported Donald J. Trump since the announcement of his candidacy, today's inaugural speech made no apologies and offered no refuge from the populist message he has conveyed without refrain or neglect of those he proudly represents: the marginalized masses of political contempt. In the brooding face of media elites and plotting Democratic foes, the billionaire bulldog spoke with unflinching resolve and a majestic sense of duty dedicated to honoring the country he loves and reforming a hostile government willingly bereft of common sense and culpability. Not only were his words powerful, his convictions refreshingly candid, it's clear his vintage charter of "America First" will scuttle the globalist agenda in favor of reclaiming our economic vitality, restoring the rule of law, defeating Islamic barbarism, and embodying the spirit of the American exceptionalism so tirelessly suffocated by progressive malcontents.

Despite mocking his every nuance or constitutional affirmation as divisive and dangerous on this day of national revelry – a characterization egregiously lacking from the unvetted Marxist beliefs, Islamic loyalties and anti-American associates of one Barack Hussein Obama – the press continues to operate under the delusion they are anything but a yellow stain of petulance on the road map to progress. When your pulpit of propaganda crucifies a man's reputation and true intent, incites people to the point of fracture over an "incomprehensible" election result, the cross of betrayal is yours to bear alone. The truth is, after enduring 8 years of executive deception and pardoned corruption, Donald Trump shouldn't have to mince words solely to coddle the tears of melting snowflakes or tread lightly to protect the fragile egos of the status quo simply because so-called educated pundits are now incapable of objective discourse, or at the very least, identifying the unrivaled source of our ills and societal division.

If putting 'America First' is such a radical and foreign concept, why do we vote, pay taxes, have borders, sing the national anthem or celebrate the Fourth of July? Better yet, before I believe China, Iran, Syrian refugees or the United Nations have our best interests at heart, I don't ever again want to witness the "radical" proposition of electing a president that doesn't love America or instinctively put the welfare of his or her countrymen first and foremost. Yes, contrary to paid protestors, it is entirely possible to lead a sovereign nation from a position of strength, a prudent platform of self-preservation, without abandoning empathy or the international community. And for those who don't agree, tell me what goes through your mind when you tuck your kids in bed at night or endlessly endeavor how to best protect and provide for your family.

The Sour Grapes of Bitter Protestors & False Allegations

Because the national press has worked so tirelessly to slander Donald Trump day and night, millions of Americans are under the delusion he is the reincarnation of Hitler; a serial rapist and unparalleled bigot bent on global supremacy. Yet, before announcing his candidacy in June of 2015, he was never labeled hateful, let alone accused of any such scandalous behavior by the media, celebrities or Republicans and Democrats alike. In fact, he was often praised and befriended by the likes of Al Sharpton, Jesse Jackson, Oprah Winfrey and even Hillary Clinton herself. And now in the aftermath of the media's reckless pandering and criminal practices, these obnoxious protestors take to our streets are a perfect example of the inevitable bitter fallout from a growing propaganda state. Yes, this is what happens when a political party knowingly colludes with the "independent" media in a shameless attempt to wage war on the truth and to demonize the same candidate they would have opposed regardless. And for what...to falsely sway public opinion, taint the integrity of our democratic process, and put people's lives at risk in the name of winning an election? For the sake of posterity and peace, the last vestiges of common sense from which our Republic dangles, let us examine what we already know about some of his accusers...

- None of Donald Trump's "victims" came publicly forward until roughly three weeks before the election.

- Nearly all of his accusers, supposedly spanning decades and from all across America, were represented by Gloria Allred; the infamous feminist attorney who took down Herman Cain on mere accusations and the same Democratic operative who lives to politicize any perceived discretion for personal or political gain. Coincidence? Of course not.

- Media surrogates and DNC officials put out Craigslist advertisements asking women to come forward and claim they were groped or assaulted by Trump. ABC producers even contacted every contestant from all of Trump's pageants trying to illicit or bribe stories of impropriety. Many attempts were rebuffed and some publicly by those who chose to speak out. Victoria Hughes, former Miss Teen New Mexico, said Trump was a perfect gentleman and that she spoke out, despite not voting for him, because "she wouldn't want false allegations made about her or anyone else". Too much logic for the media?

- A former contestant on 'The Apprentice', Summer Servos – the same one who claimed Trump made lewd advances – sent a letter to his campaign manager asking if Mr. Trump could visit her restaurant because, and I quote... "We hire a diverse crew and embrace anyone who is honest while working hard. Mr. Trump is cut from the same cloth." It was also reported Ms. Servos was offered $500,000 by Democratic donors to aid her struggling business.

- Jessica Leeds, a reported Trump sexual assault victim, was a former Clinton Foundation secretary and an associate of Hillary Clinton's. There are pictures of both embracing.

- Mindy McGillivray claimed Donald Trump groped her at Mara-Largo during a Ray Charles concert in 2003 while he was engaged to Melania. Unfortunately for her, there was no Ray Charles at Mara-Lago and he wasn't engaged to Melania until a year later. Mindy McGillivray was, however, arrested for driving drunk with her child in the car.

- Former Miss Universe and an aspiring porn actress, Melissa Machado, was angry when Trump referred to her "size" after she knowingly broke the "weight clause" agreement of a lucrative contract she willingly signed. She appeared with Hillary during several campaign-stops to address size and gender shaming.

- Another accuser who actually was a Porn Star, Jessica Drake, claimed in a televised press conference – one day before her online Adult Toy Store was to launch – she was groped by Donald Trump. She too had no proof or witnesses other than her tears Gloria Allred wiped away before rolling Television cameras.

- Katie Johnson, a reported 13-year-old rape victim repeatedly invoked by liberals during the campaign, dropped her case multiple times because she was afraid of perjury charges after the DA said there was no "anecdotal or tangible evidence to her claim. It appeared without merit or sincerity." Protestors nationwide continue to call her a rape victim.

- The picture of Donald Trump hugging a young girl in his limousine was actually that of his own daughter. Yes, fathers never hug or show affection to their children.

```
Subject: Re: Approval: Craigslist Job
Post


Just talked to Jackie — apparently
because we're talking about sexual
harassment, the defamation risk is
really high, but he hasn't been
litigious yet, so...
```

If you believe there is smoke where there is fire, well, it's obvious something stinks to high hell. As civil unrest grows across America, people's lives and property are being put at risk in the name of a lie. Considering Donald Trump is an international celebrity and billionaire, it's unfathomable not even one of these women came forward in the past to, at least attempt, sue for financial compensation. Of course, when you have zero tangible evidence or credible witnesses, how could you? These protests are the deliberate result of a smear campaign, are nothing more than political theater. Why, you ask? If Hillary had won the election, would any of these same "concerned citizens" have felt compelled to take to the streets for the welfare of Trump's supposed victims; at the very least in the name of justice? Of course not. Did they shout from America's street corners to defend Bill Clinton's rape victims or mourn the victims of Benghazi? How about the murder or rape victims of illegal immigrants hiding in Sanctuary Cities? Their sterling values and sense of feminist outrage must have been playing video games or Snapchatting that day.

The same progressive puppeteers who pulled the strings of "Occupy Wall Street" before the 2012 election and fueled the racial unrest in Ferguson to demonize police, are now mobilizing public opinion against Trump for one calculated reason: to undermine his victory and to forcibly diminish the "change" his policies will inevitably bring. Whether you call it "sour grapes" or Marxist propaganda, it is a reminder that true radicalism not only exists on the left side of the aisle, it almost solely resides there now.

"If you don't read the newspapers you are uninformed and if you do read them you are misinformed." ~Mark Twain

WOMEN IN THE TRUMP ADMINISTRATION

NIKKI HALEY
UN AMBASSADOR

IVANKA TRUMP
SPECIAL ADVISER
TO THE PRESIDENT

KELLYANNE CONWAY
COUNSELOR TO
THE PRESIDENT

SARAH SANDERS
WHITE HOUSE
PRESS SECRETARY

GINA HASPEL
CIA DIRECTOR

ELAINE CHAO
TRANSPORTATION
SECRETARY

BETSY DEVOS
EDUCATION
SECRETARY

KIRSTJEN NIELSEN
HOMELAND
SECURITY SECY

LINDA MCMAHON
SMALL BUSINESS
ADMINISTRATOR

MERCEDES SCHLAPP
WH STRATEGIC
COMM DIRECTOR

FOX
friends

Prelude to a President

What's the difference between reality and perception? Well that depends on who is taking your picture or if they're writing your obituary. Those individuals who have actually met or befriended Donald Trump overwhelmingly share the same opinion of the New York native. That is...he's a genuine, generous man who embraces and helps people from all walks of life; whether hosting a Royal Saudi diplomat at one of his prestigious hotels, aiding an ill child or thanking an everyday employee working in the shadows of his mailroom. However, because his critics love to highlight his unfiltered bravado, they immediately opt to demonize the messenger, tarnish his name to undermine his message, rather than earnestly debating the merits and validity of his message: i.e., America is being dismantled along economic, racial, and religious lines with little regard for the truth or the rule of law. For more than 30 years, well before the media and the Clinton campaign embarked on an "unbiased" crusade to paint Trump as a hateful xenophobe, he donated to both political parties and was widely praised for his social works, generosity, by celebrities and activists alike; those whose "infamous" ranks include Jesse Jackson, Al Sharpton, Oprah Winfrey, and even the once-proud 'Confederate' Clintons themselves.

As the progressive mob conspires daily to derail Trump's growing popularity – a desperate attempt to convince America he is the modern-day reincarnation of Hitler – they're omitting one-minute detail. He openly praises and encourages "legal" immigration, is married to an immigrant, and merely seeks to halt the costly epidemic of illegal immigration; something countless other presidential candidates have pledged to address for decades without their opponents ever inciting riots, silencing free speech or re-incarnating Nazi propaganda to deflect from their own failures. And yet before announcing his Presidential bid, Donald Trump...a global celebrity, entrepreneur and philanthropist...was never labeled a racist, a bigot or a "Nazi. How ironic. Not only are such assertions blatantly false, recklessly antagonistic, they belittle the memories and suffering of the countless victims who were actually murdered by a sadistic madman. Now who's being callous and obtuse?

Considering "character" was once the crux of presidential worthiness, what's more relevant in choosing a credible, inspiring leader: someone who lends his time, money and resources to help critically ill children, families of slain cops, and struggling veterans – contributing to numerous legitimate charities – or a career politician who uses her own "charitable" foundation as a presidential slush fund to defraud natural disaster survivors? Because "truth" is now a sexist term, that answer requires a full-time nurse, a liberal debate moderator and a private server. I guess when you're selling future favors at the State Department and you're personally knee-deep in Wall Street campaign vouchers, character and integrity are as expendable as the scandalous paper they're printed on. Cuban cigar, anyone? Duty and conscience free!

If Donald Trump is guilty of anything it is for succeeding in a country predicated upon innovation, making a difference in the vacuum of others' empty rhetoric and for speaking his mind without endless deception or unnecessary convolution. In my personal experiences, it is not the politically incorrect pragmatist that threatens liberty, security and prosperity, but the seasoned politician who cajoles, conspires and selectively reports the actual state of the union in order to more easily divide and conquer the voting masses. In other words, modern day progressives believe the best way to win a game of electoral chess is by sacrificing their perceived pawns; insulting voters' intelligence with stale propaganda and endlessly pandering to their state-assisted sense of "victimization". And all without ever achieving "real" change before the next election! However, when you shed the rusted shackles of blind allegiance and perceive America as a bastion of hope and opportunity, that power to transform one's life resides in our God-given rights, the free will of every individual, and not the dictated terms of forced dependence and mass conformity. The power of "you" suddenly and rightfully supersedes the unconstitutional authority of the state. I'll take an unfiltered, successful CEO over a dictator every time.

Regardless of your personal attributes or political beliefs, the sensory overload of this divisive election can be remedied by answering one inescapable question. Do you believe the best way to ensure a prosperous, united and moral America is through an undying love of liberty, a transparent government, personal responsibility, an insatiable worth ethic and a healthy respect for this nation's blessings...your fellow man? Or do you believe the U.S. is an evil empire where true progress is characterized by teaching our children to despise America, by silencing intellectual diversity in our schools, condemning police but pardoning criminality, glorifying communism at the expense of freedom, declaring discrimination as exclusive but privacy as gender inclusive, labeling Christianity as hate speech while importing Islam, and by claiming that only American borders and immigration laws are racist and unjust? If this stark dichotomy and chilling reality is by any means disturbing, a cultural conundrum, then by all means please allow me to present 'The Common Sense Case for America" before that choice may no longer duly exist. The most revealing questions are typically not the ones the mainstream media attempts to answer. The best questions are almost always the ones they refuse to ask.

Because America Matters

Can anyone here tell me, without any degree of uncertainty, that Barack Obama and Hillary Clinton love America? Isn't it about time we had a President who did, rather than one who incessantly denigrates our history, incites racial discord ad nauseam, dismisses Islamic terrorism by attacking Christianity and demonizes financial success for political gain? Truly, how can you have a country's best interests at heart when you can't bring yourself to respect and appreciate her indelible blessings: her constitutional precepts recognizing that man's natural born rights are derived by God and not the property of any man-made institution ransoming free will? This is the unwavering reason as to why I tell people I overwhelmingly support Donald Trump for President. I don't want an anti-American apologist who struggles to shake the hand of police officers or honor our military veterans, let alone salute the very symbol of opportunity and liberty that defines their ascendancy to power...our national flag. I want a leader who is more dedicated to making America great again – protecting her people and ensuring her survival as a beacon of hope, strength and prosperity – in lieu of serving any political party or divisive agenda. If this simple truth makes me a bigot so be it. I'll gladly withstand those blind epithets of political convenience to defend what centuries of our brethren sacrificed and died to protect; and are still fighting in the name of freedom, equality and justice across the globe.

An Unwilling Accomplice

Once upon a time an ambitious, educated, hard-working young man stepped forth into the world to make his father proud and honor the blessing that is America. The revered "Don of "New York" spearheaded over 500 successful business ventures, created thousands of jobs, erected renowned real estate on four continents, was repeatedly lauded by all sects of society for his philanthropic and social work, and he even won the Republican nomination for President of the United States in the face of unwavering scorn and scrutiny. However, for the first time in his 70-year-old life and roughly just three weeks before the election, this devoted husband and doting father who chose a path free from alcohol and recreational drugs was suddenly accused of harassment and sexual assault by nearly a dozen women; of which an overwhelming majority were solicited by network/party operatives hunting for any hint of indiscretion or scent of jaded associates willing to imply guilt. Hour on the hour, choreographed press conference after choreographed press conference, the tears of the victims' unsubstantiated stories were rolled out in front of cameras as feminist attorney Gloria Allred held their hands without ever once mentioning how her celebrity services were so deftly obtained – the very same political hotline used to sink and slander the campaign of Herman Cain – or if she enjoyed her trip to the Democratic National Convention in July as a Hillary Clinton delegate. Apparently "hearsay" is a billable foray.

Despite being "violated" by an international icon and affluent mogul, not one of these women filed a civil case, if at the very least, to secure a quick, lucrative settlement. Equally ironic, not a single criminal charge was ever filed by law enforcement against their alleged assailant, nor was a single interrogation ever required. To the surprise of no one, and without a shred of tangible evidence except that provided by the accused debunking claim after claim, the mainstream media viciously degraded this man night after night, 24 hours a day, engineering a blatantly false narrative that convinced millions a rising populist candidate was a womanizer, a misogynist, a pedophile and a serial rapist; a vile legacy Bill Clinton has been apathetically acquitted from by the same outraged partisans who buried a treasure trove of sexual impropriety and deceit. As a result of the media's reckless tactics and criminal indifference, riots ensued, property was destroyed, and countless Americans were assaulted for doing nothing more than honoring their civic duty and exercising their electoral rights.

Today, as part of a mass demonstration of ignorance and juvenile spite, thousands of women across this nation protested a man they never met, personally knew or ever asked a single question. In a deplorable display of bitter self-righteousness, Ashley Judd accused him of molesting his own daughter while Madonna gave a profanity-laced tirade glorifying her seething desire to bomb the White House and murder a sitting U.S. President and his family. How incredibly admirable. This cultivated hate harnessed by activists to incite such disgusting behavior is by no means a mistake, or an organic grassroots reaction, but an organized charade designed to delegitimize the greatest threat to the progressive agenda: an unwilling accomplice.

"America was never that great." ~New York Governor, Andrew Cuomo

Making America Great Again

'Making America Great Again' isn't about disrespecting our transcendent past or selectively favoring any gender, race or economic class to secure a privileged future. It's about working together to solve our most daunting challenges by rededicating ourselves to the timeless ideals – liberty, equality, limited government, faith, hard work, self-reliance, and duty – that once made this nation a beacon of hope and opportunity for all mankind. Poverty, disease, discrimination, crime, and moral apathy are not new obstacles or an unexplainable phenomenon. They're exploited realities whose corrosive effects have been exacerbated by career politicians and poisonous agendas that welcome division and discord, encourage victimization in lieu of self-empowerment, and purposely mislead the masses solely to spurn our collective struggles into voter discontent. These soulless parasites freely dispense blame to deflect from their failed policies, their true radical intentions, to ensure their own electoral survival by feeding off the misery and misfortune of the very people they sanctimoniously betrayed.

However, when our economy is strong, our schools and streets kept safe, the Constitution upheld, our immigration laws respected, and America's societal values protected from the nonsensical subversion known as progressivism – unapologetic anti-Americanism, social entitlement, race-baiting, gender/sexual identity conditioning, and Islamic indoctrination – than a new era of prosperity and robust optimism can flourish beneath competent and steadfast leadership. Despite enduring an avalanche of preposterous attacks inciting both fear and violence against his supporters, it is not Donald Trump who is recklessly threatening America's future and decaying communities. That danger exists in the false narrative of media propagandists attempting to divert attention from the true source of our country's ills: an inept, detached, self-self-serving and unchecked political establishment.

If "We the People" return accountability to government, reward ambition instead of envy, honor God and our fellow man by taking responsibility for own lives and actions, America can leave behind the destructive status quo to reclaim the sanity and ideological soul of an industrious, free republic. It is not higher taxes and shameless identity politics that make us "stronger together"; it is the fearless heartbeat of liberty, the spirit of boundless innovation, and the firm handshake of dependability. A proven leader doesn't need special accommodations and media manipulation to greet the public as disposable stage props every four years. A real executive merely needs to look you in the eye and speak the inconvenient truth; for better or for worse. A better tomorrow does not reside in the broken promises of Washington elitists or the doctored legacy and condescending rhetoric of a detestable globalist. The fate of America's future resides with you; a singular vote cast by every fleeced taxpayer, forgotten veteran, mocked Christian, marginalized minority, naturalized citizen, and 'deplorable' patriot who simply wants to live in a proud, prosperous nation free from hate, deception and federal abuse. On November 8th, 2016, the sacrificed pawns of party politics toppled the kings and queens of corruption by choosing the only candidate seeking to renew the promise of America's founding fathers every waking moment of his presidency. That man is Donald. J. Trump and unlike "the resistance" he's fighting to make America great again!

To Lead by Example

I do not deny that I love Donald Trump's "no-nonsense, get shit done" mentality of leadership. The man tackles problems with timely vigor, he consults people from all schools of thought regardless of personal differences, and he views "politics" as an obstacle to sound, lasting solutions. An effective executive doesn't lose daylight cultivating excuses – especially in the face of failure or apathy – and by no means accepts them from those delegated with his utmost trust and authority. While bitter partisans continue to cry and plot over an election result instead of protesting the egregious state of our Union – a feeble economy, reckless immigration, record debt, incited racial division, political censorship and eroding urban epicenters – the President-elect has already secured commitments for nearly 100,000 new jobs, restored consumer confidence, banned lobbyists from Washington, identified and rejected federal waste, rescinded his personal business interests and salary, donated all profits from international Trump hotels to the U.S. Treasury, and shown both cooperation and unflinching resolve in addressing our cultural differences, including the moral degradation and failing infrastructure plaguing our communities. And the man hasn't even taken office yet.

Whether you love him or despise him, you will not find Mr. Trump's tireless work ethic and love of country loitering on golf courses during times of civil unrest or spending 100 million of the people's money on lavish vacations as families struggle to provide for their children. You'll find it front and center, day or night, striving to better a nation and help her people despite continually facing endless hate and dishonesty. A legacy of change isn't born from finger pointing, orchestrated outrage and shameless rancor designed to distract from one's obvious failures and anti-American agenda. It resides in the "politically incorrect" candor and steadfast convictions of those willing to do and overcome whatever is necessary to solve our most pressing issues; to restore our forsaken founding charter of individual liberty and transparent, limited government. America doesn't need more inflammatory stigmas born from false media narratives. It needs leadership – bold, fearless, accountable – willing to expose the corrupt establishment, endure the relentless hostility of social and political parasites, in order to reinvigorate the vitality and standards of nation that have been slowly anesthetized by those who reject our heritage and openly embrace our enemies.

If you do not love America, understand those timeless principles that made her the most influential and revered nation in modern history, how can you truly have her best interests at heart? How can you tell the difference between terrorism and violence, socialism and economic liberty, equality and Islam, globalism and independence? Although mistakes will happen, and uncertainty is inevitable, it is our actions – not regurgitated excuses or bankrupt apologies – that define our character, and yes, ultimately one's legacy. I do not need a paid political rally or a choreographed news conference to realize Donald Trump was never accused of racism or rape before he ran for President. I just need to open my eyes to realize he chooses prudence over propaganda, results over rhetoric, and hope over hate. If only I could say the same about his critics.

In 1984, the New York Times proclaimed Donald Trump would be our best president.

They have yet to issue a retraction.

"The American Dream is to be Donald Trump."
~Barack Obama, 1991

The Enriched Hypocrites of Public Harassment

Those scheming House Democrats seeking to violate President Trump's legal rights by subpoenaing his tax returns, also believe proof of citizenship or a photo ID is a racist plot to disenfranchise helpless voters; except, that is, when required in Mexico, Central and South America to protect the integrity of their elections. Nevertheless, this completely unconstitutional attempt at political extortion will eventually be dismissed, albeit by a Federal Judge or the Supreme Court. As for those amoral anarchists turning our government into their personal playground for vicious vendettas, tax returns do not constitute public domain; even for elected politicians placed in the assassination crosshairs of a kangaroo inquisition without merit or shame.

Nancy Pelosi -
- admitted net worth $26.4 million
- CRP (Center for Responsive Politics) reported her net worth $58,436,537 in 2009
- CRP reported her net worth $101,273,023 in 2014
- owns up to 7 properties worth $16.5 million
- owns $5 million vineyard
- yearly salary, $193,400

Let's see her tax returns.

The fact President Trump has dutifully filed and paid his taxes every year, following the prescribed tax codes proposed and authorized by Congress itself, proves this newest chapter in their never-ending witch hunt is but another malicious, juvenile stunt. After all, where are the insatiable demands for the tax records of the 271 millionaires living high on Capitol Hill, a majority who substantially increased their net worth serving the "public interest" on a $193,000 annual salary, let alone any hint of concern over Obama's conveniently-sealed college transcripts and Hillary's 33,000 deleted emails which the FBI was denied unfettered access by the DOJ? Apparently, the penalty for federal misconduct is much smaller than the applauded jurisdiction of public-financed harassment.

Considering there are infinitely more pressing issues currently facing this nation – rampant illegal immigration, a ballooning debt, social media/internet censorship, an unprecedented coup attempt by a previous administration – it's obvious the Democratic party is fully content waging a nonstop "Get Trump" extravaganza solely to pervert public opinion for partisan gain, while an undaunted Chief Executive continues to successfully serve the American people without the assistance of a legitimate legislative branch or an honest press. Then again, it is essentially impossible to raise the proverbial bar of ethical standards for a glorified lynch mob selling cow flatulence and plastic straws as a greater threat to "truth, justice and the American way" than Islam, socialism or three radicalized Freshmen representatives who believe "impeachment" is the equivalent of swiping left on Tinder because "racist" America failed to commit suicide on the Fourth of July. If only "We the People" still had a functional government that aggressively identified and expelled those subversive agents masquerading as public servants who openly sought her demise.

The Politics of Persecution

When the Russian Collusion hoax fell apart after the release of the Mueller Report, Democrats desperately began plotting to fabricate a new "scandal". When the separation and temporary incarceration of illegal immigrant families was finally attributed to an ongoing Obama policy, mass media outrage quickly subsided. When the false claims of the fake whistleblower were debunked after Trump released transcripts of the actual phone calls, and the Ukrainian President himself denied any "quid pro quo" misconduct, Nancy Pelosi and Adam Schiff rigged the impeachment hearings to fraudulently pass Abuse of Power and Obstruction of Congress articles.

The very moment President Trump released the actual transcripts of his Ukrainian phone conversations, the impeachment hoax should have immediately ceased. Case closed, good-bye, the proof of his innocence was irrefutable. Yet, instead of accepting the obvious truth, mentally deranged Democrats went to elaborate lengths to create an absurd fiction based on personal hearsay, moot conjecture and omitted exculpatory evidence for partisan gain. If anyone deserves to be prosecuted, I nominate those "deplorable" bureaucrats who continue to conspire, shamelessly lie, recklessly incite the public's ire and unapologetically abuse their Congressional power to relentlessly harass a successful, populist leader their obsessed ranks overwhelmingly fear they cannot defeat in November.

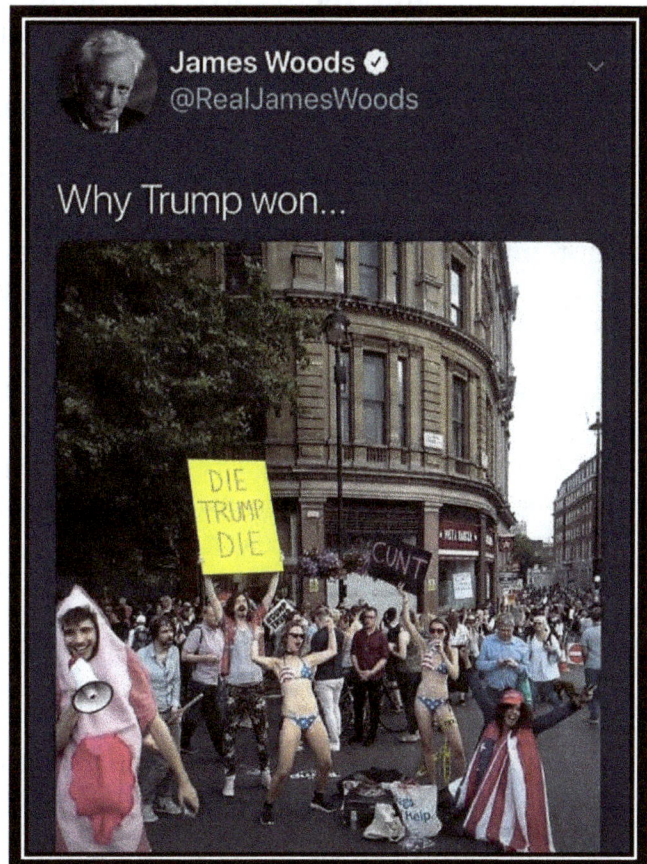

Ever since Democrats took control of the House in 2018, they have spent every waking moment undermining Donald Trump despite a robust economy, historic trade agreements, criminal justice reform, and the emergency restoration of order at the border. They are not serving the American people or this beloved country we call home. Democrats are unapologetically abusing our public institutions and tax dollars as a means to punish political opponents and consolidate power for their own radical aspirations. When's the last time you attempted to criminally frame and destroy the life of your more accomplished colleague simply because you disliked his ideas and coveted his job? Unforgivable is an understatement! If their malicious behavior doesn't sound like dereliction of duty, collusion, perjury, wrongful prosecution and treason, then the real con artists in Washington are the Democratic lynch mobs blaming President Trump for refusing to die to bury their own impeachable crimes. Our President deserves justice; "We the People" demand accountability!

Of Mice and Presidents

Unless reveling in one's own deranged desire to join the 2020 Democratic presidential rat race suddenly supersedes the extremist dogma currently infesting their party's detached ranks, it doesn't matter whether Bernie Sanders, Joe Biden, or Fake Francis O'Rourke is ultimately their preferred choice; for they all espouse a dangerously skewed viewpoint of reality, human history itself, but more profoundly our watershed Constitutional charter they all blindly endeavor to usurp and abandon with insatiable contempt.

Take for instance the beloved caricature of pardoned privilege, dare I say applauded ignorance, known as Mr. Bernie "three estates" Sanders...the 77 year-old Marxist sponge who never earned a living in the private sector, proudly leeching off the system before profiting from political endeavors showcasing his radical 60's roots, yet serendipitously claims to embody the shiny, new progressive ideology of Democratic Socialism: the same fascist farce which brought Europe and Russia to the brink of annihilation 75 years ago, routinely demonized, imprisoned and murdered political opponents to achieve political supremacy in the name of a censored, disarmed utopian society, and turned the natural born crux of individual liberty, free will and independent thought, into the confiscated property of soulless, centralized rule.

In other words, no matter which Democratic candidate rises to the dangling precipice of assured infamy, their insipid, regurgitated allegations are as baseless as their false platform of unity, prosperity and accountability. Every single one of their depraved choices disparage America ad nauseam, label all Republicans as racists, misogynists, xenophobes and greedy capitalists, decry unequal wealth but never unequal work ethic and personal responsibility, empower illegal immigration and electoral fraud, religiously mock and target our Judeo-Christian faith, and fabricate racial, gender and economic injustice solely to justify rewarding hateful, envious malcontents who believe this nation is forever indebted to those cultural terrorists openly seeking her demise.

Forgive my brazen insolence and reasoned dissent, but unless the eventually crowned snake charmer of Democratic "social justice" is going to lower unemployment to the lowest level in half a century, reduce taxes and remove excessive regulations resulting in record minority and female employment, renegotiate disastrous trade deals to stimulate economic and wage growth, reclaim American energy independence in less than years, enact sweeping prison sentencing reform for non-violent offenders, prosecute human, drug and sex trafficking on an unprecedented scale, tackle the Opioid addiction destroying countless lives, eliminate Common Core indoctrination to emphasize critical thinking skills, restore border security while honoring the founding premise of legal naturalization, withdrawal from two wars in the wake of achieving a denuclearized North Korea, seek to decriminalize homosexuality worldwide, fight systemic federal corruption, waste and partisan abuse, ban professional lobbyists and end Congressional slush funds, expose the malicious false narratives of criminal media collusion, and unapologetically represent this esteemed and enduring Republic, there is only one steward of the American Dream I want roaming the historic halls of our prescient forefathers: and that unflinching patriot is President Donald J. Trump.

THE RUSSIA RUSE

FRAMING *with the* FRENEMY

Crossfire Hurricane: The Collateral Damage of Global Collusion

If you're Jumpin' Jack Flash or a Rolling Stones fan, the struggle is the glory when you're "raised by a bearded, toothless hag" amidst the German bombing campaigns and air raid sirens of Dartford, England. If you're Donald Trump, it's perhaps the final straw of an ongoing secret war that is far more nefarious than almost anyone could have possibly imagined.

For those who don't recall, Peter Strzok was the Chief of the Counterespionage Section during the FBI's investigation into Hillary Clinton's use of a personal email server. As we all know, many of her incriminating, electronic devices were destroyed, her computer specialist granted immunity and the final report sanitized to avoid recommending prosecution. Naturally, all harmless coincidences. However, for those who remember the unmasked agent who was having an affair with fellow Bureau colleague Lisa Page – a former Clinton intern and equally-venomous Trump critic – one of their texts eluded to an "insurance policy" in the impossible scenario the brash, politically-incorrect billionaire actually won. While Trump's victory was by no means a surprise to those who utterly despised the alternative, the scope of a cross-continental conspiracy to discredit and/or destroy one man was as intricate as it was unprecedented.

"Crossfire Hurricane" was the code name for the FBI's investigation into Russian election interference. Of course, this absurd operation was set in motion long before the public had even been baptized with the leaked details of a "brewing" scandal; "details" of supposed serious, "treasonous" crimes that were only to be released, pursued, in the event Hillary lost the election. Well, the latter came to fruition and the "break glass in case of emergency" insurance policy was cashed in by not one outgoing President or minority party but perpetrated by two countries with common interests: The Obama administration and English intelligence.

Above all else, Barack Obama and his anti-American associates were terrified of a Trump presidency; an accomplished executive who stood diametrically opposed to his near every decision. In their hearts, they knew socialist Obamacare would be dismantled, skyrocketing public assistance reformed, excessive taxes curtailed, immigration laws enforced, negligent trade deals renegotiated, ties with Israel strengthened, the Iran Nuclear deal nixed, ISIS defeated, and the infamous Paris Agreement – a $100-trillion-dollar death penalty tax designed to punish American interests in the name of Climate alarmism – terminated. Many already blamed Trump's popularity, his brand of American nationalism and newfound populism, as the impetus for the unforeseen success of "Brexit"; a rejection of globalism and a rebirth of sectional independence. Therefore, in the eyes of globalists, Trump's "America First" platform would only further threaten and destabilize the future viability of the European Union. Essentially, the mere presence of Donald Trump was an unimaginable nightmare for the progressive obsession with control, forming a New World Order which would eventually absorb American sovereignty, wealth and power, would be significantly delayed, even derailed, if America rediscovered her founding charter of individual liberty, economic prosperity and limited government.

It was amid this palpable paranoia, this tangible threat to plotting globalists, Obama's CIA Director John Brennan and National Intelligence Director James Clapper secured the services of Stefan Halper: a seasoned foreign policy scholar, Cambridge professor and fellow Trump critic with deep ties within the Republican party, but most notably, American and British intelligence. Halper had a gift for identifying vulnerable targets, manipulating them to extract information, to skillfully expose and weaken adversaries. In late April 2016, multiple contacts at the U.S. Embassy in London, who identified themselves as Defense Intelligence Agency officers, attempted to befriend George Papadopoulos, an eager 24-year-old member of Trump's foreign affairs campaign team, repeatedly praising his value in shaping international affairs while grooming his views on potentially strengthening ties with Russia: a clear red-herring of baited foreshadowing.

The FBI officially but covertly opened the Trump-Russia case on July 31, 2016, based on "suspicions" Papadopoulos had prior knowledge that Russia hacked Clinton's emails, but quickly pivoted by early fall 2016 to "evidence" such as the Democratic-funded "Fake Dossier" and Trump campaign adviser Carter Page's trips to Moscow; a senior foreign policy specialist with legitimate Russian connections. It was during this juncture, Mr. Papadopoulos was contacted on September 2, 2016, by Halper via email to write a policy paper on issues related to Turkey, Cyprus, and Israel for $3,000. He also offered to pay for George's return flight from America and a three-night stay in London. The inquiry was little more than a diversionary tactic to gain his trust, for once they met Stefan coyly asked, "You know about the hacked Russian emails, right?" A meeting with a second local professor, Joseph Mifsud, masquerading as a foreign operative, informed him thousands of emails would soon be released by Russia thus implicating Hillary Clinton's illicit deeds. Mr. Papadopoulos instantly became the phishing victim of the Deep State's self-fulling prophecy to frame a future president by sowing seeds of "guilt" within his own staff.

Of course, several months earlier - armed with the intelligence orchestration of John McCain, the FBI, and the strategic research firm Fusion GPS - British music publicist Rob Goldstone lured Donald Trump Jr. into an introductory conversation with notorious Russian lawyer, Natalie Veselnitskaya; a Fusion GPS associate and former personal guest of the Obama White House who later admitted she had no such dirt on Hillary's dealings although she initially claimed otherwise. In other words, it was all about the salacious appearance of wrongdoing, the public specter of secretive meetings and foreign collusion, not the extensive efforts by conspiring agencies, personalities and countries to stop just one man.

What makes this entire charade truly fascinating is the fact John Brennan was "coincidentally" meeting with Kremlin officials while Peter Strzok was sent to London three months before the election to "investigate" various leads. George Papadopoulos was also in London and instructed to meet an anti-Trump Australian Diplomat, Alexander Downer, at a local tavern where he inevitably divulged Halper's imaginary claim and initiated a chain reaction of meticulously documented events, it's painfully clear how breathtakingly vast, complex, this operation truly was. This is also about the same time the infamous Fake Dossier was released and funneled to the FBI by Bruce Ohr; opposition research paid for by the DNC and Clinton campaign much earlier during the year, but a project which continued when Fusion GPS eventually subcontracted with Christopher Steele, a retired British MI-6 officer and Trump critic with field expertise on Russian matters, to investigate suspected dealings of foreign impropriety. As such, IRS 990's revealed Perkins Coie Law Firm, an international legal partnership with offices in Washington D.C. that represents Organizing for Action (Barack Obama's anti-Trump agitation arm) and counseled the DNC during Hillary's 2016 election run, paid Steele $160,000 to construct the infamous "collusion" narrative. And for those keeping score, Bruce Ohr was not only the DOJ contact for Christopher Steele, his wife Nellie worked for the beforementioned Beltway research firm, Fusion GPS.

> **Senator Rand Paul** ✓
> @RandPaul
>
> BREAKING: A high-level source tells me it was Brennan who insisted that the unverified and fake Steele dossier be included in the Intelligence Report... Brennan should be asked to testify under oath in Congress ASAP.

It was within this fictitious document used to illegally secure three FISA Warrants under a blatantly false narrative, a planted trail of suspicious activity American and British officials had been staging for some time, Mr. Steele concluded Donald Trump conspired with Russian officials for years in exchange for intelligence, the Kremlin blackmailed him over the existence of a sex tape with a Russian prostitute, and that Trump himself approved of Russia hacking the DNC

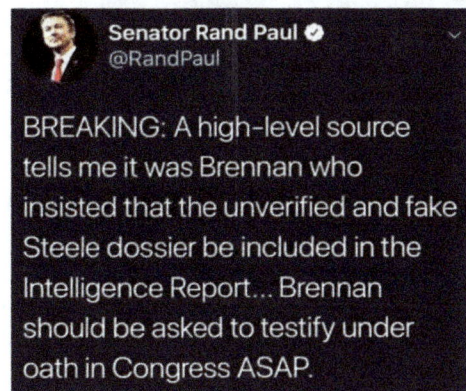

database and distributing the content of those emails through Wikileaks; a claim Julian Assange called laughable and categorically false. It would not be until nearly two years later on a Monday in July, while detractors raged over President Trump's cordial praise of Vladimir Putin during their Helsinki Summit, that Lisa Page's unreported, Congressional testimony revealed a foreign power not named Russia successfully hacked all but four of Hillary's emails and that Peter Strzok, the venerable FBI, sat on the finding to shield her during the election. In espionage terms, our intelligence community suspected China all along but allowed the American press, Democratic Party, to perpetrate this deception without condemnation or consequences.

Not surprisingly, and not to pour rocket fuel on the smell of desperation, Mr. Steele also claimed Carter Page personally conceived of the idea to leak the emails during the Democratic National Campaign to further divide the party by inflaming the fact the DNC rigged their presidential primaries. Any guesses as to who initiated "friendly" discussions with Mr. Page over a several-month period just before the election? That's right...the unquestioned, the unindicted, the unscrupulous mole named Stefan Halper. Shortly thereafter, a FISA application with no "reasonable suspicion" of wrongdoing, was granted when the Steele Dossier was presented as evidence without revealing who secretly financed the project.

A PICTURE IS WORTH A THOUSAND WORDS
CONNECT THE DOTS

Unfortunately for news conspiracy theorists, the DNC email dump was quite possibly an inside job, quite possibly Seth Rich – a party operative and ardent Bernie Sanders supporter murdered in cold blood – and Wikileaks has publicly verified the source of the breach was not from abroad. Nonetheless, there is a stark difference between partisan rhetoric and an elaborate hoax coordinated with the knowledge and extensive assistance of a foreign intelligence apparatus. How many times to I need to hear the words FBI and British intelligence before realizing the real conspiracy is but a foregone conclusion the guarded Global Estate is willing to sweep the entrails of liberty, truth and justice under the rug without hesitation. I have a hard time believing Barack Obama, James Comey, John Brennan, James Clapper, Andrew McCabe, Rod Rosenstein and Susan Rice had no idea what was truly transpiring at the highest levels of our government, the now infamous 25th Amendment 'Hail Mary' coup d'état, let alone the clearly premeditated activities of their politically motivated subordinates and associates on foreign shores. Whether the DNC was infiltrated by foreign hackers or "betrayed" by one of their own disgruntled agents, strategists knew the fallout would be swift and immeasurable. Therefore, the social barons of mass misconception did what all magicians do best: conjure a riveting illusion for an intricate ruse that would distract from their own illicit endeavors while simultaneously implicating the single greatest threat to the globalist blueprint of unrivaled "progressive" rule: Donald J. Trump.

In the wake of perhaps our government's most disturbing disaster, Crossfire Hurricane is but a Civil War metaphor for the collateral damage that ensues when power, unrelenting aspiration, refuses to relinquish the reigns of democracy because a broken establishment sanctimoniously believes it is acting on behalf of the common good. I for one, question the sanity of anyone who consciously fights to preserve the legacy of the most destructive and divisive President in our nation's history, let alone the corrupt ambitions of a bitter, career politician who bartered American security, resources, to the highest foreign bidder while pretending to be our loyal Secretary of State.

Which former CIA Station Chief in Jeddah, Saudi Arabia issued Visas to 11 of the 19 hijackers responsible for the September 11th Attacks?

John Owen Brennan

Philip Schuyler
@FiveRights
Following

Not a great situation when the man investigating the president is best pals with two of the people who attempted a coup against the president.

Raw Sushi, Bleached Servers and Russian Roulette

There is a stark difference between a rogue cyberattack on a vulnerable target, ignoring repeated warnings of imminent danger, and international election "collusion" conducted on a flagrant scale between two historic adversaries. For those drunk Sushi Chefs who have tested the wisdom of Murphy's "R"aw, if Hillary Clinton had never set up an illegal server in the bathroom closet of a small private establishment, flagrantly violating federal law and foolishly sending classified information across unsecured channels, the DNC's crooked dealings would have likely never been discovered. However, once the depraved details of their scandalous endeavors were leaked on the information super highway, the Clinton campaign panicked and hatched an elaborate hoax to both deflect legal scrutiny while simultaneously implicating the greatest threat to the re-election chances of the corrupt progressive establishment: Donald J. Trump.

Paul Sperry
@paulsperry_

BREAKING: DNC/Clinton lawyers were old friends with former FBI Director Bob Mueller's computer forensics analyst. That's why they hired him and his firm CrowdStrike to run forensics on alleged Russian hacking of DNC system. Voila! The analyst quickly concluded it was the Russians

3:05 PM - 18 Jul 2018

The moment Democratic officials refused to immediately notify the FBI of a national security breach, surrender the "hacked" server and those incriminating emails operatives destroyed to avoid prosecution – dare I say public humiliation – they not only became collateral damage to their own criminal stupidity, but have forced the American people to endure endless media hysteria over a shamelessly preserved lie, protected by a hopelessly biased FBI investigation, for almost two years. And yet if not for the twisted actions of a deplorable, deep statist, the true depths of political misconduct within our intelligence community and the now unintelligible party of JFK would still not be known today. Like the unsolved murder of Seth Rich, a suspected voice of conscious dissent surrounded by blind surrogates, coincidence may get you shot twice in the back but it rarely leaves your watch and wallet to reward your sense of naivety.

While I hate to disappoint the social architects of fake tears, my heart does not bleed for Hillary's karmic defeat, nor her insatiable apologists' appetite for coerced concessions, because their blatant, systemic deception has caused this country far greater grief than Vladimir Putin could ever dream. Unless open borders, sanctuary cities, unvetted refugees, urban crime, high taxes, socialist healthcare, illegal surveillance, gender conditioning, disrespect for our flag, vote fraud, militant activism and police shootings are somehow a Russian conspiracy app launched on a laptop in Red Square, when will those domestic, anti-American terrorists weakening this country at every conceivable opportunity be held in equal contempt for playing Russian Roulette with our collective future? I fear the rising military prowess, technological acumen and acquired U.S. debt of Communist China, the cultural subversion of Islamic supremacy, and the unchecked propaganda state of the mainstream media far more than any wrongfully maligned President's refusal to cater to the political sensitivities of emotionally bent adolescents suffering from unresolved election delirium.

Details and Denial

Were the DNC servers hacked in 2016 despite party officials being repeatedly warned of security risks? Yep.

Did it change one vote in the general election? Nope.

Were the Russians the source of those DNC emails published by Wikileaks? Sure weren't.

Did Barack Obama, Hillary Clinton, John Brennan, James Clapper, James Comey, Rod Rosenstein, Lisa Barsoomian, Susan Rice, Sally Yates, Stefan Halper, Peter Strzok, Fusion GPS, Christopher Steele and John McCain aid and abet a treasonous attempt to frame Donald Trump, members of his administration, with a fabricated dossier used to construct the knowingly-false media narrative of election collusion with the Russian government?
UNAPOLOGETICALLY & UNEQUIVOCALLY!

Dumpster Fires, Cold Trysts and Pitching Fits

President Putin inviting the legal charlatan Robert Mueller to investigate his fraudulent claim of Russian election interference is absolute gold. Why? The former KGB agent knows without hesitation it's a partisan sham based on a fabricated lie designed to deflect from the DNC's numerous leaked scandals, Barack Obama's domestic espionage and foreign policy abuses, in the face of our President's growing popularity and historic successes. The best way to deal with a coddled bully is to call his calculated bluff on an international stage where he has no power to manipulate the final outcome. Even liberal media censors were caught off guard, unsure of how to respond or proceed with their carefully preserved ruse, because no nation or leader is more aware of Hillary Clinton's scandalous past – Mueller's Deep State, underhanded dealings – than the "Pale Moth" himself. Being Hollywood loves a good bedtime story almost as much Democrats love starting a new dumpster fire every week, perhaps we'll finally learn the real-life identities of Sergei and the Seven Dwarfs. Rumor has it The Winter Soldier was too busy hacking Fitbits for the IRS.

Those deluded detractors pitching fits over President Trump's public decorum and cordial respect for Vladimir Putin, did nothing to condemn the unconscionable sale of U.S. Uranium rights to a Russian conglomerate in exchange for $145 million donated to the Clinton Foundation and remained conspicuously silent as Barry and Valerie Jarett freed $150 billion in assets for terrorist militants, secretly granted 2,500 Iranian officials citizenship and then paid another $400 million for a likely staged hostage negotiation. But we're still talking about hurt feelings, executive dignity and public appearances, right; not rampant injustice and unapologetic treason?

> "There have been times where they slip back into Cold War thinking and a Cold War mentality.
>
> "And what I consistently say to them, and what I say to President Putin, is that's the past and we've got to think about the future, and there's no reason why we shouldn't be able to cooperate more effectively than we do."
>
> BARACK OBAMA
> AUGUST 6, 2013

Because irony loves ignorance, the righteous flash mob's conscience also conveniently abstained from the Obama administration's illegal surveillance of the press and fraudulently obtained FISA warrants to spy on the Trump campaign – the first such espionage waged on an incoming administration in American history – emphatically refused to discredit Mueller's tireless witch hunt despite knowing it was predicated on a proven fake dossier, were complicit during Jim Acosta's daily tirades at White House briefings and the repeated vicious attacks on Sarah Huckabee by liberal celebrities, encouraged vigilante violence against law enforcement by selectively reporting police shootings, and even endorsed Hillary Clinton despite the irrefutable fact she shared classified information on an illegal server, destroyed incriminating evidence and shamelessly colluded with party loyalists to rig the Democratic primaries. When your fickle recollection cannot discern between criminal aspiration and mere legal political dissension, your incestuous ethics are but willing accomplices to the aftermath of real depravity and pardoned deception. The insulting dichotomy of news coverage praising a bigoted propagandist who did everything in his power to weaken and divide America, contrasted against their universal contempt for a faithful servant who works tirelessly on her behalf, the deceived and forsaken people, is nauseating to say the least.

Considering 90% of media reporting has not only been absurdly negative towards a highly accomplished and transparent President, but outright hostile to the occupational necessity of journalistic integrity, spare America the high and morally indignant routine of acceptable behavior. Network pundits will instinctively find fault with his actions regardless of the circumstances. How can any elected leader normalize relations with a former adversary, one that consciously abandoned the destructive legacy of communism, without engaging his or her counterpart in a civil, constructive manner? More profoundly, when did the facetious demands of your most bitter and belligerent domestic enemies supersede the potential diplomatic, economic and military benefits negotiated with an evolving superpower open to breaking old chains for new paths of mutual respect? I'd much rather have our President embrace Putin on the world stage as an equal to expand new markets, international cooperation, than a pandering apologist who despised America's heritage and capitulated to every abusive tariff and trade deal possible; even praising the murderous legacy of Castro himself before the entire free world.

If members of my own "trusted" intelligence apparatus were trying to end my presidency and frame my subordinates, without a single official stepping forward to expose the lurid plot, why would I publicly reject a foreign leader who also knows it to be true? In light of the left's psychotic obsession with election collusion, the fascist press lacks the necessary credibility to disparage anyone, let alone the right to claim they represent the prevailing "disgust" of the American people; i.e., those not bound to hate Donald Trump for all eternity. Their singular agenda is to destroy any person, party or ideology who threatens their stranglehold on public perception. I, for one, have far more respect for two competent, patriotic leaders wading through the endless minefield of globalist shills to lead their respected countries to the last respite of national identity, cultural and commercial independence, in lieu of being coerced into indulging the pathological ploys and gross exaggerations of politically deranged sycophants for one second longer. However, before conspiracy theorists continue to rage against the undaunted Trump foreign policy machine, let me digress. The United States has spied on nearly every perceived threat or sworn foe without progressives protesting every nuance of those Heads of State willing to graciously embrace a Democratic president's diplomatic duplicity. Who knew the difference between semantics and sedition is the company that you keep?

Shenanigans and Sheep

Despite his widely unreported disclaimer - "There is no allegation that any American citizen committed a crime: there is no allegation it changed the vote count or affected the 2016 election result" - Rod Rosenstein's very public indictment of 12 Russian operatives was announced without a shred of factual evidence but a great deal of sensational fodder for ravenous journalists. Condemning a dozen foreign agitators who will never see the inside of a courtroom for allegedly hacking DNC files reeks of a desperate political stunt to deflect from embarrassing FBI hearings right before President Trump's much-anticipated visit with Vladimir Putin in which Chuck Schumer pompously demanded a Democratic escort accompany our Commander in Chief to ensure "acceptable" negotiations. As expected, media surrogates are now demanding our President cancel the meeting entirely since such a diplomatic gesture will somehow confirm the left's stale accusation that an extensive plot existed between two "notorious" leaders determined to hijack our electoral process for personal gain. And yes, the Grinch really stole Christmas.

Of course, the DNC initially refused to report "the breach" due to publicly revealing their own illicit behavior...incriminating memos concerning Hillary's destroyed illegal server and foreign fundraising efforts, an unauthorized IT specialist granted access to Congressional accounts, the death of suspected mole Seth Rich, Donna Brazile conspiring with the Clinton campaign to defeat Bernie Sanders, John Podesta's questionable ties/activities with Kremlin bankers and child sex trafficking, inflammatory emails disparaging various voting demographics...and because top Democratic officials already knew a "Russian collusion" dossier was already being formulated through Fusion GPS, U.S. spies/informants stationed in the U.K. and the research of Christopher Steele who was previously discredited as a trustworthy source. Furthermore, both Wikileaks and Julian Assange have repeatedly asserted neither the Russia government, nor any rogue entity from that region, was the source of the "leaked" emails released to the public.

Sorry, but this announcement is clearly a publicity ruse designed to once again seize national headlines by validating Robert Mueller's never-ending investigation – which has yet to prove "election collusion" of any kind – as well as to give credence to the fictitious narrative Hillary Clinton only lost the White House due to an unprecedented plot spearheaded by Donald Trump rather than the irrefutable reality the DNC criminally colluded to nominate the most distrusted and detestable candidate in our nation's history.

Progressive strategists know the average voter is easily swayed with simplistic, sensational allegations because a majority are misinformed and/or hopelessly apathetic. How else can so many anti-American politicians touting such a radical agenda get elected to the highest levels of our government despite promising to dictate nearly every aspect of our Constitutionally-protected liberties? Without inciting hatred and discord behind the incessant smokescreens of manufactured scandal, the same bureaucrats espousing socialism, criminalizing self-defense and promoting open borders would be forced to run on the merits of their record and counter-intuitive beliefs. The incessant Russian collusion fairy tale is but another tool of mass persuasion in their prized, propaganda shed to topple the greatest threat to their political monopoly on public perception: the unadulterated truth. Apropos, if Hillary Clinton's private server was under the required protection of government security instead of hidden in a bathroom closet, her most sordid dealings would not have become public domain. Who knew karma was an absentee soul.

> **Donald J. Trump** ✓
> @realDonaldTrump
>
> ....Where is the DNC Server, and why didn't the FBI take possession of it? Deep State?
>
> 7/14/18, 2:57 AM

Whereas the Democratic Party was desperate to salvage any credibility in the wake of multiple scandals during an election year, the syndicated "Russian hacker" melodrama – supposedly perpetrated under the watchful eye of Obama's surveillance state, no less – was a perfectly timed excuse to derail public scrutiny by once again playing the helpless victim. If Mr. Rosenstein and his Deep State mentor Robert Mueller aren't too busy chasing cyber ghosts or attempting to sabotage Brett Kavanaugh's looming confirmation, perhaps they could arrest and indefinitely detain Peter Strzok, Lisa Page, Imran Awan and themselves for embarking on the most deceitful, costly witch hunt in modern American history. At least someone who is unquestionably guilty of treason would finally see the inside of a federal penitentiary.

Jordan Rachel
@TheJordanRachel

Names of 12 Russians indicted:
1. Hillary Clintonesky
2: Barrocksky Obamovich
3. Sally Yateskich
4. John Brennovansky
5. Valerick Jarretkich
6. James Comeyski
7. Peter Strzoki
8. Bruce Ohrskoh
9. McCainzi
10. Susan Ricekoh
11. Lisa Pageovich
12. John Podestinskiah

2:57 PM · 13 Jul 18

Critical Mass Manipulation: An American Casualty

Andrew McCabe lied four times under oath and now the Inspector General has submitted his recommendation to Congress for criminal prosecution. Naturally, the only real question that remains is who will he "betray" first...Rosenstein, Comey, or even the feckless Robert Mueller himself? After all, if Mr. McCabe truly has nothing to hide, why lie in the first place; let alone three more punishable instances? Either way, unless Jeff Sessions and Congressional representatives take immediate action against this ongoing Deep State coup d'état – a coordinated plot to invalidate an election result, stonewall common sense reforms and frame a sitting President – our own government will have successfully and unapologetically supplanted the rule of law.

Since the right to attorney-client privilege is longer a key cog of due process, if you're Donald Trump that is, why not also pardon perjury, absolve abuse of power, congratulate collusion, and abolish the very tangible concept of treason itself? Barack Obama, Hillary Clinton, Loretta Lynch, Susan Rice, James Comey, Rod Rosenstein, Andrew McCabe and the DNC were not only active parties to this entire Machiavellian charade, this elaborate and unprecedented ruse to sabotage an incoming administration in hopes of preserving their progressive agenda, they continue to labor under the delusion they're leading a populist uprising against federal corruption and foreign interference.

If you believe in the adage "the best defense is a good offense", that strategy is exponentially more formidable in the political arena where molded public perception can defeat the most-sound logic or rudimentary fact. While these tried and true tactics of infamous communist regimes and fascist dictators are hardly nascent activities, they are alarming indicators that America – a Constitutional Republic predicated upon limited government, Checks and Balances, and a vigilant, free press – is teetering on the precipice of becoming a propaganda state; one in which justice, equality and transparency are somehow subjective or partisan constructs because the people are too complicit or apathetic to care otherwise.

The loudest and most disruptive obstacles to effective, responsible government typically reside in those "resisting" civil servants whose ideology, political beliefs, cannot withstand honest scrutiny and impartial debate. Thus, only through an endless array of orchestrated distractions and salacious accusations are the most culpable, clearly contemptible, able to evade accountability. The fact our duly-elected President is being investigated for an imaginary crime a number of his accusers actually committed – admittedly rigging the DNC primary, soliciting Russian financing for a future presidential campaign, conspiring government agencies falsifying evidence to secure surveillance warrants, and election tampering by inviting a foreign body of illegal votes – is undeniable proof the progressive establishment's war on reality is reaching a point of critical mass.

If my observations are nothing more than gross exaggeration, in what other era would our sovereign and internationally recognized borders be deemed racist, a peaceful disarmament of a North Korean tyrant considered dangerous in the wake of Democrats negotiating a nuclear Iran, our own National Anthem derided as "divisive" and therefore preempted on national TV, the NRA absurdly slandered as a terrorist organization when Barack Obama protected/aided Hezbollah, Hamas and the Muslim Brotherhood, universal tax cuts condemned as capitalist "greed" despite billions of taxpayer dollars being spent on non-citizens, social entitlements and sworn enemies, and a resurgent economy reported as a "broken promise" despite boasting the fewest jobless claims in 45 years, the steepest manufacturing gains in over two decades and the lowest black/Hispanic unemployment in our nation's history? Together, these insulting discrepancies represent a concerted effort to destabilize our societal values, our civic obligation and sense of wrong or right, by drawing a horribly skewed account of current events. If you need to be told who to blame for a problem that may or may not exist, where does dissent end and due diligence begin?

When every detail of the news must be distorted to demonize the President, to misinform the masses to the point of welcoming open hostility solely to win an election, the very basis of a free thinking, democratic society becomes the conquered ruins of a dystopian nightmare. To conquer a country's territory, you must first raise a standing army. To silence a country's founding history, you must erase all remnants of its existence, criminalize the past and discredit any medium speaking on its behalf. The faintest flicker of an ideal, however, will always remain.

Pawns willing to sacrifice themselves for the Marxist wet dream of the "greater good" – the mere illusion of fighting injustice by empowering the unjust aspirations of anti-American globalists consuming wealth and consolidating power – are far easier to control than a lone voice wiling to brave scorn and bodily harm to defend a forsaken Declaration of Independence. Whereas ignorance will enslave itself in the face of fear, pervasive propaganda, mankind's innate desire to be free from centralized coercion, to gather strength from a higher calling and wisdom through our God-given senses, rarely makes such concessions. America, it seems, is losing its ability to delineate between "the consent of the governed" from the "carnage of the corrupt". For if we fail to act now in the face of these damning revelations, what will be left to salvage for future generations? A nation of laws is only as legitimate as the people's willingness to ensure principle over party, duty over duplicity. Without equal deference for the necessity of justice, the functional integrity of our public institutions, truth is the unreported hostage of unmistakable intent: America is under attack and we're harboring the growing list of paid accomplices.

What Lies Beneath

Peter Strzok – a vocal, anti-Trump, FBI agent who praised resisting DOJ holdovers like Sally Yates criminally leaking classified information – was allowed to question General Flynn and fraudulently changed the concluding remarks of the uninspired Hillary email investigation from "grossly negligent" to "extremely careless" – was a senior lieutenant on Mueller's partisan hit squad. He was only recently dismissed after his duplicitous ties and nefarious motives were publicly revealed. Strzok was raised in Iran and his father supported, allegedly assisted, Ayatollah hardliners during the fall of the Shah.

Andrew Weissmann, a lawyer currently aiding Mueller's Russian witch hunt to unearth any discernible crumb of vaguely interpreted indiscretion, was invited to and attended a Hillary election party in New York City.

Another attorney, Aaron Zebley, the same accessory who represented the infamous Clinton IT specialist and who actually physically smashed evidence to protect Hillary, is also assisting Mueller and Comey's vindictive campaign to evict Donald Trump by fabricating election collusion. He is still an active participant in the never-ending probe despite his obvious conflict of interest.

Robert Mueller's "grounds for impeachment" inquisition is so hopelessly biased and fatally compromised that no matter how many indictments he issues or what his final conclusions may be, any sane court of law would immediately invalidate the findings over a clear unethical breech of legal protocol and for failing to provide an objective, fair evaluation of evidence, subpoenaed testimony and wrongfully targeted suspects. Did I mention he literally coached, "colluded", with James Comey before his testimony?

How dangerous and incestuous has the Deep State community become? So corrupt that the FBI knowingly accepted/conspired on the creation of a fake Russian dossier to help the NSA obtain a surveillance warrant under false pretenses so the Obama administration could spy on a Presidential candidate and his transition team for the explicit purpose of attempting to frame an innocent man solely to overturn an election result and thwart his "America First" agenda. If treason and sedition are still crimes, there are more than one pair of handcuffs lacking an accomplished felon.

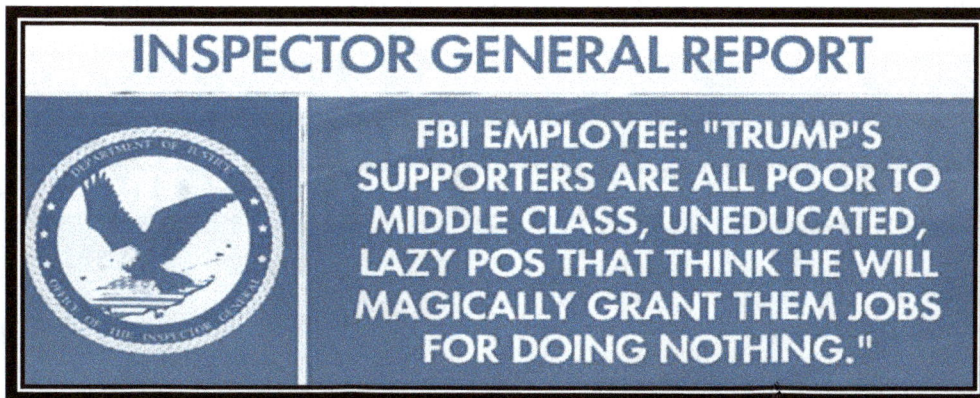

Shameless: Fidelity, Bravery, in Contempt

When a Virginia Federal Judge calls you a liar to your face and says your entire investigation is a witch hunt intended to bring down the President, it's time to close down the carnival. Robert Mueller only cares about Paul Manafort, General Flynn, Stormy Daniels and Michael Cohen — three of whom were victims of illegal surveillance, one currently detained in a Virginia prison without a trial— as far as they can cause enough collateral damage to conceal the embarrassing reality he cannot prove that which he was solely commissioned to research: foreign election collusion. One year and over 12 million dollars later, taxpayers are still being forced to watch a bitter partisan beat a dead horse for media ringmasters while his corrupt FBI accomplices continue to obstruct the public from discovering perhaps the greatest government scandal in modern politics: a vast plot by a vacating administration, loyal intelligence officials, and a Democratic nominee to invalidate a possible future election result, to frame a sitting U.S. President with fabricated evidence, and/or to demand his eventual impeachment through incited public hysteria alone.

The much-forgotten detail Deputy Attorney General Rod Rosenstein recommended the termination of James Comey – who put far more effort into his book tour than tackling real corruption – only to turn around and decry "obstruction of justice" as justification for giving Mueller an unlimited "treasure" hunting license, is as duplicitous as it is obscene. To this day, Mr. Rosenstein has yet to relinquish unredacted memos, documents, which both Congress and Judge Ellis have requested to discern our intelligence community's true level of culpability in this enduring fiasco.

The fact this farce has continued without refrain or any shred of regret, not to mention none of the actual conspirators have yet to face prosecution, God forbid fired or indicted, is a travesty in itself. If you truly care about exposing treason, fraud and collusion, ask yourself what individuals in the past decade have repeatedly tried to weaken America, invalidate the rule of law, aid and abet our sworn enemies, undermine the integrity of our elections, suffocate private business beneath the global Ponzi scheme of unfair trade, disparage our heritage, destroy historical monuments, and spread disinformation to the point of violent discord. I assure you the list is as predictable as it is unapologetically "progressive".

I RECOMMENDED IN A LETTER FOR TRUMP TO FIRE COMEY

DEPUTY ATTORNEY GENERAL ROD ROSENSTEIN

AND THEN I TOLD MUELLER TO INVESTIGATE TRUMP FOR FIRING COMEY

Dear James Comey...

If the FBI did not act improperly or collude with the Obama administration to illegally spy on an incoming President, potentially frame members of his staff and exonerate Hillary's criminal activities, why is Andrew McCabe asking for an immunity deal before his scheduled Senate testimony when he can simply Plead the Fifth? Innocent men don't need "insurance policies" unless they're desperate to avoid prison time or they're being strategically sacrificed by the swamp to silence an exploding scandal by promising legal bombshells only to deliver stale crumbs of public ridicule. Your "honorable" reputation as a classified leaker, a pathological liar and a spineless puppet will soon be immortalized in the annotated annals of political conspiracy and treasonous betrayal. Since big government is for feckless small minds, please amend your mistaken memoirs to include your Deep State merit badge and redacted memo of undeniable guilt. Denial is unapologetically foreign to forgiveness, but not to be confused with regret.

Signed,

Your signature on three fraudulent FISA warrant applications

THE GREATEST TYRANNIES ARE ALWAYS PERPETRATED IN THE NAME OF THE NOBLEST CAUSES.

THOMAS PAINE

Rogue One: A Jester Never Rests

While I could detail the numerous hypocritical parallels between Robert Mueller's raid on the office of Trump's personal attorney, Michael Cohen, and the sheer level of impropriety present in our intelligence community, there are really two overriding questions I find most disturbing. First, what in the hell does such a reckless infringement upon one's rights have to do with "election collusion"; the original, prescribed scope of the investigation which has already been debunked by the House Intelligence Committee, the Inspector General's report, as completely without merit or evidence? And two, how in the hell is the undeniably disgraced FBI – the same one that knowingly validated a fake dossier and colluded with the Obama administration, DNC, and DOJ to obtain false FISA warrants in a Deep State plot to frame a newly elected president – still participating in such an obvious partisan farce that has now lasted for nearly a year and cost taxpayers over 10 million dollars?

Searching for any hint or crumb of indiscretion to oust a common political foe hardly constitutes electoral collusion nor does it acquit the man chosen to "invent" injustice who ironically presided over perhaps the most infamous, international scandal in recent memory: The Russian conglomerate Uranium One enriching the presidential slush fund of one not so legitimate charity through exorbitant speaking fees and personal donations made by board members in exchange for one-fifth of our national reserves regarding a known nuclear trigger. But yes, by all means, more Stormy Daniels, please: an aging porn star and feminist hero who openly admitted she was neither assaulted or raped but instead paid "hush" money for a discrete, consensual encounter.

The fact Robert Mueller still has a job – tapped by former Whitewater "prosecutor" and his longtime personal subordinate, Rod Rosenstein, who repeatedly lied about internal leaks and shielded Hillary's private server cover-up from justice – is about as predictable as Lisa Page and Peter Strzok not being immediately fired for their obscene, treasonous texts eluding to an active coup against a sitting President. And yet no such raid was conducted on the office of Rosenstein's wife, Lisa Barsoomian, a longtime Clinton lawyer who received obscene amounts of cash from the Clinton foundation for her personal political campaign as Hillary was shielded from prosecution for at least 5 documented felonies of which she was never indicted for a single crime, let alone questioned under oath about her numerous conflicting statements.

Yes, "what difference does it make" that Lisa Barsoomian represented Robert Mueller three times, James Comey five times, Barack Obama forty-five times, Kathleen Sebelius fifty-six times, Bill Clinton forty times, and Hillary Clinton seventeen times between 1991 and 2017. And because the media is so skilled at ignoring smoke billowing from a raging dumpster fire, Barsoomian herself represented the "Democratically' weaponized FBI at least five separate times. Who needs ethics, checks and balances, when you have an army of smiling cronies so adept at disregarding the truth?

Robert Mueller's eternal crusade to immortalize himself has not only become a rogue threat to our country's electoral process, that which he was empowered to supposedly protect, his recent encroachment on our civil liberties proved progressivism's real totalitarian intentions by completely ransacking the judicial precedent of "attorney-client privilege"; a key cog of due process and private legal consultation in Western society. If any scorned individual or unhinged lynch mob can summarily invent "probable cause" with the nod of a deluded judge to justify such gestapo tactics, a juvenile attempt to save a floundering witch hunt by seeking the glory of national headlines, then our government would be fully justified in arresting those parading bureaucrats who are unrivaled at collusion, conspiracy, stock manipulation, false prosecution, treason and election tampering through orchestrated illegal immigration, vote fraud, in a constitutionally sovereign nation.

Or, if I may, are we still talking about jaded porn stars, the multilingual First Lady's accent and the length of Donald Trump's pants because his business associations, successes, stretch much farther than the hypocrisy of a wrongfully commissioned court jester? Perhaps if the President concealed granting citizenship to 2,500 high-ranking Iranian officials, since covertly naturalizing thousands of Russian operatives would be immediate grounds for public hanging, the cost of media prostitutes and partisan inquisitions would be tax deductible instead of wasted by obsessing over an "innocent" act of treason.

Bill Clinton paid Paula Jones $850,000 after accusations he assaulted her. Does anyone remember the FBI raiding his attorney? Neither do I.

The Usual Unconvicted Suspects

The DNC civil lawsuit against the Trump campaign, Russia and Wikileaks is not only a bad joke, it's an extraordinarily dumb one. The same collection of conniving propagandists that admitted in litigation they rigged the Democratic nomination because they legally could, are somehow livid Wikileaks exposed their entire corrupt operation by publicizing actual communications detailing real collusion: an orchestrated attempt to recruit and enrich false accusers of sexual harassment, coordinating with media networks to distort and/or selectively report current events, plotting to smear Bernie Sanders as a "sexist" extremist, seeding presidential debates with planted questions and partisan moderators, expressing their unfiltered contempt for various American demographic groups (Christians, "Taco Bowl" voters, Super Predators, Deplorables), promising donors a nation with open borders, covering-up a suspected inside leak and the likely impetus for Seth Rich's death, and touting Hillary's extensive ties with Russian donors, Uranium One, Wall Street, Goldman Sachs and Silicon Valley data pirates.

This newest yet far more desperate attempt to salvage any hint of credibility, amidst the billowing backdrop of a widening FBI fire sale, will allow Trump's lawyers to launch a counter suit after invoking "discovery" requests on DNC servers, the infiltration of the House Select Committee on Intelligence by the Awan brothers, Hillary's improperly vetted/questioned/detained foreign IT managers, and the most intricate dealings of Fusion GPS research itself; the infamous "fake dossier" paid for by the Clinton Campaign and peddled by Deep State conspirators to fraudulently obtain surveillance warrants of an incoming administration.

> **Charlie Kirk** ✓
> @charliekirk11
>
> A Obama appointed judge decided to give no jail time to Pakistani IT Staffer Imran Awan because he "suffered enough"
>
> In July, he pleaded guilty to a false statement he made on a loan application. Same thing that now has Manafort heading to prison

Suing to hopefully imbue a fabricated narrative into a nation's voting conscience is the modern-day Clockwork Orange of aspiring Orwellian gangsters. What's next...filing a federal injunction against "offensive" gun owners for exercising their Constitutional right to self-defense? But as "We the Betrayed" already ascertained, this juvenile legal stunt is really about maintaining public appearances until midterms, the illusion of an illegitimate election and President requiring a Blue Wave of retribution, to distract from a mounting listing of impressive successes and conceal the unforgivable fact Democrats willingly nominated the most corrupt, detestable politician in our nation's history. When the truth is your mortal enemy, burying the remains of your criminal intent is not quite as easy as blaming unruly Russians for getting out of your piss-stained bed. Who needs "justice" when drunk party jesters openly court revenge?

Unless sneezing unicorns are forced at gunpoint to push bleached email servers, glittering generalities and assassinated whistle blowers off the unguarded edge of a recently discovered "flat earth", the now very distant embodiment of the party of JFK wants you to believe Voter ID's are racist – except in Latin American countries or the DNC National Convention – but that millions of non-citizens casting votes, with little to no loyalty to our founding values and publicly encouraged by the Obama administration, by no means constitute foreign interference or election tampering. Of course, if five million let alone 500 Americans crossed the border to defeat Trudeau or install a conservative Mexican President somehow willing to fight illegal immigration and "unfair trade", those individuals would be arrested and made public enemy #1 by every liberal news pundit decrying a vast Right-Wing conspiracy: an egregious assault on each country's sovereignty, economy and indigenous population.

The bigger the lie, the more often you repeat it, the more likely uninformed people are to believe it. The Democratic party, by choice, has become a false flag operation...a notorious syndicate of demagoguery, a shameless instigator/agitator of societal strife to achieve radical social change, political supremacy, at any price. This transformation of cultivated discontent and warped public perception begs but one inescapable question? What's the difference between immunity, impunity and an implicated, broken establishment unwilling to testify on America's behalf? That would depend on your ability to discern between a sociopath, a traitor and a progressive activist laughing alone in a police line-up. If anyone needs to unconditionally apologize and pay full restitution for undermining the time, resources and peaceful foreign relations of two collective nations, the prescribed transparency of limited government, it's the Democratic National Committee of unconvicted suspects.

To Russia with Love: Robert Mueller

As numerous sources have alluded to previously, former FBI Director Robert Mueller was not only privy to the secret sale of 20 percent of US Uranium stockpiles to Russia, he was a key participant. And now we know why the Clinton Foundation has never been investigated for receiving a total of 145 million in "donations" from the Kremlin, including various Russian banks and businesses. Oh, and PS...even the notorious Russian Lawyer, Natalie Veselnitskaya – who was a personal guest of the Obama administration – has ties to the infamous Bill Clinton/Loretta Lynch tarmac meeting where this entire Russian narrative was set into motion as a viable distraction from investigating real criminality, collusion, and thus incriminating themselves. How deep is the swamp? Deep enough to comfortable hide the skeletons of every crooked bureaucrat, congressional kickback, awarded government contract, electoral scheme and treasonous foreign affair for over the past 100 years.

6.   (S/Rel Russia) Action request: Embassy Moscow is requested to alert at the highest appropriate level the Russian Federation that FBI Director Mueller plans to deliver the HEU sample once he arrives to Moscow on September 21. Post is requested to convey information in paragraph 5 with regard to chain of custody, and to request details on Russia Federation's plan for picking up the material. Embassy is also requested to reconfirm the April 16 understanding from the FSB verbally that we will have no problem with the Russian Ministry of Aviation concerning Mueller's September 21 flight clearance.

WikiLeaks ✓
@wikileaks

🗗 Follow

Special Prosecutor Robert Muelller flew to Moscow and gave the FSB 10 grams of Highly Enriched Uranium (HEU) in 2009
wikileaks.org/plusd/cables/0...
3:51 PM - Jul 29, 2017

To Deflect by Design

Because of the damning revelations detailing the Uranium One deal and news of the fake Russian dossier finally coming to public fruition, the "unmasked" left is scrambling to maintain their mass media illusion of Trump colluding with and soliciting Russian interference...that which Hillary has perpetrated for years with both Robert Mueller's and Mr. Comey's knowledge and/or involvement. Therefore, it is of little surprise Mr. Mueller has reportedly filed his first official charges being both politicians and pundits have called for his termination due to recent developments. My best guess is Paul Manafort, Trump's former campaign manager who was fired and replaced with Kellyanne Conway, will be indicted for completely unrelated activities – i.e., tax fraud charges he was cleared of by a lawyer named Rod Rosenstein 8 years ago – but the same "crimes" Tony Podesta was granted immunity for by Mr. Mueller to aid his partisan "blood drive". Beyond that, any possible charges implicating the President, his family or any of his cabinet would be a malicious abuse of power and obvious political stunt to salvage a rapidly sinking ship. The fact Hillary Clinton, Susan Rice, John Brennan, Rod Rosenstein, Andrew McCabe and James Comey have not been indicted for a slew of conflicts of interests, orchestrated leaks and repeated instances of collusion, is a crime in itself. What started out as a media induced hoax, a baseless investigation into alleged election fraud, has quickly transformed into a partisan witch hunt for any conceivable crumb of wrongdoing capable of toppling a man Democrats want to unilaterally impeach for simply existing.

When yesterday's definition of treasonous collusion becomes today's interpretational alibi, or "opposition research", prison somehow requires a convict's consent. Any response to these disturbing events other than an immediate investigation into Uranium One, the fake Russian Dossier paid for by the DNC/Clinton operatives and fraudulently delivered by Bruce Ohr/John McCain to the FBI, and the first ever ordered wiretapping of a presidential candidate and his campaign staff – an egregious action which presented the fake dossier as justification and continued even after his successful election – is a clear and present danger to the very concept of law and order and the absolute necessity of Constitutional checks and balances. The progressive establishment is not interested in justice or even necessarily concerned whether convictions are obtainable. Their overriding goal is to monopolize the national headlines by maintaining the false public appearance of scandal. The mere suggestion and political stigma of criminality is often far more powerful than the finality of any discernible truth.

To clarify some misconceptions...*Paul Singer, owner of the Washington Free Beacon and an open borders establishment Republican who gave freely to John McCain, was the original funding source for Fusion GPS research against Donald Trump. However, Fusion GPS research was later continued by Hillary Clinton's campaign, which was directly responsible for the creation of the now-infamous fake Russian dossier; a document fabricated by former British agent Christopher Steele, who had previously worked with Bruce Ohr, and eventually leaked to the FBI. Shortly thereafter, a British publicist set up the well-publicized meeting between Donald Trump Jr. and a Russian lawyer under the false pretenses she had damning information on Hillary.*

Vodka, Caviar and Fish Sticks

There is the foul stench of political desperation, and there is the echo of fumbling footsteps loitering in their own delusional waste. In the curious case of the American media chasing yet another Red Herring, it's hard not to pin the tail on the drunk donkey wearing a Ushanka while selling party favors in Red Square. In other words, if you can't defeat a politically incorrect capitalist with a bad comb-over who suplexed your credibility on the wrestling mat of social media, blaming a hated political rival for the identical crimes committed by your absolved constituents, why not besmirch the prodigal son who bears his very name but never ran for public office?

Not to burst the 99 balloons of Russian roulette, exactly what law did Donald Trump Jr. break; regardless of his intent or status as a private citizen? It's well known English publicist Rob Goldstone initiated contact on behalf of Russian attorney Natalia Veselnitskaya, she recently admitted to not possessing or passing any notable information during their meeting despite misreported claims of damning revelations, and the President's son freely and adamantly released all records of their so-called "scandalous" correspondence. Hmm, color me cognizant of the difference between Caviar and fish sticks, but this woman sounds far more like a political plant, a wealthy sycophant and convincing decoy used to imply misconduct, than a rogue character assassin conspiring to conquer the world with a married man from New York who religiously takes selfies with his kids in his waders.

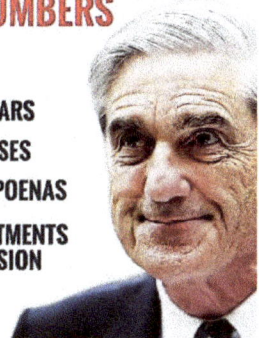

MUELLER INVESTIGATION BY THE NUMBERS

675 DAYS
$25M DOLLARS
500 WITNESSES
2,800 SUBPOENAS
ZERO INDICTMENTS ABOUT COLLUSION

TURNING POINT USA

And yet every election season, with little to no criticism or ethical standards, the DNC hires an army of lawyers and private investigators to find any crumb of usable intelligence to slander Republican candidates into submission. Not that Herman Cain would or Gloria Allred would digress! After all, just because the Clinton campaign initiated a quid-pro-quo rendezvous with Ukrainian officials last year to discuss trading Trump's dirty laundry for possible future political concessions, or Ted Kennedy begged a Russian diplomat to defeat Reagan by directly interfering with the integrity of our elections, there's no need for mass hysterics over real collusion and unpunished treason. Naturally the liberal press rarely mentions such shameless behavior because they're the DNC's proud propaganda pimps pushing an endless array of salacious narratives with zero discernible proof. Considering the Clinton's longtime ties with the Kremlin, Uranium One and Moscow banks like Renaissance Capital sponsoring $500,000 speeches – yes, no foreign government is more acutely aware of Bill and Hillary's sordid past and shoddy dealings than Russia – you would be a fool not to exhaust all leads blatantly ignored by the mainstream media when the most corrupt and dishonest candidate in our nation's history was mere months away from permanently liquidating the American dream.

This entire, nonstop Russian conspiracy fiasco is but an absurd microcosm of how desperate the Fourth Estate has become to deflect from Trump's growing list of successes and thus derail his extensive reforms loosening the grip of the Washington establishment.

If anybody needs to be investigated for consciously colluding with Russia, China, Europe and the Middle East, for intentionally demonizing America's heritage and values at every conceivable opportunity, it's Barack Obama and Hillary Clinton. Does anyone honestly believe the $100 trillion-dollar Paris climate agreement was actually about addressing global temperatures – a proposed scant reduction of .3 degrees by 2100 when solar activity alone can account for such variation in a single year alone – in lieu of perpetrating a globalist Ponzi scheme clearly designed to redistribute America's wealth, sovereignty and historical influence? Why was Iran, a radical Islamic regime and sponsor of jihad against the West given permission to "eventually" build nuclear weapons, with almost no enforceable oversight, let alone made the beneficiary of a $400 million-dollar ransom payment in Swiss Francs and Euros made out to "sorry"? Did Valerie Jarrett, a self-admitted anti-American Marxist, not possess ties to both Iran and the Muslim Brotherhood while serving as Obama's most trusted adviser in the pinnacle of our government? Apparently not.

Unfortunately for "We the Pawns" of public perception, the media isn't interested in ascertainable truth, exposing real impropriety through objective research, merely fabricating false appearances to incite further societal division and discord for the explicit purpose of destroying the President and his family by any means necessary. And to think Seth Rich's death – a DNC operative gunned down outside his home in our nation's capital – generated far less genuine concern or moral outrage than a completely legal and fully justifiable series of communications regarding one Hillary Rodham Clinton; a notorious lifelong politician and reckless reprobate whose name is synonymous with pathological deceit, inappropriate associations and personally profiteering from foreign dissent. It's a tragic failing of journalism, our national ethos, when an unsolved, cold-blooded murder of a young man "resisting" rigged primaries, or God forbid a presidential nominee using her own "charitable" foundation as a campaign slush fund to defraud disaster relief victims in Haiti or for accepting "pay-to-play" bribes from foreign governments, doesn't quite equate to the delusions of rabid partisans obsessed with chasing a figment of their imagination by 'wagging the dog' of implied indiscretion. Although there are no doggy bags big enough to dispose of the incalculable intellectual waste produced by the proud lapdogs of the progressive state, for the first time in modern history a man has dared to stick their collective noses in it. And the smell is glorious!

From Investigator to Instigator

You've probably heard of Whataburger, so welcome to 'A Big Nothin' burger where nothing is edible but costs twice as much to throw away! Despite all the political vitriol and senseless hyperbole surrounding his testimony, the Comey hearing basically confirmed what we already knew...Trump never obstructed justice and the President was never under investigation by the federal intelligence community...for anything. In other words, this entire fiasco was designed to convict by fabricating the appearance of scandal through mere supposition alone; a vindictive media circus born from sheer political malice. What we did learn, however, is that James Comey is a partisan snake who purposely tried to smear Trump by leaking classified documents to the New York Times through a longtime colleague and law professor. I find it ironic the Head of the FBI took notes regarding his conversation with Trump because he assumed the President was "lying" to gain false favor, only to give the most infamous and pathological liar in American history a free pass: Hillary Rodham Clinton.

And yet it was the former FBI Director himself who acted more out of "loyalty" to the Clintons and his former employer, the Obama administration, than doing his sworn duty of investigating and stopping real impropriety. You admitted former AG Loretta Lynch pressured you to exonerate Hillary before the election, to obstruct justice, yet no memo was leaked to the media or a nationally televised tribunal called by outraged Democrats. Why? Did your ideals ask for a recess or is Donald Trump much worthier of contempt because your hypocrisy is now a prerequisite of his guilt?

For the record, James, "loyalty" is not asking a federal official to circumvent the law to achieve an unscrupulous end for personal gain. It's a common-sense affirmation that you can trust a colleague, personally and professionally, so that you both understand what you're attempting to achieve; i.e., to faithfully uphold the Constitution and restore the rule of law without prejudice. If demanding loyalty is now a criminal endeavor, nearly every American President would have been impeached and practically every successful CEO fired for hurting their subordinates' feelings. The next time a prestigious public servant is distraught over an election result or feels unsafe due to their boss' direct demeanor, I would prefer they buy a Binky instead of wasting the people's time and brain cells with another Congressional hearing simply because they were fired for not doing their job.

A Game of Thrones

Ever since the orchestrated hysteria over Russia collusion and electoral interference emerged as a marketable excuse to better contextualize Hillary's loss, one thing is for certain: the liberal media and Democratic hierarchy are irrevocably invested in the mere suggestion, dare I say the indictable hope, of conspiracy and scandal. In fact, by pushing all their collective chips to the center of the political poker table, it's clear many progressives believe this is their last, best chance to undermine Donald Trump's reforms, but more profoundly to derail his re-election chances. The problem with playing Orwellian roulette is you must either push a known lie to the proverbial edge of the cliff, thus potentially implicating and destroying yourself, or you must relinquish your remaining political capital to your opponent who subsequently sits that much higher on the throne of public perception. As long as those bitter, conniving voices occupying the Halls of our Forefathers increasingly view public service as a vindictive game of selfish recompense rather than a solemn duty to preserve our founding values and the symbolic pinnacle of intellectual discourse, the results will mirror the malevolent nature of their despotic intent.

If Russia is now the eye of the political hurricane, Robert Mueller is undoubtedly the surly dealer with a score to settle for either partisan or posterity's sake. No matter what his true intentions or how much he tilts the odds in favor of his true allegiance, albeit for the integrity of truth or to feed personal distaste, there are basically two likely outcomes. One, he admits there is no tangible proof of Russian Collusion, i.e., a smoking gun, and concludes the Trump campaign made some questionable but innocuous contacts without any criminal intent or obvious wrongdoing. Or two, despite possessing no damning evidence of real conspiracy linking the President directly to punishable misconduct, Mueller opts for the theatricality of implied guilt by weaving every coincidence, chopped communication and circumstantial crumb into some passable pattern of misbehavior solely to support the media narrative of "probable" collusion and a complicit subversion of the Democratic process; something the DNC, Bernie Sanders and their marginalized primary voters know all too well.

Regardless of his final conclusions, I'm of the humble opinion Mr. Mueller is grasping at straws, questioning anything that moves or anyone who has ever mentioned "Russia", because a house of cards cannot withstand the faintest whisper of its own hypocrisy; including the fact two disgraced FBI agents exposed for anti-Trump activity remain on his "holy inquisition" team. Any career disciple of "Fidelity, Bravery and Integrity" who intentionally stacks the deck with Democratic lawyers and Clinton donors is either foolishly hostile to the concept of "objectivity", has no discernible regard for his own reputation and due process, or he is smugly trying to solicit a rash response from a known impulsive leader who will not hesitate to tweet at three in the morning. In other words, if Trump fires Mueller and his "Ides of November" assassins – a justifiable course of action being both James Comey and the former Head of Homeland Security testified there was no evidence of collusion – every liberal politician and media pundit would interpret such a move as a glaring admission of guilt; a desperate attempt to avoid prosecution and the impending humiliation of impeachment. When the judicial adage "beyond a reasonable doubt" is far too stringent for the foaming lynch mob, the court of public opinion requires no such logical restraints. And to think perjury, obstruction of justice and a little blue dress autographed in the Oval Office were by no means worthy of Presidential disbarment.

BREAKING: DOJ insiders have reportedly revealed that Robert Mueller and his Special Counsel team concluded in August 2018, months before the midterm elections, that there was no proof linking Donald Trump or his campaign to colluding with Russians during the presidential election

It's also painfully obvious Natalia Veselnitskaya was a private Russian citizen, not a Russian government agent, when she sought a meeting with Donald Trump Jr. under false pretenses or when the Obama administration gave her a Disney Express Visa Pass into the epicenter of our government; thus, allowing party constituents to fortuitously dust her off when needed as a prop to insinuate a massive cover-up of alleged treasonous activity.

Maybe my recollection of "collusion" or "election interference" is a bit hazy but it doesn't take a private investigator or a political scientist to realize the possibility of a Trump presidency caused widespread panic within the Washington establishment and a fair amount of doomsday planning. Then again, when your vacationing conscience forgets plotting and spending millions to taint the legitimacy of Israeli elections, flying in unvetted refugees or encouraging mass illegal immigration to tip America's electoral scales and incite a seditious culture war, you're hardly an innocent bystander or a traumatized victim of Russian deception after claiming "more flexibility" to willingly collude with our supposed enemy after your re-election. The same raucous media inquisition designed to invalidate an election result by condemning Donald Trump over mere wishful thinking, despite his unrivaled transparency, religiously ignored much more nefarious and substantiated charges levied against his obstinate predecessor. Apparently, advocacy and accountability are now entirely symbiotic in the moonlit studios of political prostitutes.

Collusion to Convict

While convening an "impartial" Grand Jury in any investigation – especially one with so little credible evidence – is largely a procedural issue to request documents or solicit testimony, it is still a convenient political tool of public manipulation. Despite the remarkable feat Barack Obama and Hillary Clinton have endured no such invasive inquiry,

> **Donald J. Trump** ✓
> @realDonaldTrump
>
> "Fox News has learned that Bruce Ohr wrote Christopher Steele following the firing of James Comey saying that he was afraid the anti-Trump Russia probe will be exposed." Charles Payne @FoxBusiness How much more does Mueller have to see? They have blinders on - RIGGED!

a thoroughly debunked meeting stemming from an admittedly fake dossier, fabricated by a known foreign political agitator colluding with a Russian lawyer (and former White House guest) who was previously and "coincidentally" awarded an emergency visa by the Obama administration, apparently now deserves the ominous specter of a Grand Jury to possibly indict Trump or his son for criminal misconduct. Yep, I concur, truly amazing. Naturally I'm completely disregarding Mueller's relationship with Comey – a clear conflict of interest with a personal friend and FBI colleague who already admitted leaking classified information – his shameless ploy to load this partisan inquisition with bloodthirsty Obama/Clinton cronies and his abusive attempt to expose all of Trump's financial records and business ties over the past 25 years. Keep in mind these are serious infractions prosecutors could not get away with in the most liberal court of law. Yes, if you can't convict a man of electoral collusion, at the very least you can legally data mine his private information to be mysteriously shared and weaponized before the 2020 election.

This fiasco has become so blatantly absurd that it's unmistakably clear Mueller is attempting to dupe Trump into dismissing him solely to imply scandal and guilt in the court of public opinion because no hard evidence exists, or the swamp has simply abandoned all sense of legal protocol and ethical behavior in a desperate attempt to overturn an election result they still cannot fathom. Yes, never mind that little legal conundrum a commissioned Special Prosecutor can't actually indict a sitting President; a pesky fact media alarmists have ignored but the DOJ itself confirmed. Regardless of the juvenile posturing, I honestly do not fear the "truth" for all formal requests for clarification have been promptly answered, or even precipitated by the willing release of any relevant correspondence, and this so-called investigation has all the hallmarks of a "witch hunt" because the left is obsessed with drowning the President's agenda and perceived legitimacy with an avalanche of obscene accusations, frivolous lawsuits and choreographed media ridicule. In the immortal words of Snuffleupagus, so be it. A lie takes far more effort to perpetuate and camouflage, than the truth requires to expose the swarming rats biting your kicking feet.

The Russia Ruse: A Red Dawn of White Noise

The greatest historical parallel between fascism and Communism is that both ideologies were exceeding efficient at one common practice: demonizing all opposition, threatening political opponents, by accusing nonconformists of what the very establishment did themselves: deceive, manipulate and seize control under false pretenses. These regimes and their supporters relied on inciting mob justice, mass hysteria, because their radical agenda and slanderous ploys would inevitably self-destruct under the legitimate scrutiny of rational thought: i.e., free speech and due process. The theatricality of fear and fabrication are powerful allies in the red fog of political assassination.

Enter Donald Trump, a brash and ruthlessly mocked entrepreneur, who ran on a populist platform of putting 'America First' by reforming a septic establishment and challenging the filtered of media. His victory so shocked the status quo – those who refused to take accountability for, let alone acknowledge, 8 years of failure, corruption and rampant anti-Americanism – they immediately sought to discredit his policies, or more succinctly, torpedo his presidency by any means necessary; that lone circling shark who poses the biggest threat to the globalist agenda and their monopoly on the perversion of the truth. Rather than embracing the fact Trump created more manufacturing jobs in 5 months than Obama lost during his entire tenure (300,000), that an unapologetic capitalist immediately created monthly budget surpluses in lieu of a redistributing socialist who doubled our nation debt, and illegal border crossings fell by roughly 70% by simply enforcing the law, elected adults became petulant children obsessed with petty vendettas and concocting sensational allegations of impropriety, instead of honorably serving their country and the Constitution they swore to uphold.

As a result of the President's immediate success and tireless work ethic, a culture of disinformation quickly ensued to cloud public perception of a competent, adept leader. The common-sense necessity of border security became a bellwether of racism, a constitutional travel ban issued by previous presidents invoked hollow cries of xenophobia, successful job creation and revitalized industry were reported as corporate greed, affordable healthcare without penalized mandates became a mandatory death sentence, and truth became fiction as mere suggestion "supplanted" honesty. In essence, the same "unbiased" press and conspiring Democratic party that tried to destroy his candidacy with numerous unsubstantiated charges of sexual misconduct just weeks before the election – smearing a known billionaire who was never formally charged or served with a civil suit by any accuser before his candidacy – revealed just how incestuously toxic they were by openly declaring war on the very man who so effortlessly exposed their blatant hypocrisy, infantile games and ill-conceived policies.

Because perception is often more powerful than reality, this entire Russian Conspiracy fiasco was hatched by the suddenly unemployed think tank of one extremely bitter Hillary Rodham Clinton; the very pay-to-play, "what does it matter", Goldman Sachs advocate of the poor who is still in utter disbelief as to how a politically incorrect, patriotic CEO somehow survived an orchestrated media firestorm, an avalanche of sordid celebrity rants, death threats from naked feminists and Black Lives Matter, attempts by the DHS to hack the electoral databases of multiple states, and a community organizer's final hour plea to illicit votes from illegal immigrants. Character assassination, voter fraud, funded protests and political witch hunts intended to overturn an undesirable election result? The concept of guilt is always subjective when proof is a Nancy Pelosi press conference and the liberal litmus of "intent" never installs a private server in a bathroom, deletes 33,000 "non-classified" emails, destroys government property, and religiously lies about it for posterity's sake. Apparently, manslaughter is now an imaginary crime because falling asleep at wheel requires a crosswalk full of irresponsible children.

And then there was the curious case of James Comey; a registered Democrat with documented financial ties to the Clintons who testified to Congress there was no proof of Russian election tampering. After being fired for failing to stop a waterfall of leaks or earnestly investigate the numerous indiscretions of Hillary Clinton and the Obama administration, he somehow produced a three-month-old "memo" less than a week after being relieved of his duties. Although withholding such information is a prosecutable crime in itself, this revelation is a disturbing reminder of how the Deep State mindset has enabled a hyper-partisan climate in which the rules increasingly only apply to one side of the aisle; i.e., those who make us feel "uncomfortable" or offend our fragile sensibilities. Perhaps this is why the FBI or anti-Trump Congressional hoard showed absolutely no concern when the Washington Post celebrates yet another leaked rumor going viral in a vile attempt to convict a President without regard to truth or context. The end always justifies the means when there are no consequences in the aftermath of animosity: to injure with extreme prejudice.

While I'd love to dismiss the schizophrenic delusions of scheming despots, I cannot in good conscience. First of all, expressing your hope that a good man and career civil servant would be exonerated is neither illegal nor unreasonable. It is a simple affirmation that pales in comparison to Bill Clinton privately meeting with Loretta Lynch on a tarmac to shield his wife from prosecution, or Barack Obama telling his former Attorney General to

"I have to ask, is the Russian collusion in the room with us...right now?"

Plead the Fifth to conceal the true nature of his Iranian dealings. Second, just because some leftover Obama loyalists have been duped by salacious propaganda into believing Donald Trump is the physical manifestation of Satan, doesn't give subordinates the right to divulge national secrets or reinvent the rules of confidentiality. Unlike those planted saboteurs within his administration, our Chief Executive has the authority to share information, classified or not, with any foreign leader that he deems worthy or relevant to the best interests of the county. Regardless, the only thing "classified" about ISIS is showing the civilized world where to annihilate the true embodiment of evil; a target Barack Obama gladly painted on America's back every single day of his presidency.

Contrary to the relentless conditioning of progressive programming, if any President or administrative appointment was going to be indicted, dare I say impeached, it was the corrosive elements with the Obama administration; those agents allowed to act with reckless impunity beneath the gloating applause of network news and the complicit silence of our intelligence community. Unfortunately for fans of equal opportunity and due diligence, no mysterious memos magically appeared to sooth hurt feelings or suggest guilt in the kangaroo court of public opinion.

If I may, where was the liberal Gestapo's acute level of concern and stringent demand for culpability when Barack Obama used government agencies to target conservatives, when his administration wiretapped the press, members of Congress and even a presidential candidate, repeatedly lied to the public and the courts to pass the single-payer Trojan horse known as Obamacare, colluded with Eric Holder and Loretta Lynch to obstruct justice in regards to Fast & Furious, empowered Lois Lerner and the IRS to harass conservative citizens, allowed the Muslim Brotherhood to infiltrate the highest levels of our government, approved Hillary's sale of Uranium to Russia in exchange for campaign donations and future speaking engagements, ignored the Clinton Foundation defrauding disaster survivors to fund her campaign, interfered with Israeli elections, transported unvetted refugees into America, granted visas to internationally red flagged immigrants, incited a homicidal war on cops, and attempted to send $221 million in taxpayer dollars to Palestinian militants as he slithered out the backdoor of infamy? The truth is if Barack Obama and Hillary Clinton were held to same, sterling standard as Donald Trump, where blind hatred superseded any tangible proof of criminality, the only organized social "resistance" would be in the form of The View decrying the assumed gender of their orange jumpsuits.

When the goal is to turn molehills into mountain ranges, turn the most innocent sentiments or routine duties into imaginary impeachable offenses, nothing will satiate the foaming lynch mob; those juvenile malcontents who embarked on a path of political sabotage to demonize a man from the very inception of his nomination. Sadly, the crass and profane behavior of media personalities, politicians and everyday citizens has not only become acceptable in contemporary circles, it is a blaring reminder of how far "We the People" have fallen as a society. America was founded upon the nonnegotiable ideals of individual liberty; a free republic that demanded open and constructive discourse from its elected officials to find lasting solutions to our most daunting challenges. Instead of a government defined by mutual respect and compromise, Washington has regressed into a street hustle where a sizable but growing faction of whining adolescents incessantly connive and conspire to seize power by any means possible. To these malignant souls, the welfare of the country and the people are mere afterthoughts, impressionable and expendable pawns to be sacrificed in their insatiable lust to control and humiliate their most hated adversaries.

Other than the obvious waste of taxpayer resources, I do not fear any investigation because I have little doubt the findings, if left untainted by the corrupt likes of Robert Mueller (**see page 168**), would confirm the obvious truth: that current political misappropriation starving the fascist engine of ignorance and paranoia. Ironically, as the masses are forced to digest hourly catcalls of impeachment and "scandal", DNC lawyers are currently arguing in court as to why they had the right to repeatedly lie to their electorate, rig their primaries to defeat Bernie Sanders, and fraudulently secure the nomination for the most corrupt candidate in American history. And yet these are the duplicitous snakes accusing Donald Trump of such grotesque wrongdoing. Democrats and the vengeful remnants of "Never Trumpers" know they do not have the necessary votes to impeach the President, or the required majority to initiate proceedings, but the persistent stigma of scandal is far more damaging than its eventual resolution.

Rather, their overriding mission is to magnify the manufactured appearance of impropriety in order to deflect from any meaningful accomplishments and thus weaken his reelection chances in 2020. By endlessly beating the drum of Russian tampering and feasting off mere inference from orchestrated classified leaks, the Red armies of intolerance will vilify and dehumanize the one individual whose unyielding nature exposed just how corrupt, divisive and destructive the media/political establishment has become to the survival of America's founding creed: life, liberty and justice without undue government interference.

I have long feared America was on the downside of history, but the unhinged behavior of political terrorists has confirmed we're spiraling towards our own self-imposed demise. While critics will denounce my assertions as presumptive and pretentious, I pose one final sociological proof. If Democrats held healthy majorities in both Congressional houses, Donald Trump would have been impeached before his sixth month in office; not for any egregious crime or unprecedented action, but for winning an election...a singular event that has revealed how detached, dangerous and vicious the modern left has become. Democracy and intellectual diversity are obviously too much of a burden to bear, so screaming tantrums, public tribunals and cultural anarchy are now the preferred charities of enlightened progressives.

I have no problem with discerning minds disliking Donald Trump for any number of reasons. Such is life. However, I have no patience for those who believe his every decision requires their explicit approval or an engraved apology carved into his tombstone. The President of the United States could literally save a school bus of handicap children from drowning in a river, or cure cancer, and his selfless actions would still be condemned as crimes against humanity. When 'right and wrong' become a political construct and justice is no longer a moral derivative of rational thought, patriotism is labeled as hate speech, rogue judges subvert the law with senseless spite, and the faintest whisper of opposing viewpoints triggers violence and accusations of extremism. I'm not interested in repeating a shameless lie until it is somehow perceived as irrefutable truth for the sake of achieving political supremacy. I'm interested in allowing the fearless leader I voted for to finish 'draining the swamp' before the country I love and the last vestiges of integrity are forever buried beneath the marginalized victims of baseless entitlement and cultivated malice.

> "
> Leaks of classified information are **serious, serious federal crimes** for a reason ... It cannot simply be tolerated.
> — FBI Director James Comey
> FOX NEWS

A Carnival of Democratic Collusion

After spending two years debunking this political charade, a sensational hoax countless politicians and famed pundits shamelessly promoted as an impeachable fact, I'm grateful the "truth" has finally been confirmed; regardless of how many reject the final conclusions. If I may, unless repeatedly and unapologetically maintaining your innocence is considered an egregious offense, how is it possible to obstruct justice when the mere accusation of election collusion was a complete fabrication from the start? Such reasoning is the crux of entrapment, a brazenly-fictitious premise, solely to imply guilt in the absence of real misconduct.

The disturbing reality this tainted process took two years, $25 million and the nation's collective sanity to verify an obvious fairy tale, to appease those deranged voters and leftist radicals who refused to recognize Donald J. Trump as their legitimate Commander in Chief, was and continues to be nothing short of a scandalous, criminal conspiracy. It's also obvious the lack of procedural integrity during this lengthy inquisition, which harassed and incarcerated several of his former associates on unrelated activities, was an attempt to bluff the Trump administration into terminating Mueller's everlasting but essentially empty reign of terror; a baited trap the President astutely avoided, despite possessing every justification for immediate dismissal, which would have only fueled media speculation of his "undeniable" guilt.

Today's released findings represent far more than just the public vindication of a populist President, but a turning point for the misled American people and an endlessly-persecuted man's quest to reclaim this country from the treasonous dealings of a failed coup attempt. Why else would a patriotic nationalist empower Robert Mueller – a known Obama operative, vocal globalist and longtime James Comey colleague – if he did not unequivocally believe in his eventual exoneration; no matter how naive his belief in "objective" justice from a biased team of Democratic lawyers? You cannot conjure collusion in the absence of tangible evidence.

Because the truth typically requires far less explanation than the feckless lies of partisan hacks, the clear lack of accountability in the incestuous swamp of Washington politics, the time has come to investigate, expose and indict those real criminals who maliciously colluded to frame a sitting President with this blatantly-false narrative: the Obama administration and Department of Justice, FBI and CIA Deep State saboteurs, the Clinton campaign, Fusion GPS and Christopher Steele, and the insidious "Fake News" establishment. Failure to prosecute impropriety on this unprecedented scale will only ensure its future application on a systemic level: a totalitarian platform of unchecked corruption once single party rule is permanently achieved.

The only question that remains is whether or not the American electorate, patronized taxpayers and betrayed citizens, will continue to entertain the adolescent antics of Democratic carnival workers instead of demanding the return of common sense and honorable public service to the occupied halls of our now disparaged forefathers.

But of course, James, for what exiting president would ever establish an obstructionist organization, "Organizing for Action", to resist his successor? Unheard of and treasonous to say the least. Both deserve to be exposed and indicted for an elaborate ruse hatched well before the election.

Clapper: Obama Was Behind The Whole Thing
Flashback to Strzok after returning from London:...
zerohedge.com

Foreign Diplomacy

& Democracy

<u>Setting A Course for Change</u>

As more details continue to emerge and evolve over due time, the historic peace agreement signed by both our President and Kim Jong-un is more or less a culmination of pressure, timing, and seized opportunity. The same hysterical liberals decrying Donald Trump was going to trigger World War III through mere rhetoric alone, are now complaining a mercurial dictator who threatened our annihilation and recklessly tested nuclear ordinance in the Pacific Ocean was brought to his senses. In other words, they're distraught over the widely hailed prospect of yet another unfathomable success for our Commander in Chief; one which his beloved predecessor either foolishly dismissed, lacked the discernible skills to achieve or found no common ground to negotiate. If the roles were precisely reversed, Barack Obama would have been anointed world savior on nearly every network before the ink from his Smithsonian archived pen could consummate his historic breakthrough. Excuses, like elections, also have consequences.

While I make no apologies for Kim's past transgressions or brutal reign, he is nonetheless the proverbial lightning rod from which all, if any, progress must emanate. As much as I welcomed his potential assassination, such deliberate action would immediately invoke widespread condemnation – from both allies and adversaries alike, most notably China and Democratic antagonists – giving Donald Trump's endlessly plotting enemies but another barb from which to skewer him with salacious accusations of murder and chargeable war crimes. And yes, there is also that distinct possibility where a justifiable, painless military operation to eliminate but one irrefutable tyrant concludes with yet another deranged family despot quickly assuming power and ultimately with the full protections of the "reinvested" global community. It's hard to stop the flood of unabridged human suffering, claim the moral high ground, when your unabashed critics left the sprinklers on for insurance purposes.

When rooting against America becomes your favorite national pastime, hoping a notorious regime retains Weapons of Mass Destruction is far less disturbing than simply acknowledging the watershed milestone of a fellow American. Regardless of the treasonous politics and shameless posturing, the progressive establishment's desperate attempt to derail any meaningful progress or perceived triumph, the past 6 months has confirmed two salient facts: President Trump is never going to peacefully accept a nuclear North Korea and the North Korean people are in dire need of immediate assistance. These destitute and forsaken families need food, healthcare, electricity, basic infrastructure, education and in due time...commercial opportunities as a gateway to a better life.

Although I by no means trust Kim Jong-un, how is consciously accepting a legacy of failed diplomacy remotely superior to protecting mankind from another armed menace? How is doing nothing any better than at least attempting to forge a brave, new path? If the 34-year-old descendant of totalitarian rulers has even the slightest hope of regaining a shred of respect from his people, not blind adulation driven by fear of death, his only true recourse was to accept peaceful disarmament, seek an end to economic sanctions by joining the civilized world, and to stop hoarding his nation's wealth for personal glory. That momentous moment our President initially withdrew from the peace summit was the very pivotal instant an apologetic North Korea fully committed to the idea her failed past can no longer dictate her present course. Whether by earnest sincerity, artful flattery or reasoned harmony, only a skilled and astute leader can potentially turn a vaunted foe into a personal confidant of foreseeable change.

Whereas America has an abundance of agricultural resources, technology and business acumen, our greatest enduring tribute is that of humanity: an innate calling to spread liberty and hope throughout the world, especially in the most inhospitable places or during unconventional times. If building a few condos or beach resorts gives a crying child his prized rattler of international allure, such trivialities will cost far less than waging a military campaign on foreign soil or cleaning up the atomic aftermath of a rogue attack on the beaches of Hawaii. Appeasement, on the other hand, is capitulating to fear, indecision, without demanding specific concessions and verifiable actions necessary for reaching an acceptable solution. Fortunately for the American people, accomplished CEO's don't deal in sentimental whims or intangible assets. You either fulfill your part of the bargain or you're liquidated in a Pyongyang penthouse by your own myopic accord. Unlike tipsy pillow talk with an undercover assassin, only one has a promising future.

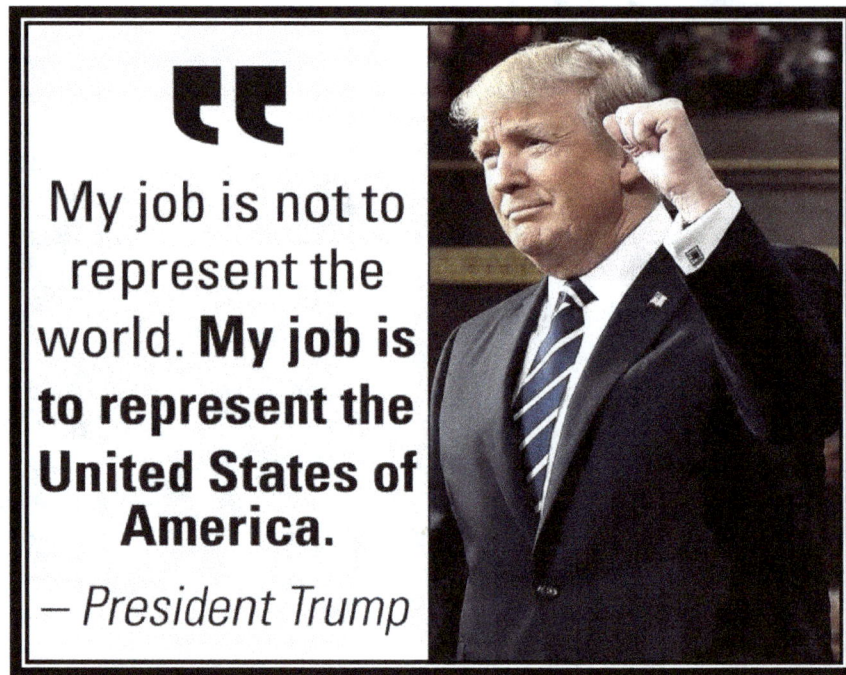

The Enduring Prize of Peace

There are statesmen, universally praised and/or bestowed with hollow accolades, because they fit the world perception of what a "progressive leader" should represent. And then there are those proven executives, resourceful pragmatists who are neither interested in politically correct platitudes or coddling global elites, who seek results by the most unconventional means. Donald Trump was repeatedly accused of being a reckless antagonist of North Korea who would inevitably trigger World War III by mere "mean" tweets alone. His relentless "Rocket Man" disparagement of Kim Jong-un – a feared, Communist tyrant guilty of countless atrocities against his own people, not to mention threatening the United States and South Korea with annihilation – was branded as unnecessary and juvenile. And yes, perhaps it was. Of course, the President was faintly concerned with appearances and foolishly embracing a policy of continuous appeasement for he was standing up to a notorious bully on an international stage; showing both a spoiled despot and the free world one man had the resolve to either reject the nuclear aspirations of a murderous regime or to peacefully bring an impoverished nation to the bargaining table for a historic opportunity to choose unity, opportunity, over futility.

Unlike his predecessor who presided over the proliferation of ISIS, did nothing to assuage the mass persecution of Christians in the Middle East, shielded Hezbollah from prosecution for drug/human trafficking, allowed a tortured U.S. student, Otto Warmbier, to die in a North Korean prison for stealing a poster, negotiated the released of five Taliban terrorists from Guantanamo Bay for a deserting, anti-American soldier, christened plans for a nuclear Iran with a 150 billion-dollar endowment for "world peace", and triggered an unprecedented war on American law enforcement through inflamed racial tensions and selective outrage, Donald Trump's legacy will never rise to the "esteemed" expectations of the modern Nobel Prize.

Nevertheless, what has been accomplished in a matter of months, if not during a singular, secretive visit by Mike Pompeo to North Korea beneath the real-time radar of media narcissists, is truly remarkable. For 65 years a number of world leaders and U.S Presidents attempted, many never even tried, to end lingering hostilities between South and North Korea. In fact, until last week, there was never an official peace agreement between the estranged countries despite an official armistice being signed in 1953. And now, despite decades of threats and not only did Kim Jong-un and South Korean President Moon Jae-in embrace in public, they agreed to begin abolishing the infamous Korean Demilitarized Zone, as well working towards the "complete denuclearization" of the Korean Peninsula. The North Korean authoritarian even personally announced the release of three American detainees, wrongfully-held prisoners, to an embassy in South Korean as a demonstration of good faith. For two nations that rarely engaged in dialogue, let alone civil discourse, this stark reversal is the equivalent of Russia collapsing from within, "Palestinians" recognizing Israel's borders and right to exist, or Elizabeth Warren wearing a "Make America Great Again" hat while hugging Donald Trump at a Berkeley press conference. It is, without pretense or prevarication, an astonishing development for a region paralyzed by endless strife and uncertainty for over half a century.

So exactly how did the President, one supposedly so politically unrefined and woefully ignorant of global dynamics, achieve one of the most significant breakthroughs in the intricate arts of foreign diplomacy? To avoid a convoluted, well-rehearsed response...short-term memory. Donald Trump is that rare breed of Chief Executive who can engage in the most divisive rhetoric with a colleague or rival, only to have dinner and drinks with that same individual or delegation hours later. While personal feelings may always linger, business is business and a seasoned pragmatist doesn't think in terms of Republican or Democrat, history or animosity. He or she creates, seizes upon, an advantageous opening to discover a common ground of mutual benefit; albeit immediate or deferred. However, unlike Mrs. Clinton who views American lives, national interests, as "bumps in the road", people are inspired by a 71-year-old patriot waiting to privately greet ordinary civilians on a tarmac at three o'clock in the morning despite having not slept for 20 hours. Since the President already and very publicly demonstrated his willingness to exert force, if necessary, to end North Korea's unchecked nuclear aspirations, my guess is he gave Kim Jong-un a much more viable option: End all nuclear testing, cultivate diplomatic and economic relations with South Korea, and the world community will end sanctions restoring some semblance of sanity in a nation where

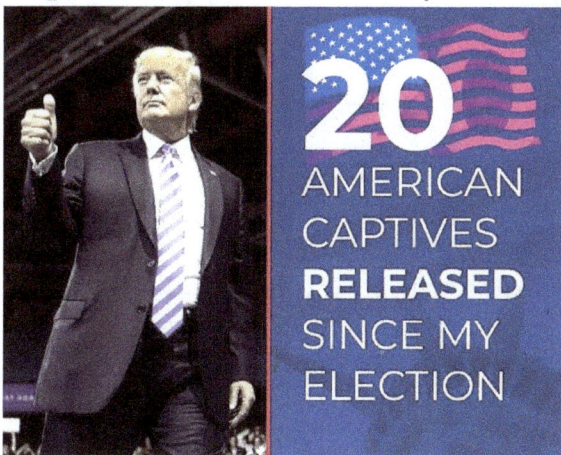

citizens still die of starvation and only the very wealthy, high-ranking public officials, enjoy basic electricity.

Although such a self-evident choice seems exceedingly obvious for most "reasonable" people, tyrants and dictators rarely think in such terms. That's what makes this diplomatic feat such a watershed moment in modern history: this unforeseen triumph was built upon the backbone of a supposed political and military failure. Because the Korean conflict failed to produce a decisive "winner", historians and media pundits still to this day refer to it as a wasteful campaign which resulted in the unnecessary loss of 35,000 American lives. While I too mourn the loss of a single life, not all victories culminate with a planted flag or a televised military parade. U.S. efforts, for all intents and purposes, eventually halted communist aggression in a region where South Korea was nearly completely consumed by intervening Chinese forces after the initial North Korean/Russian-backed invasion was repelled beyond the 38th parallel. The revered city of Seoul itself, the focal point of this violent tug-of-war for independence, exchanged hands 5 times in a matter of a few short years; the final time, her people and future prowess freed from the plotting hands of communist aggression.

If not for the valor and fierce determination of our forces, the democratic and sovereign state of South Korea – a Constitutional Republic boasting the world's 4th largest metropolitan economy, the 8th largest median household income and 11th largest global GDP – would have very likely suffered the same depraved fate as their northern counterparts. For the current 52 million residents of South Korea, including the millions more who died in their homeland after their liberation from Japan in 1945, America's steadfast commitment to the advancement of freedom, the dignity of education, opportunity and a humane quality of life, is viewed as anything but a failure. I have little doubt they are equally thankful for one man's unique ability to find hope, a pledge of future Korean unity, in one of the most inhospitable states of moral disrepair: the breached invincibility of Kim Jong-un's sheltered mind.

Emissaries, Ingrates and the Unholy State of Iran

If you don't believe in the omnipresent New World Order, a virtually untouchable yet conniving conclave of global elitists attempting to undermine American independence and influence through shadow diplomacy, look no further than the extra-curricular activities of one Barack Obama. Since Donald Trump's inauguration, the former President's administration has harassed, undermined, obstructed and sought to illegal act on behalf of a country it no longer represents. Not only is such behavior unprecedented and distinctly hostile, it's a clear violation of the Logan Act: a statute which strictly forbids any citizen not registered as a foreign agent, empowered by our government alone, to negotiate, dare I say even discuss, any official matters pertaining to existing U.S. policy.

After his historic victory in 2016, President Trump toured Europe and the Far East to inform nations he would be terminating the Paris Accord and to seek new economic opportunities in the wake of nixing any grotesquely "unfair trade" deals...such as the

Trans Pacific Pact. Shortly thereafter, Mr. Obama himself orchestrated meetings with many of the same leaders and/or diplomats. Why? Well it's obvious. Not only was he attempting to seek future concessions in the fresh face of incited, international fear regarding the election of an "American First" Chief Executive, he was undoubtedly informing them not to scrap his administration's policies because Trump's eventual Democratic successor would immediately agree to abide by the original terms. Sound remotely treasonous? Not if you welcome your neighbor renegotiating your home's mortgage or your former supervisor telling you how to do your job.

Like his aforementioned boss, I don't need to discern the exact nuances of John Kerry's visit to Iran when his entire life is a microcosm of his political ambitions: religiously disparaging America to the raucous applause and potential benefit of her of vocal enemies. From his self-aggrandizing Vietnam betrayal with Jane Fonda to aiding and abetting radical regimes as Secretary of State, there is little doubt as to where his true loyalties lie. How else could a U.S. civil servant and former Presidential candidate, a dignitary expected to act in the best interests of a sovereign nation and ultimately her people's well-being, ever agree to a nuclear Iran: a militant Islamic state whose President, Hassan Rouhani, and Supreme Leader, Ali Khamenei, have repeatedly called for the annihilation of America and Israel? Well, when your "esteemed" colleagues are Barack Obama and Iranian native Valerie Jarrett – two lifelong, Marxist detractors of the very Constitutional Republic they once claimed to serve – the answer is as infuriating as it is unforgivable.

It's a sad day for democracy, common sense, when three progressive leaders have far more affinity for a despotic country that has sponsored global terrorism for decades and denied millions basic human rights in the name of Islamic supremacy. What other creature of intellect would characterize a free nation blessed by an abundance of opportunity and individual liberty, one that has overcome injustice and sectional discord through the timeless wisdom of a watershed document, as a racist, greedy, and evil empire when contrasted against those forsaken souls forced to live amidst the rampant depravity of the Middle East. And yes, never mind all three accomplices are American educated, "oppressed" millionaires who rose to the pinnacle of power beneath their seething disdain. What else could better contrast these differences, reward true hypocrisy, than to give billions in taxpayer-money and classified technology to rabid extremists seeking nuclear armaments capable of our, if not our allies, destruction?

The Iran deal was but the desired culmination of a corrupt plot to shift the balance of military power in the region at any cost. The truth is this fraudulent agreement, hailed as a diplomatic wonder by pandering globalists, was but a calculated smokescreen to conceal the fact Iran's nuclear ambitions were much more advanced than previously thought; yes, once again, much to the delight of Obama's anti Judeo-Christian aspirations. Iran had already cultivated enriched Uranium to some degree, although the exact amount is still not entirely known. All that remained was weaponizing and developing a reliable ballistic delivery system by which to terrorize the world; a task a number of American, Chinese or Russian scientists are more than capable of helping a notorious regime achieve under the right circumstances or administration.

Naturally, President Obama was far more concerned about minimizing international outrage to consciously arming such a rogue state, mobilizing opposition against Israel's inevitable response, than the destabilizing aftermath itself. Therefore, as any proud propagandist would surmise, he sought to publicly craft the affable appearance of responsible oversight and diplomatic good will. This in-turn would pave a more receptive road until an atomic Iran came to fruition and thus potentially deter any military strikes in the face of more unified support. Of course, anyone in their right mind knows nothing would have ever stopped the Islamic Republic of Iran from pursuing weapons of mass destruction; that very same "mythic" instrument of war liberals demanded as the only justification for removing an Iraqi tyrant named Saddam Hussein who had already and unmistakably gassed thousands of innocent Kurds.

Donald Trump, the symbolic leader of the Free World and entrusted with ensuring the survival of liberty across the globe, had no other logical alternate than to unconditionally reject a nuclear Iran. To even entertain such an absurd notion was to embrace those eternally seeking our demise. During his entire 8-year tenure, almost every domestic and foreign policy decision ever made by Barack Obama was done so from an ingrained perspective of victimization and entitlement. Anglo-America was guilty for much of the modern world's struggles, economic and moral inequities, and the international community was entitled to recompense. In reality, however, a bitter son of absentee parents was the victim of a misguided education, his personal insistence upon identity politics and a glaring lack of appreciation for the unparalleled life America had afforded perhaps its most renowned and ungrateful critic of all.

The "Iron Dome" of Guarded Diplomacy

Before Barely 24-hours after the U.S. terminated its infamous Iranian nuclear deal - Barack Obama's "acceptable" timetable for a terrorist regime to stockpile nuclear arms - Iran immediately proved the wisdom of President Trump's decision by firing 20 missiles directly into Israel from neighboring Syria. Luckily, no one was hurt except the feelings of bitter globalists left to dine on the sour garnish of their stale propaganda. And that includes one Jimmy Carter whose ankle-biting criticism is about as credible as an internationally-lauded lapdog who once watched the Ayatollah Khomeini seize power and hold 52 Americans hostage for 444 days; the longest such crisis, diplomatic "neutering", in recorded history. To commemorate the victory of common sense over the Islamic caliphate's 'common good', Donald Trump just announced the capture of five of ISIS' most wanted leaders. If the President is indeed the best friend of ISIS, as Hillary so obnoxiously claims, why is their organization but a shadow of itself despite flourishing across the globe just a few years ago under her former boss' accommodating tenure? Yes, I concur, when it comes to denial and the progressive art of mass media manipulation, the truth is always a dish best served cold to those domestic combatants who forced America to eat last for nearly a decade. Who knew eggs Benedict Arnold were considered such a posh delicacy in the frigid pantheon of political betrayals?

Allies & Asterisks

Watching a fearless Chief Executive expose the inexcusable hypocrisy of NATO elitists on a global stage is nothing short of long overdue. Unless 70 year-old "allies" fighting communist aggression are knowingly content fleecing a loyal colleague that has provided international security, advanced military equipment, and vast economic opportunities for their vulnerable populaces, our feckless press should be applauding the unappreciated fact America finally has an "embarrassing" leader who refuses to politely acquiesce after years of "acceptable" exploitation by the same "sophisticated" European community our loved ones once liberated from Nazi occupation.

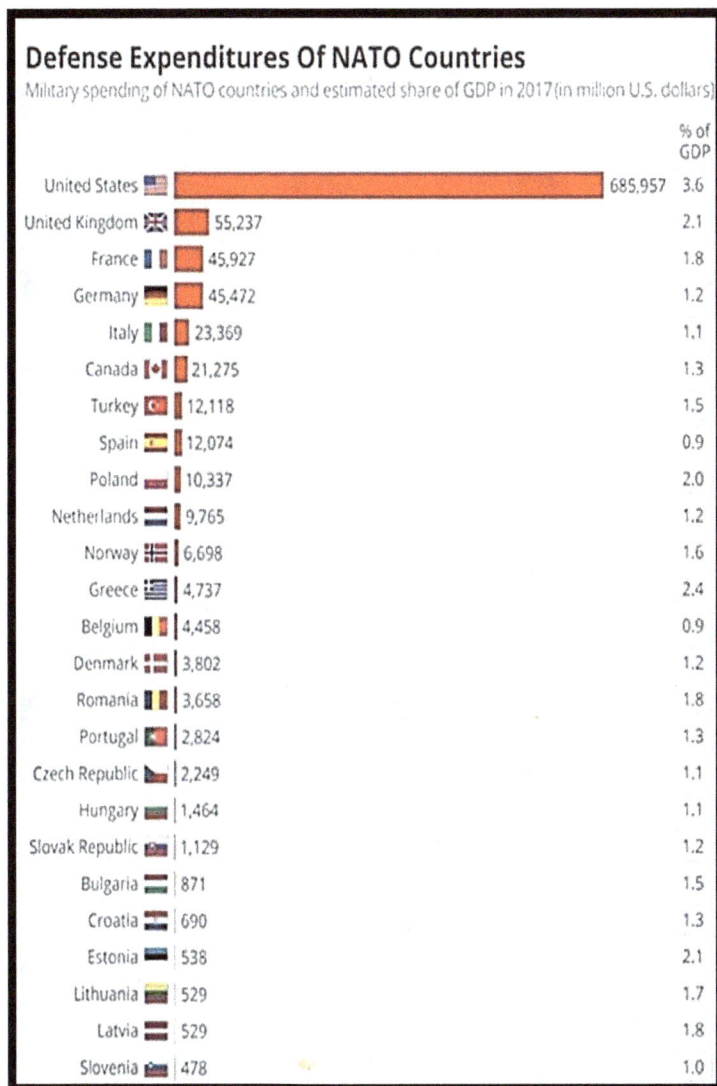

Defense Expenditures Of NATO Countries

Military spending of NATO countries and estimated share of GDP in 2017 (in million U.S. dollars)

Country	Military spending	% of GDP
United States	685,957	3.6
United Kingdom	55,237	2.1
France	45,927	1.8
Germany	45,472	1.2
Italy	23,369	1.1
Canada	21,275	1.3
Turkey	12,118	1.5
Spain	12,074	0.9
Poland	10,337	2.0
Netherlands	9,765	1.2
Norway	6,698	1.6
Greece	4,737	2.4
Belgium	4,458	0.9
Denmark	3,802	1.2
Romania	3,658	1.8
Portugal	2,824	1.3
Czech Republic	2,249	1.1
Hungary	1,464	1.1
Slovak Republic	1,129	1.2
Bulgaria	871	1.5
Croatia	690	1.3
Estonia	538	2.1
Lithuania	529	1.7
Latvia	529	1.8
Slovenia	478	1.0

For all of the lauded "fair share" rhetoric regurgitated by Bernie Sanders and Elizabeth Warren, despite the inconvenient reality corporations actually create jobs, new wealth, the top 20% wage earners account for over 90% of all income taxes, and both Senators got rich selling the liquidated lie of socialism, when did grossly disproportionate tariffs and unequal military defense expenditures serve the best interests of American taxpayers, let alone the surviving unity, safety, of the free world? Dismissive globalists offering little in return while expecting preferential treatment, financial sacrifice, are neither trustworthy confidants or faintly self-aware. Rather, it's refreshing to wake-up every morning knowing America has no greater friend, tireless advocate and astute ally, than the one constantly misrepresented man who was not only elected to restore common sense and accountability to the barricaded landfill of progressive regression, but who categorically refused to retreat from the arduous goal of his stated presidential obligation: government reform and the restoration of American Exceptionalism, even in the face of overwhelming media manipulation and escalating political hostility.

A "Mental" Refresher

See anything inappropriate here; other than the absentee rage of today's hypocrites who have no idea what real scandal looks like! More flexibility after the election, $500k speeches paid for by Russian bankers, personally profiting from the sale of U.S Uranium to a known adversary...spare me the fake outrage and orchestrated protests. Those who aided and abetted this recent hysteria are symbolic of the mindless duplicity killing this country and the people's ability to discern the most evident truths. When your most vocal critics' secrets have secrets, justice is an inside joke. Yes, Trump Derangement Syndrome needs to be officially recognized as a serious mental disorder by the American Psychiatric Association before more people get hurt or God forbid accidentally discover the truth!

A Sword in the Sand: Salvation or Suicide

Before I share my unfiltered opinion on the Syrian air strikes, I have one humble request for media and celebrity pontiffs alike: spare America your apocalyptic doom and sanctimonious drivel. Barack Obama not only launched over twice as many Tomahawk missiles into Syria with no outcry from the pacifist peanut gallery, he cajoled the America people into accepting thousands of refugees despite financing Hezbollah and Iran – both key allies of Bashar al-Assad – while simultaneously arming and lending military intelligence to the Syrian Rebels with the support of Saudi Arabia and Turkey. Why stop at "wagging the dog" when you can cook the whole damn thing, sell it as a humanitarian crisis to justify mass Western immigration and hire PETA to blame Russian hot dog vendors for feeding non-Halal meat to Sunni "freedom" fighters; that is, after the election is over when you have more leverage to hug your childhood heroes before accusing them of interference because you failed to properly rig an election Donald Trump overwhelmingly won on a populist pledge to end corruption. Those circling scavengers who believe in never letting a good tragedy go to waste are typically the most vocal, if not complicit, in cultivating the circumstances of misfortune's fate.

The problem with Syria is that it's a quagmire, a riddle wrapped inside an enigma, keenly camouflaged to keep the outside world from understanding the real roots of this geo-political, religious tug-of-war. In other words, outside of independent humanitarian efforts, it's an intersecting landmine of incorrigible interests that has very little to do with saving human lives, human rights, and everything to do with global superpowers and Islamic factions vying for control due to its proximity to Israel and the Golan Heights. Otherwise, most so-called civilized nations would simply treat it as another destitute, war-ravaged African nation. Before the rise of Islamic extremism under Iran's Ayatollah Khomeini and Iraq's Saddam Hussein, Syria had a respectable agrarian, petroleum-based economy which enjoyed 336% per capita growth in the 1970's. Now, after seven years of a devastating civil war resulting in upwards of 500,000 deaths, over 50% of their population is unemployed, 80% live in poverty and much of their infrastructure is destroyed or in severe disrepair.

Believe it or not, Syria was recently considered one of the more moderate Middle Eastern nations, touting secular laws and religious freedom. The Assad family are Alawites, a branch of Shia Islam (Shiites) that intertwines Gnostic, Islamic, and Christian elements, who publicly reject much of Sharia Law. To Islamic fundamentalists, this "heresy" is compounded by the fact Alawites account for only 11% of the Syrian population; a statistic that only fuels Muslim claims of illegitimacy.

While liberal critics are divided according to hating the President no matter what and aiding a new Muslim caliphate, approval for Trump's attack on Syria's weapon's capabilities seems to boil down to one litmus test: did Assad actually use chemical weapons on his own citizens, opposition forces, or was it indeed a "False Flag" operation? A False Flag is little more than a fabricated and/or manipulated event intended to incite outrage for the purpose of achieving social/political change that might not happen otherwise. A staged hate crime before an election, a known fake dossier used to allege election tampering, or psychological warfare convincing entrenched armies their leaders surrendered, are all varying examples of such orchestrated ruses. In short, it is little more than organized propaganda, a tool of persuasion which has existed since the dawn of civilization, the first governed city-states, to usurp power, harness rage and topple empires.

Right or wrong, the difference between perspective and propaganda is negligible without tangible proof. While I freely confess to the deceptive ploys of antagonists, I am by no means a conspiracy theorist. I do not believe 9/11 or Newtown were False Flags. There were simply too many moving parts – unrelated victims, credible motives and varying local, state and federal officials – to perpetrate and conceal these nefarious crimes. However, I do not dismiss the possibility of rogue sects within our intelligence community ignoring or even igniting potential threats, such as the Parkland shooting or the Las Vegas massacre, to sow the seeds of a "Constitutional crisis" conveniently magnified by the media's saturation of coached spectators and/or third-party opportunists. Why soil your own hands when an armed patsy will do it free? Even though some scenes of death and depravity been have undeniably been doctored during the conflict to sway public opinion, there is little doubt Syria is a war-torn hell hole defined by human atrocity.

Whether the attack on Syria was justified or prudent boils down to historical precedent or more succinctly, trust. While leftists love to mock the "fairy tale" existence of WMD's in Iraq, it's a U.N. documented fact Saddam Hussein gassed thousands of Kurds with banned chemical weapons. Furthermore, the CIA also surmised it was highly likely much of those stockpiles were transported to Syria before the commencement of Operation Desert Storm; a country which once sought to create a unified state with Iraq under the Ba'ath Party in 1978, followed by a brief period of political animosity until al-Assad took power in 2000. The probable existence of chemical weapons in Syria, the assertions of repeated attacks in 2013 which also revealed remnants of Sarin gas – stockpiles Russia claimed to have removed from their military concubine that same year – are reputable indicators of further crimes committed by the Assad government. However, for myself personally, the most compelling piece of evidence is the assurance of one General James Mattis – an unswerving patriot, decorated Marine and revered man of integrity – who is "absolutely confident" such an attack occurred last week.

Despite the strong case for military intervention, a pinpoint bombing campaign I believe was both justifiable and exceptionally planned with minimal to no loss of life, it was but a symbolic show of force that will likely do little to deter future attacks in a hopelessly hostile environment. In a perfect world where the religious fanaticism of Iran or Hezbollah doesn't exist, where Russia and America are bound by a common duty in lieu of gaining strategic leverage, and where Israel's homeland is not in daily distress, the entire globe would stand in unison to ensure the dignity of every human life and the majesty of natural born liberty. Unfortunately, because we do not yet live in a world community where reason trumps rhetoric, history precludes hypocrisy, a red line must periodically be drawn in the sand; that ethical boundary which personifies moral obligation. The only real question that remains is who will cross it, what will be the consequences and how many will be paid to look the other way? When fighting one injustice requires appeasing another, martyrdom becomes the most democratic form of hostage negotiation. We cannot truly help the Islamic community, alter centuries of systemic strife in the Middle East, until they universally seek to assimilate to a more humane way of life.

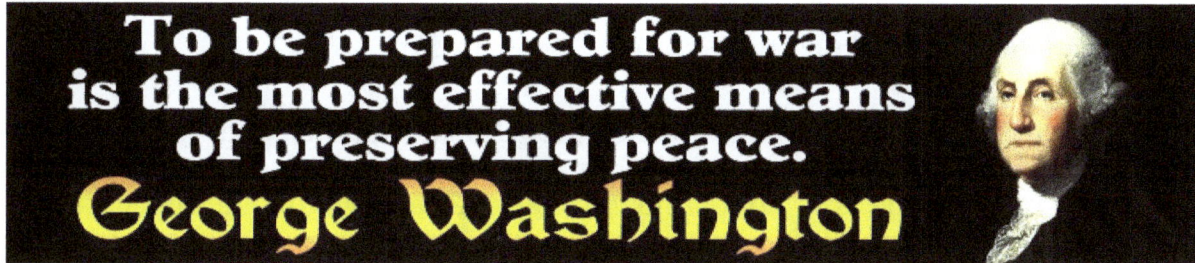

To be prepared for war is the most effective means of preserving peace. George Washington

Straws, Spitballs and the Coordinates of Kim Jong-un

History is littered with the human aftermath of tyrannical regimes and aspiring dictators who sought global power, coerced adulation, at the expense of the oppressed. And yet the only revelation more hypocritical than the "civilized" world's willingness to appease such evil is their concerted effort to marginalize the suffering of their victims; so-called statistical aberrations too often relegated to the triviality of banned history books.

Kim Jong-un is far more than the mindless byproduct of neurotic nepotism compensating for a Napoleonic complex and a bad haircut, he is a displaced relic of the Cold War. While a petulant child wastes billions-of-dollars pursuing his recurrent wet dream of a nuclear arsenal – a singular intercontinental ballistic missile that can reach American mainland – the North Korean people toil in poverty, lack basic amenities including a functional infrastructure, and are incarcerated, even terminated, for the slightest signs of dissent or acts of misconstrued disrespect. For a country that allocates the least per capita on healthcare in the world, wastes millions brainwashing children with history revisionism and the mandatory deification of a tyrant – the very man responsible for their unapologetic suffering – it's of little surprise the North Korean Education Minister was executed for not sitting properly during a cabinet meeting. Who needs critical thinking skills, universal standards of basic human decency, when native children are taught Kim II-Sung used teleportation to single-handedly defeat one million Japanese? More profoundly, who knew Star Trek wasn't science fiction?

The Korean Demilitarized Zone, considered the most dangerous strip of land in the discovered world, is but a microcosm of the institutionalized denial present in Western Society. Whereas media propagandists and detached progressives love to morally equivocate Donald Trump with Adolf Hitler, a mass murderer guilty of some of the most grotesque atrocities in human history, their love of Marxist principles leaves their ranks almost completely oblivious to the true nature of Communism. Who in their right mind would tout Cuba as a 'progressive", modern state – an indigent, totalitarian cesspool its citizens are fleeing in makeshift rafts – let alone acquiesce to the insatiable demands of

Iran and North Korea – barbaric and intolerant manifestations of fascism – to grant a homicidal madman the means to murder millions in one rash moment of unbridled hate? Sadly, their identity is as unmistakable as it is treasonous: they are the same delusional 60's radicals and entitled millennials who need safe spaces from accountability, who religiously attack free speech on college campuses and who still linger under the academic delusion Communism is the ethically superior choice for a Constitutional Republic predicated upon individual liberty and limited government.

I find it insulting, morally irreconcilable, the United Nations and self-proclaimed humanitarian organizations such as WHO and CAIR zealously demonize America for enforcing its immigration laws, combating terrorism and preserving its citizens' right to defend themselves against all forms of tyranny, only to consciously dismiss and politically pander to jihadists and tyrants guilty of unyielding crimes against humanity. Yes, those disregarded transgressions that far exceed denying 'transgenders' a dress on the battlefield or the unique gender privilege of using the bathroom of their choice; requests that would result in their imprisonment, torture or execution behind the very fortified walls of those bloodthirsty rulers globalists spitefully protect. Rather than encouraging these tormented populaces to rise-up and reclaim their homeland, restore the dignity of all human life and their natural born rights, the New World Order is content pardoning murderers and thieves to procure the downfall of Western values.

In the early 1980's, unprovoked terrorist attacks rippled across Europe targeting civilian cafes and nightclubs, which culminated in the deaths of 241 sleeping American servicemen after their barracks in Beirut, Lebanon were bombed. President Reagan, acutely aware of the state sponsors of Islamic militants and their ties to the Kremlin, bombed Libyan military installations and even the palace of Muammar Gaddafi himself under the veil of night. Unbeknownst to critics, the perpetrators of these "mysterious" attacks immediately ceased. Kim Jong-un, if he so foolishly desires, can conduct missile tests and hurl spitballs at America's geographic sense of security until he turns blue in the face. However, know this truth; for every singular missile that can reach our mainland or strike our allies, the United States possesses the means to annihilate North Korea with a solitary launch for the next 4,000 consecutive days without refrain. If you're going to tug on Superman's cape solely to solicit a pre-emptive response of unrivaled recompense, do not decry the results when your research facilities, missile silos, secret bunkers or your lavish living quarters are buried beneath the midnight rubble of pinpoint bombing campaigns; an ability your scientists can faintly fathom.

Like the unwavering "Peace through Strength" doctrine of Ronald Reagan, Donald Trump, General Mattis and Chief of Staff John Kelly do not believe the best way to defeat unrelenting evil is by apathetically waiting for the inevitable body count of senseless appeasement. Therefore, in the immortal words of "The Gipper", I leave Kim Jong-un with one final straw of prophetic advice: "They counted on America to be passive...they counted wrong." If self-preservation requires no explanation, the unannounced reminder of our resolve will be as short lived as your vile legacy.

Return to Sender

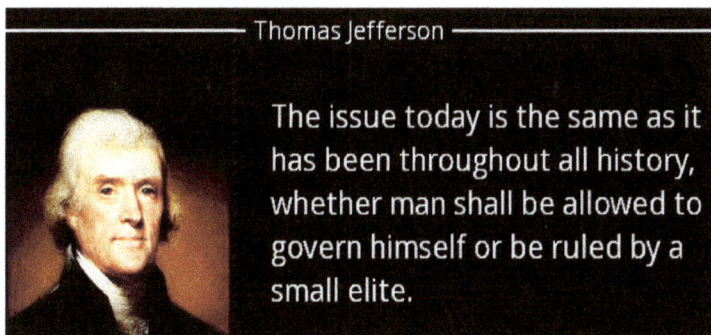

Thomas Jefferson

The issue today is the same as it has been throughout all history, whether man shall be allowed to govern himself or be ruled by a small elite.

For anyone critical of the decision to divert 5 billion in UN funding back to the American people, there are countless strangers, sketchy amoral neighbors, more than happy to cash your check or loiter in your inviting living room without rhyme or recourse. From border security, to renovated infrastructure, education, child homelessness and veteran benefits, I can think of countless needs more pressing than subsidizing the anti-American, anti-Semitic goals of bent globalists who embrace collectivism over individual liberty, excuse Islamic intolerance at the expense of Western Civilization, and justify state censorship in lieu of free speech and government transparency. Only the most spiteful, myopic partisans would viciously besmirch a loyal pragmatist who chooses the everyday interests of America and the welfare her people, over bankrolling the generational regression of the United Nations: now but an antithetical shadow of its founding mission, the open rejection of Judeo-Christian ethics, by catering to the devious subterfuge of Marxist ideologues.

For those unfamiliar with Agenda 21 and the vainglorious New World Order, their demographic blueprint includes enabling large scale immigration from underdeveloped, impoverished countries into North America and the European Union for the explicit purpose of more "equitably" redistributing economic resources, but more importantly, permanently shifting the electoral balance of power in favor of progressive rule by migrant invasion: foreign populaces that are neither loyal to their host nation's heritage, identity, or fluent in our founding ideals. The raucous cheerleaders of open borders who smugly dismiss the increasing prevalence of vote fraud in America as Right-Wing paranoia are completely indifferent to the disturbing reality there were nearly 3.5 million more registered voters in the 2016 election than the total number of living adults of legal voting age. It is also of little surprise that liberal bastions like San Francisco are granting illegals the right to vote and influence the most consequential decisions of our governing bodies, a privilege specifically reserved for U.S. citizens. I find it obnoxious Russian conspiracy theorists readily believe a handful of anonymous hackers somehow helped Trump win the presidency, despite not changing one vote in a virtual electoral landslide, but 20 million illegal immigrants incessantly incited by Democratic race-baiting and entitlement rhetoric have absolutely no bearing on our electoral process.

Unless these criminal ploys are immediately struck down by the Supreme Court, those rogue civic and state legislators arrested for purposely subverting the Constitution of the United States, the only remaining course of action is to revoke the Union charter of each offending state. America cannot survive as intended when the imported baggage of political agitators, hostile malcontents or appeased opportunists is allowed to tip the sovereign scales of American independence.

From Abraham to America: The Divine Capital of the Judeo-Christian State

For the sake of posterity, not indulging the baseless claims of revisionists and anti-Christian antagonists, I'll try to be as credibly concise as possible. The theological, geographic roots of Judaism stretch back over four thousand years – or three times greater than the first documented revelations of Mohammad – and Canaan, better known as modern-day Israel, represents a covenant between God and Abraham to consecrate a "Holy Land" for a "sacred" people. Likewise, the birth of Jesus in Bethlehem to his transcendent Sermon on the Mount near the Sea of Galilee until his mourned crucifixion in Golgotha, the divine source for our natural born rights, serves as the moral basis of our Constitutional charter and the very ideological foundation of Western Civilization itself. To claim Islam or modern-day "Palestinians" have any legitimate claim over Israel's ancestral homeland, the newly and rightfully recognized capital of Jerusalem itself, is to disregard history itself.

In 624 A.D., Mohammed plundered an Arabic caravan and murdered 70 Meccans for material gain. Between 630 and Mohammed's recorded death in 632 AD, Muslims conquered the bulk of Western Arabia and southern Palestine through approximately a dozen separate invasions and bloody conquests. These clashes were in large part "Holy Wars", debunking the popular myth the Crusades were "The First Holy War", as if Christians nefariously invented the mere concept of religious conflict. Immediately following Mohammed's fall, the new Muslim caliph, Abu Bakr, launched Islam into nearly 1,500 years of perpetual imperialism through invasion, war and forced subjugation; a blueprint Islam still follows to this very day.

The lust for Muslim conquest stretched from southern France to the Philippines, from Austria to Nigeria, central Asia to New Guinea and included over 1,000 incursions into Europe alone which predated the onset of the "Crusades"; that infamous Christian "Holy War" which is routinely depicted by academia as an unprovoked campaign of intolerant, brutal aggression. While I will not deny the fighting was undeniably vicious and some European armies made no distinction between Muslims and Jews, the Crusades were clearly calculated reciprocity, not unsolicited hostility.

Headquartered in Arabia, the Muslim goal was to first erect a central government in Damascus, followed by Baghdad and later at Cairo, Istanbul or any other advantageous Islamic center. The local governors, judges, of these distant colonies were appointed by central authorities, Islamic law was introduced as the absolute decree of their newfound rulers. In essence, two classes emerged in these newly captured territories: the native, tax-paying residents and their colonialist dictators...the Islamic Caliphate.

Predominantly populated by Jews and Christian Monophysites, "Palestine", the prophesied "Promised Land", was the first Western, non-Arab region invaded by Muslim imperialists. At the time, Palestine was in great decline under the rule of the Byzantine or Eastern Roman Empire, a Greek speaking people. The Muslim annexation of Palestine began with the battle of Yarmouk in August of 636 AD with an estimated 75,000 soldiers. With the help of local Jews who initially welcomed the Muslims as liberators due an underlying hatred of their current despotic leaders, these Islamic invaders eventually conquered the remainder of Palestine but were unable to capture Jerusalem. Beginning in July 637, Muslims laid siege to Jerusalem, which lasted for five months, and concluded with its surrender in February 638 AD. And although Arabs did not ransack the esteemed city, the attack was but a taste of Islamic tyranny which in due time would illustrate many trademarks of Muslim oppression. In short, only Christian and Jewish people were made to pay tributes and neither could bear arms, ride horses, proselytize (preach their faith) or build without Muslim permission. Baghdad also used these colonial wars of conquest to provide the Caliphate with a steady stream of slaves, many of whom were turned into eunuchs.

Beginning in 725 A.D., after nearly a century of Muslim occupation, the centralized Islamic government was subverted by a rise in extremist factions which deemed Arabic the official language, demanded the conversion of all "infidels" to Islam, and systematically drained the wealth and economic vitality of Jerusalem. In approximately 750, the reigning Caliph destroyed the walls of Jerusalem, leaving it defenseless, only to later be rebuilt in time to defend against the Crusaders. During this period, Jerusalem and its Christian/Jewish majority suffered greatly during alternating periods of peace and war. The countryside of Israel (970-983 AD) and that of Jerusalem (1024-1077 AD) was repeatedly laid waste and local resources pilfered. The Caliphate ordered the wholesale destruction of Christian churches – although Islamic mobs independently unleashed their own ruinous wrath – and in 1020 the Caliph of Cairo ordered the cultural genocide of Jerusalem by building small Mosques over existing Christian churches, robbing Christian pilgrims traveling from European countries and by attacking Christian processions in its city streets.

WAYNEDUPREE.COM
AOC Calls For Ending U.S-Israel Relationship In Fundraising Letter
SHARE

Not until 1099 AD or after roughly 450 years of uninterrupted Muslim rule was Jerusalem briefly recaptured before changing hands on numerous other occasions. All in all, Jerusalem has been destroyed at least twice, besieged (surrounded) 23 times, attacked on 52 separate instances, and captured/recaptured an astounding 44 times. The "City of David" – including Eastern Jerusalem's subsequent Christian proliferation and the West Bank remnants of Islamic infiltration – was not fully returned to the rightful descendants of Abraham until the victorious culmination of the Six Day War in 1967 when Israel decisively repelled the combined advances and undying aspirations of Jordan, Syria, and Egypt. Furthermore, a number of today's self-proclaimed "Palestinians" currently occupying the Gaza Strip, the same archaic militants defined by incessant depravity, are most likely the direct descendants of 12th century, seaborne Philistines indoctrinated into conquering Islamic tribes.

For those anti-American apologists who adamantly disagree with President Trump's decision to recognize Jerusalem as Israel's capital and the proper home for our foreign embassy, claiming it will destabilize the Palestinian "peace process" and compromise their right to a sovereign homeland, please allow my "Islamophobia" to digress. The very basis of Islam is the unconditional submission and forced conversion of non-believers. Nothing during the past 1500 years has led mankind to believe their sordid mission has changed or reconciled the Quran's belligerent teachings, inhumane practices, with the societal values of the civilized world. Even during the renovation of Jerusalem's famed walls and city infrastructure under Suleiman the Magnificent, the occupation by the Ottoman Turks between the 16th and 19th centuries, the subsequent rise in Mosques and Islamic symbols were specifically commissioned to commemorate a "great victory" over a conquered indigenous people and their native religion. Assimilation was little more than a sharpened ultimatum without an address.

JERUSALEM BELONGS TO ISRAEL!

THIS IS KING SOLOMON'S FIRST TEMPLE IT STOOD FOR 410 YEARS 832BCE

1433 YEARS BEFORE ISLAM

"Peace and Palestinian sovereignty" is an oxymoronic fallacy that is as prevalent in anti-Semitic circles as it is historically obtuse. After all, when the Babylonian King Nebuchadnezzar II pillaged Jerusalem and its sacred Temple – one of three great exoduses of Israelites into Egyptian bondage – it was populated by Jews, not Palestinians. Why, you ask? Because "Palestinians" were not invented yet. Yes, I concur, a most troubling revelation. Regardless of these omitted facts and the Islamic incarnation of such cultural misappropriation, America and Israel are forever intertwined by an unbreakable premise. America was established upon the moral cannon of Judeo-Christian principles – the indelible ideal our Constitution was forged solely for a moral and religious people – and the Biblical account Christians are called upon to defend the "Holy Land" for God's "chosen people"; or more succinctly, the salvation of all mankind.

A Court Without A Ball

Note to Lavar Ball...It is not uncommon for perpetrators to spend 5 or even 10 years in Chinese prisons for crimes that would normally constitute misdemeanors in the United States. Not only are their communist courts notoriously hostile towards foreigners and love to make examples of smug Americans who knowingly break their laws, many suspects are deprived due process and adequate representation; let alone ever granted a jury of their "peers". It's not a matter of lavishing President Trump with undue praise but instead showing a little damn appreciation for the fact that your spoiled son who drives a $250,000 Ferrari wasn't left to rot in a diseased cell while awaiting trial with two other players for shoplifting from three stores; most notably, a pair of designer sunglasses any self-respecting teenager could afford with a minimum wage job. Your predisposed hatred of the President's selfless gesture by no means pardons your reckless ignorance and juvenile need for national attention. Who knew "Big Ballers" lacked the necessary skill set to realize convicts wash their prison blues below the rim?

The Anatomy of Entrapment

For those unfamiliar with the Logan Act, it is little known piece of legislation that prohibits private citizens from acting on behalf of the United States in disputes with foreign governments. It also became the preferred form of entrapment when the Obama administration obtained a warrant from the FISA court under false pretenses to illegally wiretap a presidential candidate, the eventual nominee, and unmask his transition team; a first in American history. If Flynn is guilty of violating the Logan Act for simply engaging a Russian diplomat, with whom he had a relationship with for years, to discuss United Nations policy concerning Israel, what exactly has Barack Obama been doing for the past year by shadowing President Trump around the globe and holding private meetings with foreign dignitaries concerning global warming, immigration and free trade? Perhaps my definition of intentional subversion, impersonation or even treason is a bit hazy. Regardless, telling a lie to conceal a harmless act was Flynn's only real mistake. It's even more silly when you realize Martha Stewart was charged for the exact same thing, lying under oath, only for those charges to be dropped because her most significant indiscretion was insider trading...a much more serious transgression.

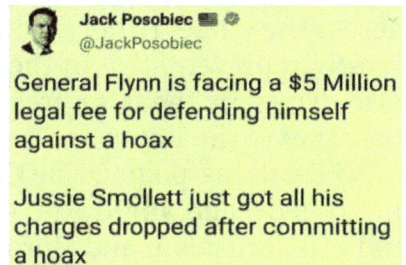

> **Jack Posobiec**
> @JackPosobiec
>
> General Flynn is facing a $5 Million legal fee for defending himself against a hoax
>
> Jussie Smollett just got all his charges dropped after committing a hoax

If this entire media induced hysteria over Russian election collusion never materialized – a false narrative the scandalous Clinton campaign concocted to pardon her failed candidacy and, in the process, undermine Trump's legitimacy – an honorable man who dedicated his entire life to serving this great country would not be disgraced by those who disparage America and our military on a religious basis. For those keeping score of these petty games and who grow tired of con artists fabricating injustice and exploiting mere technicality, that also means the President never obstructed justice...he merely exposed the laughable hypocrisy of the intelligence community and fired a failed FBI director who leaked memos, faked investigations and routinely ignored real corruption.

Iran & The Cult of Progressivism

Dear John Kerry...

If your Muslim neighbor – the same frothing madman who cursed your very existence daily – incessantly told you he was going to kill your family and rape your daughter, would you give him a gun, your checkbook and the keys to your house? Of course not! So don't give me that inane nonsense "they don't really mean death to America and Israel" because your blatant anti-Americanism, anti-Semitism and disdain for the Judeo-Christian values of Western Civilization leads you to blindly defend the counter-intuitive policies of progressivism. I don't need to pretend to believe in unicorns, magic rainbows and nuclear good tidings, when my enemy reminds me exactly who he is every waking moment of my life. Not only was 9/11 the worst terrorist attack in our nation's history, a callous and vile display of inhumanity, thousands of other potential plots are foiled every year by our intelligence community; many identical to that fateful day, as well as Fort Hood and Chattanooga, that your beloved media sweeps under the rug and the White House refuses to label as "terrorism" to avoid giving your precious "Islam" a bad name. Yes, please don't forgive me for characterizing the Koran for what it truly is: a hateful and barbaric diatribe designed to exact mass capitulation to an archaic ideology forged by a pedophile, a murderer, and a polygamist. If that's the modern definition of virtue – love, acceptance and forgiveness – I'll pass without a single regret. I don't need to be a racist or a Right-Wing fanatic to resist and denounce the bloodthirsty cult known as Islam. I only need a heartbeat and an ounce of common sense to ask why you feel so ignorantly and foolishly compelled to reward their enduring legacy of hate.

For those Islam apologists, a.k.a. Howard Zinn disciples of anti-American thought, claiming Christians are just as bad as Muslims...please list one event Christians are responsible for during the past century that remotely compares to the Armenian Genocide, the Kurdish gassing, 9/11 or the current mass atrocities unleashed by Islam across the globe. Hitler acted out of fascist desire and national jingoism, while the KKK – hardly representative of the love, acceptance, and forgiveness the Bible espouses – was also driven by the false premise of hate and supremacy. In other words, read the sadistic passages of the Koran and get an ounce of perspective before you regurgitate your MSNBC & NPR talking points. The Christian Crusades – which ended roughly 700 years ago and not this decade, mind you – were a direct response to Islamic incursions and barbarism in both Jerusalem and Europe. For the past 1,500 years, which religion has never had a reformation and continues to oppress, murder and maim in the name of Allah? Islam...that militant scourge which continues to deny millions of women basic human rights, kills gays for merely existing, engages in human sex trafficking, and still religiously calls for the beheading of all infidels! Refusing to bake a cake for a same-sex couples, or vocally support homosexuality, is hardly equivalent to slitting their throats in accordance to Sharia Law. There is no debate except by those who are incapable of reason or who refuse to accept one inescapable truth: Islam is the single greatest threat to humanity.

ILLEGAL Voter ID

Racist Memes

ELECTORAL SCHEMES

☞ **Stuffing** ☜

the Ballot Box WITH Undocumented

DEMOCRATS

Dear Scheming State Legislatures... only a Constitutional Amendment can eliminate or alter the Electoral College. Since electoral delegates are already awarded based on a state's popular vote victor, you'll merely be forfeiting those appointed individuals to the declared winner. Stop wasting taxpayer money by passing ignorant laws and filing frivolous lawsuits that only further mislead an already misinformed public. As long as vote fraud remains rampant and 25 million foreign-born nationals continue to illegally reside in America, preserving the legitimacy of our 243-year-old Republic begins by ensuring every state – regardless of wealth, population or region – plays an integral role in our elections and federal government. A pure democracy is little more than mob rule where the rights of the minority party, the individual, are superseded by the tyrannical whims of the popular majority; case in point, Democratic legislatures attempting to invalidate the afforded protections of our electoral system, legalize infanticide, or by allowing noncitizens to receive taxpayer benefits and sanctuary from criminal prosecution.

The "Dream" Decision of SCOTUS

Whereas gay marriage has unlocked an inevitable erosion of our societal values and Obamacare has permanently extended the groping hand of big government, the Supreme Court's refusal to hear a state's appeal on citizenship verification could seal America's fate. According to the infinite indifference of the Supreme Court, Arizona and Kansas does not have the right to verify whether any voter is an actual citizen. Come again? That's right, you heard correctly! Illegal immigrants can now register to vote without having to show one single shred of proof of citizenship. The same court that ruled in 2014 voter ID is a perfectly valid method of ensuring the integrity of each vote, somehow believes that authenticating the actual citizenship of suspected immigrants – those who cannot legally vote otherwise – is unnecessary and discriminatory.

In what other civilized nation, let alone the nearest sentient universe, are non-citizens allowed to influence the future of a sovereign nation, tip the scales of political power, and essentially overthrow the government of their host countries by unconditionally stuffing the ballot box? It's idiotic, it's preposterous, and such nonsense allows America to be toppled by any foreign electorate that has little or no regard for our laws, our heritage, or our nation's survival. Honestly, who needs citizenship, dare I say amnesty, when any foreign body – regardless of their qualifications, loyalties or intentions – are granted the same innate privileges of natural born or naturalized citizens? So not only is Washington blocking the absolute necessity of enforcing our existing immigration laws, "We the People" can no longer validate the legitimacy of those "bribed" votes that will literally threaten our livelihoods and our God-given rights? Absurd!

Since 2008 the White House has courted, bribed and even transported illegals all across America without one congressional hearing being held or a single alarm sounded by the mainstream media. Not only did our own government break countless statutes by using federal agencies and resources to conspire to undermine the Constitution and our national sovereignty, they misappropriated taxpayer funds by giving millions of immigrants free welfare, healthcare and education. And yet our veterans, those brave souls who risked their lives to serve their country and protect our freedoms, continue to suffer from untimely and incompetent medical care while over 50,000 of their brethren remain homeless. Simply unforgivable.

The injustice of illegal immigration goes far beyond dollar signs and legal nuance; it inevitably threatens the safety and lives of every American. Because misery loves Marxism, waves of medically and criminally unvetted immigrants have reintroduced once eradicated or highly controlled diseases – the mumps, measles and tuberculosis to name but a few – into our communities and public schools, while rarely encountered strains of the polio-like illness Enterovirus-68 have crippled and even killed children. Equally appalling, despite a sharp rise in the number of murder, rape, and pedophilia crimes committed by our illegal population, our own government is helping hardened criminals escape prosecution by having them deported, an act common sense Americans demanded all along, only to have these serial trespassers re-enter our country at a later date. Yes, racism now extends to your unwillingness to be a victim or your irrational insistence on enforcing the law. Just remember to mark "undocumented" the next time you go to jail for unpaid parking tickets. Ignorance is never an excuse!

A sitting U.S. President doesn't unknowingly leave the back door to his country ajar, no more than he'd allow a complete stranger to rent a room next to his slumbering children. Such malicious actions are calculated and without remorse. Barack Obama's prime time cry for Amnesty was never about the plight of suffering children – the "bring your own family" humanitarian crisis fabricated to tug on the heartstrings of America – it was from the very inception an orchestrated demographic ruse dedicated to seizing an inexhaustible source of votes for the sole purpose of forging an unbreakable Democratic majority. And now, sadly, that treasonous dream is finally within reach because the Supreme Court – the same activist body that found it of the utmost importance to twice save the socialist leviathan Obamacare and redefine the religious institution of marriage – found it of no immediate consequence to ensure the integrity of our elections; our most sacred duty as patriotic Americans and the crux of our Constitutional Republic.

For years progressives have lied to the American populace, cajoled the judicial system, and muddled a simple issue for no other reason than to usher millions of non-citizens to the voting booth. Likewise, armed with the knowledge propaganda thwarts principle in a low-information society, Democrats have religiously shouted voter oppression and invoked 'White Privilege' by claiming minorities were mysteriously barred from partaking in elections for decades because they lacked basic identification. Hmm, I'm guessing the near 25 million undocumented foreigners currently residing in America will now have absolutely no trouble finding their license to register to vote for Hillary in 2016. It's just too bad congress or the courts never found the necessary votes to arrest and prosecute this administration for abandoning the country they vowed to protect, the rule of law they swore to serve, at every conceivable opportunity. Apparently conspiring to destroy America along racial, economic and religious lines, not resisting the radical schemes of a rogue government, is now considered patriotic and prudent. If over two centuries of proud vigilance have boiled down to an apathetic and ignorant populace allowing an anti-American President to invite our disgruntled neighbors to overthrow our country, displace our founding creed, who in their right mind could possibly complain? The Supreme Court surely isn't.

The Art of Vote Fraud: Who's Watching Who?

Because the term "vote fraud" is now reported as minority voter suppression by progressive media, the mathematicians of electoral subversion naturally offer no logical explanation or palpable concern for the disturbing fact the U.S. now has 3.5 million more registered voters than living adults. As such, I believe the greatest potential sources of vote fraud are one, poll workers, and two, the automated voting machines now utilized across America. Yes, as we all know, poll workers are human and vote too. Naturally in this supercharged era of divisive politics a number of these individuals are bound to be highly partisan. If some of these officials choose to give illegal immigrants (non-citizens) ballots, or they turn a blind-eye as fellow party members vote countless times – similarly to what recently transpired in Arizona when a single person admitted to voting over one-hundred times – who is going to stop them? Have any of these volunteers been vetted for criminal behavior, nepotism or radical activism? Do the sheer gravity and long-term implications of our elections not deserve such unfettered access and scrutiny?

For those Americans left to toil in a precinct dominated by one party – and every state has them – you've most likely heard the inappropriate conversations or witnessed the unprofessional behavior displayed by these so-called "independent" representatives. In 2012, several Philadelphia precincts actually sported Obama banners and memorabilia! What a shameful and unlawful display of favoritism. Therefore, my question is this; who is holding the poll workers accountable? Not every state uses video surveillance, let alone properly trained and trustworthy watchers. For those states that do, how many actually check every second of those recordings? It's become painfully obvious America needs a much more responsive, objective and universal set of protocols put in place to detect and deter voter fraud on a wide scale. Would have Hillary still won the popular vote if federal agents were placed at every polling station of suspected abuse? Casually uncovering these crimes years later does nothing to ensure the proper outcome of our elections today.

If modernity has taught us anything it's that machines are as fallible as the people who engineer them. Case in point? There have been a number of verified reports, some by politicians themselves, claiming their vote was wrongfully changed to the other candidate. Honestly, electronic vote fraud doesn't even need to be this obvious. If a skilled mathematician, albeit a computer programmer, inserted an algorithm to wrongfully tally every 10th, 50th or 100th vote until "Candidate A" took the lead and remained there, who would even know? And I'm not even mentioning the much more evasive scenario of fractal vote fraud. Have you ever asked yourself who owns and operates these machines? What are their political affiliations and whose campaigns have they donated to? These are relevant questions every American needs to ask and deserves to know.

Critics will quickly claim I'm suggesting people are incapable of being fair and nonpartisan. Not at all: the concept of 'fairness' now seems incumbent upon whether the dead bequeathed their posthumous right to exclusively vote Democrat. I'd just rather not take their word for it when our country, my children's future, is at stake and subject to the fickle whims of political discontent. I truly wish we all resided in a world where honesty, integrity, and the validity of our elections are at the forefront of everyone's concerns. Sadly, that is not the truth. Democrats openly encourage and invite voter fraud with senseless lawsuits and ridiculous victimization banter. Apropos, their party recently honored an Ohio woman who was convicted of fraud! For the life of me I cannot understand why all states and/or precincts do not require Voter ID – just like many impoverished central American nations – which is universally required to drive a car, buy alcohol, cash a check, apply for welfare, or attend the Democratic National Convention. If we cannot ensure the legitimacy of our elections, our greatest right and responsibility as free men and women, America has become nothing more than a third-world banana republic whose sole export is ignorance. As for me, I'd rather stand-up and demand the unconditional truth before I'll ever believe Barack Obama and Hillary Clinton have our best interests at heart.

% OF COUNTIES WITH MORE REGISTERED VOTERS THAN ADULT CITIZENS

□ % counties with over registered voters

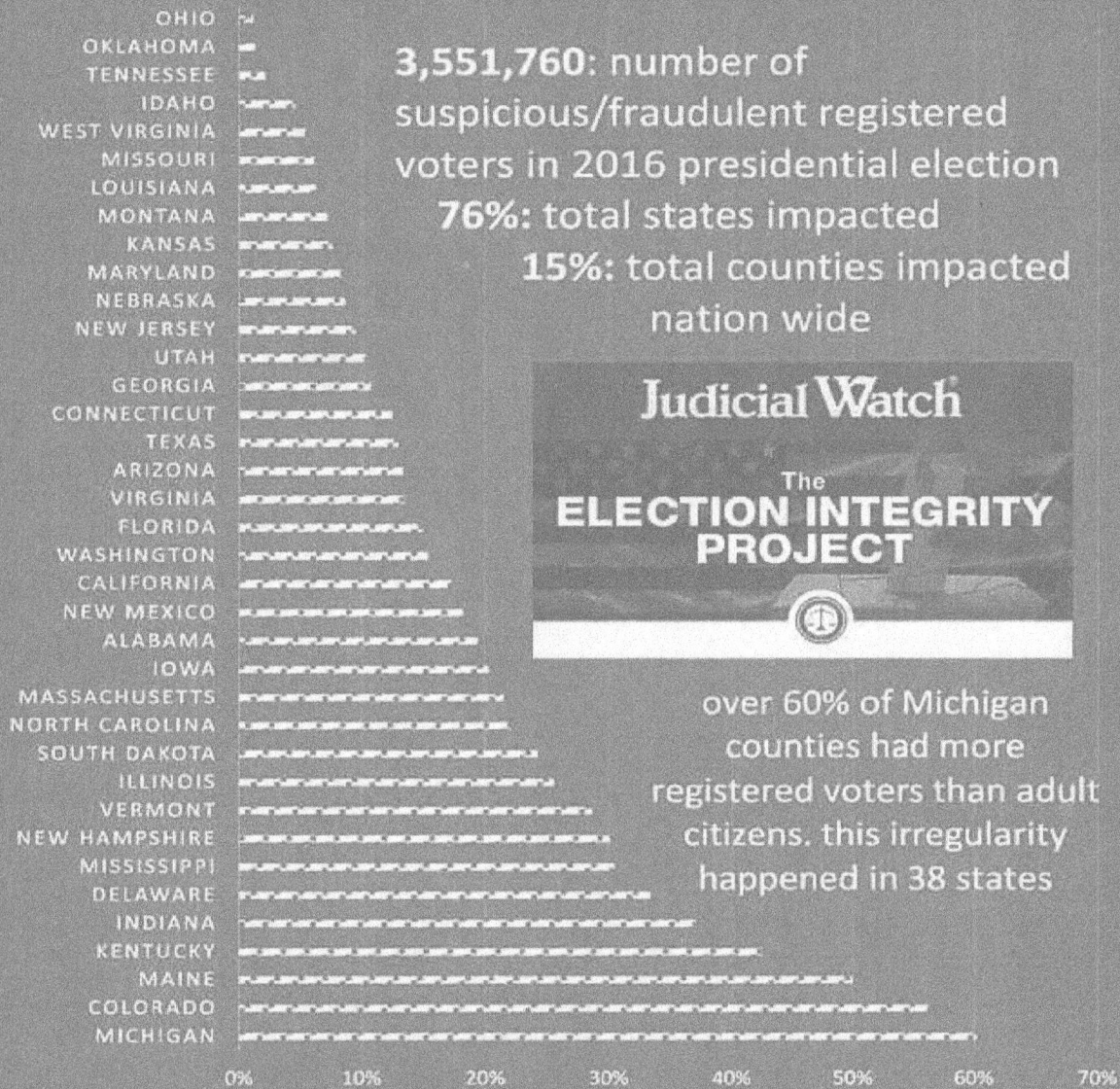

3,551,760: number of suspicious/fraudulent registered voters in 2016 presidential election
76%: total states impacted
15%: total counties impacted nation wide

Judicial Watch

The
ELECTION INTEGRITY PROJECT

over 60% of Michigan counties had more registered voters than adult citizens. this irregularity happened in 38 states

States (top to bottom): OHIO, OKLAHOMA, TENNESSEE, IDAHO, WEST VIRGINIA, MISSOURI, LOUISIANA, MONTANA, KANSAS, MARYLAND, NEBRASKA, NEW JERSEY, UTAH, GEORGIA, CONNECTICUT, TEXAS, ARIZONA, VIRGINIA, FLORIDA, WASHINGTON, CALIFORNIA, NEW MEXICO, ALABAMA, IOWA, MASSACHUSETTS, NORTH CAROLINA, SOUTH DAKOTA, ILLINOIS, VERMONT, NEW HAMPSHIRE, MISSISSIPPI, DELAWARE, INDIANA, KENTUCKY, MAINE, COLORADO, MICHIGAN

Axis: 0%, 10%, 20%, 30%, 40%, 50%, 60%, 70%

Jersey Shore Shenanigans - The same conniving Democrats attempting to violate President Trump's legal rights by requiring the release of his tax returns in order to appear on the 2020 New Jersey ballot, also believe photo identification is a racist plot to disenfranchise voters; except when buying smokes, applying for a loan or traveling abroad to dine with global elites. This completely unconstitutional stipulation and blatant attempt at political extortion will be overturned. Tax returns do not constitute public domain, even for politicians. The potential ramifications of such an unethical breach would undermine the afforded privacy of medical records or phone/internet data as well.

299

The Art of Voter Amnesia: What's an ID?

Democrats never say they are committed to stopping voter fraud, merely that they're dedicated to "everyone" voting. This slippery admission tells you everything you need to know, or in other words, nothing you didn't already suspect. The truth is Voter ID doesn't discriminate against or disenfranchise anyone. How can it when everyone is held to same standard of accountability? If you can't even verify your identity, validate and protect the authenticity of your vote, how are you a victim of anything other than your own ignorance and apathy? Without proper identification how can election poll workers stop an unregistered voter who knows your name, date of birth and address, let alone someone casting multiple votes by assuming a different identity in each precinct? People have TWO YEARS in-between elections to obtain a photo ID; yes, the very same $15 pertinence you need to win the lottery, board a plane, visit a doctor or adopt a pet! There are excuses and then there are outright lies. If our elected officials were truly dedicated to eliminating fraud and ensuring the legitimacy of our elections, our sacred duty as citizens, every American would be required to pass a computerized fingerprint or retinal scan before voting. Professional con artists like Hillary Clinton welcome and encourage voter fraud because 99% of its existence favors leftist candidates. And now you know why criminals hate red tape almost as much as they mysteriously misplace their mug shots. Apparently, cameras are racist too.

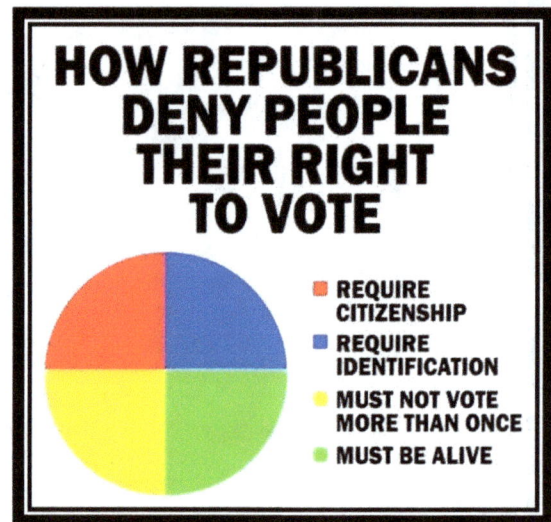

The same Democrats endlessly harping about "election interference", ironically have no interest in protecting the validity of every vote cast. Any party or politician that cannot stand on the merits of their own convictions and public service record without the benefit of voter fraud is inherently wrong for America and a disgrace to the people they claim to serve. If you need to invent injustice and incite animosity to rally support for your withering candidacy, perhaps your chauffeur can wipe the blood off your "Stronger Together" bumper sticker as you bypass the ghetto graveyard of broken promises on the way to your daughter's lavish wedding paid for with pilfered disaster relief funds. I don't need to resurrect the newly forged registration cards of the dead to realize most Democrats have little regard for the integrity of our elections, the viability of our laws or the sovereignty of this nation. If you somehow believe illegal immigrants and Islamic refugees know what's better for America than everyday, law-abiding citizens who are privy and loyal to our founding ideals, your God-given liberties, then you deserve to live in a corrupt cesspool as your freedoms, sanity and property are slowly liquidated from your naive grasp. Anyone that zealously courts or engages in voter fraud solely to win an election – albeit through absentee, repetitive or non-citizen voting – is a stain on the soul of those men and women who died to procure and protect our way of life. If I need photo identification to buy a gun, then so should those casting a vote to potentially strip me of my Constitutional right to bear arms and defend myself against all forms of tyranny; most notably, legalized lunacy.

Why is it whenever a trunk or truckful of uncounted ballots magically appear, it always benefits a Democratic candidate narrowly trailing in a critical election? Well, that's because it's common knowledge the left will go to any length to hijack any result that threatens their agenda and lust for control. Vote fraud is real, rampant and a serious threat to all Americans.

Demand a **National Election Reform Act** that universally requires the following:

--All voter registration must be physically conducted at a sanctioned County or State office requiring an instant photo and fingerprint once legal citizenship status is verified.

--Mandatory Voter ID cards must be presented at every precinct, while all electronic ballot machines instantly record/verify each voter's identity.

--Every voting machine must be fully tested for any potential irregularities – changing votes or wrongful tabulations – by an independent expert (without any political ties or funding) before voting begins, as well as examined after the election to ensure accuracy or possible coding alterations.

--End "Ballot Harvesting" and all use of provisional ballots. Any individual who is not properly registered or lacks a mandatory Voter ID card cannot vote.

--Absentee ballots must be received, verified, and fully counted before election day with the results submitted to each state's election office. Any attempt to delay this process or destroy ballots will result in termination and incarceration.

--Require independent, trained monitors for all poll workers and live cameras to record every precinct throughout the day. Poll workers must pass background checks and divulge all political affiliations and associations.

--Results from any precinct or county that indicate voting anomalies – more votes cast than registered voters, double voting, unaccounted ballots presented after polls close – will be suspended and immediately audited until the authenticity of every vote is verified.

Any voter, party official or election worker caught breaking these laws will receive a minimum penalty of 10 years in prison, without early parole, in addition to permanently surrendering all future voting privileges.

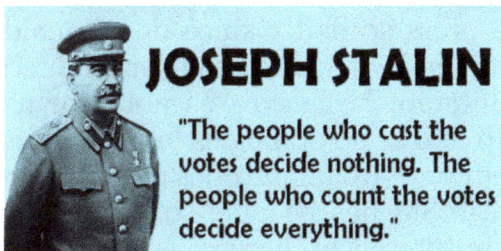

JOSEPH STALIN

"The people who cast the votes decide nothing. The people who count the votes decide everything."

Vote fraud is not a Republican or Democratic issue, but a treasonous crime that undermines the sovereignty of our nation and the legitimacy of our elections. Those activists who continue to obstruct and politicize these desperately needed reforms are either guilty of committing vote fraud or they're simply complicit with subverting the people's will.

Mass Media Manipulation

Man on Fire

Flaws and all, I haven't seen a President handle the press so deftly since one Ronald Wilson Reagan. While "The Gipper" was extremely adroit and witty, and he never relented or surrendered his convictions, the sheer level of contempt he faced was not near as caustic or juvenile as it is now. I admire the fact Trump makes no apologies for doing his job, that he's quite intuitive in-regards to people's true intentions and he does not hesitate in exposing the media's hypocrisy and hysterics. The MSM has become so hopelessly partisan and dishonest by design that these blunt, unfiltered exchanges – not those watered down, spoon-fed talking points, mind you – are exactly what America needs to hear right now. Real journalism is not predicated upon political advocacy or shameless assumptions sold under false pretenses; it's a fluid presentation of tangible and verifiable data conveyed for the purpose of informing people rather than recklessly inciting them for personal gain. How can everyday Americans ever make a prudent and enlightened decision for the benefit of their country, if not their own family, when they are routinely denied the most unadulterated details?

As an institution vital to the collective conscience of any society, journalism should embody an unconditional commitment to objectively conveying the news with an ingrained respect for the individuals/subjects covered, as well as the intelligence and well-being of their audience. Sadly, I can find few such examples of invested dignity in the media today. Rabid activism, pundits waging political vendettas with the goal of achieving a singular end, is now marketed as reputable reporting. The issue is not whether correspondents identify as liberal or conservative, for that is inevitable, as long as such beliefs are not incumbent upon needlessly distorting fact, selectively reporting current events or fabricating slanderous allegations to sway public opinion. The real crime is that culpability and consequence are increasingly viewed as naively quixotic. If the Fourth Estate cannot serve as the universal watchdog of our republic, both identify impropriety and report the truth with equal vigor, America will succumb to the same fates as many other infamous propaganda states: divided by fear, conquered by blind apathy, or dismantled according to its own complicit ignorance. Thank God at least our President got that memo.

Facebook, Fake News & "Snoping" for the Truth

When you're a multi-billionaire Social Media mogul slumbering in the plush progressive plantation of news, entertainment and education indoctrination, your perception of invincibility comes to a screeching halt after being summoned by a Congressional ethics panel to explain sharing the private analytics of your over 2 billion users with data pirates. While I freely admit such behavior was an egregious violation of Facebook's "unofficial" confidentiality agreement, it is but a symptom of a much more nefarious disease: cognitive dissonance. Those who possess far less respect for the rights and opinions of the "common man" are far more motivated by losing 100 billion in stock value, the lack of personal shower space in prison, than any real contrition for abusing the public trust. If you need "warm and fuzzy" marketing campaigns to convince the rational world you're a humble family man and not a commercial harvester of voting demographics, political censorship appeals to the human trafficker grooming sheep deep inside your virtual basement.

Whereas Donald Trump kickstarted the cultural phenomenon "Fake News" to combat the incessant disingenuous coverage of his campaign and presidency, a pretty obvious observation backed by irrefutable empirical evidence, the exposed media establishment is now aggressively targeting anyone threatening their stranglehold on public perception with but another politically-perverted medium of control. The same Mark Zuckerberg who pledged to "resist the path of becoming arbiters of truth ourselves", banning the suburban, middle-aged duo of "Diamond and Silk" for being "unsafe" and "inaccurate" – a description which aptly describes the bulk of the mainstream media – has found a more palatable means to silence political dissent and demonize conservative viewpoints: "independent" fact-checkers. Following behind the two left footsteps of Yahoo and Google

who conveniently highlight "fact-checking" websites at the top of pre-tagged search results, Facebook has contracted with "Snopes" to serve as the official face of their now more esteemed Thought Police.

Founded in 1994 by the now estranged California couple of David and Barbara Mikkelson as a home enterprise for debunking cultural myths and urban legends, Snopes eventually morphed a front for political activism packaged as factual investigation. Half owned by the ad agency Proper Media, their income is entirely derived from third-party advertisers whom they routinely placate by intentionally addressing issues relevant to their cause, politics or industry. In wine-tasting terms, that's called foreshadowing, shameless pandering, with a partisan cheese tray. Are you a fortune 500 company committed to fighting Global Warming? Why, yes; it is man-made and carbon-based lifeforms, plants, are to blame.

Amid growing complaints of favoritism, the former data-mining website called About.com, owned by the liberal tabloid New York Times, went out of its way to chastise Snopes' critics by releasing this statement: "Neither of the operators of Snopes.com has any affiliation with, has ever made a donation to, or has ever publicly expressed support for any political party or candidate." And how does such an evasive statement ensure impartiality within its ranks, especially considering the owner himself refused to confirm to Forbes whether or not a Snopes employee had run for political office? What we do know is that Kim Lacapria, Snopes' main political fact checker, modestly described herself as "openly left-leaning" despite slandering Tea Party members as "teahadists." And here I assumed an unwavering commitment to objectivity, factual integrity, demanded adhering to the strictest standards of professionalism, transparency and accuracy. Ironically enough, unlike the "Occupy Wall Street" movement and fascist benevolence of masked Antifa militants, Tea Party members held massive rallies in support of federal reform without advocating violence and discord, let alone triggering widespread arrests for loitering, theft, destruction of property, assault, rape or drug possession.

I have no problem whatsoever giving everyone the benefit of sincerity, but I cannot give much credence to any investigator who touts the journalistic resume of CNN and ABC, only to lambaste "conservatives" as conspiracy theorists by insisting Barack Obama has no ties to the Muslim faith; even despite the proven fact his step-father, Lolo Soetoro, enrolled him in an Indonesian school in Jakarta as a Muslim during his youth. Barry himself referenced memories of Koranic studies at the school in his autobiography, "Dreams from My Father", and once made the infamous Freudian slip, subconscious affirmation, "My Muslim Faith" during a televised interview. Either way, regardless of his current religious affiliation, anti-Semitic views or antagonistic comments toward Christians, it's facetious at best to claim Barack Hussein Obama has no historical ties or affinity for Islam when his life's journey, personal associations, scream otherwise.

Sadly, the more recent incarnations of Factcheck.org and Politifact are not much better in terms of focus or reputation. They are all, however, extremely adept at deceptively selecting the most controversial obsessions of right-minded voters, falsely stereotyping such views as standard Republican paranoia, to inevitably cast a "Red Herring" or shadow of doubt on much more legitimate digressions. During a presidential debate in the 2016 election, Politifact once deemed Donald Trump's assertion that Hillary Clinton was for open borders as "mostly false": similar to the cultivated hysteria over the infamous "Clinton body count". There was only one small problem with their "astute" findings...her mouth. The Duchess of Duplicity once gave an overpaid speech where she prophetically uttered, "My dream is a hemispheric common market, with open trade and open borders." Hmm...now I may not be Sherlock homes, a skilled translator or a lauded historian, but I'm going to certify their "scientific" conclusion as complete and utter bullshit or "categorically false". In honor of the Snopes family, William Faulkner would be proud!

No matter what the issue or the researcher of choice, one salient detail is clear: the unlicensed doctors of Truth or Don't You Dare are adamant about defending Democratic leaders, their ingrained ideologies, but twice as quick to dispute any conservative claim or candidate threatening the progressive narrative on issues like gun control, immigration, Islamic terrorism, Christian "radicalism", police brutality, transgenderism and Russian election tampering. I'm also willing to bet the barb wire media plantation that if I walked in any of these "independent" firms at any given moment, 90% or more of their research staff are registered Democrats or voted for Hillary Clinton in the 2016 election. Although we all carry weighted predispositions, I don't need the partisan baggage of a sponsored editorialist telling me mine is too heavy to appreciate the hidden agenda of his. My value as a sentient being does not require any "official" validation or "fake" notice of eviction.

Animals & Anathemas

The perpetually offended media has no problem with Democrats and celebrities slandering the NRA as terrorists and killers – Constitutional advocates with zero ties to criminal behavior and a 147-year-old organization that doesn't even sell or manufacture guns – but it's completely unacceptable for our President to call M13 gang members "animals": those heavily armed, violent thugs guilty of mass murder, human, weapons and drug trafficking, rape, extortion, larceny, money laundering and universally targeting law enforcement. And yet these outraged critics are the same anti-American hypocrites who can't figure out why people's trust in journalism is so historically low and Trump's popularity so inconceivable high. Perhaps today's detached, "politically correct" propagandists would like to be the shock beneficiary of a psychological intervention hosted by the grieving loved ones, shattered families and surviving victims of one of North and Latin America's most notorious crime syndicate. Critical thinking skills, a sincere concern for the welfare of one's fellow countrymen, is obviously a foreign concept to "educated" activists who struggle to rationalize the immutable concepts of free speech and self-defense over the public assistance benefits of remorseless convicts.

Emotions neither prove nor disprove facts. There was a time when any rational adult understood this. But years of dumbed-down education and emphasis on how people 'feel' have left too many people unable to see through this media gimmick.

- THOMAS SOWELL
@ThomasSowell

Mr. Brightside
@MrBrigh21239717

I feel like the left just sits in a room spinning a bingo cage wheel with problems that have been around for decades... they pull one out once a month, blame it on Trump, offer zero solutions, then act like they're saving the world because they're upset all of a sudden.

Media Blackouts and Alabama Beheadings

Illegal Immigrant Beheads 13-Year-Old Girl in Alabama – Media Blackout

My heart literally breaks for this young girl who was forced to watch the murder of her grandmother before being driven into the backwoods and beheaded by an illegal alien who belonged to a Mexican drug cartel. Obviously only jaded strippers, Russian conspiracies or an anti-Trump balloon flown in the UK are worthy of national media attention. This is but one of countless reasons why 'Open Border' advocates are out of their collective mind. Contrary to pandering globalists, the immigration dynamics of the modern world is wrought with far greater dangers than the late 19th century or even the mid-20th century when grateful "legal" immigrants almost exclusively came to America seeking a better life and to protect their newfound blessings, not to demand social entitlements, undermine our electoral process or perpetrate unspeakable hate crimes.

Sadly, several months ago a German mother was stabbed to death and her 1-year-old baby beheaded by the father, a Muslim immigrant, in a Hamburg train station. Prime Minister Merkel, in all her infinite wisdom, forbid the German media from even acknowledging the child's death, including reporting the disturbing details. When speaking an uncomfortable truth – protecting your fellow countrymen from the well-documented evil your leader naively invited – draws more contempt and consequences than ensuring the survival of a murderous lie, you've officially surrendered your dignity, humanity and God-given liberties to an elected executioner of Western Civilization. This is the tragic but avoidable aftermath of "progressive" policies that criminalize common sense and turn border security, the mandatory enforcement of existing laws, into racist conspiracies.

The Paper Sword of Perception

If the media spent as much time investigating the illicit activities and scandalous ties of Hillary Clinton as they do the crass or "mean" words of Donald Trump, she wouldn't be allowed anywhere near a ballot; for Treasurer of the PTA, no less. As long as the press continues to act with such reckless favoritism, a blatant disregard for the truth and the integrity of our elections, it is only a matter of time before some of the disgruntled masses take matters into their own hands. No, I'm not advocating or defending vigilante violence by any means. However, considering such negligent behavior can literally alter the course of history, the future of the people's children and the country they love, many feel as if they are left with no other alternative except to exact some degree of responsibility.

When network correspondents knowingly collude with political parties and exchange text messages with politicians in an orchestrated attempt to bypass scrutiny or muster support, the skewed result is inept healthcare legislation, reckless Islamic immigration, coached focus groups or partisan inquisitions marketed as conclusive debates. Thus, only one final question remains: who's fact checking the fact checkers of supposed reputable journalism? Or are "We the People" simply content leaving our most vital civil servants to destroy phones, emails, and private servers for the betterment of mankind? If only those peasants going to jail for unpaid parking tickets could harness such spontaneous immunity! The fundamental charter of the press is to question everyone and everything without duplicity or refrain; not to be the drooling lapdog of the status quo.

Without real checks and balances, a universal standard of accountability that demands objectivity and differentiates advocacy, the media can embody perhaps the deadliest form of tyranny. Propaganda's greatest weapon is that it literally can overthrow a country's founding ideals, demonize anyone who challenges the ruling party's stranglehold on public opinion, without ever raising a fist or firing a gun. Regimes have been toppled and the kindling of war set ablaze by the mere provocation of flammable words. The power of suggestion, the art of fabricated outrage, can incite race riots, falsely justify cop shootings and glorify anthem protests to cultivate widespread anti-Americanism by selectively reporting the race of tragedy or grossly misrepresenting the records of the accused.

The purpose of our Constitutional republic – an elected government with prescribed limitations – is not to influence/mold public opinion to the point of ignorance or to seek mass capitulation to any singular agenda. Its purpose is to ensure transparency in all its dealings so the people, the individual voices of the electorate who are the legitimate owners of representative government, can make informed decisions without ever being branded the enemy of truth or deemed 'deplorable' by aspiring dictators. The more we make allowances for those media activists distorting discernible facts, regardless of whom such deception benefits, the quicker we willingly digress into a propaganda state of spoon-fed relevance. And in case some are a bit hazy on their history, the Orwellian thought police aren't exactly interested in safeguarding due process, free speech or tolerance as recompense for surrendering 'control'. Just ask the statistical anecdotes of fascist Germany, Communist Cuba, North Korea or the increasingly censored collegiate campuses of America. The slippery-slope of rationalized deceit rarely self-corrects itself amidst the gravitational pull of blind ambition.

The Yellow Yahoos of Fake News

The Senate acknowledging the obvious reality Russia played psychological war games on social media to incite hysteria among the voting populace of a known adversary – similar to the Obama administration's extensive efforts to sway Israeli elections to defeat Benjamin Netanyahu and spoil Marine Le Pen's presidential bid in France – is not the same as "election collusion" between two conscious participants. Tainting actual election results, like rampant vote fraud committed by undocumented immigrants, is distinctly illegal whereas "trolling" the weak-minded is certifiably juvenile. Thank you for once again proving the true meaning of misleading reporting: i.e., Fake News!

THE DEMOCRAT PARTY & MAINSTREAM MEDIA

Susan Rice — Obama Admin	**Ian Cameron** — ABC News
MARRIED	
Ben Rhodes — Obama Admin	**David Rhodes** — CBS News
BROTHERS	
Liz Sherwood — Obama Admin	**Ben Sherwood** — ABC News
MARRIED	
Tom Nides — Clinton Admin	**Virginia Moseley** — CNN
MARRIED	
Jay Carney — Obama Admin	**Claire Shipman** — ABC News
MARRIED	
Katie Hogan — Obama Admin	**Matthew Jaffe** — ABC News
MARRIED	
Valerie Jarrett — Obama Admin	**Laura Jarrett** — CNN
MOTHER & DAUGHTER	
Jim Sciutto — Obama Admin	**Gloria Riviera** — ABC News
MARRIED	
Andrew Cuomo — Dem Governor	**Chris Cuomo** — CNN
BROTHERS	

A Slanted Tale of Two Photos

Q: WHICH PHOTO DID YOU SEE?

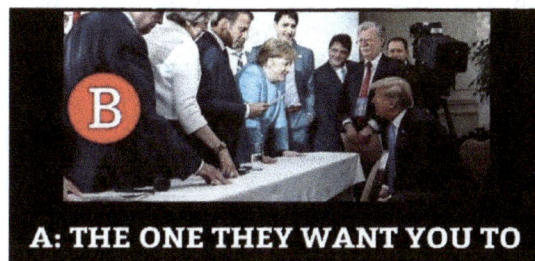

A: THE ONE THEY WANT YOU TO

Just remember, the press has no other agenda than reporting the unfiltered, unadulterated, unbiased truth for the betterment of the American people. And if you snort that magical pixie dust, welcome to the Orwellian oasis known as Club Alcatraz: an idyllic beach resort for your imprisoned, spoon-fed mind where Marco 'water' Polo requires a key and escaping requires a celebrity red scarf or invisible jet skis.

For Entertainment Purposes Only

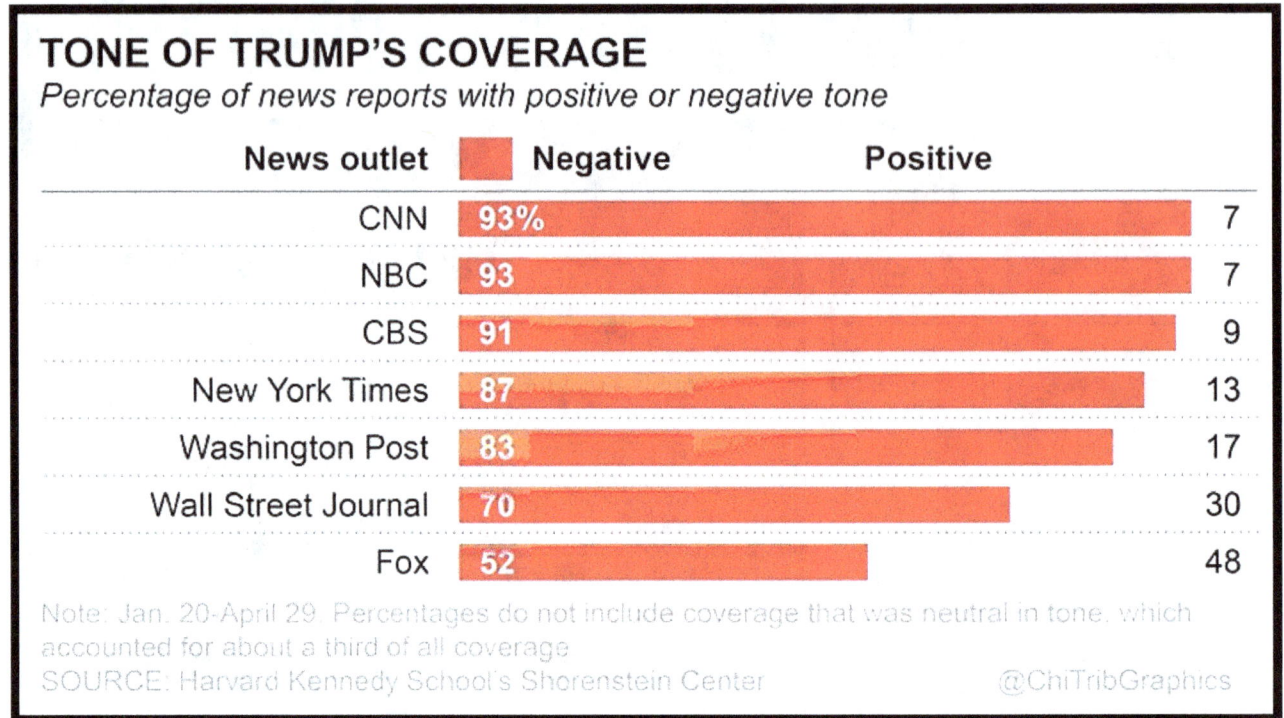

TONE OF TRUMP'S COVERAGE
Percentage of news reports with positive or negative tone

News outlet	Negative	Positive
CNN	93%	7
NBC	93	7
CBS	91	9
New York Times	87	13
Washington Post	83	17
Wall Street Journal	70	30
Fox	52	48

Note: Jan. 20-April 29. Percentages do not include coverage that was neutral in tone, which accounted for about a third of all coverage
SOURCE: Harvard Kennedy School's Shorenstein Center   @ChiTribGraphics

CNN: It's illegal to go through Hillary's emails detailing real criminal activity but OK to run stories of unproven harassment allegations, election collusion and discrimination.

Right! Our government, at its most rudimentary level, has two innate responsibilities: to provide transparency/accountability in all its dealings and to protect people's rights without refrain or prejudice. When you work for the State Department, let alone set up an authorized server to collude with the President, DNC officials, foreign donors and the media, you've officially entered the realm of public domain and waived your right to privacy long ago. As for unsubstantiated allegations, when was it acceptable for the national media to relentlessly report and give credence to unsubstantiated, defamatory charges – without making any credible efforts to debunk such claims or dare I say question their motives – and willingly become a supermarket tabloid or the political reincarnation of Jerry Springer? Once again, there is a stark difference between reporting the news...not gossip or partisan plots, mind you...and real criminality. It's time all media outlets were either officially designated as entertainment/advocacy - a glowing label slapped on the corner of every broadcast or atop any publication - or if they so choose, given their official press credentials from an independent watchdog for consistently demonstrating a commitment to unbiased, principled and responsible journalism.

Mob Rules and Marked Jurors

I understand legal posturing and petty gamesmanship is commonplace in the courtroom, but for a third party, major media network to sue for the right to publish the names and addresses of Manafort jurors during an ongoing trial is as outrageous as it is a coup waged against the ideal of justice itself. Such behavior is nothing short of political thuggery; a blatant attempt to pervert due process through fear and public coercion being these actions serve no other purpose than explicit intimidation and criminal extortion of common citizens fulfilling their civic duty. Yes, it's a sad day in America when the presiding judge himself requires continuous protection from U.S. Marshals due to escalating death threats from unhinged spectators. CNN, but more succinctly the entire progressive establishment, is completely out of control and needs a serious reality check. Putting people's lives in danger so you can aid and abet a prosecutor's crusade to falsely imprison political associates of the President is not only illicit in every sense of the word, it's fascism disguised as freedom of the press. At least taxpayers take comfort in the unreported fact Mr. Manafort is being tried for many of the same "crimes" he was exonerated of nearly a decade ago, but "forgivable" acts Tony Podesta was recently granted immunity by one Robert Swan Mueller.

> **Donald J. Trump** ✔
> @realDonaldTrump
>
> Social Media is totally discriminating against Republican/ Conservative voices. Speaking loudly and clearly for the Trump Administration, we won't let that happen. They are closing down the opinions of many people on the RIGHT, while at the same time doing nothing to others.......

A Clear & Progressive Danger

The progressive strategy is clear: to declare every public statement and policy decision made by Donald Trump as an unforgivable crime against humanity and immediate grounds for impeachment. The question is, where was this hyper-sensitive sense of duty for the past 8 years when Barack Hussein Obama abandoned Americans in Benghazi, aided and abetted terrorist regimes, redistributed earned income ad nauseam, lied repeatedly to pass socialized healthcare, authorized federal agencies to target conservatives, denied Christian businesses religious freedom, wiretapped the press and political opponents, encouraged mass illegal immigration for electoral gain, incited racial animosity and civil unrest, validated violence against police officers as social protest, aggressively imported radical Islam, and flushed our economic vitality and national sovereignty down the toilet at every conceivable opportunity? Without double standards, how would a liberal journalist ever know the difference between an aspiring despot and a conniving traitor? Simple, they voted for both twice instead of the leader who just deported a Nazi death-camp guard while admonishing all forms of hatred. When millions are perfectly content with a bitter propagandist who put America last for nearly a decade, they cannot handle the culture shock of an undaunted patriot who instinctively fights for her first every waking moment of his political life. Sorry but only one man owes the American people an engraved apology and it's not the one dutifully determined to restore our pride, prosperity and non-negotiable commitment to homeland security.

Dogs, Serpents & Poisonous Divas

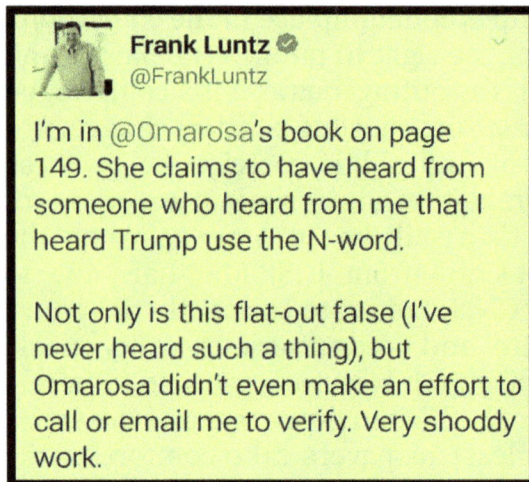

> **Frank Luntz** ✓
> @FrankLuntz
>
> I'm in @Omarosa's book on page 149. She claims to have heard from someone who heard from me that I heard Trump use the N-word.
>
> Not only is this flat-out false (I've never heard such a thing), but Omarosa didn't even make an effort to call or email me to verify. Very shoddy work.

For those who are unaware, Frank Luntz is an independent pollster and political analyst who is by no means a Trump ally or apologist. It's also ironic how quickly people forget Omarosa is a notorious diva who eagerly rode the President's coattails ever since embarrassing herself on "The Apprentice", even begging him for an entry level position in his administration, only to purposely ignore the fact she repeatedly praised his civil rights advocacy and leadership months after the election. Not surprisingly, the suddenly "offended" media that wouldn't give her the time of day when she worked for the White House is now more than happy to give her baseless vendetta a national platform of implied legitimacy despite knowing damn well she was banished from four jobs in two years while serving the Clinton/Gore cartel. What other "respectable" institution would roll out the Red Carpet for a glorified criminal guilty of illegally recording and grossly distorting the private conversations of colleagues in those confidential corridors designed to protect national security? Who could possibly have more credibility than a woman who once offered Piers Morgan sex as a bribe to win "Celebrity Apprentice"? When the unrelenting goal is to critically wound a highly-effective Chief Executive without condition or regret, any sacrificial pawn will do. If I may, other than improperly identifying a treacherous serpent lurking in his midst, how is calling a lying ingrate a "dog" worse than those Hollywood activists and honorable athletes publicly fantasizing over Donald Trump's death, disparaging his son as an autistic "retard" or advocating for Melania to be sexually assaulted? And yet the political engineers of "Fake News" who continue to justify and praise the brutality of fascist AntiFa still can't figure out why millions of disgusted voters view their crooked ranks as the enemy of the American people. They've rightfully earned that truthful distinction.

The Resistance of Real Journalism

Oh mercy, please! Nothing is more laughable than CNN decrying "juvenile" behavior, begging for partisan media solidarity, when they have lied, manipulated, solicited criminal leaks & peddled reckless conspiracy theories ad nauseam. Are we talking about a cable network's "two scoops" of investigative excellence, applauding a Broadway play repeatedly stabbing the President, or just selling a "big nothin' burger" as confirmed by Van Jones? You deserve far more than a "body slam" on the virtual concrete of the Twitter universe. Karma is an incessant tantrum's ass publicly exposed and the mainstream media's spanking has been long overdue. Now put on your footed pajamas, Jim Acosta, and write "Fake News is not Real Journalism" 1000 times in crayon on the racist wall of your padded Romper Room.

The Yellow Stain of Red October

In yet another carefully choreographed attempt to capitalize on Trump's infamous locker room banter, insinuating mere words somehow indicate an unearthed history of sexual harassment, the ultra-liberal New York Times is now claiming he inappropriately touched a handful of women who magically appeared overnight as if hired stage props on a lost episode of Project Runway. Naturally the fact the election is mere weeks away and the media used similar tactics to end Herman Cain's candidacy – a strong black candidate who threatened their stranglehold on the minority vote – has absolutely nothing to do with this latest charade of yellow journalism. After all, where were these victims for the past several years, or dare I say months ago during the primaries, when they were so traumatized and concerned about the future of our nation; before, that is, the MSM put out an A.P.B. for anyone with even the faintest repressed memory of usable impropriety against Mr. Trump? Hmm, and if I may be so bold, have the editors of the Times ever called a press conference showcasing the over ten women who have come forward claiming sexual harassment, assault and/or rape against Bill Clinton...a number who actually filed police reports? Perhaps the New York Tabloid, in all their infinite wisdom, should also run a story detailing how a close associate of the former President claims Mr. Clinton made an astonishing 26 trips to "Pedophile Island", an underage prostitution retreat for wealthy men, and that one of the encounters was even reportedly filmed. Of course, that would require real investigatory journalism, a clear case of nonpartisan objectivity, unlike those quick hit pieces broadcast for the sake of swaying an uninformed and gullible public.

The media has not only become a criminal empire of incredulity, a subsidiary of state-run propaganda, they're single-handedly the biggest threat to this country's survival. It is absolutely insulting, if not unforgivable, the press is devoting all its time and resources to wage vindictive smear campaigns on a man threatening to hold Washington accountable for a bevy of abuses and failures, while remaining completely oblivious to the reality Hillary has violated national security protocols, defrauded disaster relief survivors though her "charitable" foundation, sold political favors to radical regimes in exchange for campaign donations, "misplaced" 6-billion-dollars of taxpayer money while at the State Department, sold vast amounts of uranium to Russia, and perjured herself before the FBI and the House Select Committee. And what did the fabled watchdogs of this Republic, the stalwarts of a free and independent press, do to address this obvious blatant disregard for our laws and the welfare of the American people? They called a news conference claiming Trump grabbed someone's butt...with zero tangible evidence or plausible motive except to further slander his name in hopes of winning an election. And that, my friends, is exactly why this nation is in such dire straits. If you can't filter dirt from water, tell the difference between a pebble and a boulder, you'll never recognize the truth drowning beneath those dregs poisoning the drinking supply.

50 Shades of Media Hypocrisy

As both a parent and a spouse, am I disappointed by Donald Trump's past, crass comments? Unequivocally. Regardless of the circumstances they were wrong and inappropriate. However, his critics can stop claiming the moral high ground because their orchestrated outrage is an absolute farce. The media, including the Democratic party, associate with and support the vile Kardashians, the shameless Miley Cyrus, the career sexual predator named Bill Clinton, and Islamic nations that enslave and deny women basic human rights. And as for the "offended" public and outraged women everywhere...who exactly bought the over 80 million copies of the erotic and perverse '50 Shades of Grey'? How many of their husbands, if not their teens, are weekly visitors to Porn Hub or some other adult site? Are women being grabbed by their bible in those mediums, respected for their intellectual attributes, or am I missing the jest of the secular joke? Yes, once upon a time there was moral fortitude in America, a universal respect for God and our neighbor, but now it is more of a Sunday roll call or a campaign pit stop on the way to a night of infidelity in Vegas. And to think we're talking about "hurt" feelings; those very same anomalies that were painfully absent when Ann Coulter was recently called a "cunt" on national TV in a front of a roomful of applauding liberals.

Sorry but it's a sad indictment of our society when crude words supersede actual crimes, indecent acts, corruption and a radical anti-American agenda. Once again, the media has accomplished its goal of completely disregarding real impropriety, tangible threats to the survival and vitality of our country, solely to demonize a man they already hated with an unbridled passion. Meanwhile, Hillary openly admits to breaking law, selling favors while at the State Department, pilfering disaster relief funds for personal use and shaming the censored victims – over 10 reported instances of lewd advances, assault or rape – of Bill's sexual indiscretions. If Trump is unfit to serve and lead this nation...so be it. Just don't tell me the Clintons are any better and should be allowed to go anywhere near the White House because a decade-old recording of male vulgarity somehow exonerates two lifetimes of philandering, deception and collusion. I'm sick of the blatant, destructive and insulting double standard that has defied common sense and made a mockery of journalism for far too long. Accountability is a two-way street, not a kangaroo court of partisan hacks sentencing a jaywalker to a public hanging for their personal pleasure.

If Two by Taxes!

Congratulations to Rachel Maddow and MSNBC for turning their foolish obsession to criminalize Donald Trump's wealth into a legal fiasco that brought the White House one step closer to identifying the actual culprit guilty of releasing private federal documents. After all the media's sensationalist banter and divisive class warfare, the leaked returns revealed Donald Trump paid 38 million in taxes in 2005...or roughly more than the combined duties collected from Nancy Pelosi, Chuck Schumer, Elizabeth Warren and Bernie Sanders over the course of their disgruntled lifetimes. Not only was his 25% tax bracket higher than Comcast's 24% rate, the very liberal conglomerate that owns NBC and the esteemed patent on "fake" news, but the proclaimed capitalist "devil" even eclipsed the Social Justice Warrior himself, Barack Obama, who paid 19% of his earnings in the name of the 'common good' or Marxist 'community organizers' everywhere. And naturally, in the misplaced annals of partisan memories and due process, I'm excluding the offensive reality the supposed reincarnation of Adolf Hitler gave over 10 times more money to charitable causes in the name of hate, misogyny and blind malice. Who knew St. Jude's Hospital and those cancer-stricken children in such dire need of assistance were a fascist gateway to apocalyptic evil and global genocide?

Unless I'm horribly mistaken or otherwise allergic to the hypnotic aroma of a baited trap, the omnipotent mainstream media just got played, again, by the very man they claim is so hopelessly ignorant and dangerous to their detestable status quo. While the bitter resistance of common sense and accountability cajole, manipulate and twist every crumb of information to deflect from the aggressive reforms of the President, they're proving exactly why Hillary Clinton lost the election. A majority of the American people are sick and tired of juvenile games.

The Democratic choir of celebrity egos and collegiate activists aren't psychologically unraveling because they are deathly afraid of Donald Trump failing. Rather, they're desperate to destroy any discernible fact or societal perception that he is succeeding despite their sincerest efforts to convince us otherwise. And while we're on the subject of synchronized duplicity, please identify which limousine liberals do not exploit every legal tax loophole available to avoid paying as much taxes as humanly possible to a corrupt government that funded terrorist regimes, aided illegal immigrants and spent over $100 million of the people's money for the purpose of marketing failed socialist healthcare and protecting Barack Obama's "unremarkable", sealed past? Since when was repeatedly paying squandered or excessive taxes a patriotic act, let alone a catalyst of independence and the Constitutional sum of good government? Apparently, the moral high ground is now below sea level where the uncooperative truth keeps bubbling to the reclaimed surface of American sovereignty.

Respect and Reprobates

KOREAN WAR SOLDIERS COME HOME
MSNBC No Live Coverage
NBC No Coverage   CNN 58 seconds
CBS No Coverage   ABC 24 seconds

While the smug media dismisses our President's selfless gesture to donate his salary to repair and renovate military cemeteries, simply because he is wealthy, who among his critics is donating $400,000 to honor our fallen servicemen and women's sacrifice to this country? Even better, how many of these "noble" networks spent a single minute, if any time at all, covering the historic return of our soldiers' remains from North Korea; a foreign policy feat the ten previous Chief Executives failed to achieve? The smallest measure of gratitude, respect, doesn't require an agenda or a political affiliation, just the slightest hint of perspective. It doesn't take a Rhodes Scholar to figure out why Donald Trump has a 50% approval rating despite facing a daily avalanche of negative press. Leaders who actually care do the little things to make a difference regardless of any personal benefit. Now that's a priceless lesson the condemned Fifth Estate should take to heart if they want more than 20% of the unimpressed public to trust their dying profession.

A New York Times Kind of Racist!

Candace Owens
@RealCandaceO

Black people are only fit to live underground like groveling goblins. They have stopped breeding and will all go extinct soon. I enjoy being cruel to old black women.

The above statements are from @nytimes editor @sarahjeong. I simply swapped out the word "white" for "black".

If a conservative journalist made these racist statements, every news outlet, celebrity loudmouth and civil rights group would be demanding her head on a platter. While we're on the subject of liberal privilege, who would have guessed Sarah the South Korean migrant, a nation liberated from communist oppression by "dumbass" white men, was the loving by-product of Portland, Berkeley and Harvard all rolled into one bitter palate of insatiable animosity? Regardless of one's politics or occupation, this type of hateful ignorance is completely unacceptable and has no place in our society. Of course, such unethical behavior perfectly encapsulates the New York Times' ethnically-warped view of current events and the American electorate. When Whoopi can call the Lebanese Jeanine Pirro a "sand nigger" and Ms. Jeong can disparage an entire race without repercussions, there is officially no standard of professional conduct except that of malicious duplicity.

For Whom the Press Tolls

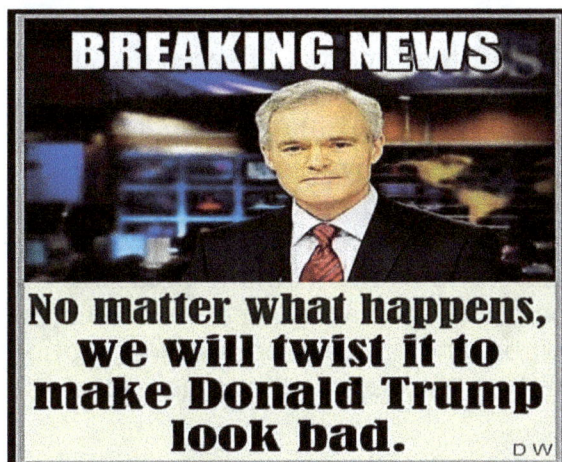

Presidential debates are not about the obvious slant of corporate media or the personal grudges of ambitious moderators. They're predicated upon vetting the records and ideas of both candidates with equal vigor. The time has come to once again honor that simple, nonnegotiable premise so the people – those voters who must responsibly decide the fate of this country – can have access to the unfiltered truth rather than the trickle-down talking points of political advocates. The greatest threat to America, our founding ideals and hallowed way of life, is neither Donald Trump nor Hillary Clinton. It's a conspiring media that is complicit in deceiving the very nation and populace they once swore to protect in the name of liberty and integrity. If transparency is now our enemy because it does not fit our fragile sense of progress, our personal political utopia, then what's the price of living in a propaganda state that interchanges fact with opinion and human rights with righteousness? Sooner or later, whether by force or by fallout, the marginalized masses will rebel against a system that neither respects their intelligence or takes accountability for its selfish, destructive actions. I do not fear the inconvenient truth...those competing viewpoints that invoke honest and earnest discourse to arrive at the most sensible conclusion. I fear watching everything I love evaporating beneath a fog of cultivated ignorance and indifference because no one stood up to realize the blessing of a free and moral society is incumbent upon our desire to protect it from all enemies, both foreign and domestic. Sunshine is not, nor will it ever be, a censor for subjugation and the media has been 'throwing shade' at the people for far too long.

The Mass Graves of Media Deception

Unemployment dropped to a paltry 3.8% in May (the lowest in a generation), median household income rose 1.8% to $61,400 last year, worker compensation hit the highest level in a decade, public assistance recipients fell to 40 million, another 225,000 jobs were added to the workforce, and black unemployment fell to a record low 5.9%. Excuse my "petty" penchant for factual observation, but are "We the Beneficiaries" of limitless opportunity still talking about the Fake News smokescreen of Russian collusion, stale charges of bigotry and the pornographic portfolio of Stormy Daniels, or appreciating a prescient President who embraces the liberating blessing of capitalism, fights for both American industry and labor, and earnestly comprehends how a market economy works? The same hyperventilating liberals who once predicted the economic chaos and spontaneous genetic mutations would ensue if Trump was somehow elected, now defiantly claim he has nothing to do with its sudden and historic resurrection but everything to do with what is undeniably wrong in America.

If you've ever been confused as to which elected representative truly loves America and cares about even her most inconsequential interests, it's the tireless executive and dutiful civil servant who restores government transparency, reduces wasteful regulations and ends abusive oversight, respects the work ethic and private property of fleeced taxpayers, deprives dictators and terrorist regimes nuclear concessions and foreign aid, rejects "unfair trade" and global wealth redistribution, pardons "wrongfully convicted" citizens regardless of their race or political convictions, restores religious freedom and our Constitutional belief in God, provides equal opportunities for women and minorities in his administration, honors our forsaken commitment to veterans, active military members and first responders, enforces our immigration laws without breaking the founding promise of America as a beacon of hope for all humanity, and embodies the fearless idealist who braves scorn and slander to expose the rampant political corruption and media subversion poisoning our national unity, public institutions and electoral process.

The Deep State stalwarts of mass deception, those shameless propagandists and plotting bureaucrats whose unwavering loyalties reside within a destructive, anti-American agenda and the treasonous allure of uncontested control, can deceive, cajole, and incite discord until their baroque hearts are fully content. Yet, no matter how hard their seething hatred of one man conspires to erase reality and obstruct real progress, the tangible results will inevitably speak for themselves; thus, tarnishing their malicious and seditious efforts all the more. During times of universal prosperity, renewed patriotism and restored trust in government, the only electoral wave present in American history has traditionally been one of welcomed optimism and electoral gratitude. And that, my discounted friends, is the one salient truth the clamoring critics of "America First" are striving daily to deny the coerced voting masses: their unconditional right, without threat of partisan hostility or societal contempt, to choose an effective, loyal and unapologetic leader of this betrayed American Republic.

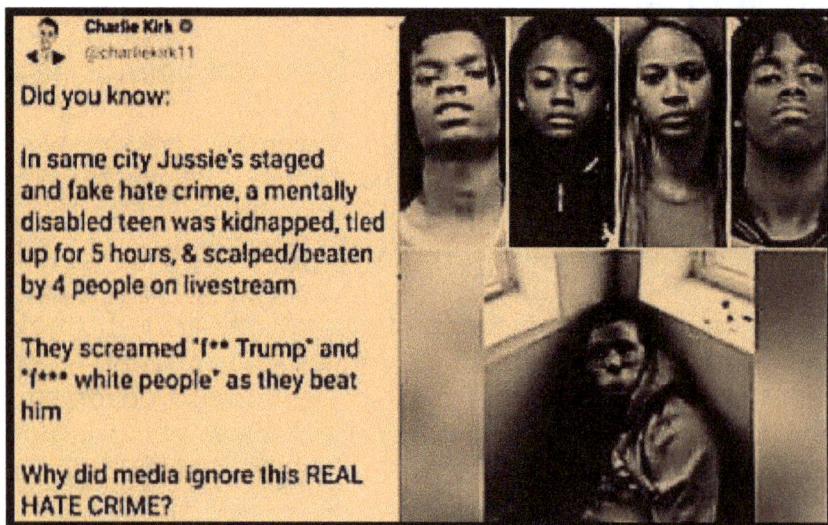

Charlie Kirk 🔵
@charliekirk11

Did you know:

In same city Jussie's staged and fake hate crime, a mentally disabled teen was kidnapped, tied up for 5 hours, & scalped/beaten by 4 people on livestream

They screamed "f** Trump" and "f*** white people" as they beat him

Why did media ignore this REAL HATE CRIME?

Hollywood and the liberal media immediately jumped to politicize Jussie Smollett's premeditated fake hate crime, with zero corroborative evidence, but remained unforgivably silent when a Facebook video emerged of a helpless handicap man being held hostage and brutally tortured in a Chicago apartment by four soulless bigots proudly mocking Trump supporters. Completely unethical.

The Muted Majority

Whether the issue is border security, abortion, taxes, gun rights, religious liberty, transgender conditioning or free speech...liberal activists make the most noise, organize raucous demonstrations and weaponize the press, because they want to give the impression they are the empowered majority fighting injustice when in reality they are the radical mob, the greatest ideological threat against this country, recruiting/bribing millions of foreign nationals to bolster their subversive ranks as a contrived means of public consent. Many of the anti-American left's most counter-intuitive beliefs would not survive honest scrutiny, let alone fair elections, otherwise.

Kellyanne Conway ✓
@KellyannePolls

The absurdity in one spilt screen:

Nick Sandmann, 16 years old, of Covington, says NOTHING and is derided & nearly destroyed in a nanosecond.

Ilhan Omar, 37 years old, of Congress, repeatedly & unmistakably spews hate speech, is praised, excused, unpunished.

Conservatives, on the other hand, tend to be much more subdued or even pedestrian in their political approach. While I whole-heartedly endorse the necessity of civility and mutual respect, constructive discourse requires an equitable platform to engage the masses without having to overcome education indoctrination, media censorship and celebrity narcissism. This nation's most fundamental and nonnegotiable Constitutional ideals, once enthusiastically embraced by both parties, are now a dire contention of unilateral, social control. Without a concerted effort and accessible, visible presence to reach an already sheltered electorate, any alternative message is essentially powerless; no matter how crucial or compelling.

All concerned, right-minded Americans who are fed-up with the violent threats, endless propaganda, destructive double standards and cultural decay of modern progressivism need to become better organized, more outspoken and equally adamant in their convictions. America, our most indispensable values, will not survive if we do not embody the unwavering fight to avoid repeating the same pitfalls that toppled some of the most transcendent, enlightened civilizations in human history. And that's exactly what globalists are counting on.

THERE ARE 1500 NEWSPAPERS, 1100 MAGAZINES, 9000 RADIO STATIONS, 1500 TV STATIONS, 2400 PUBLISHERS, **OWNED BY ONLY 3 CORPORATIONS.**

"The Resistance'
of Cognitive Dissonance

On the Left, the 1932 flag of the paramilitary wing of the Communist Party of Germany. On the Right, the 2017 flag of the paramilitary wing of the Democratic Party of America.

" IF FASCISM EVER COMES TO AMERICA, IT WILL COME IN THE NAME OF LIBERALISM "

RONALD REAGAN

...IT'S HERE

Sticks and Stones and Assassination Prose

Free speech does not cease in a nation predicated upon individual liberty, nor does it inevitably qualify as a "hate crime" simply because you disagree with or are deeply offended by the personal beliefs of others. There are no 'safe spaces' from the self-inflicted micro-aggressions of reality...i.e., one's own insecurities or deep-seated biases. Tolerance, disregarding the newly socially engineered version that slanders or threatens divergence with now disturbing regularity, is a prerequisite of free will and the fundamental crux of open and constructive discourse; a Socratic ideal colleges should be obstinately preserving rather than forcibly constricting in the name of fostering political uniformity.

Students, our own sons and daughters, should never be afraid to speak their mind out of fear of condemnation or retribution in our institutions of higher learning, let alone in the sovereign confines of a constitutional republic that openly rebelled against intrusive government, religious persecution, and the oppression of mankind's natural born rights. If the immediate goal is to label all conservative views as hate speech, then the ultimate objective is the dissolution of our nation's founding premise and the justified demise of due process. Tyranny goes by many names and you don't have to be a philosophy student to matriculate into the baited den of madness. One merely must realize that totalitarianism is a futile endeavor because human nature, regardless whether America is buried and replaced by the most progressive state, will always challenge the limitations of any authoritative society that seeks to stifle our unique faculties and man's innate desire to be free. While freedom of speech does not guarantee freedom from consequences, nor does it pardon terroristic threats, those activists attempting to suffocate the rights of unwelcome perspective, using "racism" as a justifiable alibi to incite violence and civil unrest, represent a far more nefarious threat to America's survival than those brash voices willing to speak their coarse minds and openly face their detractors. The first step in accepting tyranny or unconditional subjugation is to rationalize why you must first surrender your rightful independence.

Although I have no love, respect or earthly need for white or black supremacists, ANTIFA, La Raza, the Muslim Brotherhood or Marxist-Leninists, no one sect or ideology should be less entitled or more accountable for their actions. To quote Voltaire, and to rejoice in the "Common Sense" of Thomas Paine, I may disagree with what you say but I will defend to the death your right to say it. Democrat, Republican, liberal, conservative, Christian, atheist, white, black, gay, straight, rich, poor, Donald Trump or Hillary Clinton...to bask in the light of liberty, the transcendent gifts of humanity's intellectual prowess, spiritual and empathetic capacity, is to shed the shackles of coerced silence. Those beliefs which cannot stand upon their own merits and withstand the natural rigors of honest scrutiny, will in due time wilt beneath the unsustainable of their own hypocrisy. When confronting "hate speech" requires the political distraction of false accusation, juvenile antagonism and welcomed brutality, the so-called justified response becomes far more deadly and divisive than an annual parade of fools or the mere deployment of words. I am far more wary of those lost souls who are willing to adopt the morally bankrupt premise of senseless rhetoric, then those who merely speak of it to solicit attention.

Right or wrong, I would much rather embrace the uncertainties of individuality, encourage the open exchange of competing ideas to challenge my convictions and unearth the best possible solutions, than to faintly exist amidst the blaring stigma of stereotype to justify mass conformity. Progress, our insatiable thirst for excellence and innovation, isn't born solely from the comfort of serenity or the pulpit of self-righteousness; it is most often forged from the fires of failure, dissent, necessity and most notably, self-discovery. If people are not willing to discern truth from fiction, volition from fascism as sentient beings, then perhaps it is the media's job to tell us what to think, feel, eat and drink. Two and a half centuries of Americans didn't toil and sacrifice so their tepid descendants could bite their tongue and recoil in fear amidst the Orwellian tactics of glorified political terrorists. They risked their very lives and the welfare of their children so the flame of freedom, the very First Amendment of our inalienable Bill of Rights, would endure without condition. These unfiltered voices of free will knew what it meant to be an American; more succinctly, they overwhelmingly understood their liberties were a birthright, derived from the grace of God, and not ransomed by any government decree or bloodthirsty movement.

As long as the media wastes more time and resources manipulating public opinion to needlessly demonize or potentially "assassinate" our President – his repeated recognition and clear rejection of hate in all facets of America – instead of equally exposing the actual instigators and perpetrators of mob violence, hate will grow in congruence with society's unwillingness to identify racism without the prism of political consent. Inflaming century old racial tensions simply to selectively report hate exists, does nothing to alleviate its existence or to responsibly condemn intolerance in any of its sprouting forms. Even if ANTIFA, the KKK and the sponsored armies of fascism beat their perceived enemies into submission, they would merely ensure the reciprocal means of their own demise. You can no more command the dead than a tyrant can earn the respect of the brutally oppressed. When "tolerance" requires bloody knuckles and hateful epithets, flash mobs of masked thugs assaulting political dissent, America is the first casualty of partisan contempt. Anarchy, however, eagerly invites them all.

The AntiFa Police State

The reason the Supreme Court recently reaffirmed that hate speech constitutes protected free speech is because putting limits on self-expression inevitably invites further censorship, and if left unchecked, legalized tyranny. It is common knowledge the left wants to punish and even criminalize those political deviants who do not believe in global warming, gun control, abortion, illegal immigration or who refuse to address transgenders by their adopted pronoun of choice; and in some instances, some states and institutions have already sought to impose such nonsense. While I despise the racist rhetoric of the

THE LEFT SUPPRESSES CONSERVATIVE THOUGHT

BECAUSE THEY CANNOT COMPETE WITH CONSERVATIVE THOUGHT

KKK, BLM, or La Raza, their right to do so is the crux of maintaining a free republic founded upon individual liberty. However, with that being said, please allow me to strongly digress. There is a stark contrast between detestable free speech and those who incite violence or seek to silence others through brutal oppression. The best way to confront the oxymoron known as AntiFa – the anti-fascist, fascist gang of partisan anarchists who oppose white supremacy with racial bigotry and defend democracy with death threats – is to confront them with overwhelming numbers wherever their hateful ranks seek validation through chaos. Only by recording their vile stupidity – their reckless assault on police, political dissent, patriotic Americans and the Constitution itself – can we defeat this rising tide of millennial fascism and educate the public, our children and future generations, as to the true destructive nature of the intolerant left.

The more the Democratic Party and the applauding media justifies the dissolution of discourse and all civility, the more likely these sponsored domestic terrorists are to exact further bloodshed and torment our communities. Nevertheless, as a fellow citizen and concerned friend, I must urge great caution. Never confront these masked cowards alone or without possessing some means of self-defense. The backpack brigade of college dropouts, gender militants, unemployed Marxists, and self-entitled video game assassins reside in a detached bubble, or quite possibly their parents air-conditioned basement, where reality and empathy no longer exist. Any organization that is willing to drag an old woman with our flag, weaponize their bodily fluids against law enforcement, cut a pregnant mother, or ransack a public official's home, obviously possesses no soul or any semblance of human decency. Because there is strength in numbers, but more profoundly providence by embodying unwavering resolve, "We the Everyday People" who come from all walks of life, who love our country and respect the rule of law regardless of our differences, will no longer be intimidated or accept living in a decaying state of perpetual moral depravity. Without coercion or needless savagery, our voices and mass demonstration of unity must dwarf any wandering band of sadistic malcontents or screeching bullhorn of blind contempt. The armies of ignorance who seek mass conformity to a regressive agenda, to demonize liberty and the voters of any election result they violently reject, represent the worst type of hate; fear born from the false propaganda of an aspiring police state. The only fate worse than living in a totalitarian nightmare is refusing to recognize the unopposed beginnings of one.

The Iron Fist of Infamy

When a scheduled Patriot Prayer Rally is reported as a white supremacist assembly by the media and therefore must be canceled due to security concerns, we're no longer living in America – a country predicated on Judeo-Christian values and an indelible love of liberty – but George Orwell's dystopian nightmare "1984". Instead of Democrats and Republicans alike uniting in a civil setting for a peaceful demonstration of tolerance, a much-needed refuge from the orchestrated hostility gripping our nation, AntiFa terrorists were allowed to harass and assault innocent bystanders as local police were once again nowhere to be found. Considering these brutal attacks would result in immediate arrests and an equal display of force by law enforcement on any other day, no excuse, degree of denial or apology will suffice. The only crime more hypocritical and egregious than hateful militants beating fleeing victims under the false flag of "stopping hate", is for those officers who vowed to protect and serve our communities to consciously stand down in the face of such imminent brutality. When political allegiance or disdain for a President trumps common sense, duty, and any remote sense of remaining decency, the result clearly mirrors the madness. Only the deranged mainstream media would equate unhinged fascists with combat soldiers or heroic freedom fighters.

Despite facing real injustice and oppression, Martin Luther King Jr. never hid behind a mask because true "social change" never validates violence, animosity through anonymity, it demands moral strength through visible courage. Those false accusers who blame the abused to justify smothering free speech or coerce undue concessions are by far the greatest embodiment of hate, societal division and civil unrest. The precedent we unwittingly set, or apathetically allow to endure, is the fire in which today's children – America's future – inevitably burn.

If progressives are not going to unconditionally condemn this proliferation of Marxist style propaganda and Nazi Gestapo tactics – justifying violence by fabricating fear and demonizing all political dissent as immoral extremism – it is only a matter of time before the oppressed bear arms against those seeking to put them, and their inalienable rights, in a permanent body bag. And on that perilous note, I call on President Trump, the FBI, and the Department of Justice to restore order, make arrests and to indict the unapologetic perpetrators of domestic terrorism. The single, greatest trick the media ever played was convincing millions of Americans "extremism" only pertains to the right side of the aisle, when in fact the intolerant left, the Democratic Party, is still the single greatest embodiment of radicalism in America today. How else can a political party built on racism, seduced by communism and now an adopted anti-American sanctuary of malcontents that increasingly moralizes mass conformity through the iron fist of fascism, continue to exist? Only in the alt-reality of disposable history, where indoctrinated ignorance and celebrated bliss converge to embrace the most notorious forms of human tyranny, are liberty and logic labeled as hate crimes for attempting to loosen the grip of tangible evil. The staged theatricality of blame and bigotry are powerful agents of deception in this escalated progressive war on truth, patriotism and ideological sovereignty.

Anyone who physically attacks Free Speech, terrorizes peaceful political rallies, should permanently lose their right to vote. Actual jail time/community service (no less than 30 days) and fiscal compensation should be dependent upon the severity of their crimes.

The Real Resistance

If last night was a referendum on the Presidential election, the tireless accusations of Russian collusion, "illegal" travel bans and Executive obstruction, I'd venture to say America is tired of the bullshit. Excuse my adopted Georgia Bulldog. You don't win the respect of voters by spending almost 10 times more than your opponent and running a candidate that cannot even vote in the same Congressional district he claims to wholeheartedly represent. You earn hard working people's respect by clearly and passionately articulating your ideals without needlessly berating your opponent to incite hatred and false judgement. Taxpayers and concerned citizens want America's most pressing problems remedied, not worsened by media campaigns designed to siphon our liberty, prosperity and security solely to fulfill a radical social agenda forged upon racism, moral apathy and entitlement. Unless you're "resisting" the numerous failed policies and clear anti-American zeitgeist of the past 8 years, your detached notion of "injustice" represents the undisputed impetus as to why the marginalized masses elected one Donald Trump. The real "resistance" spoke over 7 months ago on November 8th when half of your current campaign volunteers cried in their parent's basement without the aid of a

Snapchat filter. Sadly, no such tears were shed for the approximately 5 million illegals allowed to vote in integrity's stead.

Contrary to the intolerant left, lasting reform requires dedicated and reasonable professionals working together to find the best possible solutions, regardless of the Congressional majority; not kicking and screaming juveniles triggered by a name or threatened by the mere thought of differing opinions. If your beliefs discourage constructive discourse and cannot weather earnest scrutiny by simply standing on their own merits, instead invoking conspiracy theories and partisan paranoia for political capital, then you're merely a used car salesman riding the bus to cash your donor's check at the next Antifa crime reunion. In layman's terms, please send Mr. Soros my regards and a pair of overalls....and not the pre-stained, $400, Velcro variety decorated with the blood of American sovereignty. Perhaps someday he'll have the courage to do his own dirty work rather than sending a smug pajama boy who majored in European socialism, is the textbook progressive definition of 'White Privilege' and who boasted 5 months of National Security experience as a staffer. After all, public service should never require a Hollywood entourage and a Google map to find your gerrymandered state of residence.

The Enemies of Humanity

Burning the flag, beating Trump supporters, defacing monuments, rioting in the streets, threatening Presidential assassination and to kill all white people...this merely confirms the radical left is by far the greatest threat in America. And yet people wonder why Trump, the law and order candidate, was elected. Look around and you'll see liberal fascism is alive and flourishing in the land of the "free". These anarchists aren't Americans; they're militant "snowflake" adolescents who refuse to accept the results of an election and the fact people have the right to freedom of choice...intellectual diversity. This is what happens when the media, political propagandists and educators fill people's minds with such vicious lies and exaggerations. Sick and unacceptable. The corrupt establishment that supported Obama's divisive agenda and Hillary's failed candidacy created Trump's success and now bitter voters are lashing out at the inevitable results? These actions are an insult to the indelible truth every man and woman has unalienable rights and we as Americans live in a nation built upon those freedoms; those natural born liberties so often denied by tyrants across the globe. Although I have friends and colleagues with diametrically opposite beliefs, we openly accept that reality without hate or violence. To not defend and embody tolerance is to declare yourself an enemy of all humanity.

Two Scoops of Sanity

While Kathy Griffin's disgusting actions are not worthy of the 'shock value' attention some celebrity degenerates so desperately crave, they are disturbingly symptomatic of the mindless hate engulfing our country. In essence, her behavior is the toxic byproduct of an antagonistic culture, "fake news" and triggered fascism if you will, that rejects intellectual diversity and ruthlessly demonizes a man every waking minute of every single day without any regard for the truth, the welfare of America and the safety of her people. When constructive discourse is stripped of merit in favor of feeding a political lynch mob, college professors can keep their jobs after advocating genocide, racist students are actually allowed to organize "A Day Without Whites" as they verbally assault and physically threaten non-minority professors, a popular talk show host profanely berates the President with homophobic slurs but without consequences, a 10 year-old weary child is mocked as 'autistic' for braving the morning hours of election night, and highway billboards depict Donald Trump as a Nazi for opposing illegal immigration – laws created/ratified by both parties and a prosecutable crime in nearly every developed nation – and seeking to temporarily ban unvetted immigrants from Middle Eastern countries that either lack the resources or moral fortitude to document militant elements; an executive action exercised by previous Democratic Presidents without the faintest public whisper of party opposition. Maxine Waters kindly said it best…"if Hillary proposed the ban, I would fully support it." Somewhere, facts still matter more than the syndicated newsrooms of fabricated outrage or the indoctrinated campuses of mob justice.

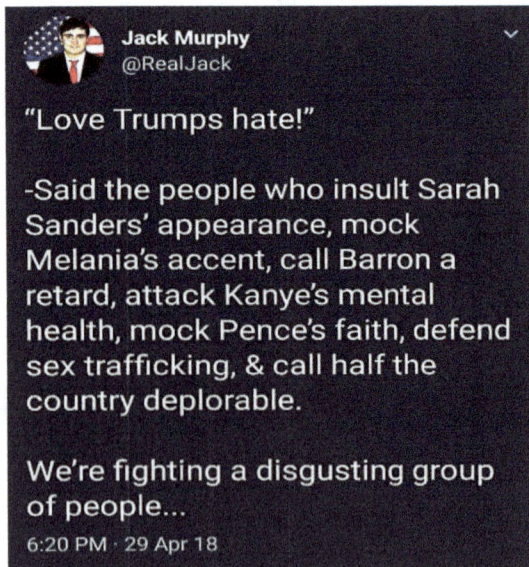

> **Jack Murphy**
> @RealJack
>
> "Love Trumps hate!"
>
> -Said the people who insult Sarah Sanders' appearance, mock Melania's accent, call Barron a retard, attack Kanye's mental health, mock Pence's faith, defend sex trafficking, & call half the country deplorable.
>
> We're fighting a disgusting group of people...
>
> 6:20 PM · 29 Apr 18

Oh, and by the way, Nazi merchandise that symbolizes authentic genocide is still available on Amazon while Confederate figures are being condemned and destroyed whether or not they partook in human servitude – a global institution practiced by only 1.6% of Americans before the Civil War – but needlessly continues to flourish across Africa and Asia today without notable protest or tangible international action.

Not only are these reactions devoid of rationale thought or any semblance of dignity, they are being actively cultivated and justified by political elites for the sake of overturning an election result that symbolizes our founding struggle to live as a Constitutional Republic free the historical ravages of intolerance and tyranny. Yes, who needs media accountability when the revisionist anchors of the Islamic creed, those "humanitarian" voyages and ruddy seas ransomed by the Tripoli pirates, are somehow magically sown into the iconic tapestry of the American dream? If America is truly dying, it's because "We the People" have become too sick and self-indulgent to notice; let alone inconvenienced enough to care.

I am not going to hypocritically proclaim I embraced Barack Obama or Hillary Clinton as honest, moral contemporaries worthy of my respect. I did not. However, my disdain for their political rhetoric and unscrupulous dealings never morphed into literally calling for their heads, threatening their supporters' rights, using obscene gestures to voice my opposition or rioting in the streets of futility. Common decency and basic decorum, philosophical benchmarks of any civilized society, never constitute mocking our fallen heroes on Memorial Day or moralizing the number of scoops of ice cream a 70-year-old man has for dessert rather than unmasking the juvenile exploits of Antifa anarchists who are funded by some of the same commercial sponsors as their so-called 'esteemed' networks. That, my friends, requires a spoiled, detached and much less evolved mind.

"I won't sit there and be lectured by (Jeanine Pirro) Trump's sand nigger."
~Whoopi Goldberg, ABC's 'The View'

Suspending the Truth

"The level of hatred toward the 45th president of the United States is beyond anything we've seen in **American history.**"
— Judge Jeanine Pirro

The increasingly-progressive Fox News hasn't been on my radar for some time. Sorry, Judge Pirro was astute and 100% correct when concluding Ilhan Omar's loyalties were to Sharia Law instead of the United States Constitution: that which she was elected to serve unconditionally. Why else would a foreign refugee demand special privileges to wear a Hijab on the House floor when no such exceptions have been made in 182 years after all Congressional members were banned from wearing headwear in 1837; not even for cancer patients? Furthermore, her anti-Semitic and treasonous comments have made her loyalties painfully obvious. The truth has become politically incorrect "hate speech".

A Political Hit

When Loretta Lynch, the former Attorney General of the United States, personally suggested "more marching and blood in the streets" was necessary to further political change, did liberals truly believe not a single agitated Democrat would interpret her reckless plea as a literal call to arms"? This morning's shooting at a GOP baseball practice for a charity game is but a sad reminder of how politically toxic and morally destabilized America has become. The insatiable hostility being waged against Trump supporters, during public events and now against nonconformist elected officials, is almost entirely a product of mass hysteria forged by a dysfunctional educational system, an unhinged celebrity class and a malicious media that has incessantly demonized right-minded Americans for decades but more specifically on an unprecedented scale over the past year.

> ### James Woods ✓
> @RealJamesWoods
>
> "Argue with people, get in their face." "If they bring a knife to the fight, we bring a gun." - Barack Hussein Obama
> #AlexandriaShooting
>
> 3:37 AM · Jun 15, 2017

The liberal establishment literally has millions of conscious adults believing Donald Trump is the antichrist; a prophesied world destroyer who rapes women, hates minorities, enslaves immigrants, poisons the environment, abandons the sick and starves the poor for the mere sadistic pleasure of personal entertainment. Excuses be damned, this avalanche of absurd rhetoric is directly responsible for ushering in an era of hyper-partisan paranoia and violent opposition. Since 2008, mass shootings have increased by 800% as the increasingly belligerent left sought to trigger a militant culture war that was specifically designed to "get in the face" of all voters who opposed their anti-American, social justice platform known as "hope" and "change". And yet these are the bitter malcontents that are still perplexed as to how a young woman who labeled the white race a disease and voiced her desire to burn down the White House was arrested for leaking a "Top Secret" document regarding Russian conspiracy theories. In their eyes, she is a hero guilty of absolutely nothing for the end justifies the means. In the annals of human history, "crazy" never sleeps. And therein lies the problem; also known as modern progressivism.

328

The moment the public can no longer employ reason or basic intuition, to discern fact from fiction amidst a tidal wave baseless hyperbole, then the very ethical constructs of any civilized society become servile to the slightest subjective whims of political opportunists. When discrimination depends on ideological affiliation and articles of impeachment merely require unsubstantiated accusation, the results are as bankrupt as the intentions of the accusers. Likewise, those parading parasites who immediately invoke guns after a senseless tragedy, rather than demonstrating sincere concern for the victims themselves, are a microcosm of this antagonistic culture which rejects accountability and civility in hopes of inciting disdain and discord for political gain. Once again, individuals are accountable, as are those perverted institutions of public trust...most notably those celebrity mouthpieces and educational mediums that divide America into mindless warring factions to achieve an immoral end. Anytime an enraged partisan fires over 100 bullets into a field of innocent bystanders, it is neither a mistake nor a victimless crime. Sadly, the same can be said for those journalists who hijacked the somber anniversary of tragedy – those roughly 50 innocents murdered by an Islamic terrorist at an Orlando nightclub – to protect Islamic intolerance by blaming an inanimate object, or by proxy those who support the right to defend yourself in the face of such barbaric aggression. If what we say is as important as how we act, America is quickly becoming a playground for moral degenerates and radical political terrorists. Historically speaking, such tyranny, whether by subversion of one's values or by forceful oppression, has only been defeated by those fearless voices willing to stand in the path of its hateful premise. The right to bear reason is not incumbent upon the permission of those who refuse to accept its necessity.

The Riot Act: The Cost of Ignorance

Violently protesting the results of a legitimate election...silly, selfish and criminal. If only that same level of outrage was present when the DNC and Hillary Clinton joined forces to subvert the people's will and the integrity of the Democratic primaries. Or how about when police officers were hunted and (continue to be) executed in multiple states because the media routinely demonized cops with their selective, race-based reporting? Surely these same "morally conscious" activists held nationwide protests when it was revealed Planned Parenthood – a modern-day "baby chop shop" – was selling human remains on the black market for profit? No...not once. Obviously losing an election is far more egregious than the loss of actual human life. Oh well, at least justice was served when the "partisan" whistle-blower was charged with altering a government ID. Priorities.

As for those "highly-educated" Hillary voters rioting in the streets, winning 306 of the required 270 electoral votes isn't a crime. It's a geographic landslide, an undisputed path to winning the presidency, not to mention a proven method of ensuring every state has an indelible voice in this Constitutional Republic. The minute jaded politicians scrap our electoral system is the moment 90% of the nation – our values, economy and rights – permanently succumb to the whims of urban progressives: those cities overflowing with illegal immigrants, intrusive government and indoctrinated anti-Americanism. Circulating a petition to end the Electoral College is like trying to change the size of a field goal because your kicker missed the winning kick. Apparently blame is far more convenient than accountability. Sorry but coffee house petitions do not override the 229-year-old wisdom of Constitutional precedent or change the fact the press lost all credibility when it collectively chose to disregard their journalistic obligation – vetting both candidates with equal vigor and distrust – in lieu of running a daily political tabloid designed solely to illicit sticker shock appeal. Regardless, when you have four years to campaign, register new voters and make your case to the American people with the shameless assistance of the liberal media, the only fault required is that of your own.

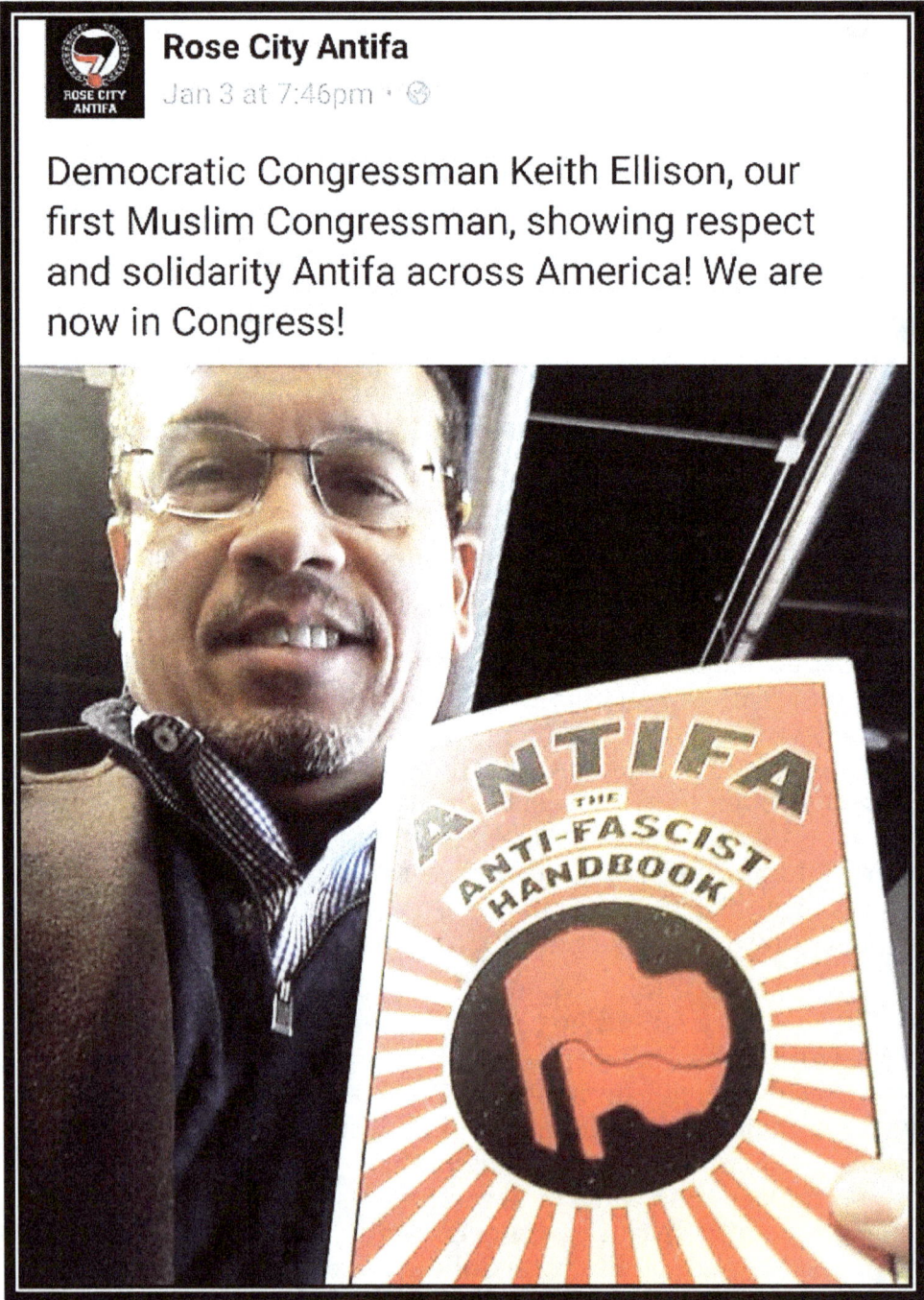

Rose City Antifa
Jan 3 at 7:46pm · 🌐

Democratic Congressman Keith Ellison, our first Muslim Congressman, showing respect and solidarity Antifa across America! We are now in Congress!

The anti-AntiFa 'Defense of Liberty' Guide

1) When confronted, threatened or attacked by a hostile Democratic Socialist, remove fascist coward's mask because "innocent revolutionaries" should never be required to conceal their "honorable" identities

2) Take a picture or record a video of said "anonymous" criminal perpetrator(s) with the assistance of friends and/or like-minded associates. There is nothing illegal about defending yourself or identifying your assailants

3) Confiscate backpacks filled with AntiFa propaganda, weapons and other potentially unlawful pertinence

4) Document all materials for publication on an internet database entitled "AntiFa Unmasked" to expose militant thugs and warn fellow Americans of impending danger

5) Turn all acquired evidence into the police, along with signed affidavits of assaults, to secure indictments or at the very least provide law enforcement with an acute awareness of active anarchists and other radicalized suspects

6) Return to the scene of disbanded AntiFa hate, sing God Bless America and embrace/shake the hands of all willing pedestrians: regardless of gender, creed or color. Unity born from natural volition is never defined by uniform submission to fear or coerced conformity but achieved amicably through a universal respect for liberty – the indispensable necessity of intellectual diversity – and by equally protecting all peaceful applications of dissenting opinion.

Only by standing together against the violent aspirations of organized hate, by demanding accountability and embodying civility in our communities, can decent, law-abiding Americans defeat the armies of intolerance – the applauded terrorist wing of the Democratic "resistance" – and restore our country's founding premise of individual liberty for all and freedom from all forms of tyranny: both foreign and domestic.

The Red MAGA hat is the new 'White Hood'. ~ Alyssa Milano

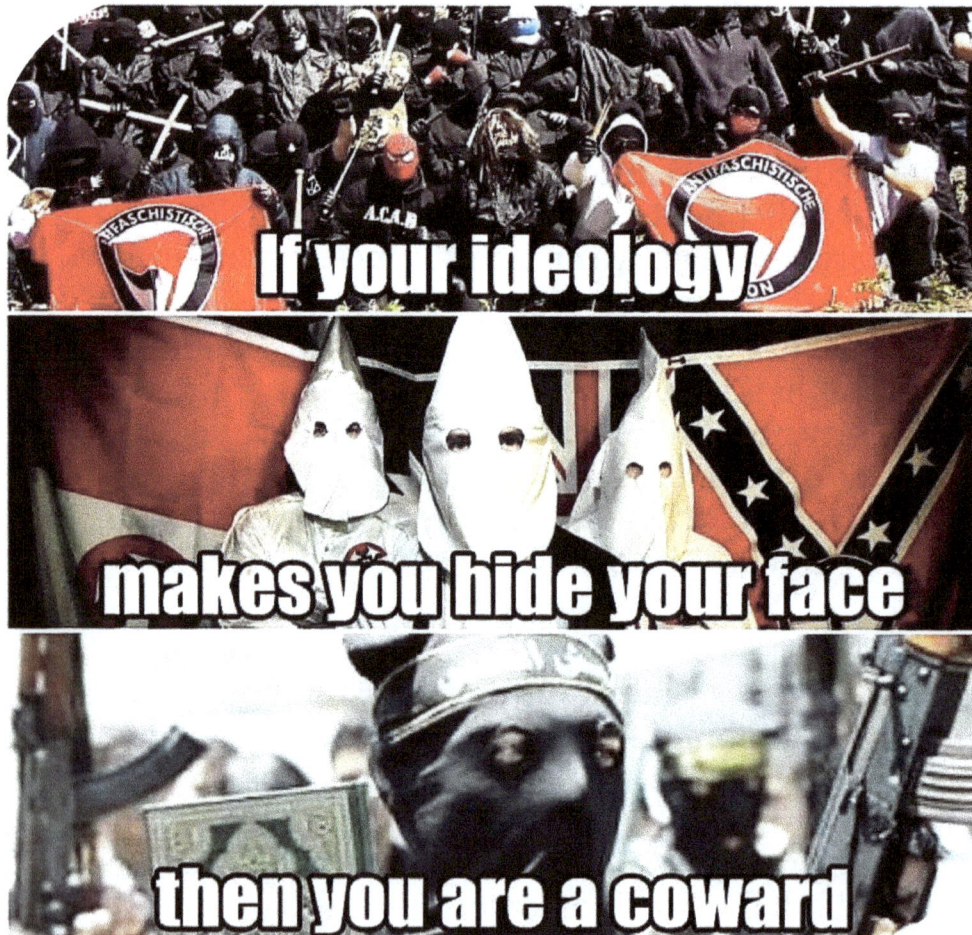

If your ideology
makes you hide your face
then you are a coward

A CALL TO ARMS

Banning Self-Defense

AMERICA

The original safe space.
Created by men with guns.

The Revolver of Reason: Reloading the Constitution

Any mass shooting in America, let alone a single murder, is without a doubt a grotesque reminder of the evil that lurks in our communities. However, as much as I unconditionally grieve for the victims and their families, I refuse to blame an inanimate object rather than the actual lawbreaker. The weapon on choice is moot for criminals will always find a means to unleash their hate. Liberals live to shamelessly politicize such tragedies – immediately blaming the NRA or Tea Party – hoping our Second Amendment rights will be ripped away by an inescapable vacuum of mass hysteria and mob justice. The same Constitutional terrorists who can't keep gangs off the streets, or drug dealers out of our schools, would leave "We the People" at the mercy of thugs and lowlife opportunists, not to mention vulnerable to government tyranny; Thomas Jefferson's most profound reason for preserving our right to bear arms. History proves tyrants prefer unarmed citizens for the same rationale criminals target defenseless victims: disarming the populace is the final lynchpin in securing uncontested subjugation and unconditional rule.

Contrary to leftist fodder, defending gun rights isn't about big trophy hunting or drunken rednecks shooting at watermelons. Its necessity is born from one immutable truth: human beings still die from the same proverbial hands of oppression and hate as they did in 1789. Career criminals, aspiring dictators and plotting terrorists rarely, if ever, follow gun laws. Why would they? Chicago bears some of the strictest gun control measures in the nation and also one of the highest murder rates. The real tragedy in this endless debate is that the media never reports how often firearms save lives, foil crimes, feed families and safeguard freedom around the globe. I could not imagine lying awake at night knowing my family was at the mercy of some deranged intruder and that I was powerless to protect them. I'm an American, a patriot, a law-abiding citizen, and there's a reason why I keep a Glock 20 beside my bed: I refuse to be a statistic like the politically correct dead. And just in case you wanted one...over 80 million-gun owners did not commit a crime last night. You do the math.

In this New World Order where logic is a form of white Supremacy, Right-Wing hyperbole, I'm still waiting for the MSM to report Global Warming is directly responsible for a rise in gun violence and terrorism. Oh wait, they already have! This is how utterly ridiculous and irreconcilable American politics has become. These insufferable hacks would have you believing pens misspell words and that homicidal cars drive drunken philanderers named Ted Kennedy off bridges if it meant preserving their backwards, victimization platform. It's not about the truth, the heartbreak, or the victims; it's only about how sensationalism can be spun into a perceived gain for a political agenda. Naturally, the media will never report how the U.S. has fewer mass shootings per capita than many developed countries; including France, Norway and pacifist Switzerland. Regardless of a perpetrator's political affiliations or beliefs, I would designate such callous acts as horrendous crimes committed by disturbed individuals. It is highly irresponsible to blame guns, the Second Amendment or any political party for the indiscretions of the few. The question isn't why are guns still legal; the question is why are so many people comfortable ending a human life? No, America doesn't have a gun problem...it has a decaying values problem. There are no 'safe zones' from the crosshairs of a corrupted soul!

An overwhelming majority of gun owners are not opposed to basic background checks – those necessary safety precautions that already exist – they rightfully suspect any additional legislation is but a prelude to the radical left's true goal: eradicating the Second Amendment. Despite swearing an oath to defend our Constitutional liberties, a disturbing number of Democrats freely admit they would outlaw firearms in a heartbeat if given the opportunity. My response? Until the day comes you can guarantee every single criminal is stripped of every possible conceivable weapon, that our government will never abuse its power and usurp our freedoms, that you can prove no one uses a rifle to provide food for their family, or you find the necessary votes to amend the Constitution of the United States, don't waste my time! And even if by some miracle those improbable events do converge, my answer is still, "Hell No!" Because human nature will never change – the vain, political and illicit aspirations of mankind – neither will the need for the Second Amendment. My God given and natural born rights, my right to self-preservation, do not require your validation or permission. Besides, your pen would probably just misspell my name. There's no 'asterisk' in freedom.

"It will be found an unjust and unwise jealousy to deprive a man of his natural liberty upon the supposition he may abuse it." ~George Washington

"The right of self-defense is the first law of nature: in most governments it has been the study of rulers to confine this right within the narrowest limits possible. Wherever standing armies are kept up, and the right of the people to keep and bear arms is, under any color or pretext whatsoever, prohibited, liberty, if not already annihilated, is on the brink of destruction." ~St. George Tucker

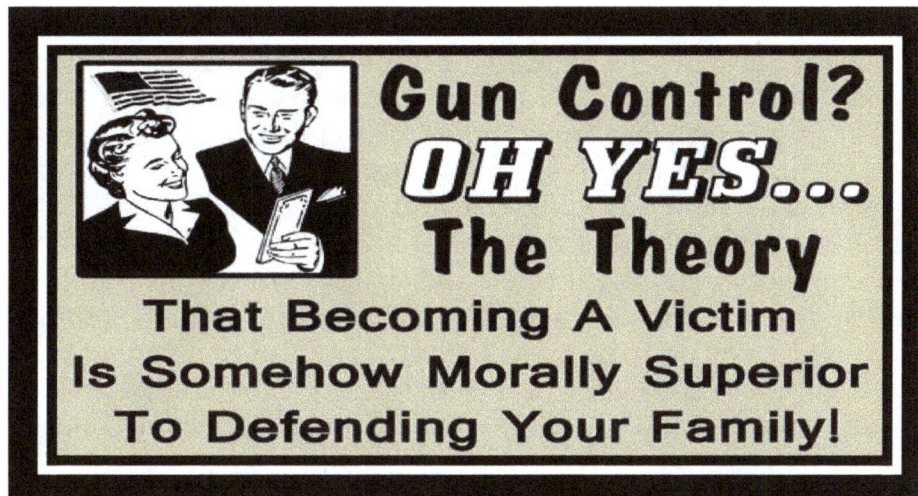

A "Santa Fe" State of Mind

Whether a single child is injured or there are multiple fatalities, school violence is entirely unacceptable. No student should fear for their life or watch their peers die within the halls of our educational institutions. Unfortunately, no matter how much I despise modern America's current mindset – her moral decay, decadent culture and glorified lack of respect for human life – there are no easy answers. Strict gun control is far more of a fallacy, an urban myth, than a proven course of action in a country predicated upon individual liberty and self-defense. Advocating harsh, new restrictions to combat mass shootings is a political ruse, a public disservice announcement, for bureaucrats cannot account for the estimated 300 million privately owned guns in circulation. Although I do accept the need for background checks and age verification, gun confiscation is largely the manifestation of orchestrated opportunism repeated at every conceivable tragedy rather than acknowledging firearms save just as many lives as those universal limitations supposedly protecting them.

Regardless of the prevailing narrative, it's common knowledge criminals, terrorists and unsuspected strangers will always find a means to unleash their hate if they truly so desire. And, as today's shooting clearly confirmed, the guns fired were legally owned by the suspect's father and the 17-year-old boy himself had constructed multiple explosive devices which, thank God, were never detonated. Whether you smuggle and assemble explosive compounds on campus, wield a machete in the parking lot, disperse a toxin in the cafeteria or bring lighter fluid and a match to school, the threat of unforeseen harm will always exist. Therefore, lasting solutions must be built around treating the actual problem, the psychological and behavioral triggers of a human being's conscious decision to kill, not endlessly debating the diabolical attributes of an inanimate object for talk show ratings. Whereas respect for God, the rule of law and our fellow man was once the common thread in nearly every American home, deception, rage and petulance are quickly become the adopted virtues of a nation in distress.

Personal disagreements aside, every demographic in America should be united in our inherent obligation to keep our sons and daughters as safe as possible. While it is true human nature cannot be regulated or entirely prevented, we all must commit to constructive discourse, creative problem solving, instead of tiresome third-party blaming or seeking to score immediate political points after every senseless loss of life. Arming teachers is a promising start, but those individuals must still locate and successfully confront armed intruders before innocents are murdered. New technological advances such as easily-deployable door blockades are affordable and effective, if alerted in time, and impenetrable classroom shelters can repel military-grade machine guns, raging fires and hurricane force winds. Yet, as expected, the cost is daunting or roughly $25,000 per room for each unit required. Then again, if we can afford to send $150 billion to Iranian extremists, it's a matter of priorities. No matter what the final remedy, or how much communities are willing to spend, it's clear a national protocol must be implemented to deter as many future attacks and save as many lives as our collective concern allows.

If security is so paramount at airports and courthouses, why aren't the same precautions not taken at our schools where there is far more potential for mass casualties and "political" statements? No matter where you're from or how peaceful the people, all public schools should be required to implement body and bag scanners by armed, trained personnel, as well as functional cameras monitoring both around the outside perimeter and inside the property. Furthermore, all foot traffic going entering and leaving each building should be limited to one or two access points, with all other exits only being accessible to those fleeing the premises due to an emergency or eminent danger.

For those who decry the momentary inconvenience or the invasion of their teenage privacy, I have a single, comforting affirmation. You're in a public facility, not your home, and if you're physically able to complain about such trivialities then the good news is you're not dead. As for the inevitable cost for such protections, if our government can waste millions on a legal slush fund for political sexual indiscretions or donate billions to terrorist regimes, surely we can find the means to protect our children, our most precious resource, even if that endeavor requires raising local or state sales taxes by a quarter or one-half of a percent; a small price to pay for a clear conscience and an empty grave.

While increased safeguards are self-explanatory and many districts have already taken aggressive measures, the current state of mental health in this country, especially among disgruntled adolescents, is a daunting proposition. What is it that leads so many of our youth to believe, specifically boys, that their high school experiences are an inescapable harbinger for their remaining lives? How does killing others, indiscriminately or not, redeem their unfulfilling lives or assuage their lingering pain? Only in the deluded heart of a lost soul would such a proposition even exist. Individuals are ultimately accountable for their actions, just as spectators can intervene or ignore the forsaken signs of festering depravity.

Identifying and preventing bullying is a powerful tool in our classrooms and the omnipresent playground of social media, but giving kids a sense of identity and self-worth, an ingrained confidence to cope with the inevitable pressures and disappointments of life, is far more valuable. Parents, teachers, friends and neighbors must all become more invested in the mental wellness of our younger generation, their struggles and needs as well as the unknown reality of countless dysfunctional homes, if these horrific atrocities are ever to become the exception rather than the norm. More than ever our communities need role models, not complicit bystanders crucifying the NRA or law-abiding gun owners for the aftermath of their apathy. Unless we as a society are satisfied with shameless Hollywood celebrities contributing to a detached culture of moral disrepair, then perhaps the time has come to once again foster well-adjusted kids who can still discern between the human toll of violence, and the live death toll of a video game.

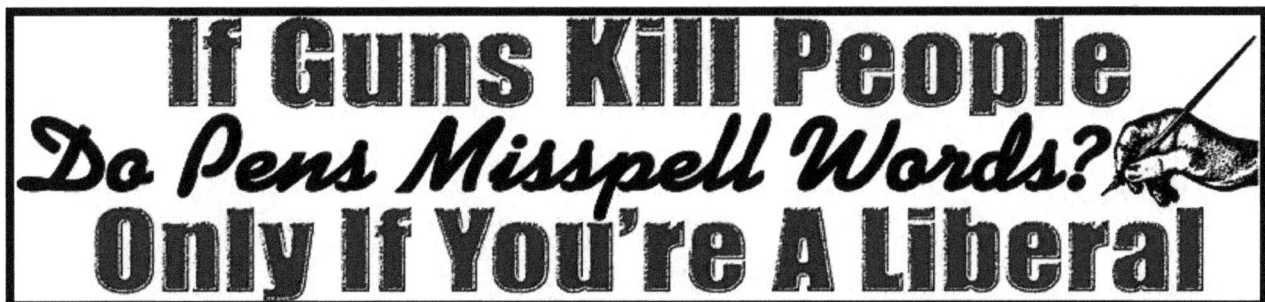

If Guns Kill People Do Pens Misspell Words? Only If You're A Liberal

Children of the Scorn

David Hogg lecturing newly-elected NRA President Oliver North on terrorism and the tyranny of private firearms is the equivalent of Paris Hilton selling General Mattis on the aesthetic benefits of open-toed combat boots. When 15 minutes of parasitic fame somehow bequeaths a smug teenager with a Criminal Justice degree, an honorary PhD in syndicated penis envy, hostile ignorance becomes the most acceptable form of psychological torture. In other words, save the history-revisionist blanks for Chicago's Cook County coroner because unarmed victims don't give speeches for the same reason Communist censors don't give refunds: dead twerps can't tweet!

The Human Cost of Denial

If students truly want to stop mass shootings, they must first begin by protesting their most inescapable threat: themselves. Before Columbine, classrooms and campuses scantily experienced such horrific atrocities. Guns haven't changed...kids, families and America have simply lost their way. Judging by the hostile/perverse content of social media and the detached reality of our celebrity obsessed culture – an erosion of basic decency, the rejection of traditional values and a pedestrian concern for the sanctity of life – it's hard to be a victim of the virtual minefield your very silence, political contempt or contributing behavior exponentially breeds. When more and more of our communities are defined by misery and envy rather than gratitude and pride, youthful discontent will inevitably sow hate's restless seed.

The exploding mental instability of violent crime engulfing this country is not a coincidence, or an aberration, but the gradual convergence of an impulsive, antagonistic, and immoral environment that seeks indulgence over discipline, vengeance over virtue, by pandering to dysfunction, immediate gratification, instead of unearthing and eradicating its toxic roots. Political correctness, student marches and stale narratives won't save our sons and daughters from themselves, let alone the materialistic, instant fame-driven world in which they so willingly reside. The invisible bullet of imminent danger will always exist, whether or not society finally decides to open its eyes before another lost child from another absentee home, failed by education's soulless decay, dies from yet another self-inflicted wound. The greatest "safety" from future, senseless tragedies are not found in prescription drugs or obsessive gun control measures, but the intervening conscience of a young shooter's own unlocked humanity; a lasting commitment morally-bankrupt politicians are rarely willing to make.

When Tantrums Aren't Enough: Protesting the Wet Beds of Unarmed Statistics

Has the NRA ever committed a single murder, let alone planned or applauded one? No, not one? How not ironic. The only ones who have blood on their hands are criminals, the mentally ill and those subversive agents who tirelessly encourage disrespect for the law, America and their fellow man through the increasingly antagonistic, amoral mediums of pop culture, mass media and public education. If standing-up for the necessity of the Second Amendment, the Constitution and Supreme Law of the United States, is now synonymous with murder, what do you call former Senator Joe Biden introducing "Gun Free Zones" which would inevitably leave millions of our children and loved ones defenseless to deranged militants; or better yet, lying and ambivalent bureaucrats seeking a counter-intuitive end for political gain?

Pretending evil does not exist – believing human nature can be cajoled by partisan rhetoric, staged protests or wishful thinking – will not save one soul from its wrath. Such ignorance will merely ensure logic, freedom, dies at the hands of armed propagandists whose real objective is to increase the historically low Democratic turnout during midterms and somehow impeach a President they failed to frame with their own treasonous plot. The same progressive zealots who conjured the fictitious term "assault weapons" to recruit a gullible public on the need for extensive gun control, despite the fact common hunting rifles like the Ruger-Mini have the same magazine capacity as an AR-15, want you to believe drugs, drunk drivers, medical malpractice and poor diets don't kill exponentially more Americans in spite of widespread government regulation and individual self-awareness. Or if I may, is liberal academia still suggesting "throwing rocks" at armed campus intruders or "peeing" on rapists as viable solutions? Unless you truly believe gun abolitionists have your family's best interests at heart, only to aid and rationalize the terrorist regime of Iran's quest for nuclear armaments, pay no mind to the tactically trained and fully armed detail of Hillary Clinton, Bernie Sanders and Barack Obama. Clearly, not all lives matter.

In other words, never mind the FBI and Florida law enforcement egregiously failed their job and the American people by ignoring over 39 warnings of a mentally disturbed individual planning mass murder. The NRA, a predisposed target of radical leftists for decades, must be blamed and brought before mob justice so rabid critics can politicize another tragedy to demonize the President while a handful of profane Parkland teenagers tour the liberal news circuit, pose for magazine covers, hire publicity agents and are flown to a national rally that never once condemned the actual criminal. Agendas? Never! Do you actually believe selfie-obsessed students organized nationwide school walkouts as "unsuspecting" principals and educators alike eagerly joined the rehearsed chorus; even punishing those independent voices who abstained or disagreed in lieu of halting unruly children hijacking our tax-payer funded institutions for an obvious political stunt? And to think superintendents now regularly obsess over the tyranny of patriotic t-shirts or excessive snow days. When facts no longer matter, the historical dangers of a disarmed, coerced and powerless populace disavowed by the executioner of free thought, the only trigger being pulled is that of "justifiable" fascism.

If 'Enough is Enough', as socially conscious millennials love to proclaim, why is modern America so willing to embrace violent movies, video games and the absurdly perverse nature of social media? If 'Enough is Enough', why is the traditional family paradigm being derided as outdated and misogynistic – only for open marriages, transgendered or same-sex parents to be celebrated as enlightened and courageous – as dysfunctional and single-parent households continue to proliferate? If 'Enough is Enough', why are kids, celebrities and politicians mired in a clear culture of disrespect, bullying and entitlement instead of embodying temperance, civility and personal culpability? If 'Enough is Enough', why is it OK for the free press to distort and selectively report the news, recklessly incite discord and prevent the public from making informed decisions, by knowingly pushing a hopelessly biased and often vindictive narrative? And if enough is truly enough, I'm sick and tired of glorified hypocrites slandering, silencing and physically threatening anyone who dares disagrees with or denounces their juvenile, belligerent behavior. Without decorum, a mutual respect for all people and viewpoints, democracy cannot endure.

Rather than educating our youth to respect and properly use firearms, restoring basic values, teaching coping skills and instilling a universal love of life and liberty, political activists are breeding hatred, intolerance, through the intentional misinformation of mass hysteria. Then again, when eroding gun rights is a prerequisite of your totalitarian aspirations, distraction is always key. While the NRA and an overwhelming majority of gun owners support thorough background checks and universal registration, preventing violent felons and the mentally ill from purchasing weapons, no such level of outrage or demanded accountability has been bestowed upon grown adults mobilizing a rebellious student populace to conceal the fact parents, politicians, school administrators and a politicized intelligence community are the greatest contributing forces to enabling mass shootings. After all, if some of strictest gun control measures in America failed to deter the over 3,000 shootings and 650 homicides last year in Chicago alone, perhaps the secular humanists of urban decay should begin by disarming hardened criminals before asking law-abiding citizens to apologize for believing in the "offensive" notion of self-preservation.

> **Thomas Sowell**
> @ThomasSowell
>
> "Activism is a way for useless people to feel important, even if the consequences of their activism are counterproductive for those they claim to be helping and damaging to the fabric of society as a whole."

The moment playing the National Anthem or reaffirming there are only two biological genders is far more of a concern than unearthing the contemporary roots of gun violence, is the moment you realize your life is the expendable garnish of conspiring globalists and your Constitutional rights the main course. The greatest trigger of hostility, death and tyranny resides not in the mindless finality of an inanimate object, the preferred weapon of choice, but in a regressive culture's refusal to accept responsibility for its own unresolved failings. And that includes exposing the deceptive ploys of parading opportunists poisoning the founding creed of a once vigilant, proud and industrious society solely to sow the seeds of a distinctly anti-American, statist agenda: complete subjugation to the moral degradation and economic disrepair of absolute progressive rule.

The Weapon of Choice: Death

The minute we learned the Orlando nightclub attack was Islamic terrorism, the left's gun control narrative self-imploded. In fact, it was inexorably insulting. After all, "a gun" just doesn't walk in and slaughter over 50 human beings without a trigger finger, a motive and any number of contributing factors. If we're searching for actual answers, the 9/11 hijackers were Muslim, the Fort Hood gunman was Muslim, the Boston bombers were Muslim, the Chattanooga gunman was Muslim, the Paris assailants were Muslim, and the San Bernardino shooters were Muslim. Sorry, Mr. President, but I believe we have a Muslim problem. Can we stop their incessant aggression; or at the very least halt the reckless flow of thousands of unvetted refugees? Of course not, because you empower, empathize and recognize their cause as your own: to dismantle traditional America by any means necessary. Much like yourself, Mr. President, Islam is hate and hate breeds violence against any person or beacon of liberty that chooses tolerance, individuality, over forced subjugation. You're the living embodiment of why the Second Amendment was created in the first place: to ensure our God-given right to defend ourselves against all forms of tyranny, both foreign and domestic.

Blaming guns for mass murders is like accusing cars of kidnapping drunk drivers. Until we somehow remember to respect our neighbor and value life, teach our children morals rather than brainwash them with soulless pop culture, the weapon of choice is moot. Better yet, it's garnish for the logically impaired. Criminals rarely follow gun laws and will always find a way to unleash their hate. 9/11 is case in point...a terrorist plot carried out with nothing more than box cutters. When mass death is the objective you could drive a semi through a parade or public gathering and instantly kill hundreds without blinking an eye. Critics refuse to invoke morality, let alone God, because they'd rather exploit death for political gain, fulfilling a predisposed campaign agenda, than address the actual source of the problem: the rapid decay of our most basic societal norms and a glaring lack of respect for our fellow man.

I'm not foolishly claiming guns are the solution to all our problems, not by any means, but they're a necessary liberty and viable defense in a world rife with crime, danger and tyranny...or better yet, human nature. Ultimately, these inanimate objects are only as "evil" as the souls pointing them. Accountability, America's founding Judeo-Christian values aren't revolutionary ideals; they're abandoned ones in the name of "progress". If Christians are evil bigots for merely opposing gay marriage or special privileges for "transgenders", what's it called when the fastest growing ideology preaches death to all homosexuals for merely existing? Perhaps if some politicians didn't constantly preach class, race, and religious warfare, the world would be a better and safer place. How many more have to die before humanity accepts the truth? How long before Islam is held accountable and the civilized world, including our abetting President, demands the "religion of peace" reforms its most hateful tenets and violent practices? The American people are tired of waiting for the last vestiges of common sense to pull the trigger of logic.

"I would like to see every woman know how to handle firearms as naturally as they know how to handle babies." *~Annie Oakley*

For Your Entertainment

As America mourns the horrific aftermath of 26 murdered in cold blood and over 20 seriously injured – in some cases entire families wiped out while gathering in peaceful worship – little is more insulting to their memories and grieving loved ones than eager opportunists once again attempting to blame such calculated carnage on an inanimate object. If guilt is no longer reserved for the actual lawbreaker, a deranged family member and reported Antifa sympathizing atheist seeking mass death to fulfill a personal vendetta, I condemn the systemic moral degradation of our most basic societal values in film, music, video games and television; those mediums which not only desensitize millions of impressionable minds to the actual human toll of violence, but glorify bloodshed, validate vengeance, fantasize about presidential assassinations and mock Christianity as a legitimate and lucrative form of entertainment. And yet how many domestic mass shootings, plotted and carried out by unsuspecting individuals devoid of known criminal enterprises, occurred 50 or even 25 years ago?

The United States is 3rd in murders throughout the world.

If you remove
#1- Chicago
#2- Detroit
#3-Washington DC
#4-St Louis
#5-New Orleans

the United States is then 189th out of 193 countries in the entire world.

PS–
All 5x Cities have STRICT Gun Control Laws

Today's homicidal mentality is a disturbing reminder mass murders skyrocketed under Barack Obama by nearly 300% or roughly a number equal to all mass shootings between 1981 and 2009. But yes, by all means, let's blame a tool of ignorance and pray the perpetrator is a white Republican to fulfill the left's unending goal of eradicating the historical necessity of the Second Amendment in lieu of addressing the hostile aftermath of political agitators inciting class, race, gender and religious warfare in nearly every crevice of America solely to achieve a morally bankrupt end; the secular supremacy of progressivism in all phases of our daily lives. When the unsung actions of everyday role models are buried beneath the deafening applause for the false idols of pop culture, our children blinded by the almighty glare and avarice of Hollywood's golden calf, real heroes who transform countless lives for the better are incessantly lectured by celebrity hedonists, Red Carpet narcissists and aspiring political arsonists.

Unless a gun or any weapon of choice is not equally capable of saving a life and foiling an indeterminate number of crimes – including the armed citizen who courageously stopped Devin Patrick Kelley – what is the intangible difference between the two fates? There is no greater instrument of death than that of ideology, indoctrinated and insatiable hate: albeit Islam, radicalized academia or armed fascist activism. Pretending evil does not exist will no more save us from its wrath than legislation can prevent the infinite triggers of human nature. Changing this insidious course of extreme violence can only be achieved in our homes, classrooms and our eroding community standards of acceptable behavior. Instead of treating the victims of gun violence as political pawns used at the most opportune moments, drowning the underlying causes of such soulless brutality with those fake tears shed by media chameleons for public consumption, let us renew our societal obligation to teach our sons and daughters the value of human life – respecting the law, America, our elders and fellow man – rather than asking the contemporary price of admission to dehumanizing and ending one.

Just a friendly reminder

*Adolf Hitler confiscated guns before killing over **13 million people.**

*Joseph Stalin confiscated guns before killing over **20 million people.**

*Mao Zedong confiscated guns before killing over **45 million people.**

*Pol Pot confiscated guns before killing over **2 million people.**

Julian Assange

THE FREE THOUGHT PROJECT

OFFENSIVE

FLAGS *of our* FATHERS

THE WAR TO INDICT AMERICAN HISTORY

The Scorpion and The Frog

For those who believe removing monuments has nothing to do with whitewashing history along partisan or racial lines, allow me an antiquated moment of indulgence. Although institutionalized remnants of Hitler and his infamous Third Reich were rightfully removed across Deutschland, there are countless young Germans today who know of his reign but are completely oblivious to the numerous atrocities committed by Nazi Germany. Many of their native citizens still do not believe concentration camps existed or that 6 million Jews were even exterminated as part of the Final Solution. Due to national embarrassment and/or fear of further retribution, these inconvenient truths were commonly omitted from their classrooms and history books; which, ironically, parallel the attempt by some U.S. educators and historians to conceal the Democratic party's racist roots, insistence upon slavery, legacy of obstructing civil rights and indoctrination of Marxist/Islamic beliefs.

Until progressives accept that light and darkness innately exists in us all, for only our choices ultimately delineate our past from our future, their refusal to condemn their party's tainted symbol and sordid history should be far more offensive than any weathered memorial that doesn't reduce a man's contributions to whether or not he associated with human servitude. Otherwise, please explain how an intolerant ideology founded by a glorified pedophile, misogynist, murder and thief has nearly two billion ardent followers today without the civilized world demanding a single reformation of its most barbaric practices and beliefs? Rather, now the executioners of American history are demanding Western xenophobes assist the unapologetic immigrants of Islam's destructive creed.

If removing Confederate artifacts has nothing to do with sanitizing history or discrediting our heritage – subverting our founding values by demanding concessions through incited racial conflict – please explain how the besieged memories of George Washington, Thomas Jefferson or Abraham Lincoln are suddenly the American equivalent of Adolf Hitler or even Vladimir Lenin: a ruthless communist dictator guilty of genocide against his own people who Seattle currently honors with no less than 7 statues. And yet in this epicenter of progressive thought and social justice, not one, angry, offended soul has defaced them or demanded their removal? Although the Egyptian pyramids are universally revered as one of the seven wonders of the world, a monumental achievement of our ancient ancestors, I can find no condemnation by world leaders or organized protests over the fact they required prolonged slave labor, the forced conscription of peasants, and mass death. Do their lives or rights not matter or is history essentially a platform from which to evolve, dissect and understand, not posthumously adjudicate for political gain in order to justify mob violence hundreds of years after such injustices occurred?

Does the fact New York City harbored more slaves than any other city (except Charleston) and was founded by Dutch slave traders warrant its dissolution; a thriving metropolis that now resides over a notorious "Negro Cemetery" because black slaves weren't deemed worthy of being laid to rest with Christian whites? No, not even one toppled statue or public accusation of White Supremacy? Hmm, how not ironic. As expected, not one of liberal New York's historical sites or erected personages of pride was vandalized to resurrect the forsaken or seek recompense if only for posterity's sake.

Without perspective and unbiased reflection, it's disturbing how quickly basic decorum morphs into AntiFa militants impersonating ISIS henchman by cursing free speech, assaulting innocent bystanders and destroying anything that contradicts or poses a threat to their hateful agenda. As "We the People" now wander aimlessly in this weaponized cloud of orchestrated deception, how many campaign issues that were so crucial to voters and Congressional candidates in November have resulted in meaningful discourse and earnest cooperation during past sixth months? The same public servants, citizens, elected to fulfill their solemn duty of working towards solving America's most pressing issues in a civil environment, are now fully content spending every waking moment spreading absurd accusations, trading juvenile aspersions and waging petty vendettas that merely deepen partisan distrust, impede lasting progress and allow our government to toil in a perpetual state of dysfunction and undeterred corruption.

When politicians refuse to acknowledge the most glaring hypocrisies and toxic ploys used to suffocate common sense and poison unity, everything America has fought to overcome is surrendered to her salivating enemies as the social decoys of sexism, racism and inanimate objects are religiously blamed to justify the aftermath of false allegation. In a nation predicated upon helping the oppressed escape the unjust whims of tyranny, who needs the annoyance of anecdotal history when pointing the sanctimonious finger of mass hysteria is sufficient enough for triggering cultural euthanasia.

"Let us not seek the Republican answer or the Democratic answer, but the right answer. Let us not seek to fix the blame for the past. Let us accept our own responsibility for the future."

-John F. Kennedy

A Human Trademark

When I watch a staged mockery of kneeling U.S. veterans weeping at the feet of modern tribal leaders, basically begging for forgiveness amidst a media circus of cultivated resentment for actions they did not commit, witness or entirely understand, it is nothing short of disgraceful. Such shameless propaganda validating Hollywood stereotypes merely inflames lingering tensions by seeking the blessing of those who willingly portray themselves as the living remnants of unprovoked American aggression – i.e., the helpless and unsuspecting victims of Anglo-Saxon brutality – but never as the descendants of ruthless predators who routinely embodied animosity and death to conquer any vulnerable target or perceived enemy without fear or reservation.

As someone who has studied Native American history, the Trail of Tears and the legacies of Pontiac, Tecumseh, Sitting Bull and Chief Joseph, I take great umbrage with pundits who claim America was nothing more than a bloodthirsty invader who can never atone for its past transgressions. I make no excuses for our government's measured betrayals or those rogue generals who sought glory and fame through the crosshairs of hate. Such grotesque violations were wrong and unequivocally beneath our nation's founding charter. However, if we're merely being objective observers, and not coerced apologists, Native Americans were hardly the benevolent and peaceful "victims" of European imperialism as portrayed by cinema and liberal academia. Vicious tribes like the Apache, Comanche, Cheyenne and Lakota butchered each other in droves – attacked settlements, federal outposts and mere common transients out of spite – and even kept defeated enemies as trophy slaves; routinely engaging in human trafficking with other tribes or French, Dutch and English traders.

It is also of little coincidence that nearly all Indians were highly adept in the art of human suffering. From the infamous practice of scalping men, women, and children – which colonialists later adopted as proof of successful kills – to removing the organs of captured adversaries while they were still alive, the sheer animosity and distrust of competing civilizations, let alone neighbors, merely fed the incessant brutality of the day. If you can imagine being buried up to your chin in the desert or left to rot beneath the glaring sun as a sacrificial snack for ants, scorpions, or snakes, "injustice" is hardly a historically exclusive term. It's a human trademark.

The rise of the American Indian population was eerily similar to colonial expansion in that they displaced other supposed "invaders", earlier nomadic cultures, by "infringing" upon their lands and/or using brute force to establish supremacy. In other words, those more adept at killing and conquering their enemy survived for sovereignty was only as relevant as the strength of your spear or the aim of your arrow. And unlike the countless victims of Indian hostilities, which are too often disregarded by history revisionists, many of these tribes received monetary compensation, land grants, and tax abatements...which modern day descendants now use for commercial ventures such as casinos and mining ventures, or via subsidized college tuition. If equality demands equal treatment and unconditional respect, why aren't all victims viewed or paid the same? To say any sect of humanity owns the political rights to human suffering in a world defined by universal hostility is to claim one form of terminal cancer is far more tragic than another. Educating all subsequent generations and foreign creeds to unite against such senseless brutality, however, is far more beneficial to the moral evolution and survival of mankind than any misguided attempt at financial recompense.

Contrary to misconception, the so-called derogatory term "Red Skin" was first adopted by Indian delegations as a term of endearment and solidarity when meeting with then President James Madison, rather than a callous epithet created solely to belittle an entire race. Like our newfound Republic, they sought strength in numbers to survive an inevitable battle of attrition. Regardless of how we judge one another through the spectrum of history, I will always revere Native Americans as fiercely independent, skilled survivalists who instinctively found a symbiotic relationship with nature. Although they were deeply spiritual and highly perceptive, their way of life inevitably succumbed, like so many others before them, to an even greater force of nature: technology, or more succinctly, the mind of man. While both groups adopted and assimilated advantageous aspects of each other's culture over the centuries - horticulture, horses, medicinal applications, tactical weaponry - the supremacy of any civilization has always resided in its capacity for war.

Unlike those European countries that evolved from perpetual warfare, American Indians simply lacked the numbers and technological advancement necessary to defeat a more powerful and versatile foe. And if they by some chance repelled the rapid proliferation of Western society, who knows how different the world would be today in the extensive wake of America's absence, economic prowess, military might, transcendent discoveries and immutable ideals. Otherwise, in a parallel universe of political correctness and mandatory guilt transference, the rightfully proud society of surviving Native Americans could very well be asked to apologize to the victimized descendants of European colonialists for being the historically superior nation or for instinctively guarding their borders to preserve their country, their culture and their very lives. In other words, placing an asterisk on an epitaph marking historical injustice is as pointless as asking your newborn baby permission to forgive you for being born a white male who must now atone for his genetically inherited sins. We all possess an inherent right to forge a life free from the burden of assumed obligation and the wrongful allocation of past strife.

Last Man Standing

Contrary to contemporary paranoia, I do not have a problem with nationalism – a fierce respect and undying love for one's country, its welfare and survival – as long such reverence is not based upon the violent oppression or senseless discrimination of any sect of society. Racial supremacy, however, is a pointless, naive and entirely self-destructive endeavor. Even if one's claim of racial superiority was rooted in incontrovertible fact, it's of little relevance in a country as diverse as America, let alone one predicated upon individual liberty and tolerance. Refusing to "coexist" is as much of an attack on our founding values as coercing free will into mass conformity. Furthermore, attempting to silence or limit free speech, the most fundamental manifestation of our natural born rights and the cognitive domain of sentient beings, merely justifies the very form of tyranny censorship inevitably invites.

The greatest contention I have with the chaos in Charlottesville or anywhere else for that matter, besides the grotesque display of inhumanity and needless loss of life, is that professional political agitators like Antifa and BLM solicited protesters, distributed detailed "playbooks" and transported hundreds of militants into Virginia with the explicit purpose of ensuring confrontation and exacting bloodshed. These radical organizations have repeatedly called for the death of police, even proclaimed a need for white genocide, with little to no outrage from the mainstream media or our elected representatives. Since when did unabashed bigotry and orchestrated anarchy not become worthy of being declared hate crimes, or dare I say recognized terror threats, in this hyper-sensitive age of political correctness and publicized mass murder?

Being the KKK has been designated a hate group for over half a century, and rightfully so, shouldn't the Black Panthers receive similar treatment for their vile rhetoric and cultivated animosity towards millions of white Americans, the very political party that ended slavery and our law enforcement community? Unlike Barack Obama who immediately exonerated and racially exploited Trayvon Martin, Michael Brown and Freddie Gray, triggering riots and a national wave of police assassinations, the President has made no such malicious assumptions or "call to arms" to fulfill a bitter, divisive agenda. He simply denounced the horrific hostility unfolding on national TV and made a renewed plea for mutual respect among fellow Americans; regardless of our skin color, political beliefs or inevitable differences.

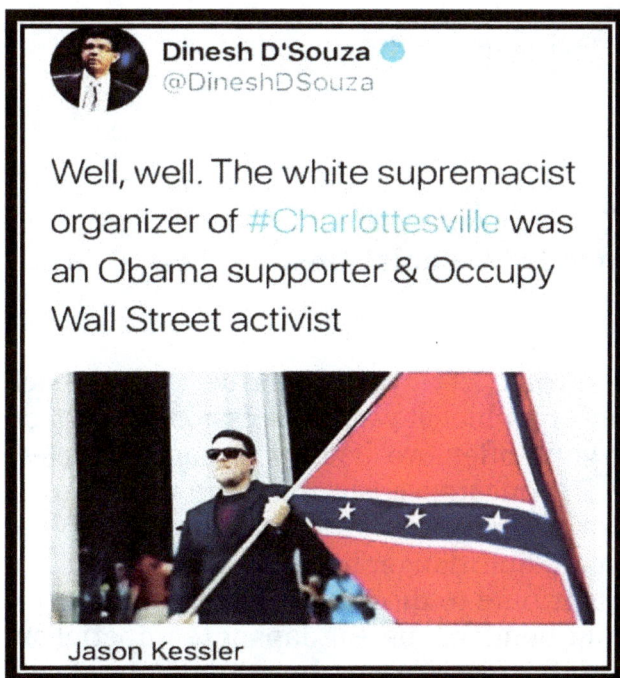

Dinesh D'Souza
@DineshDSouza

Well, well. The white supremacist organizer of #Charlottesville was an Obama supporter & Occupy Wall Street activist

Jason Kessler

This entire political melodrama reeks of an orchestrated ruse for two reasons. First, the "Unite the Right" march organizer, Jason Kessler, was a known Occupy Wall Street participant and a vocal Obama supporter who held many traditionally liberal views: such as, but not limited to, gun control, abortion rights and socialist healthcare. He is no more a voice for right-minded Americans than I am for Antifa. Second, no self-respecting conservative, libertarian, Independent or traditional Republican would align themselves with the KKK, white supremacists, knowing how tirelessly the media has worked to paint Donald Trump as a lifelong racist and Nazi sympathizer since the inception of his campaign. While I do not deny hate groups have held public events for decades, it's obvious this specific gathering was targeted and hijacked by prodding leftists with the explicit intent of instigating violence and manufacturing national outrage to further undermine the President's endlessly besieged credibility. Why else would local police from a known Democratic state stand down in the face of eminent hostility, anarchy and potential loss of life? If it smells like fire but looks like arson, the most plausible explanation typically resides in the spark of false accusation emanating from the sponsored bullhorn of those critics who unapologetically wish for your death.

Much of the discord currently enveloping America is a choreographed fire sale to give the illusion the country, if not the world, is coming apart because of one man's ill-conceived policies and contemptible nature; or in layman's terms, his resolute rejection of the corrupt, prejudiced and failed status quo. Despite his well-documented past of social philanthropy, accolades and praise received from the same civil rights leaders now invoking racism, it's obvious progressives are far more concerned with linking Donald Trump to white supremacy – yet another shameless ploy to disparage his name and discredit his presidency through false association – than fostering amity by addressing the true source of these avoidable hostilities: liberal fascism.

When societal apathy, clear political favoritism, allows criminal malevolence to fester and operate with reckless impunity, tragic events like Charlottesville are hardly aberrations...they are the acceptable aftermath of pardoned hypocrisy. Freedom of speech only becomes a buried anecdote when political charlatans preaching "unity and social justice" implore their followers to belligerently "get in the face" of anyone who disagrees with their partisan aspirations. As repugnant as some views are, our response to those ideas can be equally appalling if not even more obscene than the mere exchange of words. When the battle of ideas recuses civility and the merits of one's convictions for fisticuffs and homicidal threats, ignorance is always the last man standing.

Home is Where My Flag Resides

Dear College Administrators, Homeowner Associations, & Proud Anti-American Apologists....

How is the American flag a tangible threat to anyone, let anyone offensive and a breach of public decorum when it wavers in the republic for which it was commissioned? Instead of veterans and everyday citizens tolerating your offensive ignorance and shameless hypocrisy, I suggest that you somehow find it in your nonsensical wisdom to recognize Islam – those responsible for the bloodiest terrorist attacks on American soil and despised for mass human atrocities abroad – as the most credible danger to our homeland and that of all humanity. The American flag, an indelible tribute to those who fought and died for our freedom – whose colors bled to end human bondage, defeat Japanese imperialism and liberate Europe from the fascist grip of Nazi Germany – is a threat to no one except to subversive militants who stand in direct contrast to our founding ideals and hallowed way of life. Perhaps the time has come to declare yourselves as domestic terrorists, enemies of a free and civilized state of mind, who are irrevocably hostile towards any notion of patriotism, gratitude, or historical precedent. The only actual crime committed here is by the likes of you; those intolerant bigots so hopelessly lost and twisted by a myopic predisposition that their radical factions have been reduced to attacking, childishly burning, and attempting to ban an internationally recognized symbol of liberty rather than standing up for the universal hope it inherently espouses! On behalf of the American people, the forsaken heroes who bravely toiled and sacrificed their lives so you may freely spew your vile hate...good day and good riddance! Home is where my flag resides and Old Glory shall forever wave in the corridors & courtyards of God's undying grace.

The Roof is on Fire

Amid his racist and disturbing diatribe, Dylann Roof admitted he hated the American flag and patriotism. Hmm, such blind rage rings eerily similar to that of the radical left – the progressive narrative inciting a fervor of anti-Americanism, paranoia and moral depravity – than those conservatives who simply want to return government to its prescribed Constitutional limits. After all, it was the supremacist creed of the Democratic Party that forged the KKK as their terrorist wing to keep blacks from voting; only now to engineer their dependency, blackmail their voting base, fuel their historic discontent, and ignite the inflammatory concept of 'White Privilege'. Regardless, nine innocent people are dead while our own President and his media puppets continue to accept no accountability for using misinformation and selective reporting to incessantly divide the people into warring factions: rich vs poor, business vs. labor, white vs black, illegal immigrants vs. "racists", Christian vs. Muslim, cops vs. citizens, gay vs. straight, and women vs. men. And yet we're the ones labeled as hateful bigots who are incompatible with "change"? Just don't act surprised when you put every conceivable segment of the American populace at each other's' throats only to seem completely baffled when such horrific tragedies occur. It insults our intelligence and merely guarantees further discord and senseless bloodshed. How else can you possibly explain blaming inanimate objects, guns and the Confederate Flag, for your callous disregard and orchestrated discord? More than ever America needs a strong dose of unity, leadership, and self-respect; more than ever America needs God.

The Offensive Flag of Truth

Calling for the removal of the Confederate Flag from South Carolina's Capitol in the wake of a national tragedy, the assigned symbol of one man's hate and paranoia, is ironically both defensible and predictably shortsighted. What rabid activists conveniently forget is that the Confederate Flag – which still wavers at the behest of state law – was never derived as a proud beacon of slavery; after all, even at the height of the Antebellum period less than 2% of all Americans owned slaves. Slavery was a means to an end, an economic mechanism utilized to compete with foreign competitors and northern industrialization. And let's not forget that slavery, an abomination in any age or form, was a product of cultural relativism that stretched from the heart of Africa – the custom bartering practices of African tribes – to the known fact Thomas Jefferson procured them for his vast estate. Luckily the Constitution, the single greatest document ever conceived in our nation's history, and not the flawed cultural norms of the times, provided the blueprint to overcome society's most daunting challenges and glaring injustices.

The Confederate or Rebel Flag so widely commercialized today, that which replaced the original "Stars and Bars" of the Confederacy in 1863, was merely the battle flag of the Northern Virginia Army under General Lee. It later became the official embodiment of state sovereignty and a charter for self-rule in the face of excessive and intrusive federal power; a struggle that continues today in the form of growing statism and unapologetic unilateralism under Barack Obama. If the truth be known, the "Dixie Flag" was symbolic of a revered way of life, the fierce independent spirit of southern pride still loyal to our founding creed of limited government, rather than the sole product of those racist attitudes prevalent throughout the world in the 19th century. And how ironic is it no one is asking the Dutch, the English, Portugal or Spain, nations who streamlined slave trading to the New World, to surrender their recognized colors of civility? Regardless, because the Confederate flag is naturally synonymous with the sordid legacy of slavery and suffering, a sizable segment of America is opposed to its public display. Yes, that's common sense and to be expected. However, if we're going to be historically accurate in this politically correct centrifuge of adjudicating justice, shouldn't America give equal credence and outrage to those symbols, leaders and organizations that bear equally, if not more horrific, legacies?

If I'm not mistaken, the Democratic Party forged the KKK as the terrorist arm of their party to keep blacks from voting and opposed nearly every civil rights reform from the Emancipation Proclamation to the Civil Rights Act of 1964. If Dylann Roof is guilty of being an unapologetic racist, the twisted disciple of the KKK, Democrats are undoubtedly his founding father. The black flag of ISIS, an internationally despised symbol of religious intolerance and hatred – guilty of denying women basic civil rights, killing gays for merely existing, and beheading nonbelievers at will – has been spotted in Muslim communities across America and its representatives have even been invited to college campuses; the supposed safe harbors of enlightenment for our youth. Does embracing such hatred not enable terrorism, degrade our societal ideals and incite more death? The faces of Che Guevara, Vladimir Lenin and Karl Marx, infamous Communists and/or known mass murderers, have become a fashion statement of leftist activism and the preferred décor of liberals and educators nationwide; yes, even splashed on the walls of the election headquarters of the reigning President of the United States. If I may so boldly ask, where is the outrage; the acute awareness and engrained sensitivity for mass injustice?

If people want to blame a flag that has flown for 150 years for the misguided actions of a deranged individual driven by hate and psychotropic drugs, so be it. There is both tangible guilt and cultured misconception. But know this; taking down a colored piece of nylon will not stop similar, future tragedies nor will it assuage this culture war of orchestrated division and disdain progressives are waging to achieve their political goals. It is but a convenient scapegoat camouflaging America's true ills and moral decay. No, I'm not absolving the South for past misgivings, just putting them into perspective. There are millions of decent, compassionate, law-abiding Southerners who aren't racist or murderers, who proudly bear the colors of the Confederate Flag to honor their ancestors, and who also unconditionally weep for those nine men and women viciously gunned down in a South Carolina church. If the enduring struggle of racism and mass violence can be pinpointed to the existence of an inanimate object and not the rogue acts of disturbed individuals, then we should rejoice in the naïve delusion that wiping the enduring images of Islamic fanaticism and Communist oppression off the face of the earth will eradicate their destructive creeds. Or is their survival simply a matter of historical context and personal choice? Well that depends on whether or not you're the Presidential disciple of radical Marxists and Muslim sympathizers living in a land predicated upon liberty. To each his own beneath the offensive flag of truth

A Hitchhiker's Guide to Hypocrisy

As we sit in the midst of this progressive purge of our heritage, judging every instance of historical indiscretion beneath the microscope of political correctness, perhaps the most relevant question has yet to be asked: what would our forefathers think of America today?

Yes, what would the architects of our liberties, values and government think about abortion, gay marriage, transgendered parents, internet pornography, strip clubs, drug abuse, urban poverty and violence, communism, media collusion, Hollywood, pop culture, video games, public education, petulant youth, absentee parents, modern feminism, Barack Obama, Hillary Clinton, Benghazi, disparagement of military personnel, public surveillance, censorship, affirmative action, race riots, government dependency, illegal immigration, Amnesty, flag burning, Islam, 9/11, Sharia Law, the IRS, Obamacare, fast tracking legislation, voter ID, the national debt, cultivated hate for police, vulgar speech, racy attire, lack of basic decorum, and the fact a majority of Americans know more about their iPhone and the Kardashians than the most intimate details of American History, the Bible and the Bill of Rights? And yet offended activists have the audacity to claim the moral high ground?

Some of our founders' opinions on these subjects we already know; some we never will. Either way, I'm sure their ethical scrutiny of the country they risked their lives for – the future of their families – to forge the last bastion of hope and liberty, would be far more damning and scathing of our soulless culture than any misgivings they may personally harbor. This Constitutional republic has fallen so far off their timeless blueprint for a free, moral and vibrant society that our GPS is asking for directions to the last sentient being. If the old adage "let he who is without sin cast the first stone" rings true, "We the Politically Correct" are going to have to lift a whole damn mountain to atone for the cultural rot destroying the very foundation of Western Civilization.

History was never intended to cater to anyone's revisionist senses when the values of its modern-day detractors cannot distinguish between a Christian baker and ISIS, abortion rights and animal rights; our journey is but a road map from which to learn and grow through introspection and keen application. Human bondage was wrong; our faith overcame it. Denying women suffrage was myopic; the Constitution restored it. America doesn't need to apologize for an imperfect past – posthumously dispense guilt to the innocent – let alone blame an artifact, its descendants, for the misguided actions of any individual or rogue group living today. It needs to reclaim its future by holding everyone accountable for turning a once proud and transcendent nation into a dysfunctional, morally depraved minefield of excuses, ineptitude, and shameless opportunism. As you embark down the fiery road of restitution and victimization, Mr. President, I feel obligated to warn you objects in the mirror of antiquity appear more learned, wise, honorable and respected because the context of their legacy, not your empty rhetoric, fills the sails of humanity.

Without the vision, integrity and sacrifice of their "White Privilege" spawning the proliferation of the most affluent, powerful and revered nation on earth in less than a mere two centuries – all while Africa continues to toil in poverty, tribal slavery, disease and death beneath the nose of your excused apathy – you wouldn't have a people to divide and a country to destroy. Perspective, not progressivism, is the key to unlocking real progress and lasting unity.

When Blood Matters

During the Battle of New Orleans in 1815, roughly 4,500 ill-equipped southerners repelled a sizable fleet of the Royal Navy and 11,000 British soldiers to preserve our fledgling republic. Although the port and city of New Orleans was feared lost before hostilities even began, only 55 of Andrew Jackson's men lost their lives during the near three-week siege. The American force was largely composed of militia from Tennessee, Mississippi, Kentucky and Louisiana, as well as local pirates, Choctaw Indians and free blacks. In the spirit of political correctness, perhaps the time has come to honor Al Sharpton, Barack Obama and the liberal media by removing all notable monuments and commercial memorabilia commemorating this historic victory in order to accommodate the "Black Lives Matter" campaign of concerned citizens. Furthermore, the English Empire has expressed great interest in accepting the Old South as fair compensation to resolve this revisionist debt. Ironically, a memorial has yet to be erected to memorialize the over 7,000 victims of black-on-black homicides each year. There is no blueprint in place, or notable public outrage by civil rights leaders, to competently address or prevent such future tragedies from happening. Angry souls make eager voters and racial harmony denies political parasites a host.

Truth, Fame and the American Flag

Disregard those excuses claiming Donald Trump's "divisive" rhetoric is to blame for all the conflict in America and turmoil in the sports world. This nonsense has been escalating since 2008 and he is one of the few high-profile names who actually had the courage to expose their duplicity without mincing words. The truth is, despite all the partisan finger pointing and anthem publicity stunts, the President was embraced as a positive force of change by Democrats, Republicans, racial activists and even liberal Hollywood for over 30 years. He was a welcomed guest at their private soirees, regularly hosted celebrities/dignitaries at his hotels and resorts, won awards for his social philanthropy, was applauded for his random acts of kindness, appeared on nearly every syndicated talk show, garnered fans from all segments of society and routinely interacted with many of his most vocal critics from today on a first name basis. To suddenly proclaim he is the scourge of humanity is to condemn his newfound adversaries by their willing association and unmistakable admiration.

It wasn't until Trump announced his candidacy, or more profoundly when he won the presidency, that Democratic operatives and the media establishment viciously conspired to paint him as a racist, radical xenophobe who kicks puppies on Christmas and rapes women for entertainment. Before the man sought political office, he was never condemned as a white supremacist, let alone called a bigot or once questioned by police regarding a single, alleged sexual assault. These shameless tactics were nothing more than a desperate attempt to slander his name and cripple public support for the extensive change his populist reforms would inevitably bring.

Likewise, this entire National Anthem fiasco, which began long before his campaign ever ensued, simply gave those critics who already hated him and America to begin with but another platform to claim injustice beneath the public spectacle of "racism". Donald Trump is not responsible for the disproportionate amount of crime in urban America, the number of single parent households, the prevalence of drug abuse, a protected foreign workforce or a growing lack of respect for the law, America and our fellow man. That distinction overwhelmingly belongs to the incessant victimization narrative of pandering lawmakers who would rather collect a paycheck then demonstrate the competence and resolve necessary to exact meaningful, lasting change. Just because political opponents and ignorant athletes choose to believe such sensational propaganda, hardly makes it true or excuses coddled athletes for refusing to stand at attention for a mere 60 seconds before every game to honor the very country and those brave individuals who make our way of life possible; including those black Americans who fought in the Civil War and every subsequent war to protect this nation and secure freedom around the globe.

The American flag and the national anthem were never truly politically contentious until Marxist cultural terrorists sought out to destroy anything that conveyed patriotism or remotely honored America's "imperfect" heritage. The fact not a single American flag was initially visible at the 2016 Democratic national convention and their delegates successfully voted to exile God from their platform in 2012 before party leaders sought to quell public outrage, leaves little doubt as to the sheer level of radicalization that has destroyed the once proud party of JFK. As long as "We the People" possess faith in a higher power, a steadfast belief in a set of indelible ideals that supersede any man-made, oppressive state seeking to dictate every aspect of our lives, progressives know they can never fully achieve their goal of erecting a dependent, obedient populace that is more concerned with earthly pleasures, entitlements, than any virtuous calling that defines progress as the character of individual liberty.

The escalating racial discord and civil unrest engulfing America is hardly by accident, and by no means a coincidence, for it is a cultural coup of subversive design. The systematic unraveling of the traditional family unit, attacking our founding Judeo-Christian values and the increasingly crass and obscene behavior of violent activists are but a political means to an immoral end. As long as political agitators can hide behind false accusations of racism, homophobia and sexism as the media selectively reports the truth – immigration laws are cruel, only black lives killed by white cops matter, gay marriage will never legalize polygamy, gender conditioning is not child abuse, Obamacare is not an unmitigated failure, natural disasters are proof of unnatural global warming and patriotism is unchecked racial supremacy – they avoid having to engage in substantive debate, earnestly educating voters or being held accountable for their extremist views and endless litany of failures. Although freedom of speech and tolerance are always paramount, freedom from consequences and culpability are not human rights. They're cracks in the foundation of any evolved, self-aware society inviting tyranny, dysfunction and corruption to conceive under the same roof.

Because the modern left knows it cannot logically defend a majority of their claims, not to mention their "moralized" fascist tactics, they attempt to create a sensational distraction by which to permanently polarize the masses and demonize anyone who dares expose their hypocrisy. If the American flag and national anthem are the unrivaled enemies of the black community, generations of minorities who now claim to be the sole victims of mass injustice and unfairly oppressed despite ample opportunities and special accommodations such as affirmative action, what exactly is Africa to all her descendants and indigenous people; a continent which continues to enslave, murder and impoverish millions of Africans with frightening efficiency and international indifference? Appreciation for one's lot in life, respect for their country, would never duly exist if such conclusions were incumbent upon eradicating all dissenting opinion or politicizing every injustice and tragedy. Perspective is not a matter of favoritism or forced concessions, but a lesson in humility and personal reflection that demands our participation.

America is only forsaken when we take her for granted by allowing conniving malcontents obsessed with judging her past to divide us into bitter, warring factions incapable of reason or rationale recourse. Black and white, man or woman, rich and poor, gay, straight, or aspiring citizen; our strength is not in the brute totality of our numbers, but in the undying ideals we embody and our collective support for the one nation that tirelessly fights for their survival. If the struggle is indeed the glory and our journey a testament to how far we have come as a diverse and resilient people, the American flag has more than earned the right to fly free from politicized scorn or false strife on native soil. To protest or teach hatred of a respected symbol of freedom is to welcome the demise of the very country and natural born rights one claims to fraudulently represent.

Forward: The Sole of Sedition

Am I surprised a Department of Defense website is calling the Constitution a flawed document that promotes racism and sexism? Not at all, for progressivism is an Orwellian ideology, a deceptive means to obtain and maximize control, which requires unabashed propaganda to conceal one absolute truth: The Constitution, the backbone and genesis for the American Republic, is based on conservative ideals and Judeo-Christian values. Morality morphed into the ethical framework of our laws, communities, and liberty gave birth to capitalism, the innovative and competitive engine that pushed 13 rogue colonies to the pinnacle of economic and global power. And it is within this beacon of hope and humanitarianism, not sheer wealth or might but a philosophical bridge paving the way to unparalleled progress, that common sense tells us any person or party standing in direct contrast to the building of a free, accountable and just nation is both inherently radical and undeniably anti-America. Sound like anyone you know?

Because propagandists like Barack Obama and Hillary Clinton conceal their lies and radical intentions behind the guises of bigotry, it's of little surprise when leftists once again try to subvert the message by attacking the messenger. Yes, Thomas Jefferson did own slaves but he never denied it and a number of our founding fathers vehemently disapproved of its existence. Yet, it was the single, greatest document ever conceived in our nation's history, the U.S. Constitution – not the myopic practices or cultural norms of the times – that provided the blueprint to overcome society's most daunting challenges and gross injustices. The indelible precepts of natural rights and "all men are created equal in the eyes of God" would eventually serve as the ideologically and moral bastion to abolish slavery, ensure women's suffrage, protect religious freedom, demand due process and end segregation. How does the action of one man, let alone 1000, negate the wisdom of a transcendent piece of paper? Truth should be timeless, unlike the racist and sexist ploys of aspiring traitors who seek to silence free speech to avoid judgment.

In the past 25 years alone there has been more slavery and human trafficking in Africa than that which ever existed in America. Why has nothing been done? For centuries on end Islam has denied women basic human rights; murdering and maiming mothers out of sheer hateful spite, mutilating the genitals of young daughters in the name of Allah. Where is the outrage; the demand to end the real 'war on women'? And these are the crimes, religion and regimes, the left embraces with its apathetic absence and silent consent? Oh, it's not that America is devoid of shame or injustice or hypocrisy; not at all. We've simply learned, and continue to learn, such discord and discrimination are pointless endeavors that undermine the cornerstones of civilization; the attributes of a virtuous, fair and enduring society.

The reason such unforgivable atrocities exist in this day and age is because it's only racism or sexism when America is to blame. If progressives can't exploit it for political gain, demonize their detractors, it's acceptable collateral damage. How else can you justify rewarding the anti-Semitic, misogynistic, Iranian Islamic state with $150 billion in seized capital and the "reasonable" timetable to build nuclear weapons? How else can you equate distorting the death of a community menace, Michael Brown, to ignoring the countless Africans currently suffering under the auspices of slavery and depravity? When you despise the country you claim to serve, propaganda turns principle into an enemy of the state. When you have to conjure racism and sexism to wash the dirt and blood of real injustice off your shoes, you tell the inquiring masses to just keep moving "forward".

"The only thing necessary for the triumph of evil is for good men to do nothing." *~Edmund Burke*

THE FIRST AFRICAN-AMERICAN TO RECEIVE THE MEDAL OF HONOR IN THE CIVIL WAR WAS SGT. WILLIAM HARVEY CARNEY WHO, DESPITE BEING SHOT IN THE FACE, SHOULDERS, ARMS, AND LEGS, REFUSED TO LET THE AMERICAN FLAG TOUCH THE GROUND.

RACE

The Pawns of Progressivism

Donald Trump has been in the 'Public Eye' for over 30 years but was never accused of racism until he ran against a Democrat.

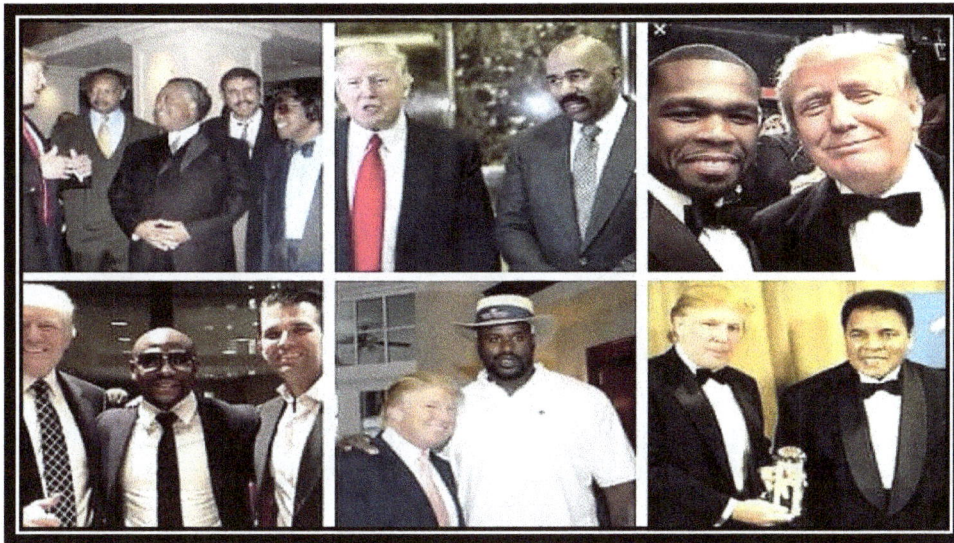

A Legacy of Hate, Race, Division and Discord

I find it amusing Donald Trump is routinely derided as "divisive" and hateful when his predecessor set race relations back by 50 years and weakened/disparaged America at nearly every opportune moment. For those rabid critics who "misremember", it was Barack Obama who mocked middle-America voters as bitter, small town xenophobes needlessly clinging to their guns and bibles. If I may, when did supporting the Second Amendment, LEGAL immigration and honoring our nation's founding Judeo-Christian values become a radical concept? And yet it was under his explicit direction the IRS admitted to singling out businesses and community organizations that identified as conservative, patriotic or even Christian. Yes, once again, nothing remotely discriminatory here. Why again did Homeland Security place proud, law-abiding citizens on the Terror Watch list by declaring "liberty lovers" as America's greatest terrorist threat...in a country predicated upon liberty and amidst the horrific aftermath of 9/11, no less? The same government operatives who never punished Islamic businesses over their marriage beliefs and ignored the terror radicalization occurring within American mosques, harassed Hobby Lobby and Catholic churches for refusing to provide birth control or insurance coverage for abortions; a procedure that violated their faith and religious freedoms. Still not convinced yet? Of course not.

As much as Obama's election was a watershed moment in American history, his proclivity for racial discord has been exponentially greater. He immediately politicized the cases of Trayvon Martin, Michael Brown and Freddie Gray, with little regard for the evidence or their criminal records, resulting in riots, destruction of property and further loss of life. Sadly, the former President made no such emotional tributes or pleas for justice after 25-year-old NYPD officer Brian Wilson was shot in the head or when Kathryn Steinle was murdered in San Francisco on July 1, 2015 by an illegal immigrant with seven felony convictions. In response, Democrats publicly vowed to save Sanctuary cities. Barack Obama sent sizable delegations to the funerals of all three black males, personally and very publicly mourned the passing of each individual but failed to even mention the tragic death of American sniper Chris Kyle in February of 2013. Rather, the White House issued a statement commemorating the death of Whitney Houston later that month. When you're busy bribing millions of minorities with free "Obama phones" using taxpayer money, who has the time for such colorblind statesmanship, or better yet, basic human empathy?

Anytime a sitting Commander-in-Chief plays golf during the funeral of General Harold Greene – the highest-ranking service member killed in combat since Vietnam – no imagination is required to decipher his true loyalties. Mr. Obama's incessant race-based rhetoric eventually gave rise to militant groups like Black Lives Matter and AntiFa, but more profoundly incited a partisan war on police which triggered an unprecedented wave of assassinations against law enforcement; including 5 officers gunned down in Dallas, Texas. Instead of bringing a troubled nation together, one increasingly fractured by his cynicism, anger and clear racial favoritism, he was content praising Colin Kaepernick for his "courageous" decision to kneel during the national anthem only a few months following the traumatic bloodshed. The same man who illuminated the White House in LGBT colors to spike the proverbial football of social justice, found no such nerve to honor those fallen officers murdered in cold blood while serving their communities.

Not to question the unifying theme of "Cops are Pigs" socks worn by a celebrated racist athlete, but did Barry ever condemn a single case of police brutality regarding a white, Hispanic, or Asian victim, justified or not, let alone publicly decry (without media coverage) a single cop murdered by a drug dealer or due to a violent suspect resisting arrest? No? I guess we should just be satisfied the media's former Uniter-in-Chief spent hundreds of billions providing for and protecting illegals while our veterans slept in the streets or died waiting for inadequate medical care. Does it even matter the Obama administration denied the request and visa applications of countless Christians attempting to flee oppression in the Middle East and Indonesia in favor of transporting thousands of improperly vetted and/or tracked Muslim refugees into cities across America; many under the veil of night? After all, what American president in their right mind wouldn't honor tyrannical Cuba as a progressive state, green-light extremist Iran's nuclear aspirations – a country that vows to annihilate America and Israel on a daily basis – attempt to illegally transfer $221 million to the militant Palestinian Authority just before leaving office, characterize the murderous exploits of ISIS as the amateur actions of a "JV team", or dine with the racist leaders of la Raza and the Muslim Brotherhood?

Any offended critic claiming Donald Trump is the most racially divisive and inflammatory leader in recent memory, must have been completely oblivious, asleep or complicit to the toxic rhetoric and subversive dealings of Barack Obama. At no point in our 241-year history has the needle of American politics moved as far left as it did during the course of his 8-year tenure. In fact, if his Marxist upbringing and radical beliefs received the same level of media scrutiny and hostility as his successor, he never would have even been nominated. Unless I'm completely foreign to the true nature of division and discrimination, nearly all of those who benefited from Obama's ill-conceived policies and personal associations were either non-white, non-Christian/Jewish, openly hostile towards America, or all of the above. Are we talking about an equitable, patriotic leader defending the interests of all people – most notably the survival and sovereignty of America – or a bitter, divisive bigot who despises America's heritage with his every breath and still seeks atonement by judging everything through the prism of race and wealth distribution? Until everyone is held to the same standard of accountability, offered the same level of innate respect, racism, sexism, and all other forms of hate will endure unchecked; especially when such distinctions are now repeatedly wielded as weapons to attack any dissenting opinion. It's just too bad so many supposedly "educated" men and women at the forefront of our national media, entertainment world and social activism no longer have the desire or the decency to admit the difference because they're still too preoccupied crying over an election.

Coffee & Cream: The Forgotten Dream

It has long been suspected America is on the downside of history; often a self-inflicted spiral delivered by the hand of incompetence, corruption or irreverence. That being said, I cannot ignore a fundamental truth that is at the very heart of the rhetoric dividing our communities and destroying our nation. The real reason there is such a high degree of cynicism and distrust along racial lines is because of the unpleasant realities people either completely ignore, carefully avoid or foolishly justify. Call them clues or outright statistical proofs; just know they are the symptoms of our country's impending peril.

How can you proclaim to the embodiment of hope and change when you can't even properly diagnose a problem, let alone admit to the actual cause? Instead of wasting countless hours and resources decrying racism and convincing their brethren they're helpless victims of circumstance, Barack Obama, Al Sharpton, and Jesse Jackson would be much better served by addressing the very source of their ills: the black family. Whereas towns, communities and neighborhoods signify the prevailing attitudes and norms of America, our families are the epicenter of our values. Our very perception of right and wrong, respect for authority, educational goals and our work ethic all inevitable stem from our upbringing. But when our homes become riddled with dysfunction – promiscuity, poverty, drugs and violence – the results, or the statistics, speak for themselves.

Despite comprising for 13% of the population, black Americans account for one-third of all assaults and rapes, as well as 50% of all robberies and murders. These are staggering statistics that far outweigh the most juvenile slights and misrepresentations. Even more damning, African Americans are responsible for over 90% of all black homicides. Considering the KKK lynched roughly 3,500 blacks in 86 years – an unforgivable number in any context – what's the significance and collective outrage when 7,000 black Americans die at the hands of their own peers each year; by far the greatest source of violence and injustice against the black community? Whether you're killed at the hands of a white cop or a black stranger, intentionally or not, how does it make it anymore discriminatory or less tragic? Does the fact twice as many white suspects are killed by police, with little media coverage or outrage, alter the actual prevalence of crime or lessen the potential consequences of resisting arresting? Racism exists in all facets of society and no one is immune from its effects, but its inevitability does not excuse or deny anyone the opportunity to accept responsibility for their actions and life. If black lives matter, and all inherently should, it seems that statement serves more as a hypocritical oath than a grounded truth.

Forget pointing the finger of futility and giving endless speeches to promote your political brand, civil rights activists and politicians should be asking the questions their pride and pocketbook somehow prevents them from asking. Why are so many black fathers missing in action; those positive male role models who provide love, wisdom, discipline and the financial stability all families innately need? Why are black women, those who represent the highest percentage of single mothers in America, having more children when a growing majority fails to emotionally, morally or financially provide for the kids they already have? Why are schools being asked to lower both their academic and behavioral standards, handicapping the potential of black youth in the name of affirmative action, only to pave the very path to their demise? And why go to church, hear the testament and calling of Jesus Christ, if your actions in no way honor his life's teachings? Women aren't bitches and hoes and when did Jesus hate anyone, let alone fault them for his choices?

When 40% of all black youth are unemployed and a majority have no other discernible ambition than to look good, get laid, get high or be famous – only to settle for standing on the corner, collecting welfare, and invoking racism for their plight – these are the depraved results; the sown seeds of an increasingly soulless and hostile society. Adolescents drop f-bombs faster than their grades, quarreling mothers exchange profanity and fists as they hold their toddlers on their hip, massive brawls breakout at the most innocuous events, and cops are accused of racial profiling when black America commits an extremely disproportionate amount of crime in America. Even at the height of the civil rights movement and segregation, Black Americans did not debase their values and self-worth by "acting a fool". They had pride, worked tirelessly, and knew they alone, regardless of the prejudiced attitudes of the day, were responsible for making a better life.

Did you know from 1900 to 1960, despite living in a period much more hostile to their aspirations and rights, African Americans had an equal or higher workforce participation in America than whites, while black teens had an equal or lower unemployment rate as their white counterparts? And how can that be? Fast forward to the apathy and entitlement of today where the black community now accounts for the highest unemployment demographic (12%), the highest percent of Welfare recipients (40%), the lowest home ownership in the nation (48 %), and you'd think "racism" would be the least of liberals' concerns. Perhaps the time has come to turn "blame" into a "blueprint" that actually works and "hope" and change" into something other than a decaffeinated conversation at Starbucks. Propaganda, like Saccharin, is a piss poor substitute for reality.

No, it's not that I believe there are no positive examples of well-adjusted and accomplished black Americans today; quite the contrary. The problem is they're pushed to the background of obscurity, deftly hidden from the urban victimization front, making these success stories the exception – a winning lottery ticket of in a celebrity world of white privilege – rather than the prevailing norm of perseverance and accountability. When liberals consciously choose to give more credence and exposure to the likes of Michael Brown and Freddie Gray in lieu of the extraordinary exploits of self-made men like Dr. Ben Carson, Thomas Sowell and Col. Allen West, there is little doubt to their duplicitous and destructive agenda. And when these reputable individuals do achieve a high degree of success, respect the law and love their native country, how does "the streets" congratulate them? By calling them white, sellouts, or Uncle Toms! Since when did having values, diligence and appreciation for opportunity become a racist thing? If toiling for a better life makes you white, then what do you call scheming to steal one, or dare I say, actually believing you're owed one?

Yes, it's much easier to cast aspersions and blame the object of your disdain, your invented enemy, than to dedicate your time and faculties towards understanding and fixing the actual problem. If you want to incite true change, transcend hope from a bumper sticker to changing a forsaken life, led by example and become that which you seek. I don't want to witness African Americans, or anyone for that matter, kneeling during the national anthem or smugly stopping on the flag while cursing the symbol of freedom so many died to protect. I want to see a proud American grab Old Glory, hoist it high, and chastise his neighbors for disrespecting the very source of their liberties! Anytime a flash mob attacks innocent bystanders for no other reason than blind hate, or a gloating thug knocks out an elderly man solely to play a "game", I want to see those colorblind pillars of persuasion leap to his aid and thwart injustice. If citizens riot, loot and threaten innocent lives, I want to see an equal number of their outraged peers rise to protect the rights of others. And when someone says, "that's racist" – hides behind the stereotypical banner of convenience – ask them how such a claim, whether true or not, absolves them from being liable for their future and overcoming the inevitable obstacles life poses to all. Opposition to such destructive behavior and blatant misconceptions doesn't require sainthood or a Vatican decree; it merely requires having a conscience and seeing yourself in all things. Jesus didn't wash the feet of a prostitute out of spite. He did so because he wanted to shield her from disparagement and the wrath of hate. One soul with courage is always a majority.

In the arena of competitive sports, it's universally accepted championships are won through hard work, meticulous preparation, and most of all, teamwork. Yet when it comes to solving the problems of poverty, crime, and social strife, grown adults – elected leaders, mind you – would rather disperse guilt and tout the failed party line than admitting real change goes far beyond bankrupt rhetoric and blank checks. The black community isn't suffering from a crisis of race; it's plagued by a crisis of culture. This erosion of values is not exclusive to any one race or creed, for it has inevitable seeped into every facet of America: white and black, rich and poor, Democrats or Republican, men and women. However, pretending these empirical facts aren't at the crux of a decaying society – the eye of the storm engulfing black community – is the equivalent of throwing a menial government check at the problem, organizing a march, or calling it good as long as it ensures your re-election every four years.

AnOmaly
@LegendaryEnergy

In the 1900's when racism was rampant, the left supplied it.

In the 2000's when racism was nearly gone; the left manufactured it, manifested it, created it & promoted it non-stop.

Without racism, the left has no power or platform.

As much as everyone may detest stereotypes, a number are actually rooted in statistical proof. Therefore, just like a doctor attempting to diagnose a malaise, it's only natural to search for the primary cause of such societal strife. That's common sense; that's real-world pragmatism. Addressing the crime and poverty rates among African Americans isn't an attempt to belittle them, rather an honest desire to empower and unite all Americans. The proven path to safe neighborhoods, a strong black community, and a robust economy isn't by riots, blame, and reverse racism. It's achieved by erecting a culture that unconditionally recognizes morality, respect, education, and an indelible work ethic do not require wealth or a particular skin color, merely a desire to grab the reigns of personally responsibility and change the world for the better. If you embrace the intrinsic wisdom of the timeless adage 'no one can help you until you help yourself', an entire generation of Americans are perfectly content wallowing in the bottomless pit of self-pity and perpetual discontent because political parasites require a bitter, distracted host in order to remain unscathed in the never-ending fog of their own systemic failure; more commonly marketed as, "social justice". Victims make the most loyal voters because the unvarnished truth – i.e., all lives matter and all should be held equally accountable – is no longer welcome in the shiny new corridors of re-institutionalized segregation.

Abraham Lincoln once uttered the prophetic verse, "A house divided against its self cannot stand!" These are also the ominous words of Mark in the New Testament. The house of our Republic cannot stand when a significant portion of America's own citizens desire nothing more than to burn it down in the name of justifiable injustice or ransomed guilt. As long as over 150 years of progress and liberty are sacrificed on our President's altar of false entitlement and hate, to fan the flames of racial animosity and national discord, the only change necessary will be the notation in a forgotten textbook. History doesn't suffer fools: mankind does.

"Every man must decide whether he will walk in the light of creative altruism or in the darkness of destructive selfishness."

~Martin Luther King, Jr.

364

The Unpaid Pawn Stars of Slavery

Every time I hear someone invoke slavery or demand reparations, albeit a politician, academic or unhinged activist, I literally cringe. Unless I'm mistaken, the Emancipation Proclamation was issued over 150 years ago, only 1.6 percent of the American populace owned slaves at the height of the Antebellum period and nearly 400,000 white soldiers died to procure their freedom; not that race should ever discern the value of a human life or disregard an abolitionist movement spearheaded by white, evangelical Christians. It is also common misconception the Civil War was fought solely to end slavery when in reality it was far more about state sovereignty (as intended by our Founders), economics, the rapid industrialization of the North, a lack of railway access in the South, and tariffs. Likewise, it is obviously of little concern to reparation revisionists that no living American breathing today "is" or ever has been a legal slave of this Republic.

For anyone, black or otherwise, to consciously compare themselves to lifelong servants – those who toiled, suffered and died under the auspices of slavery – is offensive and illustrates a complete disregard for these victims' horrific plight. If the millions who were sold into bondage had the liberties every American enjoys today, there is no dollar amount that could quantify their sheer joy and appreciation for reclaiming their God-Given rights and forging their own destiny as equals. Martin Luther King Jr. didn't identify as a Republican out of some misplaced or partisan need to bury the truth. The civil rights icon knew that if not for the efforts of the anti-slavery party founded in 1854, the dignity of every black sentient being would have remained shackled to the fields of Democratic apathy for years to come.

Not to question the sterling anti-American credentials of the United Nations, but why has no official condemnation or financial recompense been sought in memory of the astounding 5 million African slaves transported to toil in Brazilian gold mines; a sum 10 times greater than the number brought to America between 1750 and 1860? And while we're on the subject of globalists posthumously adjudicating white guilt, why haven't the Spanish, Dutch or Portuguese governments been implored to pay reparations for sponsoring and harboring notorious slave trading operations for centuries on end? Furthermore, unless thousands of Irish families have unceremoniously received a check as compensation for their ancestors being starved, driven from their homes and forced to work as indentured servants in English colonies, perhaps I'm confused as to the true definition of crimes against humanity worthy of absentee enrichment.

Between 1641 and 1652 alone, half a million Irishmen, women and children were murdered by the Crown and another 300,000 were sold as "white" slaves in the West Indies and New World, causing their native population of 1.5 million to plummet to 600,000 in less than a decade. Yes, numbers far more daunting than the estimated 3,000 blacks lynched in America; a grotesque atrocity regardless of the totality. Apparently "victimization" in the modern theater of social justice requires an invitation to sequester an equally detached alibi to not give a damn.

History was never intended to serve as a politically correct blueprint fortuitously spared from the ravages of human vice, conflict and folly; rather it is a road map for mankind to consciously elude the missteps of an imperfect past to forge a universally beneficial future where the innovative prowess of the human mind is as poignant as its cultivated respect for the lives, welfare and rights of others. If I may be so brash, how does paying blood money to disjointed descendants who have little or no knowledge of their own legacy – let alone a respectable appreciation of the opportunities their ancestors' pain made possible – honor or alleviate the gross injustices committed against the actual victims? Simply put...it doesn't. Such an exploitative ploy would merely reward those shameless opportunists seeking a free paycheck while punishing innocent taxpaying citizens who never owned a slave or supported its vile existence in any manner whatsoever.

Considering how much the U.S. Government has doled out in public assistance and disingenuous disability claims over the past 25 years, not to mention the eight and nine figure bank accounts many black athletes and entertainers now command, I'd venture to say the term "slave" is about as irrelevant as a black president in a White House. It's just too bad the modern-day pawn brokers of historical "injustice" are so incredibly immune to the human trafficking epidemic that continues to plague the Middle East, Asia and Africa because the perpetrators lack the proper nationality for an indictment of racial iniquity. Who knew the allure of the almighty dollar, appeasing America's "unpaid" political detractors, is just enough moral recompense to dull the contemporary screams of unchecked human suffering?

"Blacks were not enslaved because they were black but because they were available. Slavery has existed in the world for thousands of years. Whites enslaved other whites in Europe for centuries before the first black was brought to the Western hemisphere. Asians enslaved Europeans. Asians enslaved other Asians. Africans enslaved other Africans, and indeed even today in North Africa, blacks continue to enslave blacks."

~THOMAS SOWELL

The Bloody Rags of Righteousness

While radical leftists dust off their 60's and 70's Marxist yearbooks, don their holy Che Guevara t-shirts, wave the black flag of the ISIS JV team, desecrate century-old memorials, dig-up Confederate soldiers and remove the last traces of common sense from the American frontier in a brazen attempt to rewrite their own politically-incorrect deeds, perhaps the time has come to ban the most pervasive and offensive embodiment of racism in America: The Democratic Party. Not only did Democrats embody the beating heart and unrelenting face of human trafficking in America – streamlining commercial operations with European slave traders – they wrote the infamous Jim Crow laws, forged the KKK to lynch and dissuade blacks from voting, and endlessly fought to maintain segregation up until the landmark case of Brown vs. Topeka Board of Education; a decision Republican President General Eisenhower supported and rightfully enforced with federal troops.

In fact, the progressive party of prejudice resisted the passage of every civil rights law right up to the watershed Civil Rights Act of 1964 and the Voting Rights Act of 1965. Yes, there is a reason why Martin Luther King Jr. identified as a Republican and despised the Democrat's rampant legacy of hate: history, that same living, breathing tapestry of intent documenting the GOP's "Philadelphia Plan" which sought to breach the racial barriers of construction unions keeping blacks out of trades in the 1970's. Just ask Charles Sumner about the bloody toll of 'tolerance'. Liberal academia's feeble theory the two parties "switched" is as pathetic as their attempt to bury their sordid heritage; especially when Republicans didn't hold a majority of Southern Congressional seats until 30 years after the Civil Rights Act passed, and only one of the 21 Democratic Senators who voted against the watershed bill actually crossed the proverbial aisle. Over a century and a half later after the abolition of slavery, the descendants of Democratic injustice have merely shed the ruddy chains of bondage for the cultivated fields of financial dependence and electoral blackmail. The old habits of proud racists die hard beneath the billowing fog of fear and misplaced anger.

If the millennial goal is to unearth every conceivable crumb of indiscretion and punish any notable personage, organization or monument even remotely associated with the vile trade of human servitude and enduring bigotry, the righteous few have nearly two centuries of guilt to dispense and justice to adjudicate in the name of political narcissism. After all, if the Republican Party was founded as the anti-slavery party – and it was – and their evangelical base spearheaded the arduous movement to end its deprave practice – and they did – then conscientious citizens must find, humiliate, and/or destroy anything living, inanimate, or dead remotely linked to these posthumous crimes against humanity by stripping the rights and dignity of anyone who opposes the "truth". Lest we forget, nearly 400,000 white men died to free roughly four million blacks incarcerated by the Democratic protected institution of slavery and not a single elected Republican owned slaves on the eve of Civil War in 1860. Therefore, in accordance with the culture cleanse currently enveloping our communities solely to systematically discredit and purge our founding ideals, "We the Offended People" must begin by punishing the greatest source of racial strife and hypocrisy plaguing America: The Democratic Party. Because there are literally so many books to burn, symbols to ban, businesses to boycott, resignations to demand, graves to disturb, and lives to ruin in the name of political correctness and mob justice, time is of the essence and due process is of little consequence. Shall we begin this harmless and justifiable endeavor, together, for the sake of peace?

THE TWO PLATFORMS.

The Democratic Platform IS FOR THE WHITE MAN. | The Republican Platform IS FOR THE NEGRO.

"I think one man is just as good as another so long as he's not a nigger or a Chinaman." — **Harry Truman**

"I'll have those niggers voting Democratic for the next 200 years." —**Lyndon B. Johnson**

"It remained necessary to prove which side you were on, to show your loyalty to the black masses, to strike out and name names." —**Barack Obama**

"I will stand with the Muslims should the political winds shift in an ugly direction." — **Barack Obama**

"When was a young militant, he used to say all white folks were going to hell. Then he mellowed and just said most of them were. Now, he said, he is back to where he was.'" — **Joseph Lowery, benediction at President Obama's inauguration**

"I mean, you got the first mainstream African-American who is articulate and bright and clean and a nice-looking guy. I mean, that's a storybook, man." —**Joe Biden**

"You cannot go to a 7-11 or Dunkin Donuts unless you have a slight Indian accent." —**Joe Biden**

"A few years ago, (Barack Obama) would have been getting us coffee." —**Bill Clinton**

"You fucking Jew bastard." —**Hillary Clinton**

"Mahatma Gandhi ran a gas station down in St. Louis for a couple of years. A lot of wisdom comes out of that gas station." —**Hillary Clinton**

"America was ready to embrace a black presidential candidate, especially one such as Obama — a 'light-skinned' African American 'with no Negro dialect, unless he wanted to have one." —**Harry Reid**

"Rather I should die a thousand times, and see Old Glory trampled in the dirt never to rise again, than to see this beloved land of ours become degraded by race mongrels, a throwback to the blackest specimen from the wilds." —**Former Klansman and US Senator Robert Byrd**

"I do not think it is an exaggeration at all to say to my friend from West Virginia [Sen. Robert C. Byrd, a former Ku Klux Klan recruiter] that he would have been a great senator at any moment. He would have been right during the great conflict of civil war in this nation." —**Former Democratic Senator Christopher Dodd**

"The white man is our mortal enemy, and we cannot accept him. I will fight to see that vicious beast go down into the lake of fire prepared for him." — **Louis Farrakhan**

"White folks was in the caves while we [blacks] was building empires ... We built pyramids before Donald Trump ever knew what architecture was ... we taught philosophy and astrology and mathematics before Socrates and them Greek homos ever got around to it." —**Al Sharpton**

"Hymies. Hymietown." —**Jesse Jackson's description of New York City**

"Old white people need to die!" —**Oprah Winfrey**

"The white race is the cancer of human history." —**Susan Sontag**

"Tainting the tea party movement with the charge of racism is proving to be an effective strategy for Democrats. There is no evidence that tea party adherents are any more racist than other Republicans, and indeed many other Americans. But getting them to spend their time purging their ranks and having candidates distance themselves should help Democrats win in November. Having one's opponent rebut charges of racism is far better than discussing joblessness." —**Mary Frances Berry, former Chairwoman, US Commission on Civil Rights**

(On Clarence Thomas) "A handkerchief-head, chicken-and-biscuit-eating Uncle Tom." — **Spike Lee**

"I give interracial couples a look. Daggers. They get uncomfortable when they see me on the street." —**Spike Lee**

IF YOU DON'T KNOW:

13th Amendment ABOLISHED SLAVERY		15th Amendment RIGHT TO VOTE FOR ALL	
100% REPUBLICAN SUPPORT	23% DEMOCRAT SUPPORT	100% REPUBLICAN SUPPORT	0% DEMOCRAT SUPPORT
14th Amendment GAVE CITIZENSHIP TO FREED SLAVES		Civil Rights Act 1964	
94% REPUBLICAN SUPPORT	0% DEMOCRAT SUPPORT	80% REPUBLICAN SUPPORT	61% DEMOCRAT SUPPORT

PLEASE KEEP QUIET

The Urban Warfare of Endless Welfare

As a conservative, the supposed heartless epitome of capitalist greed, I'm repeatedly asked if I oppose helping the less fortunate. The truth is, in a nation as advanced and blessed as America, assisting those less fortunate in need is incumbent upon our values, if not our survival. However, the key variable to this entitlement equation is the workable definition of "need". There are millions of disabled Americans, albeit physically or mentally, who are suffering because they are neither capable of helping themselves or providing for their families. There are also a number of diligent couples and single parents who incessantly labor for a better life but still struggle to put food on the table. Not only do these individuals embody the conceptual crux of "need", the functional glue of true hope and change, they are worthy of respect, compassion and assistance.

Where I draw the proverbial line of provision is at the doorsteps of those career parasites that endeavor only to work the system; those able-bodied Americans who can work, contribute to the moral and vibrant society, but choose not to due to laziness or a misguided sense of victimization. Such manipulation is not only unworthy of sympathy or assistance of any kind, it personifies the callous culture of entitlement that has absolutely no regard for America, hard-working taxpayers, and most of all, the institution of integrity. Having more kids solely to collect more welfare, when you refuse to provide a proper home for those children you already have, is nothing short of criminal...if not nauseating. It should also be a recognized form of child neglect. Instead of rewarding these fraudulent schemes, allowing politicians and their puppet organizations to openly solicit the public as to how to defraud the system, our government should be indicting these shameless con artists, seeking restitution, and banning the perpetrators from ever receiving public assistance again. After all, if working Americans are convicted for failing to pay their taxes due to insolvency – a lack of money but not earnest intent – why shouldn't those gainfully unemployed parents who steal from the public's treasury suffer the same fate?

"Dependence begets subservience, bribery and corruption, suffocates the germ of virtue, and prepares fit tools for the designs of ambition." *~Thomas Jefferson*

With roughly 50 million on welfare – a number that has nearly doubled since 2008 – a record 95 million citizens out of the workforce, America is not only teetering on the precipice of economic ruin, it's suffocating beneath the unsustainable weight of Barack Obama's entitlement utopia. Common sense will tell you using money as a means to a means – (employment), not as a means to an end (welfare), is the only proven path to prosperity and fiscal responsibility. When breathing is the first order of survival, escaping the confines of leftist ignorance is your first order of business.

The heartbeat of America has always been business: risk, work, reward! Capitalism is the very genesis of our wealth and blessings, the competitive engine of innovation, and its entrepreneurial impetus has provided a quality of life few nations can comprehend. You don't need to infinitely raise 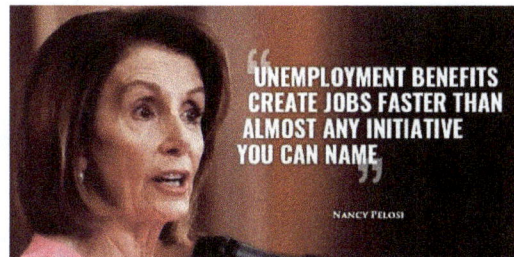 taxes to sustain runaway government or a reliant populace. Texas is proof positive an environment conducive to commercial success will naturally yield both higher profits and increased tax revenues. However, this unmitigated truth requires two nonnegotiable necessities; an ever diverse and robust job market, and skilled workers with an insatiable work ethic. Rather than indoctrinating an industrious and self-sufficient workforce, watering the roots of responsibility, Washington is feeding the masses of cultivated dependence, enabling the stale excuses of envy, by stealing bread from the mouth of honest labor. America cannot survive, let alone thrive, if the senseless politics of guilt, class and race victimization are allowed to flourish.

Detroit and Baltimore are hardly aberrations of neglect or favoritism. They're the direct result of a progressive doctrine that breeds poverty, contempt and discord by absolving their respected communities from the inevitable duties we all bear as members of society, but more profoundly, humanity: contributing to a better tomorrow. Attempting to bribe those impoverished Americans who fail to be accountable for their lives, solely to win their voting loyalties, does nothing but foster an enduring legacy of discontentment, ineptitude, and ingratitude. Those who show no concern for the bridge of their economic liberation, the property and livelihoods of others, have no intention of coexisting whatsoever. Why? A moral compass, their supposed innate sense of self-respect, should have motivated these individuals to act on their own behalf and that of their "decaying" communities in the first place! The best way to break the bonds of indigence is to realize welfare was only intended as a temporary reprieve, a crutch to restore personal balance, for prolonged

371

usage merely ensures poverty and the apathetic expectations plaguing subsequent generations. No, welfare reform isn't a racial ruse; for Americans of all ethnicities have become ensnared by dependency's false promise of hope. It's a colorless mentality that rejects the liberal proverb most are predestined to lose the lottery of life, rather than seizing the dignity of escaping the subsidized liquidation of their dreams, or more succinctly, potential. The best social program and pathway to liberation remains a job.

Whether you're white or black, a capitalist or a Marxist, don't expect working class Americans to be emotionally invested in your plight, the systemic ravages of urban poverty, when you don't give a damn about yourself or anyone else for that matter. And don't expect those who scratch and claw for the most unceremonious necessities of life to fund your victim complacency campaign. No, there is no shame in needing assistance time to time; most inevitably do and that is the unique blessing of living in a country that boasts the resources and affluence of America. Regardless, such compassion was never intended to imply welfare as a career opportunity or a perceived right without conditions. If you refuse to help yourself, your own children and meet society's benevolence halfway, you're only deserving of the depravity you inflict upon yourself. Failing to obtain and keep a job within a year's time, or dare I say during your entire adult life, isn't a humanitarian disaster or symptomatic of discrimination in any sense of the word; it's the inevitable consequence of criminal negligence and serial selfishness.

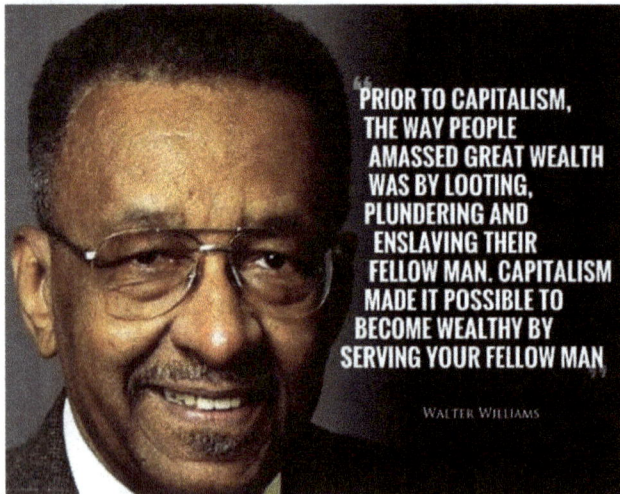

"PRIOR TO CAPITALISM, THE WAY PEOPLE AMASSED GREAT WEALTH WAS BY LOOTING, PLUNDERING AND ENSLAVING THEIR FELLOW MAN. CAPITALISM MADE IT POSSIBLE TO BECOME WEALTHY BY SERVING YOUR FELLOW MAN."

WALTER WILLIAMS

In the 1960's, Lyndon Baines Johnson's "Great Society" was hailed as a visionary blueprint for doing little more than pandering to racial stereotypes by promoting large-scale public assistance: i.e., Big Government. His real objective, however, was to "keep niggers voting Democrat for the next century" by ensuring minority's dependence on welfare, and with it, a permanent culture of disrepair within the United States. The fact millions able-bodied Americans, regardless of race, are now content living off of the taxpayer dime, without remorse or refrain, is insulting and an affront to the premise of America itself. Couple this injustice with the knowledge scores of Illegal immigrants are receiving benefits – non-citizens, mind you – while thousands of veterans are homeless and lack proper healthcare, and you can finally begin to appreciate the crisis on conscience that is destroying American exceptionalism, private enterprise, and the moral infrastructure of our urban epicenters. The most revered and powerful nation on Earth wasn't built upon the transcendent merits of handouts, the spoils of guilt or the electoral promises of endless entitlements; it was built by men and women, often destitute and without pity or scorn, who refused to take freedom and opportunity for granted. It was built by those who would do anything to provide for their own flesh and blood beneath the whisper of self-respect. Obviously, some truths are best unheard rather than unearned.

To Hue and Back

For those who are appalled at the Justice Department's decision to review the aftermath of affirmative action, please allow me to colorfully digress. Before the concept of affirmative action was introduced and implemented via Executive fiat by John F. Kennedy in 1961, discrimination was plainly prevalent and racism institutionalized throughout America. After all, segregation ended but a mere 7 years earlier and the Civil Rights movement was just beginning to gain steam; as noted by MLK's Letter from a Birmingham Jail and his iconic "I Have a Dream Speech" during the March on Washington in 1963. While the introduction of these protections was justifiable, whether or not critics agreed, there was little doubt black citizens lacked equal opportunities in many facets of American society.

Unfortunately for the pallbearers of good intentions, 56 years of affirmative action has turned into a vindictive platform to exact social justice; that modern-day construct used to consciously discriminate against people of non-color because of assumed "privilege", an unpaid historical debt or to simply inflame racial tensions. Essentially, rather than judging everyone based on the merits of their accomplishments and the content of their character, universities, our government, and even humanitarian organizations themselves have used race as a determining factor to reject more worthy candidates.

Now I'm not going to sanctimoniously decree every minority hired under affirmative action was unqualified or that some businesses do not consciously seek to favor white employees or students. Not at all. Humans are highly subjective creatures by nature and the ideal of racial harmony requires equally invested partners. I'm simply stating it's wrong to deny an Asian American entrance into Harvard, or any race for that matter, simply to accommodate a Native American given preference due to historical transgressions which neither party were victimized by or guilty of committing. Empowering underrepresented segments of the population to find the means to succeed in the workplace or the classroom, albeit by individual mentoring or financial scholarships, is vastly different than giving a promotion to someone who is much less experienced or qualified solely because of the color of his or her skin. In fact, it's legalized racism and moralized reverse discrimination stemming from an exceedingly false assumption: it's needed. Oddly enough, despite the reality Irish and Italian immigrants were the routine victims of violence or cultural bias, no special edicts or state sponsored sanctuaries were declared to ease their plight.

Whereas common sense doesn't require a political affiliation or agenda, obviously acceptance does. Until every member of society is held to the same applicable standard, regardless of one's heritage or biological attributes, the concept of equality will remain as hollow as it forever will become unachievable. Considering 1960's black America boasted higher employment numbers and lower crime rates than their contemporary counterparts, despite facing much more daunting challenges, I'd say the only crutch today's generation needs is the one that spanks their sense of apathy and entitlement. Dysfunctional homes, absentee parents, and eroding family values – a glaring lack of respect for oneself and others – has contributed to a society that somehow believes oppression involves being required to do homework, respecting differing opinions or not spewing profanity in public, in lieu of being forced to use a separate bathroom, beaten for being black or forced to only apply for demeaning, menial jobs.

This grotesque lack of perspective and appreciation is as unforgivable as it is now justifiable in pop culture. If being chased by the Paparazzi and living the celebrity lifestyle of adored athletes and entertainers is the only cure for perceived prejudice, I deserve to play center for the Boston Celtics because 13% of the population constitutes 75% of the NBA and I twice beat my 10-year-old sister at "HORSE" while hungover. As long as the guardians of affirmative action continue to indulge this divisive fantasy rather than equally recognizing the efforts of all who sacrifice and aspire to achieve, "racism" will forever become a politician's word used to feed off the buried cries of a hopelessly broken system.

The Dark Politics of "White Privilege"

In the latest chapter of the left's ongoing campaign to immortalize the grandfather clause of social justice, but more specifically to permanently compensate America along racial lines, comes the politically convenient creation of "White Privilege". Because the word "racism" obviously doesn't denote enough singular intent to indict white America as the sole purveyors of hate, victimization has now evolved into blaming the pale subjects of suburbia as the greatest impetus for urban crime, poverty, civil unrest, and societal division. If "White Privilege" is truly designed to infer advantage or favoritism, then why did I grow up in a blue-collar home, wear hand-me-down clothes, rarely have health insurance, never receive a college scholarship, get turned down for better paying jobs, repeatedly fail to qualify for loans, and suffer the consequences for the smallest infractions of the law like any other American? And how on Earth is it remotely possible I would literally not change one of these inconvenient truths: those perceived "injustices" that made me respect my family all the more and instilled the values that made me the man I am today? Without "struggle" do we ever truly appreciate the reward of perseverance or gain wisdom from the penniless gift of perspective? Apparently not.

If the ignorant stereotype "White Privilege" is meant to suggest millions of successful Caucasians didn't sacrifice for their education, work tirelessly for a better wage, teach their kids right from wrong, and honor the country that affords them a level of opportunity few can fathom, then I'm assuming the even millions more of impoverished white Americans who did the exact same thing only to struggle incessantly also share your rightful claim to economic justice? I find it incredibly ironic minority entertainers, athletes and entrepreneurs making seven figure incomes are "getting paid" and the embodiment of the American dream, but those who fail to reach such levels of achievement are "slaves" and the victims of "White Privilege"? Just because everyone doesn't get a blue ribbon, or enjoy the same blessings, doesn't mean you're a victim of discrimination or owed anything; it simply means "the pursuit of happiness" holds no guarantees and personal envy by no means requires a civil rights march or a bill for reparations to assuage the anger of those who were never slaves. When you sleep with an anchor named self-pity, labor under the delusion equal rights dictate equal outcomes, reality is the biggest obstacle to your own success. The only thing we are truly owed is that which we must do for ourselves; regardless of era, difficulty or circumstance.

Detroit and Baltimore are hardly irrefutable microcosms of racial oppression and "White Privilege", but rather a prime example of how liberalism breeds dependence and animosity by refusing to use sound economic principles, an unwavering standard of culpability from all citizens, as a proven means to erect a vibrant and prosperous society. You can't fault businesses for vacating urban epicenters that are rife with moral depravity, racial division, and decay, no more than you would tirelessly endeavor to remove your family from those dangerous exploits. Until people prove they're ready to seek a better life through empowerment, education and hard work – to honor the law and respect others regardless of their heritage, beliefs or economic disposition – the results will reflect the barren nature of their fruitless intent. No obscene amount of money, no unending number of government bailouts, will topple the status quo until the people themselves are willing to personify the change they supposedly so desperately desire. You cannot liberate able-bodied individuals from the psychological ravages of misplaced anger and societal apathy by offering them a permanent crutch to compensate for their shortcomings or inevitable misfortunes; you must help them realize the crutch is the very source of their ills.

The real tragedy in this progressive ploy to use race as an excuse to eradicate personal responsibility, to displace equal opportunity with equal outcome, is that liberals have stereotyped and reduced minorities into a helpless group of malcontents who are incapable of pursuing an education, succeeding in the workplace, obeying the law, raising children within wedlock, building vibrant communities, respecting White America, and loving a country that does far more for their future prospects and civil rights than any African nation has ever done for its indigenous population. In other words, Democrats have disgraced generations of minorities into believing their greatest ambition in life, or obligation if you will, is to be compensated via a menial government check and to repeatedly vote Democrat because a majority are not capable of anything more due to "White Privilege". Yes, I concur, how utterly racist and insulting. And if you may, how has either changed their lives for the better? Ensuring an endless cycle of poverty and an inexhaustible source of voter discontent does nothing to help the black community seize the wealth of opportunities America inherently affords. Such bankrupt propaganda merely keeps progress shackled to an exploited legacy of mass injustice that no longer exists; except for the callous purpose of inciting violence through media hysteria to ensure the electoral aspirations of their proven historical nemesis: The Democratic Party.

As a Christian who loves America and embraces people from all walks of life, I have grown tired of discussing race, refuting senseless rhetoric, and defending the color of my skin. It literally tears at my soul to repeatedly speak negatively about the country I love or any sect of society that includes many my own friends and associates. However, I also cannot sit idly and watch liberty burn in the name of immoral politics and false supposition. I don't care whether you're black or white, rich or poor, gay or straight, a Democrat or an atheist: if you show equal regard for my life and family, judge me solely according to my actions, I will unconditionally return such respect with equal vigor and gracious humility.

If I am truly the beneficiary of "White Privilege" and not the unique product of my efforts and struggles, then my critics are undoubtedly the festering product of "White Hatred"; or in presidential vernacular, institutionalized racism. What else can you call the malicious slights of a former President of the United States, one Barack Obama, who didn't attend or send one delegate to the funerals of Prime Minister Margaret Thatcher, Major General Harold Greene (killed in Action), or murdered American hero Chris Kyle, but somehow managed to deploy multiple representatives to the memorial services of Michael Brown and Freddie Gray; known convicted criminals and proud street thugs? What else can you call giving millions of illegal immigrants free welfare, healthcare and shelter from criminal prosecution – those non-citizens who have little regard for our laws or survival – at the cost of homeless veterans and those taxpayers struggling to make ends meet? Non-White Privilege? Affirmative action via racial entitlement is now the greatest form of discrimination in contemporary America.

.@EricHolder: "Exactly when do you think America was great?"

Instead of focusing on inspirational stories of decent, industrious Americans who do everything in their power to make the world a better place, minority or otherwise, an antagonistic media continues to give preference to the brokers of race in order to drive a wedge in the institutions of logic, but most notably, the streets of America. "We the People" can either strive to eliminate these numerous misconceptions and punish those who applaud anarchy or invoke racism where none exist, too often at the expense of real discrimination, or this nation can continue to succumb to the destructive relics of distrust, hatred and discord. When color is king, character is but a pawn sacrificed under the fluttering flag of blind allegiance. America doesn't need more pious politicians claiming dominion over the historical inequities of race, nor does it require safe spaces absurdly seeking re-segregation to fulfill a never-ending victimization narrative. It needs a national intervention to illustrate the true victims of bigotry – those who needlessly suffered or died under unparalleled cruelty – would be appalled by their "privileged" descendants screaming racial injustice at life's every misfortune or disappointment because God's greatest gift, freedom, is now incumbent upon the bartered price of self-respect.

"Like an unchecked cancer, hate corrodes the personality and eats away its vital unity. Hate destroys a man's sense of values and his objectivity. It causes him to describe the beautiful as ugly and the ugly as beautiful, and to confuse the true with the false and the false with the true." *~Martin Luther King Jr.*

Smoke Signals and War Paint

Sorry, Elizabeth Warren, but being called "Pocahontas" isn't a racial slur when it refers to a white pathological liar who really isn't a Cherokee native, but routinely plays the historically oppressed victim of Anglo-American aggression on TV. Actually, when you factor in your refusal to take a DNA test, it's downright hilarious! The fact the President had the brass to share your repeated "cultural misappropriation" in front of a group of Native Americans – honorable World War II veterans, Navajo Code Talkers, who proudly served their country – is no less than an epic form of social justice. After all, if "White Privilege" is so unbearably rampant in modern America as you love to proclaim, why did you repeatedly misrepresent your heritage to advance your education and career? To collect a seven-figure, permanently paid vacation for self-identified martyrdom? The next time you feel the "privileged" need to wear your Harvard headdress to a job interview or shamelessly pander to ethnic voters for the fleeting hope of exploiting their racial plight, have the courage to accept your just desserts before you fraudulently contribute one more "family" recipe to a culinary collection featuring the descendants of the Five Civilized Tribes. My guess is your newfound trail of liberal tears flowing down the "you didn't build that" Marxist driveway of your multi-million-dollar home will find no such sympathy among the displaced remnants of the Choctaw, Chickasaw, Cherokee, Creek and Seminole nations.

If you play your gender Tarot cards correctly, Pocahontas, perhaps you can even cash in on the newest "me too" fad by falsely claiming the ghost of Andrew Jackson chased you around your prized Ted Kennedy-autographed-desk because he mistook your Khrushchev Kachina doll for a third-string "Redskin" linebacker; a self-adopted term of respect, ferocity and unity among Indian delegations who despised traitors, government treaties and duplicitous politicians just like yourself. In the meantime, keep taking a knee on the Constitution, the real victims of bigotry and the intelligence of the American people because karma is a public dish best served cold.

"The Marines made us yell "Geronimo" when we jumped out of planes & that didn't offend us either!" *~Thomas Begay, decorated Navajo Code Talker*

E Pluribus Unum

As Texas begins the arduous journey of recovering from the horrific aftermath of Hurricane Harvey, it is heartwarming to see so many complete strangers from different walks of life – regardless of race, wealth, or political affiliation – come together to selflessly help those in need. Although some critics will always attempt to politicize a natural disaster because they're far too infantile to grasp the gravity of the situation or too callous to care for the true victims of misfortune, the courage and compassion shown by volunteers from across America are an inspiring reminder that it is not politicians or agendas that bind us, but a mutual love for life, liberty and an unwavering desire to protect our loved ones. And while we must not forget to grieve for those who died or to identity those soulless dregs who chose to loot property amidst the ongoing cries of human suffering, Texas is proof that a strong, independent spirit can also serve as the epitome of empathy and love. Just because fanatical factions within both parties tirelessly strive to dehumanize one another, to convince us hate, greed, and privilege are the most common modalities in society, by no means requires everyday people to accept their destructive premise or to follow the hollow prose of divisive parasites. For the moment we choose to abandon our humanity and God-given capacity to reason, to perceive one another as mortal enemies rather than innately seeing ourselves in all people and plights, is the moment America is forever lost. America is not a gender, a race, an economic class or the sum of a myopic two-party system where bitter pundits seek to drown our senses in misery and paranoia. It is the only country I want to call home. Tragedies like 9/11 or Hurricane Harvey should never have to remind us what it truly means to be an American; they should instinctively make us feel eternally grateful that we all are one.

The Progressive Plantation & the Barbwire Lights of Conformity

The inability of Republicans to connect with Latinos – yes, those of the natural born or legal variety – is painfully symbolic of their inability to dispel decades of senseless leftist propaganda and victimization banter. Before progressives poisoned the minds and souls of minorities and fatally fractured America along racial, economic, and religious lines, Latinos had far more in common, and still do, with their so-called conservative enemies than those liberal agents of entitlement who wish to keep their communities impoverished, dependent, and perpetually angry. However, if the truth be known, most Latinos are extremely hard working, family oriented and unapologetically proud of their Christian faith; of which a clear majority support the necessity of keeping God in our schools and public institutions; a key cog of our nation's founding that the media has turned into a Right-Wing conspiracy of religious fanaticism.

Is it not common sense for minority families and entrepreneurs to want to keep the bulk of their hard-earned income through low taxes and minimal federal regulation? Who doesn't want to own their own home, to be able to afford their own transportation and quality healthcare, and raise their children in a morally rich environment devoid of hate and government control? Can a menial welfare check, the bitter rhetoric of absentee politicians regurgitated every four years, achieve any of these goals? George Bush knew this indelible truth all too well for in 2004 he garnered a record 44% of the Latino vote; a decisive and key component in his re-election bid. The reason why Democrats fear minority conservatives is because their party's agenda, their racist ploys and monopoly on public perception, cannot survive even if one-third of minorities flee the progressive plantation and speak out against the left's false narrative. It is literally a death sentence for Democrats, both electorally and ideologically. If the GOP simply learned how to articulate and funnel their message into a universal beacon of liberty and prosperity – employed unflinching perspective to address these divisive issues and expose the futility of Democratic bigotry – then "We the People" may very well be surfing this cultural tsunami of discord rather than drowning beneath Barack Obama's orchestrated demographic tidal wave of proud anti-Americanism.

Hate is Hate

According to the unbiased media pundits and self-righteous soldiers of unity, Antifa represents "tolerant" revolutionaries, terrorists aren't real Muslims, BLM advocates murdering police to end "racism", the Democratic Party founded the KKK to politely educate black voters, Barack Obama empathized with race rioters in Ferguson/Baltimore to save lives, feminists urged the rape of Sarah Palin and Melania Trump to protect women's rights, Hollywood fantasizes about Presidential assassination to promote compassion, gender conditioning empowers child transvestites by encouraging pedophilia, la Raza celebrates diversity by intending to demographically conquer America, but somehow a twisted faction of parading supremacists confronted by leftist militants speaks for Donald Trump, 63 million of his voters (including minorities) and all patriotic, white Americans? Naturally. What other insipid, irresponsible conclusion would I expect from the divisive, fake news, alt-truth, violence inciting media establishment?

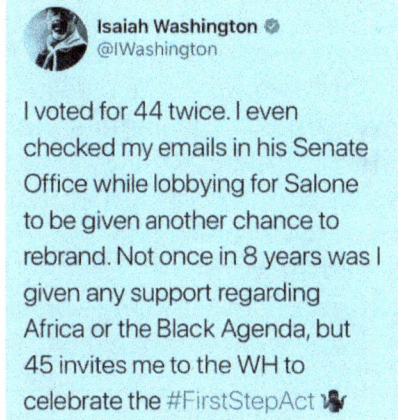

> **Isaiah Washington** ✓
> @IWashington
>
> I voted for 44 twice. I even checked my emails in his Senate Office while lobbying for Salone to be given another chance to rebrand. Not once in 8 years was I given any support regarding Africa or the Black Agenda, but 45 invites me to the WH to celebrate the #FirstStepAct 🙏

Burning America to the ground will not make the world a better place, or right past wrongs, it will merely reaffirm who truly despises our way of life and seeks to divide us according to the identity politics of race, gender or any variety of "victimized" plights. Instead of unanimously agreeing hate is hate and holding all parties equally accountable without making reckless accusations designed to inflame tensions, partisan politics and petty vendettas are destroying any hope of racial harmony. When your only goal is to destroy Donald Trump and the common-sense reforms so many Americans desperately crave – especially after the distinctly prejudiced and unapologetically anti-American policies of the past administration – anything will make sense to the millions of malcontents still conspiring to overthrow an election result by any means necessary.

The Forsaken Dream

As we celebrate the life of Martin Luther King Jr., it deeply disturbs me how so many have distorted the legacy and intent of the most influential civil rights leader in modern history. In the face of true injustice and bodily harm, Dr. King never wavered from his convictions as he spoke with a vigor and eloquence that could sway the most obstinate critic. No matter how perilous the situation or egregious the crime, he symbolically and literally embodied non-violence, the struggle for racial equality, by refusing to abandon the belief that people of all creeds and color deserved to be treated in the same light as they were created: as equals in the eyes of God.

Despite the media's otherwise sensational claims, the same man who endured hatred and death threats daily never would have embraced the Ferguson or Baltimore riots, he never would have stood idly by as crime, drug abuse, unemployment and broken families ravaged the black community, he never would have invoked slavery or poverty to justify brutality, and he never would have demanded special treatment, for anyone, not already afforded to all Americans. Above all, the son of a former pastor preached accountability born from an acute self-awareness that rejected self-pity or entitlement. Failing to hold everyone to the same standard, especially oneself, meant succeeding in discriminating. Martin Luther King did not want to be seen as a victim, to shout racism at every perceived misfortune or disagreement; he merely wished for every soul the inalienable right to live the life of their choosing, to prosper according to their own unique gifts, without undue scorn or prejudice. Sadly, those voices claiming to be faithful disciples of Dr. King's profound and indelible teachings – hovering parasites like Al Sharpton and Jesse Jackson – have exploited tragedy, invented injustice, and incited animosity ad nauseam almost exclusively for personal gain. Their presence has done little to assuage the actual plight of black Americans, the moral and economic erosion of our inner cities, because such a proposition requires principle over press conferences and sacrifice over sentiment. Change does not occur by raising a singular fist to protest a perceived injustice; it resides in the positive impressions made by loving parents, the resourceful faith of fortitude, and those overlooked contributions made by everyday people willing to act without malice or reward.

MLK's dying wish was not that we continue to be defined by race but that all Americans would demonstrate an insatiable desire to live in harmony, to educate and empower our children, to thrive and contribute to a vibrant society, and most of all, to grow free from the destructive shackles of violence and hate. Progress is not measured by the number of times race is invoked or celebrated. It is personified by the number of lives liberated from its requirement. Before Barack Obama, Eric Holder and Loretta Lynch bent the scales of social justice, I honestly believed America was on a path to achieving that iconic

FIRST BLACK REPUBLICAN SENATOR: 1870

FIRST BLACK DEMOCRATIC SENATOR: 1993

dream. No, race relations were not perfect, bigotry will always exist in some form or facet of America, but more and more people simply realized that character, not the color of one's skin, was the greatest measure of our humanity. Now, in the growing shadow of a luminary's absence and the fading dream of his forsaken wisdom, this nation is as polarized as ever. As long as "We the People" allow bitter politicians and hostile hate groups like BLM or the KKK to dissect the world according to race - encouraging self-segregation, ransoming peace and flaunting color as a commodity - this country is destined to succumb to distrust and discord rather than forever bound by the inherent needs, hopes and dreams that should inevitably unite us all. As a white man whose heroes span the likes of Jackie Robinson, Michael Jordan, Ben Carson and Thomas Sowell, or better yet a proud Christian who embraces the handshake of brotherhood over the militant crescendo of fear, Rest in Peace, Dr. King....you are not forgotten.

"Darkness cannot drive out darkness; only light can do that. Hate cannot drive out hate; only love can do that." ~Martin Luther King

A "Progressive" Betrayal

The progressive movement has no real regard for the rights, intelligence and well-being of American minorities, merely an insatiable desire to incessantly cajole and mislead their communities with false racial animus; regardless of the potential ramifications. Their first inclination is always to manipulate and deceive, create a permanent state of disrepair, not to educate and empower through personal accountability. Even Barack Obama, our first minority President who promised "hope and change", did little to revitalize urban decay, increase economic opportunities and unite America; instead opting for racial propaganda that hid his historic failures and fueled civil unrest. And yet in only two years, Donald Trump, a supposed white supremacist, initiated a national advisory board for urban renewal, created investment opportunity zones for distressed communities, passed prison reform for nonviolent offenders, sought to end the mandated separation of families at the border, designated a national park for MLK, personally honored Rosa Parks, pardoned Alice Johnson and late boxer Jack Johnson, sparked a 400% jump in minority-owned businesses and presided over the lowest black and Latino jobless rates in U.S. history. Minority voters are nothing more than prodded pieces of disposable property to the 227-year-old Democratic plantation.

Dinesh D'Souza ✓
@DineshDSouza

The recent pardons of @realDonaldTrump don't exactly support the left's claim that he's a racist & white supremacist

POLICE & POLITICS

2016 FATAL SHOOTINGS BY POLICE
The Washington Post

- WHITE: 324
- BLACK: 173
- HISPANIC: 111
- OTHER/UNKNOWN: 98

When Facts Matter

How can 'black lives' matter when they don't even matter to black America? Despite comprising for 13% of the population, black Americans account for one-third of all assaults and rapes, as well as 50% of all robberies and murders. These are staggering statistics that far outweigh the most-petty slights and misrepresentations. Even more damning, African Americans are responsible for over 90% of all black homicides. Considering the KKK lynched roughly 3,500 blacks in 86 years, an unforgivable number in any context, what's the significance and collective outrage when 7,000 African Americans die at the hands of their own brethren each year? Whether you're killed at the hands of a white cop or a black stranger, intentionally or not, how does it make it anymore discriminatory or less tragic? Naturally that's completely disregarding the realization approximately twice as many whites are killed – some justified, some not – annually by police; and all without one mass protest or riot. Apparently common sense, not arguing with, running from or assaulting law enforcement, is too difficult of a solution to comprehend because these "victims" feel the insatiable need to escape the consequences of their "lawful" actions. If race is truly the culprit, not culture, why is a police officer 18.5 times more likely to be killed by a black American than a cop killing an unarmed black person? Because facts matter.

Does police brutality exist? Of course, it does. And all cases should be treated with the utmost concern and diligence. But there are far more cops dedicated to serving their communities with honor and dignity by doing their jobs the right way, than those abusive agents who have zero regard for people's safety or the rule of law. Perhaps the next time a suspected incident of excessive force garners national attention, elected leaders and media activists will consciously choose to act like adults by waiting for the facts to be divulged, due process completed, before recklessly stoking the fires of racial animosity for political gain and primetime fame. If a lot more of our youth complied with the simple instructions of law enforcement and actually put their "hands up" to fight in a court of law, a lot more "statistics" would be alive today to tell their side of the story. And God willing there would be no other story to tell than that of a routine traffic stop, ticket or arrest. Our men and women in uniform come from all walks of life and risk their lives daily for our protection; not to fulfill a racial vendetta that could ultimately cost them their lives or their freedom.

When death is exploited solely as a platform to demand financial and political concessions, rather than working tirelessly to avoid future tragedies and address the true source of urban decay – the broken black family, an erosion of basic values, a systemic cultural disdain for authority, and an absentee work ethic – nothing will change except the names and dates. If 'black lives matter', and all inherently should, it seems that statement serves more as a hypocritical oath than a grounded truth. After all, nearly 500,000 black babies were aborted last year and no one batted an eye. Truth, unlike victimization propaganda and racist banter, does not require 'safe spaces' from accountability. It merely requires an inescapable dose of reality.

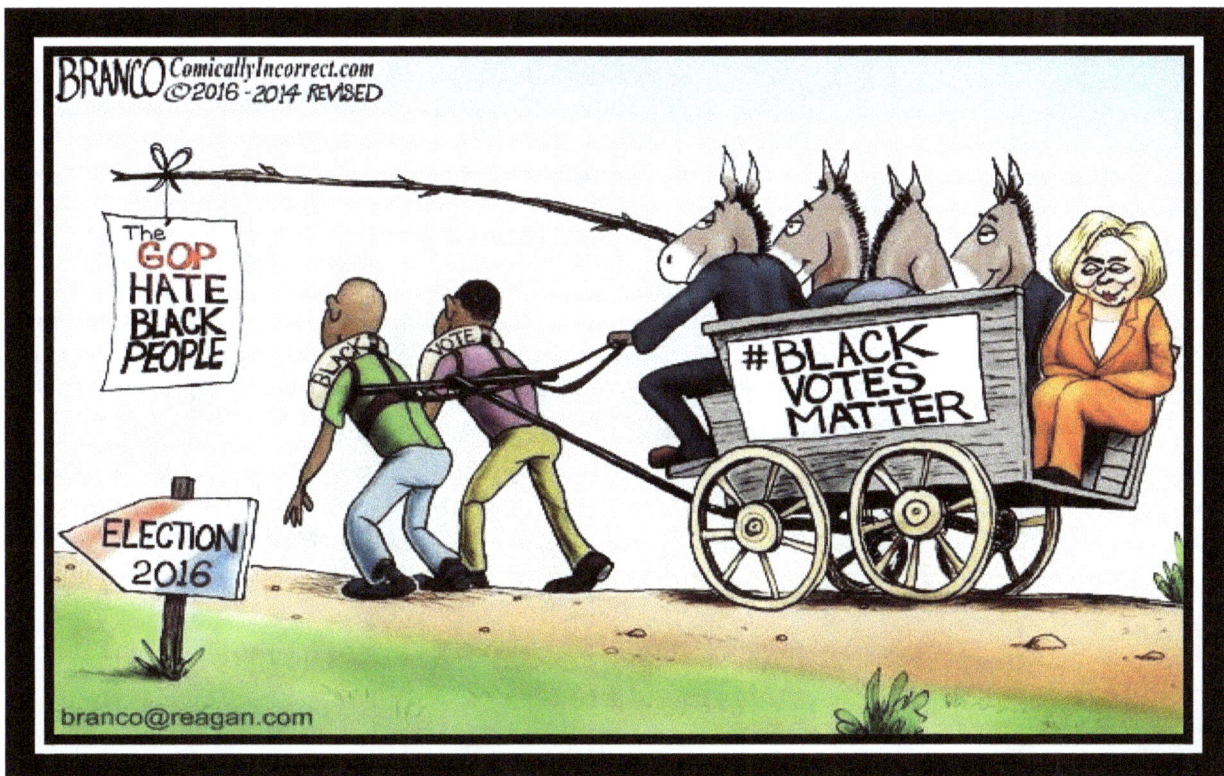

The Riot Act of Reverse Engineered Racism

There is a stark contrast between civil disobedience, principled defiance which Henry David Thoreau advocated in the face of foolish and intrusive authority, and the manufactured exploits of opportunistic anarchy for the sole purpose of selfish gain. One seeks to spiritually transcend or liberate man from unnecessary and ill-conceived government, the other merely uses misfortune and blind inference as a catalyst to steal, destroy, and incite endless chaos. And this is what happens when millions of Americans are taught to have no respect or regard for God, the rule of law, or their fellow man. This is what happens when a generation of discontented youth roam the streets, have no tangible ambition to better themselves or provide for their families, and solely endeavor to blame society or another race for their life's misfortunes. When individuals fail to sacrifice and toil for the blessings in their life – the roof over their head or the food on their table – they find it that much easier to steal from the mouth of labor and the handshake of good will. Even worse, they take for granted the very freedoms and unparalleled opportunities few nations can provide, let alone fathom. If you somehow need to live in Haiti, Nigeria or Iran for but a single month to understand you've never been a slave and that America is not your enemy, then the sheer depth of your political delusion and self-imposed depravity is as vast as the irreconcilable chasm you call color.

I don't care if you're black, white, brown or purple; there is never a justification for pillaging, looting and threatening the lives and livelihoods of the innocent. That's not justice...it's theft, barbarism and murder veiled beneath the guise of social equality. Just because you're fed-up with the prevailing system – albeit one or 100 documented cases of excessive force – doesn't give you the right or a blank check to declare war on America, white cops, or the city whose streets you occupy. There's a civilized way to question authority in a free country, inspire meaningful change, and it never requires smashing one car or lighting a single match. It merely requires fact, eloquence and peacefully rallying people to engage in open and constructive discourse through the political and legal institutions afforded to all citizens. In other words, how can you demand justice when you personally embody hate and tyranny? How do your obscene and criminal actions give your cause credibility, hold the "suspected" culprits accountable or honor any notion of justice? Believe it or not, there are numerous white, Hispanic, and Asian victims who suffer at the hands of police brutality; not to mention an endless litany of police officers purposely slain by criminals. But are their families and communities resorting to mindless mayhem and opportunistic anarchy as a means of recourse? Of course not, for such debauchery degrades any sense of higher moral ground and ultimately defeats the refuge of justice you seek. Yes, how can you demand justice when you fail to respect anything or anyone but yourself; when you can summarily deprive others of life and property without the slightest regret or hesitation? Appealing to humanity first requires being a member of the human race.

The Michael Brown and Freddie Gray riots are far less redolent of a systemic racial conspiracy – as media pundits and militant activists would have you believe – than they are representative of a much more vast and insidious movement that is literally destroying America from the inside out. Oh, there are racists, bigots and unjust forces in all facets of our society, just as there decent and honest cops dedicated to helping people from all walks of life. However, this self-evident reality becomes a moot point when we as a people, a civilized society, are irrevocably broken from seeing the world for what it is; not as black or white, Republican or Democrat, but as rationale and responsible adults committed to obvious universal precepts. Our very sense of right and wrong, our desire for a vibrant and industrious society, has been fatally compromised by those who thrive on fear and disinformation in lieu of accountability and integrity. The truth is no longer an independent institution defined by objectivity, empirical evidence and critical thought. It has become what the leftist media and our government declares it to be; political Silly Putty that is hopelessly skewed towards a self-serving agenda...an insatiable hatred for traditional, conservative America. There's a much more infamous term for such destructive and unilateral thinking: it's called fascism.

The gradual rise and proliferation of liberal fascism has driven God out of our institutions of learning, hijacked core curriculum to vaccinate our youth against common sense, turned the definition of "is" into a valid point of adulterous contention, exonerated record debt and economic failure by espousing dependence, valued the criminality of illegal immigrants over the rights of actual citizens, and turned success into the racist equivalent of envy. As disturbing and incredulous as these developments appear, they're symptomatic of our greatest cultural decay. The traditional and nuclear family paradigm of Western Civilization, once the epicenter of our values and the embodiment of the American dream, has been sabotaged in the name of gay marriage, malformed to embrace transgendered parents and children, ridiculed by feminists who celebrate abortion over the devotion of stay-at-home moms, and abandoned in favor of the bankrupt teachings of social media and the inherent "shock" value of pop culture. Is it therefore really of any surprise that porn now has more societal appeal than the Bible or that opposing homosexuality, a sin and destructive precedent in the tenets of nearly every major religion, is the new benchmark of bigoted extremism in America? Once one ethical boundary is eclipsed – one bastion of our Judeo-Christian and Constitutional values – what's to stop the next one from suffering the same fate? Nothing. When the armies of intolerance are manning the gates of freedom, truth is only as relevant as your reverence to their opinion.

Forget that Michael Brown and Freddie Gray possessed rap sheets longer than Pinocchio's nose or that minorities comprise a majority of the Baltimore Police Department. "Newsworthy" crime is now defined by race, political affiliation and religion; or lack thereof. Although every death is a tragedy, including the unnecessary and inexcusable death of Eric Garner, what does it say when the media obscures truth and incites violence, when an elected president's legacy is riddled with racial hatred, and so-called civil rights activists rarely-if-ever come to the unconditional aid of white, Christian, conservative victims? When grown men and women, supposed enlightened leaders, cannot even admit to or hold themselves accountable for such obvious failures and prejudices, how are they qualified, let alone given a national platform, to perilously affect the lives of innocent Americans and bring an entire nation to the precipice of civil war? The reason why such incessant race-baiting and senseless capitulation faintly exists in Europe is because they refuse to cater to ransomed guilt or those political ploys designed to topple logic with the circus of reverse engineered revolt; individuals are accountable today, not personally responsible for the improprieties of their ancestors. And these are the nations, openly embraced by American liberals, who knowingly bartered for and brought slaves to the New World.

Whether we like it or not, there will always be future victims of excessive police force, albeit under the flag of a national police force or local law enforcement, and those perpetrators must always be held responsible as individuals. Not everyone is racist and not everyone is guilty. Likewise, rioting, looting and anarchy are never an acceptable means of protesting legal matters or perceived wrongs; especially those instances heightened by racial tension and stereotypes. If you repeatedly remain silent as African Americans gun down one another in droves, the greatest source of transgressions against the black community, such depravity does not automatically become an unspeakable tragedy and a call to arms because a white, Hispanic or Asian suspect is involved. Your race is not your career and your life is not defined by race; not unless you choose to make that myopic distinction. The best way to ensure a culture of hate and instantaneously dissolve over two centuries of racial progressive, paid by those who physically suffered and died under the auspices of injustice and persevered to dream of a better tomorrow for all, is to become the lie that guarantees America will regress into a soulless state of justifiable bloodshed and politically convenient paranoia. Sadly, that's exactly what the voices of liberal fascism desire: to deflect blame, divide the people, destroy our values, and use any means necessary to silence opposition on the altar of secular subjugation.

If you believe your natural rights, individual liberty, are derived from the wisdom of God and transcend the cultivated walls of hate and ignorance prescribed by Big Government, uncontested statism, then you're also blessed with the ability to discern truth from fiction and skin color from sadism. Love of life, not immoral opportunism or the political manifestations of unscrupulous leaders, is what separates good from evil. Free will is not only a gift; it's a moral obligation to unite all creation under a banner of hope and progress rather than to descend mankind into a perpetual state of death, distrust and chaos.

"We do not want the men of another color for our brothers-in-law; we want them for our brothers. If you want to lift yourself up, lift-up someone else."
~Booker T. Washington

Sicko: The Paper Mache Gun of Madness

If Michael Moore wants to disarm all police, my suggestion is that his Paper Mache, firearms crusade first and foremost begins by stripping all criminals of weapons; unless, that is, the biggest hypocrite of hyperbole wants to personally patrol the inner city of Detroit, defend the streets of Baltimore, or thwart violent crime in Harlem for the rest of his life without the aid of a television crew or an army of civil rights militants. Oh, and while you're at it, please do not forget about ensuring the abolition of government tyranny once and for all; the most fundamental justification for the creation of the Second Amendment. Because human nature will never change, the unjust and oppressive schemes of vain and ambitious leaders, neither will the need for self-defense. Sorry but I give absolute no credence to a radical activist who demonizes those uniformed men and women defying death daily to protect and serve civilized people, whose untimely deaths and inflicted injuries are also a tragedy, only to unconditionally embrace those criminals who destroy, loot, and threaten the lives of innocents at the slightest hint of indiscretion or societal strife.

Rewarding opportunistic anarchy and unapologetic lawlessness isn't progress; it's a death wish. Demanding the release of violent criminals and drug dealers from prison solely because of their race, while deeming conservatives, Christians and capitalists the real enemies of the state, isn't justice; it's madness! Contrary to progressive semantics, a Christian baker isn't going to rob your home and shoot you because you're gay, don't have a job or voted for Barack Obama. They're going to ask why you're listening to a lying socialist filmmaker – worth over 50 million dollars and living under the protection of an armed bodyguard – who somehow believes Cuban socialized heath care is fair compensation for the millions toiling and dying under the oppressive boot of communism. When progressives start holding all Americans accountable as individuals for their actions and livelihoods, rather than excusing envy, crime and apathy under the banner of "white privilege" and justifiable rage, then perhaps that Paper Mache gun of progressivism can shoot them a copy of the Constitution and directions to a free, just, and prosperous country. If the goal of leftists is to ensure one sect of society can no longer be arrested, let alone questioned, and that economic inequality has nothing to do with hard work or personal responsibility, then they are well on their way to destroying the last, best hope of mankind. Tyranny never requires a turn signal; it merely requires an unarmed victim.

To Protect & Serve

I frequently get asked why I so adamantly defend law enforcement. My response? Law and order is nonexistent without boots on the ground, a principled backbone, to keep our communities a safe harbor for our children to grow and prosper. It's a duty that requires sacrifice, patience and is rarely appreciated because cops are the embodiment of our laws...the proverbial "dark side" of authority people love to hate. I freely admit I've had occasional run-ins with overbearing, unpleasant officers. However, I've also met a number of decent human beings who are just trying to make a difference in their communities by protecting hardworking Americans from the ravages of crime. What critics too often overlook is that police deal with hardened criminals, con-artists and serial idiots every day; those who lie without remorse, have zero regard for the law, and who pose a credible danger to the safety of both young and old. Yet these brave men and women are still expected to be professionals – give suspects the benefit of the doubt – even though their compassion and indulgence may actually cost them their lives. How many other jobs can boast of such a dynamic, let alone comprehend the dire consequences? Few if any.

I used to scoff at the idea of putting mini-cameras on every officer because I thought it was too intrusive and would open a Pandora's Box of frivolous lawsuits over the faintest interpretation of indiscretion. But the more I think about it, I love it. Yes, I embrace the demand touted by rabid liberals because I have little doubt these devices – which already exist in most cop cars – will exonerate countless law enforcement agents from an exploding culture of baseless media attacks, as well as shield them from the shameless ploys of career race-baiters. In fact, these video records could potentially prevent much of the senseless riots and mob violence plaguing our urban centers. After all, if rhetoric matched reality, the number of white deaths at the hands of police brutality was nearly double that of black victims in 2014. And as for those cops who do operate above and beyond the law? Such a move will make them think twice before violating the rights of citizens, or it will help put them behind bars where they belong. Either way, society is the better for it because nothing would be a greater threat to our lives, our freedoms, than a national police force under the Marxist control of Barack Obama or Hillary Clinton. I shiver at the mere thought.

Regardless of your predisposed attitudes towards police, I implore you to give them the same respect as our military personnel. Take a few minutes out of your day to introduce yourself, shake their hands, and thank them for their service. For without their dedication and sacrifice, their willingness to protect life at the risk of losing their own, America would resemble a banana republic that exports sunshine for subjugation. Our liberty, your right to due process free from mob justice and political exploitation, is not for sale.

Anatomy of Self Defense

Famed forensic pathologist, Dr. Michael Baden: "There is a legitimate concern as to whether the shooting was an overreaction." Anytime someone is shot six times I don't have a problem with such an observation. However, if a 6'4", 300-pound man – who moments earlier robbed a convenience store, strong armed the owner and assaulted Officer Darren Wilson in his own car – is charging your position despite continued warnings to stand down, in a violent neighborhood no less, you're likely to shoot repeatedly...especially if the first shots were of no deterrence. Throw in the fact preliminary reports now show Michael Brown had marijuana and alcohol in his system, not to mention an extremely bitter attitude, and the ingredients of fear, anger and confusion make for an explosive cocktail.

Did Officer Wilson overact? Was it necessary to shoot six times? Perhaps; perhaps we'll never know. But then again, none of us, including Dr. Baden or the St. Louis County Coroner, witnessed the events unfold. What we do know is that the wounds were front facing, indicative of a face-to-face confrontation, and that a man obviously felt provoked and feared for his life. The first four shots were likely to the right arm, as illustrated by the autopsy graphic, and thus, intended to wound/deter Mr. Brown. When that strategy failed, a result often quite telling of the suspect's size and determination, lethal force was used by the officer to neutralize the threat and ensure his own survival; standard protocol for nearly all law enforcement agents.

If the Trayvon Martin tragedy taught us anything – other than a racist President and activist media trying to unduly convict an assault victim for defending himself – it's that no common-sense individual is willing to become a statistic to appease the politically correct left's victimization agenda. Regardless of the incessant politics and posturing, may justice be done and the forces of hate and demagoguery be held accountable for the destructive aftermath they unapologetically incited.

A Media "Brown" Out

Has Barack Obama or Eric Holder ever personally called for an investigation into the wrongful shooting death of a white, Hispanic, or Asian teenager; especially if the perpetrator was a cop or of another race? Not even once?

I'm a white man - in a supposed "white establishment" society - but if I repeatedly ignore a cop's orders, let alone physically assault one with the intent to do serious harm, I unconditionally expect to be shot. It has nothing to with race or favoritism; it's common sense. The right to self-defense, police officer or not, supersedes any notion of color. If politicians and the mainstream media actually educated people by presenting both sides of the story, not just pushing their victimization agenda with a wanton disregard for the truth and rule of law, then there would be no doubt as to what is acceptable behavior and what conduct would likely result in lethal action. Otherwise, the destruction and chaos unleashed in Ferguson, which has nothing to do with honoring justice or the life of Mike Brown, will be but another link in an ongoing legacy of senseless violence and racial propaganda.

If Trayvon Martin or Mike Brown never attacked George Zimmerman or Darren Wilson, they would be alive today. End of story, good night, Good Morning America! That's the real tragedy. Why is this concept so difficult to understand? If a black cop shot a white man charging him with the intent to do bodily harm, no one in the black community, the White House or the leftist media would have a problem with it. So why do they now? Excuse my English but that's called racism where I come from. Self-defense is self-defense; no garnish, riots, or hypocrisy required!

For no-nonsense Americans, the national debate engulfing the violence in Ferguson isn't about rooting for Darren Wilson or Mike Brown. It's about wiping away the poisonous media slant and escaping the lynch mob mentality of activists and mercenaries who are inviting chaos without even being privy to all the facts. Far too many celebrities, media pimps, and politicians are throwing their own personal baggage into a volatile situation to somehow atone for whatever imagined slights they supposedly suffered at the hands of law enforcement or the so-called white establishment. If these hypocrites opened their eyes and tried to be objective for one solitary second, they'd realize there are white, Asian, and Hispanic teenagers who are killed every day...by cops or blacks...and no one is rioting and looting in the name of injustice. Why? Because such idiocy has nothing to do with justice or the victim's misfortune; it simply makes a mockery of every ideal you supposedly stand for. If a leader, a movement or a race wants to be taken seriously, respected by all walks of life without refrain, then give society a reason to do just that. Not everything is a damn conspiracy or a hate crime. Michael Brown isn't an angel and Darren Wilson isn't infallible. No matter what the outcome, I only pray that peace is restored, the verdict isn't trivialized by hateful ignorance, and that this shameful haze of racial opportunism is lifted from the brow of America. Everyone must be held accountable to an acceptable standard of behavior, universal respect, and any lasting change must begin with the smug politicians and media puppets pulling the strings of racial discord!

When Fact Becomes Fiction

According to the official autopsy findings, Freddie Gray's death was the result of incidental trauma caused by the rapid deceleration of a police van, and not the assumed result of homicide. So, basically, the countless hours and resources dedicated to stoking public hysteria, the destructive litany of rioting and looting of private property, the endless rhetoric spewed by professional activists – including the likes of the city prosecutor, Barack Obama, the Black Panthers, Al Sharpton and the DOJ – was all based on a false narrative, a media driven myth, a lie. And how many businesses were destroyed, lives ruined, and people unnecessarily put in harm's way by orchestrated unrest enveloping both Baltimore and Ferguson?

Does police brutality exist? Without a doubt. And all cases should be treated with the utmost concern and diligence. But there are far more cops dedicated to serving their communities with honor and dignity by doing their jobs the right way, than those abusive agents who have zero regard for people's safety or the rule of law. Perhaps the next time a suspected incident of excessive force garners national attention, grown men and women will consciously choose to act like adults by waiting for the facts to be divulged, due process completed, before recklessly stoking the fires of racial animosity for political gain and prime time fame.

If a lot more of our youth complied with the simple instructions of law enforcement and waited to fight for their rights in a court of law, a lot more "statistics" would be alive today to tell their side of the story; and God willing there would be no other story to tell than that of a routine traffic stop, ticket or arrest. Yes, all lives innately matter but so does the truth. Our men and women in uniform – those who put their lives at risk daily only to be the never-ending objects of ridicule and societal scorn – have earned the right to receive the benefit of the doubt until a thorough investigation is completed, in lieu of giving absolute credence to a man arrested over 20 times for drug possession, distribution, and burglary. Or do those leaders and media pundits so blinded by their own bias and disdain even care anymore?

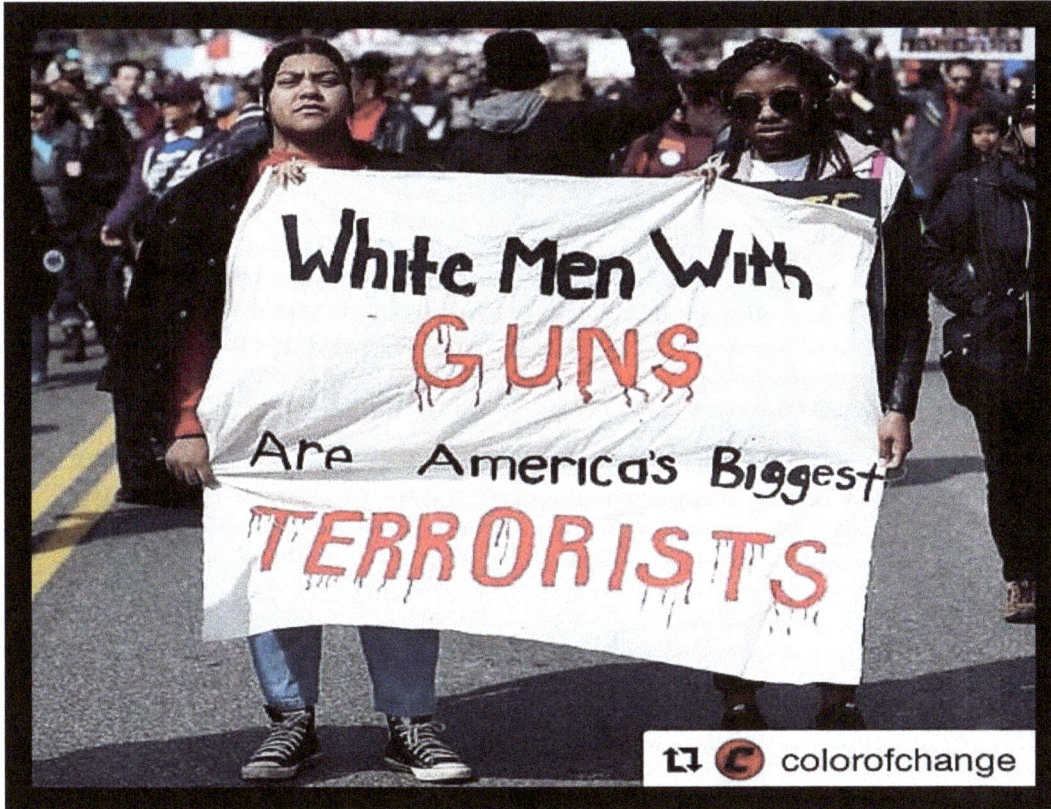

Murder of blacks and whites in the US, 2013

(per 1,000,000 members of the murderer's race)

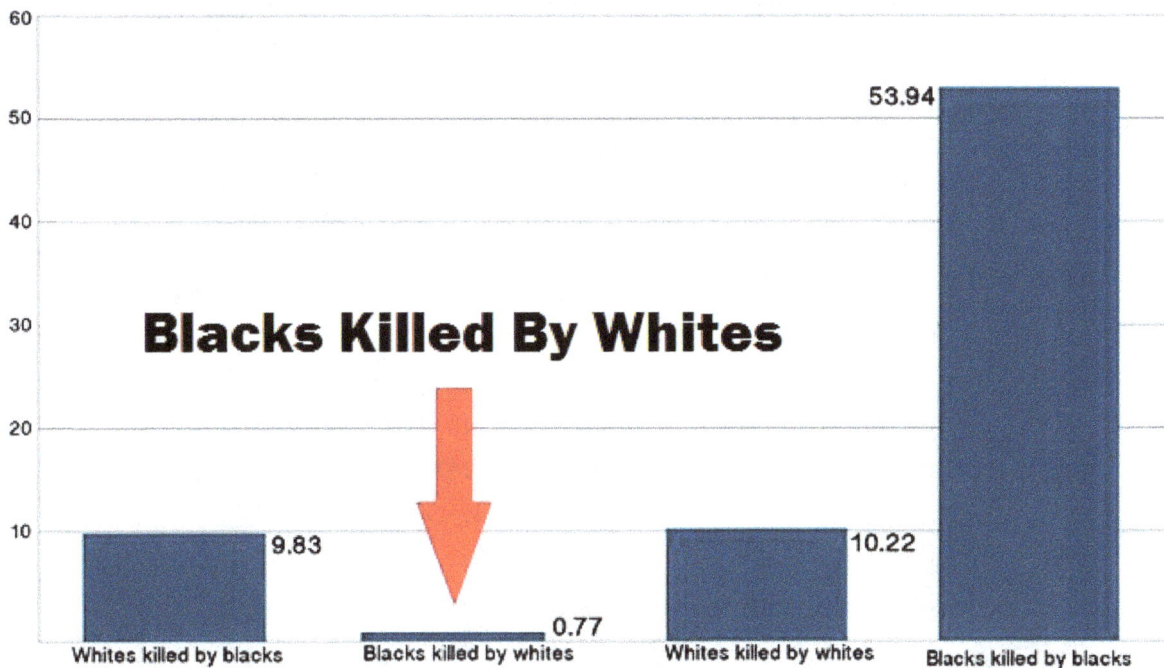

Blacks Killed By Whites

9.83	0.77	10.22	53.94
Whites killed by blacks	Blacks killed by whites	Whites killed by whites	Blacks killed by blacks

Source: **2013 FBI Criminal Report**

A Bridge to Nowhere

"We're not looters. We're liberators! We are not burners. We're Builders!" *~Al Sharpton*

There's only one problem, Reverend. You're already free, just not free from the auspices of the law, God and common sense; nobody is! And if you're legitimate builders, not community "disorganizer", please show us the blueprint to anything you've constructed other than racial discord, bigotry, crime, ignorance and apathy. Oh, we've seen the urban decay, vacant lives and sheer contempt for civility festering in the Democratic epicenters of Detroit, Chicago and Ferguson. If you truly desire to help the black community, lead society to previous unattainable heights of enlightenment and unity that Dr. King courageously personified, stop blaming the white man and start holding your own people accountable: for raising and educating their kids, teaching and embodying real values, finding and keeping a job, and not using any imagined or fabricated slight to riot and invoke racism. Oh, there's a blueprint for erecting a prosperous, moral, and liberated society...from men much more wise, honorable, and industrious than you...you simply chose to profit from the political capital of hate, division and senseless entitlement rather than fostering a deep-seated appreciation for the unique privileges America innately offers all her children. At the very least, any discernible vestige of love for your own people - or better yet, humanity - should always empower you to act astutely on their behalf in hopes of building a bridge to a better tomorrow. Sadly, nothing could be further from the truth.

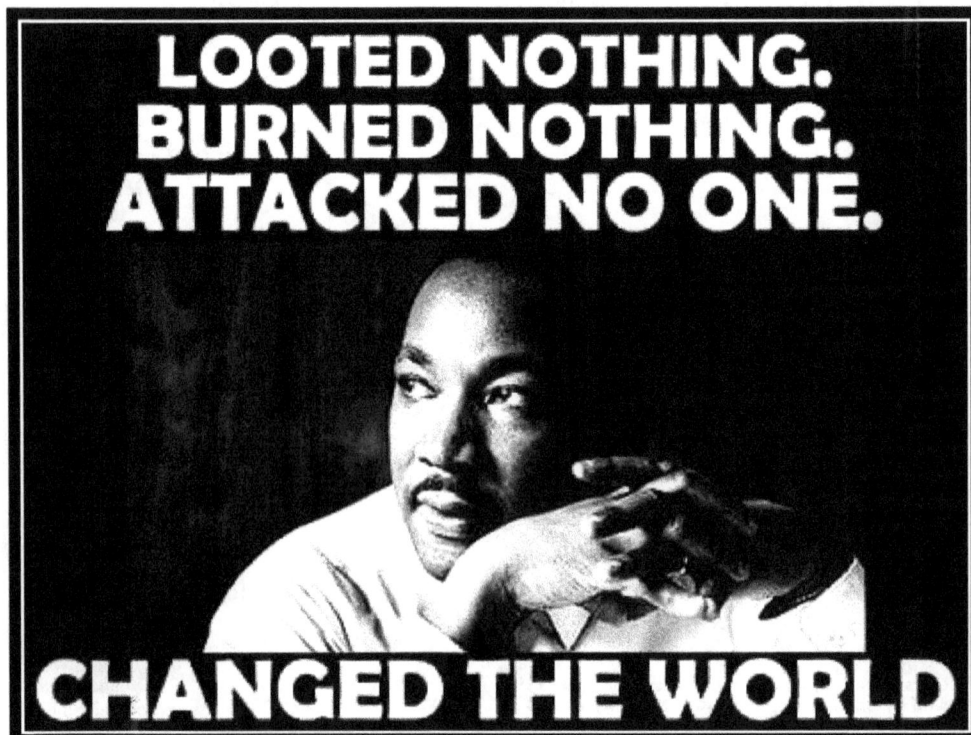

LOOTED NOTHING. BURNED NOTHING. ATTACKED NO ONE. CHANGED THE WORLD

Law & Disorder: Resisting Race & Apathy

When claiming racism and unjustified police brutality, it's important to familiarize oneself with the exact details and circumstances. For instance, Terence Crutcher – the reported unarmed Oklahoma man killed by police – had a long criminal record and history of aggression: including an "intent to kill" charge, drug trafficking and resisting arrest. In the tragic case of the Charlotte shooting, there was a black police chief, a black officer, and an armed black man who refused a simple request to drop his weapon. Unlike Eric Garner, whose death was clearly a result of excessive police force and negligence, most arrest-related deaths are completely avoidable when suspects use basic discretion.

What's really racist and unjust? Rioting, death threats, assault and looting in the name of social justice! I grieve for these men and their families, I truly wish all suspects could be disarmed with nonlethal force, but one moment of hesitation can be your last. If law enforcement acts rashly and inflicts bodily harm without reasonable cause, they should be held accountable without remorse or special accommodation. Period! However, when everyday Americans, regardless of race or disposition, refuse to follow simple instructions and therefore pose a legitimate threat to an officer's survival...i.e., demonstrating erratic behavior or wielding a gun...they too are accountable for such unwise actions. Yes, believe it or not, cops lives matter too and they die every day with little media attention or national outrage. Their families simply do not resort to mass anarchy and opportunistic theft to assuage their grief out of respect for the law, their country and their neighbor.

If politicians, athletes and celebrities spent as much time pleading with the black community to obey the law and to never resist arrest as they do inciting hatred of America and violence against police with their reckless accusations and divisive rhetoric, countless lives could be saved and our communities made all the safer. After all, there's no acceptable excuse for anyone not to comply with basic instructions when it will prevent unnecessary confusion, severe injury or death. Unfortunately, preserving human life is not at the top of the victimization agenda otherwise such prudent actions would have been taken long ago. Leadership, real quantifiable change, requires effort, responsibility and a great deal of selflessness. It's not a symbol, an NFL demonstration or a soundbite on the 5 o'clock news to increase your sagging jersey sales. Modern day activism, on the other hand, merely requires raising a fist and claiming injustice in the wake of your own apathy and ignorance. Citizens have inalienable rights just like an officer has the natural right to self-preservation. And like it or not, our differences be damned, we all must learn to coexist in a world where sensationalism is now more acceptable than self-effacing truths and holding people accountable for their actions is a prosecutable form of discrimination.

Universal Rules of Civilian Conduct When Confronted by Police

1. Follow instructions. It's not a debate!

2. Never resist arrest. It's a crime!

3. Never point a weapon at a cop or make threatening gestures. Also a crime!

4. Be honest or exercise your right to be silent! Lying raises the suspicion of officers, heightens tensions, and could result in further charges.

5. See #1 because you're accountable for your actions...regardless of what the liberal media selectively reports!

Failure to abide by these common-sense standards of behavior may result in serious bodily harm and/or death: regardless of your age, gender, race, religion or political affiliation. No, police aren't perfect, or even saints, but how does breaking any of these rules – the law, mind you – help your cause or ensure your safety? There's a time to fight for your rights, your presumed innocence or any instance of police brutality, and it's always in a court of law! How many lives would be saved, protests made irrelevant, if everyone acknowledged these simple truths? Educate your children and please remember denial is not a riot in Egypt! It's now a politically convenient excuse accepted in newsrooms across America!

RONALD REAGAN
1981   UNITED STATES PRESIDENT   1989

We must reject the idea every time
a law is broken society is guilty.
It is time to restore the
American precept each individual
is accountable for his actions.

When Life Is Not a Game

If athletes, the media and racial activists want to claim injustice and oppression at every conceivable turn, shout racism from every corner, so be it. But if they truly want to make a difference and invoke meaningful change for millions of our youth, then America needs to have an open, honest conversation about crime and the countless lives, both victims and perpetrators, being destroyed on a daily basis. As someone who has friends from all walks of life, races, and economic dispositions, I'm by no means implying whites don't commit crimes or that the prevalence of poverty, absentee parents, and a lack of education do not contribute to systemic, generational crime. Of course, they do. And while it is not my intention to seem insensitive or haughty, these statistics are so damning and unacceptable that we as a diverse, civilized society can no longer be afraid to speak uncomfortable truths simply because they may offend others. There is simply too much at stake. More than ever, this country and our inner cities need role models with an acute sense of accountability, community, not grandstanding players/owners dedicated to publicity stunts or political vendettas that do nothing to address these failings or assuage the suffering of so many people. Giving children hope begins by giving them a sense of pride, moral obligation and an unbreakable belief in themselves that transcends all barriers or racial narratives. The intersection of crime and race is not a juvenile matter of screaming "I told you so" or solved by "taking a knee", but represents a grave threat to the safety of our communities, the unity of this country and the future of all our loved ones. Denial, albeit by refusing to act upon this crisis of culture or by mastering the accusatory art of political deflection, is no longer an option.

There are dramatic race differences in crime rates. Asians have the lowest rates, followed by whites and then Hispanics. This pattern holds true for nearly every crime category and virtually all age groups. All statistics were provided by "**The Color of Crime: 2016 Revised Edition**" from *Edwin Rubenstein* of the New Century Foundation.

- The evidence suggests that if there is police racial bias in arrests it is negligible. Victim and witness surveys show that police arrest violent criminals in close proportion to the rates at which criminals of different races commit violent crimes.

- In 2013, a black was six times more likely than a non-black to commit murder, and 12 times more likely to murder someone of another race than to be murdered by someone of another race.

- In 2013, of the approximately 660,000 crimes of interracial violence that involved blacks and whites, blacks were the perpetrators 85 percent of the time. This meant a black person was 27 times more likely to attack a white person than vice versa. A Hispanic was eight times more likely to attack a white person than vice versa.

- If New York City were all white, the murder rate would drop by 91 percent, the robbery rate by 81 percent, and the shootings rate by 97 percent.

- In an all-white Chicago, murder would decline 90 percent, rape by 81 percent, and robbery by 90 percent.

- In 2015, a black person was 2.45 times more likely than a white person to be shot and killed by the police. A Hispanic person was 1.21 times more likely. These figures are well within what would be expected given race differences in crime rates and likelihood to resist arrest.

- In 2015, police killings of blacks accounted for approximately 4 percent of homicides of blacks, or approximately half of the total number of whites killed by law enforcement. Police killings of unarmed blacks accounted for approximately 0.6 percent of homicides of blacks. An overwhelming majority of black homicide victims (93 percent from 1980 to 2008) were killed by blacks.

- The great majority of people who died at the hands of the police fit at least one of three categories: they were wielding weapons, they were suicidal or mentally troubled, or they ran when officers told them to halt.

- Both violent and non-violent crime has been declining in the United States since a high in 1993. In 2015, however, a disturbing rise in murders in major American cities was associated by some experts with "de-policing" in response to intense media and public scrutiny of police activity.

- Roughly 6 - 7% of black Americans, mainly males between the ages of 20-40, constitute 38% of the federal prison population and 35% of local jail inmates.

When "The Future" is not that bright...

Alexandria Ocasio-Cortez PAC
@Ocasio4Congress

Follow

I hear a lot of Trump supporters talking about black on black crime. Well, what they don't know is white supremacy is the reason for black on black crime.

9:14 PM - 8 Jul 2018

The *Ransomed* Arenas of POLITICAL AGENDAS

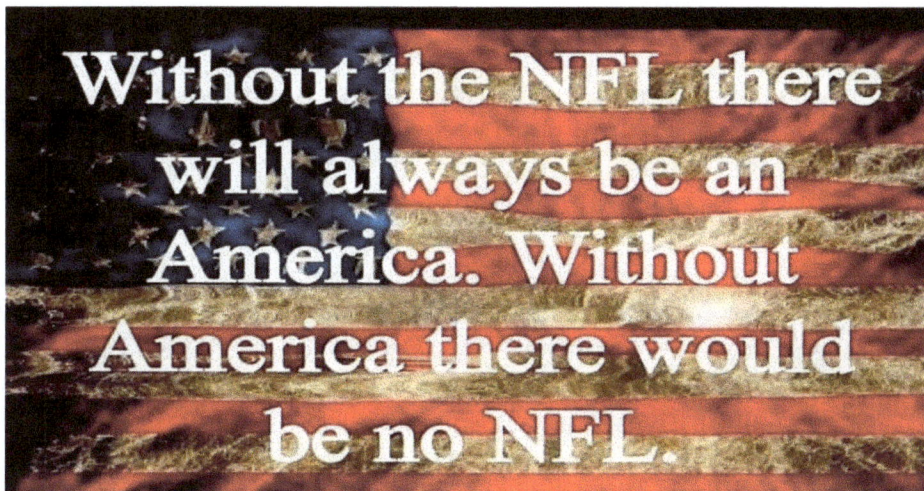

Without the NFL there will always be an America. Without America there would be no NFL.

"Playing the national anthem before a game is "interjecting" politics into sports." ~ESPN Max Kellerman

How can the flag and national anthem be labeled "political" interference, offensive, when they represent the liberties that allow grown men to play a boy's game for millions of dollars? And for the record I love sports. Having an appreciation for the opportunities America affords, the sacrifices made by those before us and now, doesn't require a political affiliation. It merely requires an ounce of respect and the slightest hint of perspective. I never hated Colin Kaepernick because he chose to express himself. I merely hated the disrespectful manner of political grandstanding he chose. If the man simply spoke his mind before or after the game, pursued social change outside the lines, he'd still have a job today. No sane team owner is going to support a product that insults its fans and drives away good paying customers. People don't watch sports to be lectured or their country ridiculed; they do it for the love of the game and to enjoy what little free time they may have with family and friends. Freedom of speech does not guarantee freedom from consequences.

Celebrity Slaves & Stale Political Stunts

Now that the NFL is losing millions in ticket sales, merchandising and advertising revenue, Commissioner Roger Goodell has come to the miraculous conclusion players should indeed stand for the National Anthem; after, that is, the NFL bribes activist players with a promise to invest millions in urban neighborhoods. In fact, after watching the NFL's favorability rating plummet to below 50%, he recently sent a letter to all 32 owners suggesting the phrase "players should stand" in the official league handbook should be changed to "required to stand" for the National Anthem. Naturally, such a self-evident and rationale revelation stirred racial parasites like Al Sharpton who are now calling for an all-out player revolt if this new language is adopted, while ESPN commentator Michael Wilbon even had the gall to call Cowboys owner Jerry Jones a "slave owner" for already requiring his players to do so. Excuse my penchant for historical perspective, basic human decency, but when did millionaire athletes become "slaves" and exactly which employers allow workers to make the rules – dictate or rewrite the terms of their employment – let alone encourage them to insult good-paying customers with such reckless abandon? Whether you work at a convenience store or head a Fortune 500 company, every staff member is required to follow a universal code of conduct. If you don't like it...quit, find a new job or buy your own damn team. Then again, even owners who purchase a NFL franchise must adhere to league guidelines or they too will be forced to sell their team. That's not discrimination, that's not racism, that's common sense!

WE CAN SURVIVE WITHOUT THE AMERICAN ATHLETE

WE CAN'T SURVIVE WITHOUT THE AMERICAN SOLDIER

Comparing overpaid, pampered players to lifelong servants who toiled, suffered and died under the auspices of human bondage – victims of real oppression and injustice, mind you – is morally grotesque and blatantly obtuse. If I may, when did slaves own Malibu mansions, drive Ferrari's, wear $100,000 suits, tweet to millions of adoring white fans or safely conceal the numbers of their "side bitches" on their back-up, gold-plated iPhone? I think not. Many slaves were lucky to eat a decent meal or God-forbid enjoy clean drinking water. In contrast, today's affluent athletes refusing to stand at attention for 60 seconds to honor our National Anthem, despite basking in the immense blessings America affords, are either too ignorant or hateful to realize they're living a life few will ever experience for doing little more than playing a little boy's game. I don't need to watch a condescending, self-indulgent video showcasing the homophobic, obscenely profane, recreational addict and serial misogynist known as Eminem – the same hypocrite who religiously raps about killing his mom, partying with "niggas", shooting enemies and violating women – to know these protests are nothing more than a leftist orgy hijacking yet another national venue to express their insatiable hatred of Donald Trump; a man they were predisposed to reject regardless.

This media orchestrated movement to turn Colin Kaepernick into a glorified martyr by encouraging similar anthem demonstrations, recruiting and teaching participants as young as grade school to despise America in the name of a syndicated lie, is far more about seizing every conceivable opportunity to further demonize America's heritage and viciously slander all Trump supporters as white supremacists than fighting any semblance of true oppression. The same intolerant celebrities who can't tell the difference between an undaunted Chief Executive challenging modern identity politics and a genocidal war criminal from the Third Reich, want you to believe they sincerely respect the military, first responders and uninfringed freedom of speech; well, except on college campuses and nationally televised award shows. Not surprisingly, a clear majority of those "brave" kneeling athletes and plotting activists claiming they simply want an honest discussion on real societal issues, label anyone who quotes crime statistics, blames eroding societal values or invokes a need for personal accountability as racist, sexist or a Nazi Republican. Truly, there is no greater bigot than someone who judges everything through the subjective political lens of race, sexuality and gender.

Refusing to control your political impulses in entertainment forums that once allowed families a much-needed escape from political discord hardly constitutes discrimination or a matter automatically worthy of immediate concern. Furthermore, shamelessly attempting to politicize the American flag to further fracture an already divided country merely confirms a clear lack of regard for the time, money and rights of others. Any self-respecting citizen who truly loved America and supported our unsung heroes would never disrespect, publicly or privately, the very symbols of hope and opportunity so many lost their lives defending and still sacrifice to preserve today; regardless of their political views, economic class or skin color. A reasonable adult would have simply concluded Colin Kaepernick was an unapologetic, anti-American opportunist who still refuses to accept the consequences of his foolish actions. If workers from all walks of life are fired every day for the slightest infractions – failing to be punctual, dressing improperly, or unnecessarily imposing their personal beliefs on others – what makes a football player immune to being held responsible for alienating millions of consumers and rightfully proud Americans? Unfortunately for the future prospects of America and the forsaken sanity of sports fans, truth is no longer a commodity accepted in the real world.

Pulpits and Playgrounds

Nearly 1,000 protesters descended upon the NFL's headquarters in New York to demand Colin Kaepernick is signed by a new team. Yes, the very same man who turned the football field into his personal political playground and who forgot he was paid to play a sport, is somehow now a victim of racist owners who refuse to lose more paying customers by indulging his wanton disregard. Yet, not one of these outraged activists have organized a single demonstration (let alone mentioned) concerning the 7,000 black homicide victims of annual black crime, the roughly 40% on welfare, the highest unemployment rate of any racial demographic in the U.S., or the fact less than 50% of blacks currently own a home. Raising a fist of solidarity through social media or kneeling during the National Anthem does nothing to assuage the true source of urban America's struggles: the moral decay of our communities, absentee parents, rampant crime and drug abuse, insufficient higher education and job training, a crumbling work ethic and a glaring lack of respect for ourselves, our fellow man and America itself. If only players had the same level of outrage for the over 855 times their police-hating peers have been arrested since 2000; or in criminal justice terms, the 215 instances of DUI, 99 drug arrests, 96 cases of domestic violence, 71 charges of assault and the two murders auspiciously missing from all their protests. Not a bad stat sheet for disgruntled employees claiming the moral high road.

I don't need a crystal ball to realize if Colin Kaepernick was a white player not one protest would have been held to validate his foolish actions. In what other universe can an athlete insult his fellow countrymen, disrespect their native flag, and not be attacked by fans, let alone keep his lucrative job? These volatile public displays concocted in the name of "social justice" are little more than opportunistic grandstanding designed to seek pity, fame or undue concessions through mass coercion, rather than getting in the unoccupied trenches of societal change and working tirelessly towards solving these perennial problems. Unfortunately for the resumes or Mr. Kaepernick, Jesse Jackson and Al Sharpton, real "hope and change" requires responsible, competent leaders willing to lead by their actions – getting their hands dirty in the absence of fawning cameras and political agendas – without giving endless speeches, shouting racism at every misfortune and self-inflicted wound, or cashing seven-figure checks to further one's professional aspirations. If you're going to pawn off another decade of celebrated moral decadence, racial division and urban blight to the next sold-out generation of affirmative inaction, at least have the gall to admit the circus comes to town only once every four years. At least then the black community will know what the going price is for used stage props.

Glen Coffee
- Born in 1987.
- Played for the San Francisco 49ers.
- Drafted in the 3rd round of the NFL Draft.
- Gave up millions of dollars and an NFL career to serve his country.

Colin Kaepernick
- Born in 1987.
- Plays for the San Francisco 49ers.
- Drafted in the 3nd round of the NFL Draft.
- Refused to stand for the National Anthem because the American flag "oppresses black people."
- Makes $19,000,000 per year.

Who's the real hero?

In Living Color

ESPN prevented Asian American Robert Lee from announcing a Virginia college football game out of fears his birth name was "racially insensitive" but the very same network has allowed Jemele Hill to continue working despite calling President Trump and his supporters white supremacists and Nazis. Not surprisingly, the same "idealistic" colleagues defending Miss Hill's unabridged right to voice her opinion outside of work were rejoicing when Curt Schilling was fired for sharing his support of North Carolina's transgender bathroom law or when Country music icon Hank Williams Jr. was removed from ABC's Monday Night Football for criticizing one Barack Obama. Sadly, such unforgivable hypocrisy is hardly coincidental considering the "The ESPYs" once gave their annual Arthur Ashe Courage Award to a 65-year-old, cross-dressing celebrity instead of a female college basketball player who eventually died battling cancer or a double-amputee war veteran turned champion triathlete. There is syndicated propaganda and then there is choreographed political terrorism masquerading as social progress. Change the channel, cut your cable cord or end your ESPN subscription until their producers no longer justify insulting millions of sports fans – the very country that affords us the opportunities to enjoy such sporting events with family and friends – while religiously honoring an unemployed quarterback who calls all police officers "pigs" and America "racist" for not celebrating a jaded, millionaire bigot who proudly mocks our national anthem, ignores the unrivaled ravages of black-on-black crime and incites civil unrest with unbridled glee. No show is worth your dignity, the universal values we teach our children, let alone those innocent lives lost amidst the violent aftermath of such irresponsible rhetoric. Hate doesn't need a misguided sports anchor to confirm its existence; it merely requires a morally bankrupt medium to spread the false narrative that injustice is a one-way street. Until Jemele Hill is fired and this incessant glorification of Colin Kaepernick ends, I refuse to even consider watching another second of their shameless political subversion of the games I have loved since my childhood.

The Yellow Flag of Rancid Journalism

Although I'm admittedly not a New England Patriots fan, I find it completely obnoxious that reporters – most notably pseudo sports networks like ESPN – are harassing Tom Brady over his friendship with Donald Trump. Forgive my constitutional acumen but no American citizen, renowned athlete or not, is required to validate their personal acquaintances or justify their political beliefs simply because someone vehemently disagrees with said choices. This is not Red China or Nazi Germany where citizens must surrender their liberties, explain their every action or liquidate every aspect of their private life so it can be judged under a microscope of mass conformity. If Hillary had won the presidency and Democrats retained the White House, the silence from these liberal sycophants would be deafening; and all despite being ever cognizant of the fact the Clintons are drowning in a cesspool of scandal, deception and bigoted remarks. If I may, have any black athletes ever been hounded by journalists for publicly supporting or befriending Barack Hussein Obama - an undeniable anti-Semite, both in tone and action – or for praising rappers who espouse misogyny or the assassination of our President?

Likewise, did the same "principled", unbiased press ever demand an explanation from Obama justifying his countless radical associates, let alone every time he praised the murderous legacies of Islam or Castro? No? Not once? How convenient and how utterly expected. If Colin Kaepernick can kneel during the national anthem to the thunderous applause of "progressive" networks invoking his unalienable right to free speech, certainly Tom Brady doesn't need to ask permission for refusing to publicize his.

Just because the "activist" media now routinely "fakes" the news and keeps half of America within a progressive bubble of spoon-fed paranoia...i.e., Donald Trump is Hitler, an aspiring slave owner and a serial rapist...doesn't require the rationale free world to cater to their sanctimonious insecurities or change their adult diapers in times of psychological distress. Unless playing a game is now the equivalent of running for office, there is a distinct difference between public domain and civil harassment. The truth is, other than providing for his family, paying taxes and honoring the contract he signed to play football, Tom Brady doesn't owe anyone a damn thing; especially the noble "thought police" at E'SS'PN. And if that singular concept is too difficult to understand, well, congratulations on finally discovering the sole source of your pungent hypocrisy. Just remember not to sit in one place for too long. Such prolonged debasement will only further cloud your limited ability to realize why so many sickened sports fans have already changed the channel.

ESPN & The Courage of Crossdressing

The annual ESPY awards are regarded as a joyous and tearful celebration designed to honor notable team champions and those incredible feats of individual fortitude. From the immortal "Don't Ever Give Up" speech delivered by an obviously frail Jim Valvano – the terminally ill coach who inspired millions with his emotional and defiant plea to find a cure for cancer – to the poignant final words of Stuart Scott – the recently deceased ESPN anchor, husband, and father – the ESPY's have embodied the physical prowess and perseverance of the human spirit for 22 years. In essence, they are the Oscars of the athletic world; attended by the biggest names in sports, if not all of society, and watched by insatiable fans from across the globe. Sadly, none of that mattered Wednesday night when legacy descended into madness and a disgraceful display of gender-bending bigotry ensued. Bruce "Caitlyn" Jenner, the LGBT community, and progressive programmers were not to be denied their prideful place in infamy. After all, they "earned" it!

Giving the Arthur Ashe Courage Award to a 65-year-old cross-dresser instead of a young woman who continued to play basketball while dying from cancer, or a double-amputee war veteran who has persevered to succeed in marathons and CrossFit events, is irrefutable proof liberals possess absolutely no shame, common sense or respect for the people of this nation. Yes, America, why recognize and celebrate freedom, God, and the indomitable spirit of true role models when you can place gays and transvestites on a primetime pedestal of worship for your children to emulate and adore? Who knew wearing your momma's clothes 39 years after competing in the Olympics, or a collegiate football player sleeping with the same sex – i.e. Michael Sam, last year's award recipient

– was such an arduous and miraculous achievement worthy of our highest praise? ESPN and ABC should not only be humiliated by their tactless display of nepotism, they should profusely apologize to Noah Galloway and the family of Lauren Hill for turning a moment of gratitude and remembrance into a political farce of historic proportions. If Arthur Ashe were alive today he would be disgusted by the crass exploitation of his memory and even more so by the complete lack of respect shown towards two genuine heroes who truly embody sacrifice, grace and courage; regardless of their sexuality or preferred dressing habits. As a lifelong sports fan, but more importantly as a proud American, I salute these two inspirational souls for reminding us limitations are merely those obstacles we place before ourselves. God Bless you both and may Lauren forever rest in peace.

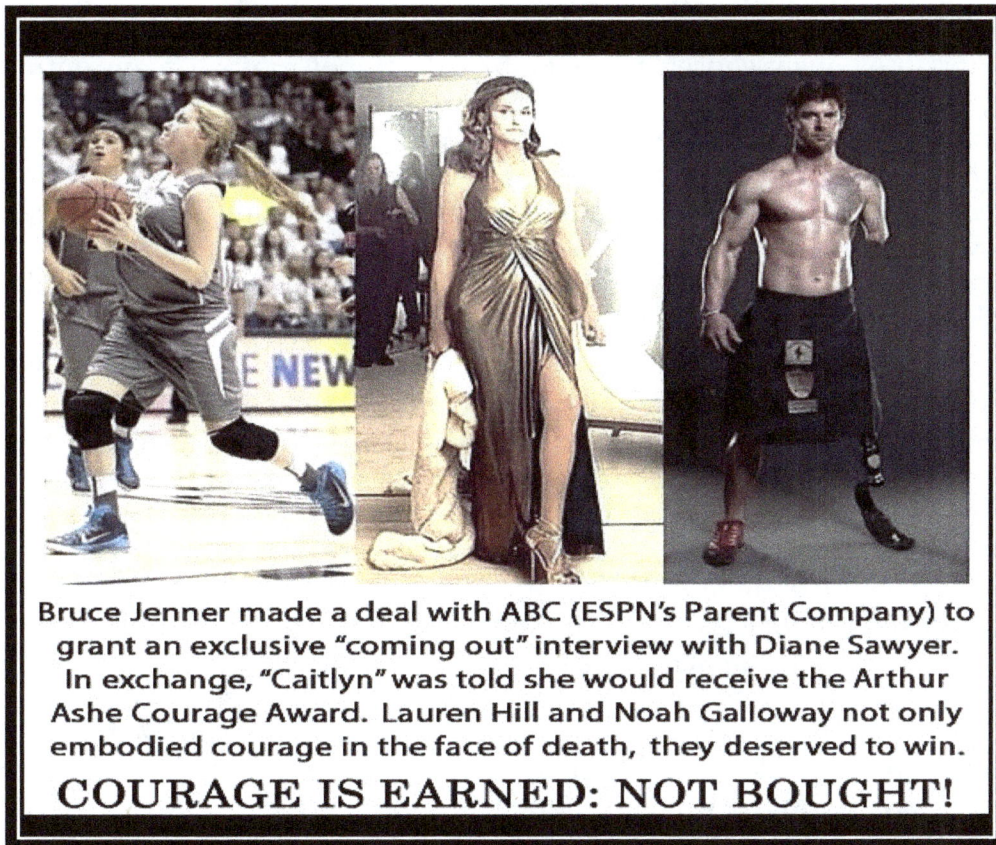

Bruce Jenner made a deal with ABC (ESPN's Parent Company) to grant an exclusive "coming out" interview with Diane Sawyer. In exchange, "Caitlyn" was told she would receive the Arthur Ashe Courage Award. Lauren Hill and Noah Galloway not only embodied courage in the face of death, they deserved to win.

COURAGE IS EARNED: NOT BOUGHT!

A Deeper Shade of Shame

According to ESPN's Max Kellerman, Tiger Woods is not qualified to be black because he refuses to criticize President Trump. If that insulting assertion isn't as racist as hell, NFL Hall of Famer Jim Brown must be a white supremacist for supporting both the President and the National Anthem. Better yet, if a conservative host made the same comment about a black celebrity, on a "sports" talk show no less, there would be mass media outrage, boycotts of sponsors, and a petition for his immediate termination. The cultural hypocrisy of liberal fascism never stops. Swing away, Tiger; America was founded on intellectual diversity, freedom of thought, not blind subjugation to pompous media bigots.

The Progressive Pigskins

In the latest chapter of political correctness versus the sporting world of common sense, our triumphant leader's return from the land of misfit confederate toys, Barack Obama is now threatening to play money ball and block public funding for the Washington Redskins new stadium. Why you ask? It's all about a political agenda, a victimization platform, designed solely to incite discord by grossly misrepresenting the fabled history behind one of the NFL's most recognizable franchises. If you recently fell off the turnip truck and landed in Nancy Pelosi's plastic garden for the not so historically fresh, the term 'Redskins' was obviously chosen to cheer a professional football team onto victory by conveying the rousing concepts of racism, bigotry, and white toast; just never the spiritual embodiments of courage, bravery, and the legendary ferocity of Native Americans. Likewise, because liberals have no concept of honor, strength, or voter ID – just race baiting, record deficits, anti-Semitism and endless entitlements – they refuse to explain why or how a team moniker, firmly entrenched as common nomenclature for well over half a century, is suddenly so offensive and unacceptable; not that a gay bondage parade in front of young children in broad daylight should draw a yellow flag.

The fact progressives show more outrage over a football team's nickname, than our government consciously abandoning America's border or the White House using the IRS and EPA to target political opponents, speaks volumes to their priorities and subsequent inability to reason. What the lapdog media conveniently buries are stories of the Washington Redskins repeatedly consulting, hosting and honoring Native Americans throughout the tenure of their proud history. Naturally such an admission by the gridiron gestapo would require being honest and not unearthing hatred where it's nowhere to be found; except in the imaginary minds of culture warriors. If you absolutely want to discover the truth about the legitimacy of this movement, ask yourself one simple question: why are a clear majority of those most vocal about the "Redskins" name not Native American? It's called conditioning, political brainwashing, the public scalping of perspective. Perhaps that's why the famed Shawnee Chief Tecumseh used the term "Redskin" himself in his writings when referring to his own people; because it's just so darn offensive.

If I was a Washington fan, even for a day, I'd chant "Redskins" as loudly and irreverently as humanly possible every second of every play. The only way to defeat the fascist fertilizer of political correctness is to incessantly mock liberals with the very object of their cultivated disdain; the stench and sound of their own stupidity. Then again, being sacked by JJ Watt while wearing a straightjacket with a leather helmet wouldn't hurt either!

The Legend vs The Lobbyist

The reason the media is obsessed with crowning Lebron James as the greatest player of all time – despite his lack of title, success, defensive discrepancy, and assembled "super" teams – is because Michael Jordan wasn't and isn't the political lightening rod, civil rights ambassador, the entertainment and political establishment desperately wanted him to be. The North Carolina alumni stuck to his athletic passions, his family's private life, and discretely contributed to various humanitarian causes or charities. Lebron, on the other hand, has been duped into believing police brutality is a racist epidemic and Donald Trump is a white supremacist instead of addressing the uncomfortable fact black America, the Democratic party, are by far our minority brethren's greatest adversaries.

A flash of lore
A contour of light
A shadow of awe
A birth of flight

A leap of faith
A hardwood prayer
A tongue smitten
A signature of air

A game to envy
A will to win
A court to rule
A child of the rim

A legend of ball
A shoe of flight
A world palmed by
A swoosh named Mike

Swoosh

As for those politically-motivated sports history revisionists, Michael Jeffery Jordan has the highest career regular season and playoff scoring averages, he's a 10-time scoring champ, a 9-time All-NBA defensive team selection, he won 6 Finals MVPs, 5 regular season MVPs, led the league in steals 4 times, owns the best Performance Efficiency Rating in NBA history at 27.91, had 2 "threepeats" with the same team, and MJ basically shot 50% for his career as a guard in an era when defensive physicality, body checking, was the norm. And he basically did it in 12 seasons, before his second retirement, despite nearly missing a full season with a foot injury and taking a year and a half off to play baseball. Sorry but his greatness is a tad bit more than "just" a 6-0 finals record. Most of LeBron's statistical records are due to volume of games, not due to unrivaled excellence. The media's newly crowned GOAT has never won a title without an assembled "Big 3" and even if you erase the Cavs lopsided losses in the last two NBA Finals against Golden State he still brandishes a 3-4 record in title series...2-5 if not for a last second three by Ray Allen against the Spurs. There's reality and then there's a media-driven lie continuously repeated until enough people actually believe it. LeBron James is a tremendous basketball player, the best of his generation, but there is only one Michael Jordan; and fans weren't marginalized or needlessly subjected to any insulting partisan tirades. They paid their hard-earned cash to watch a legend in flight, not to be lectured by a lobbyist on the mic!

Targets and Tiaras

For those who are unaware, last year Lebron James called the President "a bum" on Twitter with zero outrage from sports and media pundits. Then last night he joined the race-baiting, anti-Trump antagonist, CNN's Don Lemon, for another political dogpile in which the Anthem protests were lauded as justifiable and courageous while Donald Trump was lambasted for using sports to divide America. Should our nation's leader have taken the high road? Yes, for neither are worth the effort or the predictable backlash. However, everyone knows if you continuously call him out with misleading accusations or personal epithets, chances are he's going to respond. And how many truly horrible things have been said about his family and loved ones, including threats of violence? It's simply not in his nature to ignore the endless barrage of hate being he has lived nearly his entire life as a hard-nosed, New York CEO and not a politically correct politician. I find it humorous "the President" is using sports to divide America when ungrateful NFL players are the ones continuously disrespecting our flag, our fallen heroes and fans' hard-earned money? No, LeBron, you're clearly confused by the unwelcome interruption of pointless political grandstanding, over-indulged athletes holding America's arenas hostage, to protest Donald Trump whenever their Hollywood 'state of mind' and rampant culture of racial contempt needs public validation. While I commend your philanthropic efforts to exact social change in Akron's youth despite "promising" to leave taxpayers with 80% of the annual bill, those kneeling players perpetrating these shameless publicity stunts are making no effort to accept the real root causes of poverty and discord in their communities – black crime, broken homes, apathy – or to discredit the lingering misconceptions you continue to validate with such misguided rhetoric. Just don't whine, cry and play the victim, "King James", when you repeatedly mess with the bull only to finally get the horns. Karma does not care about your feelings or your imaginary crown.

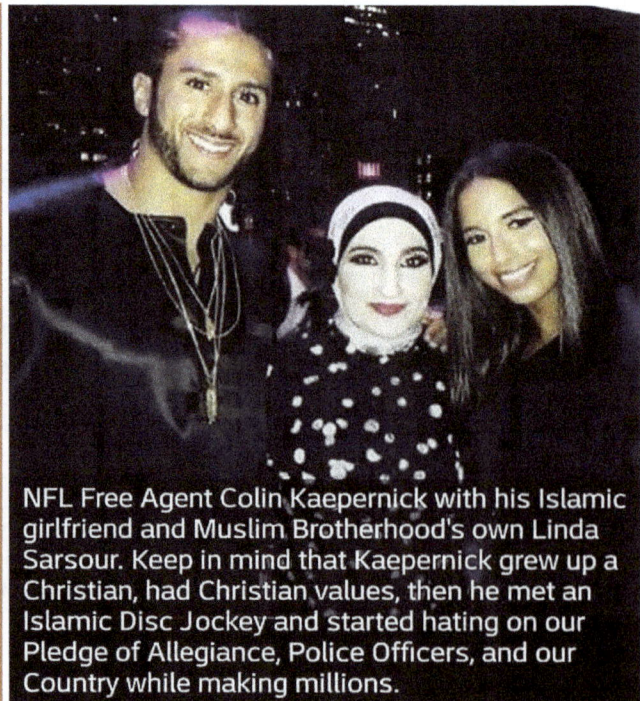

Candace Owens ✔
@RealCandaceO

To think that your ability to dribble a ball, throw a football, and/or decline a White House invitation makes you more a hero than the bodies that are sent home in coffins laid under OUR American Flag is why DONALD TRUMP WON!

I've had enough of these overprivileged athletes!

NFL Free Agent Colin Kaepernick with his Islamic girlfriend and Muslim Brotherhood's own Linda Sarsour. Keep in mind that Kaepernick grew up a Christian, had Christian values, then he met an Islamic Disc Jockey and started hating on our Pledge of Allegiance, Police Officers, and our Country while making millions.

Dear NFL Executives

If more spoiled athletes refuse to honor the flag, respect our veterans/fallen heroes and recognize the countless blessings America innately affords all people, I suggest playing the national anthem before players are introduced or can even take the field. Why give a growing faction of ungrateful millionaires a national stage to needlessly politicize sports and thus feed the cultivated myth injustice is the private property of any sole ethnic group? Just because some foolishly choose to believe the senseless propaganda claiming a majority of Americans, Donald Trump voters and police officers are white supremacists, doesn't make it so. It makes overpaid, fully-grown men recklessly paranoid and ostensibly gullible.

This country, those families spending hundreds of dollars just to attend a single game, deserve far better than such a grotesque display of ignorance and coddled lack of appreciation. Since when did insulting generations of loyal fans become an acceptable form of entertainment? The same whining activists currently threatening to protest NFL games because Colin Kaepernick is now unsurprisingly unemployed, were eerily quiet when Tim Tebow – a former Heisman trophy winner who won 6 games consecutively and beat the Steelers in the playoffs during his first season as a starter – was routinely mocked for his religious beliefs and couldn't even secure a roster spot as a back-up quarterback on a last place team only one year later. Perhaps if he beat his girlfriend, wore socks portraying cops as pigs or partied with escorts on a yacht in Key West, he would have generated enough "street cred" to win the support of the anti-American establishment.

It's an ominous failing of our culture, our most intrinsic values, when reciting a universally inclusive prayer during a nationally televised game would garner far more contempt from the media than those applauded opportunists inciting hatred of our country, the law enforcement community, with their misguided actions and morally select outrage. Until 70% of NFL players realize less than 10 percent of the population accounts for 50% of all violent crime in America – the fact a black athlete is 30 times more likely to be murdered by another black man than shot by a "racist" police officer – the only flag anyone should be protesting on Sunday is that of the yellow variety. Although bigotry and injustice will always exist in some form or facet of society, a hypothetical future forged upon the replayed cards of racial distrust and adopted victimization will inevitably falter beneath the collective weight of endless accusation. United we stand, but divided humanity falls.

SERVICE & SACRIFICE

The Folded Flags of Freedom

Courage, bravery, honor, valor...are but a few of the timeless tributes used to memorialize the charging silhouette of the American soldier. Yet these fabled words pale in comparison to the greatest embodiment of our Armed Forces: love. Love is the saluted colors of unwavering loyalty, the intrinsic calling of a sacred duty, and the solemn oath of an indelible creed. Love of country, love of family, and most of all, love of liberty – God's most precious and nonnegotiable gift – moves ordinary men and women to confront the most unconscionable forms of evil, to stand guard amidst the growing shadow of tyranny, when most would flee or kneel before the ruddy sword of subjugation. And despite the willingness of these selfless souls to lay their fleeting lives upon the altar of freedom, to die so hope and humanity may endure, there are still those Americans who blissfully desecrate the flag, disparage their native homeland, or callously mock the deaths of our fallen brethren; the etched names and fading faces of liberty's flickering light. Whether out of opposition to war, political ideology or economic plight, these voices of discontent neither appreciate nor comprehend that without conscious sacrifice, a steadfast conviction to risk physical harm and withstand societal scorn, neither America nor the rights of the righteous few would duly exist; those shameless critics shouting injustice from the comfort of their couches or cheering the opportunistic cowardice of ignited anarchy.

America goes far beyond the tangible boundaries of recognized sovereignty or the disputed legacy of any politician; the perilous struggle for freedom is forever synonymous with the fighting spirit of Bunker Hill, stretches beyond the unbreakable Allied lines entrenched across the Ardennes Forest, and dwells beneath the conquered Naval waters of Leyte Gulf. The future of this invaluable Republic resides in the indomitable ideal we are all born free, for better or for worse, and any attempt to usurp that dignity is a threat to all mankind; to our children, our hallowed way of life. This often-forsaken obligation resides in the folded flags of everyday citizens who put principle before politics, love before hate, and democracy before despair. It survives in the beating heart of the American soldier. God Bless our fallen heroes and God Bless America; forever, and still, that shining city on a hill.

Now and Forever

The American soldier is the backbone of our liberties; the rock upon which tyranny must break. Without their sacrifice, their unwavering commitment to this nation and the ideals it espouses, this republic not only would have fallen but its beacon of hope would have been extinguished long ago beneath the smoke-ridden battlefields of Lexington, Bunker Hill, or Yorktown. Tragically, despite the fact millions of Americans bask in the opportunity and affluence of their God-given rights, those procured by the unassuming few, the sacrifices and struggles of our veterans too often go unappreciated or unnoticed; especially by those with the most blessings or disagreeable political beliefs. Many needlessly suffer from debilitating physical injuries or undiagnosed mental illness, countless are unable to find work or sufficiently provide for their families who faithfully endured sleepless nights, and a disturbing number of our veterans – roughly 40,000 without shelter and an estimated 300,000 lacking adequate food – roam the littered streets of modern apathy without proper healthcare or even the faintest gesture of concern. And yes, there are those forsaken souls who commit suicide, one veteran nearly every hour of every day, to escape a hell most civilians could scarcely conceive.

The next time you stand in line for the newest technological marvel, complain about traffic or the everyday contrivances of modern inconvenience, remember that these brave men and women represent the forgotten, the nameless, the silhouette of bravery manning the gates of freedom; the billowing breath standing steadfast in the darkest corners of the world so that America, war's widowed children, may peacefully slumber beneath the unfurled dawn of liberty's light. Duty, valor, honor, God, country? These are not commercial taglines left to bleed off a bumper sticker or fade from a politician's neglected promise. They are the timeless values, the intrinsic calling, the undying creed of United States veterans; those fathers and friends, brothers and brethren, who proudly served so the huddled masses may continue to breathe. Veterans Day is not just another day of empty revelry and convenient celebration. It's our unbridled privilege, our inherent obligation as free men and women, to stand beside those heroes who restored our faith in humanity. It is our nonnegotiable responsibility to thank our veterans, not on any singular occasion or nationally ordained day of recognition, but to seek out those who have fallen into the callous cracks of society's indifference and restore their faith in America. It is our sacred duty to honor theirs, now and forever!

September 11th, 2001: The Watchtowers of Freedom

America was not forged with the red hammer of conformity, nor was our revered way of life preserved by the idle hands of modern entitlement. This republic was erected as an ideological bastion from which to harbor ordinary men and women from the historical remnants of injustice and to protect the indelible liberties of all mankind. As a sovereign nation defined by stringent geographic boundaries, our founding creed has no such limitations for life, liberty, justice and the pursuit of happiness are universal birthrights derived from the dominion of God's grace, creation and wisdom. And while it is true America cannot serve as the moral police of the world – bear the human cost of fighting every battle to free every forsaken soul from the clutches of oppression without their willingness to recognize and defeat tyranny themselves – there is no respite from the conscious aftermath of acquiescing to human atrocity.

Reducing our defenses to the point of non-existence, albeit for economic gain or misguided policy, is to leave ourselves at the mercy of malevolence. I do not subscribe to the pacifist conundrum that by burying our head in the sand, ignoring the atrocities of totalitarian states or Islamo-fascists, "We the People" make our country safer & the world a better place in which to reside. It is simply the equivalent of watching a rape across the street & doing nothing to stop it. Frankly, we are better than that. There is courage and then there is cowardice; no excuse will ever suffice in the annals of history or before the eyes of God. When our nation's resolve was baptized beneath the ruddy carnage of Pearl Harbor our military was so vulnerable & neglected it took years of nationalizing private industry to rebuild our feeble defenses. For far too long the United States of America – the supposed fearless leader of the free world – callously hid behind a policy of isolationism as World War II raged on & millions were lost beneath the boot of German fascism & Japanese imperialism. In essence, by casting a shadow of weakness, our calculated indifference eliminated any hope of deterring or preventing such a horrific tragedy. Truly, how many more lives could have we saved? More profoundly, what if our families were the victims of Holocaust, the Ukrainian Famine or the Armenian genocide? Should I even have to ask such a selfish question?

Pretending evil does not exist, failing to prepare for its inevitability, will not save us from its wrath. Likewise, blaming America for 9/11 is but to embolden our enemies for they will never cease in their lust for our demise. If ISIS or North Korea can speak openly of their bloodthirsty hatred for Western Civilization, cultivate their culture of unapologetic brutality, why should this "last, best hope of mankind" cower in the politically convenient shadows of capitulation and appeasement? America is but a name, for it is freedom, tolerance, and our Judeo-Christian ideals they despise. To lower our guard out of some misplaced sense of guilt or to seduce political favor is to sentence this nation to that which we are already guaranteed: death. I do not fear death; I fear watching my loved ones needlessly suffer beneath the rolling fog of blind apathy as any chance for recourse or valor fades beyond the autonomy of my fingertips. For the sake of my children and the country I call home, I would rather fight for the soul of creation – the last vestiges of decency and hope – than to kneel before the soiled blade of subjugation. May God Bless the heroes and victims of September 11th, 2001 and may humanity forever honor its intrinsic duty to eradicate such unrepentant evil where ever it may exist.

Land of the Free, Home of the Homeless

It is well known ample public housing exists for the poor all across America. Therefore, why not build housing communities for homeless veterans near military bases or VA hospitals? Even closed bases could be renovated to shelter and care for these forgotten heroes' needs, including the creation of skill centers offering potential educational and job opportunities to those who are still of able body and mind. In a nation as resourceful and wealthy as America, it's unfathomable so many of our brave servicemen and women – those who risked their lives and stood vigil for freedom in the darkest corners of the world – are now eating scraps of leftovers and sleeping in alleyways like discarded newspapers. Simply unforgivable and unacceptable. If our government has the money and "moral" obligation to build modern detention centers for illegal immigrants, or to transport and provide for thousands of Syrian refugees, then our veterans deserve nothing less.

The "Evil" Embodiment of Betrayal

Apologizing for America's "evil" actions that ended a costly war and defeated the ruthless aggression of your once insatiable enemy is like asking forgiveness from the man who murdered your sons; or more profoundly, apologizing for them even being born. And yet, this is exactly what your smug hatred of America did when you apologized to the remnants and descendants of bloodthirsty regime on the very same weekend we memorialize our fallen heroes; many who died defeating tyranny so you could freely desecrate their memories by displaying such disgraceful and treasonous behavior. It is common knowledge that your ingrained disdain for European colonialism and American Manifest Destiny is your very impetus for weakening and embarrassing this transcendent nation in every conceivable manner. However, despite your juvenile spite and so-called unwavering humanitarianism posing as your political mandate for changing the country you claim to serve, you publicly absolve the imperialistic aftermath of a Pacific power that treated life as an annoyance in its singular desire to expand its borders and natural resources. So much for principles and the people.

If you must know, Mr. President, dropping the bomb saved in upwards of over 500,000 lives from an inevitable mainland assault because Japan made extensive preparations to fight down to the last man, woman & child. Considering the Battle for Okinawa resulted in over 150,000 combined casualties, the amphibious assault required to capture the heart of their homeland would have been undeniably catastrophic for both armies. The fact the Japanese Emperor still refused to surrender after Hiroshima illustrated the degree of their suicidal resolve. And let's not forget, in a matter of hours Japan murdered over 1,000 Americans while supposedly negotiating in good faith, crippled roughly half of our Pacific fleet and committed horrific atrocities against the Chinese and Filipino peoples.

To this day, the Rape of Nanking remains one of the most brutal and egregious assaults in modern history. Civilians (including children) were tortured, raped, and/or beheaded, while entire platoons of soldiers, buried up to their necks, died as their heads were crushed beneath the tracks of slow rolling tanks. Must I even mention the sheer moral depravity and endless human suffering of the Bataan Death March? Yes, unbeknownst to everyone but the leader of the free world, the Japanese were anything but victims. It's a shame the same cannot be said about the millions of Americans, past and present, who have been dishonored, threatened, and minimized by your destructive and morally bankrupt agenda that can proudly honor a man in a dress demanding access to the women's restroom, defend the misogynistic and violent legacy of Islam, but not those who sacrificed everything so "We the People" may live free from the ravages from hateful and hopelessly twisted individuals like yourself. Rather than unconditionally condemning the unforgivable evil perpetrated by the Empire of Japan, memorializing those brave soldiers who died so liberty may live, you chose to pander to your own rancid obsession with fostering American guilt. Mission accomplished.

Barack Obama during the week of Memorial Day: "We must never repeat this evil again" - referring to America's bombing of Japan. And yet the President used no such negative labels to describe the countless atrocities committed by the Japanese. With our Commander-in-Chief, it's always tone, suggestion and subtext to smugly degrade America in every conceivable manner possible. Were Bunker Hill, Antietam or Normandy all booked-up, or just not worthy of honoring history in the proper context?

Of Mice and Men

Nothing speaks more to the blatant ignorance of liberalism than to hear radical leftists belittle our country and military on a national day of mourning and remembrance. Believe it or not, most conservatives despise war – view its necessity as an absolute last resort – for we too have fathers and mothers, sisters and brothers, sons and daughters. By that same token, right-minded Americans simply refuse to bury their heads in the sand and pretend evil does not exist in order to magically appease our innate desire for global harmony. Whether a Christian is beheaded in Syria or your neighbor is shot in his own backyard, how does that change the nature of the crime or excuse the absence of your concern; of our humanity? It's no different than watching a rape across the street and doing nothing in the name of fostering "peace". The politics of the aggressor or the nationality of the victim is irrelevant for that which you condone, the nature of the injustice, will undoubtedly serve as the instrument of your own demise. In the game of life there are no time outs; merely regrets and repercussions.

Were the Vietnam and Korean Wars avoidable? Sure, that is, if you believe "avoidable" is a stagnant term without tangible borders or dates. Those same "invisible" Communists our fathers warned us about and fought against have incredulously infiltrated the highest levels of our government, the White House, and now conveniently serve as the ideological basis for the Democratic platform; in a country predicated upon individual liberty, no less. And those same Marxist "ghosts" whom liberals deride as figments of Right-Wing paranoia are currently responsible for countless deaths and human rights abuses in China, North Korea and Cuba. Joseph McCarthy may have been zealously misguided in his tactics and criminal overreach, but not in his suspicions. Ignoring evil doesn't eradicate its wrath, pardon your indifference or even necessarily save lives; it merely allows you the luxury of pretending everyone basks in the same light of free will as you raise the anarchist fist of history revisionism without spilling your Mocha Grande.

Was Operation Iraqi Freedom an unnecessary and murderous campaign? Absolutely, that is, if you think it's morally reprehensible – an unwarranted risk – to depose a ruthless dictator who gassed 5,000 Kurds (nearly double the victims of 9/11), denied his people universal rights, indiscriminately launched Scud missiles into the Jewish populace, and watched as his Republican Guard raped Kuwait and threw babies from incubators or hospital patients out of high rise windows. Do such atrocities require raising the trophy of WMD's – spiking the football – or do the heinous actions of a sadistic leader speak for themselves? I guess that depends if you call nerve gas a weapon of mass destruction or if your wife and child are the ones found lying in a rotting, deathly embrace. No, I do not equate "murder" to killing those soldiers and radical Islamists who defended a tyrant in the name of a blood thirsty and subhuman cult. I believe the correct term is called liberation. Our greatest failure, or miscalculation if you will, was naively believing the Iraqi people would fight for their liberties and that the U.N. – acting out or pragmatism, not spite – would oversee the transition to a free and democratic government. When fear and distrust are engrained for millenniums on end, so must your resolve. Our end game, not our intent or justification, was ill conceived.

The question isn't so much who we were fighting in the jungles of Vietnam or across the barren desserts of Iraq; it was the fundamental principle of what America was fighting for: liberty, dignity, justice, hope. To recuse yourself as a member of the human race, to ignore the suffering of others as you sit high on your ideological perch, doesn't make you "righteous" or even remotely an instrument of peace. It makes you an accessory to a crime; nothing more, nothing less. If anti-war progressives actually did more to preemptively confront and denounce evil rather than to absolve or enable the most insidious threats against America – Marxism and ISIS – than our military, those brave men and women they so eagerly defame and degrade without remorse, wouldn't have to consistently put their lives on the line, the welfare of their families, to protect the rights of an ignorant minority who are so intent on spewing such hateful propaganda. "History, it seems, is not without a sense of irony!"

American Sniper: Aiming for the Heart

Anti-war leftists will freely wave the white flag of capitulation as tyrants and Islamists murder countless innocents, but they're infuriated beyond measure by a cinematic adaptation that chronicles both the inevitable ravages of war and the indelible spirit of a man who routinely risked his life to defend his brethren. Ironically the same foaming progressives who are desperate to discredit the unprecedented success and cultural impact of American Sniper – a supposed Right-Wing celebration of individual mass murder and unabashed jingoism – were somehow unmoved when 12 unarmed civilians at Charlie Hebdo were gunned down by Islamic cultists over a satirical cartoon and their basic right to free speech. Naturally our progressive government couldn't even stand with the international community by condemning such an obvious, horrific act. When Saddam Hussein gassed tens of thousands of Kurds, killing women and children in the streets, or his Republican Guard stormed Kuwait and ripped babies from incubators only to toss them out windows like dirty rags, where was this same intrinsic obligation to secure a just and moral world that the media is using to slander Clint Eastwood and Chris Kyle? Or is murder suddenly not murder without postcards of WMD's? Right and wrong, truth and justice, does not magically appear at your beckon call and thus fortuitously conform to your malformed political whims. After all, if you're impervious to thousands of Africans being butchered at the hands of Boko Haram because it doesn't fit your warped notion of religious victimization or racial injustice, how does attacking those who merely expose or attempt to confront such blatant atrocity disarm the real hand of hypocrisy?

War is never black and white, it is not politically correct, and it involves making snap decisions with imperfect information. Failure to act decisively and with unflappable conviction is often at the cost of your own demise and that of your fellow soldiers. Muslim fanatics don't recruit women and children because they have no other choice. These sadistic thugs use them as human shields and suicide bombers because it creates a no-win scenario for our troops; a moral dilemma and form of psychological warfare that maximizes death and incites outrage in political circles. And guess which side our media chooses to chastise as callous and criminal? Although Michael Moore and his pacifist revisionists may find it convenient to label snipers cowards, when have they ever stood in harm's way or watched an entire village slaughtered in the name of a bloodthirsty ideology? That's because, in their minds, 9/11 was an aberration, America is to blame, and Islamic terrorism is an overblown, Right-Wing conspiracy. Then again, these same multimillionaire activists who continue to warn us about the inequities of capitalism and the vile nature of war, find more in common with anarchists and looters than those veterans who are denied the same compassion and health care afforded to illegal immigrants.

If American Sniper is truly nothing more than Nazi propaganda, as Seth Rogen so ignorantly described it, then whom may I ask liberated Europe from Hitler's tyrannical grasp and how many American citizens, including those snipers with hundreds of enemy kills, risked life and limb to restore some semblance of civility and hope to the epicenter of mass murder; or in other words, the mass genocide of his native Jewish people? Chris Kyle was an ordinary man, a soldier, and whether people want to embrace him as a hero or not is entirely of their choosing. However, unlike his politically righteous critics, he endured the lasting ravages of war, a pain few can fathom, for nothing more than the insatiable desire to defend a universal ideal that if breached ultimately threatened his own family and our homeland. The same anti-American sycophants who will try to convince voters their individual success and possessions are solely the product of the angry and envious "collective", somehow want you to believe that the U.S. military – i.e., the timeless sacrifice of everyday patriots like Chris Kyle – is in no way whatsoever responsible for procuring this republic, our natural born rights, or Hollywood's ungrateful and lavish way of life. How quaint. Unlike their celebrity antagonists, our fighting men and women do not require a Red Carpet, designer pajamas, or a photo-shopped facade to facilitate a seven figure, narcissistic view of the real world. They simply need an opportunity to serve the country and the people they love without condition. May God Bless Chris, comfort his family, and watch over those who continue to man the gates of freedom.

The Real Price of Sacrifice

Believe in something. Even if it means sacrificing everything.

"Believe in something, even it means sacrificing everything": and that's exactly what millions of selfless servicemen and women, fathers and mothers, sons and daughters, have done for generations. I have two words to explain why I will never again buy any Nike products...Colin Kaepernick. I refuse to give one cent to a company that glorifies an anti-American racist who praises Communism, justifies killing cops and equates Islam with love, only to demonize his critics as Christian extremists and white supremacists. Then again, Nike's Asian sweatshops tell us everything we need to know about their hypocritical brand of business ethics. Give millions to a self-aggrandizing antagonist; pay pennies on the dollar to foreign laborers who struggle to feed, house and educate their children. Excuse me for believing sacrifice entails a tad bit more than a (now unemployed) millionaire athlete taking a knee to disparage an entire nation beneath the political camouflage of his own bigotry. Colin Kaepernick's adopted persona as a morally-conscious symbol for social change, racial harmony, is as legitimate as Louis Farrakhan advocating for the future civil rights of Anglo-Saxon babies. They just don't do it!

From Sea to Shining Sea

As we prepare to honor America for the 241st time since its iconic inception – those brave souls who fought for liberty and those servicemen and women who continue to selflessly sacrifice for our freedoms today – it's equally important to recognize the unsung heroes who tirelessly contribute towards a better tomorrow: the proud parents, devoted single mothers and fathers, emergency responders, educators, social workers, engineers, researchers, mechanics, construction workers, truckers, farmers, cooks, entrepreneurs, manufacturers, janitors, volunteers...and yes, those unwillingly unemployed, ill, injured or handicapped patriots who love their country but are struggling to live the American dream. Without everyone's efforts and unique attributes, America would not survive as it was intended: a beacon of hope and opportunity for people from all proverbial walks of life. Regardless of our race, gender, sexuality, ideological beliefs or economic disposition, there is literally nothing we cannot achieve or overcome when hard work and accountability serve as virtue's transcendent light. For it is not our disagreements that ultimately define us, but our humanity and compassion; how we bridge our inevitable differences through constructive discourse and a mutual respect to heal our wounds, join our hands, and collectively reach heights previously thought unattainable. Although I have family, friends and associates with vastly varying beliefs and lifestyles, I am grateful for their existence and religiously pray for their success, happiness and well-being. Without the beauty of diversity, the fertile tree of liberty and the non-negotiable necessity of tolerance, America, but more profoundly civility, would cease to exist. Despite the discord incited by those misguided malcontents who will incessantly seek to divide mankind, we are all brothers and sisters, guardians and God's children. May America continue to harbor the poor and the persecuted, the aspiring and the afflicted, and may God forever bless all of you.

REAL HEROES DON'T WEAR CAPES

Illegal Immigration

Give me your Huddled Masses, your Unvetted and Poor, Behold a Sanctuary of Sedition, Casting Votes upon our Shores

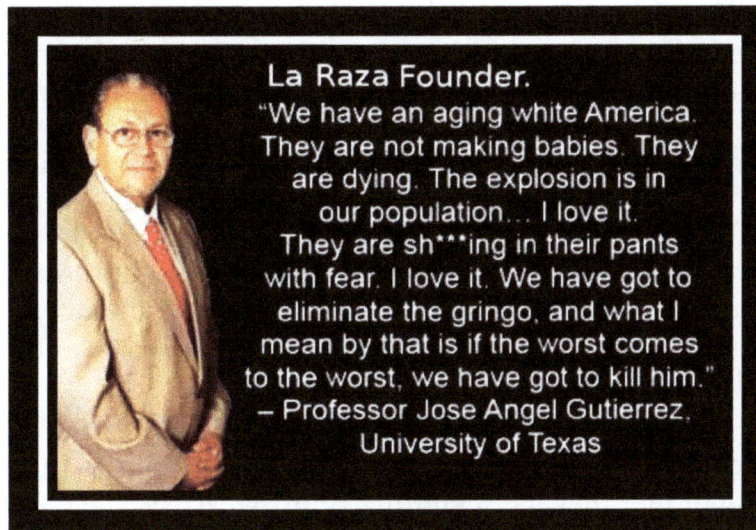

La Raza Founder.
"We have an aging white America. They are not making babies. They are dying. The explosion is in our population... I love it. They are sh***ing in their pants with fear. I love it. We have got to eliminate the gringo, and what I mean by that is if the worst comes to the worst, we have got to kill him."
– Professor Jose Angel Gutierrez, University of Texas

The RAISED Standards of Immigration Reform

Before 1965 roughly 200,000 immigrants were approved annually to reside in the United States; largely to pursue professional opportunities and/or to reunite with estranged family members. Regardless of their circumstances, these individuals had to demonstration a willingness to assimilate to our culture and provide for themselves without harboring any undue animosity towards America. In fact, applicants were required to demonstrate a working knowledge of our founding ideals, government procedures and laws, in addition to formally pledging allegiance to America while denying serving as a foreign spy or Communist agent. In essence, citizenship was a privilege with firm requirements and stark expectations. Not only were our immigration laws viewed as fundamental necessities designed to protect America's interests, her citizens and sovereignty – yes, legislation written and ratified by both political parties – they were routinely enforced without any organized protest, media outrage or inflammatory rhetoric from duplicitous politicians plotting to grant Amnesty to an additional 25 million Democratic voters. Immigration was universally accepted as a matter of prudence, non-partisan pragmatism, not a destructive platform to invalidate intellectual diversity through electoral supremacy.

Since 1970, but even more so during the past 15 years, immigration has divulged into a chaotic dereliction of duty that now accounts for over one million immigrants entering America each year; a majority of which are illegal, unvetted, harbor almost no loyalty towards America but somehow were awarded federal benefits, healthcare and education at taxpayer expense. If this astronomical trend continues, 40% of all children in the US will have come from foreign born parents by 2060. To make matters worse, elected public servants who once swore to uphold our laws and the Constitution itself, including one Barack Hussein Obama, have purposely muddled an elementary issue of national security for political gain. "Hope and Change" were obviously the misunderstood, monosyllabic cousins of "Confuse, Conspire and Conquer".

Despite the disturbing reality illegal immigration costs America approximately 150 billion annually, increases the prevalence of crime and threatens the integrity of our elections through the auspices of voter fraud, sanctuary cities are absurdly attempting to sue the Justice Department for upholding the law and doing their sworn job. Illegal aliens account for roughly 25 percent of the current U.S. Prison population, with each inmate averaging 12 criminal offenses and 8 arrests for a total incarceration cost of 7 billion taxpayer dollars per year...ironically almost the same "unaffordable" price tag of building a border wall, minus the cost of deporting repeat offenders. Yet by some unintelligible form of "progressive" reasoning, our President is a radical supremacist for specifically ordering the deportation of career criminals and violent gang members who pose a threat and financial drain to all sects of society; including other illegals, and both naturalized and natural born citizens? Naturally!

Considering Los Angeles alone has spent an estimate 1.6 billion in the past two years providing for and shielding illegals, including offering driver's licenses, tuition waivers and free legal assistance to sue actual American citizens, bankrupt California is the epitome of the detached bureaucracy attempting to dismantle America in favor of a globalist socialist utopia that criminalizes common sense and seeks to euthanize any concept of self-preservation; if you're a patriotic, Christian American with a job, a gun and an acute awareness of history, that is.

Under the Trump administration's new "RAISE" program, common sense will replace political chaos and points will earn the privilege of residing in America. Immigrants seeking work visas and/or citizenship will be given special preference according to their job skills, knowledge of the English language, and willingness to assimilate as productive, law-abiding members of society. In other words, the reignited "Don't ask what America can do for you, but what you can do for America" creed of John F. Kennedy will help filter out those aspiring burdens who are more concerned with handouts, exploiting both the system and struggling taxpayers, than working towards the betterment and preservation of a free, independent and economically vibrant nation. And yes, these reaffirmed goals of naturalization will also help better identify those bitter transients who despise America and have no regard for her people or survival. Unless burning the American flag, cursing our heritage and attacking Amnesty opponents are now acceptable behavior for foreign guests – smugly waving the symbol of their native countries which so egregiously failed them – such unapologetic logic is long overdue and sorely unappreciated.

The problem with enacting policies rooted in reason, historical precedence, and beneficial to the U.S., is that progressives are bound to protest anything that makes too much sense. Despite the knee-jerk "resistance" prescribed by Democrats, the liberal commune of Canada utilizes a similar merit-based system and routinely denies or delays migrants entrance into their country for both economic and security reasons; despite Trudeau's mindless proclamation "all refugees are welcome" to assimilate naïve Westerns. Of course, you will hear no such admission by the mainstream media for truth is not welcome in the production meetings of mass manipulation. When buying cigarettes or applying for a loan requires more screening and due diligence than stepping across the unguarded border of a sovereign nation, in a post 9/11 world no less, the insane asylum has obviously mastered the art of absentee voting.

If you thought Sitar music was the annoying aftermath of lazy indigents attempting to become existentially enlightened through hallucinogenic horticulture – the Marxist love child of Bernie Sanders and Elizabeth Warren – the red Armies of Entitlement fed by the wealth redistribution scheme of the Obama administration quietly doubled our national debt by nearly 10 trillion and triggered the first two credit downgrades in American History; an astounding figure nearly equaling the accumulative debt accrued by all other Presidents combined. And to think publicly funded abortions and sex changes, albeit for prisoners and incarcerated illegals deported multiple times, are now being promoted as natural born rights by social activists.

Whereas his predecessor recklessly distributed over one million green cards each year, using them primarily as a criminal means to help illegals escape deportation, Donald Trump will limit that number to 5000,000 or less and require all approved immigrants to wait at least 5 years before qualifying to apply for public assistance. If you're outraged by one man's attempt to restore accountability and fiscal responsibility to a politically hijacked matter of national security, but you're completely ambivalent towards the treasonous ploys of an anti-American propagandist seeking to supplant our founding values and electoral balance through an orchestrated demographic invasion, you definitely flunked Ethics and hate your grandparents' powers of observation. How else can an American Governor, bound by the state ratified supremacy of the Constitution and subject to the jurisdiction of the Department of Justice, refuse to release election data when 11 of his counties cast more votes than citizens or legal voting age? Could Democrats still win the popular vote with ICE agents placed at every precinct with such irregularities?

When the argument is lost and all credible options of opposition are exhausted, one word always remains in the progressive pantheon of victimization: racism. Luckily for civilization, outside the regurgitated excuses of the irrational mind where photo identification is somehow the most unattainable form of pertinence but a nonnegotiable necessity to attend the Democratic National Convention, lies the single greatest manifestation of the real world: consequences. If a white American stood in the heart Mexico City, demanded the right to vote and free entitlements, all while waving the U.S. flag and cursing those Mexican "bigots" who dared to disagree, how long would it be before he was beaten, jailed, or buried? Would I be offered "sanctuary" for committing larceny, assault or raping a Mexican child? No? How quaint. Apparently, logic has a passport with an undocumented carry-on of tuberculosis.

There are numerous cases of Americans jailed in Central and South American countries for imaginary or pedestrian infractions, corrupt nationals ransoming their life savings as recompense for their reclaimed freedom, with almost no public outcry of "racism" from those very critics demonizing our right to protect our borders. Yes, it is true, a border wall will not stop all illegal immigration, but such an ominous edifice, fortified by the public knowledge of our recommitment to enforce our laws, will discourage and stop far more people than it entices. I openly welcoming those individuals and families seeking a better life by contributing to a moral and prosperous America, as long as they respect the process and accept the inherent responsibility of becoming a citizen. I simply refuse to provide the kindling for opportunistic malcontents who would gladly watch America burn, bleed her dry behind the veil of political correctness, before lifting a finger to act on her behalf. If thousands can successfully immigrate from Asia, Europe and Australia without organizing a single protest or demanding a billion-dollar door prize, our contemporaries South of the border shouldn't require need a translator to explain why houses have locks and bank cards have pin numbers. Likewise, if the pompous Pope can lecture America behind a 1167-year-old wall designed to repel pillaging invaders, why can't America build one to weed out aspiring terrorists, disgruntled anarchists and uninvited parasites?

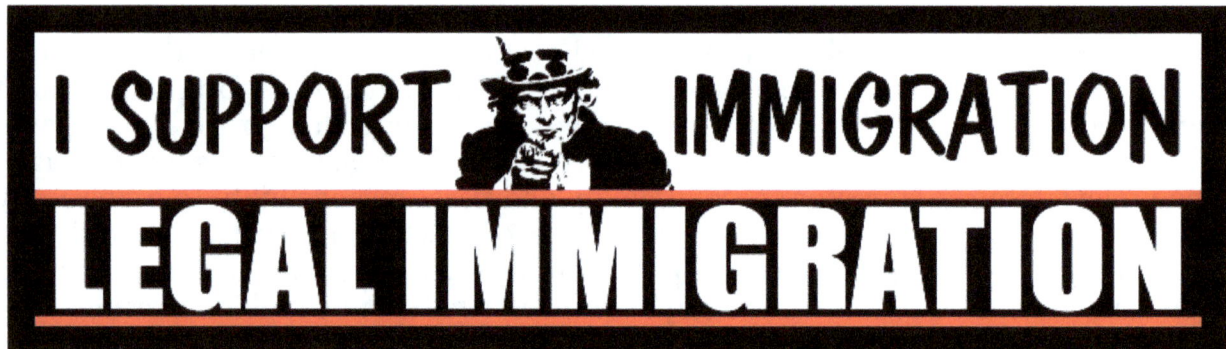

A Hazy Shade of Shameless

When the economy is too good to criticize, a notorious North Korean dictator agrees to denuclearization and returns wrongfully imprisoned Americans, terrorist regimes are no longer favored, the constitutional precept of limited government is restored, and the confirmed details of a damning IG report must be upstaged to conceal widespread Democratic corruption, leftists conveniently orchestrate national hysteria over a decades-old immigration policy their own party consummated and publicly enforced during previous administrations. And yet unbeknownst to most liberal partisans, except the elected engineers of social injustice, the physical well-being of undocumented immigrants is of little consequence to their ranks. Why, you ask? Because even if Donald Trump graciously agreed to grant amnesty to all illegals currently residing in America and lingering in our detention centers – under the caveat they had to work, pay taxes and could never vote in a U.S. election – the entire progressive establishment would immediately balk without reservation. Apparently a "humanitarian crisis" really isn't an emergency unless it can be exploited by shameless propagandists for personal gain and political favor. But just in case you need one, over 63,000 Americans have been killed by illegal aliens since 2001: a sum now greater than all U.S. war casualties in Vietnam.

Kamala Harris ✓
@SenKamalaHarris

A reminder this Fourth of July: it was eight immigrants who signed the Declaration of Independence. Happy Independence Day.

5:38 AM · 04 Jul 18

Ann Coulter ✓
@AnnCoulter

Following ⌄

Forty-eight of the 56 men who signed the Declaration of Independence were born in America. The other 8 were British or Dutch, same as our entire colony/country for about 200 years.

Kamala Harris ✓ @SenKamalaHarris
A reminder this Fourth of July: it was eight immigrants who signed the Declaration of Independence. Happy Independence Day.

Custody & Consequence

Immigration activists suddenly and vociferously demanded trespassing families be kept together at the border, which our President has graciously agreed to despite the Obama administration's unquestioned failure to do so, but now their jaded court jesters are refusing to afford the necessary time for DNA testing to ensure children aren't being smuggled by sex trafficking pedophiles pretending to be a parent or guardian. So much for "humanitarianism" when political semantics makes no genuine effort to curtail the multi-billion-dollar global empire of human trafficking. In other words, disregard the detestable fact the "terrorist organization" known as ICE arrested 4,818 gang members and apprehended illegals responsible for 1800 murders and 76,000 drug offenses in 2017, let alone the 904 children rescued from mass exploitation. As long as Mexico, Central and South America, have no discernible interest in fighting real depravity, I'm going to assume they don't have the time or moral fortitude to cash any additional foreign aid checks out of respect for the safety of soulless, "racist", American taxpayers. The ethical euphemism for progressive intent is voluntary rape in the subsidized House of ill repute.

If "invested" politicians spent more time educating the public and supporting our immigration laws, not fundraising off half-truths or inciting discord solely for self-aggrandizement, this overblown debacle would be void and moot. When did it become a humanitarian crisis for migrants to follow the prescribed naturalization process or responsibly seek asylum at a recognized Point of Entry? No crimes would be levied or families divided due to such reckless actions. Of course, it's common knowledge gang members, drug mules, serial convicts, those with communicable diseases and generally unqualified applicants purposeful skirt detection because they or a member of their caravan would never be granted entry into America regardless.

> **Black Women 4 Trump**
> @TallahForTrump
>
> The difference between legal immigration and illegal immigration is the same as shopping at a store versus robbing a store. One adds value to this country, the other does damage. We are a nation of immigrants, LEGAL immigrants.

Just in case the melodramatic media needs an academic reminder, foreign nationals apprehended at the border are not owed any due process whatsoever...that which Congress must officially and specifically designate. Rather than enabling costly lawsuits and endless legal maneuvering making a mockery of our immigration laws by invoking imaginary rights of trespassing non-citizens, the Executive branch has the full authority to process and swiftly prosecute illegal aliens apprehended within the United States. Immediate deportation without lengthy detainment, including a mandatory criminal conviction barring any chance of future citizenship, is by far the best course of action until and after an effective border wall is constructed. When 8.4% of the population accounts for 42.4% of kidnappings and 31.5% of all drug convictions, failing to act decisively is as absurd as declaring the word "illegal" inhumane. Political semantics have become the costliest if not the deadliest form of collateral damage.

The moral conflict of natural-born liberty isn't simply unadulterated "choice", but the glaring lack of equitable consequence absent in its wake. How else can the apoplectic advocates of social outrage rejoice over the 60 million babies legally separated from their biological parents since Roe v. Wade, or consciously support the sale of healthy baby parts by Planned Parenthood? If moonlighting "humanists" refuse to make any concessions regarding our civilized obligation to combat drug, sex and weapons smuggling – human servitude and slave labor markets in the year 2018 – then I fully support our President taking whatever actions are necessary to act in the best interests of the American people and on behalf of those innocent children used as pawns by crime cartels or callous parents with no regard for the rule of law, or God forbid, human life. Lest we become the "means" to end this absurd political ruse of unchecked immigration, fabricated concern and false contrition to conceal the unreported aftermath, our border might as well serve as the last sovereign checkpoint of surrendered self-respect instead of a mutually-respected path to a better life. I hear the forgotten names of victims aren't near as valuable as the electoral body count of bartered flesh.

Immigration Laws

1. The government will allow entry only to foreigners who will be useful to society.
2. The government will keep track of every single immigrant.
3. Foreigners who enter illegally will be fined, imprisoned, and/or deported.
4. Those who help illegal aliens enter the country will be considered criminals.
5. Non-citizens are forbidden from participating in political life.
6. Foreigners have no property rights.
7. Foreigners are not guaranteed equal employment rights.
8. Foreigners may never become federal lawmakers, cabinet secretaries, or Supreme Court Justices.
9. Citizens will be protected from "undesirable aliens".
10. Foreigners may be expelled for any reason and without due process.

Too strict?

The above laws are current immigration laws of **MEXICO!**

Borders, Blueprints & Elastic Heartstrings

The only ones tearing apart migrant families at the border are those individuals who refuse to recognize and consciously abide by our prevailing immigration laws: the very same family "separation" protocol Democrats helped pass, Bill Clinton signed in 1996 and Barack Obama never scrapped despite the benefit of a Congressional majority in 2008. And never mind that in March of 1993 the U.S. Supreme Court ruled, in Flores vs. Reno, minors couldn't be incarcerated with adults accompanying them illegally across the U.S. border. The landmark decision settled a long-running dispute on how to best care for these children while their guardians were detained for criminal proceedings, whereas a subsequent 1997 ruling from the 9th Circuit Court of Appeals stipulated minors must be placed in a safer environment where they could receive education and other normal life cycle amenities that imprisoned individuals typically do not. As for the social media firing squad, their erudite scholars failed to explain how a revered real estate mogul managed to orchestrate this cruel "separation of state" some 20 years before he was elected.

Naturally, these detention centers are only now being absurdly characterized as "Nazi death camps" because Donald Trump is President; a man the left conspires daily to denigrate and remove from office by any means necessary. Regardless, how is it suddenly a horrific injustice when foreign children of imprisoned illegal aliens are detained until they can be transferred or deported to a suitable home, when for generations the offspring of American citizens are sent to foster care or a relative's residence until their parents' sentence is fully served? Unfortunate, yes; unprecedented, no. Families that belong together should have stayed together in their home countries until they had permission to legally enter the United States.

1. Entering the U.S. without permission is a crime.
   - 1st time is a misdemeanor. 2nd time is a felony!

2. When 'Immigrants or Americans' get busted committing a crime, they go to jail!

3. 'Immigrants or Americans' are separated from their kids when they're in jail!

4. Having kids is not a "get out of jail free" card!

5. Those being separated at the border are the ones busted for having crossed into the U.S. ILLEGALLY!

SIMPLE! NO CRIME = NO SEPARATION!

Selective semantics aside, illegal immigration is far more than just a harmless instance of trespassing for public advocates also enable drug, weapons and human trafficking opportunists. Unlike the shameless victimization ploys of pandering politicians and media muckrakers, these essential laws have existed for over a century to protect the American people and preserve our national sovereignty; well before the evolving threats against America multiplied in complexity, frequency and ferocity. Reform is a political ruse for only blanket amnesty, open borders, will ever truly satisfy the globalist hoard.

REMEMBER WHEN BILL CLINTON AND JANET RENO SENT MEN WITH AUTOMATIC WEAPONS TO KICK A CHILD REFUGEE OUT OF AMERICA AND DEMOCRATS CHEERED?

Immigrating caravans and families are not only aware of our existing enforcement procedures, they refuse to turn back despite being warned by Border Patrol agents they will be jailed and separated from their children if they do not leave immediately. As for those televised "crying kids" who showed up with strangers or God-forbid by themselves, do you honestly believe that was mere coincidence or by design? Better yet, is brazen "child endangerment" still a crime? When U.S. taxpayers are having to shelter and feed an average of 250 new adolescent arrivals per day, at cost of $35,000 per immigrant each year, their parents' negligence is but confirmation a border wall is needed more than ever to dissuade such reckless and irresponsible actions. If I may, where is the choreographed concern for the roughly 550,000 homeless, law-abiding Americans living in squalor; or in "humanitarian" terms, the 43 million men, women and children currently living below the median poverty line of $21,000 on their own native soil? Until a single offense of illegal immigration results in a permanent loss of citizenship eligibility and possible felony indictment, little will change for the foreseeable future.

Many of the same livid activists blaming Donald Trump for decades of trespassers consciously ignoring our national sovereignty and the inevitable consequences, dismissed or even laughed at the heartless reality Planned Parenthood has been dissecting countless aborted babies and profiting from the "separation" of their healthy tissue. Selective semantics aside, illegal immigration is far more than just a harmless instance of trespassing for public advocates also enable drug, weapons and human trafficking opportunists. Despite the shameless victimization ploys of pandering politicians and media muckrakers, these essential laws have existed for over a century to protect the American people and preserve our national sovereignty; well before the evolving threats against America multiplied in complexity, frequency and ferocity. Although the President just announced an Executive Order allowing families to be detained together, unlike his hypocritical predecessors, reform is a political ruse for only blanket amnesty, open borders, will ever truly satisfy the globalist hoard.

Attempting to demonize the White House for simply enforcing the absolute necessity of border security, law and order, is as ignorant as ignoring the reality American citizens are currently imprisoned in Central and South America for violating similar legislation.

Becoming a legal citizen is not a racist conspiracy, merely a universal process of prescribed requirements designed to ensure due diligence, mutual respect and safety, without the subversion of partisan interference: i.e., divisive identity politics and criminal electoral schemes. Corrupt bureaucrats survive, often thrive, by demanding sympathy and feeding off society's indulgence of their destructive excuses. Sorry to disappoint the contemporary critics of common sense but accountability is not a revolutionary concept; it's the modern ideological Kryptonite of mindless progressive hostility.

Reflections & Revisionists

Since media-induced hysteria has turned common political practice and basic legal protocol into crimes against humanity, behold a 2014 picture from an Arizona detention center during Obama's tenure. Where are the crying journalists and rabid celebrities demanding his arrest, assassination or public tribunal? Something tells me such a farce will cost far less than to collectively shelter the over 10,000 illegals occupying our border, with 250 new child arrivals every day, at an estimated price tag of $35,000 per individual each year. And to think countless Americans are currently in jail for unpaid parking tickets and trespassing on private property. Who needs borders when drug, weapons, and human trafficking cartels have such vocal allies protecting their honorable trade?

Ironically, due to the inflamed reactions created by Democratic hypocrisy and history revisionism regarding border security protocols, the left unknowingly just helped our President fight chain immigration. His new Executive Order now ensures families that are detained together, can also be deported together. Deliberate duplicity is not without a sense of karmic fate.

The left's lynch mob behavior regarding such an obviously manipulated issue is but another ominous example of how it has literally become impossible to coexist with modern progressives; those hostile malcontents who are neither interested in truth, universal accountability or easing the burden placed on actual American citizens. Until a border wall is built, foreign parents are held responsible for their callous actions and a single instance of illegal immigration results in a permanent loss of eligibility for future citizenship – a mandatory felony indictment and significant fine – only the names propagating this never-ending debacle will change. Using children as political pawns for sympathy does not entitle anyone to special privileges. If a family truly wants to become U.S. citizens and dine at the table of American liberty, economic independence, then simply fill out the paperwork, complete the required process and protect the abundant opportunities this nation proudly offers all who respect her Constitutional sovereignty.

Aiding & Abetting Sociopaths

Those Philadelphia officials responsible for aiding and abetting this horrific crime, Mayor James Kenney specifically, should be arrested, charged and forced to sit across from the child's distraught loved ones on live national television. Combating illegal immigration and tracking known fugitives from justice is not a harmless game of political charades. It's a grave matter of public safety. There are real-life dangers and consequences which activists seem content believing do not exist or pertain to their ignorant, callous ranks.

> **Charlie Kirk** ✔
> @charliekirk11
>
> Unacceptable:
>
> An illegal alien raped a child in Philadelphia after the city refused to comply with an ICE detainer request & released him back into the city
>
> Sanctuary city mayors should be arrested for defying federal immigration law & be held civilly liable for these incidents

Shock Treatments & Socialist Demigods

Since America apparently no longer needs ICE or border patrol agents to enforce our immigration laws – to prevent the proliferation of crime, infectious diseases or terrorism by combating human, sex, drug and weapons trafficking – why do we need Congress; those deceitful, bureaucratic dregs who profit from legislative kickbacks, reckless propaganda and incessant partisan games? Hell, while the so-called egalitarian left teeters on the precipice of sponsored anarchy and visualized economic ruination, why does anyone need the police, a standing military or a judicial system? No wonder the IRS admitted to harassing law-abiding conservatives only to disperse refunds to Illegals who never paid taxes...because it makes so much sense to betray the very country, loyal citizens and rule of law your "loving" political neurosis so predictably but ignorantly despises. What could possibly be more redeeming than transforming the United States into a national sanctuary for trespassing indigents, fugitives from justice and anti-American agitators whom liberals already tirelessly groom and shamelessly favor in educational opportunities, government jobs, and public benefits? Or is equality in the eyes of God and the blind wisdom of activist judges still an affirmative action program with complimentary gift bags?

I'M AN OPEN SOCIALIST
I WANT SAFE PASSAGE FOR ILLEGALS
I WANT TO ABOLISH I.C.E.
I DON'T BELIEVE IN BORDERS OR NATIONS
I WANT A "MARSHALL PLAN" ($ Billions)
    FOR CLIMATE ISSUES
I WANT MEDICAID FOR ALL
I DON'T BELIEVE IN FREE MARKETS
I WANT TO IMPEACH THE PRESIDENT
I WANT AMERICA TO MIMIC VENEZUELA

ALEXANDRIA OCASIO-CORTEZ IS THE NEW FACE OF THE DEMOCRATIC PARTY

The moment "resisting" a President's mounting achievements and populist reforms requires abandoning reason for madness, the mere prospect of facing reality turns elected statesmen into kicking and screaming delinquents at the slightest hint of accountability. Better yet, when the DNC chairman zealously proclaims Alexandria Ocasio-Cortez is the future "gold standard" of the Democratic party's silver bullet, a privileged but "victimized" millennial possessing far more socialist hyperbole and racial angst than real-life experience or acquired expertise, sanity is the hidden, dissenting elephant euthanized in the romanticized media narrative of the "honorable" Bronx zoo. Unfortunately for the common man caught in the cultural cross-hairs of clueless Marxist ideologues, including "oppressed" debutantes raised in Yorktown Heights of Westchester County, reality and regurgitated rhetoric rarely cross political paths in the same plane of existence.

Pay no attention to the undaunted pioneer trailblazing towards a limitless horizon of self-actualization, welcome to the cognitive re-calibration asylum where recognized (U.S.) borders are a form of illegal enticement, unearned entitlements are a human right, basic civility is a tool of Right-Wing fascism, where universal tax cuts promote poverty, and profit-producing businesses must relinquish the private fruits of ambition, professional skill and personal sacrifice to the mandatory custody of the bloc-voting welfare state. Unless these absurd agendas and insipid insinuations poisoning our most fundamental ideals are denounced as clear and present dangers to the rationale world, that symbolic yet indomitable American spirit breaking free from oppressive rule will inevitably become a blasphemous metaphor for breaking the untouchable glass motives of Democratic demigods. I, for one, am tired of false idols and glorified carnival tricks.

Black Pots, White Lines and Brown Paper Bags

A startling majority of immigrants who come to America, many with little more than the shirts on their back, do so to escape the extreme poverty, corruption, oppression and inept leadership plaguing their native countries. Sadly, having three meals a day, let alone a high school education or a functioning hospital, was and still is considered a luxury. As someone who has personally known and befriended people from Mexico, El Salvador, Haiti, Venezuela, the Dominican Republic, Cuba and Uganda, I couldn't help but ask them one inescapable question: "If you had the opportunity, other than to visit your remaining family or friends left behind, would you return to your homeland?" Their unflinching response? "Hell no!" These individuals and their loved ones literally lived in dilapidated "hell holes", routinely watched people die of starvation, violence, rampant pollution or non-existent healthcare, and therefore chose to do everything in their power to escape the depravity of these dysfunctional regions.

Whether or not a known politically incorrect President actually made these truthful remarks is actually a petty and moot point considering the harsh reality millions are facing and fleeing on a daily basis. Rather, it is incumbent upon our government, our founding charter as a beacon of hope for all people willing to respect and preserve America's abundant opportunities, to find an equitable balance between properly/diligently documenting the skyrocketing numbering of immigrants seeking our shores, a better and more humane life, and how to ease their suffering through the auspices of responsible, legal immigration. In a world where shock value is no longer shocking and FBI collusion commendable, I'm far more offended by the now acceptable obscene, profane and immoral content of pop culture and social media – a supposed feminist icon and crooked presidential candidate that used her "humanitarian foundation" to siphon millions in donations from disaster survivors in Haiti – than an unfiltered CEO who views progress by results, pragmatism, instead of the pampered sensitivities of shameless propagandists who cry racism and sexism every time someone disagrees with their fragile, ignorant and distinctly Anti-American beliefs.

Walls, Whims and the Border Less Traveled

DACA was never about saving a handful of wrongfully persecuted "Dreamers" from the xenophobic pitchforks of Right-Wingers. It was and still is about shamelessly exploiting the plight of roughly 800,000 adolescent illegals, a majority of which are now adults, to justify cultivating an additional 3.2 million relatives: i.e., an untapped expanse of eager Democratic voters. In fact, according to a campaign memo co-authored by Hillary's former Communications Director, Jennifer Palmier openly admits "the Democratic Party needs to protect illegal immigrants brought here by DACA in order to ensure those additional votes"; which, of course, was the unwavering contention of conservatives all along despite the media's exhaustive efforts to paint such allegations as heartless and false. Even if "Donald Trump the White Supremacist" allowed all DACA families to remain and prosper in the United States, contingent upon forever relinquishing their right to vote as recompense for their illegal status, Democrats would still cry injustice despite his willingness to pardon their incontrovertible crimes so they could pursue a better life without fear of arrest or deportation.

> **Charlie Kirk** ✔ @charliekirk11 · 1h
> Facts:
>
> Between 2001 and 2013, George W. Bush and Barack Obama used their national emergency authority 18 times to authorize 18 different military construction projects—All to benefit other countries
>
> @realDonaldTrump is using it to protect AMERICA.

Once you factor in the realization 40% of Hillary's votes came from states which rejected Voter ID laws and currently house over 5 million illegal immigrants of voting age – many of whom harbor negative, exploitative or even hostile views towards this country – it doesn't take a rocket scientist to realize the Democratic Party has almost zero regard for America's sovereignty, ideological and fiscal survival, let alone the rule of law. If over a century of immigrants from across the globe managed to respect our borders and fulfill the naturalization requirements under the most-dire circumstances, surely a handful of "dreamers" and their tailgate-crashing relatives can understand the need for a wall, if not a moment of silence for those Americans denied the same level of impunity, economic entitlement, by "racist" Central and South American governments. That's right...who needs easy lighting briquets when U.S. bureaucrats will provide a bonfire burning the effigy of American gullibility.

It is common knowledge, except for millennial marshmallows inviting themselves to a free lunch, the Marxist minions of cultural suicide have conspired for decades to undermine our immigration statutes by encouraging mass migration, shielding trespassers from prosecution and even giving preferential treatment to those perpetrators over actual citizens; including those individuals with extensive records or radical associations. And because victimization indoctrination is the affirmative action appetizer professional propagandists, progressives have fabricated a humanitarian crisis to pull on the heartstrings of America and thus justify their reckless, if not emphatically criminal behavior. DACA, in all its misappropriated glory, is little more than an extension of this inexcusable endeavor. Not only is Obama's electoral trafficking program completely unconstitutional, as recently confirmed by the Supreme Court because it was never ratified by Congress and his executive order violates existing immigration law, the 9th Circuit Court of Appeals futile attempt to force President Trump to honor such an abusive, non-binding farce is the equivalent of a slumlord decreeing every new tenant must sleep in the previous owner's pissed stained sheets.

Until these spiteful judicial obstructionists are put on trial and impeached for their pronounced abuse of power, choosing to collude with pandering plaintiffs by placing shared partisan hatred over legal precedent, the President should either openly disregard and/or bypass these obscene rulings which are completely antithetical to any sense of moral obligation. After all, the sheer level of lawlessness prevalent in the Obama administration would make such a principled stance, dare I say, seem revolutionary. With the unapologetic assistance and/or convenient indifference of the DOJ and FBI, Obama's regime was able to auction off nuclear grade uranium to a known historical adversary, finance Islamic terrorism with unauthorized ransom payments, absolve Hillary's countless transgressions with admitted preferential treatment, instruct DHS agents to distribute millions of green cards to unvetted recipients despite federal court injunctions, weaponize the IRS to target conservatives, empower the BLM to terrorize ranchers or needlessly confiscate state/private lands, and validate a knowingly fake dossier used as justification to wiretap a Presidential candidate for the first time in U.S. history, the crime syndicate now known as the former party of JFK could use a double dose of reality, better known as, accountability.

The growing crescendo to end DACA and to build a wall are both justifiable and crucial to restoring responsible immigration. However, even as a staunch conservative who has advocated swift action for years, desire doesn't always dictate with the complexities of legislative reform. It is true, within several months, DACA will expire on its own accord without further intervention. And yes, I'm confidently assuming the Supreme Court will once again vacant the 9th Circuit's newest display of masturbatory lunacy. Unfortunately, erecting a border edifice over 2,000 miles by navigating between three separate, polarized but intertwined branches of government is not nearly as simple as many mistakenly assume. While it is true the cost of constructing a wall pales in comparison to the annual $150 billion price tag of harboring approximately 25 million illegal immigrants, funding requires Congressional approval. Republicans hold but a narrow 51-49 advantage in the Senate and a number of GOP Senators – McCain, Flake, Collins, and Murkowski to name but a few – have expressed resistance to the idea of a border wall, let alone any agreement/compromise that doesn't include explicit protecting "dreamers; that political manifestation which turns logic, rightfully enforcing existing immigration laws, into genocidal hyperbole on the five o'clock news.

Before "We the People" vow to abandon arguably the most persecuted and daring President in our history, a man whose family has withstood an endless barrage of hateful epithets and criminal partisan schemes to confront a corrupt ruling class, let us remember that unity – unrelenting faith in the face of the most trying circumstances – and not ultimatums, is what nurtures success. How many angry voters lamenting the repeated failed attempts to repeal Obamacare, myself included, actually predicted a sweeping tax bill would essentially remove the individual mandate and thus cripple Barack Obama's

Trojan horse intended to usher in an eventual single-payer system? The more plotting leftists know Donald Trump is left isolated with little flexibility or recourse, the more their unscrupulous ranks will feel compelled to sabotage his aspirations with the added leverage of our discontent. Honestly, what other Republican nominee would have achieved half as much, let alone survived the incessant onslaught of public humiliation, media duplicity and unprecedented degree of Deep State collusion? Patience isn't a virtue because fear demands immediate reassurances from the unforeseeable means of achieving closure. Patience is often the conscious revelation that one must open a new door to remove the greatest obstacle hindering progress: our closed minds.

"Foreigners will generally be apt to bring with them attachments to the persons they have left behind; to the country of their nativity, and to its particular customs and manners. It is unlikely that they will bring with them that temperate love of liberty so essential to real republicanism.

The influx of foreigners must, therefore, tend to produce a heterogeneous compound; to change and corrupt the national spirit; to complicate and confound public opinion; to introduce foreign propensities. In the composition of society, the harmony of the ingredients is all-important, and whatever tends to a discordant intermixture must have an injurious tendency.

To admit foreigners indiscriminately to the rights of citizens, the moment they put foot in our country, would be nothing less than to admit the Grecian horse into the citadel of our liberty and sovereignty."

ALEXANDER HAMILTON, 1802

The Tree of Liberty

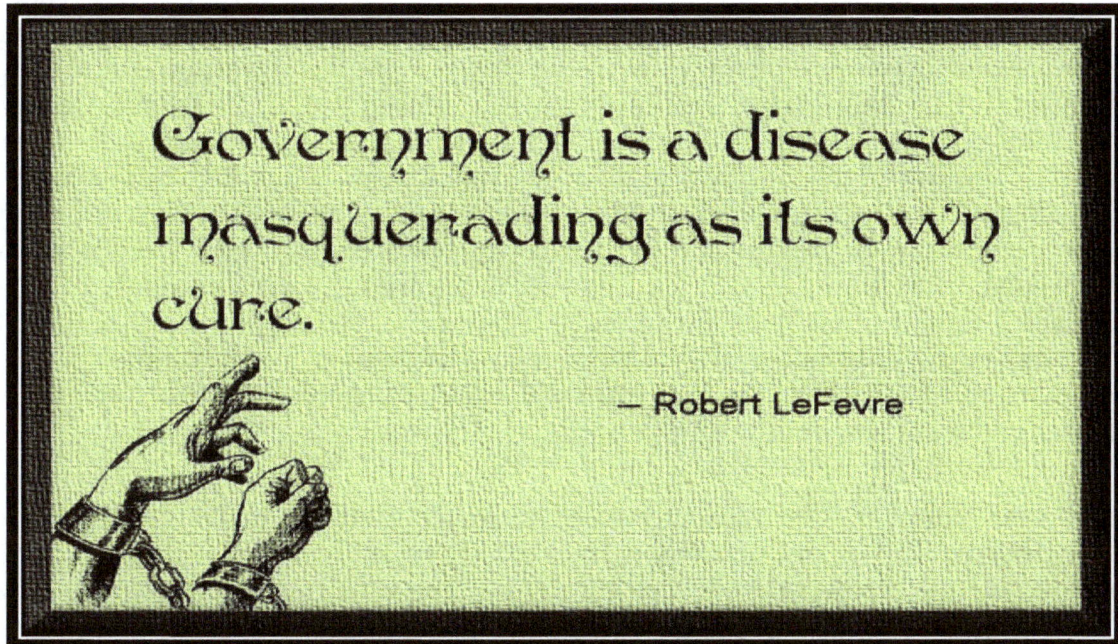

Government is a disease masquerading as its own cure.

— Robert LeFevre

For those who oppose or are outraged by President Trump's decision to end DACA, or Deferred Action for Child Arrivals, I have one question: when does a lie built upon another lie suddenly become an unjust truth? As an Executive Order issued by Barack Obama right before the 2012 election, DACA was never legally binding let alone whimsically constitutional. While any President can issue Executive Orders that expound on existing law or direct certain federal agencies to act in a prescribed manner, our Chief Executive cannot use this inherent power as an attempt to bypass Congress, unilaterally write new law or invalidate current legislation. In other words, "illegal" immigration did and still does denote a punishable crime according to federal statutes.

The failure of Congressional Democrats to both ram and coyly sneak Amnesty by their Republican constituents on multiple occasions merely emboldened an already rogue President to further abuse his powers. Considering the Obama administration was later ordered by a federal Judge in 2015 to cease and desist distributing millions of Green Cards through the Department of Homeland Security as part of his Executive Amnesty plan, an oxymoron also known as Deferred Actions for Parents of Americans (DAPA), it's evident DACA was the first stone cast in a series of calculated distractions designed to specifically circumvent jurisprudence with the intent of triggering an unprecedented wave of unchecked immigration. When your goal requires using grown children as media props to deflect criticism in order to achieve De facto Amnesty for entire families – i.e., protect countless illegals from deportation until Congress officially issues a reprieve or sanctuary states like California fraudulently grant them the right to vote – the Constitution, the welfare of actual citizens, is obviously of little concern in the Kangaroo Court of public opinion.

As someone who fully appreciates and supports the premise that is America, I openly welcome all legal immigrants who respect our sovereignty and complete the required naturalization process to pursue a better life. However, there is a stark difference between political exploitation – pardoned ignorance or indifference to achieve a corrupt political goal – and equal deference in the eyes of the law. Illegal immigration is not simply a harmless matter of trespassing that is needlessly blown out of proportion by white, patriotic xenophobes. In today's climate of global terrorism and rising anti-American sentiment, illegal immigration represents a tangible threat to our national security, the functionality/survival of our schools and hospitals, and an undue burden on taxpayers; those men and women, in addition to competing with an influx of foreign labor for American jobs, must now account for the over $150 billion spent annually to care for impoverished immigrants or to incarcerate those criminal perpetrators among their ranks. Sound reasonable or remotely equitable...regardless of one's nationality, creed or color? Or, if you like, just ask the survivors of Hurricane Harvey who now must reclaim their lives amidst the aftermath of $150 billion in devastation.

While I do not blame children for the wrongful misconduct of their migrating parents, such conscious choices do not negate a crime's existence or change the nature of our laws. I for one do not and have never believed that a child born on American soil to non-citizens, especially ones conceived by illegal immigrants who knowingly disregarded our laws, is a natural born citizen. That, in my opinion, is purely wishful thinking born from false assumption. Whereas some believe the term "anchor baby" is a derogatory term used to wrongfully describe mere extenuating circumstances, I believe the acronym DACA is even more offensive once you realize a former President, ever fearful of losing his re-election bid amidst sagging approval numbers, concocted a completely illegitimate program that was actually designed to save immediate or extended families of illegal children from deportation by pulling on the heartstrings of America. The fact DACA has existed this long without being struck down by the courts, dismissed by states or defunded by Congress is an absurd failing of our government's clearly enumerated checks and balances. Since when did false appearances and corrupt intentions warrant concessions to the very pandering bureaucrats responsible for this enduring mess?

The Obama administration knew quite well most American voters with kids, or God forbid anyone with a soul, would not want to witness families being torn apart once a child was granted a protected status. Likewise, because most illegal aliens are not at risk of deportation, unless they're felons, militant agitators or identified gang members, I believe Donald Trump's pledge to delay ending DACA by six months so Congress can rightfully take action and "do their job" is both prudent and compassionate. Any subject matter as vast as immigration reform should always include the input and approval of all necessary parties and government branches. Not only have conniving politicians muddled a simple procedural issue of due diligence for decades, but in what other country can my "American or white privilege" receive immunity for illegally entering a sovereign nation; not withstanding committing robbery, assault, rape, tax or welfare fraud while claiming to be the victim of racism? And yes, excuse my common sense, but why aren't Asian, European or Russian immigrants also marching under the hollow cries of injustice? As a firm believer in Karma, or more profoundly respect, accountability and honesty are the antidote for 99% of our ills both as a country and a species.

Despite the devious ploys of Democratic "Dreamers" and anti-American agitators, sympathy should never be a fabricated crisis molded into political capital but rather a sincere reaction born from true concern or mistreatment. For those DACA participants seeking to remain in America past the program's termination despite lingering claims of "victimization", I have no problem granting such a request as long as these individuals are fully vetted, abide by all terms of their "guest" worker/student status, are barred from receiving federal or state assistance during their stay and permanently denied voting privileges unless they leave the country, apply for re-entry and are granted citizenship under the new RAISED standards of naturalization. If DACA was truly about allowing "Dreamers" a chance to appreciate the countless blessings America affords to all – and not some bankrupt, partisan scheme to subvert our laws, discredit our founding values and forever tip America's electoral balance – than hard work, earned trust and ample opportunity should more than suffice for those seeking to escape the depravity of their native countries to dine from the preserved tree of liberty.

Kate Steinle: A Victim of "Privilege"

How are you not guilty of murder, let alone involuntary manslaughter from "accidental negligence", when there's a dead body, gunshot residue on your hand and you admit firing the weapon that killed her; a firearm stolen from a federal agent, no less? When political hearsay replaces logic and common sense becomes a micro-aggression! Apparently if you're an illegal immigrant living in California, shielded by the sheer lunacy of Sanctuary Cities, the law is secondary to the warped perceptions of bitter social anarchists. It's obvious a sizable percentage of judges and jurors are incapable of delineating fact from identity victimization propaganda; i.e., the growing mindset in extremely progressive states that politics trump judicial obligation because illegals are obviously helpless victims of a racist American society and therefore worthy of special considerations. Sorry to disgrace the "honorable" court but "intent" does not magically exonerate criminals from the consequences of their actions.

A conviction of guilt doesn't require three bystanders filming a suspect standing over a bleeding body while holding a smoking gun. You simply have to prove there is no other likely, plausible explanation within the scope of the evidence at hand. Regardless of your personal opinion of the verdict, the fact liberals are rejoicing over this historic injustice, claiming Kate's Law should now be nullified to allow similar future tragedies, illustrates just how shameless, morally bankrupt and dangerous the left has become in the wake of such a senseless loss. It's painfully absurd to call yourself a "feminist" or a champion of women's rights after celebrating the unpunished murder of a callously marginalized life.

Sorry to disappoint the Jose Garcia Zarate fan club, but I never viewed our legal system as a color-coded game of partisan contempt – white versus black, man versus woman, Christian versus atheist, Democrat versus Republican. Rather, I recognized the concept of "justice" as the most sacred duty of a sovereign, constitutional republic to reassert the rights and value of a human life. For once our judicially system is irreconcilably compromised, tyranny and mass injustice are merely a formality. If we as a nation of laws cannot demand accountability, deliver legal recompense with damning proof and grieve for an innocent woman gunned down in the prime of her life by a trespassing non-citizen with 7 felony convictions and deported 5 times, this nation is no better than a banana republic that claims witnessing a rape is a violation of one's right to privacy. And if that's now the universal standard of prescribed innocence, Europe would like to share their secrets of culture capitulation by teaching unreasonable Americans how not to trigger foreign militants into robbing, assaulting or killing their loved ones. As long as subjective advocacy perverts the rule of law and tangible evidence no longer indicative of guilt beyond a reasonable doubt, "justice" will remain the battered political hostage of detached apologists who actually correlate forensic science with white privilege and "racism".

No Mas: A Sanctuary of Stupidity

In honor of defunding sanctuary cities and the soon to be passed Kate's Law – posthumously named after the young murdered woman whose final words were "Help me, Dad".

Once upon a time, immigrants from all corners of the globe respected America, honored our laws, and appreciated the innate opportunities liberty affords. For well over a century, millions of foreigners filtered through our ports and industrialized epicenters seeking a better life under the auspices of freedom, private enterprise and limited government. Despite enduring much harsher conditions with little to no assistance, they did not smugly demand concessions out of self-pity, degrade their new host with blind hatred or derision, and they did not muddle the simple issue of immigration for personal gain by ignoring the legal requirements of the naturalization process. These impoverished individuals and forsaken families merely thirsted for a chance to become Americans and forge their own destiny with their own two hands: no regrets, no excuses. They were, and many continue to be, the salt of the earth and the heart of American exceptionalism. Now, amidst the modern-day zeitgeist of race warfare and wealth redistribution, this new generation of overwhelmingly "illegal" immigrants – Latino and Islamic transplants zealously recruited by our government as part of Obama's demographic coup d'état – religiously slanders America, openly pines for her demise, gleefully desecrates our flag and extorts entitlements under the hollow cries of racism. Sadly, these usurpers would rather help liberals turn this blessed land into the bankrupt and morally corrupt socialist cesspools they are instinctively fleeing, solely out of spite for America's heritage and rapid ascendancy, instead of fighting to preserve the founding ideals that keenly molded the most revered, affluent and transcendent nation our ancestors died so desperately seeking.

The dichotomy of these two diametrically opposed eras, in terms of mentality and intent, could not be more evident. If asking those seeking the privileges of citizenship to recognize our national sovereignty and fill out the necessary paperwork to legally immigrate to America is too inconvenient or unreasonable, then please don't bother completing the necessary forms for welfare, subsidized housing, obtaining a driver's license, enrolling in school or taking your child to the emergency room. Why should America bear the financial and permanent electoral fallout from obliging the needs of her sworn detractors when those same brash guests have little or no intent of obliging the common courtesy of our immigration laws and functional culture? In other words, don't disparage the very source of your salvation, the universal formalities of our hospitality, simply because your native country repeatedly failed your brethren without refrain. That doesn't make the United States racist or an evil, capitalistic empire; it makes your government woefully inept and millions like yourself ignorant to the true source of their incessant ills. Mexico didn't build a fence to stop Guatemalans from enjoying the spoiled fruits of crime, drugs, pollution and rampant poverty. They did it to preserve the integrity of their borders and their national identity...to discourage and control the influx of illegal immigrants. Apparently "trespassing" still doesn't require an interpreter with a degree in social justice.

Do Latinos not want REAL jobs and business opportunities so they can afford a respectable home, transportation, quality healthcare or to send their kids to college? Unequivocally, for Hispanics are some of the most hardworking, family oriented, religious people you'll ever meet. Well, according to the dregs of socialism, Latinos obviously want nothing more than to work menial jobs the rest of their life and/or to barely scrape by each month on government welfare. What patriotic Americans really want is to create a vibrant private sector – where commerce, jobs and opportunity flourish for all races and creeds – so the American dream can once again become a reality for those who truly want it. Economic freedom has, and always will be, the heartbeat of America. "We the People" of these United States welcome all people who seek safe harbor on our shores, the promise of America our forefathers swore and died to protect. However, in return, we expect all immigrants to have this nation's best interests at heart and to respect our nonnegotiable need to protect our borders and safeguard our citizens without condition or juvenile threats. If all foreigners respected our immigration laws and the Obama administration physically enforced them, Donald Trump wouldn't have to introduce the "radical" idea of building a wall to preserve the last vestiges of common sense. How else can a 10-billion-dollar solution to a 150-billion-dollar annual epidemic be hailed as an unjustifiable expense?

Are everyday Americans tired of the incessant race-baiting and victimization propaganda spread by social justice parasites? Are 'We the Privileged" blessed with designated safe houses to escape legal prosecution? No, not even for unpaid parking tickets or drunk driving? Yes, semantics aside, I'm offended by those duplicitous opportunists who have no regard for our intelligence and who refuse to recognize America's right to self-preservation. I proudly embrace the natural beauty of diversity, the indelible premise that America is a beacon of hope and opportunity for all, but I refuse to abandon the principles of jurisprudence as media puppets pardon treason in the politically correct theater of the absurd. When did our national security – the safety, Constitutional rights and fiscal burden of actual citizens – become a Shakespearean tragedy of celebrated stupidity? More profoundly, when did we so willingly surrender our soul to the sanctuary cities of progressivism that are more outraged over the forced fluidity of transgender bathrooms than a child being raped by a repeatedly deported criminal or a woman murdered by an undocumented fugitive from justice? Obviously the morally bankrupt excuses of political relativism work best when you try not to think for yourself because the end always justifies the means in the lion's den of impunity; especially when trying to topple your native country with an inexhaustible army of illegal votes.

Mexico's Enduring Legacy of Failure

If Mexican President Enrique Nieto truly believes Donald Trump is a bigot for not welcoming millions of medically and criminally unvetted illegal aliens with open arms and a check made out to "cash", then why does Mexico have stricter immigration and foreign work laws than "racist" America? Every civilized nation recognizes the absolute necessity of securing their borders and maintaining the integrity of their immigration programs. It's the type of common sense that requires no apology or gratuitous reminders. Perhaps if the Mexican government wasn't so adept at destroying its own country with an endless cycle of incompetence and corruption, their own flesh and blood would not be fleeing their native homeland with nothing but the clothes on their back. And yet these are the same hypocrites who have the nerve to denounce America as greedy capitalists; that transcendent beacon of liberty, opportunity and prosperity so many thankful souls have legally immigrated to from across the globe for over a century.

Contrary to conspiring globalists, good neighbors don't sneak across sovereign borders, seek sanctuary from criminal prosecution or demand free benefits at taxpayer expense. Respect the immigration process and America will respect you. The fact the Obama administration spent more per illegal immigrant than the average social security recipient or U.S. veteran is unforgivable. Trump didn't facilitate the necessity of a wall...he merely exposed those who abandoned the truth, the rule of law and the welfare of actual citizens. Actions have consequences and adults are not children.

Mr. Nieto, if you may, please explain how America is obliged to help those illegals who mock our generosity, disregard our laws and threaten our nation's survival – if not the lives of our loved ones – simply because they refused to properly apply for the privilege of being an American citizen? In other words, respect is given when trust is earned! When a majority of your own towns lack basic infrastructure and sanitation, your crime ravaged populace is considered fortunate to possess an 8th grade education, the only injustice being committed against the Mexican people is that you're even given a platform to speak, let alone paid to be an unmitigated failure on a never-ending list of unapologetic failures. Sorry if "We the People" do not jump at the opportunity to become a third-world, socialist cesspool out of some misplaced duty to bailout an elected slumlord in the name of political correctness. Until you clean up your house, don't ask for the right to rob ours!

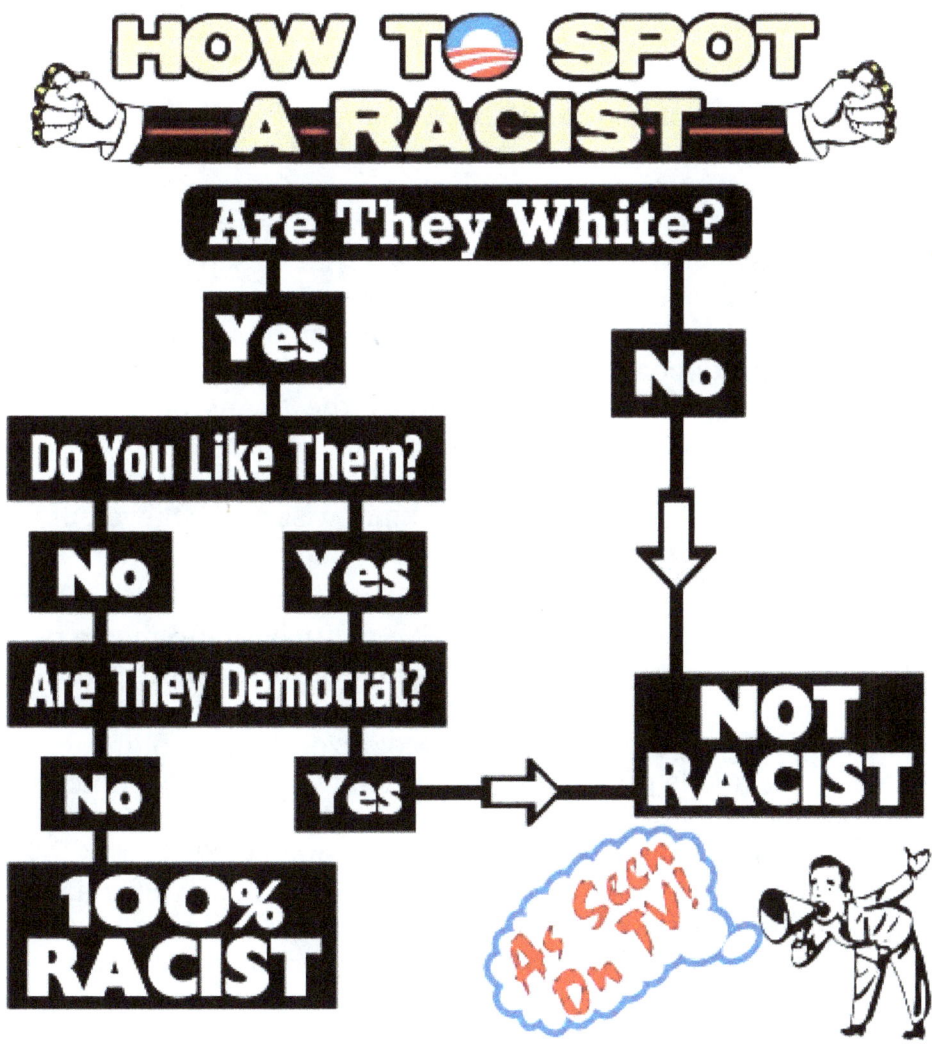

The American Refugee

California is bankrupt, losing even more federal funding for refusing to repeal Sanctuary Cities, and what's their solution for restoring order and solvency? Create a single-payer healthcare plan for illegals, mandate free tuition for "Dreamers" and grant suffrage to all driver's license holders; which now includes any willing, warm body. Behold the madness where employed, taxpaying citizens are treated with less regard than those illegal immigrants who verbally abuse our nation, burn our flag and assault Trump supporters on American soil to the complicit silence of plotting progressives. Spare my petty indulgence but if I went to Mexico City, publicly cursed their country, demanded free benefits and waved the American flag with unbridled spite, in what cemetery or prison would I reside? Would their educators speak English for the benefit of my child or offer them free lunches to the exclusion of their own? Better yet, would any of their citizens hold a nationally organized march on my behalf demanding justice or an officially recognized safe space from criminal prosecution...that my rights and financial well-being superseded that of the Mexican populace? Of course not, for belligerent, subversive guests who seek chaos in lieu of cooperation or electoral supremacy in lieu of preserving our founding charter – the timeless catalyst of their economic and liberation – should never be given preference to law-abiding, loyal citizens who toil and sacrifice on her behalf every day.

As a transcendent beacon of hope and liberty founded for all of humanity, Americans are not opposed to "legal" immigration; those documented procedures of safety protocols ratified by both political parties that have duly existed for over a century. "We the People" merely reject those who seek entitlement over assimilation or breed enmity over unity. Contrary to the racist narrative of DREAMERS, the Geo-political theater of the world today is a far cry from the mass influx of foreigners so synonymous with Ellis Island. Yes, once upon a much saner time, millions flocked for our shores seeking or asking for nothing more than an opportunity to forge a better life with their own two hands; an intrinsic desire to prosper – proudly grabbing the reigns of accountability – and to respect, if not fiercely protect, the limitless blessings America afforded. They had little to any discernible interest in toppling America, the very source of their salvation, let alone murdering 3,000 innocents in the name of a kind, wise and benevolent God.

And now? Now an entire new generation of immigrants, guided by the regressive Red Carpet of American apologists, i.e., progressive politicians and media propagandists, are being baptized by a growing tide of mindless malice; that immigration laws designed to safeguard American lives and interests are supposedly intolerant relics of greed and hate...despite the fact every civilized nation recognizes their absolute necessity. If America is truly driven by insatiable prejudice over principle – and bankruptcy, crime, terrorism and riots are but figments of our xenophobic imagination – why would so many risk so much to journey to such a universally despised harbinger of injustice? Why would entire families cling to the faintest hope of a new beginning in makeshift rafts drifting upon the rogue currents of inescapable death? Simply put...they wouldn't. The death certificate to the American Dream is the relinquished deed to American sovereignty.

The prescribed path to U.S. citizenship is not a Republican conspiracy nor an offensive impetus for a weekly civil rights march. It's both a course of due diligence and due process exercised for the benefit of all parties involved; including the rights and welfare of its most obstinate critics. However, failing to abide by these elementary terms or evade prosecution does not constitute a humanitarian crisis born from bigotry. It is a crime of conscience, choice, and little more. When completing mere paperwork, pledging allegiance to the survival of your newfound home and fulfilling the nonnegotiable steps required to pursue a civilized life becomes an unconscionable burden, what's the cost of remaining in your native country that so egregiously failed you? The only sanctuary from common sense and the inevitable consequences of one's actions is under the extreme auspices of the unvetted liberal mind. And if that's too difficult or radical to comprehend, then please leave your front door unlocked, your checkbook on the table and the birth certificate of your children on the nightstand next to the unchecked baggage of reason's latest refugee.

Private Property and Lost Privileges

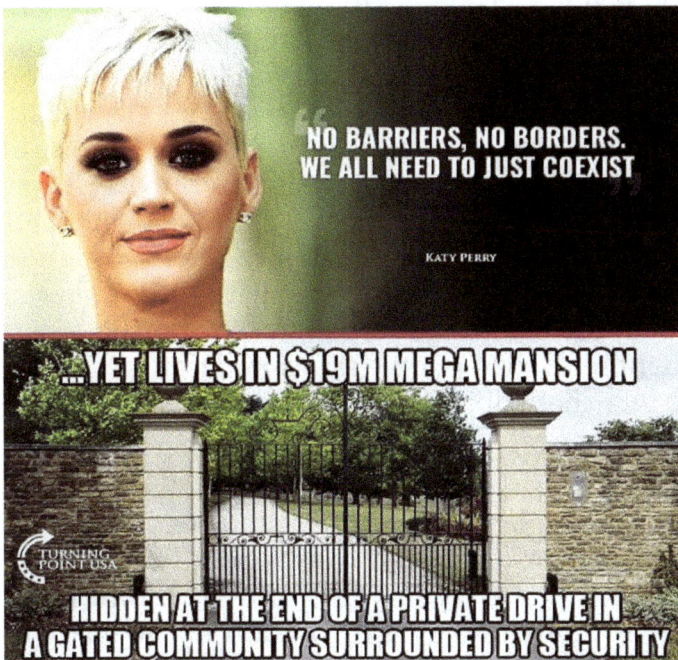

"NO BARRIERS, NO BORDERS. WE ALL NEED TO JUST COEXIST

KATY PERRY

...YET LIVES IN $19M MEGA MANSION

TURNING POINT USA

HIDDEN AT THE END OF A PRIVATE DRIVE IN A GATED COMMUNITY SURROUNDED BY SECURITY

I'm not a mathematician or a border patrol agent but when a sovereign nation is infiltrated by over 25 million illegal immigrants costing taxpayers $150 billion a year, accounting for 25% of felony incarcerations, reintroducing previously eradicated pathogens to a vulnerable populace, and disrupting the integrity of our elections with millions of uncovered illicit votes, I'm pretty sure these developments constitute a State of Emergency. Our Southern border alone serves as an entry point for over 90% of drug trafficking flowing into North America, but more profoundly, our homes, schools and communities.

Of course, who needs such trivial details when Blue states are providing sanctuary to wanted criminals, offering free college and preferential social services to noncitizens, and charging law-abiding citizens for their abortions and sex-reassignment surgeries while somehow labeling any vocal, outraged American as racist or xenophobic for simply demanding accountability. I, for one, am sick and tired of the double standards, insulting rhetoric and complete disregard for the rule of law. Since "legal" immigration is apparently no longer regarded as a privilege or a respected means to pursue a better life, then all aspiring trespassers and sponsored caravan invaders can enjoy the new view of wasted opportunity after "We the People" rightfully remind them why their homes have doors and walls and locks. Citizenship, unlike theft, must be earned.

The Why "Not" of Illegal Immigration

If Donald Trump is a "racist" and supremacist for illustrating the disturbing truths about illegal immigration, then the time has obviously come for his "offended" detractors to answer a few inconvenient questions about their own bigotry and convenient indifference.

Why is it OK for our elected leaders to NOT enforce our immigration laws and to allow millions of medically and criminally unvetted trespassers to cross our border? Why is perfectly acceptable for the White House to encourage and even orchestrate illegal immigration, transport undocumented and radicalized "refugees" to unsuspecting cities all across America, and grant illegal aliens free welfare, healthcare, and education at taxpayer expense; those hard-working Americans who are already struggling to find work or make ends meet? Why is it not a dereliction of duty, a prosecutable offense, for the President and Congress to abandon our borders in a post 9/11 world, or any era for that matter? Why are liberals allowed to invoke "racism", muddle a simple issue of national security, and disregard the fact every civilized nation has strict immigration statutes – including Mexico, Central and South America – designed to protect their people and ensure their national sovereignty? Why is it not a crime, a threat to our heritage and survival, for Democrats to incessantly scheme, manipulate public perception, and mislead the judicial system to find any conceivable way for millions of non-citizens to vote and subvert the integrity of our elections? Why is it tolerable for Barack Obama and Hillary Clinton to dine with, solicit donations from and/or voice support for La Raza – a group of racist militants who have called for the extermination of white people and the overthrow of our country through a demographic coup d'état – while Donald Trump is ridiculed for merely highlighting their laughable hypocrisy? And when will our President, Congress and the media – those most critical of his unfiltered comments – visit with the families of those Americans who were murdered, raped, molested, beaten and robbed at the hands of illegal immigrants because our government refused to put the safety and rights of actual citizens over its treasonous plan to ensure an exhaustible source of foreign votes?

If the adage "no human being is illegal" is as true as activists love to proclaim, why do we have borders and immigration laws in the first place; those very statutes Democrats helped author, pass and have duly existed for over a century? Has federal oversight of immigration not existed since 1891; first through the Treasury and now via the BCIS? If anyone should be protesting in the streets and threatening a revolution in the name of mass injustice, it's the citizens of this republic who have become afterthoughts in the progressive war on traditional America. The appalling fact our government spends more money per illegal immigrant than on actual citizens, even those social security recipients who worked and paid taxes their whole life, is criminal and insulting to say the least. If Democrats consciously honored our existing laws, recognized the prescribed process of naturalization every civilized nation demands and admitted their socialist schemes are bankrupting this nation both fiscally and ideologically, then Donald Trump wouldn't have to suggest the "radical" concept of building a wall to stop and confront the even more radical Democratic concept of overthrowing America's sovereignty and electoral balance to achieve a permanent state of political supremacy.

I proudly embrace the beauty of diversity and sincerely welcome those who seek the life-changing privilege of being an American. However, considering a well-known path to citizenship has existed for well over a century and millions of law-abiding foreigners had the common sense and innate respect to follow it, consider me officially offended. America was founded as a beacon of liberty and optimism for all mankind; not as a paid refuge for opportunists, a safe house for known fugitives or as a political oasis for cultivated anti-Americanism. As a nation of laws, we spend more time forging alibis for and making concessions to the illicit behavior of grown adults than we do recognizing the moral fortitude and character of conscientious children. If politicians and illegal aliens can now pick and choose which laws they want to follow, then "We the People" are obliged to invoke that same right. An enemy of America, the rule of law, is no friend of equality or justice.

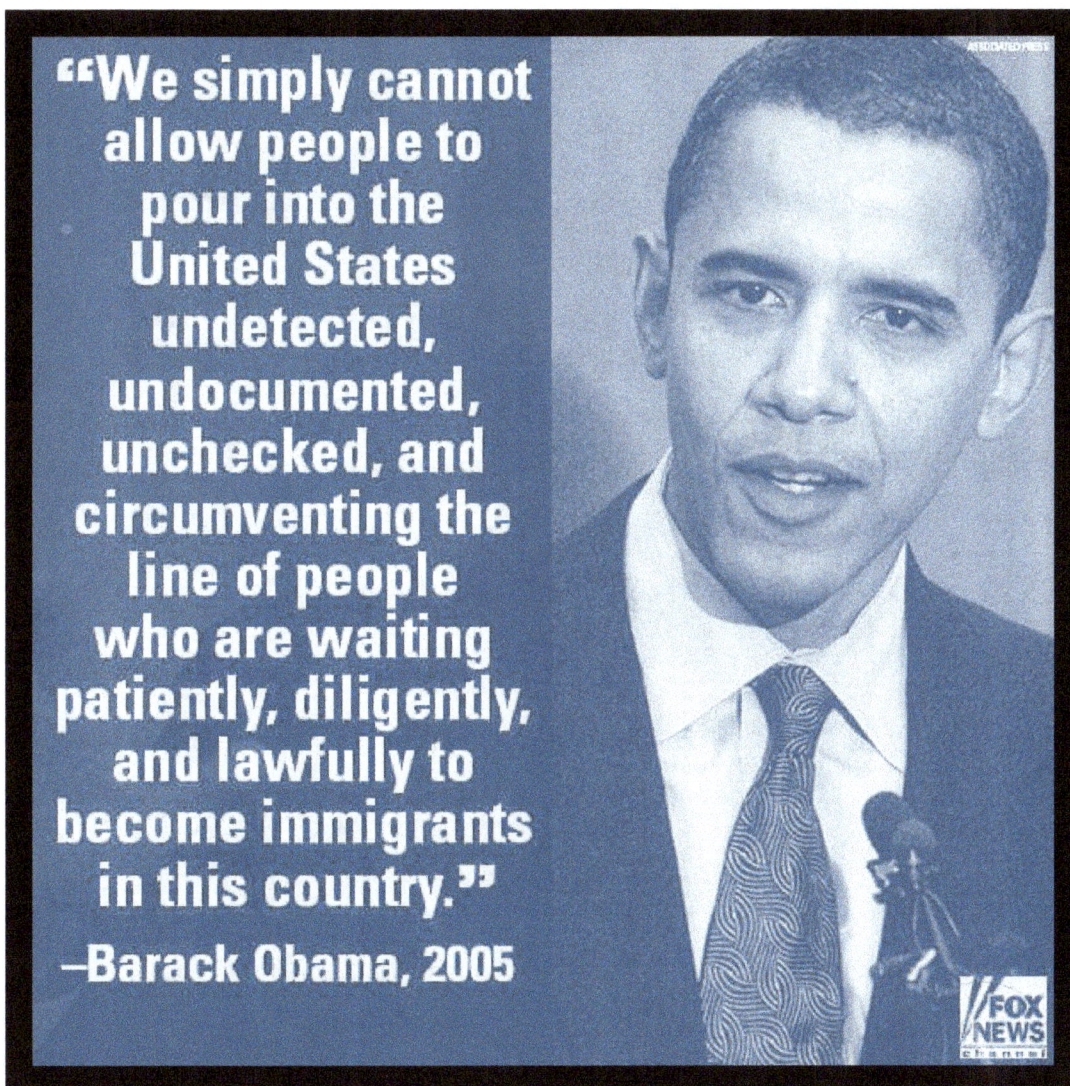

"We simply cannot allow people to pour into the United States undetected, undocumented, unchecked, and circumventing the line of people who are waiting patiently, diligently, and lawfully to become immigrants in this country."
—Barack Obama, 2005

ISLAM

THE SWORD OF SUBJUGATION

ISIS & RADICAL ISLAM's DAILY DEVOTIONAL

Qur'an 2:191- *Slay the unbelievers wherever you find them.*

Qur'an 3:28 - *Muslims must not take the infidels as friends.*

Qur'an 3:85 - *Any religion other than Islam is not acceptable.*

Qur'an 5:33 - *Maim and crucify the infidels if they criticize Islam*

Qur'an 8:12 - *Terrorize and behead those who believe in scriptures other than the Qur'an.*

Qur'an 8:60 - *Muslims must muster all weapons to terrorize the infidels.*

Qur'an 8:65 - *The unbelievers are stupid; urge the Muslims to fight them.*

Qur'an 9:5 - *When opportunity arises, kill the infidels wherever you catch them.*

Qur'an 9:123 - *Make war on the infidels living in your neighborhood.*

Qur'an 47:4 - *Do not hanker for peace with the infidels; behead them when you catch them.*

askdrbrown.org

Erasers for Islam: The Excuses Edition

The three most common ploys used by progressives to defend Islam and denounce the necessity of immigration restrictions.

"The seven countries chosen for the travel ban have produced no terrorists and none of the 9/11 attackers hailed from these regions."

Unless "profiling" is a relic of the Cold War, I'd venture to say this flunks the smell test. At least 20 individuals who committed terrorist acts on American soil have immigrated from these temporarily banned populaces; and yes, let's not discount those who tried and failed or waged acts of terror in other countries. Whether invoking the roughly 50 Islamic attacks in America since 2001 or the hundreds more perpetrated worldwide, attempting to "moralize" evil on pervasiveness alone discounts the singular greatest factor of all: what is the one common denominator in this global pandemic? Due the ubiquitous nature of Islam and the limitations of tracking undocumented backgrounds, Donald Trump knew the arduous task of protecting lives had to begin somewhere. Therefore, despite the false narratives and tearful protests of knee-jerk contrarians, he merely chose the most radicalized regions already identified by the Obama Administration; the very same notorious Muslim sympathizers and enablers of an Islamic caliphate. The fact Saudi Arabia refused to accept these "helpless" refugees and has enacted travel bans for years, despite having the resources to house their Arabic brethren, speaks volumes to the imminent threat. Sadly, there are far more Christian refugees at risk of imminent death in the Middle East than the reported "homeless" Islamic militants persecuting them and seeking paid passage to our shores as a reward. These families represent both the sacrificial pawns and buried casualties of selective media reporting.

Yes, it is true, none of the 9/11 attackers emanated from the "Militant 7". Then again, it was September 11th where nearly 3000 people were slaughtered in a matter of hours by a handful of unarmed jihadists. Intent is everything and without the benefit of geography America would experience a far greater prevalence of terrorism. Failing to do everything in our collective power to prevent any loss of life at the hand of malice, whether a lone airport security guard or an entire metropolis, constitutes gross negligence and a callous disregard for our safety. These restricted regions are but a microcosm of the cultivated hate which incessantly festers and threatens our communities on a daily basis. In the end, their point of origin is a moot point for they embody a cruel culture of antiquated intolerance that is consciously allowed to flourish beneath the afforded indulgence of globalists. Nevertheless, the inherent and unavoidable difficulties in eradicating terrorism – names, harbingers, accomplices – do not absolve our elected leaders from their constitutional duty and moral obligation to protect us from its ravages. The only thing extreme about restricting Islamic immigration and demanding extensive vetting, is the extreme opposition to employing common sense.

"Terrorism pales in comparison to the number of domestic shootings."

But of course, it does. We are a nation of over 300 million people and a criminal element exists in all societies. However, such depraved actions are overwhelmingly the property of rogue individuals targeting a specific person or institution out of sheer disdain. Other crimes are completely random and a product of frustration, a break from reality, with no specific target or reason. The Newtown shooter was mentally ill, Dylann Roof was an aloof racist who targeted black Christians, and the Columbine shooters were jaded teenagers obsessed by a cinematic culture of glorified violence. There is a stark difference between acknowledging the inevitable pitfalls of human nature, anger or mental illness, and a religion of indoctrinated hate that preaches martyrdom as the highest aspiration to its near 2 billion followers. Likewise, the inevitable existence of criminal misconduct within our native population does not infer we must welcome, without prejudice, death and destruction from beyond our sovereign borders. Such reasoning is plain absurd. The problem with violent crime in America doesn't reside in an animate object, as conniving pundits love to naively proclaim, but in the systematic decay of our societal values; those fundamental Judeo-Christian cornerstones of Western Civilization progressives have worked so tirelessly to undermine. So, in a not so ironic twist of fate, or a defiant lack of accountability, progressivism and Islam are symbiotic cancers eating away at the moral fabric of modern society. Their desire to enable and protect one another stems from a clear commonality: an insatiable lust for control and a mutual hatred for both America and Israel.

"Christianity is no better than Islam: The Crusades, the Inquisitions."

Only a fool would deny that nearly every faith is tarnished by some degree of historical injustice. Because religion is practiced by flawed and fallible believers, the true delineation between good and evil is best achieved by filtering the dregs from actual dogma. The Crusades, in all their demonized misconception, were a direct reaction to the over 900 hostile incursions made my Muslims & Turkish Moors into Europe. While the brutality of both factions cannot be condoned, the Crusades were by no means an unprovoked campaign of blind aggression. Rather, they viewed the rapid expansion of Islam as a grave threat to their faith, or more succinctly, an innate calling to save the ancestral birthplace of Christianity and thus ensure their people's survival.

The infamous Inquisitions, on the other hand, were sordid tools of righteous paranoia, Christian doctrine perverted by moral relativism, designed to exact loyalty through fear and thus eliminate perceived threats to the monarchy. However, unlike its obstinate Islamic detractors, Christianity willingly partook in a formal reformation over 500 years ago and learned over time that senseless bloodshed in the name of God was a fruitless endeavor that neither honored his commandments or the hopes of humanity. On the contrary, you'd be hard pressed to find another religion that comes close to the sheer depravity and death toll achieved by Islam in the past 100 years; from the Armenian genocide to widespread human rights abuses and the endless acts of terror carried by its devout followers today. To dismiss such soulless crimes as rogue aberrations is to deny the root philosophical affirmation of Islam: you cannot pervert that which is already pernicious by nature.

THE TRUTH ABOUT THE CRUSADES

ISLAM IS NOT A RELIGION OF PEACE

The First Crusade began in 1095

460 years after the first Christian city was overrun by Muslim armies. 457 years after Jerusalem was conquered by Muslim armies. 453 years after Egypt was taken by Muslim armies. 443 after Muslims first plundered Italy. 427 years after Muslim armies first laid siege to the Christian capital of Constantinople. 380 years after Spain was conquered by Muslim armies. 363 years after France was first attacked by Muslim armies. 249 years after the capital of the Christian world, Rome itself, was sacked by a Muslim army. and only after centuries of church burnings, killings, enslavement and forced conversions of Christians. By the time the Crusades finally began, Muslim armies had conquered two-thirds of the Christian world.

So much for being the victim

Whereas Christians have universally adopted the virtues of love, forgiveness and tolerance exemplified by the life of Jesus Christ and praised by the New Testament of his disciples, the same cannot be said of contemporary Sharia Law; that which has never swayed from the barbaric practices espoused by the hateful tenets of the Quran. Although there are undoubtedly decent and compassionate Muslims throughout the world, these voices of moderation too often fade into the obscurity of silent consent when confronted by the unrelenting shadow of unapologetic evil. As for those immoral acts committed by people who merely identify as "Christian" – pastors who abuse boys or poisonous sects like Westboro Baptist Church spewing judgement – such duplicitous actions are not validated or celebrated by the Christian masses, nor do they represent the moral canon of Judeo-Christian ethics. Unfortunately, even after 1400 years of endless human suffering, Islam still justifies beating/disfiguring disobedient women, sentences homosexuals to death, encourages sexual/marital relations with children, and seeks global supremacy by conquering, enslaving and/or killing all non-believers. If fear of malevolence is discrimination, the torchbearers of Islamophobia have more than earned that right.

Do you honestly believe Muhammad, a documented thief and polygamist, would have washed the feet of a known prostitute and embraced his enemies as his brethren – as equals in the eyes of the Lord – or sought salvation through the virtuous servitude of all mankind? Not even by decree of death. My goal is not to hoist the flag of Christianity and piously claim providence over the throne of divinity. My sincerest hope is to shed the shackles of distrust and discord to one day live among all faiths, without marches and martyrs, and share in a divine salvation not built upon bricks and beams but found in the hearts and souls of noble human beings. Regretfully, until that day comes, you cannot break bread with those who want to remove your hand for simply offering to coexist.

The Aftermath of Appeasement

So, it's "big city livin'" when jihadists murder Westerners but the same depraved act suddenly qualifies as a "horrific tragedy" when Muslims die at the hands of an English assassin who targeted a mosque with suspected terrorist ties? Yes, make no mistake about it, London Mayor Sadiq Khan is a disgrace. For the record, I condemn all acts of senseless aggression...regardless of one's nationality, race or religion. The man and any possible accomplices who perpetrated this brutal plot are criminals and should be shown no mercy in a court of law. However, when the British people endure attack after attack only for globalist activists to sweep such systemic radicalism under the rug in the name of unity, or more succinctly encourage submission to the hateful, intolerant and historically

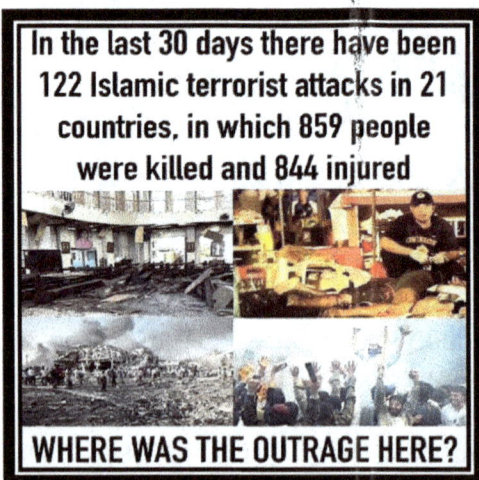

In the last 30 days there have been 122 Islamic terrorist attacks in 21 countries, in which 859 people were killed and 844 injured

WHERE WAS THE OUTRAGE HERE?

unaltered diatribe known as Islam, what do the Marxist merchants of "One World, One Government" truly expect? Simple: a slow, complicit death of our culture, sovereignty and values.

If the continuous onslaught of premeditated acid attacks targeting innocent pedestrians were not enough to leave an impression, London's recent wave of knife attacks have helped "Old Smoke" surpass the homicide rate of New York City for the first time ever. When the defenseless allure of gun confiscation fails to deter insatiable evil, knife control, not to be confused with the identical utensils to cut your meat or decapitate the ham eating infidel, becomes the newest political stunt to avoid invoking logic or deporting moral depravity. Unless your loved one is murdered, maimed, blinded or repeatedly sexually violated, apparently your only recourse in progressive Europe is to admit being a hateful, xenophobic bigot seduced by Donald Trump's rebellious hair. Just ask famed English activist Tommy Robinson, the recent recipient of an absurd 13-month prison sentence by a UK magistrate, who was jailed for refusing to abide by a gag order preventing exposing the undaunted epidemic of Muslim gang rape. Who needs free speech when court mandated ignorance graduates the greatest number of expendable victims? Feeding the vagrant viper swallowing the soul of your national identity, Western values, is much easier when racist lab rats are oblivious to their awaiting fate.

In the growing prevalence of such callous indifference, it's only a matter of time before the sacrificial lambs slain by Muhammad's soldiers become the unchained lions of liberty defending their fellow brethren and threatened homeland. While the media rejoices in selectively identifying the "worthy" victims of terrorism, they conveniently forget that assimilating to the societal norms of the civilized world is not a rhetorical question, a "get out of jail" free card or an open invitation for endless political debate to justify misogyny and martyrdom. It is a universal affirmation of human dignity that must not be abridged or broken to appease anyone regardless of your political preferences. And nor should it ever be disregarded when millions of Islamic immigrants supposedly weep for the opportunity to flee the depravity and desolation left by over 1400 years of Islamic oppression and indoctrination. If all we seek is the exploitation of death by marginalizing tragedy to manipulate the voting masses, then the innocent blood spilled during last night's rampage is also on the hands of those who treated the countless Anglo-American victims of Islamic terrorism, for well over a decade, as arbitrary 'bumps in the road' to a New World Order; one that obviously doesn't manufacture "Stop" signs in Arabic.

Once upon a time Western Civilization was a beacon for hope and a road map for securing human rights; now we willingly make excuses to protect those who silence, rape and beat women, who punish free speech against Islam as hate crimes, and who defend pedophilia, genital mutilation, as freedom of religion. Forgive my disgust, but where have all the feminists and humanists gone? Obviously to sleep…to protest a Judeo-Christian, capitalist, "patriarchal" society that ensures their economic, sexual and civil liberties in the face of such unrelenting evil. In Machiavellian terms, never confuse taste with tantrums when equality is a corpse and a cappuccino best served cold.

If you must dance naked and scream anarchy in the streets of "injustice" to condemn those who value the sanctity of life and free will, only to empower those militants who seek to religiously cover your face and demand your unconditional obedience, you're earning less money and daily respect because you obviously misunderstand the relevance of "choice". Gender is not an adopted identity of real victimization and human suffering is not a self-aggrandizing march eagerly embracing modern profanity and ignorance by pardoning a millennium of cruelty and intolerance to celebrate your heartless misappropriation. It is, however, most commonly the jagged aftermath of incited hate, dismissed circumstance and blind apathy colliding in history's frozen wake. Only so many can needlessly die, without repercussion or remorse, before the abandoned prey become the undaunted predators of self-

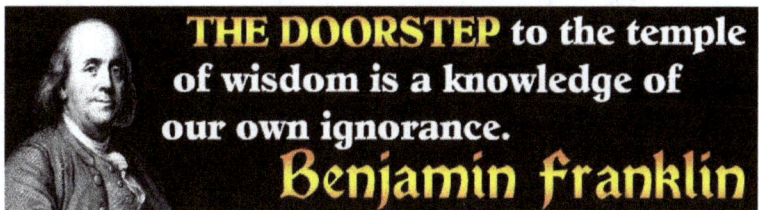

THE DOORSTEP to the temple of wisdom is a knowledge of our own ignorance.
Benjamin Franklin

preservation. May God comfort the dead's grieving loved ones and may he give mankind the unwavering courage and moral fortitude to save far more lives than those acceptable casualties eulogized by the part-time tears of political thespians.

Enabling Islam & the Fairy Tale of Peace

The senseless machete attack at Ohio State University by Somali refugee Abdul Razak Ali Artan is but another disturbing reminder of the ideological evil that lurks in our communities and all across the globe. Although many Muslims live, work and go to school in the U.S. without incident, the left's incessant efforts to demonize America inevitably inflames or reawakens the predisposed animosity many of these individuals harbor towards a Christian, free nation; i.e., those same hateful Islamic tenets so prevalent in their native countries that breed intolerance, violence, and celebrate martyrdom. When your supposed salvation is incumbent upon converting or killing nonconformists, "infidels", the Western ideal of assimilation is as foreign as a convenient political incubator for these historically destructive beliefs to fester and come to fruition. The Quran itself emphasizes the practice of "Taqiyya" or Islamic deception. Devout Muslims are taught from an early age to lie whenever necessary in order to exploit the tolerance, political correctness, of Western societies and thus further the spread of Islam by infiltrating the homelands of their perceived enemies.

The question the civilized world should be asking isn't whether we can coexist with a fanatical religion that has never a reformation; a formal condemnation of its most barbaric practices and teachings. The question is, "what would become of the civilized world if the rabid followers of Muhammad rose to power in societies founded upon liberty, equality and due process?" If Muslim women are beaten for speaking or dressing inappropriately, children deemed worthy of marriage, sexual intercourse, and homosexuals condemned to death for merely existing, no imagination or exaggeration is required to paint such a bleak future. Sadly, these perilous details are of little consequence when the liberal establishment is much more despondent over whether a gun was used, yet another opportunity to blame Right-Wing America and harvest votes, in lieu of any genuine concern for the actual victims abandoned by a reckless policy that cultivates ignorance and invites insatiable evil to dine on the open wounds of history. According to these distraught "humanists", if the American people just hugged the angry assailant, ignored his hateful posts & took away his imaginary firearm, all would be safe from the endless ravages of Islam; or more succinctly, 1500 years of uninterrupted misogyny, rape, slavery, murder and oppression. Apparently education, or lack thereof, is secular bliss.

Considering Islamic terrorist attacks in America have risen by over 400% since 2009 and our government seems far more content aiding and excusing the endeavors of known radical regimes – not to mention labeling all concerned citizens as "xenophobic" nationalists – the only leap of faith necessary is the exact time and date of logic's demise. Any man or woman who denounces Barack Obama, Hillary Clinton and leftist academia as willing Muslim sympathizers, enablers, are immediately discredited as racist extremists by mainstream media puppets. However, when everyday people fear speaking an uncomfortable truth to avoid enduring the blind epithets of political activists, "We the People" risk much more than losing our loved ones to the bloodthirsty blade of an antiquated cult; we risk our duty as Americans, human beings, to delineate between right and wrong and defend the universal charter of common decency, free will. For nearly a millennium, or simply during this century alone, no other religious faction has accounted for more mass death and suffering than Islam itself; not even Christianity during the Dark Ages or amidst the much-politicized Crusades which were a direct response to the over 900 incursions made by the Moors and other conquering Muslim armies into Europe.

Islam is, by definition and unyielding action, the most despotic, intolerant, and xenophobic movement in the world today. With over two billion ardent followers bent on global supremacy, Islam's growing threat to peace and basic human rights has only been surpassed by a handful of elected individuals sworn to protect the civilized world, their vulnerable populaces, but who instead chose to shield a comforting lie: Islam is a religion of peace and Muslims are not terrorists. Unfortunately, not all fairy tales are harmless and welcomed invaders are not helpless refugees.

Bigotry and Blame: Democrats in Denial

Kimberley Strassel
@KimStrassel

So just to be clear: A Somali-American Democrat engages in repeated anti-Semitism, and Democrats pass a resolution that condemns "white supremacists" (and gets in a reference to Charlottesville).

Rather than simply admitting Ilhan Omar and Rashida Tlaib are racist Islamic radicals who have no place in our government, their religious beliefs grossly incompatible with our Constitutional values and their sworn Congressional duties, House Democrats simultaneously condemned "white supremacy" and Islamophobia to deflect attention away from the rampant anti-Semitism poisoning their own ranks. It's also worth noting, anyone who vocally criticizes their policies and/or supports President Trump is routinely labeled a white supremacist by media pundits, celebrities and leftist politicians. Therefore, by proxy, this resolution is actually a formal condemnation of 63 million Americans who dare have the audacity to question progressive hate, lies and intolerance. Appalling.

Giving Terrorism A Chance

Sayfullo Saipov, the jihadist arrested in NYC for using a rental truck to kill 8 pedestrians on a bike path, was a Uzbekistan immigrant who entered America via the Diversity Visa Program; i.e., the honorable "lottery" system of undeclared intent. And, of course, let us not forget the unreported tidbit of journalistic integrity he was inspired by instructional ISIS propaganda. To add insult to the additional 15 individuals reportedly injured, Saipov was supposedly interviewed and cleared by federal investigators in 2015. Enlighten me again as to why America doesn't need immediate immigration reform or extreme vetting protocols for the explicit purpose of our safety? When properly investigating or denying potentially radicalized agents from known hostile regions is considered racist, dare I say "xenophobic", what excuse suffices for the epitaphs of loved ones murdered by Washington's clear dereliction of duty and obstinate indifference?

Once again, this is not 1800, 1900, or even 1984 where America was far more revered by migrants than despised by contentious factions indoctrinated by the incessant conditioning of leftist academia or a globalist press relentlessly demonizing our affluence, influence and founding heritage. There is a vast contingent of anti-American zealots – albeit Islamic supremacists, disgruntled dissidents or professional agitators – who want nothing more than to fatally wound this nation to satisfy their misplaced sense of entitlement, ideological duty, or insatiable lust for the West's expedited decay. Failing to take every precaution possible in a post 9/11 world, both to protect our citizens and our blessed way of life, is a wanton criminal act of ignorance, if not complicit treason. I find it morally repugnant progressives are far more offended by teaching our children to pledge allegiance to the flag or requiring millionaire athletes with rap sheets to stand for the national anthem, than decrying any detectable manifestation of foreign terrorism, or more profoundly any legitimate attempt to confront its proliferation. Then again, it is no coincidence a majority of terrorist acts and mass murders committed in the U.S. are perpetrated by Muslim extremists and/or hyper-sensitive Democratic enablers triggered by everyday socio-political events.

While I do confess a majority of immigrants are merely pursuing a better life, seeking to partake in the abundant opportunities liberty offers, that does not abstain our elected officials from thoroughly disseminating the countless threats against this nation and preventing as many agents of malevolence as humanly possible from ever crossing our sovereign borders. Yes, I'm perplexed as to why a Constitutional Republic defined by laws and prescribed privileges of citizenship is obligated to "give terrorism a chance" – i.e., welcome known foreign catalysts of death and destruction – simply because Americans kill Americans. One is an unavoidable circumstance of birth, the inevitability of native crime, the other is choosing to risk further bloodshed by ignoring the fact militant Muslims kill, assault and rape far more natural born Westerns in unprovoked acts of cultural aggression than Islamic visitors slain by American civilians. If a millennium of unabridged brutality has taught us anything, other than Western Civilization being the sworn infidel of the Muslim faith, it's that hate is Islam's undying creed. "Islamophobia" is not a baseless fear of a religion itself, but a rational distrust and united opposition to loved ones needlessly dying at the hands of an unevolved ideology that has never had a formal reformation of its most barbaric practices and antiquated beliefs.

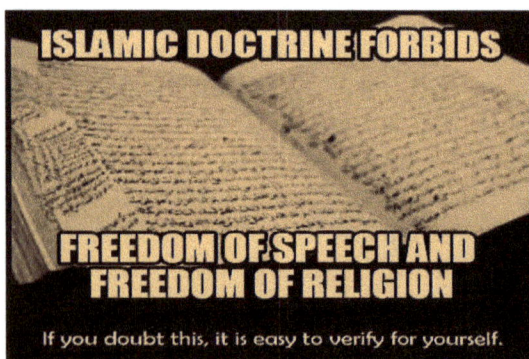

ISLAMIC DOCTRINE FORBIDS
FREEDOM OF SPEECH AND FREEDOM OF RELIGION
If you doubt this, it is easy to verify for yourself.

Banning or severely restricting the flow of immigration from certain geographic regions, ideological backgrounds or ethnic populaces is only unjust to those who refuse to recognize the aftermath of historical anonymity, let alone the fact American cultural apologists are intentionally watering the seeds of sedition. Besides, how many Orthodox Russians, Hasidic Jews, Buddhist Asians or impoverished South American families declare "Death to America" on their route to greener pastures? Assimilation, loyalty and tolerance are not optional conveniences, they're the required price of admission to the civilized world; specifically, our homes, this nation and liberty's inalienable rights. If America is to remain a transcendent beacon of hope for all people, from all reaches of the globe, then it must be equally defended against those virulent malcontents religiously endeavoring to extinguish her flame.

Banning Islam vs Offending Amnesia

AL-TAQIYYA: **The dutiful act of concealing or disguising one's beliefs, convictions, ideas, feelings, opinions, intent and/or strategies for the future advancement of Islam.**

Funny how quickly the "offended" masses forget that a liberal Democrat, Jimmy Carter, barred all Iranian immigrants and Shiite Muslims – he even expelled college students – over eminent security concerns during the Iran hostage crisis. Unlike Washington and the history revisionist media, at least Donald Trump has the public fortitude to confront the problem rather than hide behind meaningless platitudes and political correctness as the body of Islamic extremism count grows exponentially.

This President's bleeding-heart aches for Islam/ISIS because they're the proverbial tip of the spear; the executioners of his insatiable hate for the West and our heritage. Likewise, because they both despise America, Christians, Jews, and liberty, Barack Obama will never fully commit to recognizing the true degree of their global threat or take the necessary steps to fully defeat these subhuman factions. If it wasn't for the massive public outcry, even from within his own party and the media, Mr. Hussein would be fully content bowing to foreign dignitaries, vacationing with 1% elitists and signing away more of our national sovereignty; yes, the same notorious critic of indulgence occupying the Oval Office and who literally poses the greatest risk to this country's security, vitality and unity.

America's most decorated apologist is obviously more concerned with exploiting these tragedies to push his gun control agenda, to paint all immigration opponents as violent xenophobes, than the fact GAZA schoolchildren are staging mock Jewish hostage raids and sharpening their decapitation skills. Apparently, one's unwillingness to become a statistic, to trust the harmless benevolence of Islamic terrorism, results in an automatic invitation to public suicide and career ridicule. Acceptance, your family's survival, is obviously of no consequence. The last time I checked Barack Obama has blood on his hands, not Donald Trump. He's the one who has abandoned our borders, openly encouraged illegal immigration and unilaterally brought thousands of radical Islamic refugees to America with no regard for the consequences or the rule of law. He's the bigoted lunatic America should be fuming about.

"We have 50 million Muslims in Europe. There are signs that Allah will grant Islam victory in Europe — without swords, without guns, without conquest — and turn it into a Muslim continent within decades."

MUAMMAR GADDAFI, 1975

An Arranged Marriage

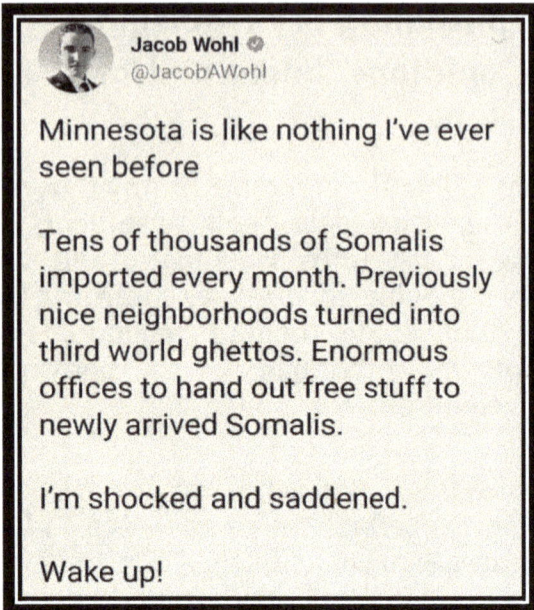

Jacob Wohl
@JacobAWohl

Minnesota is like nothing I've ever seen before

Tens of thousands of Somalis imported every month. Previously nice neighborhoods turned into third world ghettos. Enormous offices to hand out free stuff to newly arrived Somalis.

I'm shocked and saddened.

Wake up!

The hateful, extremist intentions of Omar Ilhan and Rashida Tlaib were never painstakingly concealed or shrouded in doubt, for both are the radical byproduct of Democratic strongholds with large Muslim contingencies; otherwise, neither would have likely won their respective Congressional races. Each victory can be traced to the choreographed relocation of largely non-assimilating "refugees" across pre-selected regions, i.e., Dearborn and Minneapolis, which eventually ensures the election of naturalized or natural-born Islamic ideologues to our clearly incompatible form of government. This arranged marriage is exactly why their newly adopted party – which harbors similar anti-American, anti-Semitic views and religiously slandered Israel while aiding terrorist regimes under one Barack Hussein Obama – openly embraced each candidate in their shared quest to fundamentally transform American culture, global demographics and Western values.

Only during times of billowing national outrage and potential electoral backlash, do progressive leaders denounce the most undeniable cases of Democratic bigotry before casually returning to business as usual by dining with the vitriolic likes of Louis Farrakhan, Linda Sarsour, Valerie Jarrett, La Raza, the Palestinian Authority, Hamas, Hezbollah, the Muslim Brotherhood, CAIR and the infamous Republic of Iran. Regardless of how contrite or coerced these apologies may seem, their unified goal remains unchanged: to redistribute the wealth, influence and sovereign independence of this American Republic – our Constitutional liberties born from Judeo-Christian ethics – for the competing yet co-opted totalitarian aspirations of Sharia Law and Marxist rule.

SO OBAMA IMPORTS 70,000 SOMALI IMMIGRANTS AND PARKS THEM IN MINNESOTA, WHERE ALMOST ALL CLUSTER IN A SINGLE AREA, SPECIFICALLY THE FIFTH CONGRESSIONAL DISTRICT.

THAT DISTRICT RECENTLY WAS IDENTIFIED BY THE FBI AS AMERICA'S TERRORIST RECRUITMENT CAPITAL, AND IS REPRESENTED BY ILHAN OMAR, WHO IS CALLING FOR DISSOLUTION OF AMERICA'S HOMELAND SECURITY. ARE YOU CONNECTING THE DOTS YET?

Catering to Madness

Who needs real leadership when the "fake news" turns the temporary ordered cessation of refugees from 7 terrorist dense nations into a complete Muslim ban? Furthermore, who needs standards when there are currently 16 countries that forbid the entrance of Israeli passport holders; and all without a single peep or threat from the progressive lynch mob? But of course.

Thousands of Muslim immigrants – including Islamic travelers from the likes of India, Pakistan, Turkey, and even Saudi Arabia – are still being granted visas and/or the opportunity to complete the naturalization process. Unfortunately, such omitted details are of little consequence to a press that is much more interested in fueling further paranoia until fear destroys property, threatens lives and erects a permanent state of Trump "triggered" anarchy. It is therefore of little surprise an Obama appointed judge once again spitefully bypassed the law and issued an immediate stay restricting those powers explicitly granted to the Chief Executive by a former act of Congress. Not only will the Federal Appeals Court annihilate this embarrassing decision, they will reaffirm refugees are not entitled to the same rights/privileges as citizens and a sitting U.S. president is fully within his or her authority to cease, limit or alter immigration from those populaces and nations deemed a credible threat. Just ask Jimmy Carter, Bill Clinton and even the Social Justice Warrior himself, Barack Obama, who exercised such expressed powers six times; including barring anyone under a U.N. travel ban. Being it's literally impossible to properly investigate the backgrounds of refugees from a number of destitute, radicalized regions, why would our safety protocols suddenly cease to exist? For the sake of political correctness and kickstarting their bitter presidential aspirations for 2020? Ignorance is bliss until someone gets killed; for which the media will inevitably blame Donald Trump.

"When Muslims are in the minority they are very concerned with minority rights, when they are in the majority there are no minority rights"

– *Winston Churchill*

It's unfortunate progressive zombies are still beguiled as to why American voters overwhelmingly rejected the Democratic relocation program. Their unyielding desire to subvert our electoral process and demographically terraform our founding values does not override our desire to exist; or better yet, to prevent terrorism in our communities. If politics instinctively catered to prudence, America would be fully justified in banning all Muslim immigration until Islam formally rejects its never-ending legacy of violence, discrimination and intolerance. Or perhaps said protestors would like to bury the future victims of Islamic jihadists with their own soft hands of calloused apathy. I'm sure the grieving families will understand that 9/11, Fort Hood, Chattanooga, the Boston Marathon, San Bernardino and Orlando – to name but a few costly "bumps" on the toll road to globalism – were just misreported figments of America's xenophobic imagination. To hijack Robert Frost...I welcomed the guests least hostile and it made all the difference. When did self-preservation require an explanation, let alone a dinner invitation to our own demise? Complacency is obviously not very fond of quoting history because it can't pronounce "evil". And therein lies the problem.

Resisting the Logic of Self-Preservation

**Statutory Authority of the President
to keep out anyone**

8 USC §1182:
Whenever the President finds that the entry of any aliens or of any class of aliens into the United States would be detrimental to the interests of the United States, he may by proclamation, and for such period as he shall deem necessary, *suspend the entry of all aliens or any class of aliens* as immigrants or nonimmigrants, or impose on the entry of aliens any restrictions he may deem to be appropriate.

Those critics who foolishly believed Donald Trump's travel ban was unconstitutional, an unprecedented hate crime against humanity, were clearly duped by the same "Russian Conspiracy" hysteria that has triggered mourning millennials into licking toilet seats or pledging to remove their beta-male genitalia for proper submission to alpha-Islamic jihadists. And for the record, October's hearing is but a formality otherwise the Supreme Court would have clashed over maintaining the Appeal's Court ruling.

If the President was guilty of anything, other than opposing the reckless immigration policies of his anti-American predecessor, it was for exercising the same authority and discretion Barack Obama, Bill Clinton, and Jimmy Carter invoked to restrict travel from specific nations or populaces without any such opposition from their fellow constituents; most notably, those Democratic officials who encouraged partisan judges to "resist" explicit law in favor of pursuing personal vendettas over an election result. Despite the fact these individuals knew Trump's travel ban was completely legal and historically relevant, their intent was to once again fabricate the appearance of scandal – using mass media to paint the President as a reckless supremacist mired in Executive overreach – with the real goal of delaying his order or defeating his resolve to implement such a "controversial" action. And here I thought the safety and security of the American people, not childish games and political sabotage, were of paramount importance to our elected officials.

Immigrants, especially those hailing from known tumultuous regions, can no more dictate the terms of their entry into a foreign country than a child can choose his or her biological parents. Unless "Give Terrorism a Chance" is America's new lottery motto, did 9/11 and the over 90 terrorists incidents perpetrated on American soil since that horrific day never happen or are we still debating whether knives, guns, trucks and planes murder the "infidel"? Has the new European playground of militant Islam sounded any bells of civilized concern over unvetted radicals or are "We the People" still believing "moderate" Muslims share our values, respect human rights and possess a mutual commitment to the survival and sovereignty of America? The reason Poland and Japan have not become a complicit statistic is because both refuse to accept refugees and believe there is a direct correlation between Islamic terrorism and Islamic immigration. Yes, logic burns the short fuse of Democratic outrage, or more specifically, the powder-blue ploys of electoral supremacy. Apparently, the progressive brain trust of "Pelosi and Schumer" did not share that memo because plotting globalists must extinguish the light of liberty before their victims can read the paper it's printed on.

Lost in Translation

There are military veterans – poorly paid, callously cared for and gravely injured in combat – who have never complained about their country or their circumstances; despite having every right to do so. Now we have foreign residents, temporarily detained in airports or delayed from returning to the U.S. in the comfort of their own homes until their visas can be cleared, claiming to be unjustly inconvenienced and the unmistakable victims of Islamophobia. Considering there have been over 50 Islamic terrorist attacks on American soil since 2001, imagine how many forsaken souls would eagerly reclaim their lives, limbs or their waning health if it meant being briefly inconvenienced by the unbearable tyranny of a safety protocol. The inevitable dissatisfaction experienced by a small fraction of international guests is a small price to pay for potentially saving the lives of thousands...including their own ungrateful existence. If you're going to cry me a river of mass media victimization, make sure it's a biblical flood of such visceral magnitude that it redefines human suffering rather than ingratiating the type of omitted entitlement that involves impatiently eating a sandwich on a sofa while watching TV or posting annoyed emojis on your bored Snapchat selfie. A tragedy and irrefutable act of xenophobia is exactly what transpired on September 11th, 2001. Your momentary inconvenience is our unyielding desire to never again repeat that fateful day. Or perhaps you'd like to see the immortalized images of true depravity or the haunting last words of unspeakable injustice. Unlike yourselves, the grieving families of these marginalized victims will forever be "inconvenienced" by picking up the unidentifiable remains of their lost loved ones. For that, even as a natural born citizen, I would gladly give one year of my life for a fleeting hope to assuage 3,000 lifetimes worth of suffering.

The Blindfolded Victims of Political Injustice

There is the inevitable ignorance of detached moral relativists drowning in contemporary pop culture and there is political radicalism masquerading as due process and equality in the eyes of the law. How can a man receive a 15-year sentence for placing bacon on the door of a Mosque, regardless whether it was a foolish prank or a malicious act, when no one was physically hurt or any financial losses incurred? If the mere designation of a "hate crime" warrants such a harsh sentence, how are four Chicago teens only given probation for kidnapping and streaming the torture of a terrified handicap boy? How are street thugs spared prison, the obvious designation of a hate crime, after assaulting and knocking out innocent bystanders in public, including women, senior citizens or those peacefully leaving political rallies? And how can an illegal immigrant with 7 felony convictions who was deported 5 times not serve a day in jail for murdering an innocent woman, whether intentional or not, while repeatedly fleeing extradition from federal agents?

When it's no longer uncommon for a rapist or pedophile to be incarcerated for less than a year for physically assaulting and/or sexually violating another human being – such as the recent verdict of a Stanford athlete upset over serving 3 months of an imposed 6-

month punishment or three Muslim refugees spared incarceration for raping a 5-year-old girl in Utah – I'm confused as to what constitutes an egregious act or who isn't a danger to society.

If the legal adage "the penalty should fit the crime" is still a self-evident maxim, do you sincerely believe an atheist smearing animal blood on a Christian church door in today's America would be given 15 years in a penitentiary, plus an additional 15 years-probation? Not by a long shot for such an ignorant act would most likely be adjudicated as petty vandalism. How about a Muslim baker or jeweler who declined to serve or poisoned any homosexual customer; those who are routinely condemned to death in Muslim nations for merely existing? Is it not also a "hate crime" when a couple specifically targets a Christian bakery for the explicit purpose of suing an owner who respectful declines service, resulting in the loss of their business or even bankruptcy for simply exercising their religious freedoms?

Make no mistake about it, this obscene double standard and clear disregard of jurisprudence is far more synonymous with Sharia Law – a hyper-fanatical punishment of any perceived blasphemy against Islam – than any semblance of equal application of American law. Even more disturbing, the same modern-day progressives, "ardent secularists", who have become increasingly hostile towards Christianity are overwhelmingly indifferent or outright supportive of Islam; despite its unending legacy of indoctrinated hate, violent intolerance, and unapologetic goal of global supremacy. The more political subjectivity pervades and supersedes our judicial ideals and institutions, dare I say the decaying faculties of common sense and Western Society, the closer America is to becoming an unrecognizable, lobotomized vagabond wandering aimlessly in its own ransacked home condemned for the use of logic.

A House Without Neglect

Barack Obama himself reluctantly admitted it was essentially impossible to properly investigate the backgrounds of Muslim refugees or track their ranks once they arrived in America. Unfortunately chanting 'Death to America' on an almost daily basis in their native countries just wasn't enough to stir the banished institution of logic in progressive propaganda. If Donald Trump is truly a misogynist and bigot as unhinged leftists love to proclaim, what exactly is Islam; that antiquated diatribe of hate which oppresses millions, brutalizes women for merely dressing inappropriately or speaking without permission, instinctively preaches intolerance, and unapologetically seeks to both conquer and violently punish all non-believers? How can you faintly welcome or freely trust that which refuses to assimilate; to recognize your unconditional right to exist? A civilized nation cannot assist the alleged victims of theological and economic carnage by endeavoring to enable the very culture of radicalism that so egregiously failed them. In a post 9/11 world, it's absurd and a clear dereliction of duty when our elected government investigates American citizens, potential employees or political adversaries, far more rigorously than migrants from the most notorious regions of the world.

Unless "We the People" have forgotten what constitutional ideals America was forged upon – individual liberty, equality, due process, religious freedom – President Trump represents a fleeting speck of dust in a never-ending desert of Islamic depravity. Temporarily banning Muslim refugees from the most notorious radicalized regions shouldn't require an explanation or a media inquisition for its necessity is self-evident. It's also a stark reminder as to why our original Continental Congress failed; it lacked the necessary resources, collective fortitude and derived authority to more effectively protect our rights, lives and national sovereignty. Islam is not only grotesquely incompatible with our values and way of life, it represents the most tangible threat to the ideological basis and survival of Western Civilization. In a nation as blessed and transcendent as America, these once non-negotiable precepts are now racist fodder for those scheming politicians, media pundits and opportunistic anarchists who are increasingly bitter over an election result, rather than indelibly committed to the non-partisan welfare of America, her people and the liberty she espouses. The human toll of Islamic barbarism can never be fully enumerated or internalized; especially by those who deny its sadistic charter or live free from its ravages. But it can be swept under the carpet of our slumbering senses, our unsuspecting children, by those who seek to undermine everything we built and ultimately sacrificed to protect: our home. To that end there is no amount of political subversion to which I will bend or ask permission.

I Am the Infidel

The only way for mankind to survive the ideological plague known as Islam is to systematically remove the radical roots of their uninterrupted culture of hate. Otherwise, just like minimally invasive bombing campaigns or PR campaigns warning native citizens not to trigger their misunderstood foreign assailants, we're merely putting a political band-aid on unadulterated evil. If you're going to tout your imaginary War on Women, begin by challenging every single Muslim to eradicate their misogynistic and medieval practices that deny females their God-given rights, if not their lives. If you're going to admonish Chick-fil-A for merely voicing their opposition to Gay Marriage, stop financing, let alone recognizing the legitimacy of Islamic nations who torture and stone homosexuals to death for merely existing. If you incessantly plot to deny Christian business owners and organizations the right to religious freedom, the very First Amendment of our Constitution, then publicly condemn the barbaric and discriminatory tenets of Sharia Law your administration is consciously allowing to infiltrate our public institutions. And finally, how can anyone expose and defeat an ideological movement that liberals embrace more than America itself because sympathizing Democrats refuse to differentiate between conservatism and Islamic genocide? One questions tyranny and corruption without refrain or capitulation, the other invites it to appease their hatred of America's Judeo-Christian ideals...our individual liberties, economic prowess and hallowed way of life.

ISIS is ISLAM. There is no distinction for death is glorified, human life trivialized, and hate justified in the name of honoring a violent diatribe of antiquated intolerance. Its billions of ardent followers, scattered across almost every sect of society, can overwhelmingly be characterized into two groups: the tip of the sword or the muted voices of consent lurking in the shadows of civility's tolerance. Their singular goal is not to conform or coexist with Western Civilization – those seeking enlightenment, peace and happiness in hopes of living a more fulfilling life – but to threaten, terraform, and assert its septic lust for global domination. Whether beheading innocent children in the Iraqi desert, exploiting the naive invitations of globalist leaders or attempting to biologically overrun free and Christian nations the likes of Great Britain, Sweden and Germany, modern Islam has no other noteworthy accomplishments – albeit educational, technological, or economic diversity – other than that of religious subjugation. Israel, from the seize of Jerusalem in 637 to the Seven Day War of 1967 and the Munich games massacre, knows this conundrum all too well for Jews have toiled and died for millennia on end battling the Islamic caliphate; that which now seeks a glorious, universal return to power.

Oh, it's not that Christianity and Judaism do not bear their share of historical black eyes for practically every religion has them; their believers simply evolved and learned that bloodshed in the name of any ideology or God was a senseless and fruitless endeavor. Islam, however, hiding behind human shields in the religious squalor of the Middle East to plot terrorist attacks against our civilian epicenters, continues to wage war on humanity in lieu of reforming its most vicious practices and destructive beliefs. Therefore, those souls remaining at the table of the civilized world have but two choices: cut off the calloused hand of unapologetic hate, that which religiously celebrates the Holocaust and 9/11, or embrace evil to the sound of their own demise. Any other suggestion is an ignorant exercise in futility.

The Serpent and The Soul

Under Egyptian Law, Dzhokhar Tsarnaev would be placed in an empty room and a pressure cooker bomb detonated by his feet. Or, because equal justice demanded equal outcomes, unexpectedly shot in the head and neck like 26-year-old police officer Sean Collins, executed in cold blood solely for his firearm. Instead of respecting the abundant blessings America affords, a beacon of liberty and opportunity as a proven path to a better life, the Chechen immigrant elected to emulate his militant brother and become seduced by a murderous ideology that advocates death to all nonbelievers, venom over virtue. April 15, 2013 was far from just another day; it was an international celebration of unity, applauded excellence and perseverance, used as a public minefield for a private war. Limbs were shredded, lives ended, and the fractured dreams of innocence slipped through the callous hands of unquenchable hate. No eight-year old child deserves to die on the beloved streets of his hometown; his ruptured and lifeless body covered with white tablecloths from an adjacent restaurant, guarded for 12 hours until investigators could reassemble a portrait of evil in the aftermath of the injured parents' unimaginable plight. If you abandon all regard for humanity and cut the last vestiges of empathy, moral discernment, you neither understand nor deserve the slightest hint of compassion derived from true human temperance.

None of the families Tsarnaev hurt, the lives he changed forever, ever knew or spoke ill of his name. The horrible atrocities committed against these individuals were no different than if a complete stranger, guided by the false pretense of divine righteousness, tossed a grenade beneath his parents embrace and reveled at the inevitable carnage that ensued. Who could even witness such a grotesque injustice? Who would dare inflict it? Whether you feel like an outcast in your newly adopted home or discontent compels you to dehumanize the object of your scorn - your perceived enemy - you're merely at war with yourself; for you alone have the power to exact change without destroying that which makes you unmistakably human...a soul. Justice isn't about revenge but rather equality under the law; restoring balance to an imperfect world and giving comfort to those remaining loved ones who will never be whole again. And for that, Dzhokhar Tsarnaev should forever crawl in the afterlife haunted by the inconsolable screams of his victims because he sure as hell will never hear them in the comforts of a federal prison. Mercy is for those worth saving, not the wrongfully breathing.

A Fear of Ignorance

While globalists and the media conspire daily to protect and enable Islam's destructive creed, it's refreshing to have a President who possesses the conviction and courage necessary to expose their hateful, violent intolerance of Western society. The only thing "shocking" or "inappropriate" about those disturbing videos he shared is the disgusting fact so many progressives continue to blindly defend the vile behavior of those Islamic immigrants who tirelessly seek our submission – albeit through economic collapse, cultural coercion or demographic attrition – to a barbaric ideology that is unquestionably incompatible with our founding ideals. Rather, it's "shocking" Western leaders have never demanded a formal reformation of Islam's most barbaric practices and regressive beliefs despite an unyielding legacy of bigotry, misogyny and death.

If over a millennia of mass oppression and human atrocity is not convincing enough to stoke the fires of international concern, then we deserve to suffer the same fate as those European nations currently inundated with acid attacks, sexual assault and public battery, pedophilia and incessant terrorism. It's not simply a matter of weeding out the "bad apples", for those who are not the proverbial "tip of the spear" are either steadying the hand plotting our demise or applauding the victorious aftermath of evil. Rejecting all forms of malice, albeit Islamic supremacy or domestic crime, is incumbent upon our ability to combat and differentiate the two. One is the product of our society's decaying moral values and encouraged political hostilities, the other extends from openly inviting nearly two millenniums of unrepentant "Jihad" to freely walk through our door without a care or legitimate suspicion.

Do you honestly believe it was a coincidence the Obama administration enabled Iran's nuclear aspirations, illegally gave radical regimes and organizations billions in foreign aid, condemned Israel with spiteful regularity or transported as many unvetted refugees into our slumbering cities as possible? Hardly. Even more telling, if you were a destitute foreigner from a war-ravaged region living under a host country's grace and generosity, would you deface their sacred monuments, attack handicap kids, murder gays or gang rape children and women? Not a chance in hell unless you were a sadistic cult which neither had the sanity or basic decency necessary to appreciate the opportunities, life sustaining amenities and safety, afforded to your people! Linda Sarsour and Valerie Jarrett have repeatedly disparaged and threatened this nation – the exploding Muslim community in Dearborn, Michigan waves the ISIS flag and shouts "Death to America" – despite basking in those liberties and protections they would not find in any glorious Islamic caliphate. How many so-called "moderate" Muslims have condemned these ungrateful actions or marched in our streets to demand accountability, cultural assimilation, as a means of preserving their newfound blessings? More profoundly, how many Islamists truly love America, respect our Constitutional sovereignty or unconditionally recognize our right to exist, if at all? So few you would need to detect a muffled whisper beneath a roaring train fleeing an advancing avalanche during an earthquake!

Winston Churchill...on Islam

"How dreadful are the curses which Mohammedanism [Islam] lays on its votaries [faithful]! Besides the fanatical frenzy, which is as dangerous in a man as hydrophobia [rabies] in a dog, there is this fearful fatalistic apathy."

"A degraded sensualism deprives this life of its grace and refinement; the next of its dignity and sanctity. The fact that in Mohammedan law every woman must belong to some man as his absolute property - either as a child, a wife, or a concubine - must delay the final extinction of slavery until the faith of Islam has ceased to be a great power among men."

"Individual Moslems may show splendid qualities...but the influence of the religion paralyses the social development of those who follow it. No stronger retrograde [backward] force exists in the world. Far from being moribund [becoming obsolete], Mohammedanism is a militant and proselytising faith."

The River War, first edition, Vol. II, pages 248-50

No, contrary to politically correct accessories, defeating Islamic tyranny is very much a grave matter of having the fortitude and wisdom to realize if Muslims were the dominant populace or in control of our public institutions, to what end would they unleash their wrath on our families and unsuspecting communities. Whether "We the People" acknowledge the lion in the room is of no consequence because predators do not recognize the rights or screams of their prey. Rather, they feed on their victim's ignorance, vulnerabilities and false sense of security. "Islamophobia" is not a racist or mindless fear of the world's 1.6 billion Muslims. It is an educated and rational response to anyone who is acutely aware of Islam's teachings, history and unbridled aspirations to harm our loved ones and topple this beloved Republic's enduring creed; a beacon of hope from despotic rule and religious persecution.

Islam is, and always has been, the mortal enemy of modern civility, our capacity for human empathy and the divine concept we are all born equal, blessed with inalienable dignities, to live free from the soulless depravity of forced subjugation; that which still breathes in the Middle East, Africa and Asia without refrain or global condemnation.

The Ire of Islam

Islam condemns non-believers to death, openly advocates murdering all homosexuals and strips women of basic human rights – denying females education, forcing them to cover their bodies and brutally punishing those who speak or act inappropriately – and the Department of Justice wants to prosecute those individuals who expose these blatant abuses for hate speech? Come again? Truly, what is more offensive than Sharia Law in a country forged upon the prescribed necessity of liberty, equality and due process? All lives matter regardless of religion, gender, race, or sexual orientation.

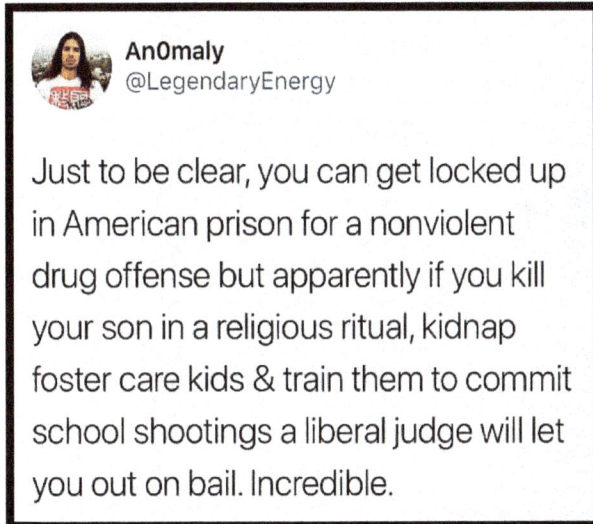

An0maly
@LegendaryEnergy

Just to be clear, you can get locked up in American prison for a nonviolent drug offense but apparently if you kill your son in a religious ritual, kidnap foster care kids & train them to commit school shootings a liberal judge will let you out on bail. Incredible.

Our forefathers founded this nation to escape the perils of religious persecution and to erect a nation predicated upon individual liberty; not government persecution based on subjective tolerance. Who hasn't been verbally disrespected, insulted or angered by another? But that doesn't give me Carte Blanche, a 'get out of jail' free card or automatic political pardon to gun down innocent people in a sadistic rage of vengeance. In other words, freedom of speech doesn't come with an asterisk and your sensibilities may be offended, but murder is universally despised. Blaming an unflattering video for the terrorist attack on Benghazi is like blaming a broken toaster for kicking your dog. You're still accountable, all garnish aside. Nearly all religions, at some time or another, are guilty of grotesque transgressions. That fact is irrefutable. However, you'd be hard pressed to find one in the past century that surpasses Islam in terms of body count, ongoing human rights abuses, and sheer mass depravity. Perhaps this is also why the Islamic world has never had a reformation...a formal questioning and rebuke of its most antiquated, hateful and violent tenets. Muslims are overwhelmingly not interested in assimilating with the civilized world; merely conquering and converting humanity in the name of Allah.

If I'm going to be prosecuted for speaking an uncomfortable truth about Islam, that which is literally supported by the Koran – the ideological basis of Islam itself – how long is it before Washington jails or silences American citizens for their personal political beliefs: whether or not they support abortion, believe in climate change, or advocate the Second Amendment for the purpose of self-defense? Are atheists being arrested for mocking Jesus or degrading Christianity in the most perverse and offensive manner imaginable? Is right and wrong, acceptable or punishable, simply dependent upon whether a Republican or Democrat is in office? If we allow this nation to begin sliding down this slippery slope of aggravated subjectivity, silencing dissenting speech and attacking freedom of thought, then "We the People" must be prepared to watch our God-given rights, if not our Constitutional Republic, vanish beneath the fog of excused tyranny. If I may, when did common sense, dare I say individuality, require a permission slip?

The last line in the speech at the unveiling of the Statue of Liberty, October 28, 1886

"There is room in America and brotherhood for all who will support our institutions and aid in our development. But those who come to disturb our peace and dethrone our laws are aliens and enemies forever."

LIBERALISM
PROGRESSIVISM
COMMUNISM

"Communism is not love. COMMUNISM IS A HAMMER which we use to crush the enemy."

— MAO ZEDONG, Communist Dictator of China (1945-1976)

PragerU

Progressivism is about control – an aversion to America, free will and God. It removes the power of the people, demonizes individual achievement and thought, and usurps our natural born rights in the name of an elite/wealthy ruling class that freely exercises...that's right...their own freedoms. Progressivism requires an ignorant and dependent populace conveniently distracted by class, gender and race warfare to avoid holding their government accountable for its numerous failures, lies and abuses. It's a political Ponzi scheme that blackmails low information voters with their own taxable money under the guise of the 'common good'. It is, unequivocally, a comforting lie, a paradigm of propaganda, born from the anecdotal ashes of Communism to ensure a singular goal: mass conformity to a secular and totalitarian government.

From Revolution to Regression: Conservatism, Classical Liberalism and the Malaise of Modern Progressivism

"I always consider the settlement of America with reverence and wonder, as the opening of a grand scene and design in providence, for the illumination of the ignorant and the emancipation of mankind."
~John Adams

The journey from "Classical Liberalism" to the social upheaval of modern-day progressivism is as pronounced as it is unnerving. Classical Liberalism, weary of the endless religious prosecution and human inequities that defined European monarchies, viewed government as a minimal construct to defend one's rights and property from other individuals, to protect a sovereign nation from foreign invaders, to uphold common law, and to maintain the necessity of public institutions and civic infrastructure required for everyday life. Essentially government was a framework for maintaining civility, commerce and national defense. Classic liberals like Thomas Jefferson believed the "pursuit of happiness", not just the preserved titles and property of feudal lords, required limiting government interference by recognizing individual rights, economic liberty, as the greatest harbinger of personal independence and upward mobility. After all, no other financial system has liberated more people from the depths of despair, orchestrated dependence, than the mechanism of private enterprise; also known as capitalism.

Although the term "Free Markets" is often synonymous with Laissez-Faire (hands-off) economics, it did not entirely preclude taxation or minimal regulation to ensure public works, services, and in due time, public education: a conservative theory encouraging universal enlightenment as a path to a more law-abiding, productive and self-sufficient population. Giving individuals the tools to succeed was a direct repudiation of a permanent welfare state, wealth redistribution, which usurped the property and power of the governed. And while this commercial free reign was seen as the most sensible catalyst for rewarding the ambition, ingenuity, of corporations and private businesses, labor was also viewed as an "open market" in which the acquired skill or experience of an individual could dictate his or her monetary worth through the practicality of "supply and demand". Unfortunately for the common working man, coercion and scarcity of opportunity were also determining factors in the never-ending quest to merely survive or potentially flourish.

"So that the record of history is absolutely crystal clear. That there is no alternative way, so far discovered, of improving the lot of the ordinary people that can hold a candle to the productive activities that are unleashed by a free enterprise system." ~Milton Friedman

Much like Constitutional Conservatism, Classical Liberals feared pure democracy, majority rule, because there is little to stop the dominate faction from enriching themselves or dissolving the rights and property of the minority populace. Whereas communism seeks to rule by force, the disarmed facade of socialism enslaves by vote. This belief, in theory, was the basis for "Checks and Balances" to prevent centralized abuse or "legalized" tyranny, as well as the genesis for the "equal representation" premise of the U.S. Senate or the wisdom of the Electoral College system: granting a voice, a degree of significance, to all invested/affected states no matter how small or restrained by resources. Thomas Hobbes, on the other hand, advocated unilateral rule over a secondary class of citizens – a social contract granting government exclusive control over the Executive branch, courts and the military to guard against man's nefarious nature – just not the means to repel the innate flaws or aspirations of their adopted rulers.

Without such constraints placed upon the plurality of mob rule, it was feared "purely democratic institutions, whether sooner or later, would destroy liberty, civilization or both. Either the poor would plunder the rich, causing civilization to perish, or a totalitarian government would ensue to ensure order and prosperity in which liberty would ultimately perish." As a result, unscrupulous politicians or scheming parties could manipulate, threaten or bribe the electorate with other people's property, privileges. This delicate balance between individual freedom and the afforded degree of oversight has been the ideological battleground of citizens, statesmen and scholars for thousands of years.

"Natural Rights", the "utility" and well-being of all sentient beings, became the crux for forging an ethical society defined by reason; the rationalization of a universal, pre-existing standard of behavior as espoused by famed-philosopher Immanuel Kant. Whether the source of liberty was legislated and defined by man-made institutions or derived by the grace of God himself – the steadfast contention of most Christian conservatives – ethics do not require any religious affiliation; although its tenets are most often synonymous with Judeo-Christian values. Right and wrong, injustices and inequalities, humanity's moral state resided in its resolve to confront the immoral practices, cultural relativism, of regressive regimes and militant religions. In the words of Jean-Jacques Rousseau, man is most civil when he is in a natural state of co-existence or equilibrium, an instinctive disinclination to witness suffering, not one defined by fear, decadence or ego-centrism. And so goes the birth of the "noble savage".

"The man who asks of freedom anything other than itself is born to be a slave." ~Alexis de Tocqueville

In Kant's estimation, lasting peace could only be secured by universal democracy and international cooperation...a collective consciousness that gave rise to the United Nations. Unfortunately, this global assembly has been little more than a symbolic gesture, a noble but naive notion perverted by bitter agendas, double standards and appeasement, in lieu of aggressively confronting the historic adversaries of Western Civilization, but more succinctly, mankind: the inhumane and uninterrupted legacies of fascism, communism and Islamic extremism. Man's undying penchant for atrocity – human, sex and organ trafficking currently so prevalent in Africa and Asia – is a reflection of our failure to embrace universal responsibility, natural law, as an "evolved", sentient species. Neo-Classical Liberalism, commonly referred to as Libertarianism but negatively stereotyped as Social Darwinism, reflects the challenge to bridge both the limitless blessings and the inherent pitfalls of unhinged liberty due to a lack of individual accountability amidst the inevitable choice of malice, discrimination, and discord.

Social or Modern Liberalism, born from the destitution of the Great Depression, the depravity of World War II, is basically an oxymoron when contrasted to its current manifestation: Progressivism. Liberals from this 1930's and 40's endorsed a market economy, were distinctly patriotic, did not assail or needlessly disparage Christianity, of which many practiced, and they rejected the divisive practice of gender, class and race warfare which defeated their goal of expanded civil and political rights, social unity and human dignity. It's also a misnomer this form of liberalism was the ideological property of Democrats when evangelical Republicans, a party formed on the abolition of slavery itself, spearheaded the movements to end human servitude, grant universal suffrage and secure equality. This intrinsic duty to respect and empower all sects of society would eventually succumb to the Marxist and Gestapo tactics so prevalent in progressive circles today.

Of course, the other philosophical cornerstone of "Modern Liberalism" was that government had a legitimate claim, obligation, to address issues such as poverty, health care and education. Once again, these were not unilateral concerns, but how our nation went about alleviating or improving these respected plights differed; i.e., welfare is not hammock but a springboard to get back on your feet. The black family survived centuries of global slavery and generations of Jim Crow, only to disintegrate in the eventual creation of the American welfare state. Nevertheless, contemporary socialists, statists, routinely hail Franklin Delano Roosevelt's New Deal as a luminous success in the darkest aftermath of the stock market crash in 1929. Although the President's federal work programs did help assuage the immediate problem of hunger and widespread poverty, it actually prolonged the Great Depression.

The Great Depression, triggered by the crash itself, was rooted in rampant over-speculation, a lack of banking/stock market safeguards and a stagnant, constricted monetary supply in the face of the expanding economic needs of a growing populace. This, in turn, resulted in a lack of capital and extreme deflation as $14 billion in personal securities was lost in a single day. Without investment/consumer capital to generate new or reciprocal wealth generated from manufactured goods and new business, a means to a means, millions had little other option than to survive. If not for the outbreak of World War II, the historical economic boom from armed conflict, America's financial woes could have lingered well into the 1950's. A country that does not instill ambition, cultivate opportunity, reward hard work and expect its people to provide for themselves is doomed to collapse beneath the collective weight of their idle existence. Under Socialism and Communism, you're either a ward of the state or a disposable means to an end. As such, FDR and "The Red Tsar" Joseph Stalin shared a warm relationship, mutual respect, rooted in the centralized confluence of common ideology.

"People will not look forward to posterity, who never look backward to their ancestors." ~Edmund Burke

In the curious case of the Democratic party, how did their contemporary descendants migrate from the "ask not what your country can do for you but what you can do for your country" political thesis of JFK – a platform predicated upon low taxes, robust industry, unwavering patriotism, faith in God and defeating the scourge of communism – to profanely demanding an unearned living wage, single-payer healthcare, coercing "white guilt" by portraying racism/slavery as a singular purveyor, labeling patriotism and respect for the flag as white nationalism, defending the sale of aborted fetuses over a child's unabridged right to life, attacking intellectual diversity/protected free speech in our schools and communities, compromising the fundamental duty of an independent media, destroying the living history of national monuments while praising murderous ideologies, tyrants and terrorist nations, decriminalizing illegal immigration for electoral advantage, obstructing the integrity of our sovereign elections, and placing the welfare of non-citizens, even enemy combatants and unabashed opportunists, over the rights and safety of actual Americans?

If irony was indeed a curtain, it would posthumously reside over the mortified face of a weeping Lady Liberty. There is the inevitable disagreement among like-minded colleagues, the fluid evolution of one's convictions, and there is the complete abandonment of duty, love of country, and reason. The systemic subversion of our founding ideals, the Constitution, and our hallowed way of life is not a new occurrence for socialists and Marxists have lived among us for over century; a number have or continue to hold office. Senator Joseph McCarthy was in theory correct, he simply allowed his paranoia to wrongfully accuse disliked political adversaries and randomly threaten due process. The Port Huron Statement was much more than a drunken idealistic binge by leftist students, it was an ominous ode to the "peaceful overthrow" blueprint for exacting political and social change from within.

"What 'multiculturalism' boils down to is that you can praise any culture in the world except Western culture – and you cannot blame any culture in the world except Western culture." ~Thomas Sowell

This organized assault on our national interests, enduring sense of pride, has increased in ferocity and scope as a disturbing number of progressives now hold a negative or outright hostile view of America. It really wasn't until the counter-culture of the 1960's – a rebellious, discontented generation inflamed over Vietnam, racial unrest and traditional societal norms (like getting a job) – that the radical likes of Saul Alinsky, Richard Cloward, Frances Piven, Bill Ayers and Frank Marshall found a receptive ear to assist in their treasonous aspirations; much like naïve millennials who are more concerned over access to social media, liquidating liberty for the promise of a free lunch and gun-free zones, then the dismissed historical parallels of Stalin, Hitler, Hirohito, Mao, Guevara or Castro.

Regardless of common misconceptions or ingrained biases, elements of Classical Liberalism, Conservatism, Modern Liberalism, and Progressivism are present in both political parties. No matter how similar or diametrically opposed, the true measure of trust is that of intent. What is the intent of Republican and Democratic bureaucrats, the collateral targets of their respective policies, and what is the path chosen to achieve these goals? Debating the merits of a Federal Reserve is a reasonable debate; justifying FBI corruption is not. From the recent rise to militant activism, intolerance, to a rapidly eroding respect for the law and our fellow man, America's values have clearly been corrupted from within. This now visible malaise has clouded common sense to the point of contempt upon contact. Any political movement incumbent upon dividing citizens into warring factions, using mass hysteria/misinformation to negate constructive discourse through fear or violence, and perverting the role of public education – choosing political indoctrination over individual thought and failing to give students an objective understanding, detectable appreciation, of America's blessings – is no friend of this republic or her people.

"There is a difference between happiness and wisdom: he that thinks himself the happiest man is really so; but he that thinks himself the wisest is generally the greatest fool." ~Sir Francis Bacon

Progressivism has become a starry-eyed, storybook euphemism for a scorched-earth campaign against the family paradigm, Christianity, accountability, self-rule, and the founding charter of the American dream. The prudence and practicality necessary to protect fundamental freedoms, the prerequisite of truth and transparency in a representative government, is now an acceptable casualty in the rush to claim political supremacy. The intentional infusion of propaganda into nearly every facet of society, specifically our elected institutions for political gain, has betrayed the people's assumed ability to discern fact from fiction, conviction from hate. Reality is not nor should it ever be reported as a conservative or liberal viewpoint, but as an unfiltered journey to wisdom beyond any singular, self-serving end.

Rather than selectively highlighting past transgressions to wrongfully condemn the present, critics should applaud America for its moral fortitude to create a more just and civil society. Instead of reducing the empowerment of women to naked feminists shouting profanities in our city streets before the eyes and ears of impressionable children, recognize their priceless prowess as strong matriarchs and esteemed professionals without the debasement of political condescension. Why degrade the traditional family's proclivity to produce more well-adjusted and content generations, only to turn the innate strengths of natural biology into a self-fulling prophecy where social activists relegate "individuality", dare I say progress, to the proven destructive dysphoria of gender conditioning?

Contrary to pundits and media puppets alike, an overwhelming majority of conservatives are steadfast supporters of equal rights, those existing laws and avenues of recompense readily available to their own affected friends and family, they simply reject inventing injustice or courting madness to further divide America for the public spectra of partisan spin. While it is true no party is without fault or sin, misjudgments or misgivings, the American people solely bear the burden of questioning any ideology that is incompatible with those inalienable rights necessary for "the pursuit of happiness", but more so for posing a tangible and grave threat to the very country, which by nature, entertains the most inhospitable guests or unworthy, entrusted patrons seeking her fall. To quote those progressive soldiers guarding the unlocked backdoor, "The Russians are coming; the Russians are coming!" Forgive my intrusion, but they're already here.

They have been...for years.

"If Tyranny and Oppression come to this land, it will be in the guise of fighting a foreign enemy." ~James Madison

Cuban Dictators and American Communists

How exceedingly twisted and self-destructive has the American political landscape become? To the point of freedom's fracture and truth's partisan demise. For months now, the media establishment has viciously slandered Trump as a racist, terrorist and xenophobe, only to proudly celebrate centuries of tyranny as its Red army of progressive thinkers characterize Fidel Castro as an unsung hero and visionary! Come again? If I may, when did a communist dictator who oppressed, impoverished and murdered generations of innocent Cubans become a hero; let alone worthy of any discernible praise whatsoever? I'm guessing the countless men, women and children who bravely risked their lives and fled their native homeland in makeshift rafts did so because communism is so utterly benevolent, painfully misunderstood, while the timeless ideals of liberty, limited government and capitalism – the upward mobility of manifest destiny and the transcendent prowess of individuality – are so utterly unjust and discriminatory? Are the civilized requirements of basic sanitation, sufficient food resources, competent health care, higher education and self-sustaining employment opportunities a Right-Wing conspiracy or a free pass in the catered newsrooms of six-figure enlightenment? Hmm...how about due process, democracy or the cognitive human condition known as free speech?

Perhaps our professors of humanitarian revisionism have spent too much time spoon-feeding each other Starbucks memos of 60's academia rather than tasting the sheer depravity of the Ukrainian famine, recreating the horrific imprisonment and torture of Cuba's most vocal dissidents who vanished from loved ones without a trace, or witnessing China's mass executions of its disarmed populace under Mao Zedong. Just imagine the "dire" consequences if the collective conscience of media humanists never worked so tirelessly to remind "ignorant" voters that Donald Trump is on equal footing with the most notorious, bloodthirsty villains in modern history. Without "fake news" from "honest hacks" where would true progress ever begin?

It's physically nauseating, politically cancerous, when so-called educated activists can no longer delineate between hope and hate, poverty and opportunity, freedom and fascism. When I say the leftist establishment despises America's founding creed, blames us for age-old global inequities and would gladly denounce all political dissent as hate speech to welcome autocratic rule and thus ensure their progressive utopia, this is case-in-point. Sadly, it's only a matter of time before these subversive radicals brainwashed at the altar of Karl Marx and Howard Zinn have the electoral supremacy to ensure the government has the power to dictate every aspect of your surrendered dignity: what you eat, how to think, your child's true gender identity, that ambition is greed, Islam is virtuous, abortion ethical, skin color a privilege, accountability racist, exhibitionism empowering, and that sex is inherently sexist.

How else can any rational parent explain, dare I say fathom, as to why nearly half of all millennials are growing up under the delusion Communism is a superior alternative to our nation's founding and hallowed way of life? The disturbing reality is that we as a nation are openly embracing historical infamy as the propaganda state of cultivated division and justifiable mob violence grows exponentially with each passing day. This election has proven that integrity, if not objectivity and civic duty, is only as relevant as the desired end it serves. Once society empowers corruption as its rightful king, the "means" to alter any inconvenient outcome, truth or obstacle becomes perception's unquestionable queen.

KARL MARX

NEVER RAN A COMPANY
NEVER HELD POLITICAL OFFICE
WAS NEVER SELF-SUFFICIENT
NEVER EVEN HELD A JOB

EVERY APPLICATION OF
HIS THEORY HAS ENDED
IN MASS MURDER

DESPITE ALL THIS,
HE IS IDOLIZED
BY THE LEFT

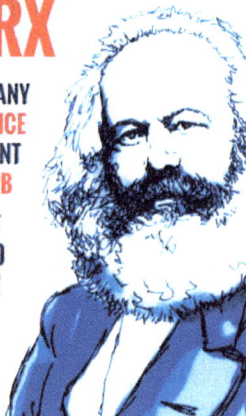

Communism was never about equally sharing a country's resources or resolving the inevitability of income inequality. It is, and always has been, about a despot, an elite few, a unilateral ruling party using the political constructs of blame, discord, fear and mass dependency to maintain control over a compliant citizenry. Marxism is an economic ruse, a victimization campaign drive, designed to prey upon the calloused hearts and jaded minds of human misery. Surprised? Proletariat, please! What does defy convention is as to why humanity must experience these brutal lessons every 25, 50 or 100 years in order to realize tyranny's victims are far more than anecdotes in a condemned textbook, they are a stain on the living sanctity of choice...that which so many today are willing to ransom and take from the mouths of their own children to feed a regurgitated lie.

As for the joyous news of America renewing its resolve to secure a free Cuba, I stand with the Cuban people and their native brethren whom have suffered and died for over half a century – and continue to toil beneath the iron fist of totalitarianism under Raul Castro – while soulless politicians and media pundits who did nothing to assuage the Cuban people's plight actually have the gall to praise the very political mechanism responsible for such moral atrocities. The world doesn't need more political prisoners or incestuous decrees legalizing the intolerance of sanctimonious bigots. It needs a champion of free will, not just of flesh and frailty, but an immutable beacon safeguarding everyone's natural born right to pursue the life of their choosing without the shackled burden of indoctrinated fear and mass conformity. Yes, our forefathers, in all their infinite wisdom but especially amidst the cultural imperfections of their era, knew it was possible to kill a man or vanquish an entire army but that no earthly force can conquer an ideal that stirs the indelible spirit of conviction and answers only to the divine throne of reason. To that ethereal end, liberty for all or may justice be done though the heavens may fall.

Imprisoned homosexuals, executed dissidents, burned books, restricted free speech and association.

LOVED BY THE LEFT

THE TWISTED LIBERAL MIND

Dr. Jill Stein
@DrJillStein

Follow

Fidel Castro was a symbol of the struggle for justice in the shadow of empire. Presente!
6:46 PM - 26 Nov 2016

2.062   2,957

fb.com/HostilityAgainstTyranny

Jill Stein

I Oppose the Death Penalty!

#GoPublic

Fidel executes prisoner

The Psychological Warfare of Marxist Identity Politics

The goals of Marxist identity politics are the epitome of psychological warfare turned deadly public inquisition: divide, demonize, conquer. Whether you're a Republican, a Christian conservative or an independent Trump supporter, the intolerant left will immediately brand you as a racist, a white supremacist, a misogynist, a homophobe, xenophobic and a Nazi purveyor of hate rather than rationally and respectfully debating the merits of your beliefs. It's impossible to properly address our most pressing issues, constructively collaborate to find the best possible solutions, when civil discourse and common decency have been displaced by academic censorship, media propaganda and militant coercion. And in the United States of all places; that astutely-crafted Constitutional Republic founded upon individual liberty, due process, as a refuge from religious persecution and the historical tyranny of unilateral control.

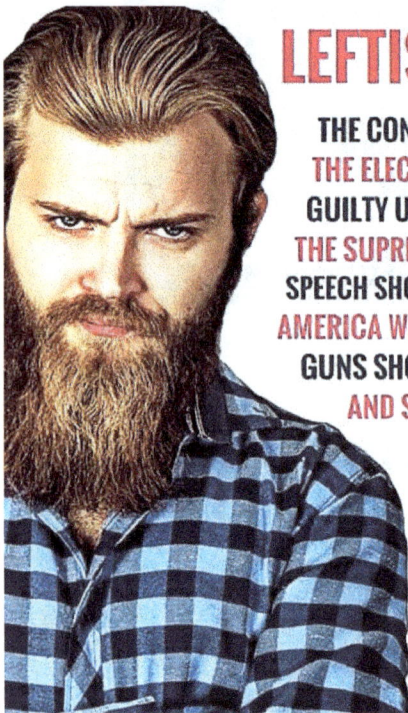

LEFTISTS BELIEVE:

THE CONSTITUTION IS OUTDATED
THE ELECTORAL COLLEGE MUST GO
GUILTY UNTIL PROVEN INNOCENT
THE SUPREME COURT IS A SHAM
SPEECH SHOULD BE CENSORED
AMERICA WAS NEVER GREAT
GUNS SHOULD BE BANNED
AND SOCIALISM CAN WORK

...AND IF YOU DISAGREE, YOU'RE A RACIST, SEXIST, XENOPHOBIC BIGOT!

TURNING POINT USA

If it's perfectly acceptable to be a proud black or Latino immigrant, but not a vocal white citizen, let alone a strong Christian leader, then we are willingly shaming millions of children into hating themselves and their own country. And yet the same people encouraging and praising multi-culturalism – a delicate balance which at the very least demands some degree of assimilation or equal respect for a host nation's heritage and way of life – are incessantly attempting to discredit or exclude America's history, sovereignty, and most revered traditions.

The "seek and destroy' politics currently defining Washington but more precisely our fractured society as a whole, are poisoning every facet of our communities and systematically killing any chance at a meaningful future. Without independent thought, intellectual diversity, freedom cannot exist....and neither will America. A fatal fact her conniving enemies know all too well. Unlike those 'Rules for Radicals" twisting our most indispensable values and religiously inciting discord, most right-minded Americans have no ulterior motives or subversive agenda; merely an innate desire to prosper according to their own two hands, to protect their family, property and home, and to live free from cultural hostility and undue government interference. But according to career liberal malcontents protesting common sense, natural born liberty, "We the Patriotic People" are just too damn extreme to peacefully coexist.

Commie California Dreamin'

Disturbing, yet so utterly predictable being California is now eagerly confirming what "We the People" already knew...the American left enthusiastically embraces Marxist principles and/or they're sympathetic towards a potential Communist revolution. I'd expect nothing less from a resource-rich, progressively-backwards state with some of the highest poverty, crime, tax and homeless rates, not to mention record debt, government waste and self-inflicted environmental disasters. If you live in California I suggest planning a mass exodus...and soon.

The once prosperous, respected home of Ronald Reagan has collapsed into an anti-American cesspool of liberal indoctrination where hard working, law-abiding, patriotic citizens are the marked enemies of sanctuary cities, armed criminals, drug addicts, eco-terrorists, cultural Marxists, gender sadists, Hollywood hedonists, academic censors and affirmative action globalists. The once "Golden State" has been forever lost to a tidal wave of political correctness, electoral corruption, victimization entitlement and fascist intolerance, also known as Democratic Socialism. What Communists fail to properly explain is how their historically-debunked fairytale of a perfectly equitable, harmonious society requires depriving millions of their natural born rights, lives and property, including that universal liberty which is most synonymous with the dawn of humanity: conscious free will. Obviously the brutal, tyrannical legacies of Mao, Stalin, and Castro have failed to educate enough California voters about the single, greatest threat of unopposed Democratic rule. Willful ignorance.

Once socialism culminates in economic collapse, moral degeneracy and widespread civil unrest, communism will be the modern left's long-sought solution to restoring order, nationalizing industry, silencing opposition, and ensuring political indoctrination through mass propaganda. And that is why the unmarked grave of human history never truly dies. The truth is the immortal enemy of the unholy state.

The Final Countdown

Pardon my candor, but I love Alexandria Ocasio-Cortez, Rashida Tlaib and Omar Ilhan. Let me repeat, I LOVE this new vitriolic trio of fearless Democratic freshman. I love their petulant antics and unfiltered intolerance because they are zealously confirming what right-minded voters have reiterated for decades only for the complicit media to tirelessly discredit as Right-Wing paranoia, white privilege, corporate greed and systemic racism.

With their radical, ignorant and undeniably treasonous intentions now entirely front and center, it's only a matter of time before the Democratic party completely rejects our founding charter, the Constitution itself, to institute socialism by taxing successful businesses and wealthy Americans at a 70% (or higher) rate, terminate private insurance for single-payer government healthcare, enact radical environmental reforms (eliminate fossil fuels, combustion-engine travel, meat consumption, animal-based products, water/forest mismanagement), champion open borders and unlimited immigration, legalize infanticide and euthanasia, embrace Islam and Sharia Law over Judeo-Christianity and religious freedom, remove all "hateful" historical monuments and "false" teachings of American history, issue federal reparations for distant relatives of slaves and trespassing immigrants detained/separated at the border, abolish the Electoral College, declare mandatory LGBT education and gender acceptance guidelines, discourage/punish "toxic masculinity" in favor of toxic feminism, abandon Israel as a Middle Eastern ally while aiding militant Islamic regimes, censor free speech and advocate state-controlled media, confiscate guns by any discriminatory means possible – veteran status, social media history, prescription usage, political affiliations – and impose extensive affirmative action protocols for commercial and government positions, as well as public education.

The ominous fate which awaits America is no longer up for debate, let alone an ambiguous matter of personal supposition. It is fact. The only question that remains is when; when will an iconic refuge from tyranny and mass privation, one predicated upon individual liberty, free enterprise and limited government, officially abandon reason for madness.

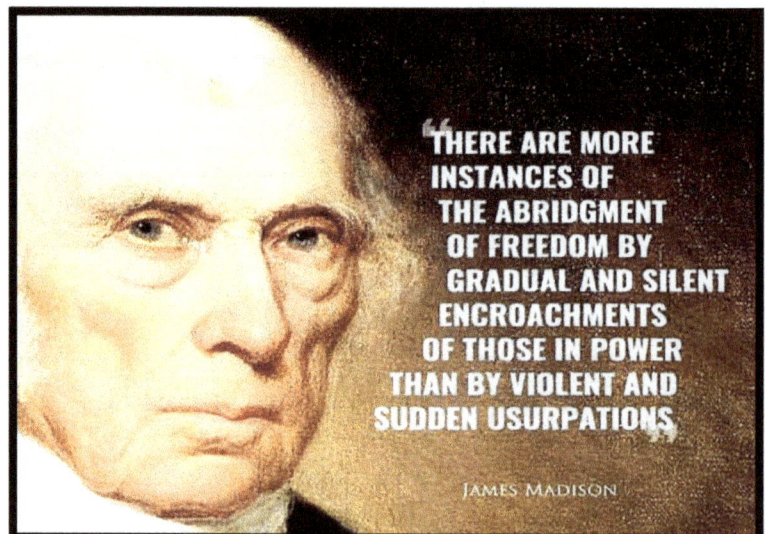

"THERE ARE MORE INSTANCES OF THE ABRIDGMENT OF FREEDOM BY GRADUAL AND SILENT ENCROACHMENTS OF THOSE IN POWER THAN BY VIOLENT AND SUDDEN USURPATIONS"

JAMES MADISON

The Great American Experiment: To Rise Before the Fall

For a number of years now, scholars have surmised America is spiraling towards the dustbin of history. Every great civilization, no matter how refined or transcendent, have all shared one inescapable similarity: the inevitable decline of their power and global influence. Although the impetus for their fall may have varied – from apathy to corruption, the conquering hoard of war or unforeseen misfortune – their fates were, more or less, forever linked to the failings of human nature. It is therefore of little surprise more and more Americans believe the most transcendent nation in modern history is now beyond saving; a fractured shell hopelessly adrift from its once liberated intent. The two-party system is so irrevocably broken that incessant "bipartisan" warfare has eviscerated public trust in government, reduced the media to party jesters, and incited hostility in every corridor of America. With increasing numbers of voters unable to discern fact from fiction, freedom from fascism, a disturbing percentage of Americans are now far more concerned with partisan supremacy than the actual survival and State of the Union. And yet despite these indelible truths, 50% of all millennials recently declared, dare I say believe, they would prefer to live beneath a socialist or communist regime. Ignorance is bliss until you're reminded starvation, censorship and the spontaneous decree of death are not Right-Wing fairy tales in the guarded squalor of Venezuela, Cuba or North Korea.

If the elections of 2008, 2012, and 2016 taught us anything, it's that the lapdog media will say or do anything to toe the party line: regardless of any perceived consequences, the subversion of our own government, the future viability of the rule of law. In this cantankerous, political era where rabid activists double as objective, award-winning journalists, no lie is too big, no manipulation too shameful, no association too infantile. From blatantly misrepresenting economic data, to concealing treason and even blaming Donald Trump for "racist" natural disasters, nothing is too inane or inappropriate in the pursuit of manipulating public perception.

Not discounting the shock value of such vile propaganda, what does this proliferation of absurdity reveal about us as a people, an "evolved" nation, when grown adults of varying mindsets and diverse backgrounds can no longer engage in constructive discourse without resorting to slander and stereotypes; i.e., labeling patriotic Republicans – those who actually ended the abomination of slavery, Jim Crow laws and opposed the KKK to grant citizenship and suffrage – as slave masters, Nazis or white supremacists? How can our American Republic solve the most pressing issues plaguing this nation, work in earnest cooperation, when we cannot agree on the problem let alone look one another in the eye without utter disdain and blind contempt? Better yet, in what hijacked country are we living in when real collusion and widespread impropriety are purposely disregarded by the press, absolving fellow partisan constituents, in favor of pursuing a false judgement based on fabricated evidence solely to remove a political opponent beneath the fog of incited public hysteria? For the life of me, I cannot recall a single, outgoing President, other than an anti-Semitic Marxist who routinely mocked America's heritage and presided over the worst economy since Jimmy Carter, forming an organized resistance to his successor before that leader even took the Oath of Office; especially one elected on a populist platform to reform the many failures and abuses of an increasingly corrupt and detached ruling establishment.

Our media and educational institutions, perhaps the two most indispensable mediums in sustaining a vigilant and vibrant free republic, have become so ingrained with anti-Americanism and a feral disrespect towards their fellow man, that objectivity and justice are becoming frighteningly synonymous with partisan intolerance. Therefore, amidst the supposed glory and enlightenment of modernity in the year 2018, "We the People" are literally living in a propaganda age where truth and the intent to deceive are intrinsically one. How can you coexist with those who believe America is an evil empire forged upon greed and hatred, human trademarks that still flourish across the globe, rather than a refuge from the historical ravages of government oppression and religious persecution? How can we protect the best interests of our national sovereignty, the welfare of actual citizens, when enforcing our immigration and voting laws, passed by both parties, is now reported as a hate crime? More profoundly, why would anyone acquiesce to those treasonous agents of discontent seeking to weaken America without refrain, instead of appreciating and preserving the unique opportunities she innately affords?

The fact our two political parties cannot even agree on a core set of common sense principles – a balanced budget, lower taxes, free enterprise, government transparency, individual liberties, religious rights, a secure border – is ominous to say the least. Because the political pendulum of power sways every 4 to 8 years, our government is constantly, and often abruptly, changing directions: economically, culturally, ideologically. If any business operated under this paradigm, i.e., those who cannot print their own money or blame capitalism, they would be bankrupt and out of business within a year. It is nothing more than an unmitigated recipe for financial disaster. Yet, we continue to embrace this cycle of insanity as our country, the Constitution itself, is literally torn apart by this incessant tug of war. When elected representatives can no longer pass a bill on its own merits without stuffing it full of kickbacks and highly questionable legislation that would not pass otherwise, "the system" is irrefutably broken and the people made to bear the burden of glorified incompetence.

The problem with contemporary Republicans is that too many try to be even-handed out of some misplaced duty to indulge dangerous leftist principals, instead of drawing an ideological line in the sand they know damn well cannot be crossed without severe consequences for America. They would rather surrender to the "status quo" for future votes than to stand and fight for what is right. As someone who truly loves America, I would never abandon her to those circling wolves salivating at the mere thought of her demise. I also cannot deny this nation is on the precipice of rejecting free speech, individuality, for the sake of the so-called "common good". For the sake of self-preservation, but more profoundly to contrast these two diametrical opposed views of "progress", I feel deeply compelled to propose the "Great American Experiment".

I recommend, for a moderate duration and to be reviewed upon completion, allowing like-minded states to form peaceful coalitions; that is, granting those states still dedicated to our founding charter – freedom/free enterprise, limited government, faith, family, hard work and duty – an opportunity to secede and thrive under a renewed constitutional union. Those remaining states, who are content to continue to accept the decay under unapologetic progressivism – intrusive government, social/economic justice, secularism, political correctness, history revisionism, race-baiting, rampant poverty/crime – can remain under the collectivist banner of the Democratic Party.

Of course, as we all know, the militant left would never agree to such an amicable split, even if but a temporary reprieve, because they rely so heavily on the political capital of identity politics – anger and fear born from division, blame, distraction – rarely the relevance of proven or even reasonable policies. Their incessant need to dictate and control the everyday lives of others, specifically dissenting conservative voices, would immediately negate any hope of an agreement. Therefore, it's clear the only way such a bold initiative could begin, possibly succeed, would be under the auspices of a Republican president acutely aware of a scorched-earth campaign currently waging war on the American dream. And because time is dwindling as fast as basic civility, decorum, fades beneath the fallout of political militants who believe the end justifies the means, these next few years may very well represent the final opportunity to contrast these two vastly incompatible ideologies by embodying a revered way of life millions are willing to ensure without excuse or prevarication.

In the end, no matter what the duration or inherent difficulties, I have no doubt the results will be stark in terms of economic vitality, bureaucratic competency, national unity, and a renewed sense of moral obligation to our communities. This new union of faithful states, dedicated to the ageless attributes of virtue and natural born rights, will be vast and influential. As common sense is restored to the forefront of government, entrepreneurs will be allowed to thrive, God can rightfully return to our public institutions (not just our prisons), our borders will be secured through the reciprocated respect of legal immigration, and people will once again be held responsible for their livelihood and their actions. Now, that's not to say assistance won't be available those individuals/families in need, only that such aid wouldn't represent a career opportunity; rather, we would proudly endeavor to compassionately assist the needy, the disabled and the elderly without indulging the apathetic, entitled or the lazy.

In short, this philosophical departure would mean no more endlessly arguing with liberals over the definition of a human life, the necessity of voter ID, the right to bear arms and eliminating exploitative taxes. No more political malcontents telling us what to eat or drink; no more Global Warming alarmism and pseudo-science regulation; no more attacks on the sanctity of Christmas or Christianity; no more destroying historical monuments and erasing our nation's imperfect but invaluable history; no more mindless social regression through the destructive constructs of gender identification, conditioning; and no more degrading the brave service of our Armed Forces by needlessly burning the American flag and kneeling during the national anthem. Yes, all are welcome to remain and prosper according to their own ambition and abilities, regardless of race, religion or personal disposition, with the understanding our founding values are non-negotiable and cannot be voted out by any political scheme or electoral advantage.

Although open and meaningful debate would still be required to finalize the specifics of America's surviving ideals, these fruitful exchanges would by no means represent the current mockery that placates our government; a despotic desire to cajole and dissuade the misinformed as an immoral, statist agenda is forced down the American people's throat without cessation. By choosing to stand for what is right, no matter what the cost, hope and opportunity will flourish for countless generations to come.

Likewise, when given complete autonomy over their own willing subjects, Blue State oligarchs will finally be free to fleece every successful business owner and native citizen to the point of bankruptcy, illegitimacy, to impose affirmative action to the precipice of unbridled discrimination, to prosecute self-defense and disarm law enforcement, and to systematically denigrate every Judeo-Christian ideal America was predicated upon. Thus, when the dust clears and the hearsay of hyperbole crumbles, the destitute, dependent, decadent masses turn on one another, progressives will have no one left to blame but themselves: not big business, not white privilege, not religious extremists, not "fake" or Fox news. And then, perhaps, if only for one fleeting moment, the masses will realize they have forsaken the two greatest catalysts in human history: freedom and those of faith who have the courage to act upon its behalf.

I love my country, my family, and God with all my heart. That being said, I cannot sit idly by as the coming demographic tidal wave engineered by globalists permanently drowns the last vestiges of American independence, exceptionalism, beneath a socialist cesspool of progressive rule. I cannot sit idly by and watch everything America stands for – the wisdom and sacrifice of our forefathers who toiled as condemned traitors so we may eat from the tree of liberty – suffocate beneath the echoing footsteps of moralized fascism, only to be eulogized by the Marxist indoctrination of liberal academia and the smug moral relativism of Hollywood elites. Our children deserve better, centuries of men and women who fought and died for this nation deserve better, and lastly the civilized world deserves better...this "last, best hope of mankind". This is why I would unequivocally support organized secession, albeit short or long term, if only to illustrate just how far this forsaken nation has fallen.

While some will find my observations exceedingly dire or entirely too presumptive, I have but one final request. When you're forced to apologize for your very existence, your identity methodically erased and private property marked as public domain, when right becomes wrong and logic a liability, and your every move is judged through the oppressive prism of class, gender or race, what will be left of America worth saving? Sometimes, the slumbering masses need to be reminded of the cost of breaking the promise that was once America. Sometimes the cost of sacrificing the comfort of the status quo is far less than the unpaid price of failing to stand for your convictions.

"America will never be destroyed from the outside. If we falter and lose our freedoms, it will be because we destroyed ourselves."
~Abraham Lincoln

"Brexiting" the New World Oligarchy

Oligarchy: (noun) a form of government in which all power is vested in a few persons or in a dominant class or clique; government by the few.

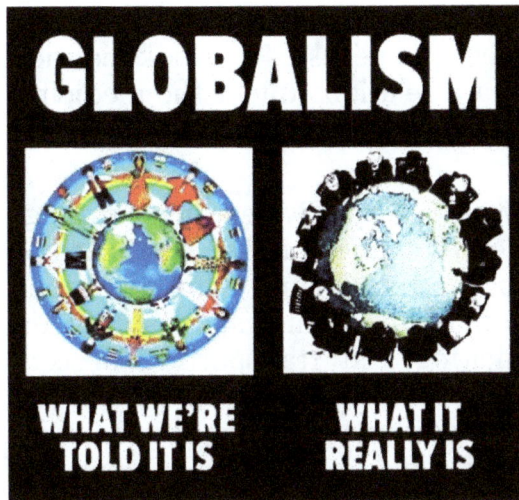

Globalism was never about bringing the fundamental constructs of modern society – responsible government, liberty, commerce, infrastructure and education – to the impoverished, corrupt and war-torn corners of the world. It was, and remains, a veiled coup by radical leftists to diminish the influence, wealth and values of Western Civilization by siphoning our sovereignty and resources in lieu of dysfunctional nations that have failed their people and increasingly harbor anti-American sentiments. Historically speaking, the easiest way to achieve this Orwellian goal is to blanch the lines of distinction and achievement, those benchmarks of economic and military superpowers, by erecting one government under the glittering premise of creating a better world rather than attempting the arduous task of convincing independent and vibrant nations to leverage their rights, security, and somehow willingly consent to their own demise. In other words, lie; because old collectivists, usurping socialists, Islamic supremacists and whining millennials all know what's best for you and your family. That's correct, mes amis...disregard the royal court of conspiring ideologues pushing a counter-intuitive agenda for personal gain and kindly leave your keys and checkbook on the chopping block of global judgment. Only foreign votes matter.

It is hardly a coincidence that capitalism, Judeo-Christianity, and gun rights have come under fire across the globe; from world leaders to media activism and even the Pope himself...a man who publicly disparages and sacrifices our natural born liberty, our belief in God's divinity, on the immoral and oppressive altar of statism. It's also no coincidence that we have basically endured a global recession since 2008 as private enterprise and manufacturing – that which creates individual wealth, jobs and fiscal solvency – is flailing beneath excessive regulation and incessant taxation. The fact both America and much of Europe are suffocating beneath historic debt due to excessive social programs and immigration is but a surefire recipe for economic collapse and the globalists' primary objective: capitulation to the New World Order due to manufactured mass dependency on centralized government.

The same Barack Obama who once said raising the debt by one cent was patriotic, is now sitting on a 20 trillion deficit – double the accrued debt of all other Presidents combined – while the once most revered and diverse economy in the world has not had a single annualized GDP of 3% in seven consecutive years; the first ignominious distinction since the Great Depression. When you preside over the first two credit downgrades in U.S. history, 7-11"Manager of the Year" is not in your future. If I may, do you actually believe

481

"Free Trade" was designed to help self-sufficient nations continue to push the world engine of innovation and growth? It was primarily forged to help Latin America, Pacific and other third world nations – those riddled with slave labor, inept governments and nonexistent environmental safeguards – tilt the playing field at the cost of our companies and economic vigor. Whether you call it reparations or affirmative action, the left's obsession with white imperialism and "capitalist greed" knows no bounds: except when data-mining with their Google glasses, using iPhones to peruse Facebook political algorithms or asking Starbucks' baristas to improve race relations under the medicinal aroma of a Double Chocolaty-chip Frappuccino.

The final lynch pin in procuring the downfall of America, Western Civilization, is through immigration and the political art of distraction. Little has changed in the destitute and war-ravaged Middle East in the past 8 years, including the Obama administration's shadow support for the reemergence and potential clout of one Islamic state, so why the sudden urgency? Western leaders are openly soliciting and transporting obscene numbers of Muslim and Latin immigrants with the overriding intent of diluting the influence, ideals and eventually the electoral clout of traditional citizens; those British and American nationals desperate to preserve the heritage and Constitutional identity of their respected countries. Furthermore, a sizeable faction of these foreigners has little regard for their host countries, the opportunities afforded within, as countless openly disparage and opine for their fall.

How else could a radicalized Muslim of an immigrant family murder 50 homosexuals in Florida only for Washington to blame guns and Republican hate, or a raucous hoard of illegals in California pledge on prime-time news to "Make America Mexico Again" – an impoverished, incompetent, crime ridden nation – as the bloodied victims of their unprovoked aggression flee for their lives in the background of liberal indifference? In what alternate reality are European women chastised by their own native government for not assimilating to the Islamic culture of rape, misogyny and assault? And these are the overwhelmingly ungrateful and unvetted "refugees" our tax dollars are enabling at record amounts at the expense of our independence and safety? Yep, because promising to "Make Mexico Great...err Spain Again" would mean more jobs, drinkable water, and fewer El Chapo threats against racist America. For a nation of laws, the American people spend more money per illegal immigrant, or roughly $18,000 for every NWO mercenary, than we do per capita on our own veterans and the average Social Security recipient.

Logically impaired globalists know there is no way to confront the factual outrage of their restless detractors, so they resort to hyperbole, slander and the polarizing charges of prejudice to deflect from their indefensible actions. Thus, by fueling animosity and clamoring in the streets to foster some sense of collective anger – labeling their European and American detractors as xenophobes or neo-Nazis – these propagandists attempt to give the illusion they are the voice of the majority when in reality they're the raucous, indignant few victimized by their own reckless stupidity. If respecting one's desired identity is now the King and Queen of social 'genderfication', redefining Mother Nature and reconditioning grade school children to society's detriment, why is the natural act of being proud of your nationality, the personal desire to preserve your country's identity and functional integrity, bigoted and hateful? Succinctly put...it's not.

All are welcome to partake in the innate blessings of our respected homelands, as long as they respect our heritage and laws. Sadly, as the ashes of pragmatism gasp beneath the tidal wave of anti-Western animosity that progressivism incestuously breeds – demonizing Christians, justifying anarchy, and demanding special treatment for bitter belligerents – that proposition is becoming exponentially unrealistic and a gateway to self-assured ruin. Just kindly ask the passive-aggressive, European victims of political correctness how their guests are acclimating to their new "civilized" surroundings. Too bad pillaging and rioting, molestation and mass murder, are now considered the acceptable collateral damage of voiceless, culture terrorists on state assistance: both foreign and domestic. Where else is nationalism, self-preservation, reported as callous hate and economic assimilation a form of cultural enslavement because "progress" demands "privileged" German taxpayers publicly embrace supporting over 700,000 unemployed, volatile Syrian migrants living solely off government benefits? Or if you're a careless, disposable daughter of Denmark, only a sadistic supremacist would dare invoke the forgivable fact 83% of all rapes, or 100% of group related sexual assaults, are committed by misunderstood migrants and their morally depraved descendants.

Make no mistake about it, Globalism, the New World Oligarchy, is a singular campaign bent on forging a genderless, borderless, Godless society – secular souls are easier to conquer and cajole – that will blindly support a handful of progressive demigods bent on destroying the traditional cornerstones of civilization; those ideals that innately threaten their totalitarian ruse. The new CEO's of few good intentions, the 'common man' heirs of the 1% lifestyle, the "armed" rich and famous but never those marauders of the evil "corporate" variety, know it's much easier to institute mass change when all the pawns, whether in agreement or not, are corralled under one unretractable roof of legislated order. Yes, it's also equally convenient to punish those who dismiss Global Warming as a natural climatic cycle and who believe eating meat, or God forbid a doughnut, is a personal choice and not murder; a blameless designation now reserved for Islamic terrorists, La Raza subversives or BLM militants.

Naturally, the only way to get people to freely surrender their individual freedoms is to convince them they are sacrificing for the 'greater good', a world free from hate, greed and senseless achievement, when in reality their self-respect and the institution of choice, individuality, become embers in a Machiavellian bonfire. Why else would a rational, sentient being consciously abandon their natural born dowry of God's grace and submit their human dignity for approval to conspiring strangers when "We the People" explicitly believe the limited power of transparent government is derived from the will and consent of a moral, industrious people? Unlimited porn and Pokemon Go? Regardless of any plurality fabricated under false pretenses, any entity that does not defend liberty, demand accountability, foster self-reliance, respect authority and recognize due process, is not only an enemy of humanity but the primary accomplice of an antiquated cult called denial. Why again is the UN tirelessly scheming to disarm "bloodthirsty" Americans, only to turn a blind eye to the rogue stockpiles of weapons terrorizing the Middle East and Africa? Or perhaps a nuclear Iran is more of a threat than 80 million law-abiding gun owners protecting their families? Distraction and division are powerful allies in the War on Reality; especially when grooming an ignorant and apathetic populace.

In theory, erecting one global family where we all get along, are genetically devoid of malevolence, are equally average and humanity equitably divides the earth's wealth and renewable resources all sounds quite magical and reassuring. Until, that is, you realize someone will always have "more" of everything, ambition sparks innovation and independence, much of the world doesn't recognize our right to exist or share our most basic ethical norms, leftist academia believes intellectual diversity isn't as natural or as necessary as social diversity, and the international media shamelessly censors truth, ridicules dissent, to achieve their Orwellian dream of crafting one ring to rule them all. You don't have to ride shotgun in a renegade truck plowing through helpless pedestrians to realize it's not the banned weapon of mass distraction killing common sense but a poisonous ideology that destroys the rights, hearts and minds of "homeless" men. And if you're perfectly fine with Barack Obama, Chancellor Merkel, Raul Castro, Hillary Clinton, or the Saudi King telling you what to eat, think, and how to feel…for their own betterment and twisted agenda…then I'll hold the "Enter" sign to your own impending demise.

I, on the other hand, will expeditiously "Brexit" any point of order, corrosive creed or ruling class that dismisses "Death to the Infidel", "Kill Cops", or "Make America Mexico Again" as the innocuous culture appropriation of imported hostiles, only to deem any native citizens who love their county – those who reject such subversive barbarism and work for their life's blessings – as racist, national supremacists. There's a reason why proud Parisians, Germans, Italians and Danish nationals are taking to their streets in droves to protest the New World Order's demographic coup d'état and destructive policies. It's called loving your home, your children's lives, and honoring those who fought and died to preserve some semblance of liberty and civility. The key to the front door is no longer under the "Welcome" mat. It's inside an absentee ballot buried at the corner of sovereignty and sanity in the middle of the progressive minefield known as "global-assisted suicide".

Triggers, Trolls and Wolves in Sheep's Clothing

In upwards of 100,000 immigrants (aided by progressive groups and donors) are attempting to illegally enter the U.S. each month, illegal immigration costs taxpayers over $100 billion annually, non-citizens constitute nearly 25% of our entire prison population, and somehow leftist legislators only feel compelled to condemn any hint of objection, justifiable outrage, with their usual barrage of baseless accusations and stale epithets. Rather than dutifully declaring a national emergency to assist the overwhelmed security capabilities and civic resources of border states, these so-called public servants dine on chaos and smugly applaud the "bravery" of cultural arsonists desecrating the flag, dishonoring the Anthem and tarnishing any prominent vestige of national pride - the countless sacrifices made by centuries of our fallen brethren - to ultimately demand the removal of any "offensive" reference to America's founding heritage under the media-conjured banner of fighting "White Supremacy". In what deluded daydream does reducing loyal, law-abiding Americans to secondary citizens, incessantly labeling half the electorate as racist, sexist and homophobic, not constitute a clear and present danger to their lives, livelihoods and Constitutional liberties?

Equally disturbing if not entirely predictable, how does educating the public with these incontrovertible facts, unresolved realities, make one an accessory to neurotic, rogue killers when the liberal establishment gives almost no credence to fellow Americans slain, raped, abducted or robbed by immigrant fugitives and smuggled gang members in order to preserve the "scandalous" myth Homeland Security persecutes helpless women and children; individuals who are still subject to our naturalization statutes and asylum requirements? The deadliest attacks are not the blood-stained eulogies penned by salivating wolves for prime time ratings and party fundraising emails - heartbreaking tragedies which still pale in comparison to daily crime statistics, cancer deaths and common household accidents - but the continuous erosion of a nation's identity, economic vitality and willingness to confront corruption in all its enduring and nefarious forms.

Giving foreign criminals sanctuary and special privileges in the wake of dehumanizing ICE officials risking life and limb to protect our communities, including spurring acts of public retaliation after calling for their immediate eradication or incarceration, is the epitome of an orchestrated political insurrection; not that Deep State saboteurs hatching Russian fairy tales for wrongful prosecution stings need any reminder or incriminating memos. But yes, by all means, please lecture Trump "plantation owners" about who's literally inciting mass hostility with irresponsible rhetoric, a 24/7 syndicated parade of hate-filled propaganda, to conveniently camouflage their own treasonous actions with zero outcry or accountability from colluding Democrats. Or, if I may, is Antifa fighting imaginary fascism with real fascism, courageously concealing their true identity behind black masks and cowardly Gestapo tactics, so future generations of disgruntled dregs, Twitter anarchists and social misfits can assault anyone who dares offends their Marxist sensitivities and pardoned culture of violent entitlement? The "brown shirts" and "white hoods" of Democratic supremacy have a long, lurid history of color-coding hate, national elections, for the supposed benefit of humanity.

Being the pajama pitchfork brigade is largely a byproduct of the contrived anti-Trump hysteria tirelessly flooding every facet of America, perhaps the families of the mass murder victims in Dayton, Ohio should ask why Elizabeth Warren and Bernie Sanders have yet to be charged for scaring the huddled sheep into "resisting" the reported Aryan ghost of Adolf Hitler; a sadistic maniac who also loathed Jews, Christians, free speech and embraced state control over education and healthcare. The clamoring media is terrified of rational adults who simply recognize such heinous atrocities always require an actual perpetrator, not a sacrificial scapegoat for circling scavengers desperately searching for a shiny weapon to cripple a populist's re-election chances by any scurrilous means possible. Under no set of remotely plausible circumstances will the DNC "rigging" machine accept the President winning a second term.

Little Red Riding Hood aside, are "We the digestible People" expected to believe the steady diet of Presidential assassination fantasies echoing from the "me too" catacombs of Hollywood are just harmless parting gifts from the "love wins" humanitarians of homicidal entertainment? Rape, sex cults, drugs, and glorified death scenes always register in the fundraising coffers of liberal hypocrisy; endearing sentiments which clearly have no bearing on the lunatic lynch mob surrounding Mitch McConnell's home and aspiring to "just stab the motherf#@cker" because killing political opponents with the "obsolete" ideal of self-defense is always on the vegan menu of the unhinged left. Is it too late to stop Climate Change and ban Right Wing hate by perusing our dying planet in more private jets and celebrity christened yachts in search of Jeffrey Epstein's pedophile island? According to the commercial sponsors of Pride Month and human trafficking cartels, the Fourth of July is too long and our children's future is at stake. You don't say.

Funny how the same foaming mouthpieces painting President Trump as the genesis of all evil in a perilously-maladjusted and tone deaf world, fortuitously forget that mass shootings and terrorist attacks - Fort Hood, Chattanooga, Boston, San Diego, Orlando, Sandy Hook and Charleston to name but a few - jumped by over 400% respectively during Barack Obama's tenure. Naturally, his strong racial commentary, brash brand of social activism, were by no means lamented or implicated by the mainstream press, let alone the militant organizations of la Raza and Black Lives Matter, when cops were being assassinated in the line of duty for simply doing their job. Thank God no one in the appalled, hyper-vigilant press demanded a sitting President denounce racism and black supremacy due to Kodak moments with genocidal luminaries like Louis Farrakhan. Unlike opaque shower doors with no handicap access, obtuse selfies are clearly cheaper. Those who view and judge everything according to race are, by definition and disposition, "racist".

The "Great Beguiler", who could elegantly deceive and cajole millions as unflinchingly as Donald Trump speaks unwelcome truths, was practically deified for his abrasive "social justice" bravado despite unapologetically fueling national unrest along racial, economic and religious lines, demonizing police inundated with an urban epidemic of criminals resisting arrest, and even triggering mass riots that resulted in loss of life and property after impetuously bypassing the pertinent details of the Michael Brown and Freddie Gray cases. No wonder his lovesick voters and globalist disciples have no recollection of the "inhumane" cages his administration built to separate children from their unvetted families, or profiting traffickers, until a legal determination of "asylum" could be made in accordance with our existing immigration laws; common sense necessities both parties once acknowledged and passed.

And yet those conscious trespassers wishing to return home on their own accord were still free to do so, as they are today, without any sensational tales of Nazi torture or inane accusations of a secret Republican Holocaust. Apparently, air conditioned detention centers with free medical care and hot food are the new concentration camps of millennial historians attempting to classify Christian conservatives as terrorist agents of hate speech for choosing the Bible over drag queen story time, salvation over soulless indoctrination, and the divine blessing of children, family, over extolling the "feminist" extravaganza of abortion.

Punishing ideological dissent, the crux of free will, is the infamous calling card of every depraved totalitarian regime in history; and now, modern progressivism. Thinking for yourself has become an unfathomable hate crime to biased educators and media puppets who believe it is their moral obligation to convince the masses Islam is peaceful, "white nationalism" the root of all suffering, success the inherited privilege of greed, and borders a racist conspiracy. No, the noxious sky isn't falling amid an unquenchable cloud of gunfire from redneck militia, the pawnbrokers of projection and camera-cued tears have simply put ceiling fans on the basement floor of voters' drowning senses. Wrong is right and Big Bird can no longer fly because of "greedy" tariffs on notorious Chinese polluters and currency manipulators paying peasants pennies on the dollar for the 'greater good'. To quote the Red Star portfolio of Traitor Joe, "Orange man bad, communist oppression good!" No wonder he believes "white kids" are immune to poverty, discrimination and twisted predators; not excluding his favorite shampoo, of course.

That feral moment a campaign political bumper sticker or solitary red MAGA hat, a falsely attributed symbol of extremism and bigotry, is recklessly transformed into a public tribunal of condoned brutality, is also the day civility, discourse and the nonnegotiable premise of tolerance evaporate beneath an epitaph of regret. Would Syrians, Mexicans or the Japanese welcome their elected government placing the needs and unwarranted demands of millions of Americans over their own marginalized citizens; condemning, attacking or imprisoning anyone who exposed their deception and betrayal? How many of their celebrated athletes have knelt during their national anthem on an international stage to advocate liquidating their country's resources, laws and sovereignty to appease its plotting critics in the name of fabricated "racism", political correctness or radical "feminism"; spiteful stunts devoid of any factual argument or legitimate grievance?

Since good, old-fashioned election fraud isn't enough to tip the electoral college, social media censorship and search engine manipulation are now the most effective forms of Democratic "patriotism". And because socialism, open borders, "white guilt", "toxic" masculinity and tofu barbecues can't sell themselves to a populace armed with a principled spirit of independence - individual autonomy, ambition and self-respect born from an historical aversion to government tyranny - the only suitable alternative for progressive hypnotists is to divide, disinform and viciously slander the very embodiment of American exceptionalism: a candid pragmatist who also happens to be one of the most effective and transparent Chief Executives in modern history, if not the most hounded, underappreciated and misunderstood figure in the world today.

Distrust, party rancor and racial animosity, social constructs that have existed for millennia on end, are not new occurrences in American society; Donald Trump's 2016 victory merely triggered the true depths of their existence, and even more so his obsessed detractors' willingness to manipulate them. Shamelessly politicizing every horrific tragedy for partisan gain, only to ignore the systemic roots of escalating violence in America, does nothing to address the decaying societal values and mental health crisis fertilizing the killing fields of failed gun control havens like Chicago and Baltimore.

Whining opportunists can no more regulate the festering volatility of human nature than they can blame a trigger for pulling itself or a raging forest fire for lighting a match. But together as a concerned and sentient people, without finger pointing, public grandstanding and the condescension of corrosive identity politics - vilifying a resolute leader for correctly referring to a murderous gang as "animals", for rebuking a national soccer player repeatedly disrespecting the privilege of representing her country, or for rightfully shining a spotlight on decades of neglected urban blight and incompetence - we can restore a basic respect for life, America, and the necessity of earnest communication; a proposition which only requires time and an unwavering commitment to virtue over vice, honesty in lieu of choreographed duplicity. The mighty grandeur of Rome didn't fall in a day. Its watershed foundation rotted and collapsed beneath the weight of its own depravity and complacency long before any foreign power breached its assumed invincibility.

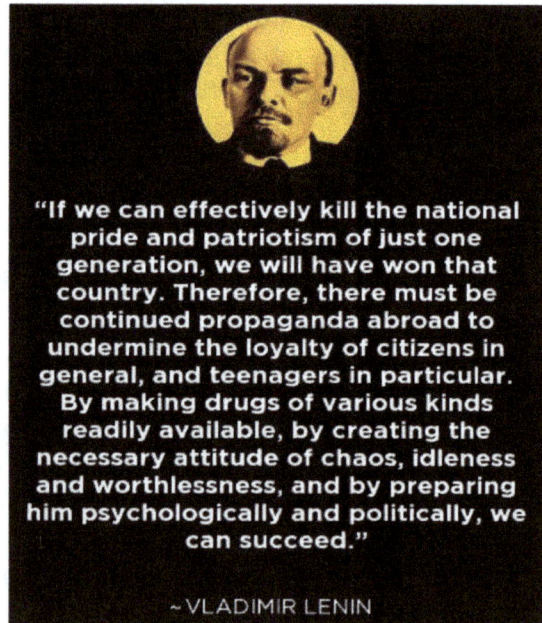

"If we can effectively kill the national pride and patriotism of just one generation, we will have won that country. Therefore, there must be continued propaganda abroad to undermine the loyalty of citizens in general, and teenagers in particular. By making drugs of various kinds readily available, by creating the necessary attitude of chaos, idleness and worthlessness, and by preparing him psychologically and politically, we can succeed."

~VLADIMIR LENIN

Those career malcontents and scheming social engineers who crave political power above all else will invent outrage, mock our faith, twist the most self-evident morals, reject reason and manipulate every inconvenient truth solely to reclaim control of the very country they so ignorantly despise and seek to dismantle; that imperfect yet transcendent Republic responsible for such an iconic degree of individual liberty and limitless opportunity that even a toxic squad of parasitic socialists, ungrateful immigrants, elected enemy combatants, unabashed bigots and clueless eco-fascists could succeed in light of undermining the very cultural and ideological pillars of Western society. Only in America. Fortunately, only your vote can simultaneously stop this blasphemous betrayal and denounce the dysfunctional disrepute of contemporary politics poisoning millions of impressionable minds with grotesque exaggerations and incendiary lies, hoping America will graciously destroy itself to restore the New World Order.

An American State of Mind

Why, yes...I am a capitalist, a Christian, a gun owner and a proud nationalist. I unapologetically embrace these quintessential American ideals because much of the world does not share our values, recognize our natural born liberties or remotely care about the survival of our homes, children and livelihoods. Does embodying these self-explanatory attributes somehow suggest that I'm racist, sexist, a Nazi or a domestic terror threat? NPR, please! Only in the syndicated echo chambers of media hypnotists and the sheltered minds of liberal academia does such absurd hyperbole exist; only amidst those depraved politicians whose divisive agenda require inciting hatred through victimization propaganda because they cannot properly articulate and defend the merits of their beliefs in the face of real scrutiny. Forgive my functioning senses, but when's the last time a prominent progressive shared their so-called vision for America without the stale, obnoxious accusation of bigotry, misogyny, homophobia, class warfare or Right Wing extremism; without religiously speaking ill of the very country responsible for their freedoms, opportunities and good fortune?

And yet a majority of these self-proclaimed "social justice" warriors who grotesquely justify the brazen censorship of conservative voices on campuses and social media, are somehow outraged by the prudent idea of placing illegal immigrants in the beloved sanctuary cities of their own home states. Why? Because globalism was never about elevating the human condition, helping millions of impoverished families by demanding an accountable, competent form of government in their native homelands. It's about control...permanently turning the red states of Texas, Florida and Arizona into deep blue cabals of uncontested progressivism just like California: to culturally transform their defiant populations and economically sabotage Republican leadership to achieve future electoral supremacy no matter what the consequences to our hallowed way of life.

Scheming opportunists like Nancy Pelosi and Chuck Schumer know damn well another massive influx of foreign nationals will increase crime, exasperate homelessness and poverty, further strain their state's overwhelmed budgets and spark an even greater exodus of taxpaying residents to greener pastures. And while I commend the President for holding the two left feet of scurrying Democrats to the raging dumpster fire of their own fertilized hypocrisy – the unresolved fact he is handcuffed by the "Catch and Release" and asylum loopholes of our current system – I do not support dumping millions more of unvetted migrants into American cities being it is only a matter of time before they migrate elsewhere, illegally vote or are granted wholesale amnesty by an unchecked Democratic Congress.

If requiring prospective immigrants to follow the legal naturalization process is just too much to ask for a chance at a better life, then why are loyal, law-abiding citizens being threatened and punished for speaking the inconvenient truth about socialism, abortion, Islamic radicalism, armed self-defense or LGBT indoctrination in our classrooms? There is nothing endearing, enlightening or patriotic about conniving politicians and colluding pundits spending every waking moment undermining the fundamental cornerstones of the most revered Free Republic on Earth: that clearly "unjust, racist, sexist and greedy" bastion of enduring hope inspiring countless foreigners to brave perilous deserts and cross vast oceans just for the opportunity to call home. Where would the conspiring global community be today without the technological advances, foreign assistance, and conscious sacrifice of the American people: that surviving spirit of sovereign independence made possible by the founding declaration of thirteen, idealistic colonies? Complacency is the living epitaph of regret.

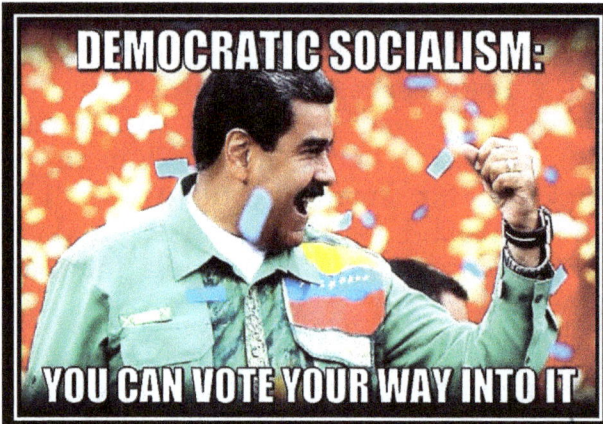

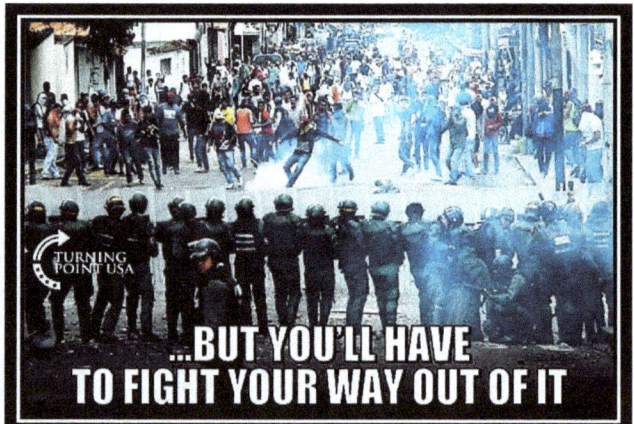

Joseph Stalin was once a hip intellectual, devout atheist and Democratic Socialist who led protests against the rich and powerful. He rose to power, promising equality, then siezed private industry leading to mass poverty and famine. He murdered 20 million of his own people.

Dear Alexandria Ocasio-Cortez…

Contrary to what your sheltered upbringing and revisionist education may have taught you in the spineless echoes of progressive indoctrination, I'm rightfully and deathly afraid of socialism. As someone who is keenly aware of the grotesque atrocities and regurgitated lies of Democratic Socialists and Marxist propagandists, I fully understand centralized collectivism unapologetically and relentlessly usurps people's liberties, property and dignity until they are permanent wards of the state. Rather, instead of rational adults simply acknowledging the inevitable inequities of human achievement – skill, perseverance, sacrifice and hard work – whining, conspiring statists like yourself attempt to suffocate ambition, individuality and mankind's innate desire to succeed according to one's own devices beneath the politically-imposed ceiling of equally-divided misery; also known as, economic fascism.

Using a nation's existing resources to assist those in need, protect its citizens or ease suffering during times of misfortune, by no means justifies redistributing wealth or forcibly seizing personal property to erect a socialist utopia of legalized theft beneath the "fair share" gauntlet of unearned social justice. Or in money laundering terms, finance the lavish lifestyles of Washington elites and Hollywood concubines dining on the liquidated ignorance of the spoon-fed electorate. Replacing incentive and self-sufficiency with entitlement and unsustainable debt is a preamble to the type of grassroots revolution that leaves a stained pitchfork in the superfluous zeros of your Congressional bank account.

History has proven time and again the larger government grows without restraint or condition – resulting in escalating waste, greed corruption and public persecution – the more insatiable their schemes become to unilaterally control every aspect of the people's lives; i.e., what to eat, think, own or even say. And since you and your newly-elected, militant colleagues have openly waged war on free enterprise, fair elections, limited government, federal transparency, independent media, the male gender, natural biological distinctions, the traditional family, Judeo-Christianity, white "privilege", wealthy citizens, sovereign borders, the sanctity of newborn life, intellectual diversity, the Supreme Court, and our Constitutional Bill of Rights, it doesn't take a political scientist to discover your true intentions are as extreme as they are repugnantly naive.

Your adolescent lust for fame, validation and uncontested power deserves every ounce of scorn and derision the forsaken citizens of this threatened Free Republic can dutifully muster. If anyone personifies a hateful quest to silence, oppress, and discriminate against a transcendent nation's diverse populace, unique blessings and founding ideals, it is you and your upstart hoard of Democratic supremacists whose blind obsession with a ruinous ideology is leading their detached party's glorious march into madness. And tragically, the American dream along with them.

Signed,

The Passed Torch of Liberty

The American Patriot

Born from the billowing defiance of a crisp December night in 1773, the Boston Tea Party was much more than an abbreviated footnote in the fog of forgotten history; it quite literally was the lynch pin of the American Revolution, the hand of fate that propelled colonists towards an inevitable confrontation with England and the capture of their once inconceivable independence. "Life, liberty, and the pursuit of happiness" became a singular, unifying thread – an unyielding desire to live as free men and women and prosper solely according to their labors – that weaved patriots from all walks of life into the most powerful and prolific tapestry Western Civilization has ever known: The United States of America. Patriots the likes of Samuel Adams and Norma Washington, the Sons & Daughters of Liberty, realized any manner of rule that did not represent the will of the people, their natural rights, was a gateway to subjugation, strife, and senseless sacrifice. And to defeat this injustice, each was willing to give his or her life. If not for their bravery and unanimous disdain for a corpulent, crowned leviathan that spanned some 3000 miles, America could very well still be "tea and toiling" under the fluttering flag of the United Kingdom, instead of the safe harbor of God's domain. And it is within this context, the eternal struggle of man vs. man, vice vs. virtue, freedom is not always won on the battlefield of valor or by the attrition of silenced heartbeats. Liberty, the dawn of democracy and the light of divinity, is also forged on the backbone of conviction, within the fire of faith and across the civilized streets of solidarity.

PATRIOTS HAVE NO SKIN COLOR

Because time is indeed the fire in which we burn, the epitaph we inexorably write, when did our revolutionary platform of natural-born freedoms, an impenetrable bastion of independence and pride, become eroded to the point of indifference, interpretation and implied consent? When did our conscience break the mirror of self-awareness, accountability, into a wielded shard of media manipulation? When did a blessed people willingly trade the American flag, the heartbeat of a nation and the sole signature of iconic leaders the likes of Washington, Jefferson, Lincoln, and Reagan, for the fascist symbol of a President so narcissistic, so consumed with a cancerous ideology, he transformed the people's government into a personal vendetta of coerced assimilation? When did handouts become synonymous with hard work, pornography replace parents, and government supersede God? Most of all, when did we sacrifice the Constitution – a clear limitation and check on government, not individual liberty – for horse blinders and a knotted whip?

Generations of immigrants who narrowly fled the spiraling decay of socialism and iron boot of communism with nothing but their lives intact are now watching their American descendants, their own grandchildren, march on each's behalf. For the sake of brevity, but more succinctly, hope, let me share this singular tenet of Tea Party radicalism: "We the People" proudly and humbly welcome all races, creeds and colors – regardless of gender, age, economic disposition, heritage, religious beliefs, or sexuality – who are dedicated to defending and restoring American idealism. Every citizen of sound mind and body owes it themselves, their family, and this country to earn a living; otherwise, America will falter and the fruits of others' labor forcefully usurped for the "common good". We universally reject, without reservation, hate, discrimination, and/or violence, those adopted constructs of liberal intolerance that violate individual liberty, or more profoundly, human decency.

If our founding fathers were alive today, leaders far more learned and accomplished than any of their contemporary critics, they would immediately be admonished as radical extremists, or more succinctly, Tea Party insurgents. They also knew, in all their prescient wisdom, that absolute "Democracy" is a legalized state of mob rule where 51% inevitably liquidates the liberties and/or property of the other 49%; unlike a "principled" Constitutional Republic which gives a voice to all citizens bound by a prescribed set of ideals, Checks and Balances. On behalf of Allen West, Dr. Ben Carson, Mia Love, Bobby Jindal, Condoleezza Rice, Thomas Sowell, Brian Sandoval, Clarence Thomas, Tim Scott, Booker T. Washington, Martin Luther King, those "racist" voices of vigilant independence and inalienable rights, I unequivocally and respectfully proclaim, "Never!" Never will I acquiesce to the disingenuous attempts by any man, mob or government decree to criminalize my peaceful convictions, erase my heritage and those blessings born from an imperfect past, or steal the bread of providence from the sovereignty of my beloved home.

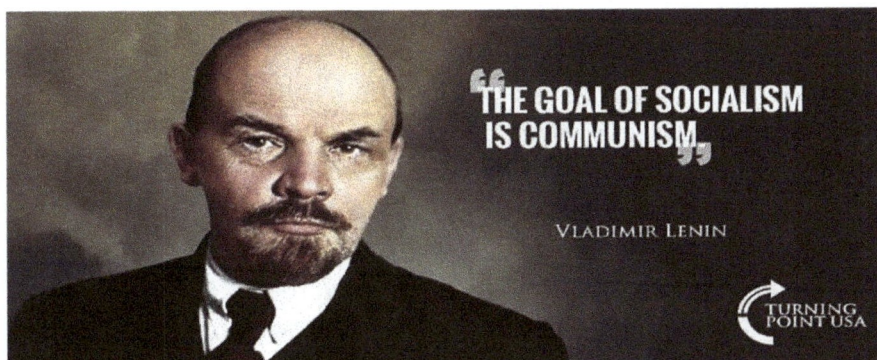

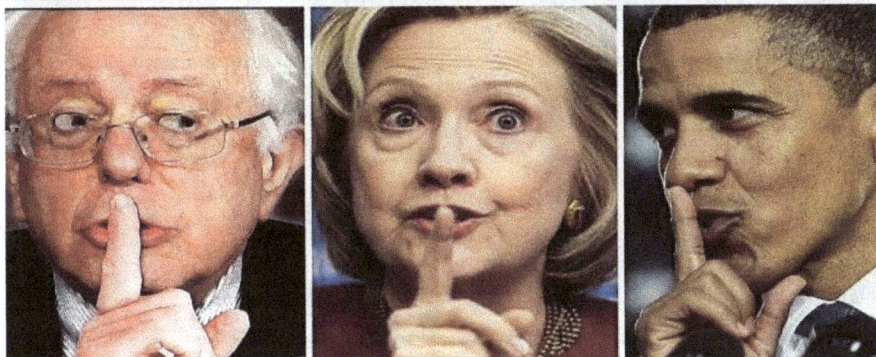

In Honor of Ronald Reagan and the New American Revolution

Ronald Wilson Reagan never apologized for being an American; he reminded "We the People" exactly what it meant to be one. The son of a vagabond shoe salesman reminded us a discounted rabble of colonial peasants once rose from the obscurity of oppression, a King's decree of death, to forge a beacon of hope and prosperity that would transcend humanity for centuries to come. His intellect, fierce convictions and unwavering patriotism rose far beyond the slanderous slights and political ploys of the partisan media. To debate him was to resign yourself to defeat; to listen was to marvel at the hypnotic prowess of his eloquent diligence. Simply become a willing guest to any of his recorded orations: from his 1964 sermon, "A Time to Choose", his "Warrior's Pledge" inaugural address in 1981, or the immutable "Mr. Gorbachev, tear down this wall" diatribe at Brandenburg Gate in 1987. "The Gipper" instinctively knew this nation would never fall to the armed might of a foreign enemy, rather America could only be toppled by the duplicitous schemes of domestic forces plotting her demise deep within our own apathy. No, Ronald Reagan didn't mince platitudes of political correctness or needlessly suffer fools; he spanked their whining agenda, put their juvenile propaganda to bed and woke the American Dream slumbering within a forsaken people. The Great Communicator was a skilled statesman, a true gentleman and a natural-born leader of mankind. He was infinitely charismatic, an insatiable scholar and a fearless bastion of strength, but more profoundly an indelible inspiration amidst the rising tide of progressive depravity, virulent discontent, poisoning the moral fabric of a fabled Republic's timeless charter. May the 40th President of American liberty forever rest in peace alongside his faithful wife, Nancy, with the eternal gratitude of his enduring country; both of whom he loved dearly without refrain.

"A nation can survive its fools, and even the ambitious. But it cannot survive treason from within. An enemy at the gates is less formidable, for he is known and carries his banner openly. But the traitor moves among those within the gate freely, his sly whispers rustling through all the alleys, heard in the very halls of government itself. For the traitor appears not a traitor; he speaks in accents familiar to his victims, and he wears their face and their arguments, he appeals to the baseness that lies deep in the hearts of all men. He rots the soul of a nation, he works secretly and unknown in the night to undermine the pillars of the city, he infects the body politic so that it can no longer resist. A murderer is less to fear." Marcus Tullius Cicero

www.ingramcontent.com/pod-product-compliance
Lightning Source LLC
Chambersburg PA
CBHW080352030426
42334CB00024B/2852

9 780692 178478